THE SEVENTIES

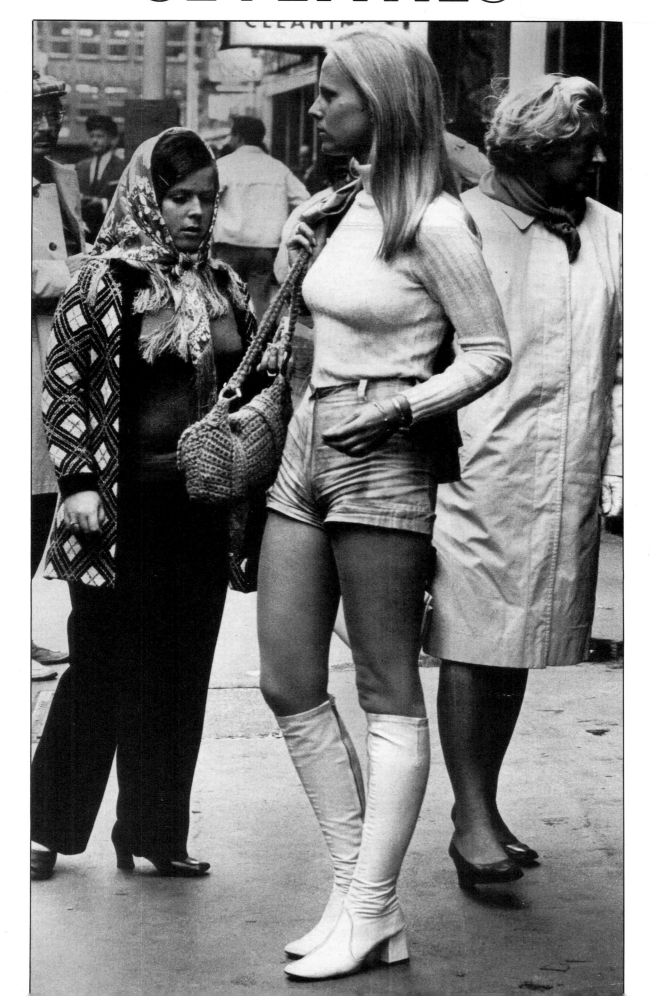

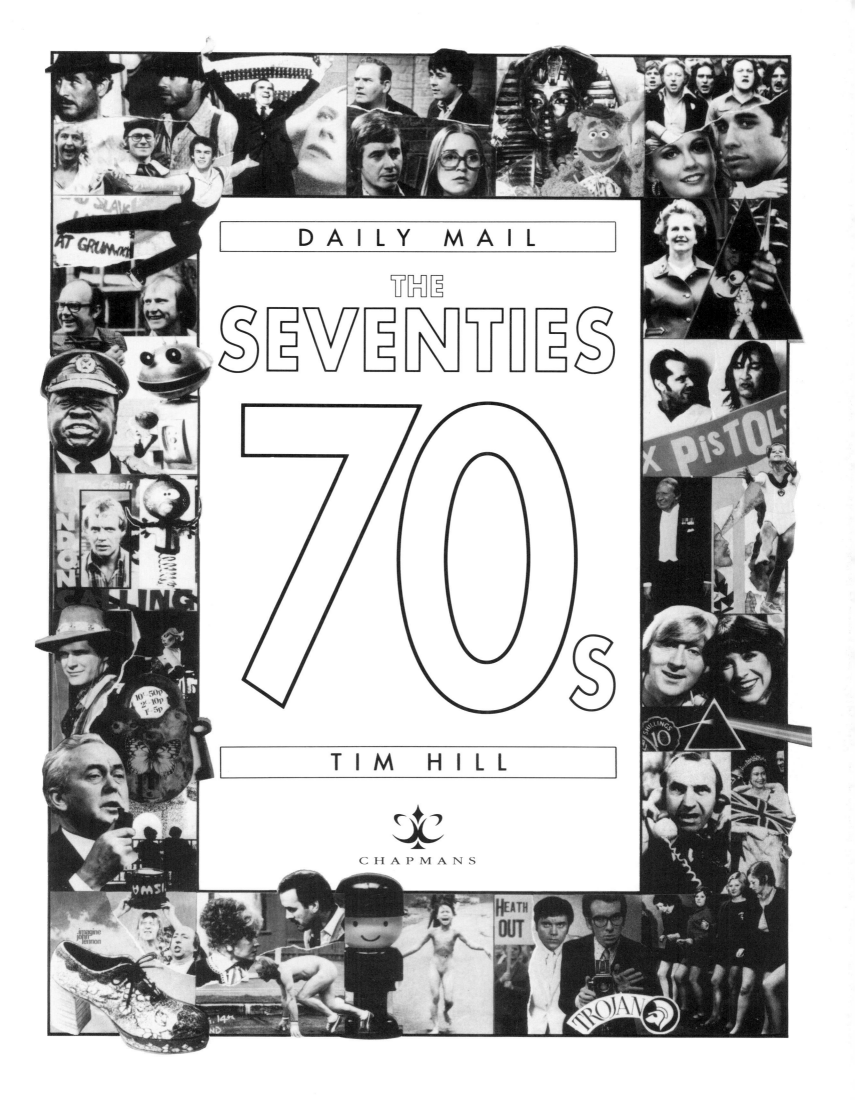

DAILY MAIL

THE
SEVENTIES
70s

TIM HILL

CHAPMANS

Chapmans Publishers Ltd
141–143 Drury Lane
London WC2B 5TB

A CIP catalogue record for this book is available from the
British Library.

ISBN 1–85592–719–5

First published by Chapmans 1991

Photoset by York House Typographic Ltd, London

Printed and bound in Great Britain by
Clays Ltd, St Ives plc

Acknowledgements

Bob Dignum
John Dunn
John Emery
Yvonne Holland
Alex Howell
Christine Hoy
George Johnson
Roger Lightfoot
John Plummer
Paul Rossiter
Cliff Salter
Dave Shepherd
Steve Torrington
and with special thanks to everyone at the *Daily Mail*
reference and picture library for making this book
possible.

For Jane, Laura and Jenny

INTRODUCTION

The inspiration behind this book lay in the anomaly of an era so rich in ideas, changes, events, yet with such a dearth of published material to do justice to it.

Only now is the decade of the 1970s assuming a cult status to rival its celebrated and idiosyncratic predecessor. It would be strange were it not so, for not only was it a decade that had a plethora of colour, excitement, drama, innovation, triumphs and disasters, icons and bogeymen, but to many of us in our thirties and forties, the 1970s was a time of growing awareness, of greater participation, of the children of the 1960s reaching maturity.

At no time in Britain has the pace of change – in all aspects of life – been so rapid and so complete over just ten years. But the 1970s wasn't just a thoroughfare between the carefree 60s and the materialistic 80s; with the immediacy of a wealth of archive material I have aimed to capture in this book the essence of a decade that had its own identity and ideals, and which is now ripe for retrospective and nostalgia.

If you lived through the 1970s, the events and images will flood back with all the freshness that contemporary reports can generate. If you didn't, I hope this book will give you an insight into what life was really like in the decade that bridged flower power and Thatcherism.

TIM HILL 1991

JAN 1970

The audience at this pop concert display a mixture of fashions and styles.

NAVY LOSES THE BATTLE OF THE TOT

Parliament's Old Salts – Tory and Labour alike – yesterday tried in vain to save the Navy's rum ration. Labour MP, Mr James Wellbelove, demanded, 'What research has been carried out into the comparative efficiency of those who take their rum ration and the temperance ratings who take their 3d.-a-day grog money in lieu?' Dr David Owen, Under-Secretary for the Navy, refused to give way, pointing out that the rum ration was equivalent to 4 single whiskies. With the additional allowance of 1 pint of beer this would put a person over the 80 m.g. mark – the breath-test limit for motorists.

AND AN AWFUL WARNING . . .

Maxi girls are worrying road-safety expert George Rutter. He would like them to revert to the leg-flashing mini as the longer hemlines make them difficult for motorists to see.

'INVITE ENVOYS,' POP GROUP TOLD

The Tremeloes pop group will invite British diplomats to their next overseas show on the suggestion of Mr Roy Mason, President of the Board of Trade. The Tremeloes had complained that they and other pop groups who earned millions of dollars abroad were snubbed by British diplomats overseas. Mr Mason claimed his department and the Foreign and Commonwealth Office are 'with it' and understood the contribution made to the balance of payments by the entertainment industry. He pointed out that his Parliamentary Secretary, Mrs Gwyneth Dunwoody, made a golden disc presentation to the group, Led Zeppelin, in recognition of £5m-worth of records sold in the USA.

HOW CAN A MINI GIRL WEAR A MAXI?

I am in a state of despair after reading Sandy Fawkes's report from Paris – that the mini is out and the maxi is definitely in!

If those of us who are less than 5 foot tall stay in fashion by wearing the maxi we will look as though we are walking below ground level!
Miss S. Reece
Chippenham, Wilts

100 m.p.h. TRAINS ROB THE AIRLINES

British Rail's 100 m.p.h. electric trains between London and the North have doubled their passengers since being introduced 4 years ago. 40% of the increase has been won from airlines, according to a BR survey. These figures will be used to persuade the Government to extend electrification from Crewe to Glasgow at a cost of £30m – the equivalent of 3 miles of urban motorway.

LAST REEL FOR *PATHE*

Pathe News will be seen by cinemagoers for the last time at the end of next month. After 50 years it has been decided that TV and other information media provide a more topical service. The only remaining British newsreel will be *Movietone News*.

IS THERE NOWHERE IN BRITAIN NORTH OF LUTON?

The choice of Birmingham as the site of a National Trade Exhibition Centre caused bitter controversy in the Commons yesterday. Mr Roy Mason, President of the Board of Trade, rejected arguments that the new centre should be sited in London. He said, 'It is really appalling to me that most people, in spite of the fact that we pretend to be British, recognize nothing north of London and they think Luton is the fringe of the continent.'

Birmingham, chosen as Britain's 'shop window' despite strong lobbying from industrial leaders, lost no time in getting the project under way; just 2 hours after the decision was made, Birmingham Council snapped up 367 acres of farmland at Elmdon – close to the city's airport – for about £250,000. The centre will cost approximately £11m.

A small boy displays his favourite sweets – sherbert 'flying saucers'.

CHEAPEST SITE FOR LONDON AIRPORT NAMED

Cublington in Buckinghamshire would be the cheapest of the 4 proposed sites for London's third London airport, says a report published yesterday. It is estimated that Thurleigh, Bedfordshire would cost £3m more; Nuthampstead, Hertfordshire £18m more; and Foulness, Essex £235m more. Foulness is the most difficult to reach by road and Nuthampstead the easiest. But measured in flying costs and passenger time Cublington emerges as first choice and Nuthampstead last.

Twenty one year old disc jockey Noel Edmonds is quite a car enthusiast. He has even built one from a Kit – a Mini-Jem – He's got a Morris 1100 and a 1965 Healey Sprite. But it's his 1964 Hillman Imp that is really special.

OFFICIAL: ROCKY THE GREATEST

Cassius Clay was knocked out in the thirteenth round by Rocky Marciano last night. A computer dictated the action between the 2 unbeaten heavyweight champions.

DECIMAL POINT KILLS BABY

A baby boy with a bad heart died after being given 10 times more than the prescribed dose of a drug at a hospital which was changing over to the decimal system, a coroner was told yesterday. Instead of giving 0.025 m.g. of the drug digoxin a nurse administered 0.25 m.g.

NICKLAUS REACHES RECORD MILLION

30-year-old Jack Nicklaus earned the fastest million dollars from tournament golf when he picked up $14,300 for second place in the Bing Crosby Classic at Pebble Beach. It took him only 9 years. The other million-dollar men are Arnold Palmer and Billy Casper. It took Palmer 14 years; Casper reached the mark 2 weeks ago after 16 years as a professional.

BEETLES ON THE MOVE

The VW Beetle – the world's best-selling car – is catching up on the model T Ford of the 1920s in sales, with nearly 12 million sold world-wide, more than 200,000 in the UK.

DAY BY DAY

1 Jan
The Family Law Reform Act lowers the age of majority to 18.

Lloyds admits women members for the first time in its 300-year history.

2 Jan
The £50 foreign-travel limit ends.

Uganda bans the MCC touring team over a decision to invite an all-white South African cricket team to Britain.

9 Jan
The Flu death-toll reaches 2,400 weekly – the highest since 1951.

15 Jan
Labour MP William Owen is charged under the Official Secrets Act.

19 Jan
The FA orders clubs to prepare grounds for the issue of first 'safety certificates' on 1 September.

20 Jan
East German leader Walter Ulbricht says the Berlin Wall stays regardless of any agreement reached between East and West Germany.

21 Jan
Johnny Prescott retires from boxing after losing to 19-year-old Joe Bugner.

22 Jan
Pan Am's 'Jumbo' Jet goes into service.

23 Jan
The world's biggest newspaper company, International Publishing Organization, is to be taken over by Reed Paper Group.

27 Jan
145 MPs sign a motion tabled by Airey Neave for the release of Rudolf Hess.

28 Jan
The Equal Pay Bill making it illegal after 7 December for women to be paid less than men in similar jobs, is given its first reading.

WHEN A FATHER DECIDES 'NO MORE BABIES'

Should men be paid a £500 bounty for agreeing to be sterilized for birth-control purposes? This novel suggestion is made by Dr Aubrey Manning, Reader in Zoology at Edinburgh University. He points out that bounties are paid in India and that Britain's population is increasing by an alarming 1,000 a day, despite current family-planning practices.

But this operation – vasectomy – although almost unheard of 4 years ago, is becoming increasingly popular without financial incentive. Some 20,000 underwent the operation last year, which may have delighted their wives, but reaction among men seems to indicate that most still find it unacceptable. Even some doctors have shown themselves sceptical and unenthusiastic when patients have expressed an interest in the operation. The cost: £15 when done under local anaesthetic.

UNION KILLS OFF RADIO POP PLAN

The BBC's bid to turn Radio 1 into a non-stop pop station has failed. The Musicians' Union would not agree to the extra 100 hours 'needle time' needed to separate Radio 1 from Radio 2 – they combine at 7 p.m. at the moment. The union feels that increased needle time would affect the amount of work offered to musicians for live performances.

BACK DOWN TO EARTH COMES NEW DOCTOR WHO

Doctor Who returns to the screen tonight with a new batch of spine-chilling adventures. The new doctor – the third since the programme was launched 7 years ago – will be 50-year-old comedian Jon Pertwee. There will be a 1980s Earth setting and the doctor will be saving modern Britain from, among others, Daleks, Yetis and Cybermen.

Stephen Lewis, Reg Varney and Bob Grant – On the Buses.

UNKNOWN HUTCHISON HAUNTS ARSENAL

21-year-old Scot, Tom Hutchison, a winger unknown in the South, took on the vaunted Highbury defence almost single-handed on Saturday. The £8,000 buy from Alloa scored the goal that nearly put Arsenal out of the FA Cup. If £90,000-Peter Marinello performs half as well for his new club, Manager Bertie Mee will be pleased.

AMONG THE NEW YEAR HONOURS

Noël Coward – knighthood
Lillian Board – MBE
OBEs for:
Kenny Lynch
Pete Murray
John Arlott
Tony Jacklin
Don Revie

CBEs for:
Kenneth More
Maggie Smith
Joan Plowright
Colin Chapman

FEB 1970

MICHAEL TOPS THE POPS AT 10

At the age of 10 Michael Jackson has become the youngest singer ever to top the Hit Parade. From Gary, Indiana, he is leader of a family group called the Jackson 5. Their record *I Want You Back* has toppled Eddison Lighthouse's *Love Grows* from No 1.

HEATH PLANS BIG SHAKE-UP FOR UNIONS

The Tories pledged themselves yesterday to a drastic programme of trade union reform after a general election victory. They promise an onslaught on the cobwebbed, rusty machinery of trade unionism that has stayed untouched for decades. Union chiefs will have the shaking of their lives as hardly any of their much-worshipped sacred cows and totem poles will be allowed to survive.

MEASLES JABS TO SAVE UNBORN BABIES

Mass vaccination of schoolgirls against German measles is expected to start in Britain within a year, effectively removing the fear of deformed babies being born. The vaccine became officially available yesterday.

PICK THE OSCAR GIRL

This year's Best Actress Oscar will be between the following:
Jane Fonda (*They Shoot Horses, Don't They?*)
Liza Minelli (*Pookie*)
Jean Simmons (*The Happy Ending*)
Maggie Smith (*The Prime Of Miss Jean Brodie*)
Genevieve Bujold (*Anne Of The Thousand Days*)

The nominees for the male award are: Peter O'Toole, Richard Burton, Dustin Hoffman, Jon Voigt and John Wayne.

Darryl Zanuck, last of the old Hollywood titans, speaking about films he has in the pipeline (*Butch Cassidy and the Sundance Kid*, *John and Mary*, *MASH*, *The Kremlin Letter* and *Patton*) comments: 'I envisage an unusually concentrated cash flow by next fall and winter.'

He also has an £8m film planned called *Tora Tora* about the Japanese attack on Pearl Harbor.

ROW FLARES ON TEST-TUBE BABIES

The prospect of test-tube babies is causing widespread conflict between those who have serious misgivings and women who desperately want to have a baby. Anthony Alment, Gynaecologists' Secretary, said that people were naturally concerned that scientific progress would escape from humanity. Father John Macdonald, adviser to the Catholic Marriage Council, said marriage did not give the partners the right to children and this practice was tantamount to artificial insemination. Leader in the field Dr Douglas Bevis said he thought the technique would not work at present, though it was possible. 'It could be next week, next year or next century,' he commented.

LP PRICES TO GO UP

Britain's biggest record company, EMI, is to raise LP prices next month. Albums with a present recommended retail price of 37/5 will go up to 39/11. The price of singles will remain at 8/6.

THE AVENGER STREAKS IN

Rootes have announced their all-new car for the 1970s, intended to spearhead the firm's fight back to prosperity. They have opted for the increasingly popular wedge shape (as recently adopted by the Renault 12 and Saab 99). Publicity will include colour TV advertising and music from The Avengers. Price range: £766 – £903.

Paul Newman and Robert Redford in a scene from Butch Cassidy and the Sundance Kid.

ABORIGINE EVONNE COMES TO EUROPE

Evonne Goolagong, an 18-year-old Aboriginal girl from Sydney, already heralded as a second Margaret Court in Australia, makes her first European appearance at Southport over Easter.

I'LL BE GUINEA-PIG, SAYS JACK HAWKINS

Actor Jack Hawkins volunteered last night to be the first Briton to have an artificial larynx developed in America. It involves having a hole constructed in the neck to plug in a 2-inch plastic larynx with a metal tuning reed. Mr Hawkins, who speaks through his stomach after having his larynx removed because of throat cancer, said, 'If they want a guinea-pig in England, I'm first in the queue. It sounds marvellous.'

DAY BY DAY

2 Feb
Bertrand Russell, mathematician, philosopher and CND campaigner, dies at the age of 97.

3 Feb
Police close theatre showing Andy Warhol's sex movie, *Flesh*, after receiving a complaint that the film is obscene.

Tories censure motion in Commons over Labour's employment record: more than 500,000 registered unemployed in 29 out of last 30 months, the longest continuous period of high unemployment since the war.

17 Feb
69-year-old Anna Anderson's claim to be recognized as Anastasia, daughter of the last Czar of Russia, is rejected by West Germany's Supreme Court. She vows her 40-year battle will go on.

19 Feb
It is announced that Prince Charles is to join the Navy, entering Dartmouth Royal Naval College next year at the rank of Midshipman. It is not known yet if he will accept the pay, £885 per year.

ITA STAMP ON 'STOP SPORTS' PLAN

A group of ITV executives led by ATV's Sir Lew Grade have had their plan to replace Saturday afternoon sports programmes quashed. The idea was to show 'family entertainment' – shows such as repeats of *The Saint* and *Dangerman* – instead. But the ITA is insisting that ITV continues to screen *World of Sport* to compete with BBC 1's *Grandstand*.

WHEN THE DARTBOARD IS EVICTED AND THE VILLAGE PUB IS BURIED UNDER AN AVALANCHE OF SCAMPI

The village pub – high-backed chairs in front of log fires, dartboards, dominoes and all – is being dragged unwillingly and unceremoniously into the 1970s. There seems precious little pub lovers can do to stem the tide of wall-to-wall carpeting, scampi and chips, chicken in a basket and piped music. Breweries now own most pubs and have decided they must be economically viable. This means plasterboard over oak beams, plastic tables, fruit machines instead of crib games, and the disappearance of the public bar. And the piano, part and parcel of pub heritage, is out while 3 selections for 1/- juke-boxes come in.

SHORT SEEKS POWERS TO FORCE ALL-IN SCHOOLS

Mr Edward Short, Education Minister, has taken the first steps towards making comprehensive schools compulsory throughout the country. In a brief bill he is taking powers to bring into line those authorities still fighting to keep grammar schools and the eleven-plus. Mr Short accuses those who wish to retain the grammar-school system of labelling 80% of the population as failures. He said, 'The bill will ensure for all our children that the goal of equal opportunity at the secondary stage of education – which should have been the achievement of the 1944 Act – will be achieved at last in our time.'

In reply, Shadow Education Minister Mrs Margaret Thatcher said, 'I believe there are some parents who would like to take the option of letting their children be assessed to go to very good grammar schools of proven excellence.'

SIXPENCE IS SAVED

The sixpence will not be abolished next February when Britain goes decimal. An all-party campaign by MPs, many of whom feared that its abolition would lead to unwarranted price increases, has won an indefinite reprieve for the coin. Conservatives have launched an attack on the Government's handling of decimalization. They say that if the basic unit were 10s instead of £s there would be no need to get rid of the sixpence.

No stars, no violence, no sex. Just one boy and his bird, Kes.

WHY I SHOOT DEER, BY PRINCE PHILIP

Interviewed on BBC's *24 Hours* last night about European Conservation Year, Prince Philip explained why he shoots red deer: 'It's got nothing to do with whether you enjoy cropping them or not; this has to be done, otherwise they would eat out their own habitat and degenerate.'

'WATCH JAPAN' ALERT FOR BRITISH FIRMS

Japan has ousted America and Germany as the country to be watched by British industry in the 1970s according to a National Economic Development Council report to be published soon.

MAR 1970

EVERYTHING BUT THE KITCHEN SINK

- Washing up without soap and water
- Cooking a frozen meal in 30 seconds flat
- Switching on the oven or heating by simply telephoning home
- Relaxing on a gently moving mattress which rocks you to sleep while you learn a language from a speaker under the pillow
- Dispensing with the iron as fabrics won't need it
- Choosing a film or TV programme from the local video library

These are just some of the features that the house of 1975 will have. It may sound like never-never land but the fact is that many of these items can be bought in Britain today – at a price. However, wide demand should make them affordable by 1975. The Japanese, for example, have already produced a microwave oven for the US market costing only £100; the current price here is £300.

DON'T GET THE NEEDLE

For those who hate sewing on buttons the task becomes a 5-second job with the new Buttoneer. Available in 10 sizes and 99 colours the Buttoneer will be on sale nationwide soon. Cost: 39/6.

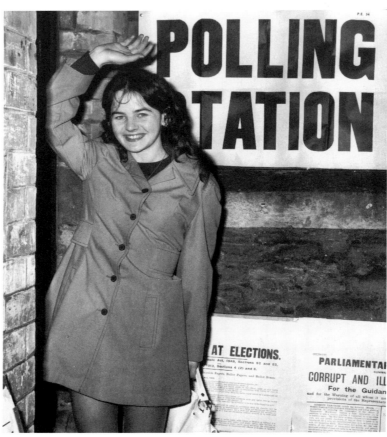

18-year-old Trudy Sellick is the first person under 21 to vote in a British Parliamentary election.

'UNFAIR TO MEN' CAR WALK-OUT

Men nightshift workers at Vauxhall's Luton plant walked out on unofficial strike after claiming women were being given lighter work. Although they receive the same wage – 10/9 per hour plus nightshift bonus – the women have been shielded from awkward jobs such as working on dashboard panels, the press shopmen say. The dispute is the first big row over women's pay since the Government's decision to bring in equal wages.

ENTER THE NEW SOCCER TYCOON

It's the age of the soccer superstar. George Best was the first to see that more money could be made off the field than on it. Now a new would-be tycoon – and speak his name reverently within earshot of Stamford Bridge – is emerging. Peter Osgood scores goals for Chelsea and hopes to help England retain the World Cup in Mexico this summer. But you might just as easily see his face in a car advertisement or on the wall of a King's Road boutique as in the sports pages. At 23, Peter Osgood is a Limited Company.

SECRETS THAT TOOK A NIBBLER TO THE TOP . . .

Next time you buy a box of Matchmakers – and with 15m boxes sold in the last year the chances are you will soon – think of the care which attended their creation. It took 4 years to perfect the 'informal nibbler' as the makers call it, the final choice coming from 7 original product ideas, 5 alternative names and 30 pack designs. From sales it looks as if the right idea won.

This is a classic example of how modern market research techniques are used to determine what the public will buy. Rootes discovered most people are only interested in fuel gauges and speedometers on their instrument panels – so they left everything else out on their new Avenger model.

WHO IS THIS MAN WHO BEATS LAVER?

Overnight Ismael El-Shafei has emerged as the Omar Sharif of world tennis. Suddenly everyone is talking about the handsome 22-year-old Egyptian who has beaten world champion Rod Laver twice within 6 weeks of turning professional.

A meeting of Ted Heath's Shadow Cabinet.

COUNCILS TOLD TO PUSH UP SPEED LIMITS

Against the will of some local authorities, the Government is asking them to review current speed restrictions. Whitehall feels that higher limits would not increase the number of accidents and might even reduce the figure by improving traffic flow. The Ministry of Transport says, 'Realism is the key. There is no point in having a restriction that is ignored by the vast majority of motorists.' Once local councils are won over the speed limit on many urban roads could rise to 40 m.p.h. from the present 30 m.p.h. The ROSPA supports the principle of raising limits, as does the AA, which hopes that the 70 m.p.h. limit for motorways might be increased, thereby preventing the bunching tendency associated with lower speeds. Motorways are safe roads, says the AA, and could take increased speed.

22-year-old David Essex is understudy to Tommy Steele in the pantomime Dick Whittington.

NEW LABELS MAKE DETERGENTS EASY TO PRICE

Housewives will no longer have to use mental arithmetic to find the bargains when buying detergents. Following an order under the Weights and Measures Act yesterday, powders will be marked in complete ounces only – no more fractions. To simplify matters further, only ounces – not pounds and ounces – will be shown. The 2 big detergent manufacturers Procter & Gamble (Daz, Tide, Fairy Snow, Ariel, Dreft) and Lever Bros. (Persil, Radiant, Omo, Surf) have both welcomed the new code.

'Space Oddity' hit maker David Bowie marries model Angie Barrett at Bromley Register Office.

IF IT'S CUSTARD YOU'RE SELLING, SAY SO

New laws to protect customers from misleading food labels and advertisements were announced yesterday. Under these the contents of food packages must be stated simply and clearly; labels will also have to state the ordinary name for brand goods – if custard powder is in the tin, the label must say so. Most pre-packed food will have to show a list of ingredients and there will be strict controls on false claims regarding the slimming or health-giving properties of food or drink.

The new laws will come into force on 1 Jan 1973 in order to give the manufacturers time to re-label and to use up present stocks.

ENTER A SMOKE WITH SEX APPEAL

The age of the sexy cigarette dawns this week with the introduction of a new brand by Carreras: Dunhill's Slim Size, designed exclusively for fashionable and discerning women. It seems from Carreras's research that to please women a product must be long, slim, mild, cheap and preferably packed in gold. Slim Size satisfy all these requirements at 5/5 for 20.

AIRPORT TUBE LINK ON THE WAY

Heathrow is to become accessible by tube – Airport Central on the Piccadilly Line. The station could be open by 1973, putting Hyde Park Corner just 35 mins away. When the line opens coaches running airport-passenger services via the M4 may be banned. This is one government idea for helping London Transport recover the £14m cost of the project. The fare to Hyde Park Corner: 4/6.

ROBOT BRAIN TO SPEED LONDON'S TRAFFIC

A vast robot brain aided by scores of TV cameras is to take over control of every inch of traffic in the heart of London. The most modern nerve centre in the world is being planned to house the computers and monitors which will cover every major junction within 40 square miles of the capital and adjust traffic lights in accordance with traffic flow. The system should be operational by spring 1973.

BREMNER TOPS

Billy Bremner has been named Footballer of the Year by the Football Writer's' Association. Gordon Banks was second and Peter Osgood third.

LAUREATE'S LAMENT FOR A JUNKIE

Cecil Day-Lewis's wife Jill Balcon says of her husband, 'When he became Poet Laureate he said he would be writing about contemporary issues . . . and drug addiction is something we are all talking about.'

The following poem is not based on any personal knowledge of the drugs problem; it is a reflection of the world at large.

EPITAPH FOR A DRUG ADDICT
Mourn this young girl. Weep for society
Which gave her little to esteem but kicks.
Impatient of its code, cant, cruelty,
Indifference, she kicked against all pricks
But the dream-loaded hypodermics. She
Has now obtained an everlasting fix.

C. Day Lewis 1970

APR 1970

TAX-THEM-ALL PLAN TO CUT RATES BURDEN

The idea of a local income tax to replace or reduce rates is to be put to the Government by 500,000 owner-occupiers. Every MP will be lobbied in a campaign to spread the rates burden to all earners. At present the head of the household pays an average of £47 in rates; under the new scheme this would fall to £32, the remainder coming from people currently paying nothing, thus spreading the burden from 16 million to 23 million people. The Government is not expected to consider changes in the present rating system.

IS THIS THE FACE OF THE SEVENTIES?

Glenda Jackson and Oliver Reed in Women in Love. *Having made* Women in Love *and* Negatives *and currently working on* Bloody Sunday, *and with Ken Russell's* The Devils *and* The Lonely Heart *in the pipeline, Glenda Jackson is certainly the actress of the year, if not the decade.*

QUESTION – *THE MOODY BLUES*

'I found this the most interesting record I've heard for some time. Unfortunately it's probably not commercial enough to make any real impact.'

The Vietnam War extends to Cambodia as US support South Vietnamese across frontier.

TUC DEMANDS 3 MONTHS' 'BABY' PAY

Working mothers-to-be should have a minimum of 3 months' maternity leave on full pay to bring Britain into line with standards of the International Labour Office. Plans including allowing pregnant women time off with pay for antenatal visits, ensuring rest provision at the workplace and prohibiting tasks which might be harmful to health (for example, heavy lifting, undue standing) will be discussed at the fortieth Women's TUC this week. But new laws to ban employment soon after childbirth will be opposed. Union leaders say that the decision to return to work should be the woman's, not the law's. Instead, the law should concentrate on protecting pregnant women employed in factories from being penalized if they refuse to do tasks which might be harmful to health.

BUSMEN TO GET A CUT OF THEIR TAKINGS

London busmen are to get a bonus on fares taken, in the hope of cutting down on fare-dodging and improving services. The idea is that drivers will no longer shoot past passengers at request stops and bunching will be avoided because crews at the back would be losing money. The bonus rates will be:

- 4*d.* in the £ up to £20 per shift
- 6*d.* in the £ if £30 is reached
- 8*d.* in the £ thereafter

In exchange drivers have agreed to use radio control and electronic equipment to boost takings. There are no plans for a similar scheme outside London at the moment but transport chiefs are interested.

PRIORITY FOR THE WRONG WAY BUS

An experiment giving priority to buses in many major cities is to be tried by the Ministry of Transport. Private cars may be squeezed out of parts of some city centres as various new ideas are tried including:

- reserved bus lanes, running with or even against the traffic
- selected roads closed to cars and designated buses only
- priority lanes for buses at traffic lights and junctions
- special mini-bus services for city centres.

SCRAP THE LOT!

Tory peer Lord Somers speaking in the House of Lords on progress he would rather do without:

Concorde: 'A fine achievement but a complete waste of money.'
Decimalization: 'I haven't heard a good word for it.'
North Sea Gas: 'I shall most certainly go over to electricity or oil. I'm not going to run the risk of having my house blown up.'
All-figure phone numbers: 'One can remember names, but to remember numbers is absolutely beyond my reach.'
Metrication: 'The last straw. To be logical the Government should introduce a 10-month year, a 20-hour day and a 10-day week.'

TV TOP 10, 4 APRIL

1. *Coronation Street* (Mon and Wed)
3. *The Dustbinmen, This Is Your Life*
5. *Steptoe and Son*
6. *On the Buses*
7. *World In Action*
8. *Crime of Passion*
9. *David Nixon's Magic Box*
10. *Manhunt*

GIRLS WHO ARE JILTED CAN KEEP THE RING

The House of Commons decided yesterday that engagement rings should no longer be recoverable by law when lovers split up. This reverses a 1917 Court decision that engagement rings are not the girl's property until marriage. MPs accepted an amendment to the Law Reform Bill which also scraps Breach of Promise and damages for adultery.

THE SUPER SURGERY

A revolution in dentistry will help take away the fear of the chair and make life more comfortable – and longer – for the dentist. In the surgery of the 1970s you will hardly know you are at the dentist's: drills will be tucked away; aircraft-type reclining seats will electronically put the patient into the best position; instead of hovering over you the dentist will sit behind as you lie stretched out and the drill will make only a soft whistling noise. From the dentist's point of view the awkward postures which have given such severe problems will be a thing of the past. The problem is that at £5,000 to equip such a surgery few dentists can afford to make the changes.

Richard Attenborough's son Michael announces his engagement to 19-year-old Joyce Frankenberg whom he met when she was a member of the chorus of Oh, What A Lovely War. *Joyce's stage name is Jane Seymour.*

A FAMILY AT WAR

'Watching the first episode. . . was like being shut in a carriage full of dull talkative strangers in a train that for some reason has stopped just outside the station it just left.'

ENTER THE HIGH-SPEED GAS TAXI

The days of the noisy, smelly London taxi may be numbered. Quieter, sweeter-smelling cabs could take their place if an experiment by a London firm is successful. One company is already running 3 cabs on propane – liquid petroleum gas – which is not only cleaner and quieter but adds 50% to engine life and at 3/6 per gallon compares very favourably with an ordinary fuel price of up to 6/5. The drawbacks to the new kind of vehicle are the extra 100lb weight from the fuel tanks required and the lack of outlets stocking LPG, causing a refuelling problem.

FUMES LAW WILL MEAN DEARER CARS

New regulations to cut car exhaust fumes are being considered by the Ministry of Transport. MPs were told that the aim was to reduce air pollution by curbing carbon monoxide, hydrocarbon and nitrogen oxides pumped into the atmosphere – but this could only be achieved by adding equipment which could put £30 onto the price of the car. Because of the cost involved British manufacturers are unlikely to make modifications until it becomes a legal requirement.

NEW-LOOK ZEBRAS TO CUT CRASHES

Tough new measures to make zebra crossings safer are planned by the Ministry of Transport. The area around the crossing will be forbidden territory for both pedestrians and motorists. New 'matchstick puzzle' markings 20 yards each side of the crossings will forbid vehicles from stopping or overtaking, while pedestrians must walk on the zebra itself and not cut corners.

Paul McCartney – no future plans to appear or record with the Beatles. Their new album, Let It Be, *is due for release shortly.*

POSTMEN PRESS TO END DARK MORNINGS

The Government is being urged to scrap the British Standard Time and make mornings lighter. A report says that accidents to postmen on the morning round have doubled since BST began. Tom Jackson, Secretary of the Post Office Workers Union said: 'We hope the TUC will put pressure on the Government to drop BST once and for all.' Milkmen and builders, particularly in the north of Scotland, would also be happy to sacrifice lighter evenings for lighter mornings. The 3-year experiment with BST is not due to end until October, though Home Secretary, James Callaghan is expected to announce before then whether it will stay or whether GMT will return for the winter months.

DAY BY DAY

3 Apr
Donald Healey, 72, designer of Austin-Healey sports cars, is to take over as boss the Jensen car firm, makers of the £5,800 Interceptor.

4 Apr
Gay Trip wins the Grand National.

10 Apr
Prime Minister Ian Smith's Rhodesian Front Party wins overwhelming victory in the first general election since UDI.

17 Apr
Reverend Ian Paisley wins a Stormont seat in the Bannside by-election.

21 Apr
Black Power rebels riot in Trinidad, accusing the Government of being a puppet of British and US.

22 Apr
The campaign to fix jail terms for murderers reacts strongly to figures showing some killers released in the past 10 years served only 8 or 9 years of their life sentences.

27 Apr
The Ocean Viking oil rig makes the first promising oil strike in the North Sea.

29 Apr
Chelsea win the FA Cup, beating Leed 2–1 in a replay.

PARCELS ARE THE WEAPONS IN JUNGLE WAR

A confidential report accuses the 4 state-owned parcel delivery businesses of wasting taxpayers' money by fighting each other for custom instead of integrating to improve the service. Vehicles from the 4 companies – National Freight Corporation's British Road Services Parcels and National Carriers, British Rail's Express Parcels Service and the Post Office – cover the same ground and even call on the same customers each day. The next Government, either Tory or Labour, is expected to streamline the operation or even decentralise it if a private buyer can be found.

SIMON, 15, SIGNS UP A 60–PIECE ORCHESTRA

Schoolboy Simon Rattle got the go-ahead from a charity to put on a fund-raising musical evening. Officials were thinking in terms of a small concert but 5 weeks later Simon turned up with a 60–piece symphony orchestra. Simon will himself conduct at next month's concert at Liverpool College, Sefton Park where he is a sixth former. 'Once I started it just snowballed,' said Simon, who is also a tympanist in the National Youth Orchestra. Top musicians are appearing free and it is hoped ticket sales at 4/- each will raise £100 for Liverpool Spastic Fellowship.

MAY 1970

DOWN GOES ROOTES

The name Rootes is to disappear from British motoring after 53 years. From July the Rootes Group will be called Chrysler (UK) Ltd after its US parent company. In spite of the successful launch of the Avenger, the company has sustained large trading losses recently.

Rival to the Avenger – and a close relative – is the Simca 1100. Both come from firms in the giant Chrysler Group but they could not be more unlike. Whereas the Avenger is conventional and almost old-fashioned in its mechanical layout (front engine, rear-wheel drive) the Simca typifies the new breed of 5-door saloons – along with the Austin Maxi and the Renault 16 – having front-wheel drive and a rear tailgate.

£7.5m CHANNEL FERRY PLAN

British Rail has announced it will build Kent's second cross-channel car-ferry terminal at Folkestone. The buildings will cost £1m while £6.5m will be spent on two new ferries which will operate from Folkestone to Boulogne and Calais. The service should be open in 1972.

STARS EVICTED FROM *CORONATION STREET*

New life is to be injected into *Coronation Street* while several of the regulars are to disappear. It began last week when Dickie Fleming (Nigel Humphreys) packed his bags and left his young wife Audrey (Gillian McCann). She walked out of the series last night during Lucille Hewitt's twenty-first birthday party. Policeman Cyril Turpin (Bill Moore) is to leave the show, too, as are three other as yet unnamed members of the cast.

HERE'S SOMETHING TO SLEEP ON . . .

Should a newly wed, working housewife spend time making beds in the morning? Or any housewife for that matter? The answer could be to sleep under a Slumberdown – a light and warm Continental-style quilt filed with down which needs no blankets to support it. The makers say that it follows the contours of the body during the night, holding in natural body heat, and in the morning you simply pat it down.

PRINCE ATTACKS ROBOT 'SIR'

Prince Charles joked about technological advance in a speech to the Cambridge Union. He said it could reduce humans to 'what one can only call awe-struck serfdom,' and the stage could be reached where schoolboys would call their computers 'Sir'. The motion being debated was: This house believes that technological advance threatens the individuality of Man and is becoming his master.

Shorts replace the mini.

TOP OF THE WORLD BUT STILL ON TRIAL

A reputation as the world's best pop guitarist is rather like being known as the fastest gun in the West, says Eric Clapton. 'There's always this chap round the corner who reckons he's a bit better.' The 25-year-old, whose music has received standing ovations rather than screams, says he has often been conned into a studio merely to prove himself. Since the supergroups Cream and Blind Faith – with whom he became a cult – disbanded he has been playing intermittently with John Lennon and Yoko Ono and Delaney and Bonnie, but he has plans to form his own group. 'I shall have to start working regularly again soon; I need the bread,' he says.

THE SWEET SELL

The idea of telephone sales has proved successful in the USA. People, it seems, find it just as hard to slam down a phone as they do to slam a door in a salesman's face. The idea has now spread to Britain. In the past 4 weeks, for example, 3,000 London women have been called and offered the *Good Housekeeping Cookery Book* for 6/11.

SCHOOL CHIEF WARNS ON VIOLENCE IN CLASS

One of the country's leading educationists, Sir Alec Clegg, says that US-style violence may come to British schools unless our system stops treating slow learners as no-hopers. He said that the national attitude was to 'suffer little children with an IQ of 120+ to receive the best secondary education for they shall add most to the GNP.' Trouble could flare as slow learners resent a system which is failing them and the situation could become dangerously ugly in some schools after the planned raising of the school-leaving age.

Conservative Leader, Edward Heath shows off his party's manifesto in preparation for next month's general election.

American troops in action as the US makes its first incursions into Cambodia.

£3,400m TO END TRAFFIC JAMS

Transport Minister Mr Fred Mulley has put forward the most ambitious national road plan ever – 6,000 miles of new roads by the end of the 1980s. The scheme would link every sizeable town through a network of motorways and dual carriageways, thereby, he promises, ending traffic jams and frustration on inter-urban routes. The plan would double the capacity of the trunk-road system over a period in which traffic is expected to increase by 70%.

THEY CALL HIM PAPILLON

Papillon arrives tomorrow. Never heard of him? You will. He is 63, a murderer and the most explosive force to hit the literary world since Hemingway. His name is Henri Charrière – called Papillon, the Butterfly, because of the tattoo on his throat and his light-fingered touch on other people's safes. His luck ran out at the age of 25 when he was found guilty of murder and sentenced to life in the penal colonies. 13 years and 9 escape attempts later he finally got away from Devil's Island by drifting to the mainland on coconut-filled sacks. A film is to be made of his story with either Warren Beatty or Alain Delon playing him. The book is published here next week.

DAY BY DAY

4 May
Charles Forte's hotel and catering group is to merge with Trust House. The new group – Trust House Forte – will be one of the largest of its kind in the world.

Back Home tops the charts as the England squad flies to Mexico.

5 May
4 students shot dead during demonstration against US action in Cambodia.

6 May
Russia and Czechoslovakia sign new 20-year treaty of friendship and mutual aid.

Labour MP William Owen cleared of charges.

8 May
Government announces £6m rescue package for shipbuilding and engineering firm Cammell Laird and has taken 50% stake of the company.

10 May
Bombs targeting Iberia Airlines explode at 3 European airports – a fourth at Heathrow is found, believed to be anti-Franco campaign.

12 May
Brian London announces his retirement from boxing after losing to Joe Bugner.

13 May
William Hill – failed engineering apprentice who became world's largest bookmaker – retires at 67.

17 May
Thor Heyerdahl sets out from Morocco in 8-ton papyrus boat *Ra 2*; his second attempt to prove Ancient Egyptians crossed the Atlantic and discovered America.

22 May
Springbok tour called off.

28 May
Bobby Moore given provisional release and flies to Mexico.

29 May
Grand Metropolitan announces plans to purchase Berni Inn restaurant and hotel group.

BEATLEMANIA AGAIN

It's a long time since Beatlemania brought London to a halt but it happened again last night – without their going near the place. There were battles with police as 7,000 fans gathered outside the Pavilion cinema for the première of their new film *Let It Be*. It is possibly the last time people will see the group playing together; none of them turned up for last night's gala event. The *Let It Be* album has sold 4 million copies in the USA in advance of its release, making it already the biggest seller in the history of the American record industry.

MUSICIANS ACCLAIMED

25-year-old Tony Macauley was named British Songwriter of the Year by the Songwriters' Guild of Great Britain last night. His hits include 'Love Grows' and 'Build Me Up, Buttercup'. Tom Jones was named International Artist of the Year and an award for outstanding services to British music was made to Sir Noël Coward.

CAR CHIEF FORECASTS 3-WHEEL FUTURE

The Reliant motor group is to launch a series of 3-wheeler cars in the early 1970s, confident that they will become the trend-setting 'Minis' of the future. Speaking at a time which has seen a growth rate in 3-wheelers treble that of their 4-wheel counterparts during the past 10 years, Mr Ray Wiggin, Reliant's Managing Director, says, 'We are not alone in believing that the 3-wheeler is going to become an increasingly popular substitute for both the car and the motor-cycle. General Motors in the US is developing a 3-wheeler as a commuter car and clearly considers this type of vehicle has an important role to play in the 1970s.'

Next month sees the launch of the Bond Bug, a tangerine-coloured 3-wheeler which Reliant hopes will appeal to the young as a fun car, the housewife as a shopping car, and the rest of us as a city car. Prices will range from £548 – £629.

Skinhead girls 'moon stomping' at Epping Public Hall.

BOBBY MOORE HELD ON JEWEL CHARGE

England's World Cup Captain Bobby Moore has been arrested in Bogotá accused of stealing a £600 gold and emerald bracelet from a local jeweller's shop. He has been ordered not to leave Bogotá while he awaits appearance before a magistrate. The rest of the England squad has already left for Mexico.

WHO'S NEW?

New entries in the latest edition of *Who's Who* out today include:
Ken Dodd
Bernadette Devlin
Lester Piggott
Judi Dench
Sir Robert McAlpine
Joe Haines – the PM's Press Secretary

JUNE 1970

BAN ON FALSIES FOR GIRL RUNNERS

The advantage that girl runners wearing falsies have as they breast the finishing tape has been spotted. At the AAA championships this weekend Association Secretary Marea Hartman will be in the dressing room to ensure this kind of front running is stopped. 'We think it is high time that built-in curves are ruled out of international women's racing,' says Miss Hartman, who would like the ban to be extended to the Olympic Games.

This is the craze which has swept America; now the same thing is about to happen in Britain. The bicycle, called the Chopper, is made by Raleigh and costs £32.

3 GALLONS FOR 7/6

A gas revolution is about to hit the motoring world. A new type of fuel that will replace petrol and sell for a fraction of the price has not only been developed but is starting to appear on forecourts. Motorgas is liquidized petroleum gas (LPG), commonly called propane. It costs £135 to convert a vehicle, regardless of the model. The other drawback is that the only garage so far selling LPG is in Hemel Hempstead – though this will be overcome as outlets develop nationwide.

On the dashboard of the converted car is a switch which will change you over to petrol – at 6/5 a gallon – till you can replenish your gas tank. Another benefit for a society becoming increasingly aware of pollution is that exhaust gases from LPG are almost totally free from carbon monoxide. The idea is not new. Gas-driven vehicles were used in the war when petrol was in short supply and have been in general use on the continent for more than 10 years.

HEATH IN

Edward Heath after winning the General Election.

YARD TRAINS PLANE-BOMB SNIFFERS

British scientists and detectives are training dogs to sniff out bombs on board aircraft. They hope this may be the answer to the menace which has terrorized the airways in the past 18 months. If tests continue to go well it may become routine for dogs to give planes and passengers the once-over before take-off.

MRS THATCHER GOES BACK TO THE NURSERY SCHOOL

The new head of Britain's £2,000m state-education system may look the part of the successful middle-class wife – elegantly tall, evidently the woman men gravitate towards at a party – but 44-year-old Margaret Thatcher takes an almost demonic pride in showing how toughly determined she can be. And the first thing she will tell civil servants in her new ministry is to file away Labour's plans for comprehensive schools. Her own background has taught her the importance of a good educational foundation so she says that primary and nursery schools will be of far greater importance in her policy than any reform of the secondary sector.

FAREWELL ENGLAND!

Broken-hearted football fanatic Bill Curtis who threatened to emigrate if England lost the World Cup says he and his wife will be leaving their home in Denham, Bucks and going to live in Pakistan.

EYES DOWN FOR THE LAST £20,000

Saturday 27 June will be a night to remember. The last ever big money bingo game – with a top prize worth £20,000 – will take place at 8 p.m. when 54 Top Rank clubs throughout the country are linked. After that date prizes will be limited to £1,000 by government order. A spokesman for Top Rank said he did not anticipate a decline in demand when the big jackpots became a thing of the past. 'It is too much a part of people's lives now; people will still be able to win an average prize of anything between £300 and £600 any evening for an outlay of, say, 15/- to 17/6.'

SHOULD A MAN WATCH HIS BABY BEING BORN?

After going through 9 months of wondering about it, waiting for it, to be left out in the corridor when a baby is born must feel like being cheated out of a prize. This is why Dec Cluskey of the Bachelors was present at the birth of his daughter. Dec's brother Con takes the opposite view. 'You think of a woman – especially your wife – as someone elegant and lovely. To see her strapped up there in the most inelegant position of all must be horribly embarrassing for her.'

Con's wife Kay agrees. 'It must be revolting for a man to watch. I never realized how ugly a woman looks in labour.'

SIGN OF THE TIMES

The 5/- Champion sparking plug which has kept its price for more than 40 years is to go up to 6/- next week because of increased production costs.

Triumph launches a new businessman's GT express – a 120-m.p.h. car called the Stag. Priced from £1,996 it should have a wide enough appeal to embarrass Triumph who are not planning to produce the car in great quantity.

NOW BANKS MAY END LATE-NIGHT OPENING

Late opening one day a week at banks is now almost certain to be abandoned except in a limited number of branches – and whether even these will continue the 4.30 – 6.00 p.m. service is doubtful. The late shift – Thursday in most places – was introduced last year as banks yielded to union pressure to close on Saturdays.

BUT WILL IT BE A HIT?

Mr Nigel Lawson, Editor of the *Spectator* and Tory candidate for Eton and Slough is enlivening his election campaign with slogans set to music. He writes the words himself and his wife Vanessa sings them to words borrowed from John Wells's stage production of *Mrs Wilson's Diary*. Mr Lawson is diffident about his compositions. 'They sound a little banal without the music,' he says of efforts such as 'Eton and Slough, Eton and Slough, we want Nigel and we want him now.'

Tony Jacklin, 25-year-old former fitter from Scunthorpe, becomes the first Englishman for 50 years to win the US Open. In taking the title and £12,500 prize, the British Open Champion is only the third person in history to lead throughout the 72 holes.

BRITAIN MAKES OIL BONANZA GAMBLE

Licence concessions to 24 companies to drill another 8,000 square miles of ocean, mostly off Scotland, were announced by Paymaster General Mr Harold Lever yesterday. He said that if the Phillips petroleum company's claim to have found a 'giant' field off Norway was justified, oil finds could be expected nearer home. He said, 'It is as if the British people were given a free ticket in a lottery; the prize might be £2,000m or it might be nothing.'

Mike Pratt, Annette Andre and Kenneth Cope from the new detective series Randall & Hopkirk (deceased). It is a story about a detective agency in which one of the partners is a ghost.

ASCOT GIVES IN TO TROUSER-SUITS

At last trouser-suits are to be allowed in the Royal Enclosure at Ascot. The decision to lift the ban comes a week before this year's meeting and follows a 4-year battle between race-goers and officials. Denying that the new ruling has been influenced by Princess Anne's wearing trouser-suits on official occasions, an official said that until recently such outfits were considered too informal. Trouser-suits are still banned in the Stewards' Enclosure at Henley.

HERE, HAVE A SUNTAN PILL

Whatever else befell them, the scorching sun didn't beat the England team. They took a new pill which could mean more comfortable holidays for sun-seekers. Silva-sun costs 5d. per tablet and 2 a day give protection – though it doesn't mean you can lie out for hours on day one. Makers Intec claim that their product, which will be undergoing more tests this summer, also overcomes the lethargy felt when lying in the sun and can be used to treat sunburn.

PROCTER DEFIED BY TRIAL BOY

David Bairstow, an 18-year-old student playing his first innings in a 4-match Yorkshire trial, survived a gruelling test by South African star Mike Procter yesterday. Gloucestershire had Yorkshire struggling at 12 for 5 when wicketkeeper Bairstow came in. He scored 15 runs in 30 minutes and earned credit for his courage in attacking Procter's pace. 'This chap was a bit faster than anyone I've faced,' said Bairstow. But Procter had the final word, taking Bairstow's wicket and giving him 6 for 38.

ARKLE THE BRAVE IS PUT DOWN

The bravest and greatest steeplechaser of all time died yesterday. The Duchess of Windsor – Arkle's owner – was advised to have the horse put down after he failed to respond to treatment for arthritic lesions. The 13-year-old won 27 races including 3 Cheltenham Gold Cups and amassed £75,000 in prize money. Pat Taaffe, the Irish jockey who rode Arkle to most of his victories, said, 'It's just like losing an old friend.'

12 MINUTES TO GO . . . AND MULLER SCORES THE KILLER GOAL

Gerd Muller heads the winning goal to make it 3-2 and England are out of the world cup.

DAY BY DAY

4 June
Nijinsky wins the Derby.

16 June
The radio comedy *Stop Messing About* starring Kenneth Williams, Hugh Paddick and Joan Simms is sold to 20 countries by the BBC.

23 June
Foreign Secretary Sir Alec Douglas-Home scraps the embargo on arms sales to South Africa imposed by the Labour Government.

24 June
Mr Christopher Chataway is appointed as Minister of Posts and Telecommunications with a brief including the introduction of commercial radio stations.

25 June
US car giant General Motors offers £10m to German Audi–NSU group for a stake in the revolutionary Wankel engine.

26 June
Violence flares in Londonderry over the jailing of Bernadette Devlin, 23-year-old MP for Mid-Ulster.

29 June
Mrs Caroline Thorpe, wife of the Liberal leader, is killed in a car accident.

BEAUTY CIRCUS HITS END OF LINE

It is the end of the road for the professional beauty queens – girls who travel the swimsuit circuit of seaside parades. Mecca has announced that this year's Miss UK contestants must live within 10 miles of where the heat takes place and cannot use assumed names.

JULY 1970

100,000 CHEER THE *GREAT BRITAIN*

The rusty hulk of the world's first iron ship was towed home to Bristol yesterday 127 years after her launch. About 100,000 people lined 9 miles of the River Avon to greet Brunel's *Great Britain*, which arrived in the country last month. A property tycoon paid £150,000 to bring her 9,000 miles from the Falkland Islands where she was written off in 1886.

Mr Iain Macleod, Chancellor of the Exchequer, dies suddenly aged 56.

STUDENT LOANS URGED

Government loans to students repayable later on a means-test basis were suggested last night by Lord Robbins. He said in the House of Lords that students would only be expected to repay if they earned high incomes later in life, thus removing criticism that the loan would hang 'like an albatross' round the necks of the unsuccessful.

LOVERS' NOTE

The new £20-note is out tomorrow with a message for young lovers: on the back is the balcony scene from Romeo and Juliet. There is also a reproduction of the statue of Shakespeare in Westminster Abbey. The purple note, which is believed to be forgery-proof, will be the first '20' issue since 1945; there are still thought to be more than 7,000 of the old white £20 notes in circulation.

Laces and thongs are the fashion for the summer.

SCRAMBLE IS ON TO BUY COUNCIL HOUSES

Local authorities are being swamped with applications from council tenants who want to buy their homes. The rush follows a government decision 2 weeks ago to lift restrictions on council-house sales.

FROM THE BOND FILM MAKER . . . A NEW GROUP

'This is the face of Toomorrow.' No, that's not a misprint. Toomorrow is the name of a new pop group created by Harry Saltzman, producer of the Bond films, and Don Kirschner, the man behind the Monkees and the Archies. It has cost well over £1m to launch the group, £15,000 being spent to secure Olivia Newton-John as lead singer – to buy out her existing contract and pay off the girl who had originally been signed. The group's first record is released next Friday.

WHEN YOU JOIN THE LAGER SET, WATCH OUT

It is expected that we will swallow 640 million pints of lager this year. It is the boom drink, with sales rising at 30% per year. It is also the least predictably priced booze in Britain. The cost ranges from a brewery-recommended, public-bar draught price of 2/6 a pint – where you can find it in a public bar, that is – to almost 10/-, for outside the public bar the licensee can charge what he likes.

QUICK TRAIN TO PARIS

A Channel tunnel could cut the London–Paris train time from around 8 to 2 hours 45 minutes, French rail experts predict. A report says that no new capital investment would be needed in Britain for an hourly service, though a new line would have to be built in France.

PENGUIN'S SIR ALLEN DIES

Sir Allen Lane, founder of Penguin Books, died last night aged 67. He was the brains behind Britain's biggest and most successful publishing gamble. The man who said he wanted to give the man in the street books which would have been read at university launched the famous symbol 34 years ago on capital of £100. He became a millionaire 9 years ago when Penguin went public on the Stock Market.

Edward Heath with two of the members of his new cabinet – Margaret Thatcher and Quintin Hogg.

SUPERTOWN'S PLAN FOR EXTRA POPULATION

An extra 5 million people threaten to swamp south-east England by the year 2001. To cope with this influx 5 vast new areas may be created if the Government approves a planner's report published yesterday. With the idea of keeping the countryside from disappearing under an urban sprawl, these areas would be employment centres large enough to act as counter-magnets to working in London. The 30-year plan, drawn up by the South-East Joint Planning Study set up by the Government in 1968, forecasts an age of prosperity for the majority, with people working a 4-day week. However, the gap between rich and poor will be wider than it is now, and it appears there will be little room left to enjoy what prosperity there is. The five big growth areas highlighted in the report are: South Hampshire; Milton Keynes; Northampton; Wellingborough; Reading; Wokingham; Aldershot; Basingstoke; South Essex; and the Crawley, Sussex area.

'IMMIGRANTS WILL BECOME SERFS' – CALLAGHAN

Home Secretary Reginald Maudling told the House of Commons yesterday of further drastic restrictions on Commonwealth immigrants under a new bill. Immigrants will be limited to a 12-month stay initially and will have to obtain a work permit for a particular job in a particular place. Permits will only be issued where local labour is not readily available. Former Home Secretary James Callaghan attacked the bill, saying that it would give immigrants the status of serfs – afraid to leave a job for fear of deportation.

Elliott Gould, Tom Skerritt and Donald Sutherland in the film M*A*S*H.

ULSTER TROOPS MAY USE RUBBER BULLETS

Heavy rubber bullets to knock rioters off their feet are ready for use by the army in Ulster. The 6-inch projectiles are fired from CS riot gas-guns and fly at ground level in an unpredictable snaking pattern, which is why they are sometimes known as ankle-smashers.

VIDEO DISCS IN SHOPS SOON

Gramophone records which can play pictures onto TV screens will be on sale within 18 months. The video discs will be played on a special £50 record-player linked to the aerial socket of ordinary TVs. Makers British Decca Co. and Telefunken of Germany claim that video discs will be much cheaper than the TV tapes which rival companies plan to market in cassette form in the next few years.

KENNY EVERETT IS SACKED

Kenny Everett was sacked last night by the BBC for a joke told on his Radio 1 show on Saturday. He said that Transport Minister John Peyton's wife Mary had passed her Advanced Driving Test 'only because she slipped a fiver' to the examiner.

DJ Noel Edmonds, 21, a former student teacher, has been picked by the BBC to take over from Kenny Everett. The new show, from 10 a.m. – midday starts this Saturday.

PLASTIC LITTER WILL END UP IN THIN AIR

A team of British scientists believes it has solved one of the world's most difficult pollution problems – the disposal of plastic. It has produced a dye which will make throw-away plastic containers turn to dust when they are exposed to sunlight.

COMPOSER MEETS *KOMMANDANT*

Actor Werner Klemperer is in town to see his father, Otto, the 85-year-old musician. A good example of the divergent talents of father and son can be seen this week when Klemperer Senior will be conducting Beethoven symphonies on BBC 2 while Klemperer Junior will be back in Hollywood to record another episode of the show for which he is best known, *Hogan's Heroes*, in which he plays Klink, the comic POW-camp *Kommandant*.

HARVEY'S SUPER MINI

When Actor Laurence Harvey arrives in his chauffeur-driven Rolls-Royce to see how his new Mini is coming along, you might think the car is something out of the ordinary. You would be right. He could have got his Mini Cooper S on the road for £1,000; instead he is paying £3,500 to have it converted with features such as:
– a 1325cc engine instead of the usual Cooper S 1275cc.
– tailor-made hide individual seats.
– 8-track stereo tape-player.
– twin-speaker radio.
– polished wood and leather dashboard including clock, vacuum gauge, battery-condition gauge, tachometer, oil water and petrol gauges.
– cigarette lighter.
– electric windows.
– sun roof.
– underseal.
– safety belts.
– wheel trims.
– initials in gold on the doors.

Skinheads and their 'mollies' on the promenade at Brighton.

AUG 1970

BEE GEES GET TOGETHER AGAIN

The Bee Gees pop group, which split up last year, has decided to re-form. The group, which was in the £1m-a-year bracket, consists of Barry, 24, and twins Maurice and Robin, 20. Maurice is pop singer Lulu's husband. Robin started the break-up when he went solo 17 months ago.

PLEASE GIVE DORIS ANOTHER NAME

Parents are being warned by a psychologist not to call their daughter Doris. The reason? People will probably dislike her before they even meet her. Psychologist Dr Joseph Mallory-Wober from Bristol University is investigating the link between names and personality. The results of a survey in which he questioned a number of girls about the characteristics they associated with various names show that most girls thought Dorises gossipy, fat and dim. Other findings put Elizabeths and Rachels as likeable, attractive and intelligent, whereas Amandas were attractive but upper class. The survey also seems to indicate that people tend to grow into the personalities associated with their names and the doctor suggests that people needing help to change their personality should consider changing their name.

LEYLAND QUITS MOTOR SPORT

British Leyland is pulling out of motor sport. The decision, announced yesterday, robs rallying of one of the strongest factory organizations. The firm wants to channel its skill and energy into its new model programme, leaving drivers like Paddy Hopkirk to find new backers.

D-DAY BLAMED FOR FARES INCREASE

London Transport is the first major organization to announce price increases directly because of next year's decimalization. The cost of a child's half fare on a shilling journey is going up to 7d. because this is the nearest amount capable of conversion on D-Day, when the fare will be 3 new pence – equal to 7.2d.

CALL FOR 'LITTLE MAN'S' CLAIMS

A small claims court should be built into the British legal system, according to a report by the Consumer Council entitled *Justice Out of Reach*. It should be a 'genuine people's court' covering most of the law of contract and a maximum claim of £100 where settlement is made without legal representation.

Hippies swarm in their thousands onto Devastation Hill to get an illegal free view of the Isle of Wight pop festival.

POWDER HELPS TV MEN TO FACE THE NEWS

ITN newscasters Reginald Bosanquet and Sandy Gall are wearing make-up in front of the cameras for the first time. They say they've been working too hard and would look haggard without it. Extra duty started when Diplomatic Correspondent Peter Snow was assigned to the Middle East; Leonard Parkin and Andrew Gardner were already on holiday. 'We decided to ask for make-up after my 12-year-old daughter said how awful I looked,' Mr Bosanquet said last night.

BAN THE 'BOVVER-BOYS' PLEA TO CLUBS

Home Secretary Reginald Maudling told football clubs yesterday to be tougher with troublemakers and bar them from matches, also hinting that magistrates may impose stiffer penalties. FIFA President Sir Stanley Rous has suggested a ban on coloured scarves and rosettes, saying that they 'can easily be identified and can have an inflammatory effect'. A Magistrates' Association official said it had proposed daywork centres where hooligans would have to report and work all day.

PENSIONER BRENNAN

Manchester United full-back Shay Brennan was thinking over a move to Shrewsbury yesterday with the security of a life pension behind him. Brennan, 32, will receive £15 a week in 3 years' time through an annuity bought for him by the club. This long-service reward is the first of its kind in football.

YOUNG SPUR SAYS, 'I QUIT'.

While the Spurs team was playing in Majorca, one of their brightest prospects, 17-year-old Scot Graeme Souness, walked out on the club. Souness, star of the Spurs FA Youth Cup Final team, went home to Edinburgh declaring he would not return because he was being given neither enough chances nor enough money at Tottenham.

COMING UP! HATELEY'S £400,000 JACKPOT

Tony Hateley is about to complete a £400,000 wheel of fortune from which he has accumulated more than £20,000 in transfer percentages. Birmingham, his sixth League club, has listed him at £30,000 – the amount Notts County is prepared to pay to take him back to where he started. Hateley, 28, who has never asked for a transfer, claims he is worth every penny of the £375,000 for which his services have changed hands because the 5 top managers who bought him in effect said so. The moves Hateley has made and the managers who bought him are:

1963, Notts County to Aston Villa (Joe Mercer) – £25,000
1966, Aston Villa to Chelsea (Tommy Docherty) – £100,000
1967, Chelsea to Liverpool (Bill Shankly) – £96,000
1968, Liverpool to Coventry (Noel Cantwell) – £80,000
1969, Coventry to Birmingham (Stan Cullis) – £65,000

DRIVE SAFELY WITH A WHIFF OF OXYGEN, MOTORISTS TOLD

Motorists are being urged to add another item to their essential kit: oxygen. The idea is that the tired driver takes a whiff every time he feels drowsy; a few gulps from the mini-mask and he is fresh to fight on through the exhausting fumes. A portable oxygen mask has been put on the market by the British Oxygen Company at £4.15s.0d., plus 25/- for 5 refill tanks. Pocket-sized oxygen dispensers are already common in air-polluted Tokyo – their police stay on duty only 10 minutes at a time before going off for a reviving sniff and our bobbies could be doing the same thing one day.

GO ON, HAVE THAT £1,200 GRANT

A 'salesman' may soon be knocking on your door and pressing you to take £1,200. The cash comes with the Government's compliments, but the money must be spent on modernizing your home. The 'salesmen' are Housing Minister Peter Walker's idea for bringing new life into the house-improvement grants scheme. He plans to set up teams at major centres throughout the country as more than 4 million older houses lacking up-to-date amenities could be modernized or converted into comfortable flats under the plan. It will be carried out under existing arrangements in which the Government splits the bill 50/50 with the householder.

MOTORWAY FENCES TO GO UP

Safety barriers are almost certain to be installed on Britain's motorway blackspots soon. Sections of the M1 – where several people have died recently in cross-over crashes – will be first to receive them, though police chiefs and motoring organizations hope that central reservation barriers will be put along the whole of the motorway network.

HAYNES CHOOSES DURBAN OVER WIMBLEDON

Johnny Haynes, England's first £100-a-week footballer, flies to South Africa today, ending a 20-year English soccer career. 36-year-old Haynes left Fulham at the end of last season and will be joining Durban City. He yesterday turned down an offer from Wimbledon that would have made him the highest paid non-league player.

THE BLITZ THAT SAVED A TV ARMY

'In these times of violence and horror this programme shone like a beacon to ease our troubled souls.' This Churchillian tribute was just one of the many the BBC received when it decided that *Dad's Army* was to end. But the good news for the 13.5 million viewers who have become addicts is that the programme has at least earned a reprieve and more episodes of the exploits of the wartime Home Guard will be made.

DAY BY DAY

3 Aug
Government decides that a 'second force' airline, formed by a merger between British Caledonian and British United Airways, should be established to compete with BOAC and BEA.

4 Aug
The Queen Mother celebrates her seventieth birthday.

9 Aug
17 policemen are injured in clashes with Black Power marchers in London protesting about police harassment.

18 Aug
The 'afterthought' Test series ends in a 4–1 victory for the Rest of the World.

27 Aug
Citroën launches the GS at £1,050 to bridge the gap between the Ami 8 and larger models.

31 Aug
The National Youth Theatre is to get its first permanent home after 14 years – the new Shaw Theatre in Euston Road, north-west London.

BEDFORD SHATTERS 10,000-METRE MEN

David Bedford, the brilliant 20-year-old who was almost lost to athletics through injury, came back at the White City last night to win the AAA 10,000 metres in a championship record time of 28 minutes 26.4 seconds.

POP STARS PASS THE NOISE TEST

Fears that the continuous din of pop music might do permanent damage to musicians' hearing have been allayed in a new survey. Some of the noisiest groups around, including Heavy Jelly, Mighty Baby, Brian Auger and the Trinity, Led Zeppelin, The Who, Van Der Graaf Generator and Stone The Crows were tested, and, though the musicians all suffered ringing in the ears after a session, it invariably cleared after half an hour or so.

GARY SOBERS, UNDERPAID GENIUS?

In 16 years Sobers's approximate earnings from cricket have been £40,000, an average of £2,000 per year between 1953 and 1968 and £6,000 a year since then. This compares with Tony Hateley's earnings from all sources of around £70,000 in 12 years.

Gary Sobers (Rest of the World captain) and Ray Illingworth (England captain) toss for the first innings.

SEPT 1970

SKYFLATS: CHILDREN SUFFER

Future generations of disturbed children are being created by housing young families in tall blocks of flats, according to a report by the NSPCC. Children become less loved by mothers who have them under their feet all day. They live isolated lives and suffer more illness. The author of the report, Mr Bill Stewart, said, 'In some cases families would have been better off if they had stayed in tenement slums.'

ON TO THE MILLION!

Sponsorship of the Football League Championship is available to the first £1m bid, and the League Cup could go to a backer for half that price. League President Len Shipman made it clear last night that these 2 of the 3 major competitions will soon be branded with commercial trade names. The League decision to experiment with sponsorship has brought in nearly £300,000 within a year from the Watney Cup, the Ford League, and the new Texaco Cup. The Football Association, however, remains entrenched against the idea of sponsorship and is a long way from cashing in on the FA Cup.

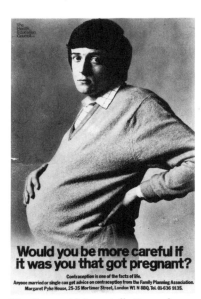

Would you be more careful if it was you that got pregnant?

Contraception is one of the facts of life.
Anyone married or single can get advice on contraception from the Family Planning Association.
Margaret Pyke House, 25-35 Mortimer Street, London W1 8BQ. Tel. 01-636 9135.

The Pregnant Man – 'effective and original' say the Health Education Council.

SINGER VAL GOES TO ITV FOR £1m

Singer Val Doonican has switched to ITV in a deal that could earn him nearly £1m. For the last 5 years he has had a regular series on the BBC; now he has signed exclusively with Sir Lew Grade's ATV to make at least 16 shows a year for the next 5 years.

RADIO LONDON WILL TURN ON TO NEWS

Radio London, biggest of the BBC's 'home town' stations, will be on the air from 6 October with 6 hours a day of local programmes. There will be 4 main news programmes: *Rush Hour* in the mornings, *Capital City* around midday, *Home Run* later in the afternoon and *Late Night London* just before close-down at around 11 p.m. Manager of Radio London Mr Peter Redhouse says, 'We will be primarily a talk station; when we are not putting our own programmes on the air then we will be taking the service from Radio 1 – things like *The Jimmy Young Show*.' Radio London is aimed at 8 million people living in the Greater London area, but only about half – those with VHF – will be able to pick up the programmes.

SEXY TIE MARKS THE HUNTER

There's a new way of telling what's on a man's mind – just look him straight in the tie. If it's 4 inches wide and covered in bright pink flowers, watch out: if you're female the wearer could be out to trap you; and if you're male you'd better hang on to your bird, for you've just come across a girlfriend prowler. A survey by the Tie Manufacturers' Association reveals that the tie is now an object of 'sexual significance'. The rule is simple: a man in a colourful tie is in a good mood and looking for fun; more conservative neckwear indicates a businesslike attitude. The under-30 age group said they deliberately chose the brightest tie possible when going to a party as a 'girl attracter'; 4 admitted to feeling jealous if they saw another man at a party in a brighter tie than their own.

BBC TO FACE RADIO BATTLE

8 commercial radio stations are expected by the end of the year under plans to be announced later this month by Mr Christopher Chataway, Minister of Post and Telecommunications. It is now clear that he wants commercial radio to be introduced as competition for local-run BBC stations.

JIMI HENDRIX IN DRUG-DEATH RIDDLE

Hendrix's own epitaph, written 2 years ago at the age of 22: 'When I die I want people to play my music, go wild and freak out and do anything they wanna do.'

SLIMMING GIRLS RUN UP FAT BILLS

Food bills for 5 girls watching their waistlines have shocked council officials. The girls, who all work and live as a family in a cottage hostel under Council care in Suffolk, get through £2.19s.4d.-worth of food each per week. Children's Officer Miss Peggy Armstrong explained, 'They are not keen to eat starchy food because of their figures – no young girls are – you have to tempt their appetites and give them plenty of vegetables and fruit and that's where the money mounts up.' The average weekly food bill for people living in a family is £2.5s.

WHY £10 GOES ON HOLIDAY BILL

A holiday company willing to charge only £39 for a 6-day trip to Athens must increase the price by £10 on government orders. This example of the burden on British holidaymakers was given by Dame Elizabeth Ackroyd, Director of the Consumer Council. The reason for the adjustment is that Britain has endorsed an International Air Travel Association ruling which states that tour operators cannot charge less for a package deal than the cost of a return scheduled flight.

RAISE TAX ON SWEETS, SAY DENTISTS

Dentists are to urge the Government to reverse the amount of purchase tax on sweets and toothpaste. This, they say, would more than pay for the whole of the National Health dental services. Toothpaste is taxed at 36.6% of the wholesale price compared with 22% for sweets. A British Dental Association official said, 'We think it ridiculous that the cause should be taxed less heavily than one of the cures.'

TV WATCH ON SOCCER THUGS

Closed-circuit TV to watch for soccer hooligans was moved into a 1st Division football match last night on the orders of Home Secretary Reginald Maudling. The spy camera was set up to keep an eye on the crowd at Derby's home game against Coventry. The system will be tested for a month at the Baseball Ground and, if successful, will be extended to other grounds.

BOOM WATCH FOR CONCORDE

Operation 'Boom Watch' stations along 500 miles of Britain's west coast are standing by for Concorde's first sonic boom. A noise typical of what the plane will produce in service will be heard today as chief test pilot Brian Trubshaw and his 6-man crew take Concorde 002 up to 1,100 m.p.h. at 40,000 feet.

EXTRA LAUGH SHOWS ON THE BBC

The accent will be on comedy this autumn on the BBC. Old favourites *Up Pompeii*, *Monty Python's Flying Circus* and *Dad's Army* will be returning, and Richard Waring, writer of *Not In Front of the Children*, has produced a new series, *Bachelor Father*, starring Ian Carmichael. Screen drama is also a mixture of old and new as *Softly Softly* and *Dr Finlay's Casebook* return for new series, while *Ryan International*, about a Paris-based lawyer, will be seen for the first time.

Hippies stream along Ryde Pier to the ferries after attending the Isle of Wight Music Festival.

DRIVERS LOSE ROAD-TAX LOOPHOLE

Thousands of motorists who drive while their application for a Road Fund Licence is in the post are breaking the law. Yesterday it became clear that they are now in danger of prosecution as a man was fined £1 with £2.2s. costs for driving an untaxed vehicle. Many people do drive with their documents in the post and the police often accept this, though they are not obliged to. A Ministry of Transport official said it was always an offence to drive an unlicensed vehicle; even the customary 14 days' grace when renewing tax was only discretionary.

LET'S OUTLAW THE CANE, SAY SCHOOL CHIEFS

Teachers in London schools are being urged to outlaw the use of the cane on young children and gradually phase out its use altogether. The first steps in the No Caning campaign were launched yesterday by ILEA, which employs 20,000 teachers.

EXPERTS PROBE A-PLANT LEAK

Scientists are trying to trace the cause of a radiation leak at Windscale Atomic Energy Plant. The leak, which has been described as small by one official, set off automatic alarms at the plant at Sellafield, Cumbria on 24 Aug. Work stopped immediately in a building used to recover plutonium from waste material. It was the fourth radiation leak in the plant's 14-year history.

BRITAIN IN 'SPACE SHUTTLE'

Concorde firm British Aircraft Corporation is to help design a revolutionary rocket-powered 'space plane'. BAC has joined with the US firm North American Rockwell to prepare a blueprint for a 'space shuttle' to be used by the US space agency. It would effectively run a 'taxi service' from ground to space.

TV BEANO FOR CHILDREN

The BBC is to spend £1m on more than 400 hours of children's TV programmes this year, the highest budget in the corporation's history. Old favourites which will be returning to the screen include *Watch With Mother*, *Magic Roundabout*, *Clangers*, *Tom Tom*, *Animal Magic*, *Jackanory* and *Vision On*.

NEW TRACTOR SAFETY RULES TO CUT DEATH TOLL

From today the Government expects to see a reduction in the number of fatal farm accidents. New regulations are being introduced to beat the biggest single killer on farms – overturning tractors, which claim 30–40 lives per year.

New tractors must now be fitted with a safety cab or frame to prevent drivers being crushed if one overturns. This regulation will apply to all tractors, old and new, within 7 years.

THE CAR THAT DIDN'T GO QUITE SO WELL ON SHELL

Teacher Terry Lickorish was so impressed by Shell's advert in which an Austin Mini Traveller does 55 m.p.g. on one gallon of Shell Economy that he switched to the petrol to see if he could match it. Unfortunately he ran dry 12 miles short of the target. Now Terry has written to Shell, Mex, BP and the RAC, who observed the test, to ask if they believe the advert to be a fair representation of a family afternoon drive. He claims it is not as it was carried out on a 4-mile circuit in the New Forest.

OCT 1970

BRITAIN GOES OVER TO TIE-BREAK TENNIS

Britain yesterday revealed its own version of the tie-breaker. The Lawn Tennis Association has decided that one ordinary game, with the serve alternating, should be played at 6–6 or 8–8 at the referee's discretion. This differs from the US system where the tie-breaker consists of 9 straight points.

The Magic Roundabout *enjoys continuing popularity with children and adults alike.*

ONCE-A-YEAR PILL WILL MAKE BIRTH CONTROL SAFER

A new type of birth-control pill containing only a hundredth of the present daily dose of hormones is being developed by scientists. The new pill, which would need to be taken only once a year, together with special 'morning after' drugs being developed, will revolutionize birth-control methods. By the late 1970s few women will be taking the pill as they know it today.

PLEDGED: CASH FOR DIRECT-GRANT PUPILS

Children whose local councils refuse to provide them with 'scholarship' places at direct-grant grammar schools are to have government help with fees. This radical move to safeguard the high-fliers was announced at the Tory Party Conference at Blackpool yesterday by Education Minister, Mrs Margaret Thatcher. The move is aimed at Labour-led ILEA, the one body which has so far announced its intention to cease aiding such children.

BOAC AND BEA TO BE MERGED

Britain's 2 state-owned airlines are to be merged to form a single giant nationalized corporation. The merger between BOAC and BEA will follow today's takeover by Caledonian Airways of British United Airways to form a second independent force to rival the new state airline.

MINX BECOMES HUNTER

The Sunbeam Vogue and the Hillman Minx disappear from the motoring scene today – but in name only. In its 1971 programme Chrysler has renamed all its middle-range cars Hunters. The name Minx has been a feature of the motoring scene for 39 years.

ICES AND CHIPS BRIGHTEN SCHOOL DINNERS

Chips and ice-cream are to replace mash and custard in some school canteens in an effort to lure back the thousands of children who prefer eating out to the 1/9 school dinner. The brighter menus will be available at selected secondary schools run by ILEA.

AD MEN QUEUE FOR *THE DALES* ON RADIO

Major advertising organizations want Britain's proposed commercial radio stations to bring back the old BBC serial *The Dales*; others are lining up for shows such as Hughie Green's *Opportunity Knocks* and Michael Miles's *Take Your Pick*. Advertisers have already put in bids to Hughie Green, the TV quizmaster who heads Commercial Broadcasting Consultants. Giving his company's plan for 115 local commercial radio stations Mr Green said that although the stations would not be on the air for at least 18 months, advertisers were already asking if they could be patrons to certain programmes. Under such patronage advertisers would agree to 'buy' the programme, but would have no editorial control and advertising would be restricted to 2 minutes in a 30-minute programme.

HEATH CHOOSES DYNAMIC DUO

2 new Tory ministers emerged yesterday with vast powers over the way we work and live when Mr Heath sent his promised wind of change whistling through Whitehall. Mr Peter Walker, 38, will head the new Ministry of the Environment which has been formed from the former Housing, Transport and Buildings and Works Departments. Mr John Davies, former Chief Executive of Shell, will be in charge of the new Trade and Industry Ministry, a combination of the old Department of Technology, Board of Trade and part of the Department of Employment and Productivity. The shake-up heralds the start of Mr Heath's intention to achieve less government and fewer civil servants.

Mrs Margaret Thatcher dancing with Roger Mountford of the LSE at the Conservative Party Conference in Blackpool.

SMOKING: SHOCK FIGURES

Smoking is killing 100,000 people a year in Britain, an estimated increase of 25,000 according to government statistics. Sir George Godber, Chief Medical Officer of the Department of Health, condemning the figures, said, 'This is no harmless indulgence but the biggest single avoidable menace to health in contemporary life.' A Royal College of Physicians report calls for a range of measures aimed at curbing the effects of smoking, including:
- warnings on cigarette packets, including tar and nicotine content.
- restrictions on tobacco advertising and promotion.
- differential taxation, with heavier taxes on the more harmful cigarettes.
- more advantageous life-insurance packages for non-smokers.
- a ban on smoking in public places such as cinemas, trains, buses and possibly restaurants.

These 2 reports herald the hardest-hitting attack yet on smoking; the first moves could be the banning of cigarette coupons and advertising in newspapers and magazines.

GOVERNMENT MOVE LEAVES WILSON IN COLD

Chancellor Anthony Barber yesterday announced a package of financial measures, most of which will come into effect in April of next year.
- income tax cut by 6d., down from 8/3 to 7/9.
- prescription charges to go up from 2/6 to 4/-.
- school meals to go up from 1/9 to 2/5.
- free admission to museums and art galleries to end.
- dental treatment to go up so that about half the cost is paid for.
- young people to pay dental charges at 18 instead of 21.
- passports to go up from £2 to £5.
- subsidized milk no longer available.
- free school milk for all primary-school children over the age of 7 to be scrapped from the beginning of the autumn term next year.

The Government also plans to scrap the Consumer Council, at a saving of £240,000 per year. This means that Britain's best-known charity campaigner, Mr Des Wilson, has lost his job before even starting. He was to have left the housing charity Shelter in February to take over as Director of the Consumer Council. Mr Wilson said, 'Naturally I'm disappointed but I am much more concerned about the loss to the nation of such a valuable watchdog . . . ' A successor for Mr Wilson's Shelter job has already been found.

2 a.m.: GUARDS CLEAR RUBBISH

Home Secretary Reginald Maudling ordered troops into London's rubbish-strewn East End early today to clear tons of rotting food. The decision came after the 4-week 'dirty jobs' strike reached crisis point in the London borough of Tower Hamlets. It is the first time since 1955 that troops have been used in an industrial dispute, though they are only removing rubbish which constitutes a health hazard.

Oz men go to court – prosecution alleges the magazine is likely to deprave and corrupt.

COLOUR TV TAKES OFF

Whatever the Chancellor does in his public-expenditure review, makers of colour TV sets are laughing. They are selling all they can produce, despite the 42 weeks' advance rental required and the £60 purchase tax on a 22-inch set costing £280. Colour TV has certainly caught on more quickly than anyone expected; 3 out of 4 homes with the 600,000 colour sets rent them.

HEATH ACTS OVER HEREDITARY PEERS

Hereditary honours are going for good. Mr Heath does not intend to revive the system, though Labour policy of awarding life titles will be continued. He has told ministers that the hereditary peer system has no place in his reforming ideas for the new Government. The news will shock supporters who have illusions of the party's obligations to class and aristocracy.

DECIMAL RISE FOR POOLS PUNTERS

It will cost more to do the pools after 15 February – Decimal Day. Littlewoods's minimum Treble Chance stake will be ½ new penny a line (1.2d.) instead of 1d. But the jackpot limit will also increase – to £400,000, compared to the present record payout of £338,000, set in 1966. In future the Pools Panel will operate when 25 matches are called off; previously the 'results' were decided for 31 void games.

3-MINUTE MILE IS ATHLETE'S LIMIT, SAY EXPERTS

Studies of the world's fastest runners show that there is an inbuilt mechanism to prevent men breaking certain barriers. Experts studied athletes such as Jim Ryun, Ron Clarke and Ron Hill to find out what stops a man from running 10 miles at the same speed as 1 mile. Hill was found to have the lowest fatigue coefficient and using him as a guide they have calculated these ultimate times for the distance events:

800 metres	1 minute 27 seconds
1 mile	3 minutes
10 miles	35 minutes
Marathon	1 hour 37 minutes

At the present rate it will take at least 100 years to achieve these times, though Roger Bannister says of the event for which he is renowned: 'I predict that a 3-minute-30-second mile will be possible by the end of the century. After that it will be up to evolution and genetics.'

OIL HOPES IN NORTH SEA

BP last night said it was 'hopeful' that it had struck oil in the North Sea. Chippings drilled about 100 miles off the Scottish coast contained hydrocarbons and an official from the company said, 'This means there is some form of deposit there.'

ENGLAND BAN CHARLTON FOR GOOD

Jack Charlton will not play for England again. The end of his international career is part of the price he will pay for threatening on TV to 'do' 2 players.

NOV 1970

Charles De Gaulle, former President of France, dies.

FOR PEOPLE WHO HATE MOWING THE LAWN . . .

Husbands who hate mowing the lawn will be delighted with a chemical spray discovered by German scientists. It prevents grass growth for several weeks, yet does not affect the lawn's colour or appearance. The spray could be on the domestic market within 2 years.

STARVING TO STAY ON TOP

Lester Piggott, 35 and 8 times champion jockey, has been ordered to rest. This comes as no surprise as for 20 years he has eaten like a sparrow to keep his weight down to about 8 stone 5. He chain-smokes cigars at breakfast-time to ward off hunger, goes without lunch and nibbles only lean meat for supper; he has also dehydrated his system so much that he has endured agonizing cramp. Dr Austin Darragh, a specialist who has helped many leading jockeys, says, 'I know of no other trade or profession that would accept physical conditions so dangerous to health.' On the positive side, Piggott has ridden more than 2,000 winners and earns an estimated £100,000 a year.

SPOT THE BALL ILLEGAL, SAY JUDGES

3 Appeal Judges yesterday ruled that Spot the Ball, the newspaper football competition, is illegal. The competition, run by the Ladbroke organization, involves a scene from a soccer match over which a grid of 40 squares is printed. The competitor has to mark the square in which he thinks the ball is most likely to be. A panel of experts led by Spurs skipper Alan Mullery also studies the picture and the winner is the one whose decision coincides with that of the panel. Ladbroke has been convicted of running a competition in which prizes were offered for forecasting the result of a future event; the judges ruled this illegal as the future event was the decision of a panel.

RAMSEY NAMES DANGER TEAM

Sir Alf Ramsey yesterday named the biggest threat to England's World Cup recovery in Munich, 1974. Everyone would quickly acknowledge the danger posed by teams such as West Germany, Brazil, Italy and Russia but, 4 years away from the next competition, Sir Alf is already alert to the side that could shock the world – Yugoslavia.

THE SEX STARS OF 1970

A *Playboy* poll reveals that the men with the most appeal for the girls are: Donald Sutherland, Jim Brown, Ryan O'Neal, Jon Voigt, Dustin Hoffman and Peter Fonda. Top of the list of girls most appealing to men were: Jacqueline Bisset, Candice Bergen, Ali McGraw and Jane Fonda. But Robert Redford, Elliott Gould and Raquel Welch get top billing as the poll reveals that they appeal to both sexes.

FREEPOST SOON

Britain's first Freepost service will be introduced in the new year. Businesses will pay a £5 a year licence fee to enable everyone writing to them to do so without using a stamp. The Post Office will then charge the firm a special rate for delivery. The new service is expected to have a wide appeal to mail-order firms, travel agencies and others now using a coupon reply service to attract new business. All Freepost mail will go second class at the new 6d. rate to be introduced next February.

SCRAP MONOPOLY ON POST, SAYS REPORT

The Post Office monopoly over letter delivery should be scrapped to allow competition from private enterprise and British Rail, says a report out today by the Institute of Economic Affairs. Mr Ian Senior, the report's author and former Post Office executive, believes that greater efficiency and cheaper postal services would be the result. 'The Post Office's statutory monopoly of the letter is not based on economic justification and should be abolished,' he says.

Schoolgirls sporting skinhead haircuts.

The ten-shilling note ceases to be legal tender.

NOW THE SEATBELT YOU CAN'T FORGET

Seatbelts which tighten automatically round the driver when the door closes may be compulsory within 2 years. Transport Minister John Peyton believes a system which would mean no one could drive without being strapped in would prevent up to 50,000 deaths and serious injuries a year. The Road Research Laboratory says in a report out today that it has perfected the system, which could give equal protection to front-seat passengers.

STARR'S THE STAR OF THE NIGHT

It was 25-year-old Freddie Starr's big night last night. The Liverpool comedian appeared in the Royal Variety performance and was the surprise hit of the show with impressions including Norman Wisdom and Mick Jagger. Freddie's manager said, 'He used to do his act in front of a pop group and I told him I didn't think he ought to go it alone.' Freddie's 'competition' in the show included Max Bygraves, Leslie Crowther and Marty Feldman.

PUPILS MAY GO TO WORK

The Government has plans for children to work in factories and offices for up to a month in their last year at school. The aim of the scheme is to cushion the shock of going out to work for the first time. Employment Minister Robert Carr and Education Minister Margaret Thatcher have started discussions with TUC leaders on a 'work experience' experiment. At present the law prohibits the employment of children in industrial undertakings, even as part of training. Under the new proposals children over 15 would be able to take part in schemes under strict supervision.

PACK UP YOUR OFFICE IN A NEW BRIEFCASE

In 10 years' time executives will carry briefcases looking very much like the ones they carry today – but what a difference inside! Instead of files and notebooks there will be electronic hardware designed for instant communication including TV screen, TV camera, fibre optics, push-button calculator and telephone. An example of a sales executive of the 80s calling on a customer would be first of all to activate the battery-operated case and connect it to his customer's computer. This in turn would be connected by electromagnetic data-link to the salesman's home office computer. In this way both salesman and customer would have all the benefit of the central computers of each company, allowing such information as specifications and delivery schedules to be displayed on a TV screen in the case.

BRITAIN STOPS HEART SWAPS

Heart-transplant operations in Britain have stopped. Mr Donald Ross, who has performed the only 3 transplants carried out in this country, said yesterday that he did not think there was any justification for going on with such operations at present. He revealed that he is now using a technique which will make the bulk of transplants unnecessary. The operation, developed in the US, consists of veins being removed from the patient's leg and grafted into the heart, bypassing the blocked or constricted blood vessels. Since 'spare parts' from the patient are used there is no problem of rejection. Mr Ross has successfully performed 6 such operations, which can save 9 out of 10 lives for whom a transplant was the only previous hope.

IT TAKES 2 CARS TO STAY ONE UP

You need 2 cars and central heating to keep up with the Joneses these days. The old status symbols of car, washing machine and refrigerator no longer count, an Employment Department report reveals. Every other family in Britain now runs a car and two-thirds have a washing machine and fridge. TV hardly scores at all – 9 out of 10 have one. But only 6% of families have 2 cars and only 25% have central heating. A telephone is a good start in the status race – only 32% of those surveyed were connected.

DON'T SCRAP RATES, COUNCILS WARN

Doing away with rates could put up income tax by 3/- in the £, councils warned yesterday. The Association of Municipal Corporations is worried that Environment Secretary Mr Peter Walker, who is examining local-authority financing, might come up with an alternative such as extra income tax or a national property tax or a sales tax which would be worse than the system it replaces. Of the rating system, the Association says it has 'stood the test of time and we doubt whether there is any alternative form of taxation which would raise the sum required more equitably, more cheaply, more effectively and with so little scope for evasion'.

The Goodies – a new late-night comedy show about a trio of well-meaning troubleshooters, written by and starring 3 of TV's brightest young comedians.

DEC 1970

THE GREAT BUSTARD IS BACK

The great bustard, Europe's biggest bird and one of the rarest, is to be reintroduced into Britain after 150 years. The birds – 2 males and 4 females from Portugal – will live in a protected pen in Wiltshire. Their wings will be clipped but their young will be allowed to fly free.

AIRPORT UPROAR

Villagers in Buckinghamshire are preparing to 'fight to the death' the Roskill Commission's recommendation that London's third airport should be built at Cublington. Under the plan, yet to be ratified by the Government, Cublington would disappear and several surrounding villages would be partly demolished. More than 160 MPs of all parties have signed a Commons motion demanding that Foulness or any other coastal site should be developed instead.

CLOCKS WILL GO BACK

British Standard Time was swept away in the House of Commons last night. MPs threw out the 3-year experiment by an overwhelming majority in a free vote. The decision means the clocks will go back 1 hour to GMT on 31 October 1971, giving an extra hour of daylight in the mornings. Summer Time – clocks going forward an hour – will be restored in 1972, giving the extra daylight hour in the evenings for a 7-month period.

CLINICS DROP THEIR ORANGE JUICE

Orange juice and cod-liver oil, which have helped keep expectant mothers healthy for 30 years, are to disappear from welfare clinics. From the end of next year expectant and nursing mothers will get all their vitamins in a single tablet; babies and young children will get their A, D and C vitamins in drops. The reason for the change is that undiluted fruit juices can be harmful to teeth.

LEYLAND DROPS 3 CARS AS UNIONS FIGHT AXE

Union leaders yesterday launched a fight for the jobs of 5,000 British Leyland workers. The big cutbacks announced yesterday will also mean that 3 cars will be axed: the Austin 3-litre, the Morris Oxford, which dates from 1959, and the Morris Traveller, first introduced 17 years ago.

SPEED LIMITS WILL NOT GO METRIC

Speed limits on Britain's roads will not go metric in 1973 and may never be changed. Transport Minister Mr John Peyton announced the decision in the Commons 18 months after a move to continental speeds was mooted by the Labour Government. It will mean a saving of nearly £2m alone on the cost of changing speed-limit signs.

RIBENA BEATS TAXMAN

Ribena – the vitamin C drink – may cost about 10d. a bottle less, the Beecham group said yesterday, because of a Court of Appeal ruling that the drink is a medicine and therefore not subject to Purchase Tax. The company says that if there is no appeal the price would be reduced by the amount of the tax plus a sum to take account of extra cost borne by customers since 1962.

CHRISTMAS CRACKERS

Scientists have found a way of preventing Christmas trees from shedding their needles by sealing them with an alginate – a seaweed chemical used in food. Next year growers hope to start winning back the million sales lost to plastic trees by the needle nuisance.

Both John Lennon and Yoko Ono have released albums with the title The Plastic Ono Band, *and despite speculation of a Beatles reunion Paul McCartney files for the legal dissolution of the group.*

COVENTRY CALLS FOR SUNDAY SOCCER

Coventry City is applying for permission to play on Sundays in a bid to boost its gates. Chairman Derrick Robins believes the game generally could profit from a move to Sunday soccer, a day when people have fewer commitments. The Bishop of Coventry, the club's President, has raised no objection. Asked how the club would tackle the problem of turnstile takings, which are forbidden on Sunday, Mr Robins said a way would be found of overcoming this if the League gave the go-ahead.

MARY IS QUEEN OF THE POPS

Mary Hopkin and Roger Whittaker are named today as top-selling solo single record stars. A *Record Mirror* survey puts Roger ahead of Tom Jones, Cliff Richard, Rolf Harris, Gerry Monroe, Desmond Dekker, Jimmy Cliff, Des O'Connor, Nicky Thomas and, at number 10, Engelbert Humperdinck. Among the women Mary beat were Shirley Bassey, Dana, Dorothy Squires and Jane Birkin in that order. Top group was Christie, followed by Blue Mink and White Plains. Elvis Presley, Freda Payne and Creedance Clearwater Revival are the top US singles artists.

Wendy Craig as Jennifer Corner with her four offspring in Not in Front of the Children.

'MAKE EVERYONE PAY LOCAL TAX'

The Government is being urged to scrap the rates system and replace it with a local income tax of 2*d*. in the £. Under the National Union of Ratepayers' Association's plan the rates burden that falls on heads of households would be spread to include all household members earning more than £500 per year. The rates system has remained unchanged for 400 years.

DOUGAN'S FREEDOM FRONT RUNNERS

Charlton, Venables, Setters, Dougan, Moncur, St John. These inspirational names on the field are, together with Cliff Lloyd, the offfield front runners in an attempt by footballers to have freedom to negotiate when contracts expire. The occasion was the Professional Footballers' Association AGM. Players were angered by the League Clubs' rejection of their bid last June and have made representations to Mr Eldon Griffiths, Minister for Sport.

KICKING OFF WITH A DEGREE

Steve Heighway BA has completed one of sport's most remarkable transfers – from Warwick University to Anfield. In just 9 League appearances the 22-year-old has set the public talking about his devastating pace and ability. He became an international for the Republic of Ireland before making a full appearance for Liverpool. The club is also happy with the form of another graduate, 24-year-old Brian Hall BSc from Liverpool University.

SEX BEATS SOCCER . . . BUT ONLY JUST

Soccer is now second only to sex as a selling force in Britain. When Esso launched its World Cup Coin Collection it sold an extra 24 million gallons. 2 years ago Stylo brought out a side-laced football boot endorsed by George Best. They expected to sell 500 pairs; in fact sales surpassed the 28,000 mark. However, campaigns based on individual popularity can cause problems. When George Best was banned for misconduct the Egg Board was tempted to take off an advert that featured him. The Milk Marketing Board faced a similar problem when it geared a pinta campaign to Arsenal's Peter Marinello only to find that he had been dropped.

SPIKE BAN TO BE LIFTED

The administrators of athletics are having second thoughts about the banned brush-spiked running shoes – the type used by John Carlos for his amazing unratified world 200-metre record 2 years ago. Athletes claim these shoes add up to 4 yards' improvement for sprinters. Each shoe has $66\frac{3}{16}$-inch spikes instead of the orthodox 4 or 6. They were not permitted at the Mexico Olympics.

BID TO BAN THE DONKEY FREE KICK

The donkey kick, anticipated as Goal of the Year, was last night branded in Scotland as illegal. Millions see this Coventry invention as a prelude to *Match of the Day*, a move that was first seen publicly in their home match against Everton on 3 October. Willie Carr gripped the ball between his feet and with a backward flip lifted it into the air for Ernie Hunt to volley home.

BIG JACK: FA COOL DOWN

Jack Charlton has been let off with a rebuke from the FA over his TV interview in which he threatened to 'do' 2 players. His international ban may now be lifted but, at 36, and with players such as David Sadler, Roy McFarland and Larry Lloyd around, he is clearly too old for any long-term England plans, a factor obviously in the minds of FA officials.

Peter Barkworth as Vincent, the British agent working in occupied France, Cyd Hayman as the Resistance worker and Alfred Lynch as the crash RAF pilot on the run from the Germans and trying to escape to Britain in London Weekend Television's Manhunt.

60-M.P.H. MEMORIES

The world's fastest rollercoaster at Belle Vue, Manchester is being sold in pieces as souvenirs. Attempts to have the 60-m.p.h. ride transferred to Whitley Bay, Northumberland, have failed.

LETTERS TO STOP AFTER MONDAY

The first all-out strike in the 300-year history of the Post Office will halt postal services from Tuesday midnight (19 January). Chances of a peace formula emerging over the next four days are slim as the Cabinet has decided that the 8% pay offer cannot be improved at this stage. The Union of Post Office Workers is demanding 15%. The effects of the strike will be immediate. All 4d. letters must be posted by tomorrow and no first-class mail (5d.) will be collected after 5.30 p.m. on Monday. Regarding telephones, all directory enquiries, personal-transfer-charge, credit-card, fixed-time and alarm calls will be suspended. All inland and international telegrams will stop, though special arrangements have been made to continue payment of pensions and family allowance.

SEX ACT ON SCHOOLS FILM

Schools throughout Britain, including primaries, have been offered a sex-education film showing a naked couple making love. The film, entitled *Growing Up*, was written and directed by Dr Martin Cole, 39, a genetics lecturer at Aston University.

SUDDEN DEATH WIMBLEDON

The tie-break gimmick will invade Wimbledon for the first time this year. It is 'worth a try' claims All England Chairman, Herman David, because of complaints about long, boring matches. It marks the first upheaval in Wimbledon scoring for a hundred years. The tie-break will be the new 12-point system operating from 8–8, except in the final set. After 8–8 the first player to win 7 points with a 2-point margin will win the set. Players will serve 2 points each in turn until 6–6 and then serve alternately.

AVENGER LINDA DRESSED TO KILL BY DIOR

Paris is going crazy about two things right now. One is shorts: French girls have discarded the midi *en masse* and are going for diminutive shorts in every fabric; the other is for our own Linda Thorson, *Avengers* girl Tara King.

BIG RUSH FOR 'EASY' DIVORCE

A queue for easy divorces started yesterday as the new Divorce Reform Act became law. Somerset House alone reported almost three times the usual number of petitions. The new act does away with the system of granting divorces because of 'offences' such as cruelty or adultery; instead the sole ground for divorce is the irretrievable break-up of the marriage. Couples who have lived apart for 2 years and agree to divorce will qualify. If one partner objects the other partner can apply for divorce if the couple have lived apart for 5 years. Some have labelled the act a Casanova's charter but most have welcomed it as a way of decently burying dead marriages which exist in name only.

The mangled terrace at Ibrox Park where 66 people were killed when the barriers gave way as spectators at the back surged forward while many other fans were exiting in the last few minutes of a Rangers-Celtic match.

TV MAY CUT THAT 'OLD-TIME RELIGION'

Sunday-night religious programmes on Independent TV may be cut. A survey has shown that viewers are switching off the programmes because they object to religion's being 'crammed down our throats'. The ITA is considering trimming the 70 minutes of Sunday religion by up to half an hour. The BBC may follow suit. The two channels have an agreement to give the same amount of screen time to religious programmes during the Sunday-evening 'closed period'.

Nanette Newman and Malcolm McDowell as the innocent, physically handicapped young lovers who struggle to come together in The Raging Moon.

NEW BALL RULE

Ryder Cup Captain Eric Brown yesterday attacked a loophole which could penalize Britain in proposed laws to give the world a uniform golf ball of minimum 1.66-inch diameter and initial velocity of 250 feet/second. According to Brown, it would mean that the Americans would not have to change their 1.68-inch ball, but simply reduce its velocity. British manufacturers, on the other hand, would have to design a completely new ball.

TRAVEL FIRMS RUSH TO BUY COOK'S

The Government set off a stampede in the travel business by its decision to sell off Thomas Cook & Son. The flag-carrier of British travel for years is being auctioned off with the Lunn Poly agency and Pickfords Travel Services. The Government is also going ahead with plans to sell off state pubs and hotels.

NEW-LOOK WORLD CUP

The 1974 World Cup winners in West Germany will be decided by a new elimination system. A committee organizing the competition has decided the quarter-finals and semi-finals will not be decided on a knockout basis. Instead, the 2 leading teams from each of the 4 qualifying groups will form 2 further groups. After a round-robin series of matches the winners of these groups will meet in the final.

MAKERS PUT AN END TO GLUE SNIFFING

Manufacturers have taken swift action to stamp out the growing menace of glue sniffing by teenagers. In the past 9 months 3 British boys have died as a result of inhaling the fumes. In an effort to prevent further tragedy, the country's two largest manufacturers have put a secret additive into their products which stings the nose and causes eyes to water when inhaled in large quantities. Commenting on the severity of the problem in America a spokesman for one of the firms said ' . . . we decided to put a stop to it before it got going here.'

BIRD NUMBER 7 FOR 007

Raquel Welch is hot favourite to land the plum role in *Diamonds Are For Ever* and become the seventh James Bond girl and 007's first American leading lady. Producers are still looking for a successor to Sean Connery and George Lazenby to play Bond. On the short list for the part are Roger 'The Saint' Moore, Simon Oates of TV's *Doomwatch* and Patrick 'Danger Man' McGoohan.

MAKE LOVE OFTEN IF YOU WANT A BOY

If you want to have a boy, make love more often, says an expert who has been investigating what determines the sex of babies. Mr William James of the Department of Biometry at London's University Hospital claims that boys are more likely at the beginning of the two or three days each month that a woman is fertile. As it is difficult to accurately pinpoint these days, couples who make love more frequently have the best chance of conceiving in the early period. Mr James found that more boys than girls are born to mothers under 25, to couples who have been married less than 18 months, and during and just after wars, all periods when couples would be making love more often.

GO-AHEAD FOR £36m LIBRARY

The Government has given the go-ahead for the British Library to be built on a 7-acre site in Bloomsbury, London. The Library, likely to cost £36m and take 13 years to complete, will house 8 million books and 250 miles of microfilm.

Glenda Jackson as Queen Elizabeth I and Robert Hardy as Robert Dudley, Earl of Leicester in the second of six plays about the Queen screened under the title Elizabeth R.

WARNING OVER NEW LUNCH-HOUR ABORTION

A new '10-minute abortion' now being tried in Britain has been criticized by a leading gynaecologist. The new operation, pioneered in America using a suction technique, could lead to severe mental stress, warned Professor Hugh McLaren. Its use in Britain on NHS patients at a London teaching hospital – where proper after-care is given – was revealed this week. 'These sprint techniques are carried out for economic reasons rather than for the good of the patient,' said Professor McLaren. Privately, the operation would cost £30, compared with £150 or more for a conventional abortion.

FEB 1971

NOW THAT I'M DEAD I CAN LIVE

Anne Reid – *Coronation Street*'s Val Barlow for the past nine years – last night watched as she was carried out dead on a stretcher after electrocuting herself. Although very emotional at leaving the show, Anne said, 'I'm 35 now and even if I don't get any work I just have to get out. Being in *Coronation Street* is like being cast adrift in a luxury liner – you're cut off from the rest of the theatre.'

IS THIS THE LAST BIG STRIKE?

Anybody thinking of going on strike these days had better be prepared for at least a month on the cobbles. With the Post Office strike a month old today, this is the lesson now dawning on trade unionists.

And the strike everyone has forgotten – the Ford car plant shutdown – is three weeks old on Friday and has already cost £25m.

These are the first two examples of the Government's 'stew in your own juice' approach to beating strikes.

BRITAIN ACCEPTS AMIN

Mr Heath angered his African critics yesterday by giving official recognition to the new army regime in Uganda. In a short statement from the Foreign Office, Britain became one of the first countries to recognize the 11-day-old regime of General Idi Amin.

'OBSCENE' POP SHOW BANNED AT ALBERT HALL

Top pop stars Frank Zappa and his group, The Mothers of Invention, were banned from playing at the Albert Hall last night on the grounds of obscenity. Song titles including 'Penis Dimensions' and 'This Town is a Sealed Tuna Sandwich' were described by Mr Frank Mundy, the Albert Hall's General Manager, as 'filth for filth's sake'.

BRITAIN GOES DECIMAL

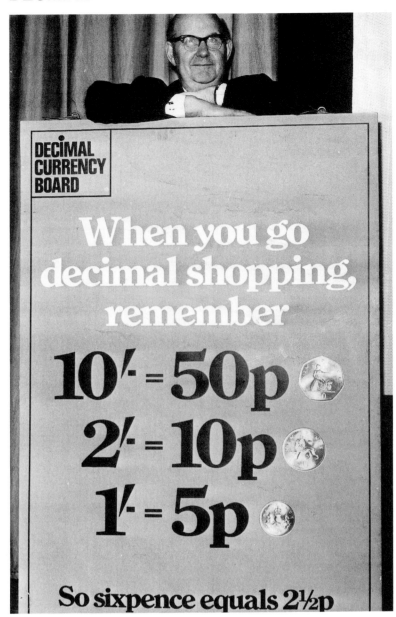

DECIMAL CURRENCY BOARD

When you go decimal shopping, remember

10/- = 50p

2/- = 10p

1/- = 5p

So sixpence equals 2½p

THINGS THEY SAID

'In no circumstances will the Government encourage or connive at unreasonable pay settlements. If it involves standing up to unwarranted strikes, then in the general interest both the Government and the nation must be prepared to face them.'
Chancellor Anthony Barber.

'We are capable of winning that treble – League, FA Cup and Fairs Cup – not only because we have a squad to overcome serious injuries, but because there isn't a man among us who doubts that we can beat anyone . . .'
Arsenal's Jon Sammels being interviewed.

'Everyone wants more money on the assumption that prices will remain static. But one man's wage increase is another man's price increase.'
Harold Wilson.

PERFECT WIFE IS WORTH 10/- AN HOUR (LESS DEDUCTIONS)

How much is the loss of an ideal wife worth? Yesterday a judge put it at 10/- an hour for a twenty-hour working week. But then he made a reduction because of the circumstances of the family which had lost its wife and mother. That brought the figure down to 5/- an hour.

The law, Mr Justice Talbot said in the High Court, could award damages only for financial loss – not for grief or loss of companionship. The husband's comment: 'How can you measure the value of a wife and mother? Twenty hours' domestic work a week? Call it 80 and you'd be nearer the mark.'

BREAKING UP THE BEATLES

The High Court: Paul McCartney, opposed by the other three Beatles, is seeking the appointment of a receiver to act as caretaker of the group's assets – more than £17m in 8½ years – pending the hearing of his action to break up their partnership.

TAKING THE ELBOW GREASE OUT OF OVENS

Cleaning the oven was always a miserable chore. But now housewives can buy cookers that do the job themselves. . . Special oven linings which clean themselves are available as an extra costing around £7.

JAMES BOND KILLS OFF POETRY

A survey into the reading tastes of boys and girls in the 16 to 18 age group from grammar and similar schools has revealed a strong preference for the blood-and-thunder of Ian Fleming and D.H. Lawrence and outright hostility to poetry. The investigators suggest that GCE examination boards should consider replacing poetry with expanded study of prose in O level English courses. The complete Top 10:
1. Ian Fleming
2. D H Lawrence
3. Agatha Christie
4. H G Wells
5. Charles Dickens
6. George Orwell
7. Neville Shute
8. John Wyndham
9. Thomas Hardy
10. Shakespeare

ROLLS-ROYCE BANKRUPT

Rolls-Royce crashed yesterday after a personal appeal by Mr Heath to President Nixon failed. The company collapsed because it was unable to fulfil its order for RB211 engines for the American Lockheed Tristar airliner without sustaining huge losses. The State will be taking over the aero, marine and gas turbine division, while the car division will be sold off to private bidders. For a Tory Government to nationalize such a large company will be seen as a blow to their supporters' morale.

NEW MINE GETS 'NO POLLUTION' CLAUSE

Mining firm Cleveland Potash was yesterday given planning permission for a £2m scheme in a Yorkshire national park on condition that part of the works would be shut down without compensation if it caused pollution. It is the first time an environmental protection clause has been included in a planning consent.

'Management must rid itself of the illusion that it can go on indefinitely running a business in conditions that don't pay.

'Unions must rid themselves of the illusion that they can go on indefinitely demanding higher wages without any concern for the effect.

'And governments must rid themselves of the illusion that you can find the way to prosperity by pouring out the taxpayers' money in perpetual subsidies for uneconomic ventures.

'All of us must rid ourselves of the illusion that we can buy our way out of the problems of today by mortgaging the future.'

Edward Heath

DAY BY DAY

3 Feb
Britain faces oil rationing as 11 OPEC states threaten price increase.

5 Feb
Apollo 14 lands on moon.

6 Feb
Belfast: the first British soldier is killed since Army began peace-keeping role 18 months ago.

8 Feb
Foreign Secretary Sir Alec Douglas-Home makes it clear that arms sales to South Africa could go beyond the legal obligation if it is in national interests. It is impossible to police trade routes of Indian Ocean without help of South African Navy, he says.

6 US helicopters are shot down as they accompany South Vietnamese troops' invasion of Laos.

9 Feb
Apollo 14 splashes down in the Pacific.

11 Feb
Britain is one of 40 countries to sign a treaty banning seabed nuclear weapons.

16 Feb
Environment Secretary, Peter Walker, announces plans for local-authority reorganization.

17 Feb
England beats Australia to regain the Ashes after 12 years.

19 Feb
Jobless total 720,000 – the worst figure since the 30s.

Sir Gerald Nabarro's bill to make health warnings compulsory on all tobacco products wins unopposed second reading in Commons.

Colin Todd joins Derby County from Sunderland at a record £170,000.

24 Feb
Under the Immigration Bill published today Commonwealth citizens who come to work in Britain will no longer have the automatic right to settle.

Inside South Vietnam, near the Laotian border; lead by three weapon and ammototing US soldiers a US army tank ploughs its way down a narrow dirt road through a forest, heading towards the Laotian border. But Gen. Creighton W. Abrams, the US Commander in Vietnam said that 'no US ground forces are or will be involved' with South Vietnamese ground combat units in Laos.

BEA BANS GIRL PILOT

Delli Gray-Fisk, 25, a pilot with top qualifications, is furious after being turned down by BEA because of her sex. A BEA spokesman said last night, 'I know of no big international airline which employs women pilots on any scale.' Mr Norman Tebbit, MP for Epping and himself a pilot till last June, criticized the blatant sexual discrimination and is to consult the Minister for Trade on the matter.

BRADMAN GOES AFTER 40 YEARS OF FIGHTING ENGLAND

Sir Donald Bradman, English cricket's foremost opponent for 42 years, retired from the fray yesterday. The batsman England feared most and the administrator who has helped choose Australian teams for 35 years announced his retirement as a Test selector.

SOCCER STAR OF 16 GOES BACK TO CLEANING BOOTS

16-year-old Trevor Francis, the £8-a-week apprentice tipped as the new Denis Law, scored all four of Birmingham City's goals against Bolton Wanderers on Saturday. He will be back at his normal job today – cleaning other players' boots.

MAR 1971

LOCAL RADIO GETS TUNE-IN ORDER

The go-ahead for Britain's first commercial radio stations to be set up has been given by the Government. Up to 60 'home-town' stations will compete with the BBC. The new stations, the first of which should be opened in 2 years, will be under the control of the Independent Television Authority, which will be renamed the Independent Broadcasting Authority. It will issue licences for 3-year periods, control advertisements and set programme standards. Revenue will come from 'spot' advertising; there will be no sponsored shows.

WHAT'S COOKING FOR THE KITCHEN OF THE FUTURE

Now that self-clean ovens are becoming a standard feature rather than an optional extra, what new developments could we see in the domestic cooker? Colours are a long way off – the manufacturers have tried bronze and chocolate and nobody liked them. Only when you begin to change your cooker as often as you change your car – every 18 months or 2 years – will colour come in in a big way. The ceramic glass hob, which has a completely smooth surface, is still in the development stage and until the price comes down will remain in the laboratories. Microwaves look as though they will only be big sellers industrially unless Britain's housewives take to convenience foods in a massive way and reheating becomes a way of life.

STONES HATE THEIR DISC

The Rolling Stones have spent nearly £700 on advertisements in the musical press to urge fans not to buy their latest album *Stone Age*. The group complain in the adverts that the record was below their usual standard and issued without their knowledge. The album comes from Decca, the company from which the Stones parted last July.

HEALTH CRACKDOWN TO HELP SMOKERS

A campaign to curb deaths from cigarette smoking has been launched by the Government. Manufacturers have agreed to print health-hazard warnings on the sides of all packets of cigarettes. They will read 'Warning by HM Government: smoking can damage your health.' Other measures announced by Social Services Secretary Sir Keith Joseph were:

– all cigarette advertisements will have to carry references to the danger warning on the packets.
– theatres, cinemas, restaurants and transport organizations will be asked to set aside much more room for non-smokers.
– life-insurance companies will be asked to give lower premiums to non-smokers.
– a committee will investigate all brands with a view to drawing up a league table of tar and nicotine content.

FADE OUT RED BARREL

Watney's Red Barrel beer won't be rolled out much longer. It is to be phased out this month and replaced by Watney's Red. The new beer will taste sweeter than the old and have a creamier head. Red Barrel was originally produced nearly 40 years ago as a long-living beer for shipment to India.

END OF 'SLAVE MARKET' IN SIGHT

A bill to end the 'slave market' assessment of a widow's marriage prospects has been given an unopposed third reading in the House of Commons. The private bill, sponsored by Labour MP Arthur Probert, said that neither the prospect nor the fact of a new marriage should be considered in judging damages under the Fatal Accidents Acts. Solicitor-General Sir Geoffrey Howe agreed that the bill answered a long-standing women's grievance.

OUT! 'ENERY LOSES AND QUITS

Henry Cooper retired from boxing last night after losing his British and Commonwealth heavyweight titles to Joe Bugner. Fans at the Empire Pool, Wembley booed and showered the ring with missiles when 21-year-old Bugner gained the decision by a quarter of a point.

'QUICK SWIG' BEATS B-TEST

Police chiefs and government departments are to make urgent moves to seal a loophole in the law which allows 'hip-flask drivers' to escape drunken-driving convictions. At present a man who has been drinking, is involved in an accident and then drinks again before taking the test, can be safe from conviction. This was shown yesterday in a test case when the House of Lords upheld the quashing of a conviction against a man who drank 3 whiskies after being involved in an accident. The man was convicted after experts claimed that even without the 3 whiskies he would have been over the limit. This decision was quashed by the Court of Appeal and that ruling was upheld by the Law Lords.

Marc Bolan and T. Rex hit number one with their single Hot Love.

The Prince of Wales is greeted by the P.M. Edward Heath when he visits 10 Downing Street to see the working of the Prime Minister's Office.

AGE LIMIT FOR ULSTER SOLDIERS UP TO 18

No soldiers under 18 will be in Ulster after next week. The 170 there now are being brought home and no more will be sent out. The decision was taken on humanitarian grounds by the Cabinet and reflects the Government's fear of a worsening situation after the murder of 3 off-duty fusiliers, one of whom was only 17. It seems probable that Northern Ireland Premier Major James Chichester-Clark must now seek some form of limited internment without trial for known terrorist leaders or face being ousted from the leadership. Demands for internment for terrorists were made after a 7,000-strong march in Belfast protesting against the 3 murders.

CUT-RATE TV BID FAILS

A plea for a cut-rate TV licence for two million viewers unable to receive BBC2 has been turned down in the House of Lords. Tory peer the Earl of Kinnoull said, 'Clearly defined areas should be exempted from paying the full £7 fee,' but government spokesman Lord Denham said that the cost of operating a two-tier system could well absorb all licence revenue.

SUNDAY SPORT KILLED

The House of Commons has killed the idea of paying for Sunday entertainment. The first reading of a private member's bill to allow admission fees to be charged for Sunday entertainment and sport was defeated. It was the fourth time in four years that a Sunday entertainment bill had been before MPs. Mr Ron Lewis, Labour MP for Carlisle leading the opposition warned: 'If we pass on to the next generation a de-Christianized Sunday, they will pass on eventually a de-Christianized Britain.'

EXIT JACK DE MANIO

Jack De Manio, 57, is to be dropped from the early-morning BBC Radio 4 *Today* programme after 12 years.

CAR-INSURANCE FIRM FOLDS

Vehicle & General, one of Britain's largest motor-insurance companies, crashed last night leaving more than half-a-million motorists without cover. The directors said the company is insolvent and should go into liquidation as soon as possible.

YETOU LEARNS TO TALK PROPER

A French girl wanting to learn English the spoken way from BBC television is having to unlearn her lessons. 20-year-old Yetou's tutors were Alf Garnett and the Steptoes. When she heard a girl running France down she called her a 'silly moo' and when a shopkeeper got his decimals wrong and gave her the wrong change she called him 'a silly old git'.

John Cleese in a sketch from the Monty Python's Flying Circus *programme which is to be the BBC's entry in the Golden Rose of Montreaux competition.*

APR 1971

'MINI-FOOD' PLEA FOR BED-SIT GIRLS

A plea for special mini-sized portions of pre-packed food has gone out to Britain's grocers. The move is designed to cater for pensioners, bachelors and bed-sit girls who buy only a little food at a time. With the trend towards selling in larger quantities to cut down on packaging costs, Minister of Agriculture Mr James Prior appealed to the National Grocers' Federation for help. There was particular difficulty in obtaining small quantities of eggs, cheese and bacon, he said. It is the first time the Government has stepped in to try to protect a minority consumer group in this way.

CITY SAYS 'YES' TO £17-MILLION ARTS PLAN

London is to get a £17-million Arts Centre after all. The Common Council of the City of London has voted to go ahead with the scheme which was first proposed in 1959. Since then it has been the subject of intense controversy but now the council has voted for culture over the cost-conscious arguments of opponents. The new complex for the Barbican will include a theatre for the Royal Shakespeare Company, a 2,000-seat conference hall and a new home for the Guildhall School of Music.

RAT POISON KEEPS WIFE ALIVE

Mrs Ethel Flear takes rat poison every day to stay alive. Doctors have warned her that if she stops her daily dose of Warfarin she might die. Warfarin kills rats and mice by causing internal bleeding but it also stops blood clots forming and Mrs Flear would be a likely thrombosis victim if it were not for the rat poison. 'I thought my leg was being pulled when a nurse first told me that I would have to take rat poison for the rest of my life,' said Mrs Flear. 'When one of the doctors at the heart hospital heard I was going to take it he laughed and said, "So you're joining the Dracula Club?"'

'The absolute limit' – a woman in hot pants outside Buckingham Palace.

EXPERTS URGE A CHARTER TO SHIELD CHILDREN'S RIGHTS

Children should be shielded from bullying teachers and parents, leading educationalists urge today. They will call for a charter of rights which would give young people from 5 – 18 the same protection against personal harassment that adults take for granted. Children should have:

- freedom from physical assault, including caning (Britain is the only major Western industrial nation which still has corporal punishment).
- freedom to take complaints about adults to an ombudsman.
- the right to dress and wear their hair as they wish without being 'victimized' (recently some boys have been told they would be deprived of the chance to take GCE exams unless their long hair were cut).
- the right to be free from religious or political indoctrination and to have access to full knowledge about such matters as sex, contraception and drugs.

HOVERCRAFT PIONEER QUITS

Hovercraft inventor Sir Christopher Cockerell, 60, has finally accepted a government pay-off of £150,000 for his pioneering work, ending a 3-year dispute. 'I had to take what I was offered. It's no big figure when you look at what was given to the inventors of radar and the jet engine in their day, but I've been living on air for some time now. . .' Sir Christopher commented. Sir Frank Whittle, jet-engine pioneer, was awarded £100,000 in 1948; Sir Robert Watson-Watt, father of radar, £50,000 in 1952.

HUNDREDS MOURN THE RIVER THAT DIED

Easter Sunday became a day of mourning for hundreds of country lovers. They erected a cross and laid wreaths beside a Lincolnshire river in which every living thing has been killed by pollution. Fish, river animals, birds, insects and microscopic organisms all died when a chemical was discharged into the River Till.

Cadbury's popular chocolate bar.

CENSUS SUE STRIPS IN THE NAME OF PRIVACY

Sue Rogers is worried about her privacy. To prove it yesterday she stripped to her underwear in front of holidaymakers on Plymouth Hoe, part of a 'burn the census' protest by 400 Young Liberals against the 1971 census form. The differences between this census and any before are that it asks for:

- the date of marriage, and of birth of each child (this applies to women under 60).
- the birthplace of parents.
- the number of A levels or equivalent qualifications.
- a person's occupation one year ago.
- a person's whereabouts 1 year ago and 5 years ago.

BOYCOTT NYLON, SAYS THE DOOMWATCHER

The world's top Doomwatch scientist, American Professor Barry Commoner, has urged housewives: 'Vote with your purse for a better life.' He warned that unless plastics, nylon, artificial fertilizers and pesticides were prevented from polluting the environment the world's entire life-cycle could break down. Housewives should bring about change by refusing to buy products such as nylon shirts, plastic bottles and biological washing powder, whose materials could pollute the environment.

Environment Secretary Mr Peter Walker has ordered an investigation into the possible danger of the amount of lead released into the air from vehicle fumes.

SIR GORDON RICHARDS, STEWARD OF THE COURSE

Gordon Richards made a habit of being first. He rode his first winner 51 years ago, came first a further 4,069 times and was champion jockey 26 times before turning to training in 1954. By then he was Sir Gordon, having become the first professional jockey to be knighted. He is also the first former professional jockey to be invited to become an honorary member of the Jockey Club, the turf's ruling body. Four months after that honour, 66-year-old Sir Gordon was standing this week as a Race Steward at Newmarket, the headquarters of flat racing – another first for an ex-professional rider.

ALF'S NEW NOBBY

England's long search for a new Nobby Stiles has won Peter Storey his first call to international honours. Sir Alf Ramsey, who has for 2 years been on record as seeking a successor to Stiles, named Arsenal's Storey in his squad for the European Nations Cup Match against Greece.

And Mother Makes Three *is a new television situation comedy starring Wendy Craig.*

SIR KEITH PLANS 'PASSPORT' FOR STATE-AIDED FAMILIES

A 'passport' to enable less well-off families to get all kinds of social-security benefits is planned by the Government. The aim is to cut out the variety of means tests and apply a single test for all forms of state aid. Sir Keith Joseph, Social Services Secretary, intends to issue the first identity documents in the autumn before the introduction of the new Family Income Supplement. Families receiving FIS will automatically qualify for free welfare food and milk, free school meals and exemption from prescription and health charges.

PARKING FOR DISABLED

Disabled car drivers will soon be given exemptions from parking restrictions under the Chronically Sick and Disabled Persons Act. Regulations will be laid before Parliament in the next few weeks giving local authorities powers to grant disabled drivers exemption car badges.

'TELL ADOPTED CHILDREN' PLEA

Adopted children should be able to apply for the names of their natural parents, according to the National Council for Civil Liberties. In a survey of adopted children's rights, the NCCL urged that all children should have the 'short' birth certificate containing only their name and date of birth to end the stigma of illegitimacy. But the certificate should note that the child has the right to apply to the registrar for information about his parentage. At the moment it is virtually impossible for an adopted child to find out who his natural parents were unless the adoptive parents are prepared to disclose the child's original name, according to the report.

BREARLEY GIVES UP GOWN FOR LORDS

Mike Brearley MA has given up the cloistered security of life as a university lecturer in philosophy to captain Middlesex. 'I realize it is a risk,' said 29-year-old Brearley, whose 2-year contract with the county, which finished sixteenth out of 17 last season, will mean a drop in income and a gamble on his future. On his ambition to captain England he commented: 'I have my doubts that I am a good enough batsman. . . '

MILITANT HAIN TAKES OVER YOUNG LIBERALS

Mr Peter Hain, 21-year-old student who led the campaign that stopped the South African cricket tour last year, has become Chairman of the Young Liberals. Mr Hain promised 'a militant lead in radical politics' and a crusade to help urban society 'to meet the uncontrollable chaos which is developing there'. Other protests would include the Immigration Bill and arms sales to South Africa.

MAY 1971

Dirk Bogarde in Luchino Visconti's film of Thomas Mann's novella Death in Venice.

SUNDAY SHOP MAN SAYS, 'I'LL GO TO JAIL'

Shopkeeper Patrick Happell-Mooney faces a jail sentence because of his one-man war against the Sunday trading laws. He was fined £3 yesterday at Derby for selling a tube of cement, a sheet of glass paper and wall plugs on a Sunday morning at his hardware store. Mr Happell-Mooney, who said that his wife could keep the shop open while he was in prison, declared himself morally innocent but the chairman of the magistrates, although sympathetic, declared that he was bound to act within the law.

THE LAST SONG OF DICKIE VALENTINE

Singer Dickie Valentine died in the blazing wreckage of his car on a 'death-trap' bridge in South Wales early yesterday (6 May) with his drummer and pianist, who were also killed in the crash. He was driving from a club date when the car hit a parapet of a narrow stone bridge between Abergavenny and Crickhowell. The 41-year-old singer's last song had been 'My Way', including the words 'And now the end is near and so I face the final curtain. . . '

BIG DRIVE TO DESIGN CHUNNEL

Government scientists are looking for 200 motorists to help them design the Channel Tunnel. All they will have to do is drive in and out of special railway wagons, for which they will be paid 50p per hour. The Road Research Laboratory is advertising for its 'guinea-pigs' as they anticipate drivers will sit in their cars as they speed under the Channel by rail.

Two 'Jimmy Hills' on Aquarius *when John Cleese impersonates Jimmy Hill in a comedy soccer sketch.*

TV MAN CHOOSES JAIL

Television reporter Bernard Falk has chosen to go to prison rather than name an alleged IRA leader he interviewed in a BBC *24 Hours* programme. Falk, 28, yesterday abandoned his appeal against a 4-day sentence he received in Belfast and was later taken to Crumlin jail.

CALL FOR EQUAL PAY IN POLICE

Equal pay for Britain's policewomen is being demanded by the Police Federation. At present women get 90% of the men's rates, though if the claim is conceded policewomen will have to work more shifts and longer hours.

Arsenal's Charlie George and Ray Kennedy hold the FA Cup after beating Liverpool 2–1.

44 – THAT'S THE LIMIT

A man waving a flag may start a disorderly rush for the £60,000-plus Derby prize on 2 June, the most open Blue Riband of the Turf since its inception in 1780. Stewards of the Jockey Club met yesterday and have decreed that the number of starting stalls can be increased by 2, making 33. If more than 33 go the race will be started by a flag. There can be no barrier start – a tape across the course – as the French visitors would not know what it was. A further complication is that the width of the track does not permit more than 44 to congregate, even before a man with a flag. Only if the field exceeds 44 would stewards consider elimination, and that would be based on past performances, not a ballot.

The biggest Derby field was 34 in 1872.

WOOLIES GETS INTO HOT PANTS

'Woolies' is dead. Long live the House of Woolworth. That was the message when the chain store held its first fashion show to launch its summer collection. The show, at Woolworth House, London, included lots of hot pants, for the homely bastion of the High Street is going trendy. Of the company's new image a spokesman said, 'That expression "Woolies" might have to go.'

DAY BY DAY

3 May
Arsenal clinches the Football League championship as teenager Ray Kennedy scores the goal in a 1–0 win over Spurs.

Walter Ulbricht resigns as East German Leader and is succeeded by Erich Honecker.

8 May
Arsenal beats Liverpool 2–1 in the FA Cup Final to become only the second club this century to complete a League and FA Cup double.

11 May
The Assemblies of the Congregational Church in England and Wales and the Presbyterian Church of England vote in favour of forming a United Reformed Church.

15 May
Leigh wins the Rugby League Cup, beating Leeds 24–7 at Wembley.

19 May
The Queen asks the House of Commons to review the Civil List which, at £475,000, has not been increased since the beginning of her reign.

US poet Ogden Nash dies, aged 68.

21 May
Chelsea wins the European Cup Winners' Cup by beating Real Madrid 2–1 in Athens.

23 May
72 British holidaymakers are killed when a Yugoslav aircraft on a flight from Gatwick crashes on landing at Rijeka.

Nearly a thousand people are reported dead in an earthquake in Turkey.

27 May
Labour takes Bromsgrove from the Conservatives in a by-election.

30 May
The American Mars probe *Mariner 9* is launched on its 300-million-mile journey from Cape Kennedy.

TIED PASSPORTS STORM

A husband who shares his passport with his wife can travel alone abroad but his wife cannot use the passport without her husband. Now women MPs are asking for the joint-passport rules to be changed. Mr Anthony Royle, Under-Secretary for Foreign and Commonwealth Affairs said, however, that Britain was tied by international agreements. He added, 'Such a passport is issued to the husband and, although the wife's particulars are included as a matter of convenience for family travel, she is not the joint holder. A married woman has always been able to have her own passport to which her children under 16 can be added.'

The Arsenal Team tour Islington town in triumph following their winning of the FA Cup and League Championship.

JUNE 1971

TROUBLE AHEAD WITH GAVASKAR

India, who meet England in three tests later this season, believe they have a batting prodigy in Sunil Gavaskar, a 23-year-old student whose phenomenal success as an opening batsman was a major contribution to India's shock 1–0 series victory in the West Indies last winter. Gavaskar's aggregate of 774 runs from 4 tests was a record for a player in his first series. Gary Sobers described him as an incredible prospect.

ARE YOU REALLY AS SAFE AS YOU COULD BE?

Ralph Nader, America's 'Consumer Crusader' has turned his guns on British car makers and the British Government. He accuses them of operating dual standards in car safety, one for the models they export to America where there are stringent safety regulations, and another for those they sell to British motorists. Is he right in his indictment of British manufacturers?

These are some of the safety features already incorporated in British cars for the American export market:

- laminated windscreens, which are optional extras in this country. The government Road Research Laboratory believes it can be better for a driver to be hurled through a toughened screen than hit a laminated one.
- dual braking systems reckoned to be unnecessary by the industry here because our brake systems are far better than American brakes.
- telescopic steering columns which stop a driver being impaled in a collision. Britain's answer, produced long before America began demanding telescopic columns, is the column which breaks in two.
- emergency flashers – a system by which all four indicators flash simultaneously to warn of a breakdown or crash hazard. They are permitted in Britain but the Government says, 'What happens if the car's electrical system fails? This may not be the best answer.'

HAIL THE 155-m.p.h. SMOOTHIE

The fastest, quietest smoothest-riding train in the world was promised yesterday when British Rail unveiled its test version of the Advanced Passenger Train at its Technical Centre in Derby. The train, which goes on commercial trial in 1974, will be able to run at up to 155 m.p.h. on existing rail routes with minimum alterations to track and signalling. The APT will eventually cut the best travelling time between London and Edinburgh from 5 hours 45 minutes to 3 hours 40 minutes.

Julie Christie with 15-year-old Dominic Guard as the young protagonist in Joseph Losey's film of L. P. Hartley's The Go-Between.

WHERE ARE THEY NOW? *BRAINS TRUST* BRONOWSKI

Brains Trust and briquettes – these are the things for which Dr Jacob Bronowski is remembered. The Polish-born doctor was the man who pioneered the process of making smokeless bricks when he was in charge of research at the Coal Board. Millions of pounds were spent on research but the idea misfired because it was found that the briquettes were too fragile for easy delivery. Since 1964 he has been lecturing in America but now he is back in Britain making a £400,000 series called *The Ascent of Man* for the BBC as a follow-up to *Civilization*.

SQUEEZE IS PUT ON SMOKERS

Accommodation for smokers on London buses and tubes is to be further restricted. London Transport has decided that on the underground only two carriages will be provided on each train for smokers. This will increase the non-smoking accommodation to about 70% compared with the present proportion of 50–65%. On the buses smoking will be allowed only on the top of double-decker buses. At present it is also allowed on certain single-deck buses.

ANN SUMMERS GIVES UP SEX SHOPS

Ann Summers, the 30-year-old blonde who opened Britain's first sex supermarkets, is resigning from the board of the company she started a year ago. In a surprise statement yesterday she said, 'I realize that my resignation will give an immediate platform to the small but vociferous band of detractors that have seen my company as an opportunity to express their anachronistic views,' but added, 'Thousands of members of the public have supported my own strong personal belief in the real need for a service of this kind in Britain.'

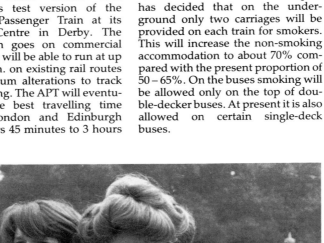

THINGS THEY SAID

'One should not be surprised to find this Philistine Government stabbing the film industry in the back.'
Alan Sapper, General Secretary of the Association of Cinematograph, Television and Allied Technicians on Junior Trade Minister Nicholas Ridley's announcement of plans to end state subsidies to the film industry.

' . . . to follow Sir Matt is like being heir to the throne.'
Frank O'Farrell after being named as Sir Matt Busby's successor as manager of Manchester United.

'I believe we are now deliberately coarsening and brutalizing sex to prove to ourselves that we are not puritans any more.'
Dr Benjamin Spock, 67, on the permissive backlash against Victorian repressiveness.

'Our new engine will be on sale next year. It will, of course, be capable of using ordinary petrol until the law is changed.'
Soichiro Honda, motorbike manufacturer, on developing a car engine capable of running on lead-free petrol.

'If Billy were alive today, he would be a skinhead or a juvenile delinquent.'
Michael Selzman, personal manager of Michael Pollard, as the actor stars in a new 'debunked' version of *Billy The Kid* called *Dirty Little Billy*.

'We've got to force industrial relations up to boardroom level. Too often top managements are not personally involved at all until there is trouble.'
Employment Minister Robert Carr.

' . . . a situation that never develops but simply runs round in ever-decreasing circles, growing less funny with every repetition.'
Peter Lewis reviewing *No Sex Please – We're British* in the *Daily Mail* – and bemoaning the waste of Michael Crawford's talent on the show.

'You can't work both sides of the street.'
David Frost on the Braden issue – and turning down a £40,000 cigar commercial to prove his point.

'The battle first, the battle second, the battle last.'
Egypt's President Sadat on his determination to ensure the return of all land occupied by the Israelis since the 6-Day War of 1967.

IT'S A TV SELL-OUT

Britain's most expensive TV series, the 24-part *The Persuaders*, has paid for its costs – £100,000 an episode – even before it is shown. The ATV comedy-thriller which will be released here in September has been sold to every country in the world with TV except Russia, China and Albania. It stars Roger Moore as a suave English lord and Tony Curtis as his wheeler-dealer American playboy chum.

THIS 'IMPOSSIBLE' CASE OF TINA, THE SLEEPING BEAUTY

Christine Houghton was quite prepared to lose her baby. For ten weeks she had felt no movement within her womb. The suspicion that the tiny life she had conceived and borne for seven months was now extinct had, in her mind and in the opinion of her doctors, become a harsh reality. Then the 'impossible' happened. An ultrasonic detector used at the last minute to confirm absence of life scanned the womb and suddenly came the feeble bleeps that proved everyone wrong. 21 weeks later the young mother gave birth to a 5lb infant, Tina, the result of a thirteen-month pregnancy. This case is a classic in British medical history, proof that the curious phenomenon – tentatively described by Birmingham obstetrician Mr Wilfred Mills, who first discovered it, as 'Foetal Hibernation' – can and does occur.

BRADEN DROPPED OVER TV ADS

Bernard Braden, the BBC's late-night television star, is being dropped because he is making television commercials. The BBC confirmed last night that there would be no more programmes for the £800-a-show host of *Braden's Week*, which has been running since 1968. Mr Braden, 51, is recording a string of margarine commercials due to start on ITV next week. Mr Paul Fox, head of BBC1, believes it is wrong for a 'television ombudsman' to sell goods on the rival channel, and *Braden's Week*'s consumer-oriented format will return later this year with a new host.

Model Vivien Neves causes a stir when this advert featuring her appears in The Times.

15 SEA-OIL AREAS UP FOR AUCTION

For the first time the right to drill for oil under the seas around Britain will go, in some areas, to the highest bidder. Sir John Eden, Secretary of State for Trade and Industry, announced last night that applications for oil-production licences were being invited for 436 ocean blocks. The experimental auction would be 'a valuable test-run' to enable the Government to decide the future system of allocation.

MARKET Q AND A . . . WHAT IT WILL MEAN TO YOU

We're in, or very nearly, but how will joining the Common Market change our everyday lives? Here is a sample of the question-and-answer analysis *Daily Mail* experts have produced – vital to every new European.

Q: Which foods will be dearer and which cheaper?

A: All foods made from milk, for example, butter, cheese and cream and manufactured products such as chocolate, soups and tinned rice pudding will cost more, so will meat, poultry, bread and eggs. Fruit will be cheaper.

Q: Will Britain's tax structure change?

A: Yes, drastically. Britain must introduce a Value Added Tax in line with the Common Market countries. This is why there will be a higher cost of living if we go in, but British Income Tax, the highest in Europe, will almost certainly come down. This is because subsidies now paid to farmers out of taxation will be abolished and the trend in Europe is towards indirect taxes.

Q: Will joining speed up the Channel Tunnel?

A: No, but it will make it more of a certainty.

Q: What will happen to the English language?

A: English will become one of the official languages and could take over from French as the working language.

Q: Which types of British business will benefit most?

A: Textiles, some building materials, toys, cars, motor components, chemicals, banks, insurance and 'City' services generally, footwear and carpets.

Q: Which types of business will come off worst?

A: Food manufacturers generally, some shipping companies, domestic appliance-makers, paper-makers and potters.

Q: Will we have to learn more languages?

A: Probably, but there will be more incentive. Most firms will now start paying extra for bilingual staff.

Q: Will our licensing hours change to conform with the continental drink-when-you-want system?

A: They are not likely to be influenced in any way by our going into the Common Market.

Q: Will there be more holidays for workers?

A: Unions will no doubt claim the longer holidays of the Community which range up to 38 days a year compared with a 21-day average in Britain.

Q: Will we be able to travel without passports in Europe?

A: Probably, but not without some form of identity card.

Q: Will there be a European Parliament?

A: There is one. It meets at Strasbourg. Britain will have 36 seats in an enlarged Parliament of 208 members. But the Strasbourg Parliament has never had any teeth. The idea behind the Treaty of Rome that there should eventually be political union has never taken root.

Q: Will there be a referendum in this country?

A: No. The Government claims it has a mandate from the 1970 General Election.

JULY 1971

BETTER SCHOOL DEAL SOON FOR UNDER 5S

Children whose fifth birthday falls after a term has started are to get a new deal in London. From September next year they will be able to start school where possible at the beginning of their 'birthday terms'. At present children are admitted to school only in the autumn and spring terms. Many do not start school until after their fifth birthday. The plan will be a big boost for summer-born children who often have a year's less schooling than those born in spring or autumn. The Labour-controlled Inner London Education Authority admitted last night that its scheme was a drastic modification of its plan 2 years ago which proposed a big expansion of nursery education. It said the main reason for the change was that any hope of legislation to provide nursery schools had disappeared. It added that priority had also been given to reducing the size of primary classes to 35 or below.

VICAR ACCUSES LONGFORD

A vicar accused Mrs Mary Whitehouse and Lord Longford yesterday of 'doing more harm than dirty books'. He added, 'If dirty books were available for everyone there would be no real problem as people would soon become bored.' The Reverend Anthony Hart-Synot of St Stephens Church, St Albans, Hertfordshire wrote in his parish magazine about Lord Longford, leader of the campaign against pornography, 'He himself is the father of eight children, a sexual achievement more harmful to the community than any number of dirty books.' Revd Hart-Synot, 64, proposed four measures to deal with the population explosion:

– abortions on demand.
– birth-control help for everybody.
– no tax relief for children born after June this year.
– an end to all immigration.

IT'S A 300-m.p.h. TRAIN BY FORD

A 300-m.p.h. train gliding along like a rocket on an invisible magnetic 'cushion' is being developed by Ford. The train, which has no wheels, would cover the 400 miles between London and Glasgow in about 80 minutes. Mr Foster Weldon, Ford's Detroit-based Research and Planning Director, announced yesterday that the US Government has awarded the firm a special railways contract to do research on the project. He said, 'We are trying to harness the principle that magnets repel. The idea is to use this energy to lift the train and to act as its frictionless wheels, then, with the train "hovering" on the magnetic field, it could be driven by linear induction motors, jet engines or turbine-driven propellers.'

COLOUR CODE FOR EGGS AND MILK

Housewives will soon be able to distinguish different grades of milk and eggs by colour codes. Mr James Prior, Minister of Agriculture, has given the milk industry 9 weeks to consider compulsory colour coding of milk-bottle caps. The proposed colours are: pasteurized Channel Island – gold; pasteurized ordinary milk – silver; homogenized – red; untreated (farm bottled) – green. Packaging colours for the four popular grades of eggs were urged by the defunct Egg Marketing Board. The Board recommended blue for large, red for standard, yellow for medium and green for small. Any move to enforce an egg colour code is likely to be delayed until the decision is made over Britain's entry to the Common Market.

ZIG-ZAG STRIPES FOR ZEBRA'S SAFETY

Sweeping new road-safety plans announced by the Government yesterday include zig-zag markings at each of Britain's 10,000 zebra crossings 'to make them more distinctive'. Overtaking and parking will be banned inside the zig-zag lines. Transport Minister Mr John Peyton outlined proposals which include:

– raising the minimum licence-age for motor cyclists later this year from 16 to 17 – the same as for a car licence – but 16-year-olds will still be able to ride mopeds.
– making approved crash-helmets compulsory for all motor-cycle, moped and scooter riders and pillion passengers.
– compelling the use of headlights in heavy rain and fog.
– a ban on stopping within 20 yards of any road junction.
– automatic seatbelts to be fitted by law in all new cars.

IT'S ALL BRITISH-MADE IN JAPAN

A flagrant Japanese copy of a British invention is likely to cost a music company many thousands of pounds in lost export orders, it was claimed yesterday. The claim was made by the head of a firm making a pocket-sized electronic organ called a Stylophone. The instrument, which has been played by Rolf Harris on his television show, was spotted in a London department store by visiting Japanese businessmen. They took one back to Tokyo and, despite a patent lodged in 1967, copied it to the last detail.

Bond is back. Sean Connery recreates the role he swore he would never play again in Diamonds Are Forever.

Australia's Evonne Goolagong becomes Wimbledon singles champion at the age of 19.

BEATLE TO SING FOR REFUGEES

Beatle George Harrison is to give a concert on 1 August, his first in 5 years. Profits from the show at Madison Square Garden, New York, will go to a special United Nations fund for refugee children in East Pakistan. Harrison's last public concert was with the Beatles in 1966. Beatles manager Allen Klein said yesterday that Harrison was prompted to do the show by Bengali sitarist Ravi Shankar, whose family remains in East Pakistan. Harrison has strong sympathy for the wartorn Bengalis. The concert format has not been finalized but none of the other Beatles will appear. Shankar and Leon Russell are known to have accepted invitations.

GOVERNMENT SELLS OFF ANOTHER TRAVEL FIRM

The Government is pulling out completely from the holiday-agency business with the sale of Pickfords Travel Service expected to be announced tomorrow. Pickfords Removals may also have to be sold because the travel side of the business operates on the same premises throughout the country.

BUMPS AHEAD – FOR SAFETY

Residents living on a 'deatn-trap' hill have built concrete ridges on the road to slow down motorists. After spending £1,200 from their own pockets on the anti-car 'bumps' they have been told by the local council that the four ridges can stay. The residents of Clumber Avenue at Arnold, Nottingham were told yesterday that the council would probably take no action because the road is privately owned. Arnold Urban Council's Works Committee Chairman, Councillor Tom Price said, 'At this stage we are proposing to leave things as they are; in fact we think the idea is a novel one.'

SPORTS CAR BAN ON SOCCER STAR

Goalkeeper John Burridge, 19, was given an ultimatum yesterday: 'Get rid of your car before reporting for training.' The order was given by Mr Bob Stokoe, Blackpool Manager, who is frightened that John's 150-m.p.h. Lotus Europa sports car will give him a 'playboy image'. Mr Stokoe explained: 'John is living away from home and it is up to me for his sake and for the sake of the club to keep his feet on the ground.' John bought the £1,500 car when he joined Blackpool from Workington in a £10,000 deal.

BARBER'S GREAT JULY SALE

Spend, spend, spend. This is Mr Anthony Barber's summer-sale policy to give Britain's downcast economy a burst of energy in time for the Common Market entry. In 18 minutes before an astonished Commons yesterday, the Chancellor pruned purchase tax on a wide variety of goods by 18%, the biggest cut in nearly 20 years. He also ended all restrictions on hire purchase and credit deals. The major group of goods affected by the cut in purchase tax includes clothing, footwear, furniture, bedding and tableware. The decrease is from 13.75% to 11.25%. The 22% rate on sweets and pet food goes down to 18%. On TV last night Mr Barber told the unions that the Government had played its part by cutting prices and boosting the economy, now it was up to the unions to moderate wage claims in return.

GRAND PRIX – IN MIDDLE OF A CITY

A plan to turn the centre of Birmingham into an international Grand Prix motor-racing circuit is likely to be given the go-ahead tonight. The city council's General Purposes Committee will decide whether to ask Parliament for permission to close part of the Inner Ring Road once a year for a Monaco-style 'round-the-houses' race. The race would be held on a Sunday and the road closed to ordinary traffic for the weekend. Already six international companies have agreed to sponsor the race and a provisional date has been pencilled in to the International Motor Racing Calendar for next year.

FALKLAND DEAL

A deal to provide better communications between the Falkland Islands and Argentina has been agreed by Britain but the long dispute about sovereignty over the islands remains unsolved, Whitehall said last night.

ROAD TAX LIFTED ON DISABLED

Disabled people who own cars but are too ill to drive them are to be exempt from paying the £25.00 road tax. The concession announced by Chancellor Anthony Barber in the Commons last night will affect about 2,000 who have adapted cars and are driven by friends. It brings them into line with the 30,000 invalids who own and drive converted vehicles.

Jim Morrison of The Doors is found dead at his Paris flat (3 July). He is buried at Pere Lachaise, Paris's celebrity cemetery.

DAY BY DAY

1 July
Learie Constantine, one of cricket's great all-rounders, dies, aged 69.

2 July
The Erskine Bridge over the Clyde is opened by Princess Anne.

19-year-old Australian Evonne Goolagong wins the Wimbledon women's singles title.

3 July
John Newcombe of Australia wins the Wimbledon men's singles title.

6 July
Louis Armstrong dies, aged 71.

13 July
In a White Paper, *Fair Deal For Housing*, the Government outlines proposals to increase rents in both council property and private, unfurnished accommodation for those tenants who can afford it. More help is to be given to the poor through a rebate scheme that, for the first time, includes private tenants. The White Paper aims to 'create the conditions for a final assault on the slums, the overcrowding, the dilapidation and the injustice that still scar the housing scene'.

17 July
Mr Wilson says the present terms for Common Market entry are not the same as those for which the Labour Government asked.

18 July
6 of the 7 Trucial States in the Persian Gulf decide to form a federation.

26 July
Apollo 15 is launched from Cape Kennedy on a flight to the moon.

Miss Nicolette Milnes-Walker arrives at Newport, Rhode Island and becomes the first woman to sail alone across the Atlantic by the northern route.

28 July
The Labour party's National Executive votes against Britain's entry into the Common Market on present terms.

30 July
162 people are killed in a mid-air collision over Japan between an All Nippon Airlines Boeing 727 and a jet fighter.

AUG 1971

ULSTER – NOW IT'S CIVIL WAR

13 people died in Northern Ireland yesterday as virtual civil war erupted. They included a Roman Catholic priest, shot as he gave the last rites to another victim in Belfast. The massive wave of rioting, shooting and looting came in the wake of the internment of about 350 IRA suspects on the orders of Ulster's Premier Mr Brian Faulkner. In Belfast, buses, corporation dustcarts and Post Office vans were hijacked at gun point and then set blazing. Protestant families were evacuated from mixed areas. As they were moved out of the Ardoyne district they left their homes burning behind them 'to prevent them falling into the hands of Catholics'. As the entire province was convulsed in the worst rioting of its 50-year history the 4,000-strong Ulster Defence Regiment, set up to replace the B Specials, was mobilized for border security work.

Mr Faulkner's drastic new measures included a 6-month ban on all marches, which means that the Apprentice Boys' March through Londonderry on Thursday is off. The Ulster Premier, announcing his internment order, said, 'We are quite simply at war with the terrorists.'

Things fall apart;
The centre cannot hold;
Near anarchy is loosed upon the world,
The blood-dimmed tide is loosed and everywhere
The ceremony of innocence is drowned;
The best lack all conviction, while the worst
Are full of passionate intensity.

W B Yeats

ENID STILL TOPS THE BOOK POPS

Old favourites that mother and father used to read are still Top of the Pops amongst school children. The most widely read books are still *Black Beauty* by Anna Sewell, *Little Women* by Louisa M Alcott and *Treasure Island* by Robert Louis Stephenson, according to a survey among 9,000 10 – 14-year-olds carried out by the University of Sheffield's Institute of Education. Enid Blyton was most often named as favourite writer.

SHELL IN £21m OIL HUNT GAMBLE

Shell and Esso, 2 of Britain's biggest oil companies, yesterday paid £21m for a bleak stretch of North Sea which they could have got for £8.5m, but they hope to reap rich profits by finding oil under the waves. Their bid was for the most hopeful of 15 100-square-mile areas being leased by the British Government for oil exploration. There were 17 other bids for the area off the Shetlands, the second being less than £8.5m. The bidders had been required to play a game of poker crossed with Blind Man's Buff. The companies sealed their bids in envelopes which were kept in a padlocked box at the Department of Trade and Industry. Mr Edward Conway, Manager of Esso Exploration, asked if anyone would be fired for making an offer over twice the figure of their nearest competitor, said, 'No comment.'

PLUG IN AND SEE TV SHOW YOU MISSED

A machine that tapes and plays back TV programmes goes on sale in Britain next spring. The video cassette-recorder can be pre-set to work while a viewer is away from home and will also tape a show on one channel while the viewer is watching another. It records and transmits colour but it may be 1973 before Britons are using it in their homes. Supplies will be limited at first, and industry and education will get priority. The machine, about 2 feet long by 13 inches wide and 6 inches high, is being made in Austria by Philips. It will cost about £300 but will be available on a rental basis. The recorder uses half-inch video tape in cassettes costing £15 for an hour's recording, £12 for 45 minutes, and £9 for half an hour's. The tapes can be wiped clean and used again.

James Irwin, lunar module pilot on the Apollo 15 mission, seen during a stay of 66 hours and 55 minutes on the moon.

Harvey Smith makes his feelings known while competing at Hickstead.

BEER RECORDS ARE BAD FOR YOU

The gargantuan habits of record pint swallowers have so worried the Guinness people that their gastronomic feats may be dropped from the famous *Book of Records*. Guinness chiefs fear someone may injure himself. They also feel that the activities of people who drink up to 65 pints in an hour by regurgitating every 5 or 6 pints is bad for the company image. Mr Norman Micherson will still try to break the 65-pint barrier later this month and he will drink draught Guinness but any record is unlikely to stand. Guinness now feels that the drink must stay down and on that strict definition the record is held by Horst Pretorius of West Germany who in 1968 drank 39.79 pints in 60 minutes.

SHOPPING TRIP ONCE A MONTH FOR MRS 1980

The British housewife of 1980 will go shopping only once a month, a food expert predicts today. The food she buys will go into an outsize deep freezer, probably separate from the house, which will supply the family's meals. If forecasts prove correct, the average person will be eating £60 of convenience foods a year by the end of the decade, Mr Allan Cameron, Head of Food Technology at Birmingham College of Food and Domestic Arts, says in a new book. The shopping expedition will involve a car trip to a major supermarket stocking several thousand different food lines.

SCHOOLS TOLD: MAKE EXTRA YEAR PAY OFF

The Government has ordered all local education chiefs to report before December on their plans to cope with next year's raising of the school leaving age from 15 to 16. Education Minister Mrs Margaret Thatcher yesterday emphasized the need to make school timetables more attractive for teenagers who would previously not have stayed for the extra year. 'Unless a school's approach meets the needs and retains the interest of its pupils, attractive buildings will not reconcile the reluctant minority to an additional year of compulsory education,' she says. Particular efforts should be made to link pupils in their final year with their future working life, for example, with visits to factories and an introduction to the operation of the social services. Teenagers whose fifteenth birthday falls on or after 1 September 1972 will have to stay on at school. This will mean that during 1973, the first year of extra compulsory education, there will be an extra 233,000 children at school.

VOICE OF SOCCER QUITS

For the first time in 22 years the BBC opened their soccer season on television without the voice of Kenneth Wolstenholme. Rumour had it that Wolstenholme, 51, had been fired, a suggestion he vigorously rebuts. 'It was all to do with the allocation of matches,' he said. 'I could still have covered games for them but they would not necessarily have been the games I would have chosen for myself.' So Wolstenholme quit. It was an expensive principle; it cost him £6,000 a year.

FILL HER UP JUST ONCE A YEAR – THE YEAR 2050, THAT IS

Atomic cars that will run for up to a year without refuelling are being planned by Ford designers for use in the middle of the next century. The designers have already built a 3/8 scale model of a car named the Nucleon. By the year 2000 Ford estimates that women will be able to go window shopping by car without looking where they are going or touching the steering wheel. Designers are working on a runabout 3-wheeler that would run on a self-guiding magnetic track. And the lorry of the future? It could have 3 air-cushion pads on legs to whisk it over any surface, land or water.

ITV HANDS OVER WORLD SPORT

Independent Television is pulling out of the fierce competition with the BBC over coverage of world sport. In future, major events like the World Cup and the Olympic Games will be treated only on news merit; but ITV sport will not suffer on the home front. Negotiations are going on for long-term coverage of British League and Cup football events, racing and wrestling. Announcing the shake-up yesterday, the programme companies said ITV's new policy was to reduce the number of simultaneous sports programmes on the 2 major channels.

Jackie Stewart becomes World Motor-racing Champion for the second time.

LIONS ROARED HOME!

Hundreds of rugby fans, mostly Welshmen, sang the British Lions home from their triumph of the New Zealand tour at Heathrow Airport last night. The tour committee had made no official welcome plans but fans took the matter out of their hands, saluting their heroes who had beaten the All Blacks 2 – 1 with 1 match drawn, scored 555 points to 204 and won 22 out of 24 games.

Stamford Bridge: George Best holds his head in disbelief after being sent off by referee Norman Burtenshaw for dissent. The incident followed a Tommy Baldwin goal for Chelsea, but Manchester United won the match 3–2.

PREPARE TO SAY GOODBYE TO THE ELM

Millions of elm trees grace our countryside and our cities but they are being decimated by a flying bug which tricks them into suicide. Science appears helpless to save the stately elm, which takes 100 years to reach maturity and only days to choke to death when its arteries have been closed by *scolytus scolytus* – the Latin name for the quarter-inch beetle which has already left 400,000 elms dead or dying throughout southern England and is spreading.

For Britain is now firmly in the grip of the deadly Dutch elm disease, so called because it was first discovered in Holland 50 years ago. The insects carry with them a fungus which produces a poison and begins to kill off the tree. In an attempt to counteract the poison the elm produces antibodies which block its sap arteries; the tree dies from a self-induced 'coronary'. Scientists are desperately racing to find a cure. In the meantime, all the helpless experts can advise is 'cut down and burn any tree under attack'.

Ernie and Bert — two of the puppet characters from Sesame Street.

LONGER PUB HOURS 'CAN LEAD TO A 40p PINT'

If Britain's pubs adopted 'continental' opening hours, beer could cost as much as 40p a pint, it was said yesterday. The warning came from Mr Harry Shindler, Secretary of the National Association of Licensed House Managers, who said at a London conference that his members were firmly against longer hours which would force up overheads. The average pub manager, Mr Shindler claimed, gets 'about 27½p' for each of his 85 hours a week. His wife worked 69 hours a week for 'about 5½p' an hour.

KER-AZY! THE TOYMAKER JUST CAN'T COPE

Toymaker Arthur Turnbull is being driven mad by the new Ker-knockers craze. Ker-knockers are 2 plastic balls on lengths of string which swing against each other with a loud cracking noise. He has been swamped with orders but he can't get enough plastic balls to make the toys. He said, 'The other day a chap pleaded with me to sell him 250,000 of them; others have arrived with thousands of pounds in their hands.' Mr Turnbull, who remembers the hula-hoop and yo-yo crazes of past years, says the Ker-knocker mania is bigger than either.

UNDER 5s SEE BANNED TV

Thousands of children under 5 in London, Scotland and Wales are to see a controversial American TV programme banned by the BBC. *Sesame Street* is an educational programme which teaches by the quick-fire techniques of TV commercials. 3 ITV networks – London Weekend, Harlech and Grampian – are to screen 13 of the programmes up to Christmas but the BBC has rejected this series, which is watched by 6 million under 5s in America, because it has serious doubts about its methods and aims. Educationalists have criticized *Sesame Street* for its essentially middle-class attitudes, lack of reality and its attempt to prepare children for school but not for life.

Adam Faith as Budgie and Iain Cuthbertson as Charlie Endell in Keith Waterhouse and Willis Hall's series.

AT 84 BARNES WALLIS LOOKS TO THE FUTURE

Dambuster Sir Barnes Wallis, 84 yesterday, talks enthusiastically of the work that keeps him busy 50 hours a week at his home in Surrey since he 'retired' from the British Aircraft Corporation last May. One project is a 1,000-foot-long airship which will carry methane gas from North Africa to anywhere in the world. Sir Barnes told the oil companies which suggested it that it was impossible. Now he thinks it can be done using carbon fibre, which is twice as strong as the toughest steel and light as a feather. 'At the end of each trip I can fill the carcass of the airship with hot air and send it back to North Africa. All that gets thrown away is a lot of hot air – a thought which pleases me very much.' It should please the oil companies, too. Millions of pounds are spent turning the gas into liquid, piping it across the Sahara, shipping it, and finally turning it back to gas.

Another project that Sir Barnes has been working on is an underwater bridge to link Italy and Sicily. This would be a giant tube suspended beneath the surface and embedded into the sea bottom. His favourite project is a 'hypersonic' airliner that would travel 5 times the speed of sound and get to Australia without refuelling.

ALF GETS A NEW DAUGHTER

Alf Garnett is getting a new daughter for the first time in his film and television career. Una Stubbs, 31, who has played Rita since the famous programme began 5 years ago, is being replaced by 22-year-old Adrienne Posta.

NO-NAME TOYS 'COULD BE DANGER'

Dangerous toys may flood into Britain because of the Government's decision to allow the import of 'anonymous goods', a toy-industry spokesman said last night. By December it will not be necessary for most imported goods, including toys, to bear any mark showing the country of origin. Toys sold to Britain have had to be labelled 'Foreign', 'Empire', or with the name of the exporting country since 1926. A spokesman for the British Toy Manufacturers' Association said last night, 'There can be little doubt that this new attitude will increase the risk of more dangerous toys being imported from countries with lower safety standards.' The Government decided the mark would not be necessary after November this year because its value to the consumer was 'limited'.

THE POOLS DYNASTY

3 people this week shared a £427,000 top prize on the pools, the biggest first dividend the pools firms have ever paid, and tomorrow, in only the fourth Saturday of the new season, 10 million punters will be waiting again for what looks like being the greatest golden carrot of them all – the £500,000 win. Only 3 years ago dividends and turnover were dropping like a stone. What turned the business round was a neat change of the rules bringing in the score draw results. Chief architect of the scheme was statistician Grattan Endicott, Technical Advisor to Littlewoods and the Pools Promoters' Association. Until Endicott's brainwave, introduced in the 1969/70 season, defensive football had brought a plethora of draws that sent dividends crashing. This year the system – 3 points for a scoring draw, 2 for a goalless draw and 1 for a home or away win – is really taking a hold.

THE DUTY OF A WIFE WAITING FOR DIVORCE

A wife has an obligation to help her husband earn as much money as he can, even though she is waiting for her divorce to come through, a High Court Judge said yesterday. Mr Justice Bagnall said that Mrs Grace Bull, who had refused to take business messages for her salesman husband, was under an obligation to 'behave in a civilized manner'. He said, 'It is to the wife's and children's interests that the husband's earning capacity be preserved. She is still his wife and should be prepared to behave in a manner in which a wife would normally be prepared to behave towards a husband carrying on business at her home.' Mr Frederick Bull, who still lives with his wife at their home in the Isle of Wight, claims that she had lost him goodwill and business contacts by being unco-operative.

WILLIS SHOCK FOR SURREY

Bob Willis, one of England's Ashes winning team in Australia last winter, may quit county champions Surrey. The 22-year-old fast bowler has turned down terms for next season because Surrey will not guarantee him a first-team place. Unless Surrey can assure him of that he wants an 'unconditional' release to play for another county with 'less bowling talent'. Willis has made his stand because he feels his opportunities were limited last season by Surrey having 2 other fast bowlers, Geoff Arnold and Robin Jackman.

DAY BY DAY

1 Sept
Old pennies and threepenny bits cease to be legal tender.

3 Sept
17-month-old Angela Gallagher is killed by a sniper's bullet meant for a British soldier in Belfast.

5 Sept
Princess Anne wins the European Individual Championship at the Burghley Horse Trials.

7 Sept
Delegates at the TUC conference in Blackpool vote against registration under the new Industrial Relations Act.

9 Sept
The British Ambassador to Uruguay, Mr Geoffrey Jackson, is released after being held prisoner by guerillas for 8 months.

11 Sept
Nikita Khrushchev, former Premier of the USSR, dies, aged 77.

13 Sept
Surrey becomes county cricket champion.

14 Sept
The Government publishes new plans for pensions, under which everyone, except the self-employed or financially independent, would receive a basic pension plus an occupational pension related to earnings. The scheme is designed to come into effect in 1975.

17 Sept
5 seamen die when the Fleetwood trawler *Dinas* catches fire in the Irish Sea.

23 Sept
Labour candidate Mr Gordon Oakes is returned with an increased majority in the Widnes by-election.

27 Sept
Jack Bodell wins the British, European and Commonwealth heavyweight boxing title, outpointing the holder, Joe Bugner, at Wembley.

30 Sept
The Foreign Office confirms that KGB agent Oleg Lyalin of the Soviet Trade Delegation in London was the defector whose information led to the expulsion of 105 Russian officials on 24 September for spying.

PARTIES TO GET TV WARNING

Politicians are to be told that party political broadcasts must stick to 'politics and policies' and not be used as fund-raising commercials. An early meeting between representatives from the TV companies and officials of the 3 main parties is planned after the outcry over Labour's controversial broadcast on Wednesday night. Many viewers complained because the programme, introduced by Party Chairman Mr Ian Mikardo, urged the audience to send donations to Transport House. It also showed products from firms which give financial support to the Conservative Party and contrasted the money available to both sides. It was the first time a party political broadcast has appealed for funds.

OCT 1971

A FAIR DEAL FOR WIVES

Marriage is unfair to wives and the law should be changed to give them a better deal. This is the conclusion of a report on family law issued today by the influential Law Commission. The Commission, whose recommendations frequently become law, recognizes that 'Women are no longer content with the system in which their rights depend on the whim of a husband or the discretion of a judge.' It proposes:

– that a wife should automatically own part of the home, often the only asset of a marriage.

– that a husband should no longer be able to disinherit his wife even if he makes a will doing so. The Commission suggests that £2,000 or a third of the estate, whichever is the larger, should go to the surviving partner. As an alternative to this plan, the Commission suggests a 'community of property'. Net assets acquired during the marriage would be shared equally at the end of the marriage either through death or divorce. Each partner's assets would be calculated and the one with the least would have an 'equalization' claim against the other.

CHIP SHOPS WILL LOSE THEIR SMELL

The smell of fish and chips wafting up the High Street is on the way out. New shops are to be deodorized. Associated Fisheries, which plans to open a whole string of bright new chip shops across the country, has discovered a way of losing the smell by using ultraviolet lights. Air from the frying range is passed into a complex of ultraviolet lamps at the back of the shop. The company says, 'The action of the rays on the fumes creates ozone, which mingles with cooled gas fumes – also filtered out by a pipe from the cooking area – to create the odourless air that leaves the shop.' Associated Fisheries also intends to sell its fish and chips in plastic containers or hygienic bags.

CALL FOR 'PAY AS YOU DRIVE' TAX

A world in which motorists will be taxed according to how much they use the roads is envisaged today by a leading transport economist. Mr J. Michael Thomson, Research Fellow in Transport at the London School of Economics, says Britain is now halfway to becoming a fully motorized society in which on average every two people will share a car. When that point is reached, within 20 years, road pricing – charging drivers for the use of road space – will be the most logical new form of motor taxation. Road pricing gets at the root of the traffic congestion problem, he says, 'by charging an appropriate price for using assets that are in great demand and exceedingly costly to expand'.

The Government Road Research Laboratory is still evaluating the feasibility of road-pricing meters that will fit family cars. Trials with electronic and clockwork meters similar to taxi meters are being conducted now. Scientists are studying an automatic unit system that would work like a household electricity meter. This would mark up units of time, the meters would be read quarterly and bills sent by computer to every motorist.

SAVED BY A SKIN ON YOUR TEETH

American dentists have developed a process which they believe can virtually eliminate tooth decay. Teeth are coated with a clear plastic adhesive which is then hardened and made decay-proof by being bombarded with ultraviolet rays. This plastic 'armour' will stay in place for up to two years but researchers believe they can perfect the process to last a lifetime. The whole process can be carried out by the dentist's assistant so that even in non-welfare-state America it can cost less than £10.

MYSTERY DEATH OF ROCK SINGER GENE VINCENT

Gene Vincent, 36-year-old American rock singer, has died mysteriously at Newhall, California. The singer, real name Eugene Vincent Craddock, was a star of the fifties and best known for his recording of 'Be Bop A Lula'. His fame diminished in the 60s in the United States but he still remained a star in Europe and until last weekend he was on a pop tour of Britain.

Daily Mail

FRIDAY, OCTOBER 29, 1971   3p

TODAY: WIN A MINI CLUBMAN —PAGE 25

❝Now we stand ready to take our first step into a new world full of new opportunities. Our historic decision has been made; the British people accept the challenge. Let us show ourselves to that new world as we would wish it to see us . . . confident, proud and strong.❞ —THE PRIME MINISTER LAST NIGHT

YES WE'RE IN BUSINESS!

Mr Heath on his night of triumph

'Right—now the first thing you had do is learn English.'

By WALTER TERRY
Political Editor

INTO Europe we go—with the Commons last night voting by a resounding 112 majority in favour of Britain joining the Common Market.

It was a spectacular victory for Mr Heath—by kind permission of a solid flank of Labour pro-marketeers determined to pursue their idealism into the division lobby.

And it was more than enough to show Brussels that Britain means business. Anti-Market MPs said it was only the start of a new fight — but so thumping a majority was a big knock for the critics who had tried so hard over the months to erode pro-Market support.

The voting figures, declared at 10.15 p.m., to a packed Commons lobby:

Yes 356

No 244

In the Lords two hours earlier, there was another hefty pro-Market vote: For 451; against 58; majority, 393.

Months of doubt, arguments and party anguish dissolved in a taut atmosphere of turbulent anger and some bitterness.

Altogether 88 Labour MPs ignored the party whip—69 voted with the Government and 19 abstained. More Tories than expected voted anti-Government — 39, with two abstentions and one MP away ill. Five Liberals voted pro-Market.

While Mr Heath was getting a standing ovation, Labour anti-Marketeers turned angrily on colleagues who voted with the Government.

Into the pro-lobby went the Prime Minister, followed by a united Cabinet, scores of junior Ministers and Mr Jenkins with his rebels.

But on one occasion, Mr Heath, who wound up the six-day Commons debate, failed to get the cross-Channel ferryboat chugging with much enthusiasm.

'Traitor'

Labour back-bencher Mr Reg Freeson shouted at Labour's deputy leader Roy Jenkins, 'Traitor, traitor. . .'

Outside the chamber earlier there had been bad feeling among Labour MPs as they talked among themselves about the insistence of so many Socialists to vote pro-Market with the Government.

And after the votes revealed the Labour rebels to be strong and united, despite so much party pressure to back down, Opposition chief whip Mr Bob Mellish hinted in a statement that he might quit.

He declared: 'I am only a care-taker chief whip. I am now seriously considering whether to resign.'

This was pique and Mr Mellish

Mostly the Tories backed Mr Heath, though the party's rebel anti-Market group stood firm and voted in the official Labour anti-lobby.

The oldest new allies voted together. Anti-Marketeers included Mr Gerry Fitt, Republican Labour, Miss Bernadette Devlin, The Rev. Ian Paisley, and Sir Gerald Nabarro.

will probably recover over the weekend. But it displayed his irritation with so much defiance of his three-line whip.

Cheering

The Opposition kept hammering at one vital point—there is not much support in the country from ordinary people for his market adventure.

In his speech, Mr Heath did not seem particularly rapturous. The last day of debate was billed as an historic occasion. But the Premier left a lot of MPs feeling a bit flat.

After the vote Tory MPs cheered and waved their order papers, Labour MPs glowered and Mr Jeremy Thorpe,

Turn to Page 2, Col 4

WHO'LL BE TV'S SUPER SLEUTH?

Television copper Charlie Barlow is in for fresh ITV opposition on the law and order scene. London Weekend's super sleuth will be a certain Superintendent Kingdom played ironically enough by John Woodvine, the actor who inherited Barlow's old 'patch', Newtown, when *Z-Cars* first returned as a serial. Superintendent Kingdom will be 'a strong character' but should put no strain on viewers' credulity. The production team are looking for a genuine CID officer to be their technical advisor and keep the series, which is as yet untitled, true to police life.

Dustin Hoffman and Susan George in Sam Peckinpah's Straw Dogs.

DRIVING LICENCES FOR LIFE

Driving licences costing £5 and valid for life are to replace the present three-year licences costing £1 a time, Transport Minister Mr John Peyton announced yesterday. The only exceptions to the 'licences-for-life' plan are heavy goods, public-service vehicles, provisional licences and those issued for limited periods on medical grounds.

AS THE PUSH FOR A FOURTH CHANNEL GAINS MOMENTUM FEARS INCREASE OVER ITV2

ITV is stumbling into the biggest backstage argument in its turbulent 16-year history over a television channel which does not exist. The Independent Television Authority says that ITV2 must be on the air by 1975 if ITV is not to fight the BBC 'with one hand tied behind its back'. This month ITA Director General Brian Young is gathering opinions and suggestions from the whole of ITV and freelance programme-makers before meeting Mr Christopher Chataway in December. Many producers, directors, writers and other creative staff oppose the idea of the present ITV set-up taking over Britain's fourth television channel, particularly since it is likely to be the last available network. They fear that the same stations will provide only slight variations on the existing ITV theme. Why not bring in new companies, they argue, and make ITV a truly original channel?

DAY BY DAY

4 Oct
Delegates at the Labour Party Conference in Brighton vote 5 to 1 against Common Market entry on present terms.

5 Oct
Emperor Hirohito, arriving in London for a State visit as part of a European tour, becomes the first Japanese ruler ever to travel abroad.

13 Oct
The Conservative Party Conference in Brighton votes by a majority of 8 to 1 in favour of the Government's negotiations to enter the Common Market.

14 Oct
The Queen opens the M62 Trans-Pennine motorway and inaugurates the Scammonden Reservoir. The dam is the highest earth embankment in Britain.

The Duke of Edinburgh and Princess Anne attend a banquet at Persepolis given by the Shah of Persia to celebrate the 2,500th anniversary of the founding of the Persian Empire by Cyrus the Great.

20 Oct
Herr Willy Brandt, Chancellor of West Germany, is awarded the Nobel Peace Prize.

21 Oct
21 people are killed when a gas main explodes in Glasgow.

The Prime Minister announces that troops in Northern Ireland are to be awarded the General Service Medal, the first time it has been generally awarded for service in the United Kingdom.

25 Oct
The UN General Assembly votes by 76–35 with 17 abstentions to admit China to membership and expel Taiwan.

31 Oct
The 3-year experiment of British Standard Time ends as clocks are put back 1 hour and Britain reverts to Greenwich Mean Time.

'WORLD'S BIGGEST BOOKMAKER' DIES

William Hill, the man who claimed to be the world's biggest bookmaker, died yesterday in a hotel at Newmarket, the headquarters of racing. Mr Hill, who was 68, founded his empire on racecourse bookmaking and on a big-money credit office in the West End of London. He told of a sharp lesson he once learned: 'You don't just stand up, shout the odds, take anybody's money and hope for the best. I did that once and finished up walking home.'

Peter Gilmore as James Onedin with Phillip Band as Albert Frazer in the drama series The Onedin Line *set against the tough world of sailing ships in the 1860s is regular Friday night viewing.*

John Lennon's Imagine *is the UK's Number 1 Album.*

'HANGOVER' BANK HOLIDAY PLEA IS TURNED DOWN

The idea that Englishmen should have 1 January off to get over New Year celebrations was turned down by the Government yesterday but in Scotland, where New Year's Day is already a holiday, revellers will get the following day off as well. Some Labour MPs have suggested that 4 extra days could be chosen from May Day, United Nations Day, Queen's Birthday, Christmas Eve, New Year's Day and Europe Day. The Banking and Financial Dealings Bill establishes 5 bank holidays in England, Wales and Northern Ireland – Easter Monday, the last Monday in May, the last Monday in August, Christmas Day and Boxing Day. Scotland will have the additional bank holiday of 2 January.

GREEDY GAZUMPERS BOOST HOUSE PRICES

A new phrase has entered the cut-throat world of house-buying – gazumping. The term, which is car-trade slang, is used by some estate agents to describe the person who sells twice, firstly to one buyer and then, as property values climb, to a second at a higher price before contracts are exchanged on the first sale. The original deal is then called off and a disappointed and angry buyer faces solicitors' and surveyors' fees. 'It is unethical but legal,' said one agent yesterday.

BRIGHTER AND SMALLER – IT'S THE IRON DUKE FIVER

A new £5 note showing the Duke of Wellington instead of Britannia on the back is issued tomorrow but a mini Britannia appears on the front together with a portrait of the Queen and a winged Victory. The French may see a bit of Common Market one-upmanship in having the Iron Duke on the note but it could have been worse for them: the Duke is portrayed in an 1811 battle scene of the Peninsular War, not Waterloo. The Duke's portrait is based on a painting by Sir Thomas Lawrence in the Wellington Museum, London. After the issue last year of the new £20 note depicting a scene from *Romeo and Juliet*, a bank spokesman said yesterday, 'Next we have a £10 note but we do not know what the subject will be.'

NIGHT CURB ON JETLINERS

No jets will be allowed to take off from London's Heathrow Airport at night during the summer. Flights are to be banned between 11.30 p.m. and 6 a.m. from 1 April to 31 October, Minister of Trade Mr Michael Noble announced yesterday. This will cover about 8 flights per night, which has been the limit for 7 years under rules that restrict aircraft 'movements' – take-offs and landings – to 3,500 during the summer.

The number of night landings at Heathrow will be unrestricted and in theory these could go up but the Department of Trade does not think this will happen. Airlines will not want to bring in a jet which is then 'grounded' for the night. Thousands of people living within 15 miles of the airport are continuing their fight to stop all-night flying.

Johnny Hamp (front) with some of the comics on his new series for Granada – The Comedians.

STAMMERING IS VANISHING

Fewer children are stammering, and the credit goes to the Permissive Society, it is claimed. The report, based on investigations of more than 20,000 schoolchildren, shows that fewer than 3 in every 1,000 youngsters stammer compared with 10 in every 1,000 recorded by other researchers 10 years ago. Most of the stammerers are boys. The report's author, Dr George Donovan, medical officer of West Glamorgan Health Division, says, 'This seems to be bound up with the Permissive Society, or can I say a non-repressive one.'

DAVIES STEPS IN TO SAVE MINI FIRMS

A special 'Minister for Small Firms' was appointed by the Government last night to protect small firms from the danger of extinction. He is Mr Nicholas Ridley, Parliamentary Under-Secretary of State at the Department of Trade and Industry. Industry Minister John Davies announced this move to save small firms, following a report on their plight from a government-sponsored enquiry committee. The report said that if the present decline continued unchecked, after the end of this century there would be virtually no small firms left in the manufacturing industry.

ODD, ISN'T IT? THEY'RE LEARNING TO EARN HALF THEIR SALARY

Clearly times have changed since Rudyard Kipling described professional footballers as the 'muddied oafs at the goals'. Many players are now looking to a second career which they can fall back on when they have retired from the game. Today's big stars have no worries about the future – George Best and Bobby Moore have vast interests outside football.

The problem arises over the players who are not going to be big stars. Coventry City footballers will be attending elocution and deportment lessons this winter to equip them for making after-dinner speeches and a number of West Ham United players are to take a course in salesmanship. Derek Parkin, Coventry's under-23 England international, is studying French cuisine; Derek Dougan, Wolverhampton Wanderers centre-forward, is already a TV star and runs his own sports programme in the Midlands; Coventry's Dennis Mortimer is taking up woodwork; and Ernie Hunt, another Coventry player, is a fully qualified hairdresser. Bob Wilson, the Arsenal goalkeeper, who is already a good TV performer, can presumably look forward to a successful TV career when he retires from the game.

FILL HER UP YOURSELF

Push-button self-service petrol is being introduced in Britain today by National Benzole. They say their system is quicker and cleaner than the present self-service. The scheme is starting at Rickmansworth, Hertfordshire, and it is planned to spread throughout the country. National Benzole expects half of Britain's filling stations to be self-service within 5 years.

Donald Sutherland and Jane Fonda in Klute.

SCHOOL FEES STORM

Education Secretary, Mrs Margaret Thatcher, was branded a 'reactionary cave woman' yesterday after she announced plans to provide an extra £2m a year to help direct-grant schools. The charge came from Labour backbencher Mr William Hamilton while Labour's education spokesman Mr Edward Short said, 'Isn't it typical that this Government should cut out our primary-school milk to save £9m and now give away the money to the direct-grant schools?' The Government's extra cash will be devoted towards reducing fees.

Mrs Thatcher also faces a storm over a plan to persuade students to attend universities near their homes to reduce the cost of grants for lodgings. At present only 17% of students live at home but Mrs Thatcher made it plain that in future many more will be expected to study at universities within travelling distance of their homes. Mr Jack Straw, Students' Union President, said last night, 'You can encourage more students to live at home but once you try to force them you start discriminating against those from poorer homes.'

RU 18 CAR GOES FOR £1,000

In pubs throughout the country imitation car number plates RU 18 have been part of the décor but the only real set was sold yesterday for £1,000 by licensee Don Batley of Hampshire. Included in the price was the 1966 Austin Cambridge to which they belong. The new owner, a car numbers enthusiast from Blackpool, expects the value of the plates to treble in 2 years.

MAUDLING NAMES NEW POLICE CHIEF

The Home Secretary, Mr Reginald Maudling, last night named Mr Robert Mark as the new Commissioner of the Metropolitan Police. The announcement of 54-year-old Mr Mark's appointment is designed to boost the morale of the force which has recently suffered many allegations of corruption.

DEC 1971

US SCHOOL BANS 16 FOR 'INSULTS'

16 American school pupils were suspended from classes indefinitely last night for 'insulting' Education Minister Mrs Margaret Thatcher. All 16 'rebels' attend the new £2,700,000 American School in St John's Wood, London NW8 – a luxurious and lavishly equipped showpiece of education. As Mrs Thatcher dedicated their school yesterday the 16 tried to interrupt her address by reading out a statement objecting to her presence at the ceremony while British children 'still had to go to slum schools'. One of the children said later, 'It was not because we bore her any personal malice but we did not want her élitist policies connected with our school.'

The protest arose from a visit some of the senior pupils paid 3 weeks ago to the Thomas Calton Comprehensive School in southeast London. There they saw the school was split over 5 sites separated by 2 main roads. The buildings were erected in 1884; plaster is coming off the ceilings; water seeps down the walls; most lavatories are outside and freeze in winter; there is an electricity sub-station in the playground; and wire mesh covers the narrow windows.

Steel-helmeted Indian soldiers man a machine-gun emplacement on the Indian-Pakistani border at Petrapole.

MALTA: THANKS AND GOODBYE

The British Government bluntly told Malta Prime Minister Dom Mintoff last night, 'We are pulling out all our troops.' It was Mr Heath's reply to Mr Mintoff's latest attempt to drag more money out of Britain. He had given Britain this ultimatum: 'Pay up a further £4,250,000 immediately for British-based facilities or get out by tomorrow night.' Mr Heath refused to pay. The fiery Socialist Premier of Malta said, 'We have told Britain to pay or else leave. They have chosen to go. The only thing to say now is, "Thank you, you can go."'

TEACHERS DRAW UP TELEVISION BLACKLIST

2 teachers yesterday listed shows which they said contributed to the concentration of trivia, sex and violence fed to teenagers through television. Mr Richard Panter and Mr Ron Taylor made a month-long survey of programmes. Their findings include:

– *It's Awfully Bad For Your Eyes, Darling*: vulgar. What wit there was concerned sex.
– *Casanova*: nudes for the sake of it.
– *Now Look Here*: unnecessary emphasis on an unmarried couple living together.
– *Tom Brown's Schooldays*: sadism under the guise of a respected author.
– *Coronation Street*: a poor reflection of public taste.
– *Cilla Black*: trite dialogue, endless confrontations with semi-articulate people.
– *Please, Sir* and *The Fenn Street Gang*: the sense of fun had sharply declined beyond the limits of decency and good taste.

These findings were made known at a meeting of the Assistant Masters' Association in Plymouth but did not meet with universal approval. Mr Peter Smith poured scorn on the blacklist, saying, 'What about *Tom and Jerry*? Is that sado-masochistic fantasizing?'

IRMA WAS DRIVING ME MAD, SAYS AXED STAR

Sandra Gough, the 28-year-old actress who was axed from *Coronation Street* at the weekend, said last night, 'I knew I was heading for the sack – it was just a matter of time.' Miss Gough, known to millions of television viewers as Irma Barlow, was sacked because of her 'behaviour over the past few weeks'. 3 weeks ago the £250-a-week star caused chaos when she suddenly flew to Spain to see her ex-husband after receiving a telegram that he was ill. Scenes in which she appeared had to be re-written to explain her absence. Miss Gough, who had played the part for 5½ years, said, 'I'm glad to be turning my back on the *Street*; Irma Barlow was driving me mad.'

Pete Duel, star of the BBC2 western series Alias Smith And Jones, *is found dead at his Hollywood home.*

£25 'CURE' FOR CAR EXHAUSTS

A device which is claimed to eliminate 97% of car exhaust fumes has been developed by ICI. British Leyland, who is to test the device, believes it could become Britain's first motor firm to produce family cars with works-fitted exhaust-control units. Cars fitted with the device, which could cost as little as £25 for a British motorist, could be on sale within 2 years.

LE MINI ROARS IN AT 84 m.p.h.

Here is the new Mini Renault being launched in France next February to challenge the British Leyland Mini. The Renault 5 is a 2-door 4–5 seat semi-estate car with a lift-up tailgate. It has a 956cc front-wheel-drive engine, giving a top speed of 84 m.p.h. The Renault 5 will sell for £727 in France. No UK price has been fixed yet.

NOW A YEARLY PENSION BOOST

The Government is to review all state pensions every year to keep them in line with the rising cost of living. The Social Services Minister Sir Keith Joseph told the Commons yesterday that the scheme will come into effect next October and will include all related benefits from industrial injuries to sickness and unemployment. Previously the Cabinet had promised to adjust pensions every other year.

LIBYA SEIZES BP FROM BRITAIN

Libya last night nationalized the British Petroleum oil company's assets in the country. The Government of strong man Colonel Muammar Gaddafi also announced it has withdrawn all its deposits, about £79 million, from British banks. The moves are in retaliation over Britain's failure to ensure protection for 3 Persian Gulf islands against Iranian occupation. Libya has renamed BP the Arab Gulf Exploration Company.

INDIA SEEKING A KNOCKOUT

The Indian Army was smashing its way into East Pakistan last night in a blitzkrieg campaign to wipe out the Pakistan forces there. If it succeeds India is poised to set up an independent state of Bangladesh immediately. Yesterday 2 leaders of the anti-Pakistan Bangladesh rebels were flown to New Delhi for urgent talks with the Indian Government. An Indian source said that the talks would be about recognition of a new state to replace East Pakistan. Once the area had been 'liberated' by Indian troops the rebel leaders would take over, India would recognize Bangladesh 'and East Pakistan would no longer exist'.

PLUMBER'S £1M PIPE DREAMS

Former plumber Kevin MacDonald's business ideas have made him a millionaire. 6 years ago, 37-year-old Mr MacDonald decided to start producing plastic wastepipes. Now he has sold his shares in the company he founded in a deal worth over £1.1m. Mr MacDonald, who lives near Doncaster, once a 35s.-a-week apprentice plumber put in £50 to start the firm and a partner did the same. His colleague dropped out but Mr MacDonald had faith in the scheme and, despite the financial squeezes of the 60s, business boomed. Copper prices hit an all-time high so more and more people turned to plastic wastepipes.

COMING SHORTLY, A FILM FOR NONE OF THE FAMILY

Stephen Murphy is in trouble again. The man who passed *Straw Dogs* has given his blessing to Stanley Kubrick's *A Clockwork Orange*. Named in America as the film of the year it is the story of a young man whose particular interests, to quote the distributor's official handout, are 'rape, ultra-violence and Beethoven'.

DOC TESTS DALGLISH IN FIRING LINE

Kenny Dalglish, the 20-year-old Celtic player who is so gifted that not even manager Jock Stein is sure about his best position, takes on a new role for Scotland against Holland tonight. He replaces the strong, experienced John O'Hare as target man in his first full game for Scotland. Dalglish, who has shown a rare brilliance both as a striker and as a midfield man for Celtic, now takes over one of the most demanding jobs on the field. Naming him in the side Tommy Docherty said, 'If it had been a World Cup qualifying game O'Hare would have been in but I must see whether anybody else can do O'Hare's job.'

SHANE – AT 15 SHE'S TOO FAST FOR OUR MEN

Shane Gould, Australia's incredible 15-year-old swimming star, yesterday shattered the women's 1,500 metres freestyle world record by 18.6 seconds. She returned 17 minutes 0.6 seconds, almost 9 seconds faster than the British men's record, to become the first woman in swimming history to hold all 5 metric freestyle world records from 100 metres to the 1,500. Shane, already acclaimed the world's sportswoman of the year, is expected to collect 5, possibly 6, gold medals at the Munich Olympics next year. Her performance yesterday was being rated as the greatest ever swim; it was fast enough to have won the bronze medal in the men's final at the Mexico Olympics.

BBC SIGNS 5 DISC JOCKEYS FOR £125,000

The BBC yesterday announced a £125,000 deal to put its leading disc jockeys under exclusive contract until 1974 – and off commercial radio. Jimmy Young, Tony Blackburn, Peter Murray, Ed Stewart and Terry Wogan have signed 3-year contracts with Radios 1 and 2. The contracts are the longest ever offered to disc jockeys; until now they have been restricted to 3, 6 or 12-month runs. The BBC is determined to give commercial radio few chances of winning listeners by buying up popular personalities.

The corporation last night also launched a shake-up of TV current-affairs programmes by bringing in a new 'Supremo' anchorman for *24 Hours*, from ITV. Austin Mitchell, former lecturer in politics, who introduces the Yorkshire Regional magazine programme *Calendar* is joining the BBC1 series next month and will be seen every evening. The present team of presenters, David Dimbleby, Kenneth Allsop and Ludovic Kennedy, will continue to appear 1 week in 3.

DAY BY DAY

1 Dec
The Government has a majority of 28 in a House of Commons motion approving proposals for a settlement of the Rhodesian dispute.

2 Dec
A Select Committee recommends that the Queen's income should be increased from £475,000 to £980,000 a year.

6 Dec
The Review Body of Top Salaries recommends that, from 1972, the Prime Minister's salary be increased from £14,000 to £20,000 a year and that of Opposition Leader from £4,500 to £9,500. MPs' salaries will be raised from £3,250 to £4,500 a year.

The Indian Government says it will recognize East Pakistan (Bangladesh) as an independent republic.

10 Dec
Britain's first hovertrain makes a demonstration run at Earith, Huntingdonshire.

12 Dec
Mr Jack Barnhill, a Northern Ireland senator, is shot dead at his home near the border with the Irish Republic.

13 Dec
The Jockey Club rules that women jockeys are to be allowed to compete in a series of amateur all-women flat races next year.

14 Dec
The Chancellor of the Exchequer announces that all outstanding post-war credits are to be repaid during 1972.

The Government of East Pakistan resigns.

15 Dec
Princess Anne is named BBC Sports Personality of the Year.

16 Dec
India accepts the surrender of East Pakistani forces.

17 Dec
Jack Bodell loses his European heavyweight title to José Urtain.

18 Dec
The Group of Ten, meeting in Washington, reach agreement over the international currency crisis.

America agrees to devalue the dollar by 7.9% in terms of gold and to remove the 10% import surcharge.

20 Dec
Zulfikar Ali Bhutto takes over as President of Pakistan in place of Yahya Khan.

21 Dec
Dr Kurt Waldheim of Austria is chosen as Secretary-General of the United Nations to succeed U Thant.

31 Dec
Mr Dom Mintoff extends the time for the withdrawal of British troops from Malta to 15 January.

The Indian Army Chief of Staff, General Aurora (l.), and the Pakistan Eastern Command Chief, Lieutenant-General Niazi, sign papers at Dacca for the unconditional surrender of all Pakistani troops in East Pakistan.

JAN 1972

ROUND-THE-CLOCK TV

The Government has scrapped all restrictions on TV and radio broadcasting hours but Britain will not become a round-the-clock TV society overnight. ITV will screen most of its new shows during the day and the BBC may not screen any extra programmes. The Independent Television Authority welcomed the freedom of unlimited hours but BBC officials said, 'Unlike ITV extra hours does not mean extra money for us.' Scrapping TV hours' 'rationing' – both main channels have been restricted to about 3,300 hours a year plus time for educational, religious and outside broadcast programmes – has taken ITV by surprise. The move is to compensate ITV for not getting a second channel but the industry expected a small extra weekly allowance rather than complete freedom.

The ITA, still anxious to prove that it deserves a second channel, is determined to keep most repeats, imported shows and old films out of extra time. It is sticking to its rules that American programmes and old movies must take up no more than 14% of total time. Breakfast shows are also causing a split. Thames in London wants them, ATV is not interested in early news programmes and the ITA 'does not envisage breakfast-time TV'.

HONOURS TO SUPERSTARS

Mr Heath gives 1972 a spectacular send-off this morning by showering honours on some of the superstars who thrilled Britain last year. Among the awards: round-the-world non-stop sailor Chay Blyth gets the CBE, motor racing's Jackie Stewart gets an OBE, Arsenal's Frank McLintock and Wimbledon's new Australian golden girl Evonne Goolagong all get the MBE. On the showbiz front zany disc jockey Jimmy Savile receives an OBE for his charity work over the years. Photographer Royal Cecil Beaton becomes a knight, Cicely Courtenidge, darling of musical comedy for generations, becomes a dame. Sports awards go to Kent cricket captain Colin Cowdrey (CBE); veteran international golfer Henry Longhurst (CBE); British Lions captain John Dawes (OBE); Britain's lone world boxing champion Ken Buchanan (OBE); long-distance runner Ron Hill gets an MBE. In the Arts, CBEs go to actor Michael Hordern, author Arthur Koestler and Hobbit creator Professor J R R Tolkien.

1,000 RIDERS ARE BARRED

At least 1,000 motor-cyclists have been ordered to surrender their licences because they are too young to ride. The age limit for a motor-cycle licence was raised from 16 to 17 on 16 December so many 16-year-olds are having to send their licences back. Legally people may apply for a driving licence in the month before the date on which they are eligible to drive. Last November hundreds of 15-year-olds were granted provisional motor-cycling driving licences to become valid from their sixteenth birthdays in December. Now these licences are being called in. Young people who have bought motor-cycles must sell them or put them in store.

ENTER ACCESS

A rival to the Barclaycard is to be jointly launched by the National Westminster, Midland and Lloyds banks this year. It will be called Access.

In one tragic hour the death toll reaches 13 on Ulster's bloodiest Sunday.

THAT JINGLE THE WORLD IS LEARNING TO SING . . .

Songwriters Roger Greenaway and Roger Cook are slightly piqued that what promises to be their biggest ever money-spinning hit is basically an advertising jingle. The song in question is the New Seekers' 'I'd Like To Teach The World To Sing', better known to millions of television viewers throughout the world as the Coca-Cola song 'I'd Like To Buy The World A Coke'. By this time next week it should be at the top of the hit parade – it is number 3 at the moment – and there are 2 versions in the American Top 20. Coca-Cola, needless to say, are delighted. Although there is no reference to their product in the rewritten lyrics of the record version the melody is instantly recognizable so, although the BBC won't play records that mention products by name, they are getting what amounts to a free advert every time the record is played on radio and television.

Demonstration march from Tower Hill to the Houses of Parliament.

HEATH ORDERS – NO RETREAT

Britain's first nationwide pit shutdown since 1926 starts at midnight with the Government ordering 'no concessions' in the £31m pay offer rejected by the miners. The tactics of Mr Heath and his Cabinet will be to let the 280,000 miners sweat it out. Miners' President Mr Joe Gormley said, 'We must get the uninhibited support of all unions so that no coal is touched. No one section of workers can beat this Government on its own.'

Rationing in the shops due to the miners' strike.

FIGHT TO KEEP THE POSTMAN CALLING TWICE

Plans to scrap the second letter delivery in residential areas are to be opposed by the Post Users' 'Watchdog' Committee. The Post Office hopes to save £13m a year by doing away with the second delivery, extending the one-delivery-a-day well into the afternoon and restricting evening and weekend collections. The Post Office Users' National Council will argue that this could mean no delivery at all when fog, ice or snow hampers postmen. Also, ending the second delivery would penalize firms in residential districts as it is not possible to separate commercial and private mail.

Gene Hackman, in Santa Claus outfit, and Roy Scheider rough up a pusher (Alan Weeks) before arresting him in Philip D'Antoni's The French Connection (1971).

BELT UP! IT COULD COST YOU IN MORE WAYS THAN ONE NOT TO TAKE HEED

There is no law to make you wear crash helmets or seatbelts on British roads. If you don't do either you are presumably willing to take the risk but could you suffer in any other way? If you think that you couldn't because you are not breaking the law you could be wrong. Recently a 19-year-old boy was knocked off his motorcycle, through the admitted carelessness of a car driver, and fractured his skull. The car driver's insurance company did not dispute liability but introduced a surprisingly new plea of contributory negligence – the fact that the young man had not been wearing a crash helmet. Despite the boy's counsel indignantly pointing out that there was no legal compulsion to wear a crash helmet, the plea was upheld and the boy's compensation was cut by 15%. After such a precedent there can now be little doubt that if it were possible to prove – or even suggest – that injuries would have been less severe had an innocent victim been wearing a seatbelt fitted to the car the same plea of contributory negligence could be upheld to reduce a damages award.

MOTORISTS SLOW DOWN FOR THE TRICK STRIPES

Trick lines painted on the road have succeeded in making motorists slow down at dangerous junctions. An experiment in Hertfordshire was so successful that drivers in 6 other parts of Britain are to be given the same treatment. 'Perceptual lines', as they are called, are a series of yellow stripes painted across the road. They start 400 yards from the roundabout and get narrower and closer together as they near the roundabout so that a driver going over them gets an impression of going faster than he really is and brakes accordingly.

MG OUSTS TWIN

British Leyland is killing off the Austin Sprite but its 'twin' the MG Midget continues in an improved form. The jaunty little Sprite sports car has been a favourite on the roads for 14 years. It started as the Austin Healey Sprite, developed by BMC and sports-car design wizard Donald Healey in 1958. The Healey connection was ended by Lord Stokes after BMC merged with Leyland and now, from today, the Austin Sprite is dead.

FEB 1972

DIM-OUT DAY EMERGENCY

A state of emergency to be declared by the Cabinet today will signal the opening of the Government's biggest challenge to the unions over wages. Advertising and window-display lights will go out from midnight tonight and there will be a ban on floodlighting. In the West End many theatre and cinema managements anticipated the ban last night and switched off a day early. Some advertisements in Piccadilly Circus were also switched off.

When the official ban starts offenders against the regulations could face £100 fines or 3 months in jail. Electricity cuts will be on a rota basis throughout the country. Powers will also be taken to move coal and oil into the power stations to ban street lighting on a selective basis and to restrict heating and lighting in every home, office and factory, but they will be enforced only as the situation deteriorates. It is the fifth week of the strike in which miners are seeking a £120m pay settlement.

Trying to make a sale by candlelight in Regent Street.

Trying to study by candlelight – a scene typical of thousands of homes as power cuts disrupt daily life.

Police and picketing miners fall like ninepins as a coke lorry ploughs through.

END OF THE ROAD FOR THE BIG TOP

Billy Smart's Circus will no longer be coming to town. The travelling show has reached the end of the road. The 16-ton Big Top, built to seat 6,000 people, is going into store. The last of the clowns are returning home to France and all the performing animals have been sold except one, Birma, the only elephant Billy Smart had when he started the circus in 1945. Mr Smart, who died 5 years ago, built it into Europe's biggest travelling show but with the 60s came decline. The Smart family tried to save the business by applying for an Arts Council grant but Mr Ronald Smart, the company's Managing Director, said last night, 'Unlike Russia and Hungary the Circus here is not considered an art. We failed to get our grant and rising costs have put us off the road.'

HEATH STAYS – BY 8 VOTES

5 Liberal MPs saved the Heath Government from catastrophe and the nation from a general election last night. With their help the Government scraped home on the Common Market issue by 309 votes to 301. In an atmosphere of near violence, with passions high and fury let loose, Liberal leader Jeremy Thorpe was manhandled. Mr Heath, the crusading European who already this week has been in the midst of his worst domestic crisis as Prime Minister, owed his victory of sorts to the element that had been ignored: the tiny Liberal Party.

President Richard Nixon and his wife with Chinese Vice-Premier Li Jsien-nien at the Great Wall. 23 years of implacable enmity begins to dissolve as the president of the greatest capitalist nation in history visits the world's biggest Communist state.

REAL FRENZY FOR HITCH

Suspense became real for screen maestro Alfred Hitchcock in his struggle not to spend a minute over 90 days a year in Britain, thus protecting his tax status. While filming *Frenzy* at Pinewood during the present financial year, 71-year-old Hitch became noticeably agitated. 'It was literally a race against time. If I stay just 1 day over the 90 I have to pay double income tax to both Britain and the United States,' he said. Luckily, the film was wrapped up on the eighty-ninth day and Hitch was homeward-bound a few hours before his financial deadline.

BERNADETTE – OUT OF CONTROL

Bernadette Devlin MP, an uncontrollable bundle of Irish fury, shattered the House of Commons yesterday by hurling herself like a wildcat at the Home Secretary. There was total uproar as she seized Mr Maudling by the hair and punched and scratched his face. Other MPs joined in to protect him and then still more charged in to the mêlée to protect the shouting Miss Devlin.

Her attack came as Mr Maudling was announcing that an enquiry would be held into Sunday's Londonderry riot. Nothing like it has been seen in the Commons for decades, yet no action was taken against Miss Devlin and that left MPs seething with anger last night. Outside the House later she said, 'The Provisional and official wings of the IRA have each said they will kill 13 paratroopers in vengeance for those who died on Sunday. That is 26 coffins coming home to England and I won't shed a tear for any one of them.'

TOUGH NEW RULES ON TYRES

New rules governing car-tyre repairs come into force today. Thousands of drivers will have to buy new tyres or risk prosecution with fines up to £50 and automatic licence endorsement. Under the BSI Standards, temporary repairs of tubeless tyres must be made permanent before the driver has done 100 miles and all temporary plugs in punctures must be red so that the police can see them clearly. All permanent repairs must be vulcanized and no repair will be considered permanent unless the tyre was removed during the job. Tyres must be scrapped if the side walls or bead are damaged, if punctures are too close together, and if they are affected by oil or chemicals. Aerosol sealants are not acceptable. Many garages are unable to vulcanize tubeless tyres, which means they will legally be able to do no more than a temporary repair.

WHISK TO BEAT POLLUTION

A huge 'egg whisk' has been set up in the Thames to put back oxygen taken out by industrial pollution. 5,000,000 gallons of water from the river are used every day by a cardboard factory at Purfleet, Essex. This is mixed with wood pulp and returned to the river; the result is a de-oxygenated, 'dead' stretch. Now the whisk – an aerator powered by a 200-horsepower motor – is floating 2 miles above the factory outflow. The aim is to whip high oxygen levels into the water before it mixes with the effluent. A company spokesman said last night, 'We're so convinced it will work we have arranged a fishing competition in the next few weeks and expect good catches for the first time.'

HEATH BACKS MRS THATCHER IN STORM

Mrs Margaret Thatcher is now more firmly entrenched than ever as Education Secretary, and all through the efforts of Labour MP Mr Gerald Kaufmann. He demanded in the Commons yesterday that Mr Heath should sack her for what Mr Wilson later called 'one of the filthiest bills ever introduced' – the ban on free school milk for the over-7s – but the Prime Minister listed Mrs Thatcher's achievements: more primary schools, the biggest ever building programme for polytechnics, the raising of the school-leaving age, and said she had earned the grateful thanks of thousands. Clearly Mrs Thatcher is there to stay.

COMPUTE A CARDIGAN . . .

A new concept in automatic knitting machines, the simple-to-operate Knitmaster 321, works on a computerized punch-card system. Made in Japan, this model knits 2 colours simultaneously in the same row. Each Knitmaster machine comes with 20 punch-cards, each offering 12 designs plus infinite permutations of colour.

Thumbs up from the Nottinghamshire miners' wives in London.

MAR 1972

'£500-CARROT' PLAN FAILS

No £520 carrots will be sold at Herbert Hardy's Furniture Store this Sunday and no more 'free gifts' of suites of furniture to go with his costly vegetables. Yesterday 3 High Court judges ruled that Mr Hardy's plan to get round the Sunday shopping laws was illegal. Carrots were being sold because the sale of fruit and vegetables was allowed on Sundays, whereas the sale of furniture was not. When a shopper saw a piece of furniture he wanted, salesmen wrote details and price on a piece of paper, the customer then agreed to buy a carrot for the same price. One customer had paid £520 for a carrot and got a 'free gift' of furniture.

TAX GUIDE FOR LOVERS

If you want to save on your next child, make love in May and June, says a report out today. A child born but an hour before the end of the tax year – midnight on 5 April – gains its parents a full year's tax saving of up to £60.06, and that makes May or June a good time to conceive, says *Money Which*, the tax-saving guide published by the Consumers' Association. It is also wise for tax-conscious couples to choose the right month for their wedding. If both husband and wife are working this is usually July, August or September and the saving could well be more than £100. The traditional March or April wedding is usually the worst from the tax payers' point of view.

The report also advises husbands to put wives out to work, even if only part-time. The reason: the wife can earn up to £418 a year and pay no tax at all. If the husband earned an extra £418 he would, in most cases, have to pay an additional £125.93 in tax. Couples in highly paid jobs can save even more by being taxed separately – an option they will be able to take up under new regulations which come in on 6 April. A well-off couple with the wife earning say £2,500 and the husband £4,350 could, if assessed separately, save nearly £200.

CHARLES LOSES HIS 1919 PRIZE

53 years ago Charles Stanley won £50 and a plot of land in a contest to name a new town on the Sussex coast. The name he suggested – Peacehaven – was chosen by the developer who ran the competition and had advertised it in the *Daily Mail* in 1916.

Mr Stanley, a boilermaker from Kent, never had the money to build on his land so it was left undeveloped. Now aged 77 and retired, he wants to claim the plot, which could be worth up to £3,000, but he has found that the title deeds, which he kept in an old shoebox, have been eaten by mice and he may lose his plot to land-grabbers who have moved in on Peacehaven.

For a long time Peacehaven was a run-down clifftop shanty town dubbed Slumhaven by planners. More recently, however, as property values have rocketed, claim jumpers have moved in.

Peacehaven, which now has a population of 8,320, was only a 'second thoughts' name for the development. The original winning name was Anzac-on-Sea in honour of the Australian and New Zealand troops who fought at Gallipoli but the developers later rejected it on the grounds that Mr Stanley's suggestion was a better commercial proposition.

MP CALLS FOR ACTION ON 'DOUBLE PRICING'

A call for enquiries into the alleged 'double pricing' of washing machines, sewing machines and lawn mowers is to be made in the Commons tomorrow. Double pricing is the practice of manufacturers fixing inflated recommended prices so retailers can advertise 'slashing reductions' and still make a normal profit. Mr Greville Janner, Labour MP for Leicester North West, will press Mr John Davies, Trade Secretary, to order the probe. Mr Janner said yesterday, 'It is the fooling of the shopper I object to. He may be getting good value but he thinks he is getting a bargain when he isn't. The price is deliberately fictitious.'

SICK PAY FOR NUDE MODELS

6 models who pose in the nude for Sheffield art students have won a sick-pay scheme. Those with more than 1 year's service who work more than 20 hours a week will be entitled to 9 weeks' full pay if they fall sick. Those with more than 6 years' service will get full pay for up to 6 months. The models are members of the General and Municipal Workers Union and a regional officer said, 'This is in line with the sickness-benefit schemes operated by the local authorities.' The union recently negotiated a 9p-an-hour pay rise for the models, raising their hourly rate to 60p.

The mask of Tutankhamun is taken out of its packing case at the British Museum.

DAY BY DAY

1 Mar
14-year-old British schoolboy Timothy Davey is jailed for 6 years in Istanbul for conspiring to sell hashish.

4 Mar
5 people die as a hovercraft capsizes in rough seas off Southsea.
Stoke City wins the Football League Cup, beating Chelsea 2–1.

8 Mar
The 192-foot airship *Europa*, built by the Goodyear Rubber Company, makes its maiden flight and becomes the first such craft to fly over Britain for more than 20 years.

13 Mar
31-year-old naval officer Sub-Lieutenant David Bingham is sentenced to 21 years' imprisonment for passing information to the Russians.

24 Mar
The Prime Minister announces in the House of Commons that direct rule from Westminster is to be imposed on Northern Ireland and the Stormont Parliament prorogued. Mr William Whitelaw is appointed Secretary of State for Northern Ireland.

25 Mar
The Eurovision Song Contest, held in Edinburgh, is won by Luxembourg. The UK entry, 'Beg, Steal or Borrow', sung by the New Seekers, finishes second.

26 Mar
Britain and Malta sign a new 7-year defence agreement just 5 days before all British forces would have been withdrawn from the island.

27 Mar
Nearly all Protestant workers in Northern Ireland begin a 2-day strike in protest against direct rule.

29 Mar
The Queen opens the Treasures of Tutankhamun exhibition at the British Museum to mark the fiftieth anniversary of its discovery.

Lord Rank, founder of the Rank Organisation leisure empire, dies, aged 83.

BRANDO IS THE GODFATHER

The king is back. After many years of indifferent films Marlon Brando, hailed by many as the greatest actor of his generation, has returned to claim his throne. Critics who have seen his performance as the aging Mafia boss Vito Corleone in *The Godfather* say it is the best thing he has done since *On The Waterfront* and *A Streetcar Named Desire* back in the 50s. As the film of Mario Puzo's best-selling novel opens it is hard to believe that the squat, sad-eyed figure in the tight tuxedo is Brando. A miracle of make-up has transformed the athletic Brando, now 47, into a man of 65. He does the rest.

CHILDREN'S HOUR RETURNS – BUT WITHOUT LARRY

BBC Radio is reviving its famous *Children's Hour* series, dropped 8 years ago because of falling audiences. With radio audiences on the upswing again the BBC is bringing back regular junior programmes on Radio 4 on Saturday afternoons when sport dominates television. But the revival this autumn will not mean the return of old *Children's Hour* favourites like Larry the Lamb of Toytown. The new series will include a feature where children could telephone questions to scientists and the *Orange-Coloured Peppermint Holiday Show*, a collection of stories, humour and do-it-yourself items introduced by comedian Bernard Cribbins. There is good news for Larry the Lamb fans, however. A new filmed series based on puppets of the Toytown characters is being launched on some ITV stations later this year.

COULD YOU STAND CHUNNEL DRIVE?

Experts doubt whether motorists could stand the mental strain of driving 30 miles underground in a Channel road tunnel, but before a high-speed car tunnel is definitely ruled out a special study is being made to determine the exact strain on drivers. Feasibility studies are already coming out firmly in favour of a car-carrying train tunnel; nevertheless experts at Rio Tinto Zinc, who are putting together the British study, have decided to collect 'balancing information'. So car designers, road scientists, motoring psychologists, doctors and eye specialists are to be consulted for their views on 'Can drivers motor safely underground for 30 miles?'

Researchers say that apart from pollution and breakdown problems the Channel road tunnel would require special regulations. Motorists would have to drive the full distance at a compulsory 50 to 60 m.p.h. in the same lane and in artificial light. British researchers studying the behaviour of drivers in the world's longest existing road tunnel – a 9-mile highway through the Alps – have found them wavering and suffering from 'psychological difficulty in maintaining a constant speed in the same lane'. The researchers also fear that some motorists could suffer from a form of claustrophobia that could lead to accidents. *The Channel Tunnel Study* is showing that an electric rail service could travel at 90 m.p.h. and the tunnel could be in service by 1980. Cost: about £350m.

It's a deal – the gifted Rodney Marsh signs on with Malcolm Allison of Manchester City.

FAULKNER TO RESIGN TODAY

Mr Brian Faulkner and his entire Ulster Cabinet will resign today. The only chance for the province now is direct rule from London. The Ulster Premier will hand his resignation to the Northern Ireland Governor, Lord Grey, this morning as soon as Mr Heath announces his peace initiatives to the Commons at 11 a.m. The Governor will be told that the Unionist Party is united and that no other members are prepared to form a government.

Mr Faulkner flew home to Belfast last night after 2 days of fruitless talks. The British plan involved an easing of internment and the taking-over of security from Stormont by Britain but Mr Faulkner and his Cabinet declared outright that they would not make any concessions on internment or security while the terrorist campaign was at its height.

APR 1972

JENKINS QUITS

Mr Roy Jenkins last night resigned as deputy leader of the Labour Party in disgust at party manoeuvrings over the Common Market. The back-breaking straw for Mr Jenkins, fervently pro-Common Market and going along with the party's anti-Market line reluctantly, was a pre-Easter decision of the Shadow Cabinet to support the idea of a referendum on the issue. 2 other members of the Shadow Cabinet, Mr Harold Lever and Mr George Thomson, also resigned. A third pro-Marketeer, Mrs Shirley Williams, wavered but decided to stay on under protest.

STRIKE LAW ON COLLISION COURSE

More than 5,000 dockers yesterday came into head-on collision with the law. They defied an order by the National Industrial Relations Court to stop blacking a firm's container-lorry fleet and they decided to extend their ban to 2 more firms. The decision by the dockers at Liverpool is the first direct challenge by a large group of workers to the Government's authority. The dockers claim that only they should have the job of 'stuffing and stripping' (loading and unloading) container lorries. Mr Robert Heaton, the lorry firm's managing director, said last night, 'Now it will be the law against the dockers and it will be a real battle.'

OLIVIA IN DRUG-DASH DRAMA

Guitarist Bruce Welch, whose 4-year engagement to pop singer Olivia Newton-John was broken off earlier this week, is in hospital suffering from a drug overdose. Olivia travelled with him in the ambulance before going on to the Prince of Wales Theatre for her part in the Sacha Distel show. Welch, 30, who became engaged to Olivia in 1968, was one of Cliff Richard's original Shadows and now plays with another former Shadow Hank Marvin in a group called Marvin, Welch and Farrar. Miss Newton-John became well known through her appearances in Cliff Richard's television series. She was recently voted Britain's top girl singer and has the George Harrison song 'What is Life' in the hit parade.

AT LAST THERE'S A PILL THAT MEN CAN TAKE . . . AND WOMEN COULD TAKE IT THE MORNING AFTER –

A contraceptive pill that can be taken by men and women is to be tried out on people this year. Tests on animals indicate that it works even if a woman takes it after intercourse. The drug is a naturally occurring compound in plant life and its greatest promise lies in the fact that it is a non-steroid – it does not contain the powerful sex hormones of existing oral contraceptives. The new pill has the effect – so far unexplained – of 'disarming' the male sperm by preventing its fertilizing the female egg. In the woman it prevents the ovum becoming implanted in the womb.

NEW LINE IN PHONES

The Post Office hopes that a new type of telephone will put an end to wrong numbers. Instead of a dial it has push buttons bearing the numbers 0 to 9. The first telephones of this type should be available from about the middle of next year. They will cost £3 per quarter extra with an installation fee of £5.

'SALT MAY CAUSE HEART DEATHS'

For years doctors have wondered why death from heart disease is more common in soft-water areas than where the water is hard. Now, 2 Cambridge University scientists think it may be because people with soft water like more salt with their food. Research showed that men from several soft-water areas had higher levels of sodium than those living in London – a hard-water area. Reporting their findings in the *Lancet* the scientists pointed out that the main source of sodium is not water but sodium chloride – salt taken with food. Dr E.M. Widdowson and Miss Joy Dauncey, who carried out the research, stressed yesterday that the idea was only a possibility which ought to be investigated further.

TOY TYCOON JOHN SNAPS UP BRITISH LION FOR £5m

Millionaire financier John Bentley has taken over the British Lion Film Company in a surprise £5m deal. The head of Barclay Securities – one of Britain's biggest toy companies – said last night that the future of British Lion as an active film-making company was assured. British Lion is the country's third largest film production and distribution company. It owns Shepperton Studios and Pearl and Dean Advertising.

ALBERT HALL BAN ON POP

The Albert Hall is to ban all pop and rock concerts because of rowdy behaviour by fans. The Council of Britain's biggest concert hall said that of 23 pop and rock concerts at the hall last year only 1 passed off without disorder. Mr Robert Patterson, who has staged more pop shows at the Albert Hall than anyone else, said, 'Where are they going to draw the line? They have told me I can't have Chicago or Ike and Tina Turner there although their concerts have passed off in the past without trouble . . . It seems likely that I shall have to ignore London in future and put the really big concerts on at Belle Vue, Manchester.'

PHONE CHEAT'S 2 CALLS COST £400

Student Duncan Campbell, 19, decided to show off his technical know-how to his friends, so he made a free call to Los Angeles and another to a student in Moscow. But the call to America – to a house of ill repute on Sunset Boulevard – proved his undoing. As he recorded the brothel's answering service Post Office investigators were listening in. In the first prosecution of its type Campbell was fined £200 with £200 costs yesterday. By using a device placed against the mouthpiece of an ordinary phone together with special codes, calls were set up which bypassed the operator. Outside the court he said, 'The code numbers are quite simply obtained. They are in a Post Office publication; any library keeps these technical journals.' He admitted that he had been freaking – the term for the free calls technique – for 8 to 9 months. One freaker said last night, 'We are not doing this to carry out any fraud on the Post Office. It's a hobby with us, just like collecting stamps or coins.'

Looks familiar? Ringo Starr's new image meant that he was virtually ignored while filming a recent concert. The 3,000 screaming fans only had eyes for Marc Bolan.

'BORROW-A-TOY-AT-THE-LIBRARY' PLAN FOR TOWN

Children will be able to borrow toys from their library free of charge in a pilot scheme approved by the Libraries' Committee at Brighton, Sussex. If the idea works, it could be extended to other towns all over the country. The aim of the 3-year scheme is to give an opportunity for deprived families to use a public service together with children and parents from more privileged backgrounds. Mr John Lee, who will operate the scheme, says, 'Children attracted to the library by toys will progress to books as a natural step from play to literacy.'

CHARLIE CHAPLIN FLIES BACK IN TRIUMPH

Charlie Chaplin flew back in triumph yesterday to America – the country that told him 20 years ago to 'Stay away until you can offer proof of your moral worth'. America has taken on national sackcloth and ashes for sending the Tramp into exile in 1952 amid McCarthy-style recriminations over his political views. White-haired 82-year-old Chaplin was too unsure of his health to say whether he would be able to fly to Hollywood to accept a special Oscar.

'GIVE STRENGTH OF BEER ON THE LABEL'

Beer should be labelled to give drinkers some idea of its strength, the Consumers' Association magazine *Which* says today. The recommendation comes in a report which confirms what many beer drinkers have known for years – that when it comes to taste there isn't much to choose between the 6 main keg beers on sale in Britain. *Which* sums up: 'We can see little reason for preferring 1 keg bitter to another and even less for preferring them to their brewers' own alternative bitters which are cheaper and in some cases stronger.' In fact 3 kegs were stronger than their brewers' own 'Best Bitters': Worthington E, Watney Red and Whitbread Tankard. Double Diamond, Tavern (Courage) and Youngers Tartan kegs were weaker than their own brewers' 'Best'. The strongest keg, Worthington E, was 3.9% alcohol. *Which* suggests beers could be classified by alcoholic content as light, medium and strong.

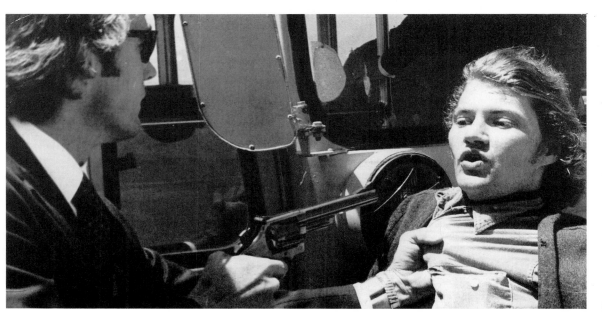

Clint Eastwood is Dirty Harry.

MAY 1972

32 INJURED AS LEEDS LOSE

32 football fans were hurt last night when a barrier gave way during Leeds United's crucial final game at Wolverhampton. Leeds needed only to draw to add the League Championship to their FA Cup win on Saturday and complete the Double, but they lost 2–1 and the title went to Derby County.

BONANZA STAR 'HOSS' DIES IN HOSPITAL

Dan Blocker, the big, bluff, likeable Hoss Cartwright of TV's *Bonanza* series, is dead. He was admitted to hospital in California 2 days ago after complaining of difficulty in breathing. He died later the same day from a blood clot in the lung. He was 43. Shooting for a new series of *Bonanza* is scheduled to begin this month.

DIVORCE BY TAPE RECORDER

Legal history was made yesterday when the rail go-slow stopped a wife getting to the High Court in London for the re-hearing of a divorce case. The case first came before Mr Justice Lloyd-Jones who heard Mrs Linda Buckland admit that she had committed adultery. The judge adjourned the case for an affidavit from her husband but has since retired. Sir George Baker listened to a 20-minute playback of the part-heard case yesterday, and both counsel confirmed that it was a true record of the proceedings. He said he was satisfied that it was proper for him to act on it and granted a decree nisi to Mr Clive Buckland.

A WATCH WITH NO HANDS

The Swiss and Americans have combined their know-how to produce what must be approaching the ultimate in timepieces – wrist-watches with no moving parts at all. Their time will be kept by tiny quartz crystals oscillating at 32,768 cycles every second. This means that the most the watches can either gain or lose will be 5 seconds a month, but the really dramatic development is the abolition of hands on the watch face. Instead an electrically activated face will show figures giving the time. Avia expect to have 500 on the British market in September and the price will probably be about £95.

DRINKING WATER DANGER AS BABIES TURN BLUE

Babies living in country areas face a danger of developing a rare blood disease from polluted water. The danger has been highlighted in a Yorkshire village where 2 babies are having to be supplied with specially delivered pure water. The disease, methaemoglobinaemia, has been confirmed in 1 of the babies. It has the effect of giving a blue tinge around the eyes and nose. The trouble is caused when there is a high level of nitrate in the water. British farmers last year used 899,000 tons of nitrogen-based fertilizer, more than double the amount used in 1961. The condition only affects babies.

GIRLS OF 14 ON PILL CAN KEEP IT SECRET

Doctors must now preserve the medical secrets of *all* their teenage patients, including 14-year-old girls on the pill. The British Medical Association has issued a new ruling that defends the interests of any child under the age of consent who asks for confidentiality. The decision, to be ratified this summer, means that any girl mature enough to take the pill or have an abortion can demand total secrecy. This decision is a prelude to the BMA's official recommendation for a reduction in the current legal age of consent – 16. It is virtually certain that 14 will now be regarded as the new age of consent and the Government will be advised to alter the law accordingly.

SPIKE AND MARTY ARE TV TOP FAVOURITES

Comedians Spike Milligan and Marty Feldman have given ITV its best chance yet to win one of the major awards in the Golden Rose Festival of TV's Light Entertainment at Montreux this week. Compiled from the best of the ATV series, *The Marty Feldman Comedy Machine*, it presented the 2 exceptional comedians at their best. The silent film skit of the 2 competitive undertakers and the Orson Welles parody of the nature film, in which the cherished animals are the last of the English aristocracy, drew the longest and loudest laugh of any show so far displayed. This year's BBC entry, *The Goodies*, is being screened today.

President Nixon and Soviet leader Leonid Brezhnev exchange copies of the signed treaty designed to halt the nuclear arms race.

VILLA FIND A FRANCIS

On the day Aston Villa clinched the Third Division Championship by annihilating Torquay they could have found the answer to their striker problem on their own door-step in the slim shape of 18-year-old Brian Little. Little burst into first-team football with the same kind of impact superboy Trevor Francis made at neighbouring Birmingham 18 months ago. Manager Vic Crowe said, 'What he lacks in size he makes up for in skill and he must have a great future.'

WOOLWORTHS STARTS AN HP SCHEME

Woolworth customers will soon be able to buy goods over £15 on hire purchase. Although only 66 shops will be selling the higher-priced goods, repayments can be made at any of the 1,100 stores in the country. A Woolworths spokesman said last night, 'We have been moving into a much higher-priced range of goods such as freezers, furniture and television sets during the past 2 years.'

THE NEW ENEMY

It is the sight the Army has been dreading in Ulster. It looks familiar: barricades and paramilitary guards have appeared many times in the Bogside and the Falls Road. But this barricade is in the Shankhill Road and the men behind the masks are Protestants. By putting up barricades the Protestants hoped to force the Army to move against similar barricades around the IRA's 'no-go' strongholds in Londonderry. There are now 2 forces lining up: the IRA and these men of the new Ulster Defence Association. And the Army is in the middle.

NOW PICK YOUR OWN ACTION REPLAYS

The Japanese have come up with the ultimate for armchair sportsmen:; a television set with a built-in memory screen. The 'memory vision' set by Hitachi has 2 screens, 1 for normal viewing and a smaller 9-inch tube which shows the same programme simultaneously. At the touch of a button, the viewer can instantly lock the picture on the small screen, press another switch and the scene is played out in slow motion while the programme continues as normal on the larger screen It will instantly end all domestic disputes about referees' decisions or racing results. The set will be on sale in Japan next month but is not expected in British shops until later.

CHRISTIE PLAY TITLE CHANGE

The title of Agatha Christie's play, *Ten Little Niggers*, is being changed for Birmingham theatre-goers to avoid racial trouble. The Alexandra Theatre will bill it as *Ten Little Indians*.

TAX POLLUTERS UNTIL THEY STOP, SAY EXPERTS

Polluters should pay a pollution tax for everything they pour into the sky or the rivers, it was suggested yesterday. The idea would be, for example, to tax a factory making smoke to the extent that it would pay the management to invest in equipment that would stop the smoke. The tax suggestion is made in a report from a working party set up by Environment Minister Mr Peter Walker. It says the tax would help to pay for the real cost in loss of amenity and health which pollution causes. It would be expensive but viable. The working party also calls for the nuclear power programme to be slowed down. If present plans went ahead there would be a vast extra amount of toxic nuclear waste to be got rid of and as yet there is no known way to do this.

AUTHORS TRY AGAIN FOR LIBRARY ROYALTIES

Lord Eccles, Minister for the Arts, came under new pressure yesterday to give authors royalties on books borrowed from libraries. A working party which he appointed examined possible systems of collecting money and distributing it to authors. It favours a system relating the amount each author receives to the amount libraries spend on his books rather than to the number of times the books are borrowed because 'it would not be practicable to collect the statistical information necessary'. Libraries might pay either by a surcharge on each book they buy or an annual licence fee. The working party does not discuss whether the money would be found from the rates or by a charge to borrowers.

An unusual sight in Love Thy Neighbour – *the Booths join the Reynoldses for a meal. From left to right: Bill (Rudolph Walker), Eddie (Jack Smethurst), Barbie (Nina Baden-Semper), Joan (Kate Williams).*

JUNE 1972

NEW... NEW... NEW...

A new pocket-sized computer, measuring 6" in length, 3" in width and just over 1" at its widest, is one of the latest and most advanced miracles of electronic engineering. Weighing 9oz, an equivalent device 15 years ago would have occupied quite a large detached house. At a cost of £199, the miniature computer will be invaluable to scientists, engineers and the like, though in 10 years' time the £5 pocket calculator will be common.

A cassette player needing as little space as a dashboard ashtray is the latest in in-car entertainment. Unlike cartridge players – often associated with cars – any part of a tape can be selected using fast forward and rewind switches. Cost: £21.50 (£32.70 for the stereo model).

A new kind of cash register for supermarkets, where the goods bear a code which is read by an electronic scanner, heralds yet another step on the road to abolishing the need for human beings altogether.

The plastic throwaway wristwatch is with us. The new watch, which has no jewels and only half the moving parts of conventional watches, has a steel case but everything else – including the spring – is made of plastic. If anything goes wrong you simply press out the movement and slot in the replacement. The watch retails at £7.25, with replacement movements £1.50 each.

THEY CAME IN THOUSANDS AS IF TO SAY 'SORRY'

Edward VIII, the uncrowned king, lies in state within a few paces of the marble effigies on his parents' tomb.

For a few days, if only in death, the troubled royal family of yesteryear are together again. . .

. . . A constant two-mile stream of humanity climbed the hill to Windsor Castle all day long to say farewell . . .

A cross-section of all Britain passed by as if to say 'sorry'. If he was loved in life, he was never better loved than in death by the patient thousands who passed by yesterday.

5 children flee their village in terror after a South Vietnamese air strike against advancing Communist troops mistakenly bombs them with napalm.

GOVERNMENT WORRIED BY JAPANESE TRADE BOOM

Mr John Davies, Minister for Trade and Industry, arrives back from Tokyo following discussions on the worrying state of Britain's trade with Japan. Not only did imports rocket by 50% last year while exports rose by less than 1%, but Japan has also raised tarriff barriers ranging up to 25% against British consumer goods.

	1970	1971	UP
Cars	2,031,000	8,230,000	305%
TVs	2,050,000	3,793,000	85%
Cameras	2,230,000	3,065,000	38%
Record players/ Tape recorders	2,661,000	6,038,000	127%

WORLD ENVIRONMENT CONFERENCE, STOCKHOLM

The need to stop the world choking and poisoning itself to death and the industrialised world's 'don't do what we did' philosophy is attracting muted reaction from developing countries, whose air is still clean and rivers still fresh but whose living standards are still lagging. To a man who considers himself lucky to get one meal a day it is illogical to argue that smoke in the air or factory waste in the water is too great a price to pay for three square meals a day and a roof over his head.

Environment Secretary, Peter Walker, yesterday proposed a worldwide satellite monitoring system together with sea sensors to counter the problem of oil tankers which dump their waste at sea.

DOOMWATCH MEN QUIT

Dr Kit Pedler and Mr Gerry Davies, co-creators of TV's *Doomwatch*, are quitting the programme and demanding their screen credits be removed after claiming that the BBC had trivialised the series. Dr Pedler, a leading expert on pollution, said that the programme had been reduced 'to a sort of poor man's James Bond'.

SMASH HIT

Roger Cook and Roger Greenaway – writers of the smash hit 'I'd like To Teach The World To Sing' – have been named songwriters of the year at the Ivor Novello Award ceremony. George Harrison received 2 awards for 'My Sweet Lord': for the biggest selling record and most performed work.

The fragments of Trident Papa India strewn across a field near the A30 at Staines.

ITV HAS A RIVAL TO *THE ARCHERS*

ITV is launching a TV rival to *The Archers*. The twice-weekly serial, *Emmerdale Farm*, featuring the imaginary Sugden family, will be shown in the afternoon starting this autumn, when unlimited television hours begins. It will join *Coronation Street* and ATV's new medical serial, *General Hospital*, to give ITV viewers three serials a week. Yorkshire TV's Programme Controller, Mr Donald Baverstock said yesterday: 'I don't think there is any danger of our reaching saturation point with bi-weekly serials.'

The serial, whose stars have not been chosen yet, has been given a firm 'life' of nine months and could run much longer. It is on offer to the national network.

LILLIE LOOKS A REAL THREAT

'The other bowlers looked average by comparison. Clearly much depends on how fit this 22-year-old bank clerk stays for the rest of the series. Lillee's pace on a surprisingly fast pitch made even Geoff Boycott hurry his strokes and we haven't seen that in this country for a few years.'
Ken Barrington, *Daily Mail*.

THE MAN WHO SAID NO TO A MILLION

Singer Don McLean has turned his back on millionaire status by his refusal to cash in on the song 'American Pie', which has become one of the greatest smash hits of all time. He even went so far as to turn down the chance of an appearance on Rowan and Martin's Laugh-In – regarded as showbiz heresy. They wanted him to sing a few bars of the song, then get a custard pie in the face. He refused.

NURSERY SCHOOLS FOR ALL ON THE WAY

Plans for nursery schooling for every 3- and 4-year-old child who wants it will be announced by the Government later this year. The scheme, which already has Mr Heath's backing in principle, would be the most important development in education since the introduction of compulsory schooling a century ago as experts now recognise that half a child's future intelligence is established before the age of 5. But there will be no extra cash and Education Minister, Mrs Margaret Thatcher, plans to raise the £100m needed to implement the scheme from swingeing cuts in the university and college sector. If the scheme starts in September 1973, it will take until the early 1980s to be fully operative.

WHERE ARE WE GOING WRONG WITH CHILDREN – BY THE MINISTER OF EDUCATION

'Many children leave school and they have never had a conversation in their lives. They get through at home on a few small phrases like 'Pass the jam' and 'Going out'.

At school they get a series of instructions from a tape recorder and have to give simple one-word answers to it.

Some children never get the chance to talk to their teacher; perhaps this is why they cannot communicate easily. . .

It could be that their home background and the vast growth of audio-visual aids means that they are losing this skill.'
Margaret Thatcher

DRIVE TO SELL COUNCIL HOUSES

A campaign to persuade more local authorities to sell council houses – aimed chiefly at Labour-controlled councils, who have so far refused to allow tenants to buy their homes – was announced yesterday by Housing Minister, Mr Julian Amery.

Labour spokesman Mr Reginald Freeson asked: 'How do you expect people living in local authority dwellings to buy their houses when prices are running at £10,000?'

Mr Amery replied: 'When discounts of 20 per cent, and even 30 per cent are allowed, subject to certain conditions, the sale represents the very best bargain available to the would-be home-owner.'

KID CONNORS CASHES IN

Jim Connors, teenage American No. 5, who is almost certain to be seeded in two weeks at his first Wimbledon, won the £1,000 first prize of the John Player Round Robin at Nottingham yesterday.

DAY BY DAY

1 Jun
Iraq nationalises the London-based Iraq Petroleum Company.

3 Jun
Burundi: Thousands are feared dead in Government reprisals after a failed coup.

4 Jun
Black militant Angela Davis is cleared of all charges of murder, kidnap and conspiracy.

6 Jun
The new 'go anywhere' ticket covering bus and Tube journeys is available later this week for the first time. Cost: £130 per year.

7 Jun
Lester Piggott wins the Derby on Roberto.

8 Jun
Rhodesia: Hopes are fading for 400+ miners trapped by a huge underground explosion 2 days ago.

10 Jun
Millitant Protestants set up 'no-go' barriers in 30 Ulster towns.

11 Jun
In a train disaster at Eltham, London, 4 are killed, 130 injured.

11 Jun
President Gaddafi claims arms, money and volunteers are set in support of the IRA.

13 Jun
There is a setback in the Government's battle to curb union power as the Appeal Court quashes a £55,000 fine on the TGWU. Lord Denning declares the union was not responsible for the shop stewards' actions.

14 Jun
The Government have a majority of 8 on the sovereignty clause of the Common Market Bill.

18 Jun
118 are killed on a BEA Trident airliner moments after leaving Heathrow.

22 Jun
The Provisional IRA announce a ceasefire – conditional upon a reciprocal response from the British Army.

23 Jun
Chancellor Anthony Barber floats the pound in an attempt to restore confidence.

27 Jun
Bodell quits as McAlinden takes the British Heavyweight title.

JULY 1972

BBC GIVES ESTHER AND THE GIRLS A NEW DEAL

Women are to have a bigger role in BBC Television's current-affairs coverage as part of a new deal for factual programmes. Esther Rantzen, the reporter from *Braden's Week*, is joining BBC1's *Nationwide* series when it is promoted from 3 to 5 evenings a week in the autumn. Jackie Gillott who came to the BBC from ITV will also appear in a new mid-week programme – still untitled – which is to take over from *24 Hours*. Brian Wenham, Head of BBC Current Affairs, denied that the move had been taken to pacify Women's Lib campaigners though he agreed that these moves would slightly redress an imbalance.

NOW YOU SEE IT, NOW YOU SNAP IT

Birdwatchers (of all kinds) can now take close-up photographs without taking their eyes away from their binoculars. The Nicnon TF is not only a pair of binoculars, it has a camera built in as well. The photograph will record all the 'circular' picture seen by the watcher plus the scene just outside the field of view. Price: about £140.

THE LORDS FIGHT A 'DINOSAUR'

The Lords yesterday took up the fight against construction of a new government building that has been called hideous, ugly, graceless . . . a dinosaur. There were demands for a public enquiry and an immediate halt to building work on the £11m, 186-foot high, 10-storey construction which is to replace Queen Anne's Mansions, Westminster. Already a private bill aimed at controlling development on the site overlooking St James's Park has been introduced by the Earl of Cork and Orrery. Yesterday he declared passionately, 'We are discussing more than a building – we are discussing proposals to change the appearance of an area extending roughly from Whitehall to Buckingham Palace, from St James's to Victoria Tower.'

CENTURIES-OLD CRAFT POISED FOR INVASION OF BRITAIN

It's called macramé – pronounced MA-KRAR-MAY – the creative art of tying knots. And if you've got a ball of string in your kitchen drawer, hold on to it, because the rate at which macramé is catching on, it may soon become a rare commodity. Although the art dates back to the Assyrians in 850 BC, it is back, fired with the inspiration of our own age. Macramé is becoming so big that 10 books have been published on it in the past 3 months. Children, old-age pensioners, Women's Institutes, men and women have all been bitten by the craze.

IT'S STARDOM AT MILL FOR VAL AND SUE

Receptionists Val Draper and Sue Sweet are to become 'stars' of a new BBC series. It will come live from the entrance hall of the BBC's new network production centre at Pebble Mill, Birmingham where Val, 25, and Sue, 22, work. The programme, *Pebble Mill at One*, will be the first BBC1 programme to take advantage of the de-restriction of television transmitting hours. It will be seen all over Britain at lunch-time on weekdays. *Nationwide* reporter Bob Langley is to host the series, which starts in October.

Going flat out for victory . . . that's Stan Smith, last year's Wimbledon finalist and favourite to take this year's singles title.

BIDS START AT £1m FOR LUCKY VALENTINE DIAMOND

The Star of Sierra Leone, currently the world's largest uncut diamond and the third biggest ever found, goes on sale later this month for at least £1m. It is about as big as a hen's egg and weighs half a pound (969.8 carats). The diamond, found on St Valentine's Day at the Yengema Mine in Sierra Leone, will be sold when sealed tenders are opened. Although tenders start at £1m the stone could fetch up to £5m and double in value when cut up.

THE FINGER OF 007 POINTS AT BURT

A new James Bond is a pen-stroke away from being announced. Expect the name of Burt Reynolds on the final contract. Mr Reynolds, you may remember, is the actor who attained stardom by appearing naked across the centrefold of the American edition of *Cosmopolitan*, since which his well-publicized frame has been sought after for countless film projects. He emerges as unexpected front runner in the continuing Bond race. He is a compromise candidate, say some, since producers Cubby Broccoli and Harry Saltzman differed in their enthusiasm for Roger Moore.

ACTORS WIN ROUND ONE

Actors won the first round of their fight for the right to operate a closed shop in the theatre yesterday. Their union, Equity, which represents 20,000 actors and actresses has had its application for a post-entry closed shop referred to the Commission on Industrial Relations by the Industrial Court. Actors feel they have a good case for exemption from the Industrial Relations Act's ban on closed shops.

FIRMS MAY HAVE TO PUT A DATE ON FOOD

Pre-packed food should be clearly date-stamped so that shoppers can tell at a glance whether or not it is fresh. This recommendation, which is almost certain to become law, was made yesterday by the Government's Food Standards Committee. Already several leading food suppliers stamp perishable food with the date by which it should be sold but the committee recommends it should not be made an offence to sell food after the date shown as, although the food may be 'out of date', it could still be in perfect condition.

RHODESIA IN GAMES ROW

Britain has thrown the issue of race into the Olympic Games by protesting at the inclusion of athletes from Rhodesia. It looked last night as if the objection may be to save the Queen and the Prime Minister from embarrassment when they visit Munich in 5 weeks' time. It also looked as if Britain were the only nation out of line. The Russians are prepared to welcome the Rhodesians, as are the Arabs. The protest was made to the West German Government, which has been thrown into confusion and alarm at the spectre of the colour issue dominating Munich.

HOME-LOAN RACKET

An MP has discovered a housing racket which, he says, is helping to push up house prices. Labour MP Mr William Whitlock said he has evidence that a man bought, with a mortgage, a house badly in need of decoration. The man then let it off in bedsitters and the tenants cleaned and redecorated the property. A year later he turned out the tenants and sold the house at a profit. He repeated the process with mortgages obtained from other building societies. Mr Whitlock, who is to raise the matter with Housing Minister Mr Julian Amery, said that building societies had rules limiting 1 mortgage to 1 person, but there was no arrangement to stop people becoming clients of several building societies. It was against their rules to let off property but there were no checks to make sure these were observed.

ALL OF A SUDDEN, BEANZ MEANZ FINE FARE

Housewife Dorothy Graham noticed a 'funny-looking' price ticket in her local supermarket yesterday, and changed her mind after 20 years. She decided that Beanz no longer meant the brand she'd been buying all her married life; instead she bought the supermarket's own product. The Consumers' Association was responsible for the 'funny-looking' price ticket which gave the price per ounce of the product as well as its retail price. A 3-month experiment into the system – unit pricing – has just begun at the Fine Fare Supermarket in Camden High Street, London. Although some products are priced in this way already Mrs Graham believes it would be a good idea if this were extended to all products. The Camden experiment will come up for discussion later this month when a unit-pricing bill enters its committee stage.

AND HEAR THIS

A record-player for the new 4-channel 'quadrophonic' records has now been developed in Britain. Made by Wilkinson/Form Electronics of Northumberland, it is claimed to be in advance of any other. Although there are 2 systems in use – 1 by Sansui of Japan and the other by CBS – the Wilkinson/Form record-player will decode and play both systems. The company is marketing a complete outfit comprising decoder and amplifier, 4 loudspeakers and a transcription turntable at a recommended price of £260.

Alice Cooper at Chessington Zoo promoting his new single 'School's Out' – with appropriately dressed models.

AUG 1972

SPITZ STARTS A GOLD BLITZ

LONDON 'ON THE BRINK OF COLLAPSE'

Civilized life is on the brink of collapse in central London, according to a bishop, and the symptoms to be found there are those of 'a sickness which is affecting the whole world'. The Bishop of Kingston, The Right Reverend Hugh Montefiore, refers to London's lack of community and dreadful tower blocks with nothing for children to do. The bishop blames the pressures generated by urban and industrial life.

FROM A FLOP TO A CULT TO A FORTUNE

They have both bought houses in the past year and they can be heard having lengthy discussions about how Andrew's wife will have to pay about £0.5m in tax if he dies tomorrow. Andrew Lloyd Webber and his friend and partner Tim Rice are the writers of *Jesus Christ Superstar*, which had its London première last night – 3 years after the West End turned them down and Broadway proved them right. *Superstar* started as a record which sold fantastically in the States but didn't go well here. It was turned into a show – a rock opera – and has been put on all over the world except, ironically, in Britain until last night.

For the authors the saga began 3 years ago when a shrewd manager called David Land told them he'd pay them the kind of salaries they'd get from training at other jobs – £25 a week – to sit down and work on a musical. They had already written *Joseph and the Amazing Technicolour Dreamcoat* for the choirboys of St Paul's and made, according to Tim, about 3/6 each. David Land took one look at Tim's lyrics and Andrew's music and said, 'All right, lads, anything but Jesus.'

AIRPORT DECISION STARTS A ROW

A storm broke last night over the Government's choice for the site of London's third airport at Maplin Sands on the Essex coast. The announcement, made just before the holiday recess, was branded 'governmental cowardice' by the main opposition group, the Defenders of Essex. A spokesman for the group described the new city, which will be part of the building programme, as a 'planned claustrophobic environment'.

I'D RISK JAIL TO KEEP BOYS FROM MY DAUGHTER

Little Sharne Pilate thinks boys are rough and horrible and her father says he is prepared to go to jail to make sure she doesn't have to mix with them at school. Sharne, 11, has been at an all-girls' convent school since she was 6 and her parents want her to go to another single-sex school when the new term starts in September but Barnet Education Department has only offered Sharne a place in the mixed Edgware Comprehensive School. Her father Victor, a 37-year-old architect from Mill Hill, North London, has threatened to keep Sharne at home until she is given a place at an all-girls' school.

Zebedee – one of the televisions most enduring and endearing characters.

SIR ALEC THREATENS TO CUT AID FOR AMIN

British economic aid to Uganda – now £4.5m a year – may be stopped if President Idi Amin carries out his threats to expel 57,000 Asian British passport holders. The warning came yesterday from Foreign Secretary Sir Alec Douglas-Home after Amin's threat had been condemned in the Commons as 'obscene racism'.

2 world record-breaking gold-medal wins inside an hour launched the Mark Spitz Olympic blitz in the swimming pool last night. First the lanky Californian slaughtered his opposition in the 200-metres butterfly final with a fantastic 2 minutes 0.7 seconds. Then, after the excitement of the medal-presentation ceremony he turned out to anchor the United States in another incredible victory in the 4 x 100-metres freestyle relay. Spitz has set his heart on taking home 6 gold medals from Munich and nobody here now doubts his ability to collect them.

Michael York and Lisa Minelli in Cabaret.

DAY BY DAY

2 Aug
Leaders of the TUC and the CBI sign an agreement to set up an independent conciliation and arbitration service.

3 Aug
A state of emergency is proclaimed, giving the Government special powers to ensure that essential supplies and services are maintained during the dock strike.

16 Aug
The Delegates Conference of the TGWU votes to end the dock strike from midnight on 20 August.

22 Aug
The International Olympic Committee withdraws the invitation to Rhodesia to participate in the 1972 Games.

26 Aug
Sir Francis Chichester dies, aged 70.

The Olympic Games open in Munich.

28 Aug
Prince William of Gloucester and his co-pilot are killed when their plane crashes just after taking off in an air race at Halfpenny Green near Wolverhampton.

30 Aug
The career of £2m-rated Mill Reef is ended after he breaks a leg in 3 places.

POMPIDOU THREAT TO SUMMIT

President Pompidou is threatening to call off the Paris Summit arranged to welcome Britain into the Common Market and plan for the future of a new united Europe. A crisis atmosphere emerged last night after emergency talks at Chequers. New rifts over economic and monetary issues plus French insistence on a firm British pledge to peg the floating pound before joining the Market have cast serious doubts about the summit, which opens in Paris on 19 October. The Prime Minister is standing firm against any commitment to end the floating of the pound by a particular date.

SIR FINDS BEING A POP STAR SO USEFUL

A schoolteacher who is turning pop star says that he is now accepted by his pupils. 'As soon as the kids in class found out I was going to make pop records their whole attitude changed,' said 28-year-old Clifford Ward. Before this relations had been difficult, with the usual situation of children who basically didn't want to learn and a teacher trying to get through to them. Mr Ward, married with 3 children, teaches English and drama at the North Bromsgrove Upper Comprehensive School, Worcestershire. After leaving school he was in a professional band called The Secrets and trained to be a teacher when the group broke up. His first record is released today and an album is due out next month.

DJs TAKE A DAY TRIP

The BBC is getting its disc jockeys out of the studios on Bank Holiday Monday to give pop channel Radio 1 an 'off-duty atmosphere'. Every day-time programme on 28 August will come from a holiday spot, making one of the longest outside broadcasts ever mounted by BBC radio. It will start at 7 a.m. with Tony Blackburn presenting his show from Bournemouth; David Hamilton's programme will come from Whipsnade Zoo; Dave Lee Travis will be at Blackpool Tower Ballroom; Johnny Walker at a Great Yarmouth holiday camp and Alan Freeman at Battersea Park, London.

BBC TELLS JIMMY YOUNG TO STOP SINGING

Jimmy Young is to stop singing on his daily Radio 1 show. BBC officials feel that his 'sweet music' songs are out of keeping with the pop service and Jim has no intention of switching to rock and roll. Mr Young, whose recordings of 'Unchained Melody' and other songs topped the British hit parade in the 50s, has been serenading housewives daily since his Radio 1 programme started in 1967.

BATTLE TO RESCUE THE GAMES

The fate of the 1972 Olympic Games, which open on Saturday, lay in the hands of the British Government last night. The Black African nations said they would walk out of the Munich Games unless the Government issues British passports to the 40-strong Rhodesian Olympic Team before they compete. The declaration came from the Olympic Committees of Africa, 16 of which have threatened to withdraw if Rhodesia competes. The Africans want the passports as evidence that the Rhodesians would be competing as British 'Colonial subjects of Southern Rhodesia'. As the British Government has opposed breakaway Rhodesia's entry in the Games, there is little likelihood of it issuing the passports demanded by the Africans.

BRITAIN'S ELEVENTH-HOUR BID TO HALT THE COD WAR

Britain is making a last minute attempt to avert a 'Cod War' starting with Iceland on Friday. That is the deadline for Iceland arbitrarily imposing a 50-mile fishing limit instead of the present 12-mile zone. In a bid to stay her hand – and keep open traditional fishing grounds in Icelandic waters for British trawlermen – the Foreign Office is offering fresh negotiations for a settlement, although the British Government refuses any terms which imply ultimate acceptance of Iceland's claim to 50 miles. British trawlermen are not stopping to await the outcome of the diplomatic manoeuvres. They are going to their old fishing grounds braced for a gunboat war.

SEPT 1972

One of the Arab terrorists that massacred 11 Israeli athletes at the Munich Olympics.

Security is stepped up at the Munich Olympics after the massacre of 11 Israelis.

WHY THE WATERGATE CAPER KEEPS ON BUGGING MR NIXON

While the presidential election grinds nearer, slumping Democratic morale is shored up by the scandal involved in the Watergate caper. This apparent Republican plot to bug and burgle the Democratic headquarters in Washington continues to embarrass the Nixon camp. Yesterday 1 of the 5 men caught red-handed inside the Watergate Hotel offices admitted his role for the first time in a newspaper interview. Cuban-born Bernard Barker, 55, said that, like most Cuban refugees, he believed Senator George McGovern's election would lead to 'Socialism or Communism or whatever you want to call it'. The Democrats have added a new dimension to the case by naming President Nixon's former Commerce Secretary Maurice Stans in an amendment to the Invasion of Privacy suit they have filed against the Republicans. Mr Stans is accused of illegally salting away £47,000 in unregistered campaign funds to mount an espionage operation against the Democrats. Mr Stans called the allegations 'a scurrilous pack of lies'.

THE AVENGERS

Before night fell on the eve of the Jewish New Year, 5733, the Israelis hit back with devastating effect against the Arabs who succoured the murderers of Munich, launching raids on 7 guerrilla camps in Syria and 3 in Lebanon. Israel's airmen paid what might be called the first deposit in settlement of the Munich account.

IT DOESN'T PAY TO BE SMART . . .

The best way of persuading a shop to accept a cheque is to have a bank cheque card, says a report in *Money Which* published today. Credit cards are 'the next best bet' but the magazine's survey revealed that some shopkeepers are suspicious of them. 1 in 4 shops would not accept a driving licence as proof of identity and 1 in 3 would not even accept a passport. Large stores generally accepted cheques from the clients of well-known big banks but the customers of less well-known banks immediately aroused suspicion. Banks issue cheque cards free to reliable customers. The cards guarantee that a cheque up to a certain amount – generally £30 – will be met.

TV'S 'LOSS LEADER' OF ALL TIME: *LOVE STORY*

Everyone knows the item in the supermarket priced down to an unprofitable figure but there as a 'magnet' to lure people on to other purchases. Loss leader is the trade phrase. The most incredible loss leader of all time has cost its purchaser – America's ABC TV network – £1,250,000. This is the amount that the network has paid for just 1 showing of the film *Love Story*. The maximum possible revenue from commercials which could be recovered during the showing is well under £500,000, meaning a bill nearing the million mark for a 1-night prestige gesture against rival networks.

CROWD JEER POWER MAN

Boos echoed around the Olympic Stadium yesterday when 2 American negro runners ignored their flag after receiving the gold and silver medals for the 400-metres final. The 80,000 crowd reacted as winner Vince Matthews stood with hands on hips and chatted with runner-up Wayne Collett during the playing of the American national anthem. Both men ignored the flag and Matthews swung his medal in the air as if it were a toy. When Collett left the rostrum he raised his fist in the Black Power salute. This is the first outbreak of this sort of demonstration, which first occurred during the 1968 Games in Mexico.

'WHY I BLIND KITTENS'

A scientist claiming to be a cat-lover yesterday defended laboratory experiments in which he makes kittens go blind by stitching up their eyelids. Doctor Colin Blakemore from Cambridge University described how after a kitten's eyes have been sealed for only a few days during the critical period of brain growth – between the third and twelfth week of life – it loses all ability to see once the eyelids are unstitched. Doctor Blakemore put the question: 'Are we born with the ability to see things or does vision depend on early visual experience?' He claims that his animal experiments could be of major value in the treatment of squint defects in children. Dr Blakemore added, 'I'm certain that my experiments are ethically justifiable. Kittens like living in the dark.'

FOR THE SUPERSTORE – A SUPER SUCCESS

Britain's first out-of-town drive-in hypermarket yesterday appealed to customers to stay away because the giant store that stocks 25,000 different lines ranging from food and clothing to hardware and household goods just can't cope. Since it opened this week outside the South Wales town of Caerphilly business at the Carrefour Hypermarket has been more than brisk. Managing Director of the group which runs the store, Mr John Fairclough, said, 'We are specifically designed for the car-owning society. Motorists can drive in, do their shopping in a trolley and wheel it to the boot of their car and then leave the trolley where it is.' As he spoke the centre of Caerphilly was like a ghost town. Carrefour expects to see 100 hypermarkets in Britain within 8 to 10 years – a third of them its own.

American Bobby Fischer beating the clock and Russian Boris Spassky to become World Chess Champion.

JOKER FOOLS CROWD

An intruder who joined the Olympic Marathon outside the main gate just before last night's finish fooled the 80,000 crowd who cheered him wildly as he sped into the stadium. Norbert Suehaus, a West German student clad in running kit, had almost completed a circuit of the track when true race leader Frank Shorter of the USA came through the tunnel and nonplussed officials, who made no attempt to stop Suehaus, realized they had been hoodwinked. The student was promptly seen off the premises. He said later, 'These Games have become far too serious and I thought it was time the crowd were given a laugh.' Britain's Ron Hill trailed in sixth behind Shorter in an event he expected to win.

DJ TERRY TO STAR IN TV SHOW

Disc jockey Terry Wogan is to become a face as well as a voice when he starts hosting his own television show next month. Terry, one of the BBC's most popular DJs, will present *Lunch-time With Wogan* for ATV every Tuesday. Terry said, 'I'm happy in radio but would obviously like to do more television. It's taken me 2 years to become a name on radio and I knew that one bad television appearance could destroy some of that so I've been patient up to now.' He will continue with his radio show.

'GUINEA-PIG' KIDS

Thousands of children are now the guinea-pigs of a 'trendy' schooling experiment which will deprive them of exam successes, claims an education expert. Mr Reese Edwards, a former Director of Education, says that bureaucratic civil servants have helped foist what are called Middle Schools – for children of 8 or 9 up to 12 or 13 – on the public for administrative and economic reasons, not for any educational advantage. This diminishes the children's chance of good CSE and GCE results because they cannot start their courses for these exams until they are 13 instead of 11 as at present. More than 50 local authorities have so far launched Middle School schemes.

ON THE BALL WITH HURRICANE HIGGINS

If you want a slight diversion from the breathless atmosphere of the Olympics, *Panorama* tonight gives a profile of Hurricane Higgins. Alex Higgins is the World Snooker Champion who has earned his 'Hurricane' nickname because of the phenomenal speed with which he sees a shot, lines it up and plays it. He's 23, Irish, and has the reputation of being as temperamental and as talented as a Best or a Fischer. He earns his money – his annual income is in the 5-figure bracket – from playing snooker competitively and giving exhibition matches.

OCT 1972

BANK MOVES TO COUNTRY MANSION

Barclays Bank is buying a mansion for its staff – and it could save the bank £1.25m a year. Soaring rents have driven part of Barclays' Head Office organization out of London into Radbroke Hall with its croquet lawn, tennis courts and 35 acres of parkland at Knutsford, Cheshire. A Barclays spokesman said, 'Rentals in the City of London have now reached between £10 and £12 a square foot, which means it costs us in working space more than £1,000 per head of staff. The equivalent figure in Knutsford is no more than £150 a year.' The Hall, used for 16 years by the Nuclear Power Group, has been bought for an estimated £2m.

BATTLE OF THE CREDIT CARDS

4 top banks today join the increasingly competitive credit-card war, having dropped something like £500m through the letterboxes of 3.5 million customers with a note attached encouraging them to spend, spend, spend. Lloyds, National Westminster, Midland and Williams Glynn have joined together in the massive launch of Access, their new credit card aimed at hiving off some of the business from the now well-established Barclaycard. Access cards have been posted – uninvited – to millions.

So far, just under 6,000 customers have sent back rejection slips. Many object to the principle of credit cards and regard the arrival of 1 as a form of 'inertia selling'. Some scorn credit cards as a 'Yankee idea'; others are worried about their liability if they should lose the card and someone else goes on a spending spree.

Access aims eventually to top 5 million cardholders, thereby nearly trebling the number of Barclaycard holders, but the 2 elder statesmen of the credit-card business, Diners Club, launched in 1951, and American Express, 1958, do not regard the young upstarts as any threat. Both organizations made the same comment yesterday: 'Ours is not a credit card but a convenience card for businessmen and worldwide travellers.'

PEUGEOT LEADS 6 CHALLENGE

A new challenger to the British Leyland Mini, the Peugeot 104, is being unveiled at the Paris Motor Show today. The new 4-door family car is the smallest model yet from Peugeot. It is expected to sell in Britain next year for about £1,000 including tax. Like the Mini the 104 has front-wheel drive, a transverse engine, a top speed of up to 85 m.p.h. and will do more than 40 miles to the gallon. Peugeot wants to be the first of the 6 Common Market countries to sell a new car in Britain after we enter Europe.

FOOD LABEL LAW WILL PROTECT THE SHOPPER

Housewives will be able to get much more information from food labels under tough new regulations coming into force on 1 January. Pre-packed items will carry labels giving a complete list of ingredients in descending order of weight. All packages will have to show the name and address of a 'responsible person' such as the packer, labeller or manufacturer. A simple trade mark with no address will no longer be enough. Packets will have to carry the 'common' name for the product and brand names will have to be linked closely with a description showing what the item is. Exceptions to the rule are brand names which have been in use for 30 years or more; it is assumed that shoppers will know what they are.

DON'T DO IT YOURSELF, TAKE A MATE ALONG

One of the most useful and versatile devices produced in years for the home handyman, or woman, is just being introduced to Britain. Those who have tried it out say it is like having an extra pair of helping hands on a job and for this reason it is known as the 'Workmate'. Basically, it is a kind of workbench which will collapse so it can be stored in a cupboard or hung on a wall. It can be used at 3 heights and incorporates a 29-inch vice which will hold practically any conceivable shape. The original Workmate was thought up by an engineer who helped design the famed Lotus cars, but Black & Decker were so impressed they bought the rights and developed a sophisticated second generation. 2 models of the Black & Decker Workmate are available at recommended prices of £19.95 and £24.95.

TAVERNE READY FOR BITTER FIGHT

Mr Dick Taverne's decision to resign his seat and fight as an Independent was taken against the advice of friends like Mr Roy Jenkins and other committed Labour marketeers. Mr Taverne, MP for Lincoln since 1962, is determined that if he has to go out of politics, it will at least be with a bang. His decision to take his martyrdom as a pro-European a step further – his left-wing constituency party executive refused to readopt him – may give Lincoln to the Tories.

Barry Foster (l.) and Michael Latimer question Edgar Wreford in Thames Television's series Van der Valk.

FILM EPIC POSES PROBLEMS FOR ATTENBOROUGH

Film directors are seldom confronted with choices as important as the ones now facing Richard Attenborough. In the next few weeks, his long-awaited epic on the life of Gandhi will begin to take shape. None of the decisions to be taken is simple. Can an Indian actor be found to portray the man who wrested India's independence from the British Raj? If a Muslim actor gives the best screen test will Hindu cinema audiences riot when it is shown in New Delhi? Could a British actor be a convincing Gandhi among 100,000 Indian extras? The role of Gandhi will not be cast until the script is finished but whoever is chosen may be asked to starve in the name of art, as scenes depicting Gandhi's fasts, which took him very close to death, will be shown.

But the major choice Attenborough must make revolves around one of the most controversial episodes of the British Empire. Attenborough has to decide whether to deal with Viscount Mountbatten's 1947 trip to India to supervise the change of power. That trip ended in the partition of the sub-continent into India and the 2 Pakistans. It broke Gandhi's heart. It is believed Attenborough will avoid re-opening old sores.

'PON MY WORD! ENOUGH TO BLOW YOUR MIND

The Oxford English Dictionary, nearly 100 years out of date, is suddenly hip, swinging, with-it and has a flip side. All these words occur in the definitions of the updated supplement to *The Oxford English Dictionary*, of which the first volume is published today. Since slang is in, the OED is full of information on going bonkers (1948), blowing one's top (1928) or one's mind along with one's cool (1966), earning one's bread (1939), pulling one's finger out (Duke of Edinburgh 1961), evading the fuzz (1929), smoking grass (1943), or even a ciggy (attributed to the Beatles, 1962). You could smoke a fag in 1888 but only take a drag since 1914. You could be dead easy or broke since the 1880s but only feel dead grotty (short for grotesque) since the *Daily Mail* first recorded this unhappy state in 1964. Girls are an interesting subject, lexicographically. In the old OED the term 'bird' was obsolete but its revived use, often disparaging, dates from 1915. There were chickadees in 1838, long before W.C. Fields; chicks only began in 1927, crumpet in 1936. Dollies were earlier (1906), but the dolly and bird were not put together until 1964.

The stars of a new drama series about the famous P.O.W. camp Colditz : *L. to r. (front row) Robert Wagner as Flt. Lt. Phil Carrington and David McCallum as Flt. Lt. Simon Carter. (Back row) Jack Hedley as Lt. Col. John Preston, Christopher Neame as Lt. Cdr. Dick Player and Edward Hardwicke as Capt. Pat Grant.*

CALL FOR A UNIFORM PROTEST OVER VAT

Mothers were urged yesterday to boycott uniforms at state schools if the Government slaps Value Added Tax on school clothes. The call was made by the Consumers' Union who said that VAT proposed for uniforms amounted to 'a special tax on education'. Wearing school uniform was not compulsory by law but many parents did not know this, nor did they want to embarrass their children by sending them to school without uniforms. Research has found that the initial cost of uniforms can be as high as £65 and is rarely lower than £30 and suggests that everyday clothes selected with good taste and common sense should be the universal rule. A new Tory Party booklet out today entitled *VAT: Fair For All* says that more than 40% of the average family budget will escape VAT.

FIGHT TO SAVE EYE OF GORDON BANKS

The career of Gordon Banks, the world's number 1 goalkeeper, hung in the balance last night. Doctors were fighting to save the sight of his right eye after the 34-year-old England and Stoke City star was in a car smash. The head-on collision between Banks's Ford Granada and a van happened on a winding road between Whitmore and Trentham, minutes after Banks had left Stoke's Victoria ground. His face was cut and his eye damaged as the windscreen of his car shattered. The van's occupants, a family from Shrewsbury, were allowed home after treatment.

'MAKE IT 7-PLUS' – HEAD

A new national examination for children of the ages of 7, 11 and 16 is suggested today. Doctor Rhodes Boyson, Headmaster of Highbury Grove Comprehensive School, London, wants 'progressive' and 'traditional' teachers to agree on basic educational standards. He says, 'If every fad and fashionable method is taken up with little or no research or monitoring, if schools break down into semi-anarchy with warring factions, no accepted curriculum, no discipline and no-one in charge and responsible, then the parents and society will clamour for a reimposition of the most repressive methods.'

Liberal candidate Cyril Smith weighing up his support in the Rochdale by-election.

SO IT'S 'GOODBYE, BANK RATE'

The 250-year-old bank-rate tradition was killed off by Chancellor Mr Barber yesterday. No longer will the voice of Government broker, Sir Peter Daniell, ring out across the Stock Market on Thursday mornings to tell the City of changes and no longer will messengers rush off to their offices with the news. Bank rate used to govern the general level of interest rates and the changes signalled the Government's desire either to squeeze or to expand the economy. In recent years commercial banks have become more independent and bank rate will now be related to the level of interest rates already established in the market.

NOV 1972

2 PENSIONS FOR ALL UNDER SIR KEITH'S PLAN

All workers are to get the right to 2 pensions on retirement, the Government announced yesterday. The 2 pension rights will be embodied in law for the first time in a bill presented to Parliament by Sir Keith Joseph, the Social Services Secretary. Pension number 1 is the basic state pension, which the Government will be obliged to review each year so that it retains its purchasing power. Pension number 2 will be earnings-related and saved for by the employee and his employer. This will be done through a recognized occupational scheme or, failing that, through a new state scheme.

DING-A-LING A SCANDAL, SAYS MRS WHITEHOUSE

Pop singer Chuck Berry's hit record 'Ding-a-ling' has upset Mrs Mary Whitehouse. She heard it on the BBC and now wants it banned from the air. Mrs Whitehouse, Secretary of the National Viewers' and Listeners' Association, has written to Sir John Eden, Minister of Posts and Telecommunications, asking him to 'decide whether it is, as we believe, a gross violation of the public duty of the BBC to include it in *Top of the Pops*'.

BOYS OF ETON LOSE THAT PENGUIN LOOK

The town of Eton is losing one of its traditional sights – the public school has decided its pupils need no longer wear their conspicuous uniform in the streets. Instead of tails, wing collars and striped trousers, the boys of £861-a-year Eton College will be allowed to wear sports jackets and flannels when they leave the school grounds. The boys are delighted. In their college magazine they write: 'This will stop American tourists capturing for immortality with Polaroid camera the depressed demeanour of a youth of 13 in penguin attire.'

THE NEW FACE OF ITN

The snappy presentation of *Independent Television News* will be strengthened in the New Year with the arrival of their first coloured reporter. He is Trinidad-born Trevor MacDonald, 33, at present an interviewer on the BBC's World Service. Mr MacDonald says, 'I think I'll be able to produce a different outlook on the news but I won't be specifically concerned with racial problems.'

OLIVIER JOINS UP

Sir Laurence Olivier is joining ITV's biggest ever prestige series, *The Second World War*, a 6-month-long documentary to be screened next year. Although Sir Laurence makes few television appearances, he has agreed to narrate all 26 episodes of the series. The programme, which is being made by Thames Television and produced by Jeremy Isaacs, is the largest documentary series ever undertaken by an independent company.

TV'S SILENT STAR IS GROWING FAST

You may not know her name but she has appeared in your house thousands of times. She is Carole Hersee, and every day her picture can be seen on the TV colour test card. Carole was 8 when she was photographed playing noughts and crosses on a blackboard with a big doll beside her. Next Saturday she will be 14 and over the years she has been seen on the screen more times than the casts of *Coronation Street*, *Dad's Army* and *Crossroads* put together. She smiles for hours at a time to help installation engineers make fine adjustments to sets. She has appeared on all 3 British channels and many overseas television services, but she isn't paid. Her only fee was the £10 she received to sit for the photograph.

LANDSLIDE FOR NIXON

President Nixon is back in the White House for another 4 years. Early this morning he was racing towards a landslide victory in the US elections. Computer projections put Mr Nixon ahead of his rival Senator George McGovern by an incredible 27 states to 1 out of the first 28 results. As the early results poured in confirming the opinion poll a sad McGovern aide said, 'You had to be a thinker to realize why America needs our man; I suppose it was too much to hope that the thinkers could make a majority.' For President Nixon it was a staggering reversal of fortune. In 1968 he squeezed into the White House by a margin of just 0.7 of 1%.

WHY I QUIT, BY DAVID ATTENBOROUGH

David Attenborough is to resign as BBC's Director of Programmes, the £15,000-a-year post he has held for 4 years because of the 'obsessive quality' of the job. His successor in the post which carries responsibility for all TV shows will be Mr Alasdair Milne, 42-year-old Scottish Controller who preceded 46-year-old Mr Attenborough as head of BBC2. Mr Attenborough said that he had enjoyed being an executive but it did not make up for being unable to travel and get back to programme-making.

IT'S A CRIME TO BREAK THE ICE

Unlimited fines could be imposed by the courts for any deliberate flouting of the Government's new 90-day pay and prices freeze. An emergency bill submitted to the Commons last night revealed that strikes for more pay will be illegal and no rent or price increases – with the big exception of food – will be allowed without special permission. On conviction, fines could go up to £400. The Industrial Relations Court will not be used for dealing with illegal strikes as the charges will be criminal ones.

SOFTLY SOFTLY EXIT BARLOW FOR NEW SHOW

Millions of *Softly Softly* addicts got the shock of their lives last night, with Detective Chief Superintendent Charlie Barlow being written out of the BBC1 series. They saw Barlow, played by Stratford Johns, leaving the programme to take a police research job with the Home Office. Although some viewers complained that *Softly Softly* without Barlow is like *Hamlet* without the Prince of Denmark, the BBC is determined to take a gamble on the 7-year-old programme which has an audience of more than 13 million. They think fans will accept Frank Windsor as 'the new boss' and Stratford Johns starts a 10-week run of his own crime thriller series, *Barlow at Large*, as soon as *Softly* ends its present season early next year.

Dennis Weaver getting up steam in Steven Spielberg's Duel.

HERMIT SOLDIER WEDS

Shoichi Yokoi, 57, the Japanese soldier who hid alone in the jungle of a Pacific island for nearly 28 years rather than surrender, married yesterday. He met his 44-year-old bride through friends after he said he wanted to get married but not to a modern Japanese girl. Yokoi hid in the Guam Jungle when the Americans stormed the island in 1944. He was still intent on obeying an order never to surrender when 2 hunters captured him early this year.

BARBARA QUITS THE FRONT BENCH

Mrs Barbara Castle has quit the Labour Party's front bench in the Commons. She made the announcement yesterday at Blackburn, her Lancashire constituency, 48 hours after being voted out of the Shadow Cabinet. Mrs Castle said that Mr Wilson had invited her to continue as the Party Spokesman on Social Services but she had turned down the offer saying that she wanted to be free to go on the back benches.

WHO IS THE MAN KNOCKING PARKY'S RATINGS?

Watch out, Michael Parkinson, a young ex-schoolmaster with the hopeful name of Russell Harty has his sights on you. In London, Parkinson's Saturday chat show on BBC1 is opposed by a similar programme made by London Weekend Television and starring Harty. LWT are pushing hard to get their show on the national network. They say that Harty's brand of conversation gets 2 million viewers – half a million more than Parkinson.

Goons Harry Secombe (l.) and Peter Sellers (r.) talk to BBC1 chat-show host Michael Parkinson (centre).

DEC 1972

£10 BONUS IS ALL ROUND

The £10 Christmas bonus will be paid to Britain's 7,000 working pensioners. The Government decided yesterday to whip through the necessary parliamentary legislation next week although Sir Keith Joseph, Social Services Secretary, admitted that the 7,000 were never meant to receive the bonus. They are pensioners who, because they earn over £18 a week, do not receive the ordinary state pension. Sir Keith said the Government had decided to relent, rather than disappoint these working pensioners.

POST OFFICES CLOSE ON SATURDAY AFTERNOONS

Nearly all main post offices will shut on Saturday afternoons, beginning next month. This is part of an economy campaign to save £250,000 a year. Only sub-post offices run as part-time businesses by newsagents and general stores are not affected. A Post Office spokesman said yesterday that local managements were being given discretion over the half-day closing. Their brief was to arrange the half day to suit the needs of local customers but the Post Office would prefer Saturday afternoons 'because it helps with staff recruitment'.

ITV TO PLAY BANNED DISC

Paul McCartney's controversial new record 'Hi Hi Hi', banned by the BBC, is to be played on ITV. BBC officials imposed the radio and TV ban after deciding that the lyrics made reference to sex. McCartney, his wife Linda and their group Wings will sing the song this Sunday in a filmed sequence in the late-night chat show run by Russell Harty. Paul claims the BBC mis-heard the lyrics.

INSURANCE WARNING FOR HI-FI MUSIC MOTORISTS

Motorists who buy expensive hi-fi tape-players for their cars could be facing trouble on 2 fronts. The booming music has attracted thieves who have ripped the sets out of parked cars. As if that were not bad enough, many insurance firms will not cover such exotic extras in their usual car policies, so a theft is often a total loss. Though a car radio is now regarded as an ordinary accessory, an expensive stereo-cassette or cartridge-player is not and thus may not be covered.

TALKING CARS WILL WARN OFF TROUBLE

Talking cars are being developed by Ford. When cars of the future need attention the vehicles will speak through a works-fitted radio and give drivers such messages as 'You are running short of petrol,' or 'Brakes need adjusting now.' Ford of Britain revealed yesterday that the talking cars are being developed in Detroit. The speaking device is called an electronic voice synthesizer. Ford says it may eventually replace the conventional dashboard instrument panel gauges and warning lights, possibly within 5 years.

UNITED THEY FALL

Manchester United rocked soccer yesterday with a sensational clear-out of their management and an announcement that their wayward star George Best would not play for them again. But before Best could be told of the decision, he wrote to the directors saying he was giving up football. Out go Manager Frank O'Farrell, his assistant Malcolm Musgrove and Club Trainer John Aston, all sacked 'forthwith' by the unanimous decision of the 6-man board.

Greg Lake, Carl Palmer and Keith Emerson making music for 'longevity'.

JAPANESE OVERTAKE GERMANS IN CAR SALES

The Japanese have overtaken the Germans in the car-sales race in Britain. Last month Datsun outsold Volkswagen at the rate of more than 10 cars a day and took third place in the foreign-car sales league behind Renault and Fiat. This is the first time that VW, now in fourth position, have been ousted from the top 3 importers.

TOP OF THE POP STUDY CHARTS – SURVEYING

One of the toughest problems facing Britain's 44 universities is forecasting the changing pattern of subjects which students want to study. Matching supply to demand is a nightmare puzzle which they can never get exactly right, for academic fashions change as rapidly as the top of the pops – and often as unpredictably. The following chart, based on figures from the Universities' Central Council on Administrations, shows how supply failed to measure up to the pressure of applications in 1971:

	Number of Applicants Per Place
Surveying	6.3
Drama	5.7
Town Planning	4.8
Hotel Management	4.74
Education	4.72
Subjects with Education	4.4
Professional Studies	4.3
Veterinary Science	4.3
Accountancy	4.2
Art and Design	3.72

SELF-SERVICE 'SHOPS' TO OPEN FOR JOB HUNTERS

Self-service 'job supermarkets' will soon be part of the scene in many high streets. People unemployed or wanting to change jobs will be able to call at new government Job Centres, identified by bright orange and black boards. Self-service displays will give full details about jobs, and looking for work will become like shopping for groceries. Gone will be the dreary queueing at employment exchanges, and people out of work will not have to collect their benefit, it will be sent to their homes by Girocheque. The Job Centres network will begin to replace the 1,000 employment exchanges in the spring. In 2 years anyone visiting the Job Centre is likely to be automatically matched by a computer to a suitable job and there could be a full computer network by 1976.

TOM AND JERRY CARRY ON FIGHTING

The MP who wants the cartoon *Tom and Jerry* banned from TV admitted yesterday that his 6-year-old son is addicted to the cat-and-mouse saga. Mr William Price, Labour MP for Rugby, said he couldn't stop his son David watching it. His wife also disagrees with him about the harmful effects of the programme. Nevertheless, Mr Price has written to Sir John Eden, Minister of Posts and Telecommunications, pointing out that the cartoons set 'the worst possible example'.

THE DEATH OF *LIFE*, AGED 36

Life magazine, the pioneer of modern photo-journalism which brought the horrors of war and the achievements of man into millions of homes, is to die. Time Inc., which published *Life* for 36 years, said yesterday the magazine had been losing money for the past few years and projections showed it would lose even more. Its 29 December issue will be the last.

DAY BY DAY

2 Dec
The Australian general election is won by the Labour party, led by Mr Gough Whitlam.

3 Dec
A Spanish charter aircraft crashes on take-off from Tenerife, killing all 155 people on board.

Legislation outlawing terrorist organizations in Ireland comes into effect.

7 Dec
Sutton and Cheam, regarded as a safe Conservative seat, is won by the Liberals in a by-election. The Tories hold the marginal seat of Uxbridge with a reduced majority.

Apollo 17, the last in the present programme of moon flights, is launched from Cape Kennedy.

8 Dec
The Amalgamated Union of Engineering Workers (AUEW) is fined £50,000 for contempt of the Industrial Relations Court in continuing to defy an order to admit Mr James Goad to union branch meetings.

13 Dec
The Distillers' Company offers nearly £5m to compensate the 342 children in Britain who were born maimed after their mothers took thalidomide as a sedative during pregnancy.

The Parliamentary Labour party decides not to send representatives to the European Parliament at Strasbourg for at least a year.

18 Dec
The United States resumes full-scale bombing of North Vietnam in an attempt to force the acceptance of peace terms.

19 Dec
Apollo 17 splashes down in the South Pacific.

22 Dec
The Bank of England's minimum lending rate rises from 8% to 9%, the highest since 1914.

23 Dec
More than 10,000 people are feared dead in an earthquake which devastates Managua, the capital of Nicaragua.

26 Dec
Former US President Harry S. Truman dies, aged 88.

28 Dec
The Birmingham Industrial Tribunal rules that a Chrysler car worker has a legal right not to belong to the AUEW.

31 Dec
Mr Heath attends the funeral in Ottawa of Mr Lester Pearson, former Prime Minister of Canada and winner of the Nobel Peace Prize.

It is announced from the White House that the bombing of North Vietnam has been called off and that peace talks are to be resumed in Paris.

Sandy Richardson, played by Roger Tonge, son of motel owner Meg Richardson is crippled in a car crash and confined to a wheelchair in Crossroads.

JAN 1973

RIP THE WORK PERMIT

The work permit, much disliked instrument of exclusion from high-paying jobs abroad, is dead. British workers may now take jobs in the other Common Market countries without asking official permission. A residence permit is usually needed, though this is a formality.

TAX ON CHILDREN MUST BE DROPPED!

MPs of all parties yesterday joined the *Daily Mail* campaign to make the Government see sense over its plans to tax children's clothing. Spearheading the politician's support was Liberal leader Mr Jeremy Thorpe, while clothing trade businessmen also joined the fight to prevent the Chancellor imposing VAT on children's wear from 1 April. Yesterday the *Mail* hit at 'this iniquitous tax' and pointed out that everything from nappies to blazers will be subject to a 10% levy when VAT is introduced. If the Government goes ahead with its plans it will be the first administration – Labour or Tory – to tax children's garments.

War in Vietnam draws to a close as the peace agreement is signed by North Vietnamese Foreign Minister Nguyen Duy Trinh.

MARK PHILLIPS GOES TO STAY WITH THE FAMILY AT SANDRINGHAM

Mark Phillips, the 24-year-old Olympic gold medallist, whose name has been romantically linked with Princess Anne, has been staying with the Royal Family. It is the first time that the Queen has invited the tall, horse-riding army officer – he is a lieutenant in the Queen's Dragoon Guards – to join her house party at Sandringham. Despite considerable speculation, Lieutenant Phillips has denied all suggestions that he and Princess Anne are to become engaged.

HOP ON A FREE LONDON BUS

Free travel for all on London's buses and on the tube is being planned. It will be promised by Labour in elections for the Greater London Council this spring. Once in power the planning of free travel will be given top priority. Mr Anthony Crosland, opposition environment spokesman, said Labour would concentrate future spending on public transport instead of building more roads. He added, 'Fares will be put on a flat-rate basis – perhaps in time abolished altogether. These positive moves to improve public transport will be combined with stricter controls of the car.'

NEW SAFE TYRES CUT OUT SPARE WHEELS

The world's first cars with tyres so safe that there is no need for a spare wheel will be on sale in Britain this year. Developed by Dunlop, the tyre is called 'Total Mobility' and a motorist can drive 100 miles with a puncture or blow-out and not realize he has a flat. Safety is due to cells of fluid – a lubricant and sealant – which discharge when the tyre is punctured. The fluid temporarily seals the puncture to retain some air.

TWO NEW BOARDS WILL CURB PAY AND PRICES WHEN THE FREEZE ENDS

New legal powers with penalties for offenders are to be introduced by the Government to back up pay and price controls after the freeze. The restraints will be administered by two boards, a prices board and a wages board. Mr Heath said last night that the Phase 2 policy would have 3 broad aims: to steady prices, to be fair and to sustain a faster rate of economic growth. Today TUC chiefs will be confronted with an ultimatum that, while the Government would prefer their voluntary co-operation, the law will be used if necessary.

AUSSIES WANT FREEDOM FROM BRITISH 'RULE'

Australia served notice to Britain yesterday that 'continuing relics of colonialism' in their relations must be abolished. The demand came from Senator Lionel Murphy, the new Australian Attorney-General. He is to have talks in London with the Government about ending legal appeals to the Privy Council and what he calls 'the remaining capacity of the British Parliament to pass laws in relation to Australia'. Mr Murphy added, 'To me it is unbelievable that 73 years after Australia became a Commonwealth, Britain still has residual legislative, executive and judicial authority over Australia.' Whitehall will raise no objections to the change.

GILBERT IS TOPS

Gilbert O'Sullivan, the 23-year-old former Swindon postal clerk turned singer/songwriter, sold more records in 1972 than any artist in the world.

Joe Frazier is completely off canvas as he goes down in the second round of his title defence against George Foreman in Kingston, Jamaica.

'FROGS' LEGS SPECIALITY OF THE HOUSE'

It's too much for some MPs to swallow: frogs' legs are being added to the Commons's menu. There will be snails, too. Well, you won't catch a Lancashire member like Mr David Waddington eating them. 'I've never tried frogs' legs or escargots and I don't intend to start now,' said the MP for Nelson and Colne, who is as Conservative in his appetites as he is in his politics. 'There are quite enough health risks in being an MP without adding to them with this sort of thing. Call me unadventurous if you like but give me beans on toast every time.' Mr Dennis Skinner, Labour MP for Bolsover, said, 'I can't imagine anybody eating frogs' legs and snails – except Ted Heath; he should be put on a special diet of nothing else until he sees the errors of his European ways.'

THE POCKET 'BRAINS' WORRY A VARSITY

Students who use pocket computers to work out complicated problems are worrying university tutors. Lecturers in science departments at Aston University, Birmingham, fear that students whose pocket money stretches to buying the £37 computers may have an unfair advantage over those who can afford only a £2 slide rule. Doctor Ronald Brewster of the Department of Electrical Engineering said yesterday, 'We shall decide next month what attitude we should officially adopt towards them if they appear in examination rooms . . . the machines are tremendously accurate and a 12-year-old child could easily learn how to use one.'

CRICKETER RACHAEL IS TV'S FIRST GIRL SPORTS REPORTER

Rachael Heyhoe, Captain of England's women's cricket team, signed up with ITV last night to become television's first woman sports reporter. Miss Heyhoe, 33, said of her new job, 'I'm no supporter of women's lib but I'm really thrilled at getting into what is accepted as a man's world.' She makes her small-screen début in ITV's *World of Sport* in which she will be covering all types of sport, not giving 'the woman's angle', but as an expert on equal terms with men. She has a 6-month contract which will be extended if she is a success and will be paid the same fees as male sports reporters – not less than £50 an appearance.

Kevin Keegan and his wife Jean.

NO KLUNK-KLIK FOR JIMMY

Disc jockey Jimmy Savile, who appears in a 'Klunk klik' TV advertisement telling motorists to 'Belt up', has been caught out. When he climbed behind the wheel of his £5,000 motorized caravan, someone spotted he wasn't wearing a seatbelt and that seatbelts were not even fitted. Jimmy, who has recently split up with Polly Brown, former lead vocalist with the Pickettywitch pop group, admitted he wasn't taking his own advice. Because his mobile home started life as a van and weighs over 13 hundredweight, he doesn't have to fit it with belts.

NOW IT'S PARENT POWER!

A headmaster suggested yesterday that parents should decide whether teachers keep their jobs. Dr Rhodes Boyson, head of Highbury Grove Comprehensive in London, said a secret ballot could be held every 5 or 7 years. Teachers approved by the parents would carry on teaching; those who did not would be retrained. Dr Boyson, who operates such a system in his own school, said, 'I would not be worried if I was coming up for re-election; I would be very surprised if they didn't vote for me.'

ROVER AND A BIT OF BOYHOOD DIE

For 50 years it put characters like Morgyn the Mighty, the strongest man on earth, into the realms of schoolboy folklore. Its heroes were whiter than white, its villains blacker than black but now the *Rover* has come to the end of the great adventure. The comic that was part of boyhood has been killed off. From now on the *Rover*, launched in Dundee on Thursday 3 March 1922 at a cost of 2*d.*, will be incorporated into the *Wizard*, another D.C. Thomson comic, selling for 3p. The last issue went out the way it came in, crammed with action and adventure. Last Minute Mitchell fought his one-man war; Lonely Larry explored his Pacific island with his pet toucan; Morgyn the Mighty rippled his muscles and Cop Capers came on with the funnies at the back page as ever. According to the youth of today it was football, the big schoolboy passion, that was the comic's downfall. Boys just stopped buying the paper and its make-believe heroes to see the real thing – superstars such as Charlie George and Rodney Marsh – from the terraces. Perhaps the most revealing observation came from a 14-year-old from London who said, 'It was a horrible comic; all words. Who wants all them words?'

NOW FOR THE GOOD NEWS . . .

The BBC is to introduce a 'good news only' bulletin on Radio 3. The 10-minute programme, *Positive World*, will go out every Sunday morning after the regular bulletin. Stephen Hearst, Controller of Radio 3, said yesterday that most news tended to be 'mainly sensational or bad' and there was room for the new bulletin, which will concentrate on significant developments and long-term trends.

FEB 1973

Marlon Brando and Maria Schneider in Bertolucci's controversial film Last Tango In Paris.

'COOKING' BEATS RUST PROBLEM

British Leyland has developed a new rust-proofing process for cars. The system uses epoxy-resin powder sprayed on the part to be protected which is 'cooked' at high temperature. The resin melts over the metal surface, but the finish is too smooth for painting or welding so only small car parts get the new treatment. Leyland are looking at ways of colouring the powder so that it paints a car as well.

NATIONALIST AIMS TO CASH IN ON OIL BOOM

Gordon Wilson believes he can carry the blue and white flag of nationalism to victory in the Dundee East by-election and that oil, countless millions of gallons of it, will smooth his way to Westminster. North Sea oil – Scottish oil, Mr Wilson calls it – will be a big issue in Dundee. He believes he can use it to set the election alight and says that the Scots are waking up to the 'fact' that they have been hoodwinked by the 2 big British political parties.

$2m! – THAT'S ROBBINS'S STARTING PRICE

Mr Harold Robbins, that master of the paperback, has just received the biggest literary advance in the history of publishing. His American publishers, Simon & Schuster, are giving him $2m in expectation of his next riveting work, *Memories of Another Day*. The one-time Hollywood studio clerk has written around a dozen books, the most successful being *The Carpetbaggers*, the royalties of which bring him at least $0.5m a year. His new book concerns a 17-year-old boy and his father, who is an American union leader. It has the inevitable ring of fortune about it. His last book, *The Betsy*, sold 4 million copies during the first 4 weeks of its publication in the US.

DOCTORS' WARNING AS 'POOR DIET' DISEASE HITS BRITAIN

There are probably children with rickets – a disease of malnutrition which causes softening of the bones – in every school in Britain, a group of doctors claims. Serious thought needs to be given to reintroducing cod-liver oil or other vitamin D foods, not just for young children but for teenagers as well, they say in the *British Medical Journal*. The doctors tested 569 children and found evidence of rickets in blood tests on 233. The number of bottles of cod-liver oil handed out to mothers and young children fell from 5,340,000 in 1948 to 610,000 in 1970. In 1971 cod-liver oil was replaced by vitamin drops.

END OF THE LINE FOR HOVER TRAIN

The 300-m.p.h. Hover Train project is to be shut down by the Government. 'No one has a use for it,' Aerospace Minister Mr Michael Heseltine explained yesterday to a Commons select committee. The Hover Train, as a link between London and the airport to be built at Maplin, Essex, was ruled out because 'the cost would be very high and the time-saving very low'. The experimental train reached 107 m.p.h. on a 2,000-yard concrete beam.

THE NEW HANCOCK

Only 2 of the 6 'possibles' tested in BBC1's latest *Comedy Playhouse* season have so far made it as a full series, which means that many stars and writers are being kept in suspense while head of TV comedy, Duncan Wood, decides on their future. 2 are safely through and set to become a 1973/74 series. One, *The Last of the Summer Wine* by misfit author Roy Clarke, concerns a trio of out-of-work middle-aged fellows played by Peter Sallis, Michael Bates and Bill Owen. The other, *The Birthday Party*, gave television unknown Gordon Peters his first star role as a loser in the Hancock tradition. He was funny enough to win cheers from the studio crew, something which hasn't happened in a long time. But the future of *Elementary, My Dear Watson* with John Cleese as Sherlock Holmes transported to the 70s, is uncertain; so is that of *Home From Home* starring Michael Robbins from ITV's hit show, *On The Buses*.

IF YOU'VE EVER SAID I CAN SING BETTER THAN THAT . . .

If you've ever warbled a chorus or 2 of a latest hit and smugly pronounced you could do better than the pop stars, you could be right. A former Soho bouncer who can't play the guitar, agrees he can't really sing, refuses to dress in extravagant stage clothes and admits to not being exactly pretty is today one of the hottest properties in the charts. He calls himself Judge Dread. He's 27, stands 6 foot 4, weighs 19 stone and talks of his lack of talent with disarming honesty. The Judge – real name Alex Hughes – is an ex-fairground wrestler, maharaja's bodyguard, debt collector and disc jockey. He has already seen his 2 records gain silver discs for sales of more than 250,000 each.

It all happened after he wrote naughty lyrics to the nursery rhyme 'Little Boy Blue' and persuaded the record company on whose behalf he was chasing unpaid debts to make a £5 demo tape. The BBC and Radio Luxembourg banned the record 'Big Six' but that didn't stop Big J. He loaded 10,000 copies of it into a van and delivered them personally to every disc shop that would take them. The record was played a few times at discos and suddenly caught on. It's been in the Top 50 for 6 months. The Judge says, 'I know my music hasn't got lasting quality. Once the weenyboppers get fed up, that's it . . . I'll just go back to bouncing or working in a disco.'

LISTEN TO HER NOW . . . THE WOMAN WHO WAS BY MRS PANKHURST'S SIDE

Nothing is worth the sacrifice of the dignity of women, said Britain's oldest surviving suffragette. 'Everything women want they can get but they must seek it in the right way otherwise it is they ultimately who will be the losers. They have the vote, we got them that, but we got it without the loss of our dignity and with the true regard for the sanctity of human life. The risks we took were our own; they endangered no one else.'

Leonora Cohen, the woman who was once Mrs Pankhurst's bodyguard, will be 100 years old this year. 'If I were born again now, with everything there is for women today – the education and the opportunities – oh, what I could have done! But this bra-burning business, it just doesn't seem right. We suffragettes advocate freedom but we should never advocate licence. Mrs Pankhurst always maintained that we should do our work with defiance but with dignity. I am not really a feminist, not at heart – how could I be with such a good husband and such a wonderful son?' Mrs Cohen regards the permissive society with anxiety and the advent of women's lib with regret. 'That is not what we were fighting for. I believed then, and I still do, that equality of opportunity would meet almost every question relating to women in a man's world . . .'

SOME MOTHERS . . .

Michael Crawford launches his first situation-comedy series with *Some Mothers Do 'Ave 'Em*, playing a young man who would make Jonah look a pools winner by comparison. The character, Frank Spencer, is summed up by his mother: 'Frank doesn't go for jobs, he just goes for interviews.'

ROW OVER GO-AHEAD FOR £600m RINGWAY

The biggest planning row in Britain's history was gathering pace last night following the Government's approval 'in principle' of the Ringway 1 motorway circling inner London. The exact route has not been settled but it would slash through Shepherd's Bush, Chelsea and across the Thames to Clapham. It is likely to cross South London partly in tunnels via Brixton to Kidbrooke.

Immediately after publication of the *Layfield Report* on London's future development a storm of protest broke on whether the roads will ever be built, for Labour has pledged that if it wins control of the Greater London Council in the April elections it will refuse to build the motorway box. The proposed Ringway 2 is rejected because it would not help end congestion in central London and because it would be too near the present North Circular Road. *Layfield* says Ringway 3 should be scrapped because it would duplicate the North and South Orbital Ring Roads which are to be built outside the GLC area. The Government is giving this further consideration.

THE FLYING SCOTSMAN IS HOME

The Flying Scotsman, one of the world's best-loved steam locomotives, was back in Britain last night. Bill McAlpine, 38-year-old millionaire railway enthusiast and grandson of the founder of the McAlpine Civil Engineering giant, rescued her from creditors in the United States and is planning to steam her out of Liverpool's Lime Street Station on Sunday. Mr McAlpine would not say what the venture was costing him but he hopes to make it pay by running special rail trips. The 50-year-old locomotive's American tour was a financial disaster for her previous owner, a Nottingham businessman.

From Saint to secret agent Roger Moore is the new 007 in the latest Bond film Live And Let Die. *Jane Seymour plays Solitaire in the eighth film to be made about Ian Fleming's super-spy.*

MAR 1973

SCANDAL OF NORTH SEA OIL

North Sea Oil – our new, possibly richest natural asset – has been frittered away, MPs reported yesterday, and the squandering has allowed the international oil giants to laugh all the way to the bank. An all-party report reveals that prospecting rights have been picked up for peanuts when they might have been sold for millions. The main target for criticism looks like being Mr John Davies who was Secretary for Trade and Industry at the time of crucial decision-taking in 1971.

Two points stand out in the report:
– 9 of the biggest oil firms can offset tax losses totalling £1,500m incurred elsewhere in the world against the profits of the North Sea operations.
– when 15 blocks of the North Sea were auctioned off for £37m no one in Whitehall had second thoughts about freezing the allocation of 267 other blocks. They went for £3m when they might have been worth anything up to £700m if they had been sold by auction instead of the sealed-bid method. The Whitehall defence was that Mr Davies was anxious to push ahead with the development of North Sea Oil.

PETE MURRAY CUT OFF IN BIG WELSH DEMO

Pete Murray's *Open House* programme on Radio 2 was interrupted by members of the Welsh Language Society yesterday. The morning show was being broadcast live in a special St David's Day edition from the Pier Pavilion in Llandudno. First, members of the society pulled out a transmitter cable, silencing Frank Sinatra's rendition of 'Come Fly With Me' for 15 seconds; then 2 girls grabbed the microphone from Mr Murray and shouted 'Welsh channel now' in Welsh – the society's demand for a Welsh-language TV station. Elsewhere members of the society got into the Independent Broadcasting Authority's office at Southampton, the Tyne Tees office in Newcastle and BBC offices in Plymouth and Manchester.

One of the victims of the Old Bailey explosion.

SMOKERS BRING RISK TO ALL

Non-smokers suffer an 'appreciable' risk to health whenever they are cooped up in a room full of smokers, a team of doctors revealed today. The doctors stress that the risk is small compared with that run by smokers but they warn that it is a hazard that the average individual could well do without. Their findings follow an experiment in which smokers and non-smokers were asked to sit in a room the size of a family lounge. The results showed that the non-smokers suffered an increase in the amount of carbon monoxide absorbed into the bloodstream which was roughly equal to the amount they would have absorbed had they smoked and inhaled 1 cigarette. They add, 'It was also of the same order as a London taxi driver takes in from traffic pollution during a whole day of driving and similar to that absorbed by London policemen after 3 hours of point duty.' The doctors describe the effects on a non-smoker of sitting in a fume-laden atmosphere as 'passive' smoking.

THINGS THEY SAID

'2 months ago when he held 1 hand in front of his face and confessed that he could only just distinguish the fingers, I would not have given him a price.'
Sports columnist Ian Wooldridge after watching Gordon Banks begin his comeback in Athens against Olympiakos.

'. . . if Donny asked me never to drink tea or coffee again then I would stop for ever.'
Julie Stevens, 14, who played truant to see her heroes leave Heathrow, having already spent several weeks following the Mormon religion.

'I can't impress enough how bad these excessively high heels and platforms are. We are already treating women with intensive physiotherapy for the painful problems these shoes have caused . . . ideally no woman should wear heels over 2 inches. Anything higher disturbs weight distribution, a third of which should fall on the front part of your foot and the rest at the back. Once you alter this you upset the whole mechanism of walking, misusing your joints and muscles. Apart from being dangerous from a balancing point of view, these shoes act as a splint, turning your legs and feet into artificial limbs with no leverage at all.'
Comment by an orthopaedic surgeon on the current trend in footwear.

M*A*S*H – the spin-off TV show from the hit film.

Mrs Mary Peters receiving her OBE at Buckingham Palace following her Olympic Gold medal win for Britain in the pentathlon at the Munich Games.

FAMILY PLANNING GOES ON THE NHS

Contraceptives will be available on the Health Service from 1 April next year, Social Services Minister Mr Keith Joseph said yesterday. He told MPs that the government decision to revise its previous policy was in answer to public opinion. The Lords have twice demanded completely free family planning for everyone but the Government thought that was going too far. The contraceptives – sheaths, the pill, loop and diaphragm – will be obtainable on the 20p prescription. This replaces the Government's original plan to limit free contraception to those in financial, medical or social need.

PUB WIVES PLAN BREWERY DEMO

Wives of publicans are to hold a mass protest demonstration outside Truman's London brewery. 82 tenants have been sacked from their Truman's pubs to make way for managers. One publican said, 'When the Grand Metropolitan Hotels Group took over Truman's they told us we had nothing to fear.' Angry at having built up a big trade over 7 years yet being offered only £5,000 compensation, Mr Keith Hall, who runs the Crown in Richmond, Surrey, says of his possible replacement, 'To him it's just another job; to us it's part of life.'

SPORTY FIAT AIMS AT MGB

A new sports car produced by Fiat and styled by Bertone will get its first public display at the Geneva Motor Show which opens on Thursday. It is the Fiat X19 designed to compete with Britain's MGB and Triumph sports cars on the American market. It is a 1290cc mid-engined 2-seater. The price has not yet been announced but is expected to be around £1,250.

VAT WILL GO ON SOME CHILDREN'S CLOTHES AFTER ALL

Children's clothes have not escaped Value Added Tax completely. Many will carry the new tax in spite of the hopes raised by Mr Anthony Barber in his budget. Details revealed yesterday show that only clothes to fit children under 12 will be totally tax free. Under the present purchase-tax laws, clothes for children under 15 are generally exempt but the Chancellor, worried by what he called 'slim and nubile young women' buying tax-free children's clothes for themselves, has told the VAT experts to work out stricter controls. The result: all clothes to fit children under 12 and those to fit children of average size under the age of 14 will be tax free; but clothes for bigger-than-average 12–14-year-olds and loose-fitting clothes for these ages will be taxed, as will all clothes for children over 14.

FEATHER'S NUMBER 2 MAY GET HIS JOB

The TUC meets this week to pick a successor to Mr Vic Feather as General Secretary. If tradition is followed the man they name will be Mr Len Murray, the present Assistant General Secretary. Mr Murray, 50, a war-time army captain, went on to Oxford, where he gained a first in politics, philosophy and economics. He joined the TUC in 1947 and became Assistant General Secretary in 1969.

DAY BY DAY

1 Mar
Dick Taverne, who resigned as Labour MP for Lincoln, retains the seat in a by-election, standing on a Democratic Labour ticket. Labour holds Dundee East and Chester-le-Street.

220,000 hospital ancillary workers take industrial action in pursuit of their claim for a £4-a-week increase, having been offered £1.88, the maximum allowed under Phase Two regulations.

Palestinian guerillas storm the Saudi Arabian Embassy in Khartoum and demand the release of Sirhan Sirhan, the murderer of Robert Kennedy, together with Arabs held in Jordan and West Germany.

2 Mar
The terrorists shoot dead 1 Belgian and 2 US envoys held hostage in the Saudi Arabian Embassy. The terrorists surrender 2 days later.

3 Mar
Tottenham Hotspur wins the Football League Cup, beating Norwich 1–0.

6 Mar
Chancellor Mr Anthony Barber announces that VAT will be at the rate of 10%, with children's footwear and clothing and all food zero-rated.

8 Mar
In a referendum in Northern Ireland, 90% of the votes cast are in favour of retaining the link with the United Kingdom.

1 man dies and more than 200 are injured when bombs explode outside the Central Criminal Court and an army recruiting office in Whitehall.

11 Mar
A state of emergency is declared in Bermuda after the Governor and his aide-de-camp were shot dead yesterday.

13 Mar
John Conteh stops Germany's Rudi Schmidcke in the twelfth round to become European Light Heavyweight Champion.

16 Mar
The new London Bridge is opened by the Queen.

20 Mar
A White Paper on the future constitution of Northern Ireland includes proposals for an 80-member Assembly elected by proportional representation; responsibility for law and order to remain with the Government in London; Ulster to remain part of the UK for as long as the majority wants; a new charter of human rights guaranteeing to prevent religious or political discrimination.

23 Mar
Gordon Liddy sentenced to serve 6–20 years in jail for his part in the Watergate affair.

26 Mar
Sir Noël Coward dies, aged 73.

Women are allowed on the trading floor of London's Stock Exchange for the first time in 171 years.

31 Mar
The Grand National is won by Red Rum at 9–1.

The fabulous Osmonds are here – (l to r) Merrill, Donny, Jay, Wayne, Alan and 9-year-old Jimmy in front.

APR 1973

BRITISH CARS ARE TOP OF THE POPS

Britain's top 20 cars are named today and mark a blow for the importers, for only 3 foreign models rate a place. The VW Beetle placed thirteenth, the Renault 12 placed seventeenth and the Renault 16 twentieth. Last month sales of foreign cars in Britain reached nearly 30% for the first time because of industrial disputes at British Leyland, Ford and Vauxhall. The 10 top-selling cars in the UK in 1972 were:

1. Ford Cortina
2. Ford Escort
3. Morris Marina
4. Austin Morris 1100/1300
5. Vauxhall Viva
6. Austin Morris Mini
7. Hillman Avenger
8. Austin Maxi
9. Hillman Hunter
10. Ford Capri

WHAT LUCY LOVES

Everyone loves Lucy. At the last count, Lucille Ball's television show was being screened in 79 countries, making its star and outright owner the richest actress in the world and the only extra who ever actually bought the studio where she once earned £30 a week. Today Lucille Ball, at the age of 61, is not only preparing the twenty-first year of *The Lucy Show*, the longest run in history, but she is also starring in the film version of the hit musical *Mame*. Of her 40 years in showbusiness she says, 'I have been out of work only 4 hours in that time – between 6 and 10 one evening between contracts.'

PICASSO DIES BEHIND THE BARRICADES OF HIS PRIVATE WORLD

Pablo Picasso, the most famous, influential, prolific, talked-about and richest painter of the twentieth century, is dead. Picasso, who had been gravely ill for 2 weeks, died yesterday from a heart attack at his barbed-wire barricaded villa at Mougins in the south of France. He was 91. With him were his wife, 46-year-old Jacqueline, and Paolo, his eldest son by his first wife, Olga Kolkova, a Russian dancer.

HYLDA IN PICKLE PROTEST

Actress Hylda Baker, who plays a pickle-factory owner in a TV series, is stirring things up over a real-life pickle crisis. She has written to Mr James Godber, the Minister of Agriculture, protesting over the proposed closure of Nottingham's last pickle firm. Jubilee Pickles has been forced to sack its workforce because of rising overheads and a world shortage of onions. Mr Ernest Smith, Managing Director of the firm, said yesterday, 'It is nice to think that Miss Baker cares enough to write to the Minister. I must say, I am a fan of her series, although it is not a good advert for the modern pickler.'

SILENCED ALI LOSES £1.4m

Muhammad Ali is 'satisfactory' – but silent – in a San Diego hospital after a 90-minute operation to wire the most expensive broken jaw in history. He was to have been paid £1.4m for a match with World Champion George Foreman in September. Now the big one is postponed indefinitely. Certainly Saturday's defeat by Ken Norton signals the beginning of the end of the greatest personality boxing has known.

Carl Bernstein and Bob Woodward, investigating journalists for the Washington Post, *uncovered the Watergate bugging scandal.*

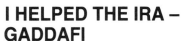

I HELPED THE IRA – GADDAFI

Libya's revolutionary leader, Muammar Gaddafi, said yesterday that his country had helped to supply the IRA in their fight against the British. The Arab strongman also spoke of his 'hatred' for the English. In an interview in the French newspaper *Figaro* Colonel Gaddafi said, 'Here is a little country which has taken up arms to defend its rights and freedom; we have given it our assistance.'

BUGGING: FBI CHIEF QUITS

The acting head of the FBI resigned yesterday as the Watergate Scandal boiled towards a new crisis. The White House strongly hinted that President Nixon himself ousted Mr Patrick Gray – hours after a press report that the FBI chief had destroyed important secret files. As pressure on the President mounted it was also reported that 2 of the men closest to him, H.R. Haldeman and John Ehrlichman, were resisting their colleague John Dean's suggestion that they should all 'save the Presidency' by telling the whole truth and risking jail sentences.

THE STARS TO BE

ITV has taken a remarkable decision in casting its latest prestige series, *Edward VII*. The title role has gone not to a major film or TV star, as the industry expected, but to Timothy West who has done comparatively little TV work and is best known for stage plays and useful supporting roles in the cinema. The part of his wife, Princess Alexandra, has been won by another outsider, Helen Ryan, who has made her reputation in the theatre and is rarely seen on television. Established stars do get a look in, of course: Annette Crosbie and Robert Hardy are playing Queen Victoria and Prince Albert, and ATV is looking for some famous actors to play cameo roles. Shooting of the £1.5m series, consisting of a string of hour-long plays covering nearly 70 years of history, starts next month.

DISC JOCKEYS GET 'A CRITICAL MENSH' FOR THEIR PATTER

Disc jockeys and the slang terms they use were criticized at a teachers' conference yesterday for introducing youngsters to a new language – 'Deejayese'. A delegate said that the language was spreading among a growing army of 'trannie tots' – children who take transistor radios everywhere. One teacher recalled how she asked the children at her school if they would like to pray for anyone who was ill. 'One little boy asked if he could have a "mensh" [meaning mention] for Auntie Dora who fell downstairs and broke her leg.' Disc jockey Jimmy Young said later, 'None of the expressions I use is likely to be harmful to young children. Who says they're slang anyway? Once they've been absorbed into the English language, surely they're part of the language?'

ROYAL HIT FOR POP MUSIC

The pop-music world wins its first Queen's Award to Industry today. The accolade goes to a firm run by 52-year-old ex-crooner Dick James, whose music company has increased its export earnings 6-fold in 3 years. One of the hits that helped that boom was a £60 record made by a session group of rock musicians. Their version of an American single, which they called 'Groovin' with Mr Bloe', was an overnight success, selling 900,000 copies. 'There never was a Mr Bloe,' said Mr James yesterday, 'but if there was I would be shaking his hand right now.' But the big moneyspinner for Dick James Music is pop pianist Elton John, who in the US alone gained $5m-worth of sales with 5 gold discs.

CLARKSONS SELLS OUT FOR A SONG

Clarksons, the package-holiday firm which lost £4,800,000 last year, has been sold for a nominal sum. The new owners are Court Line, the airline which carries most of Clarkson's holidaymakers. Under the deal Shipping Industrial Holdings, Clarkson's parent company will hand over £5,750,000 to cover Court Line against losses expected by the holiday operators in the coming year. Last night a spokesman for Shipping Industrial agreed the company was paying Court Line to take the loss-making subsidiary off its hands. He said, 'You cannot expect someone to buy a firm that's making a loss without offering some incentive.'

Above: Big moneyspinner Elton John.

The Electric Light Orchestra was the brainchild of The Move's Roy Wood who wanted to bridge the gap between pop and classical music. When Roy left, Move percussionist Bev Bevan and singer-writer Jeff Lynne led the innovative group to chart success.

MAY 1973

WHY THIS CAN'T BE JUST ANOTHER GAME OF TENNIS

As far as Bobby Riggs is concerned, his confrontation with Margaret Court in San Diego on Sunday is the most important tennis match ever played. 'It's bigger than Wimbledon, bigger than Forest Hills; it's the match of the century and the battle of the sexes.' TV will be there and the whole world will be watching to see whether he, at 55 – the 1939 American and Wimbledon champion – can defeat 30-year-old Mrs Court, currently the undisputed number 1 in women's tennis. The match is the outcome of a challenge made by Riggs to Billie Jean King last year. Mrs King had been complaining about inequality in prize money in men's and women's tennis. Mr Riggs challenged her to a match. She refused, but this year Mrs Court accepted. Riggs, who is taking 45 different sets of vitamin pills, is confident of victory. 'I can beat a woman every day of the week and twice on Sundays,' he says.

THE MOST DANGEROUS POP STAR OF THEM ALL

'I love the dead before they're cold
Their blueing flesh for me to hold.
Cadaver eyes upon me see nothing.'

An anthem of necrophilia reverberates through 20,000 watts of power as the children of America, the customers of this decadent concert fantasy, get out of their seats and rush towards the stage, frantic to be nearer the symbolic death and dismemberment. The concert amuses its thrill-seeking sub-teen patrons with disturbing visions of mutilation, torture, rape, sado-masochism and blatant obscenities. 'Am I normal? Am I adjusted? Off-stage, certainly. Away from the theatre I'm just as much a product of middle-class America as, say, Bert Bacharach,' says the protagonist on stage, Alice Cooper.

The unusual 'square' steering wheel of the soon to be released Austin Allegro 1750 Sport.

Mercury Records announce that they will soon release an album featuring a compilation from Rod Stewart's earlier albums.

RACE ROW PROFESSOR PUNCHED BY STUDENTS

A professor who claims that negroes and Irishmen are less intelligent than other races was beaten up by students yesterday. A fierce brawl started in a London School of Economics lecture room just as 57-year-old Professor Hans Eysenck, author of the controversial book *Race, Intelligence and Education*, rose to speak.

FEMAIL . . . ROAD TESTING THE BIG NEWCOMERS IN A TYPEWRITER REVOLUTION

A revolution is about to hit secretaries and girls in the typing pool. It comes with 2 brilliant new typewriters which promise to make life faster, smoother and much cleaner for the girls who use them. The novel thing about the Coronamatic (Smith Corona, available from September, costing under £200) is that it operates on a ribbon enclosed in a cartridge which is slotted in and out of the machine in a couple of seconds. If a mistake is made you just slot in a correcting cartridge and type over it.

But for slapdash typists nothing can beat the Selectric 82 (IBM, costing £314.35). Just by touching the backspace key you can miraculously erase your error. No rubber, no correcting paper, no paint – just the touch of a finger. It works on a golf-ball typing element which means you can go faster since the keys can't clash and jam up. A variety of type styles can be used simply by changing the typing element.

ANYONE CAN BUY A STAKE IN ROLLS

Anyone will be able to buy a bit of Rolls-Royce Motors, the world's most famous car firm. None of the offers in this week's 'auction' of the whole company was high enough so next week all the shares will be offered to the public for a total of £38,400,000 – the biggest sale of new shares the City has ever seen.

10CC on Top of the Pops *with their single 'Rubber Bullets'.*

CALLAN SETS JUDGE A MUSICAL PROBLEM

A judge was asked yesterday to decide whether music from the *Callan* television series is a copy of an earlier piece of music by an Italian composer. '*Sono Nostalgico*' by Italian composer Armando Sciascia was first hired out in April 1965. Rediffusion Television used it as background music to their *Ratcatcher* series. In 1967 ABC Television launched the *Callan* series and 'Girl in the Dark' was used as the theme. Mood Music Publishing Company Limited maintained that 'Girl in the Dark' and '*Sono Nostalgico*' were almost identical and are claiming infringement of rights against De Wolfe Limited. De Wolfe claims that 'Girl in the Dark' was written by Mr Jack Trombey and that the 2 tunes are not identical and any similarity is coincidental. The case is expected to last for several days.

NO WAY LEEDS CAN LOSE IT

'The sentimentalists will want to see Stokoe's Sunderland astonish us all once more; the realists, however, will want Leeds to confirm gloriously what we suspect: that they are the greatest club side ever assembled in this country. If they score first, Leeds will disappoint me if they do not make modern history by giving us a 5-goal spree to remember.'
Sports columnist Jeff Powell.

WHITE HOUSE FILES SEARCH BY THE FBI

President Nixon yesterday ordered FBI agents into the White House to guard and search vital files in the Watergate Scandal. The men were called in to prevent certain key figures in the bugging affair from smuggling papers out of the building. The move came as a new sensational disclosure established the first firm link between the Watergate conspirators and John Ehrlichman, the top presidential aide sacked by Mr Nixon on Monday. It has been revealed that Mr Ehrlichman told the FBI that in 1971 he hired 2 of the 7 convicted conspirators to investigate Daniel Ellsberg, the man who leaked secret Pentagon papers on the Vietnam War to the press.

BULL'S-EYE – AND THE SOFA'S ON FIRE!

Windows with 'bull's-eye' panes could be a fire hazard when the sun shines, a fire expert said yesterday. His comment came after the magnifying power of a bull's-eye window started a vinyl-covered settee smouldering at a house in Rochdale, Lancashire. Mrs Dorothy Gowland said, 'The sun's rays were shining directly onto the settee through the bull's-eye and the back of the settee was blistering. We have also had some pop records affected in the same way – they now look like chapatis.'

Sunderland's Bob Stokoe with Billy Hughes at the end of the FA Cup Final.

SUPERSTAR CONTEH

John Conteh is confirmed as British boxing's new superstar for the way he beat Chris Finnegan at Wembley last night. There were titles at stake. Conteh added Finnegan's British and Commonwealth crowns to the European Light Heavyweight title he already held. Big-punching Conteh could not put away his man, as he had in 16 of his 19 previous fights, but to travel the full 15-round championship distance for the first time and to outpoint by 6 rounds to 3 a man as wily and experienced as Finnegan makes the 21-year-old Liverpudlian a marvellous prospect.

JUNE 1973

'STOP THATCHER' BID BY PARENTS IN HIGH COURT

A group of parents is fighting a High Court action next week which could set back Mrs Margaret Thatcher's plans to save many of the remaining grammar schools. The group believes that the procedures used by the Education Minister to stop the schools going comprehensive are illegal. Labour-controlled Bexley Council, Kent, had wanted all the borough's 17 schools to go comprehensive but Mrs Thatcher turned down reorganization plans for 11 of them. The council has accepted the decision but it is being fought by the Parent Teacher Association at Bexleyheath School, which would lose its 2 grammar streams and become a full comprehensive. They say the law does not allow Mrs Thatcher to reject plans for some schools but accept them for others. The Chairman of the PTA made it clear that they did not object to the original plan to make all 17 schools comprehensive but are against abolishing selection at Bexleyheath while retaining it elsewhere.

Victory in the High Court would enable parents in other areas to stop Mrs Thatcher taking similar action. She has already turned down 'comprehensive' plans by several authorities. The latest government figures give the number of grammar schools as 893 against 1,591 comprehensives.

CHARLIE MAKES £20,000 GOLDEN SHOT

Comedian Charlie Williams was chosen yesterday to be the new host of the ITV show *The Golden Shot*. The new job will make the comic, who turned professional only 3 years ago, one of the most successful coloured performers on the British showbusiness scene. It will boost his earnings to at least £20,000 a year. Charlie, 43, a former professional footballer, was making £80 a week in working men's clubs when he joined the *Comedians* series. He takes over from Norman Vaughan in the autumn.

Singer Cat Stevens prepares for the release of his sixth album Foreigner.

POWELL ON THE BRINK

A whirlwind of fury descended on the unrepentant head of Mr Enoch Powell yesterday. A choice collection of epithets was hurled at him following his invitation to anti-Common Market Tories to vote against Mr Heath at the next election. Unmoved by the abuse, Mr Powell intends to go further. It is believed that he is prepared to contemplate a Labour Government for the rest of his life if this means that Britain keeps her political independence outside Europe. In a recent speech he said, 'Independence – the freedom of a self-governing nation – is in my estimation the highest political good for which any disadvantage, if need be, and any sacrifice are a cheap price.'

Dick Clement and Ian La Frenais bring Terry (James Bolam) and Bob (Rodney Bewes) back together again in Whatever Happened to the Likely Lads.

OVETT AIMS FOR 1976 OLYMPICS

Many of Britain's senior athletes are deliberately slowing their build-up this season because of the Commonwealth Games at the start of next year, but they are being pressed by a bunch of talented youngsters. 1 of the most promising is Steve Ovett, a 6 foot 1 17-year-old Brighton schoolboy. He ran a 1-minute-48.8-second 800 metres – fastest for a British athlete of his age – to finish only a yard behind the experienced Peter Browne in the Southern Counties Championship at Crystal Palace on Saturday. He has already won 2 England schoolboy titles and has lifted his ambitions this season to the AAA Championships and European Junior Championships. 'I'm still thinking about the Commonwealth Games next year but my real long-term aim is the 1976 Olympics,' he said.

BORG BOY HAS MAGIC TOUCH

7 years ago in a village 10 miles north of Stockholm Rone Borg, a clothes salesman, won a table-tennis tournament. The first prize was a tennis racquet and he gave it to his 9-year-old son. But for this obscure event the world might never have seen the most exciting phenomenon to come out of Sweden since Greta Garbo. Now, 17-year-old pin-up boy, Bjorn Borg, becomes one of the youngest Wimbledon seeds of modern times and a likely formidable opponent for Britain's Roger Taylor, who is in the same half of the draw. Though Bjorn is too young to accept prize money, he has already caused excitement and upsets in this year's major championships and is now seeded number 6 at Wimbledon.

NIXON TOOK PART IN BIG COVER-UP, SAYS DEAN

John Dean landed the first public accusation of Watergate guilt on President Nixon yesterday. With millions of US TV viewers watching, the 34-year-old former White House Counsel told the Senate investigators that the President had discussed with him every aspect of the Watergate cover-up: concealment, the danger of impeachment, executive clemency for the Watergate defendants and £40,000 in hush money to persuade them not to say where their orders came from. At the opening of his long-awaited testimony Dean said, 'With regard to the President of the United States . . . It is my honest belief that while the President was involved he did not realize or appreciate at any time the implications of his involvement and I hope when the facts come out that the President is forgiven.'

TENNIS DISPUTE GOES TO COURT

The number of top-class tennis players taking part in this year's Wimbledon tournament will probably be decided in the High Court today. Nikki Pilic, who has been suspended for 1 month by the International Lawn Tennis Federation from all their tournaments because he refused to represent Yugoslavia in the Davis Cup, is seeking a High Court injunction to have the ban lifted. The Association of Tennis Players, which includes the world's best players among its 98 members, supports Pilic and says it will boycott Wimbledon if the suspension is not lifted. Among those who say they will support such a boycott are last year's champion, Stan Smith, runner-up Ilie Nastase, John Newcombe, Ken Rosewall, Roger Taylor, Tony Roche, Arthur Ashe, Tom Okker and Mark Cox. Only Jan Kodes of Czechoslovakia has so far refused to support Pilic.

Schoolmaster and singer Clifford T. Ward, pictured with his family, releases a single, 'Gaye', from his album Home Thoughts.

DAY BY DAY

1 June
The Greek Government abolishes the monarchy and the Prime Minister, Mr George Papadopoulos, is nominated President of a 'presidential parliamentary republic'. It is also announced that King Constantine, exiled in Italy for the past 6 years, is to be deprived of his allowance and divested of almost all his property.

3 June
A Russian airliner crashes during the Paris Air Show, killing the crew of 6 and 8 civilians.

6 June
The Derby is won by Morston at 25–1, who had raced only once before.

Comedian Jimmy Clitheroe – the Clitheroe Kid – dies, aged 51.

7 June
Herr Willy Brandt arrives in Tel Aviv, the first West German Chancellor to visit Israel.

8 June
General Franco, while remaining Spain's Chief of State, appoints Admiral Luis Carrero Blanco as President of the Government, responsible for the day-to-day running of the country.

11 June
The House of Lords rules that immigrants who entered Britain illegally between March 1968 and January 1973 are liable to be expelled because of the retrospective effect of the Immigration Act 1971, which came into force on 1 January this year.

17 June
Johnny Miller wins the US Open Golf Championship.

22 June
The Security Council accepts applications by the Federal Republic of Germany and the German Democratic Republic to become members of the United Nations.

The 3 *Skylab* astronauts return to earth after spending 28 days in space, a new endurance record.

23 June
The Open University, established in 1969, confers its first degrees on students who took courses by correspondence, radio and television.

25 June
Mr Erskine Childers becomes President of Ireland in succession to Mr Eamon de Valera, who retires.

30 June
The longest solar eclipse of the century occurs, the path of totality stretching from South America to the Indian Ocean.

HERE'S A NEW GARDEN TENNIS GAME

Anyone for Dafuti? It's the new garden and beach tennis game. Just hammer the spike into the ground, get out your racquet and hit away. The ball swings round a spiral and comes back to you to be hit again. Play by yourself or with a partner. Dafuti is available by mail order and sells for £3.50.

JULY 1973

CRASH BOY: A SURGEON'S DILEMMA

A storm over the law on transplant surgery broke last night following a surgeon's agonizing dilemma. He authorized the removal of the kidneys of a 17-year-old boy killed in a road accident without the permission of the youth's parents who were abroad on holiday. The case highlights a serious conflict in the interpretation of the Human Tissues Act which governs the 'ownership' of a body. The Department of Health said that its own legal advice was that in the absence of claims by the next of kin a hospital is 'lawfully in possession' of a patient when he dies. 'As such it has the power to authorize the removal of any organs,' said a spokesman.

DOUBLE TAX PLAN TO KEEP CARS OUT OF CITIES

Motorists face the prospect of paying a double car tax if they want to drive in busy city centres. One is the present £25 for a road-fund licence, the other a new area licence that would also cost up to £25 and be similarly displayed on the windscreen. No starting date has been fixed for the scheme which is being studied as one of the methods of discouraging drivers from congested areas. Another government proposal is road-pricing meters which would charge motorists up to 5p a mile for driving along commuter roads. All cars would have to be fitted with compulsory meters costing about £5 each which would be electronically triggered by roadside toll points. The units could be dearer in London than in other cities and toll points could be closer together as required to make motoring dearer. Methods of payment are being studied. A possibility is that a car would be immobilized until it has been 'activated' with pre-purchased metal units. The units would be used up only when toll points are passed. The late 70s is the proposed introduction date for road pricing.

Sign outside a Hollywood florist's: 'Watergate carnations – with wired stems.'

HAS *CORONATION STREET* FINALLY HAD IT?

Ena Sharples has bullied Annie Walker into staying at the Rovers Return; Stan Ogden is being henpecked again – or perhaps you couldn't care less? More and more people are switching off *Coronation Street*, the world's longest-running television serial, now in its thirteenth year. Gone is the era when it took the first 2 places in the weekly top 20 of most-watched programmes. The last time that happened was nearly 3 years ago.

The programme itself betrays signs of grabbing for attention instead of expecting it by right. Stories which once developed in a leisurely way are now set up and disposed of in a couple of weeks. Soon, Joanna Lumley is being brought in as widower schoolmaster Ken Barlow's new girlfriend, but despite such attempts to restore the show's popularity, Granada knows that without Ena Sharples, Elsie Tanner and Ken Barlow millions of viewers would feel that they had been robbed of friends and switch off for good. The question implicit in the audience ratings remains, however. How much longer can they squeeze life out of the storylines?

POP IDOL BOWIE GIVES 'LAST SHOW'

Pop idol David Bowie stunned fans last night when he announced at a London concert, 'This is the last show I will ever do.' The announcement was greeted with shrieks of dismay at the Odeon, Hammersmith. Bowie was appearing at the last show of an 8-week tour in which he has appeared before 120,000 fans. The announcement of the pop singer, whose hairstyle and clothes have created a cult, is understood to apply only to live appearances.

PLATFORM SHOES CAN KILL YOU

Women drivers are being warned 'Platform shoes are dangerous.' The Royal Society for the Prevention of Accidents said last night, 'Platform shoes with high soles and even higher heels are a serious hazard to women drivers. The exaggerated thickness of the soles means that the driver has no feel for the pedals and has great difficulty in distinguishing between the brake and accelerator. In a situation which calls for swift, effective braking this could have tragic consequences.'

COULD THIS PARENT POWER SAVE YOUR CHILD?

Why does $9 + 2 = 11$? Because 9 and 1 are 10 and 1 more is 11? Wrong. The answer in the modern trendy world of new maths is: 'By definition of 2, $9 + 2 = 9 + (1 + 1)$ but because the associative law of addition holds, $9 + (1 + 1)$ equals $(9 + 1) + 1$. Now $9 + 1$ is 10 by the definition of 10, and $10 + 1 = 11$ by the definition of 11.'

That amazing piece of gobbledegook is just one example of the way in which traditional methods of teaching young children are being abandoned wholesale. It is an excerpt from an American maths lesson but in Britain the old rigorous attention to times tables and simple arithmetic is being swept aside, too, in the name of letting children discover maths principles for themselves.

Such new schemes have led to a backlash aimed at smashing the stranglehold of the progressive theorists over the way our children are educated. Parent power is still in its infancy in this country but is growing out of discontent every day. In one American experiment Californian primary schools offered courses varying from traditional 'chalk and talk' approaches to the British open-plan discovery method. The parents were given a 'voucher' for the value of a year's education which they could cash in at the school of their choice. Schools with no parents applying go out of business and the teachers are retrained and employed elsewhere. A handful of left- and right-wingers in Britain are already demanding a 'voucher' system along the lines of the American experiment.

PLASTIC OUSTS THE TOYMAKER

For 38 years Mr Harry Hunt made metal toys but when he was asked to take in tools for plastic toys he refused and was sacked with redundancy pay. Yesterday the General Manager of the Chad Valley Company, Birmingham, praised Mr Hunt's past work and said, 'He could have picked up the knowledge he needed in 12 months; he was frightened of it.' After the case, in which the tribunal dismissed Mr Hunt's claim for extra compensation on the grounds that his redundancy was unfair, Mr Hunt said, 'When I went on holiday I would see the kids on the sands playing with buckets and spades and I could say that I had helped to make the children happy, but not any more.'

WORLD CUP TEST CRICKET ON WAY

Cricket's first World Cup will take place in England in 1975, replacing the scheduled visit by outlawed South Africa. The Cup, agreed in principle last year, will be endorsed at today's International Cricket Conference meeting at Lords. Early rounds could be on a league basis, as in the Benson and Hedges Cup, with the winners moving to knock out semi-finals before a grand final at Lords. All 6 test-playing countries – Australia, England, the West Indies, New Zealand, India and Pakistan – will compete. Ceylon, with accepted first-class standards, and Holland, of almost comparable level, are likely to send teams.

AFTER BARDOT LA BISSET

The French are paying us the supreme accolade by hailing an English actress as the successor to Brigitte Bardot. Jacqueline Bisset who, despite her French-sounding name comes from this country, is being greeted as the top 'Made in France' star. She has scored a notable success as the sensation of François Truffaut's new film *The American Night*.

OOH AH AND HEY HEY HEY – THEY DON'T HALF MAKE MONEY

They have been on more hit records than Tom Jones or Engelbert or Slade put together, yet they rarely sing a word. Every week you see them on *Top of the Pops*, but despite their success their name never features in the charts or fan magazines. But you can bet that when Marc Bolan and Alice Cooper are just dim memories, the Ladybirds backing group will still be in demand. They are the 3 ladies who contribute the 'Oohs', 'Ahs' and the 'Hey hey heys' on pop records, advertising jingles and television spectaculars. 'As a kid, I dreamed of singing opera at Covent Garden,' said Gloria George, 29, the mezzo in the trio, 'and I ended up belting out "Ernie, he drove the fastest milk cart in the West." ' The other members of the trio are Maggie Stredder, 29, and Marion Davies, 28.

A suit and matching tie in brushed denim from Bilbo in the King's Road, Chelsea.

END OF THE ROAD FOR LOTUS ELAN

Lotus have killed off its famous Elan sports car. The last model has just been sold in Portugal. The Elan, one of the world's best-loved sports cars, was launched in 1962. Since then 12,224 have been produced in various forms. Now, harsher worldwide safety and pollution laws are hitting such cars and it would be too difficult to modify the car to fit the new regulations.

As a follow up to their Living In the Past *album Jethro Tull release* A Passion Play.

AUG 1973

HOW LESLIE CHARTERIS PUT THE SAINT ON AUTOMATIC PILOT

Asked why he wanted to be a writer, Leslie Charteris replied vehemently, 'I didn't want to be a writer, I wanted to be one of the idle rich.' And so he is. He hasn't written a *Saint* book personally for 7 or 8 years. They continue to appear, however, and this week's latest, *The Saint and the People Importers*, acknowledges that it is the product of a collaboration. Charteris invented Simon Templar when he was 20; they've been together now for 44 books and 45 years. In that time he has carried on never using stronger language than 'bloody', bedding the girls but never telling us about it, and providing nice clean deaths for his enemies with no dwelling on sadistic detail. Charteris is not enthusiastic about such contemporary developments. In the new book, which is about the topical subject of illegal Pakistani immigrants, there is a torture scene: the victim is made to talk by being fed with devilishly hot curry.

SCIENTISTS IN CONFLICT OVER ENERGY CRISIS

The world's energy crisis brought conflicting prophecies from Britain's leading scientists yesterday. Eminent chemist Sir George Porter assured the British Association that the tiny fraction of the sun's light that shines on the earth could meet all man's energy needs 2,000 times over; all that was needed was to collect sunlight on an area measuring 1,400 miles by 400 miles, though he warned that the technology needed to convert solar energy into power had yet to be developed and would be expensive. Dr John Pope of Aston University said the world would run out of oil within 80 years, making cars and planes 'extinct'; the only hope lay in the discovery of a new fuel, and there was no sign of that.

OLGA'S SUPER BACK FLIP

Olga Korbut's spectacular backward somersault, which thrilled millions of viewers and made her the darling of the Munich Olympics, may be seen for the last time at the European Championships at Wembley in October. Her wonder routine is one of the complicated movements which the International Gymnastics Federation's Technical Committee wants to outlaw as dangerous. Renald Knysh, writer for *Sovietsky Sport* says, 'In 20 years from now the world will regard these elements as simple and suitable only for beginners.'

REMOULDS WARNING

A coroner yesterday warned that remould tyres should not be used for high-speed driving after he heard that a van which crashed at 60 m.p.h. was fitted with a tyre that had been badly remoulded. Mr Terence Watson of the West Midlands Forensic Science Laboratory said there was no regulation about the use of remould tyres but there was a recommendation that on commercial vehicles they should not be used at more than 55 m.p.h. The tyre which burst had been buffed down too far before the new tread was put on.

THE OLD LADY DROPS HER GUARD

The Old Lady of Threadneedle Street has given up her military guard after 193 years. Security at the Bank of England has improved so much that the troops provided by the Brigade of Guards are not really needed. The tradition began in 1780 after the Gordon Riots when religious mobs rampaged through the city, pillaging and burning chapels. The Lord Mayor of London asked for men to defend the city and 50 guards were assigned to the bank.

WHAT DO ITV THINK IS WORTH £1m?

ITV is spending £1m on a mammoth documentary series that should go a long way towards explaining the generation gap. *The World at War* will trace the story of the Second World War in a way that will show the younger generation what their parents lived through from 1939 to 1945. The 6-month screening starting in the autumn is the biggest project ever undertaken by ITV in the documentary field and has entailed 4 years of research and production.

David Essex as Jim MacLaine and Rosalind Ayres as Jeanette in a scene from That'll be the Day, *in which MacLaine leaves his wife and family to pursue to the top his career as a pop singer.*

MOTHER MUST FACE THE SHOCKING TRUTH – TIM'S GOING TO BE A STAR

The last time Tim Curry's mother visited the theatre to see her actor son perform in a nude scene from *Hair* she hid blushing for the whole show. Mrs Patricia Curry is almost certain to be a good deal more shocked when she sees Tim in his new play, *The Rocky Horror Show*, a spangled piece of eroticism, which has turned into 70s sensuality all those kitsch fantasies of the 50s – horror movies, Charles Atlas muscle-bound adverts, leather-jacketed Rockers. Not since *Hair* arrived on the scene 5 years ago has a show generated so much excitement – nor one performer been so firmly tipped for stardom.

THE NEW FACE FOR A SPORTING TV GAMBLE . . .

Tony Gubba, virtually unknown south of a line between Grimsby Town and Tranmere Rovers, has landed the plum job of presenting *Sportsnight*, taking over from David Coleman when the new show returns in October. Sam Leitch, editor of *Sportsnight*, who has coached most of the top men in sporting commentary techniques admitted, 'It's a gamble, but we have to find new faces from time to time.' Tony, 29, says, 'I first realized the difference between news and sports reporting after presenting my first regional sports programme; the phone was ringing, someone shouted down it "Will you get that little runt Gubba off – he supports Manchester United!" '

THE £123,000 GAMBLE TO MAKE A SUPERSTAR . . .

CBS Records, the biggest label in the world, is gambling a small fortune in the belief that rock fans can be manipulated into turning an ordinary singer into a superstar. They are attempting to 'repackage' David Essex, the actor who plays Christ in *Godspell*, and the bill so far is £123,000, including £600 for 2 David Bailey photographs for poster promotions and £1,000 to buy air time on Radio Luxembourg to plug the new record 'Rock On'. Although he has never had a hit, CBS says, 'We are giving David the image of someone who is pretty tough really . . . but lovable too – the sort of figure who brings out the mothering instinct in the girl fans yet still retains a strong sexual appeal.'

Karen of The Carpenters who have a number one album with Now and Then.

STORM OVER NEW POP RECORD

A copyright quarrel has blown up over a striking musical similarity between 'Angel Fingers', a new song by singer-composer Roy Wood and the late Donald Peers's famous signature tune 'By a Babbling Brook'. The company holding the British copyright of the original version of 'By a Babbling Brook' (first published in America in 1927) took exception to this similarity but after a meeting with Wizzard's manager it was announced that a friendly agreement had been reached.

TOP 10 PAPERBACKS

1. *The Moon's a Balloon* by David Niven
2. *Passenger to Frankfurt* by Agatha Christie
3. *David Cassidy's Official Story*
4. *The Day of the Jackal* by Frederick Forsyth
5. *Shabby Tiger* by Howard Spring
6. *Confessions of a Travelling Salesman* by Timothy Lea
7. *Onward Virgin Soldiers* by Leslie Thomas
8. *Live and Let Die* by Ian Fleming
9. *Tobin Takes Off* by Stanley Morgan
10. *Autumn of Terror* by Tom Cullen

DAY BY DAY

1 Aug
Walter Ulbricht, founding father of Communist East Germany and the man responsible for the Berlin Wall, dies, aged 80.

2 Aug
49 people die when an entertainments complex on the Isle of Man is destroyed by fire.

6 Aug
The Ministry of Defence issues a statement saying that Kenneth Littlejohn, recently convicted of a bank robbery in the Irish Republic, was told that if he had information about IRA activities the British Government would be prepared to receive it.

Actor James Beck, Private Walker of *Dad's Army*, dies, aged 42.

9 Aug
Former singing idol Donald Peers dies, aged 64.

15 Aug
American bombing of Communist bases in Cambodia ceases.

19 Aug
Mr George Papadopoulos is sworn in as first President of the Greek republic and announces an amnesty for all political prisoners.

22 Aug
Mr William Rogers resigns as US Secretary of State and is succeeded by Dr Henry Kissinger.

31 Aug
King Faisal of Saudi Arabia warns the US of the possibility of restricted oil shipments if America continues to support Zionism.

The vogue for fancy footwear is by no means confined to the female fraternity – nor even to male pop stars.

SEPT 1973

MOTORBIKE PLANT IS CLOSED

A Triumph motor-cycle factory which employs 1,750 people is to close next February, it was announced yesterday. The firm, at Meriden near Coventry, has lost £16m in the past 3 years. The decision was made by Norton Villiers Triumph, the group formed following a merger deal with the ailing BSA concern.

Paul Newman and Robert Redford, dressed to con in George Roy Hill's film The Sting.

DES WILSON IS LIBERAL CANDIDATE FOR HOVE

Former Shelter Director Des Wilson was named last night as the Liberal candidate in the Hove by-election. Mr Wilson, 32, who was once an active Labour supporter, joined the Liberals only 3 months ago and will try to overturn the once solid 18,000 Tory majority at Hove. At the last election the Liberals didn't even put up a candidate. Now, after successes at Ely and Ripon, even Hove is considered vulnerable.

SUPERB WILKIE SPEEDS TO WORLD SWIM RECORD

David Wilkie is the World 200-metres breaststroke champion and record holder. The 19-year-old Scot's startling time of 2 minutes 19.28 seconds at the World Championships last night gave him victory over previous record holder, America's Olympic Champion John Hencken, who also got inside the old world mark of 2 minutes 20.52 to finish in second place with 2 minutes 19.95. It was Britain's first gold medal at this level of competition since Anita Lonsborough won her Olympic crown in Rome in 1960. Wilkie has been studying marine biology at the University of Miami since winning the silver behind Hencken at the Munich Olympics.

YOU CAN'T MAKE ANY EXCUSE NOW, SIR ALF

Sir Alf Ramsey yesterday talked the Football League into promising him all the help he needs to beat Poland – and with this lost his last excuse if England fails to reach the 1974 World Cup Finals. Ramsey's familiar plea that the top clubs do not give him use of their players often enough or long enough will be met by Football League agreement that League ties can be switched away from the date of the most important soccer match ever played in this country. Frankly, that does little more than strip England's much criticized manager of his last shred of self-defence if Wembley, 17 October proves his Waterloo.

THE WORLD'S MOST EXCITING STORE

It all started with a gingham shift dress just over 9 years ago and now it's a department store. That's the incredible success story of Biba which until yesterday was an internationally famous boutique but from today, spanning 7 floors and 120,000 square feet of the old Derry and Toms building, becomes probably the most exciting shop in the world. It's an event that will not only affect London, for its originality will have far-reaching influences on many other cities in many other countries. Biba is the brainchild of designer Barbara Hulanicki and her husband Stephen Fitz-Simon.

HOTEL IS HIT BY NEW FIRE LAWS

A hotel has been restricted to 6 visitors from today under the Government's new Fire Precautions Act. The Sandringham Hotel at Great Yarmouth usually sleeps more than 70 guests and staff but needs smoke detectors, fire doors and auxiliary lighting before a fire certificate is granted. Proprietor Mr Keith Shaw said, 'We believe that this is the first direct result of the new act in Britain.'

WHY I AM NOT GOING TO RESIGN

Aerospace Minister Mr Michael Heseltine last night denied that he had lied to the House of Commons. The Science and Technology Committee of MPs, furious at the Government's scrapping of the 300-m.p.h. Hover Train, quoted Mr Heseltine's parliamentary reply of 12 February that the Government was still considering whether to provide cash to continue the £5.25m project. The committee said, 'On February 14th Mr Heseltine told us the Government had decided on January 29th not to provide alternative funds. Mr Heseltine's answer on February 12th was therefore untrue.' Mr Heseltine countered, 'On February 12th . . . I was aware that Vickers were negotiating a massive contract with the Canadians . . . there were only 36 hours between what I said to the Commons and the evidence I gave the committee on February 14th and I viewed my February 12th comments as merely what you might term "a holding answer".' The 40-year-old 'Golden Boy' Minister, held in high regard by Mr Heath, says his actions were entirely justified and that the question of resignation did not arise.

Bruce Lee starring in Hollywood's first venture into the genre of kung fu movies, Enter The Dragon.

TV WRITERS: GIVE US PENSIONS OR FACE BAN

Television writers yesterday delivered ITV chiefs an ultimatum: pay us pension money or we will ban the sale of our work overseas. The demand, revealed by Lord Ted Willis to TUC delegates at Blackpool, was made by the Writers Guild in a letter sent to each ITV company. The minimum a TV writer earns for a 60-minute TV script is between £500 and £700, but 50% of Guild members earn no more than £1,500 a year. 3 current series of which Lord Willis was the creator – *Black Beauty*, *Crime and Passion*, and *Hunter's Walk* – would rapidly be hit by loss of overseas rights. Other series which he thought would be affected were *Crossroads*, *Family at War*, *Coronation Street* and *Sam*. The Guild has given the companies until the end of the year to come up with pension schemes.

IN THE HEAT OF AN INDIAN SUMMER, THE GREAT TURBAN DEMO MARCHES ON NUMBER 10

A thousand Sikhs marched on Downing Street yesterday, protesting against the law which makes it compulsory for motorcyclists to wear crash helmets. Under Sikh law a man must wear a turban at all times except in his own home or when swimming or playing a sport. They are prepared to face fines or jail rather than wear crash helmets and claim that the tightly wound turban gives protection to the head as good as a crash helmet. There was only 1 minor incident during the demonstration when an Englishwoman shouted at one of the demonstrators: 'Why don't you go back where you came from?' He replied in broad Cockney, 'That's East Barking, my old love.'

WHEN YOU'RE CERTAIN TO BE MILLIONAIRES BEFORE YOU'RE 30

They are Britain's most successful song-writing team since Lennon and McCartney. In 2 years the 18 songs they have composed have sold a staggering 20 million records. As their latest hit, 'Ballroom Blitz by The Sweet', jumps straight into the charts, they are now guaranteed to earn £100,000 each this year. By the time they are 30 they will almost certainly be millionaires. Little wonder that Nicky Chinn, 28, and Michael Chapman, 26, are envied by millions for their storybook success built on a chance meeting in Tramp discotheque. Their first record 'Funny Funny' was a Top 10 hit for The Sweet and their second 'Coco' was a number 1 for the same group, selling 2 million copies. It is an amazing success story for 2 men who can't read a note of music.

WHY MARY WHITEHOUSE AND ITV HAVE FALLEN OUT

ITV's first gesture towards censorship has run into trouble from, of all people, Mrs Mary Whitehouse. The Independent Broadcasting Authority is testing a system to warn viewers of 'disturbing' programmes. A rectangle is printed in a corner of the screen throughout such material. After a month of the year-long pilot scheme being run in the Midlands, only one programme has been stamped with a rectangle – a documentary on plastic surgery. The IBA felt that sequences showing burns victims might upset viewers. Mrs Whitehouse branded it 'a ridiculous decision; this is exactly the sort of programme people should be encouraged to see'. She added, 'The code is bound to become a kind of licence to try offensive material.'

BRITAIN'S 5 KINGS OF EUROPE

Britain's middle-distance runners are once again kings of Europe. Andy Carter won the 800 metres and Brendan Foster scored a magnificent tactical 5,000-metre victory in the Europa Cup which ended in Edinburgh's drizzling rain last night. Frank Clement's 1,500-metre triumph meant Britain gained a clean sweep in the 3 classical track races. Then there was the shock 200-metre win by Leicester's 21-year-old Cliff Monk and Alan Pascoe, defying illness, won the 400-metre hurdles. Britain topped the scoring in the track events to finish fourth behind Russia, East Germany and Germany.

The Sweet

FREEDOM HEAD DIES AT 89

Mr A.S. Neill, headmaster of the internationally famous Summerhill School where pupils can do what they like, died yesterday aged 89. Neill started his school, where children are allowed to swear, smash things up or steal, at Hellerau, Germany, in 1921. Then, after a period at Lyme Regis, he moved to the present site at Leiston, Suffolk. Neill never told the children what to do; they decided school rules for themselves in their own 'Parliament'. In Britain he was generally shunned by the education establishment but his ideas have had immense influence on teaching methods, particularly in primary schools.

YES, CADGING A CIGARETTE IS BEGGING

Out-of-work Robert McLerie asked a passer-by for a cigarette and yesterday a court had to decide whether this was begging. McLerie was arrested under the Vagrancy Act of 1824 for 'begging alms', but cigarette smoking only started in Britain during the Crimean War which ended in 1856 – 32 years after the act came into force. After studying legal books magistrate Mr Mark Romer ruled: 'A cigarette is alms, as is anything given in this way.' McLerie was sent to prison for a month.

BILLIE JEAN BEATS BOBBY IN 3 STRAIGHT SETS

The standard-bearer of women's lib, Billie Jean King, beat the professional male chauvinist Bobby Riggs in Texas early today. Bobby, 55, a former Wimbledon champion, had challenged the current Women's champion to a £40,000 winner-take-all contest to prove that men at any age were tougher than women.

'BELT UP' . . . OR ELSE

Motorists who forget to belt up in 1974 Volvo cars will be 'nagged by a buzzer and flashing light' until they have fastened their belts. This is announced today as a new feature of safer 1974 Volvo cars. Other changes are: special shock-absorbing bumpers to prevent body damage in minor collisions and special shock-absorbing steering columns to avoid or minimize chest injuries in head-on crashes.

'QUIT OR GO DEAF' WARNING TO SINGER

A pop-group singer has been warned by doctors to quit or go deaf. Phil Lynott, 22-year-old vocalist with the group Thin Lizzy is already suffering from a form of deafness caused by sustained exposure to loud music. He said yesterday, 'I kept waking up in the mornings with a piercing whine ringing in my ears.' Phil intends to carry on with the group 'but I may have to think again if I find my hearing is completely in jeopardy.'

Glenda Jackson gives George Segal something to think about in Melvin Frank's A Touch Of Class.

OCT 1973

Crisis at the yard as Fairclough and Langton are ordered to pay £200 V.A.T. on a £2000 bill which Weatherfield Plastics hasn't settled. Anne Kirkbride plays Deirdre, Peter Adamson is Len and Neville Burwell is Ray.

OIL WILL KEEP FLOWING, HEATH TELLS COMMONS

Mr Heath said yesterday that he had received 'firm assurances' on supplies from the major Arab oil states. They had declared that they had 'no wish whatever' to damage Britain and that they would take every possible step to prevent this. However, doubts immediately developed about whether petrol rationing can be avoided this winter. Whitehall rejected the idea that the message from the Arab states could be taken as a guarantee of uninterrupted supplies but Mr Heath took a cautiously optimistic view of the immediate future.

THIS COULD BE FINAL TRAGIC BLOW FOR STEWART

World Champion Jackie Stewart said yesterday that his motor-racing career was in the balance after the death of his team-mate François Cevert. Stewart spoke after withdrawing from the American Grand Prix as a mark of respect to Cevert. The 29-year-old French driver – number 2 to Stewart in the British Tyrell Ford Team – was killed instantly in a 160-m.p.h. smash during Saturday's practice for the Grand Prix.

PRINCESS ANNE WILL PROMISE TO OBEY MARK

Princess Anne will promise to obey Captain Mark Phillips when the couple make their wedding vows in Westminster Abbey on 14 November. The part of the service in which the bride promises to obey the bridegroom has become unfashionable in the face of women's liberation. Yesterday, the Dean of Westminster, the Very Reverend Eric Abbott said, 'The word obey is omitted in the Alternative Marriage Ceremony, which was introduced in 1928. However, in my view the original 1662 Service is the only legal form of marriage. Strictly speaking, the 1928 Service is not legal and it would be very strange if the Queen's only daughter did not use the form which is legally prescribed.' The Dean added, 'Captain Phillips would be a very strange bridegroom if he didn't want Princess Anne to obey him but I should be very surprised if Anne gave unquestioning obedience to her husband – it is not meant in that sense.'

GUILTY AGNEW RESIGNS

Spiro Agnew yesterday resigned as Vice-President of the United States. Then he was fined £4,000 on a tax charge and put on probation for 3 years. His letter of resignation was submitted in Washington as he was admitting the income-tax evasion charge in a Baltimore court. President Nixon expressed 'a great sense of personal loss'. The guilty plea in Baltimore concluded days of secret bargaining with government lawyers. The deal: if Agnew resigned the Vice-Presidency and pleaded guilty to one charge, the more serious accusations against him would be dropped. Attorney-General Elliot Richardson said the Government was ready to press on with the accusation of bribery but 'to have done so . . . would have been likely to inflict upon the nation serious and permanent scars'. Agnew had been under investigation since last winter on charges of seeking and accepting bribes from contractors while he was Governor of Maryland in the 60s.

John Baxter (Donald Sutherland) with his drowned daughter in Don't Look Now, *adapted from a story by Daphne du Maurier.*

Roxy Music (l. to r.) Paul Thompson, Bryan Ferry, Andy Mackay, Phil Manzanera, Eddie Jobson.

ANATOMY OF THE HOLY DAY WAR

Already it's called the War of the Day of Atonement. For it was on Saturday, on the holiest day in the Jewish Calendar at 1.50 p.m. local time, that Egyptian armed forces attacked across the full length of the Suez Canal and set up bridgeheads on territory held by the Israelis since the Six Day War ended in 1967. At the same time Syrian and Moroccan troops and aircraft attacked Israeli positions on the Golan Heights – the first time that 2 Arab countries had managed to co-ordinate an attack against the Israelis since 1948.

NIXON SURRENDERS ALL THE TAPES

In the most astonishing about-face of his controversial career President Richard Nixon last night capitulated to the courts and agreed to hand over all the White House Watergate tapes. His surrender came after Judge John J. Sirica had threatened to hold the President in contempt unless he obeyed the law of the United States.

GENESIS: THE BIRTH OF A SUPERGROUP

Charterhouse, the famous public school which stands majestically in its own Surrey grounds and charges fees approaching £900 a year, is an unlikely breeding ground for a pop group. But the school which numbers former England cricket captain Peter May, Baden-Powell and Thackeray among its old boys can add a very different name to the Old Carthusian list: Genesis. Genesis is a 5-man group whose music is a far cry from that of the school's famous composer Vaughan Williams. It is unknown to the average pop fan, it has never issued a single, yet it has 2 albums in the LP charts. Its new album *Selling England by the Pound* is at number 3 after just 1 week and the group now commands a £4,000 concert fee.

CLOUGH: WHY I QUIT DERBY IN DISGUST

Brian Clough, soccer's most controversial personality, last night quit Derby County in a mood of 'disbelief and nausea'. The end of Clough and his management partner Peter Taylor's spectacular 6½-year spell at Derby came after Clough received a written ultimatum from Chairman Sam Longson. Clough was told to stop 'engaging yourself in literary work by writing articles in the press and other publications and entering into commitments with the radio and television media'. Clough replied with a resignation letter which he wished to be effective immediately. Taylor did likewise. On their future Clough said, 'We both hope to stay in football – and it will be as a pair. We deserve to stay in the game because we are the best; only Don Revie can compare with us in terms of management and we are bound to overcome him sometime because there's only 1 Revie and there's 2 of us.'

10-EVENT OLYMPIC CUT BACK

The International Olympic Committee yesterday decided to drop 10 events from the 1976 Olympic Games in Montreal. The decision was taken by the International Olympic Committee meeting in Bulgaria yesterday. The events cut are: swimming – men's and women's 200-metre individual medleys and men's 4 x 100-metre freestyle relay; athletics – the 50-kilometre walk; shooting – 300-metre event; cycling – tandem event deleted; canoeing – 4 slalom events dropped.

CHELSEA CALLS UP WILKINS BROTHERS

Chelsea Manager Dave Sexton includes teenage brothers Graham and Ray Wilkins in a squad of 12 against Norwich at Stamford Bridge tonight and for the younger brother, 17-year-old Ray, known as Butch, the call comes only a week after he turned professional. 'These boys are very good prospects,' said Sexton.

NEW BOY BRADY MAKES IT

Arsenal 1 Birmingham 0
Heroes have been so hard to find around Highbury recently that Liam Brady's first 75 minutes in League football are in danger of being magnified out of all proportion. A fifteenth-minute substitute for injured Jeff Blockley, the 17-year-old Irish boy, brought a touch of calm and confidence to the Arsenal team and it was his intelligent pass which led to Ray Kennedy's goal.

The last chance . . . as Channon and Peters see the ball go wide in England's World Cup qualifying game against Poland.

NOV 1973

CREDIT-RATING SECRET FILES TO BE OPENED

Credit-rating agencies are to be forced to throw open their files to the millions of people on whom they hold secret dossiers. For a 25p fee anyone will be able to demand to see an agency's assessment of his financial standing. Such agencies are widely used by shops and traders when deciding whether to grant credit. The new deal for the customer comes in the Consumer Credit Bill published yesterday by Sir Geoffrey Howe, Minister for Trade and Consumer Affairs. An independent Consumer Credit Commissioner will license all those who grant credit and administer new 'truth in advertising' laws under which credit firms will have to reveal their true rates of interest. A 10-day 'cooling off' period is to apply to all credit agreements so that the borrower can have second thoughts. Touting for credit business by telephone is to be outlawed and so is the mass mailing of unsolicited credit cards. Sir Geoffrey hopes to have the new law operating by next summer.

EAR IN POST 'IS GETTY'S'

An ear sent by post to a Rome newspaper almost certainly belonged to the missing grandson of oil millionaire Paul Getty, the boy's mother has told police. A note with the ear and a lock of hair said they had been sent to impress on the family that 17-year-old Paul Getty the Third really had been kidnapped. Police have suggested that the kidnapping may be a hoax but Paul's mother, Mrs Gail Harris, is said to be more than 90% certain that the ear and hair were her son's. The note said that further parts of Paul would follow if a ransom was not paid within 10 days. Paul's parents have so far offered £700,000 to buy the freedom of their son who vanished in July, but the kidnappers are demanding 10 times as much.

STEWPOT'S POP REQUESTS ARE CENSORED

Disc jockey Ed Stewart has been told to stop playing records on his *Junior Choice* show for little Jimmy who has just passed his 11-plus. The BBC has made the decision because an education group feels it upsets children who have failed the exam. The Confederation for the Advancement of State Education says the exam is a politically sensitive subject; it also told the BBC that children in comprehensive-school areas were confused because they had no idea what the 11-plus was.

Princess Anne and Captain Mark Phillips leave Westminster Abbey man and wife.

BRITAIN SAYS 'NO' TO OIL SHARE-OUT

Britain last night refused to share her oil supplies with Holland and other Common Market countries. The message was sent to a meeting of the Common Market Executive Commission. It was called by the Dutch, who claimed their EEC partners should help with supplies following the Arab boycott on oil deliveries to the Super European Refinery in Rotterdam. Major oil companies, including British giants BP and Shell, have been told they face multi-million-pound 'fines' if they allow tankers to take their cargoes to the US or Holland, countries on the Arab boycott list.

HOW DOUGAN DISCOVERED THE MAN WHO COULD REPLACE HIM IN WOLVES' ATTACK

Derek Dougan has introduced an unknown 21-year-old striker to Wolves with this recommendation: 'I believe I may have found my successor.' Last night Dougan told how Liverpool-born Peter Withe – rejected by Southport as a teenager and made redundant when Barrow lost their Football League status – found his way to Molineux after impressive performances for Arcadia Pretoria, the South African side Dougan was playing for in the summer. When Dougan returned home he had no hesitation in recommending Withe to Bill McGarry.

MINDBENDER URI SHOCKS VIEWERS

Mindbender Uri Geller caused chaos at BBC TV last night. Hundreds of people phoned to say that watches had been 'mended' and cutlery twisted out of shape during his demonstration on the *Dimbleby Talk-In*. During the show, Uri, a 26-year-old Israeli telepath now working in the US, correctly identified the drawing of a boat in a sealed envelope, started a broken watch and snapped a steel fork simply by stroking it. It was the first time Uri had appeared 'live' on a TV show anywhere.

SPENCER TAKES TITLE IN LAST FRAME THRILLER

John Spencer won the Norwich Union World Open Professional Snooker Championship for the third time in London last night after a thrilling 15-frame final against John Pulman. Spencer won the match by 8 frames to 7 to take the £1,000 prize. Australian Eddie Charlton won the play-off for third place by beating Alex Higgins 8–5.

MOODY BLUES GROUP TO PLAY IN CHINA

The Moody Blues rock group are to become the first British pop stars to play in China. After years of condemning contemporary Western music as 'decadent and artistically barren' the Chinese have agreed to allow them to appear behind the Bamboo Curtain. The long-haired 5-man group, which has sold more than 10 million records in America and Britain, will go early next year. It will be only the second group of Western musicians to play in China in 40 years; the London Symphony Orchestra toured there last March. Their business manager Mr Jerry Hoff said yesterday, 'The Moodies are the only modern Western musicians to have their records played on Peking Radio in the last 30 years. Even Sinatra and the Beatles haven't managed that. We owe our popularity to the British Table Tennis Team who played in China last year. One of the players took along a Moodies LP and told the Chinese that the group was the finest representatives of Western music. They agreed and almost adopted the group from there.'

A TRAGEDY FOR MUSIC . . . MISS DU PRÉ'S CONCERT CAREER ENDS

A heart-rending tragedy has ended the plans of Jacqueline Du Pré, Britain's foremost cellist, to return to the international concert platform after a long period of illness. 28-year-old Miss Du Pré has been told that she is suffering from multiple sclerosis and will never play again in public. The news will stun the world of music which Miss Du Pré has captivated since her adult début at the Royal Festival Hall 14 years ago.

Chart-toppers Mud make an appearance on Granada's Lift Off With Ayshea.

'BOSTON STRANGLER' IS MURDERED IN HIS CELL

Albert De Salvo, who confessed to being the Boston Strangler, was found murdered in his prison cell yesterday. De Salvo, 42, only occupant of the hospital block at Walpole State Prison in Massachusetts, had been stabbed several times in the chest. The man who admitted murdering 13 women over a 19-month period never stood trial for any of the killings because of insufficient evidence. He was serving a life sentence after being convicted of 14 sex, burglary, robbery and assault charges. It was while he was in prison that De Salvo claimed he had been responsible for the murders which had sent a wave of hysteria over Boston from the time of the first killing in June 1962 to the last in January 1964.

GREAT CLOUGH GAMBLE

Brian Clough travels from Derby this morning to face the cold reality of life with Brighton and Hove Albion near the bottom of the Third Division. Unless Clough and Peter Taylor can work another Derby-sized miracle then both they and the club could be out of League Football in 2 years. Mike Bamber, Brighton's Chairman, has taken a big risk on the club's behalf, as have Clough and Taylor in dropping from third to sixty-third place in the Football League.

ON THE CARDS . . . THE SAGA OF EVA PERON, SUPERSTAR

The gilded musical partnership of Tim Rice and Andrew Lloyd Webber cannot be accused of a faint heart when it comes to choosing challenging subjects for their combined talents. Eva Perón has been mooted as the heroine of their next musical to follow *Jesus Christ Superstar* and *Joseph and the Amazing Technicolour Dreamcoat*. With Peronism triumphant in the Argentine these days Eva – known to the masses as Evita when General Juan Perón was last in power – seems an inspired choice. Tim Rice, 30, says, 'Before we came up with Eva Perón, we even thought of basing a musical on the Cuban Missile Crisis, but we discarded Watergate because it doesn't have a hero.' Eva, however, is an acknowledged heroine; she died of leukaemia in 1952 aged 33 and there are still repeated requests to the Vatican to make her a saint.

DAY BY DAY

7 Nov
The General Synod of the Church of England votes to retain the law forbidding the remarriage in church of divorced persons while the first partner is still alive.

8 Nov
By-elections: Tim Sainsbury and Alex Fletcher retain Hove and Edinburgh North respectively for the Conservatives. Tories lose Berwick-on-Tweed to Liberal candidate Alan Beith while Margo Macdonald of the Scottish Nationalists wins Glasgow Govan from Labour.

11 Nov
Israel and Egypt sign a cease-fire agreement.

13 Nov
The Government declares a state of emergency over the fuel crisis.

The Icelandic Parliament approves an interim agreement to end the cod war, under which British trawlers would be allowed to catch 130,000 tons of fish a year.

14 Nov
Princess Anne and Captain Mark Phillips are married in Westminster Abbey. The service is watched on television by an estimated 500 million people worldwide.

The use of electricity for floodlighting, advertising and for the heating of shops, offices and restaurants is banned.

15 Nov
8 members of the Provisional IRA, including 2 sisters, are sentenced to life imprisonment for planting car bombs that exploded in London in March.

18 Nov
Arab countries decide to exempt Common Market countries, with the exception of Holland, from further reductions in oil supplies.

19 Nov
The Government orders oil companies to cut deliveries to private and industrial consumers and petrol stations by 10%.

22 Nov
Mr Whitelaw tells the House of Commons that political parties in Northern Ireland have agreed to form a power-sharing executive and that the Chief Executive is to be Mr Brian Faulkner, leader of the Ulster Unionists.

25 Nov
Greek armed forces depose President Papadopoulos and Lieutenant-Colonel Phaidon Gizikis is sworn in as his successor.

Actor Laurence Harvey dies, aged 45.

29 Nov
Post offices begin issuing petrol coupons to car owners although the Government says no decision has been taken regarding petrol rationing.

RECORD TV PAYOUT

The ABC television network has paid a record £1,300,000 for the rights to a one-night screening of the movie *The Poseidon Adventure* shot aboard the old *Queen Mary* at Long Beach, California.

DEC 1973

'UNTRUE BROCHURE' TOUR FIRMS MUST PAY AND PAY AGAIN

Every holidaymaker who suffers because of a false description in a brochure has the right to see the tour firm prosecuted, the Appeal Court decided yesterday. 3 judges dismissed an appeal by Thomson Holidays, who contended they could only be convicted once for false information relating to a hotel in their brochure. The travel firm had described the Hotel Golden Coast in Greece as having a private swimming pool, children's paddling pool and a nightclub on the beach. A succession of holidaymakers found that all these statements were inaccurate. Following 2 separate complaints, the company was fined £450 and £1,000. Thomsons argued that they should not have been prosecuted twice for the same offence, but the judge ruled: 'The Trade Descriptions Act envisages that more than one prosecution may be brought in respect of the same course of conduct.'

TEACHERS: CHAOS IF THE CANE IS BANNED

Britain's parents are among the worst in the world at controlling their children, a teachers' leader claimed yesterday. It is because of their slack attitude that schools must keep the cane, said Mr Terry Casey, General Secretary of the National Association of Schoolmasters. He warned that a bill to abolish caning, which has its second reading in the House of Lords today, could throw school discipline into chaos. The Protection of Minors Bill is opposed by all the teachers' organizations. Mr Casey said, 'In many schools, teachers have already thrown in the sponge as far as discipline is concerned. This bill would make a serious situation much worse. If it goes through, we will advise our members to say they will no longer be responsible for a child's behaviour in school. They will become merely purveyors of lessons.'

AFTER 50 YEARS THE IRISH ARE TALKING

Two premiers and a host of other politicians will today show that miracles are still possible by holding the first meeting of representatives from north and south of the border since Ireland's partition. 50 years of religious conflict and bloodshed are unlikely to evaporate overnight at the Civil Service College near Sunningdale, Berkshire but it will herald the start of a unique effort to confound history by giving a new identity to Irish unity. Irish Premier Mr Liam Cosgrave is anxious to set up an all-Ireland council with co-ordinating powers over security, economic issues and the police. The question is whether the Ulster Unionists, led by Mr Brian Faulkner, and the new middle-of-the-road Alliance party are really prepared to go another stage in the new style of power-sharing.

GOVERNMENT KILLS SUNDAY SOCCER PLAN

The Government has turned down a plea to open the way for Sunday soccer. FA Secretary Ted Croker and League Secretary Alan Hardaker made a joint appeal to Mr Eldon Griffiths, Minister for Sport, in the hope that the Government's emergency powers would allow a switch to Sundays during the current energy crisis. The Home Office decided that such powers covered only essential services and could not be used to cancel the Sunday observance laws. These laws, which prohibit the payment of entrance fees to sporting events, have prevented football clubs from switching to Sundays. There seems to be nothing the football authorities can do about charging at the turnstiles on Sundays, though they could follow cricket's example by allowing admission by programme.

DARIN THE DISILLUSIONED

Singer Bobby Darin, teenage idol of the 50s, disillusioned actor of the 60s and reluctant drop-out of the 70s, died yesterday at 37. He had undergone his second heart operation in 2 years but failed to recover. Darin had a succession of hits including 'Splish Splash', 'Dream Lover', 'If I Were A Carpenter' and 'Mack the Knife'. He also made 9 films in 4 years and was nominated for an Oscar, then fizzled out. His marriage to Sandra Dee ended in 1968.

MY WASTED YEAR, BY SCHOOLGIRL JANE

16-year-old Jane Hilton, still at school because of the change in the leaving age, claims that the extra year is just a waste of her time. Jane, from Teignmouth, Devon, where she attends the local secondary school, says she has no proper timetable, no exams to study for and spends much of her time shopping, visiting friends and babysitting. 'They say that next year the ones who aren't taking exams will be kept busy, but we seem to be just guinea pigs,' said Jane. Headmaster Mr John Martin refused to discuss the situation.

Magpie presenters Douglas Rae, Sue Stranks and Mick Robertson dress up to present an episode discussing the latest trends in fashion.

The cast of Are You Being Served *admire Mrs Slocombe's brassieres.*

DAY BY DAY

5 Dec
The Government announces measures to deal with the fuel crisis including: a 50-m.p.h. speed limit on all roads, except where a lower limit already applies; a limit of 63°F for heating in offices and commercial premises; a reduction in the number of street lights.

9 Dec
Agreement is reached at Sunningdale between representatives of the British and Irish Governments and the Northern Ireland Executive-designate to set up a Council of Ireland during 1974.

11 Dec
ASLEF imposes a ban on overtime and rest-day working following the breakdown of talks with British Rail about wage restructuring.

13 Dec
The Prime Minister announces restrictions including a 3-day week for all industries, except essential businesses, and a 10.30 p.m. close-down for television services, except at Christmas and New Year.

19 Dec
10 people are killed when a Paddington to Oxford train is derailed at Ealing.

20 Dec
Spanish Prime Minister Admiral Luis Carrero Blanco is assassinated in Madrid.

23 Dec
The Shah of Iran announces a 100% increase in the price of oil from New Year's Day by the 6 main oil-producing countries in the Persian Gulf.

28 Dec
The electrical power engineers' pay dispute is settled.

31 Dec
More than 600,000 workers are laid off at the start of the 3-day working week.

Mrs Golda Meir's Government, the Labour Alignment, is returned in the Israeli general election.

MURDER BY NUMBERS ON THE HIJACK JET

Arab terrorists were sitting in a hijacked airliner at Athens Airport early today carrying on macabre negotiations with the Greek authorities. The gang, who had killed at least 31 people at Rome's International Airport before flying to Athens, threatened to execute 14 hostages one by one unless 2 fellow guerillas held in Greece were freed. Shooting was heard from the plane, a Boeing 737 of the German airline, Lufthansa, and radio messages announced that the first 4 hostages had already died. Just as a deal seemed likely there was an unexpected hitch. The 2 jailed Palestinians, members of the Black September, refused to join the hijackers because they belonged to a different group.

THE MAN WHO HAD 180 GALLONS

Police found 180 gallons of petrol in a company director's garage, a court was told yesterday, and when 27-year-old William Holden was told he would be reported he said to the police, 'I don't think they would believe it was for the lawn mower, do you?' Holden pleaded guilty to storing the petrol without a licence and was fined a total of £60. The magistrate ordered that the petrol should be confiscated.

CAROLINE'S RUM POSTER PAYS OFF

Model Caroline Munro has stepped straight out of a poster into a star part in a film. Caroline, the curvy girl who used to promote a brand of rum, will play the love in the life of Sinbad the sailor in *The Golden Voyage of Sinbad* which opens in London in 2 weeks.

HITLER PACT SIGNED AWAY

A treaty wiping out the 1938 Munich Appeasement Pact, which allowed Hitler to seize the Czech Sudetenland, has been signed in Prague. The agreement declares invalid the one reached by Germany, Britain, Italy and France in 1938.

CO-OP IS FIRST BANK TO SCRAP ITS CHARGES

The Co-operative Bank yesterday became the first bank to announce total abolition of charges on current accounts for customers who keep out of the red. If an account is overdrawn the charge for debits and standing orders will be at the existing rate of 4p and 7p respectively for the full half year. All the big banks, with record profits this year, have increasingly come under fire over bank charges. Co-operative Bank customers who stay in the black will enjoy free banking from 1 January.

Slade hold the number one spot in the singles chart over Christmas with 'Merry Xmas Everybody'.

JAN 1974

'NO GIFT STAMPS' WARNING

The first shot was fired yesterday in what could be a war on garages that have stopped giving trading stamps on petrol because of the fuel shortage. Shell has told one London filling station to start giving Green Shield stamps again or lose their stamp franchise. The threat to the garage, which claims it cannot afford to give stamps with petrol in the current situation, comes after Shell asked Green Shield for a list of garages that had stopped giving stamps.

Barbra Streisand and Robert Redford the The Way We Were.

THEY'RE MAKING MONEY FROM THE 3-DAY WEEK

The energy crisis and the rail dispute are providing a money-spinning bonus for some. Sales of camping gas have reached more than 4½ million refills in a month at between 30p and £1.25 a time. Do-it-yourself shops are having an unprecedented boost as husbands are using their leisure time to do all those little odd jobs around the house. Hotels are enjoying a boom as the rail dispute has led to many firms paying for their employees who can't get to and from work to stay in hotel accommodation. 1 hairdresser at Dagenham, Essex, is planning to sell cans of beans at 75p each and throw in a 'free' shampoo and set. He claims that selling beans makes him into a food shop and therefore exempt from the 3-day week.

007 GOES TO ITV IN A RECORD £850,000 DEAL

The first 6 James Bond films are to be sold to ITV for a record £850,000. The films are *Dr No*, *From Russia with Love*, *Goldfinger*, *Thunderball*, *You Only Live Twice* and *On Her Majesty's Secret Service*. Under the deal ITV will be allowed to show each film only twice and must not exceed a total of 2 screenings a year. Nevertheless, the film industry is afraid that cinemas will be empty on the nights Bond appears on television. The films are still being shown in cinemas around the country with great success and Bond pictures have topped box-office receipts in the last 2 years. As one cinema owner put it: 'Selling Bond to television is not only killing the golden goose but also auctioning off the eggs.' The most paid by the BBC for a film was £120,000 for *Bridge on the River Kwai*.

CUP TIES ON SUNDAY SCORE WITH THE FANS

Sunday soccer proved an instant success yesterday with more than 84,000 fans turning up to the 4 FA Cup third round ties. Football officials were delighted and there was no opposition from the Lord's Day Observance Society which had threatened to demonstrate. The decision was made because supporters in some areas would not have been able to watch matches without missing work due to the 3-day week. As it is illegal to charge for admission on Sunday, clubs sold team sheets at the turnstiles for the normal entrance prices.

HEATH JUMPS INTO THE LEAD

Britain's strife-weary voters want a general election if the miners do not settle soon – and the Tories can win it. This is the sensational verdict of a national opinion poll which, in the midst of the great industrial and economic crisis, gives Mr Edward Heath's Government its first lead over Labour – 3.9% – since the general election of June 1970. This could prove the decisive chance Mr Heath has been looking for on whether to risk announcing a snap election in the coming weeks.

'BATH PAY' RULED OUT

Hopes of settling the miners' dispute receded when the Pay Board ruled out the 'waiting-time' loophole which could have provided more money. The National Coal Board had suggested that waiting time – when miners are preparing for work or bathing after it – might qualify for 25 minutes overtime, worth an extra 40p to 70p a week, but this was quashed last night when the Pay Board ruled that it was not justified.

LET HOOLIGAN 16-YEAR-OLDS QUIT SCHOOL EARLY, TEACHERS URGE

Teachers appealed to Education Minister Mrs Margaret Thatcher yesterday: 'Save us from demob happy hooligans who are wrecking our classes.' In some big comprehensives rampaging bands of teenagers are smashing property and stopping exam pupils from learning, the Masters' Association's Conference in Nottingham was told. Mr David Harris of Bristol said that since the raising of the school-leaving age last year 'a lot of teachers are finding themselves with classes of 16-year-olds who have no desire to stay at school or to learn'. The Association urges that disruptive pupils should be allowed to leave before the end of the school year.

DOLLS FOR BOYS!

They are not referred to out loud as 'dolls' because that would still make them unacceptable to son and father alike. Instead they are disguised under a name and an image that evokes an aura of daring, adventure and, above all, masculinity. But dolls they are and dolls are the biggest news for boys at this year's Brighton Toy Fair, the second largest in the world. Action Man, the little male figure that made dolls possible for little boys and who came second in the Toy of the Year Award for 1973, has added to his repertoire by becoming an astronaut. He has also gained a new voice box for sending commands and receiving messages. Among the eye-catchers at the fair is Baby Alive which has outsold every other doll in the United States. This amazing doll 'eats', 'drinks' and discharges its food into its nappy.

COLDITZ TV SERIES DOESN'T RING TRUE, SAYS ESCAPER

The man who made the first successful escape from Colditz and the man who organized his break-out clashed yesterday over the authenticity of the BBC series about the prison. Mr Airey Neave, Tory MP for Abingdon, who got away by dressing up as a German soldier said, 'Prisoners look as if their hair has just been styled by Vidal Sassoon; they look well fed and their clothes are in far too good a condition.' But Major Pat Reid, Technical Advisor on the BBC series, said that great pains had been taken to create the right atmosphere though he conceded the points regarding the actors' weight and quality of clothing. He commented: 'I am told by the BBC that this is the fault of colour television; it makes everything seem a better quality.'

Elton John sometimes trains with Watford and calls himself a 'sports groupie'.

MILLION LAID OFF IN 3-DAY WEEK

The number of workers laid off because of the 3-day week will top a million today. Miners Union leaders and the Coal Board continue their search this afternoon for a formula to provide extra pay on top of the £44m-a-year deal already on offer, but neither side is hopeful of producing a solution that would conform to the pay code, which Mr Heath is determined should not be breached.

THE MARKET EMU HAS HAD ITS DAY

The life was slipping away last night from the favourite brainchild of the Common Market – Economic and Monetary Union. France's decision to float the franc dealt a potentially mortal blow to hopes that by 1980 the 9 nations would share their monetary reserves and perhaps use the same currency. 15 months ago in Paris Messrs. Heath, Pompidou, Brandt and other leaders pledged to achieve economic and monetary union within 8 years. Since then, Britain, Ireland and Italy have floated their currencies but the other 6 nations have soldiered on and named their scheme 'the snake in the tunnel'. Each currency had a maximum value represented by the top of the tunnel and a minimum corresponding to the bottom and the parity 'serpent' could wiggle as much as it liked as long as it kept between the 2. The central banks bought or sold each other's currencies as necessary to keep the snake in line. Now EMU may stay on the shelf for as long as the French franc floats.

THERE'S MONEY IN SNOOKER

Incomparable Joe Davis eyes the current explosion of interest in snooker with paternal satisfaction tinged with regret that he missed the new era of sponsorship and slick promotion. '. . . In my day there were no sponsors to put up money and colour TV has made all the difference. My TV shows were in black and white and I didn't get a penny for them.' World Professional Champion Ray Reardon, a former miner and policeman, and ex-baker's roundsman and bookie's clerk John Spencer are booked solidly until the end of March at £50 a night. Spencer believes that *Pot Black* has introduced an important new element – feminine fans. He says, 'Women were not allowed in the clubs and snooker rooms; they never had a chance to watch snooker until the game was taken into the nation's living rooms.' Top ten world rankings:

1. Ray Reardon
2. John Spencer
3. Eddie Charlton
4. Alex Higgins
5. Fred Davis
6. equal John Pulman
   and Rex Williams
8. Ray Edmonds
9. Graham Miles
10. Cliff Thorburn

NEW YEAR HONOURS

Vic Feather receives a life peerage; William Whitelaw is made a Companion of Honour; jazz musician John Dankworth and veteran actress Constance Cummings both receive the CBE, as does Bobby Charlton; Rugby Union star Mike Gibson of Ireland and Clive Sullivan, who led Great Britain's Rugby League World Cup winners, both receive MBEs.

DR SPOCK: I GOT IT WRONG

The man who told generations of mothers how to bring up their children now admits he got it wrong. Dr Benjamin Spock blames the 'brattiness' of today's American children partly on 'child psychiatrists, psychologists, teachers, social workers and paediatricians like myself'. Dr Spock's book *Baby and Child Care*, which preaches the doctrine of 'parental submissiveness', has sold more than 22 million copies since 1946 but Dr Spock, now 70, says, 'The inability to be firm is the commonest problem with parents in America today.' They were suffering the consequences of being afraid of alienating their children by imposing discipline. Dr Spock says submissiveness encourages the young only to be more demanding and awkward which in turn breeds anger and resentment among parents. 'This finally explodes in a display of anger, great or small, that convinces the child to give in. In other words, parental submissiveness doesn't avoid unpleasantness, it makes it inevitable.'

Young Dr Frankenstein (Gene Wilder) consults with his assistants Igor (Marty Feldman, l) and Ingar (Teri Garr, r). In attendance is housekeeper Frau Blucher (Claris Leachman). Mel Brooks' Young Frankenstein.

FEB 1974

Harold Wilson flanked by Shirley Williams and Ron Haywood at the Intays Conference for One Nation.

WHY SUMS DON'T COUNT

Many children can't do their sums by the time they leave school but they could tell you a thing or two about computers. Industrialists complain that trendy modern maths courses try to get pupils to understand advanced computer problems but fail to teach them about percentages or fractions. One headmaster said he could see no reason in the present age for teaching fractions, decimals, and percentages. Training Officer for Nottingham Mr Bruce Noyes gave an example: 'Ask an applicant to express the formula graphically for the classification into sets of left-handed people with warts over 32 in the Home Counties in 1936 and they'll do a perfect job; ask them to express 7/16 as a decimal and they don't know where to start.'

JURY READ *MEN ONLY*

A jury has been ordered to read copies of the sex magazine *Men Only* during a hearing in which the customs are asking that 324,000 copies of the magazine be forfeited. They claim that the magazines, seized in December 1972, are prohibited articles under a 98-year-old act, and that they are indecent or obscene. Strip club king Mr Raymond, whose organization is denying the allegation, sat in court with Miss Fiona Richmond, 26, star of his West End show, *Pyjama Tops*. He heard Mr Montague Waters QC, defending, tell the jury that the magazine had to be read as a whole and with the knowledge that it was sold for 50p and was not a children's comic.

MAN DRANK HIMSELF TO DEATH – ON CARROT JUICE

A health-food addict drank himself to death on carrot juice with an intake of between 6 and 8 pints a day. 48-year-old Basil Brown also took vitamin A tablets in spite of the fact that his doctor had warned him against his addiction to vitamin A, in which carrots are rich. The coroner's court heard that when vitamin A was taken greatly in excess of the body's requirements it was stored in the liver. Pathologist Dr David Haler, who said that Mr Brown was bright yellow when he died, told the court that vitamin A poisoning produced a condition indistinguishable from alcoholic poisoning – cirrhosis of the liver.

RONALD BIGGS IS LOCATED

The hunt for escaped Great Train Robber Ronald Biggs has ended. Good fortune and the power of money – his share of the record £2.5m haul seized in August 1963 – have kept the master criminal one step ahead of his pursuers in Britain, Australia and America. Senior Scotland Yard detectives were told last night that he had changed his name, altered his appearance and is working as a businessman, living near Rio de Janeiro. One of the first questions being discussed at the Yard is the problem of extraditing Biggs from South America. Biggs was 'sprung' from Wandsworth Prison in July 1965 having been jailed for 30 years in April 1964.

THE GREEN CARD CODE FOR EUROPE

The open road to Europe was unveiled by the Common Market Commission in Brussels yesterday. From 15 May motorists will be able to drive into 14 European countries without showing an insurance green card. The countries in the scheme are the 9 EEC nations plus Norway, Sweden, Finland, Austria and Switzerland. If a British motorist is the innocent party in an accident with an uninsured motorist in any of these countries, he will be compensated by that country's national insurance bureau. If a British uninsured driver is to blame, the other party will be able to claim from his national bureau. Holidaymakers will still need both passport and green card as in the past but will only be required to show the passport.

Striking Kent miners hoping to persuade train drivers not to deliver coal.

'SAVE PANDA CARS' PLEA FOR THE BEAT BOBBIES

A call for the ordinary PC to have his say before panda cars are abandoned in favour of men on the beat is made in the Police Federation magazine. It says that Sussex Police has taken its pandas off the road and the trend may gather impetus after forces are reorganized to align their areas with new local authority boundaries. Public reaction was not wholly in favour of panda patrols; a feeling grew that policemen in cars were not only remote from the public but deliberately inaccessible.

WINDMILL BRINGS BACK THE NUDES

Nude revues are returning to London's Windmill Theatre where they were first staged in Britain 42 years ago. Striptease king Paul Raymond, 48, has bought the lease for 114 years at £100,000 a year but there will be no place for comedians for which the old Windmill was famous. A long list of stars including Jimmy Edwards, Kenneth More, Tony Hancock and Peter Sellers were all given their first break there but Paul Raymond said yesterday, 'Our audiences are largely international and I'm afraid they wouldn't understand English comics.'

NOW RECORD BREAKER WILLIE JOHN CAPS THEM ALL

Irish captain Willie John McBride sets another record when he leads his country against England at Twickenham this afternoon. Against Wales a fortnight ago he beat the home countries record of 54 caps, held by another former Irish skipper, Tom Kiernan. Today, he eclipses the world record of 55 appearances set by the legendary All Black forward Colin Meads. This does not take into account McBride's 13 test appearances for the Lions over 4 tours, which is also a record.

FINNEGAN IS SHOCK CHAMPION

Spectators yelled, 'Rubbish' as Kevin Finnegan was declared British Middleweight Champion at the London Hilton last night. Bunny Sterling, champion since 1970, seemed to have outscored him comfortably, yet referee Jim Brimmell gave 7 rounds to 4 in Finnegan's favour with 4 even. One spectator was so disgusted with the decision that he presented dethroned Sterling with a cheque for £300.

Michael Foot and his wife in Hampstead following the General Election.

NO MORE FOOD UNTIL MY GIRL IS FREE, SAYS KIDNAP FATHER

Millionaire newspaper publisher Randolph Hearst last night took an awesome gamble on his daughter's life and agreed to give her kidnappers a defiant ultimatum. The Symbionese Liberation Army's newest demand for him to triple the £800,000 he has already provided to feed the needy of California will not be met unless 19-year-old Patricia Hearst is released. The SLA kidnapped Miss Hearst at gunpoint 18 days ago.

IT'S THE END, SAY NEW SEEKERS

The New Seekers, one of Britain's most successful pop groups, is breaking up at the height of its fame because the 2 girl singers, Lyn Paul, 24, and 30-year-old Eve Graham, are determined to be solo stars. Since the group was formed in August 1969, it has earned around £1.5m and sold almost 20 million records; its hit song 'I'd Like to Teach the World to Sing' alone sold 6 million copies. Paul Layton and Marty Kristian, who have written several of their hits, will probably continue with their song-writing. Peter Oliver plans to return to a solo career.

DAY BY DAY

4 Feb
12 people are killed, including 7 soldiers, as a bomb explodes on a coach carrying service personnel from Manchester to Yorkshire on the M62 motorway.

In the mineworkers' ballot 81% vote in support of a national strike.

7 Feb
Grenada becomes independent.

Mr Enoch Powell announces his decision not to stand for re-election as Conservative MP for Wolverhampton South-West, a constituency he has represented for 24 years.

8 Feb
3 *Skylab* astronauts splash down after a record 84 days in space.

The Labour party's election manifesto includes plans to abolish the Pay Board and repeal the Industrial Relations Act.

11 Feb
Architect John Poulson and civil servant George Pottinger are found guilty of corruption and each is sent to prison for 5 years.

13 Feb
Soviet author Alexander Solzhenitsyn is flown to West Germany after being expelled from Russia and deprived of his citizenship.

14 Feb
Bob Latchford becomes Britain's costliest footballer as he moves from Birmingham to Everton in a £350,000 deal.

21 Feb
The International Publishing Corporation, proprietor of the *Daily Mirror, Sunday Mirror* and *Daily Record*, withdraws from the Newspaper Publishers' Association, the employers' organization representing all national newspapers, in order to negotiate independently on its journalists' pay claim.

25 Feb
The Department of Trade and Industry announces a deficit of £383m for January, the biggest monthly deficit in Britain's history.

28 Feb
The general election results in no overall majority for either of the major parties. Labour win 301 seats, Conservatives 296, Liberals 14, Scottish Nationalists 7 and Plaid Cymru 2.

GEORGE BEST ON £6,000 BAIL AFTER CLUB ARREST

George Best was freed on £6,000 bail yesterday after being arrested and charged with breaking and entering. He spent 13½ hours being questioned about alleged offences committed against the reigning Miss World, 19-year-old Marjorie Wallace. He is due back at Marylebone on 27 March, accused of stealing a fur coat, passport and other property belonging to Miss Wallace.

Alexander Solzhenitsyn and his family are reunited in exile.

MAR 1974

Former athlete David Jones goes on a streak. David was a member of the famous British 'Flying Squad', which set up a world record for the 4 × 100m in 1963.

HOLIDAY FIRM PACKS IT IN

Horizon Holidays, the 24-year-old travel company, went into voluntary liquidation yesterday. The main assets and goodwill of Horizon were recently taken over by Court Line in a deal which includes the payment of £1 for every customer taken on holiday over the next 3 years.

HEATH DEFIES MUTINEERS

Mr Heath was last night hanging on to the helm of the storm-tossed Tory party as mutinous rumblings swept ominously through the lower decks. Mr Edward du Cann, Chairman of the 1922 Committee, admitted that colleagues had suggested that a contest should take place in order to confirm Mr Heath's position. Mr du Cann said he doubted whether Mr Heath would be displaced if such an election were to take place.

BOB WILSON PLANS NEW CAREER AS TV EXPERT

Arsenal's Bob Wilson, nearing 33, is planning to retire into television at the end of this season. That will leave cut-price reserves Jimmy Rimmer and Geoff Barnett to compete for the goalkeeping vacancy at Highbury. Wilson is a self-taught goalkeeper who has written a thesis on his art. He became a TV personality with the BBC but their analyst's role is now filled by Jimmy Hill. London Weekend, however, need a regular face to back up Malcolm Allison and Brian Clough, who fit in TV according to their managerial demands.

PETER REVSON KILLED IN RACE-CAR INFERNO

Peter Revson, millionaire racing driver and boyfriend of the sacked Miss World, Marjorie Wallace, was killed yesterday when his car crashed at 160 m.p.h. The car somersaulted off the Kyalami track at Johannesburg and burst into flames while he was practising for the South African Grand Prix. Last year Revson, a member of the Revlon cosmetic family, won the British and Canadian Grand Prix races in a Mac-Laren. This year he replaced Graham Hill as number 1 driver for the Northampton-based Shadow team.

Family portrait – The Waltons.

PRIMATE RETIRES

Archbishop of Canterbury Dr Michael Ramsay is to retire on 15 November, the day after his seventieth birthday. He will be given a life barony, an announcement from Downing Street said yesterday. The successor to Dr Ramsay, who became Archbishop in 1961, could be Bishop John Howe, 54, who is General Secretary of the Anglican Consultative Council. Recently an outsider has come back into the running: Dr Ramsay's successor at York, Dr Donald Coggan, who will be 65 when the appointment is made. One possibility is that Dr Coggan should be Archbishop for 5 years while the younger bishops gain more experience. Other possible successors include Robert Runcie, 52-year-old Bishop of St Albans. The final decision rests with the Prime Minister on the advice of his Appointments Secretary, Mr Colin Peterson.

MORE ASK FOR LAGER

More of Britain's beer drinkers are switching to lager, and sales this year could reach a record £300m, Allied Breweries said yesterday. In 1960 less than 1 pint in every 100 drunk was lager; today the figure is more like 1 in 7.

Relatives at a memorial service for the Japanese victims of the Turkish DC10 crash in France.

DAY BY DAY

2 Mar
Wolverhampton Wanderers beat Manchester City 2–1 in the Football League Cup Final.

3 Mar
A Turkish Airlines DC10 crashes soon after taking off from Orly, Paris, killing all 346 passengers and crew. It is the world's worst air disaster.

A British Airways VC10 on a flight from Bombay to London is hijacked by Arab terrorists and forced to fly to Amsterdam Airport. The passengers and crew are released before the terrorists set fire to the plane. Dutch police arrest the 2 hijackers.

4 Mar
The 14 Liberal MPs reject an offer from Mr Heath to form a coalition. Mr Heath resigns as Prime Minister and Mr Wilson is asked by the Queen to form a Government.

6 Mar
The miners' union executive votes in favour of accepting a deal which would give rises ranging from £6.71 to £15.51 a week.

8 Mar
The 3-day week ends.

12 Mar
Senator Billy Fox, a Protestant member of the Dublin Parliament, is found murdered. An organization called the Ulster Freedom Fighters later claims responsibility.

26 Mar
Mr Denis Healey, presenting his first Budget as Chancellor, raises the basic rate of income tax by 3p, while increasing personal allowances and pensions. Soft drinks, sweets and ice cream to be liable for VAT, while £500m is to be spent on subsidizing basic foods.

28 Mar
Mrs Barbara Castle, Social Services Secretary, tells the House of Commons that from 1 April the Family Planning Service will be available free to everyone through National Health hospitals and clinics.

30 Mar
The Grand National is won for the second year running by Red Rum, ridden by Brian Fletcher.

Admission charges to national galleries and museums, which were introduced by the Conservative Government on 2 January, are abolished.

BARBARA CLOBBERS PRIVATE PATIENTS

Private patients in Health Service hospitals will have to pay as much as £36.40 a week more from 1 April. The massive increase announced yesterday in the Commons by Mrs Barbara Castle, Health and Social Services Secretary, is a clear reflection of government hostility to private treatment in state hospitals. Many Labour MPs have demanded the total abolition of the 1,500 private beds in NHS hospitals.

BID TO KIDNAP PRINCESS ANNE

An armed attempt was made to kidnap Princess Anne and her husband Captain Mark Phillips as they drove down the Mall last night. A gunman forced the royal limousine to stop and then poured volleys of shots from a pistol through the rear side windows. As the shots spat through the royal car Mark hurled himself across the Princess to shield her from the bullets. Princess Anne and Captain Phillips were both unharmed but 4 other people were shot.

SHOPS GET NEW CURBS ON PRICES

Tough moves to curb shop prices were unveiled by Consumer Protection Minister Mrs Shirley Williams yesterday. The plan, which should be brought into effect next month, proposes a cut of 10% in distributors' gross profits; the end of price increases on goods already in the shops; and a gap of at least 3 months between price rises for the same range of goods.

BAN *THE EXORCIST*, SAY CHURCHMEN

A call to ban the controversial new film, *The Exorcist*, came yesterday from 2 churchmen who are authorities on exorcism. They say the film about a little girl possessed by the devil could be socially damaging and lead to people needing mental treatment. Canon John Pearce-Higgins said, 'I have been studying the effects of this film in America. In one week 12 people were admitted to a mental hospital in Pittsburgh after seeing it.' When the film had a private screening in London 2 weeks ago, several people were sick and some fainted at the first sight of the girl after she was possessed. *The Exorcist* is due to open in London next week after heading towards box-office records in America.

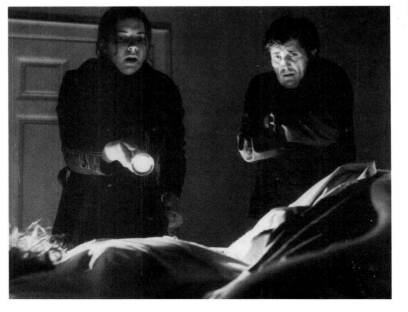

TUEART GOES TO CITY IN £375,000 DEAL

Manchester City broke the British transfer record yesterday with a £375,000 deal for Sunderland's Denis Tueart and Mick Horswill. After completing the deal Chairman Peter Swales declared, 'That's only the start; we're going all out to build the best team in the land.' Sunderland received £250,000 plus midfield player Tony Towers, valued at £125,000. Tueart was valued at £275,000 and mid-field man Horswill rated at £100,000. The price label on Tueart placed him second only to Everton's £350,000 Bob Latchford among Britain's costliest footballers.

APR 1974

Eurovision Song Contest winners, Sweden's Abba.

MEN WHO SPUN POULSON'S HUGE WEB OF CORRUPTION

The 2 men said to be the main pillars of architect John Poulson's web of corruption sat in the dock yesterday and listened as their parts in the great conspiracy were exposed. Leeds Crown Court was told how former alderman, Andrew Cunningham, and T. Dan Smith, ex-Chairman of the Northern Economic Planning Council, worked to swing contracts towards Poulson who in the 60s had built up the largest architectural practice in Europe. Mr Peter Taylor QC, prosecuting, said, '. . . the case for the Crown here is that over some 7 years these 2 men, Cunningham and Smith, used their joint power and influence corruptly to secure lucrative contracts for Poulson – contracts for housing and contracts for public building. This they did for substantial rewards from Poulson.' The case continues.

Ian Botham of Somerset CCC.

AND CHOP SUEY OUSTS OUR FISH AND CHIPS

The great British fish-and-chip shop is on the decline, ousted by Chinese take-away meals and American fried chicken. According to a survey of take-away foods, about 700 fish-and-chip shops have been closing every year for the past 4 years. If it were to continue at the present rate, there would be no fish-and-chip shops at all by about 1990, whereas a chain specializing in fried chicken has grown from 69 shops in 1971 to 215 today. One London chip-shop owner said, 'The prices are scandalous. Only a few years ago I could buy cod for 90p a stone; today it is costing me £5.90. This means that a portion of cod costs between 22p and 26p and chips have to cost 6p.'

THIEVES WARNED: ARTHUR THE TV CAT NEEDS DRUGS

Thieves who stole Arthur the TV cat were warned last night that unless he is given special drugs he could die. The fluffy white cat who scoops food out of tins with his paws in commercials was stolen from a cattery in Essex on Saturday. He belongs to Spillers, who value him at £1,000 and have featured him in almost £4m-worth of advertising promoting their pet foods. Last night detectives investigating the theft warned that Arthur, 14, was suffering from a glandular complaint and could become seriously ill if he did not get the necessary tablets. Author John Montgomery, who has been commissioned to write Arthur's life story, last night offered a £500 reward for the cat's return. He also revealed that Arthur is a she, formerly called Samantha. He said, 'Spillers decided to call her Arthur because the name is more commercial.'

DJ TONY JOINS THE WOMBLES

Disc jockey Tony Blackburn is to broadcast his Radio 1 show next Thursday from the home of the Wombles of Huddersfield. He hopes it will make up for the pestering the family has suffered since the children's programme of the same name first appeared on BBC television. The Yorkshire Wombles are fed up with jokes coupling them with furry puppets who live under Wimbledon Common scavenging litter. Diane Womble, 9, and her 7-year-old brother Paul have been teased at school and jokers ring up their home and sing 'The Wombling Song' down the phone.

ADOPTION BAN ON OVER-40S LIFTED

A ruling that a couple in their 40s were too old to adopt a baby has been scrapped by a council. Now 47-year-old Mrs Vera Sowerby and her husband Bob, 44, hope to be told that they can keep 9-month-old Wendy whom they have had as a foster baby at their Carlisle home since soon after she was born. 3 weeks ago the former Carlisle Town Council's Adoption Committee said the Sowerbys must give up the baby under a rule that limited the age of adoptive parents to 40, but then came local-government reorganization and yesterday the new Cumbria Social Services Committee unanimously voted to scrap the age limit.

BITTER TRUTH ABOUT BEER

Your search for a pub that sells real ale is over, for yesterday a group of connoisseurs launched their first publication, *The Good Beer Guide*. The authors are members of the Campaign for Real Ale, CAMRA, and in a Fleet Street pub they chose Marston's Pedigree Bitter to christen their book. They became positively lyrical as they discussed their favourite subject – where to get a good pint – for CAMRA men will drive miles rather than drink what they politely call fizzy rubbish – pressurized brews. CAMRA's growing 12,000 membership is fighting to preserve real ale which they say is stored in casks and served by hand or electric pump, not by carbon dioxide pressure.

Mr Thorpe, Mr Wilson and Mr Heath flying to Paris to attend a memorial service for President Pompidou.

TRIUMPH BIKES ROLL AGAIN

Triumph motor-cycles started coming off the production lines yesterday for the first time since September. The flow started at the Norton Villiers Triumph factory at Small Heath, Birmingham. This signalled the end of the road for the Workers' Co-operative – men who were made redundant when the firm's factory at Meriden closed under reorganization. They have been negotiating with Norton Villiers for the sale of the plant and the right to produce Triumph motorcycles. It became a race against time to see who would produce Triumphs again: the Workers' Co-operative, if the group could find financial backers, or the official government-backed combine. Yesterday the firm won and the 3-cylinder Triumph Trident 750cc started coming off the production lines.

GLENDA WINS HER MOTHER OSCAR NUMBER 2

Glenda Jackson phoned her mum yesterday to say that another 'bookend' was on its way. Her Best Actress of the Year Award for her performance in the film comedy *A Touch of Class* will join the one she won 4 years ago on her mother's sideboard in Hoylake, Cheshire. Her first Oscar as best actress was for *Women in Love* in 1970. *The Sting* won 7 Oscars, including those for Best Film and Best Director, George Roy Hill. Best Actor went to Jack Lemmon for his portrayal of a disheartened businessman in *Save The Tiger*. The Best Supporting Actress Award went to 10-year-old Tatum O'Neal, daughter of actor Ryan O'Neal, for her performance in *Paper Moon*. *The Exorcist*, which had been nominated for 10 awards, won only Best Sound and Best Adapted Screenplay.

A bobby's hat was in the right place at the right time at the rugby match between England and France when (Australian accountant) Michael O'Brien streaked across the Twickenham pitch. 26-year-old O'Brien was subsequently fined £10 for insulting behaviour.

MAY 1974

JUST CALL ME MS!

Women's libbers have won a major battle in their 'Call Me Ms' campaign. The Passport Office yesterday became the first government department to give in to their demands. Now all women who object to having their marital status identified have the option of having Ms (pronounced Miz) written in their passports. Until now women could have Mrs, Miss or no prefix at all. Other government departments were less enthusiastic last night. The Department of Education and Science said, 'When we give grants it is important to know whether or not the applicants are married.'

IT'S BACK TO STANSTED AS MAPLIN AXE NEARS

The Government is now ready to axe the £1,000m Maplin Airport project; instead London's third airport is likely to be Stansted in Essex, plans for which were killed by the Labour Government 10 years ago following an uproar from local residents. Preparations for the enlargement and improvement of Stansted Airport are being discreetly made by the British Airports Authority. The move is certain to revive the battle over the future of Stansted, originally earmarked as London's third airport. Environment Secretary Mr Anthony Crosland's plans to abandon Maplin will inevitably mean that traffic at Stansted, which has dwindled to a mere 300,000 passengers a year, will rise again to 2 or 3 million by the late 70s.

THANK YOU AND GOODBYE

'A unanimous recommendation was submitted to the Executive Committee that Sir Alf Ramsey should be replaced as the England team manager. This recommendation was accepted unanimously by the Executive Committee... it was decided that a caretaker manager should be appointed, with the approval of the Coventry FC. Mr Joe Mercer has agreed to undertake this task.' England's record under Sir Alf Ramsey: played 113, won 69, drew 27, lost 17, goals for 224, goals against 99.

BARBARA BLOCKS TORY SECOND PENSION SCHEME

Mrs Barbara Castle, Social Services Secretary, yesterday shelved the Tory Government's Reserve Pension Scheme which was to become law next year. Furious former Tory ministers immediately attacked her in the Commons but Mrs Castle maintained that the Tory 'safety-net' plan was 'wholly inadequate', discriminated against women and would mean thousands of pensioners relying on means-tested pension supplements well into the next century.

Steely Dan

ULSTER CLOSE TO COLLAPSE

The stricken province of Ulster lurched headlong into anarchy and mob law last night as normal life ground to a standstill. Ulster Minister Mr Merlyn Rees was facing what could be the ultimate crisis with industry halted, shops closed, power down to a trickle, food supplies dwindling and water rationing. As the situation worsened hourly on the sixth day of the General Strike called by the Protestant Ulster Workers Council, another battalion of British troops was hurriedly ordered in. The number of soldiers in the province has now risen to 16,000.

PATTI HEARST CHARGED

Kidnapped heiress Patti Hearst was charged yesterday with possessing and using automatic weapons. The FBI described her as 'armed and extremely dangerous', reporting that she fired at customers when making her getaway from a sports shop on Friday – the incident which led to a raid on an SLA hide-out and the deaths of 6 leaders.

AUTHORS TO GET LIBRARY FEES

Authors will be entitled to a fee when their books are lent by librarians under a bill which the Government hopes to introduce later this year. Mr Hugh Jenkins, Minister for the Arts, said he wants more talks with authors and libraries about the details. Earlier Mr Kenneth Baker, Tory MP for St Marylebone, published a private member's bill advocating a national agency to administer a monthly payout to authors. Payments would be made on each lending of a book by a library; books in reference libraries would get a royalty payment.

Brian Clough at Heathrow with children Nigel (8) and Simon (9). Speculation is increasing that the Brighton manager and his assistant, Peter Taylor, could soon be on the move.

NIXON HANDS OVER 'TAPES' THAT MAY NOW TOPPLE HIM

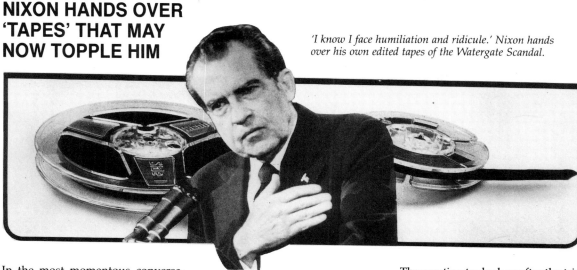

'I know I face humiliation and ridicule.' Nixon hands over his own edited tapes of the Watergate Scandal.

In the most momentous conversation of the whole Watergate case President Nixon told his White House counsel John Dean that he knew where to lay his hands on $1m to silence the blackmail of a Watergate conspirator. Today Nixon's whole future hangs in balance as Americans read the transcript of the Watergate tapes, which have been his most closely guarded secret for the last 9 months.

Yesterday, he handed 'relevant' passages from the tapes over the heads of his congressional judges to the impeachment jury he has chosen – the American people. It was immediately clear why Nixon has fought so stubbornly to keep them secret. The famous conversation with John Dean on 21 March 1973 could provide crucial evidence for the President's impeachment. One of the charges against Nixon is that he plotted with Dean to pay hush money to Watergate defendant Howard Hunt. Here is the relevant passage from the transcript:

President: How much money do you need?
Dean: I would say these people are going to cost $1m over the next 2 years.
President: We could get that; on the money, if you need the money, you could get that; you could get $1m, you could get it in cash. I know where it could be gotten. It is not easy but it could be done, but the question is, who the hell would handle it? Any ideas on that?
Dean: That's right, well I think that is something that Mitchell ought to be charged with.
President: I would think so, too.
Dean: And get some pros to help him.
President: Let me say, there shouldn't be a lot of people running round getting money.

The meeting took place after the trial and conviction of the Watergate defendants. Pressure on the White House from the resentful conspirators was mounting, and 2 days later a letter to Judge John Sirica from defendant James McCord blew open the whole case. In a sensational television appearance on Monday Nixon acknowledged that he had discussed with Dean the possibility of paying hush money and offering executive clemency to the Watergate defendants. He predicted that publication of the text would bring him embarrassment and ridicule but would finally prove his innocence of any participation in the Watergate cover-up.

MAUDLING: THE LETTER I FORGOT

Mr Reginald Maudling admitted yesterday that he was wrong when he recently denied his involvement in trying to get an overseas contract for architect John Poulson. The controversial contract was for the design by Poulson – now serving 7 years in jail for corruption – of a £1.6m hospital on the Maltese island of Gozo. In a letter dated 10 October 1966 Mr Maudling, then Deputy Opposition Leader, wrote to the Ministry of Works in Malta in his capacity as Chairman of Construction Promotion. He proceeded to give a glowing testimonial to the company's 'consultant and engineer', Mr J. G. L. Poulson. The hospital, now complete, was entirely financed by British tax-payers through a government grant. It brought the Poulson Organization fees of nearly £100,000.

I'M CHOOSING FAME INSTEAD OF MY SIGHT

Blind pop singer Lennie Peters was yesterday faced with a choice between fame and fortune and a chance to regain the sight he lost in an accident. One of Britain's most successful showbusiness stars, he has decided that his career will come first. Peters promised himself that at the first opportunity he would go to America for the costly eye operation which would give him back his sight. Today, earning around £5,000 a week, he has both the money and the opportunity but amazingly he says he dare not spare the time for the operation. Peters, with his blonde partner Diane Lee, the other half of Peters and Lee, topped the hit parade with 'Welcome Home', their first record. 'Don't Stay Away Too Long', their current release, is at number 3.

David Carradine star of the hit TV series Kung Fu.

DAY BY DAY

2 May
Britain recognizes General Spínola's new Government in Portugal.

4 May
Paintings stolen from the home of Sir Alfred Beit are found in a farmhouse in Western Ireland. This follows a ransom demand for £500,000 and the transfer to a Northern Ireland prison of the Price sisters and the 2 other prisoners, all on hunger strike and serving life sentences in Britain for last year's London car bombings.

Liverpool wins the FA Cup Final, beating Newcastle United 3–0. In Scotland Glasgow Celtic beats Dundee United by the same score.

6 May
Dr Bridget Dugdale is charged with armed robbery of Sir Alfred Beit's paintings and is subsequently sentenced to 9 years' imprisonment for receiving the paintings.

Herr Willy Brandt resigns as Chancellor of West Germany over the furore surrounding his personal aide, Guenther Guillaume, who was arrested in April and accused of spying for East Germany.

15 May
16 Israeli children are killed by Arab terrorists who held them hostage at a school in Maalot. The 3 terrorists are shot dead when Israeli troops storm the building.

16 May
Israeli planes attack Palestinian refugee camps in Lebanon in retaliation for the raid on Maalot. Between 20 and 50 people are reported killed.

17 May
23 people are killed in 3 explosions in the centre of Dublin.

18 May
India explodes her first nuclear device in the Rajasthan Desert.

19 May
M. Valéry Giscard d'Estaing becomes President of France.

28 May
The power-sharing Executive in Northern Ireland collapses when Mr Brian Faulkner and his Unionist colleagues resign after Northern Ireland Secretary of State Mr Merlyn Rees refuses a plea for talks with the Ulster Workers' Council. The Council, a militant Protestant organization, has brought the province almost to a standstill in 2 weeks of strike action.

29 May
The Government suspends the Northern Ireland Assembly and the Ulster Workers' Council call off their strike.

LABOUR: DON'T FEED THE LIONS

The Government last night delivered a public snub to the British Lions rugby team on the eve of their tour to South Africa. It announced that it had instructed the British Embassy in Cape Town not to entertain the players and to have no contact with them, either official or social. The unprecedented move, ordered by Foreign Office Junior Minister Miss Joan Lestor, follows the Black African outcry over the tour and amounts to a total government boycott.

JUNE 1974

HEATH KNOCKS WILSON FOR 9

9 votes last night sent the minority Labour Government to its first major defeat – over the planned £10m tax rebate to unions which did not register under the Industrial Relations Act. Amid the pandemonium the possibility of Mr Wilson's calling a snap July election came racing back. The vote – 308 to 299 – shook both sides, who had expected a photo finish, but 13 Liberals and 8 Nationalist MPs swung behind Mr Heath to inflict the significant body blow for Mr Wilson's 15-week-old Cabinet.

THE YOUNG ONES WARN WIMBLEDON

18-year-olds Bjorn Borg and Chris Evert are ready to give a new, young look to Wimbledon next week. Yesterday in Paris they added the French titles to the Italian crowns they collected in Rome a fortnight ago. Sweden's Borg came back from 2 sets down to beat Manuel Orantes of Spain while Miss Evert took only 62 minutes to defeat Russian Olga Morozova in a performance that has been equalled only by such tennis queens as Suzanne Lenglen and Helen Wills. Mariana Simionescu of Rumania defeated Britain's Sue Barker in the Junior Final.

ROUS SACKED AFTER 13 YEARS AS FIFA CHIEF

Sir Stanley Rous was sacked yesterday after 13 years as President of FIFA. The end of Rous, who is succeeded by Brazilian millionaire, Joao Havelange, opens up the threat that England, Scotland, Ireland and Wales may be forced to merge into a single Great Britain team in future World Cups.

STORM OVER BATTLE IN RED LION SQUARE

Home Secretary Roy Jenkins will today be asked to hold an enquiry into the bloody battle of Red Lion Square. A 20-year-old student died after the fighting between police and demonstrators in Holborn, London on Saturday. The clashes came after a march by the left-wing Liberation Movement protesting against a meeting in Red Lion Square by the right-wing National Front. The National Front's demo was against the Home Secretary's decision to grant an amnesty to illegal immigrants.

BREAKTHROUGH FOR SEA OIL PROSPECTORS

Geologists and oil companies believe they can now predict the existence of oil and gas far below the sea-bed with almost 100% accuracy. A new American technique enables scientists to 'see' a gas field on seismic charts and could dramatically cut the cost and uncertainty of prospecting. It is known as Bright Spot and uses a very low frequency airgun to blow bubbles into the water.

Jennifer Hilary and Mark McManus in Sam.

CILLA AND ROGER COULD LOSE HOMES

Singer Cilla Black and actor Roger Moore could lose their £100,000 country houses under a motorway scheme announced yesterday, but neither knows of the threat to their estates at Denham in Buckinghamshire. Cilla is on holiday while Roger Moore is on location shooting the latest James Bond film, *The Man with the Golden Gun*. The threat is the M25 North Orbital Motorway from Egham to Maple Cross, linking the M4 and M1. There is a choice of routes but the one believed most likely will slice through Tilehouse Lane, Denham, and bulldoze through both the stars' homes. BBC commentator Raymond Baxter, who also owns property which would be affected by the proposals, said that conditions had changed since he campaigned for a motorway network for Britain. 'The world supply of oil will have reached a peak by 1990 and will then decline; it puts an entirely different idea on the building of motorways as a means of communication.'

Robert Duvall, Diane Keaton and Al Pacino in Francis Ford Coppola's The Godfather Part II.

DAY BY DAY

1 June
An explosion at the Nypro chemical plant in Flixborough kills 29 people.

3 June
Michael Gaughan, serving a 7-year sentence for robbery, dies in Parkhurst Prison after 65 days without food in a campaign to be treated as a political prisoner. He becomes the first IRA hunger striker to die in a British prison since 1920.

13 June
The Prince of Wales makes his maiden speech in the House of Lords.

14 June
Russian ballet dancers Valery and Galina Panov leave the Soviet Union after a 12-year battle to emigrate to Israel.

20 June
A Conservative motion opposing the Government's plans for extending the nationalization of industry is carried with a majority of 21.

30 June
Mrs Albert King, mother of Dr Martin Luther King, who was assassinated in 1969, is shot dead while playing the organ at a church in Atlanta, Georgia.

THE VOTE OF CONFIDENCE

The flagging fortunes of the New World pop group took a turn for the better yesterday with some kind words from a judge. After they admitted taking part in a plot to send bogus votes to ITV's *Opportunity Knocks*, the Old Bailey judge hoped the prosecution would not harm their careers. Granting the 3 Australians John Lee, John Kane and Mel Noonan a conditional discharge for 2 years, the judge said, 'Undoubtedly you have talent and your act has been described as pleasant and agreeable, but you brought these proceedings on yourselves.'

The charge to which the group pleaded guilty concerned a free concert at which girls at a teacher-training college were urged to submit bogus votes in the names of friends and relatives. The judge said he accepted that the group might not have realized they were committing a criminal offence.

TRYING FOR A COMEBACK AT 14. . . THE BOY IN THE £100 SUITS

14-year-old John McNeil Cowan Reid is probably Britain's most unusual schoolboy. He often buys £100 worth of clothes at a time, has fortnightly haircuts which cost £6 a session, regularly meets girlfriends in the bar of a top Mayfair hotel, and asked about his future, says, 'I would regard an ordinary job in a bank or an office as a complete failure. . . I've just got to be a star.' At 12, Neil was a star. He made 1 record, 'Mother of Mine', which sold 3 million copies, toured the world once – singing before 30,000 people at a single concert in Mexico – and was commanding £800 a night. 2 years later he is almost a showbusiness has-been. 'My image then is all wrong for today. My record company aimed me at the mums and dads. . . I've had to change my style completely now I'm older and my voice has broken. I aim at the weenybopper market.'

LIVER BIRD BERYL QUITS TV SHOW

Actress Polly James said yesterday that she would not be playing brash blonde Beryl in BBC TV's *The Liver Birds* any more. She said she did not like the pressure of having to do a new show every week and she is fed up with being treated by members of the public as though she really is the Scouse scrubber she plays in the comedy series.

Pop idol David Cassidy, whose career was launched in the hit TV show The Partridge Family.

WHEN THE LIFESTYLE IS ON THE FAST SIDE

He's blond, 6 foot 2, good-looking and, so the experts say, likely to become Britain's replacement for ex-Grand Prix king Jackie Stewart. His nickname universally is Hunt the Shunt because he has the occasional happy knack of bumping into other cars on racetracks, but privately among the flamboyant Hesketh racing team, James Hunt is simply called Superstar.

TV BUYS UP *BORN FREE* SERIES WITHOUT SEEING IT

One of the world's most successful animal films, *Born Free*, is to be made into a television series. The story of Elsa the lioness is being made in Kenya, and ITV has bought the series without seeing a foot of the film. The series will introduce 2 American stars to British viewers, Diana Muldaur and Gary Collins who will play Joy Adamson and her game-warden husband George. *Born Free* is one of several new American series lined up for ITV viewers. They include another spin-off from the cinema – *Planet of the Apes* starring Roddy McDowell, who featured in 4 of the Apes cinema films. Also planned for ITV screening are new programmes called *Six Million Dollar Man* with a James Bond/Superman character and *The Police Story*, a series based on police records starring top names like George Maharis and Angie Dickinson.

JULY 1974

The Hopkins family (Kathy Staff, Richard Davies and Kathy Jones) comes to look over Maggie Clegg's shop in Coronation Street.

SHANKLY QUITS – AFTER CLINCHING BIGGEST DEAL

Bill Shankly yesterday announced his retirement as Anfield chief – on the day he completed his biggest transfer deal. Shankly's final act as manager was to pay £200,000 for Ray Kennedy, the 22-year-old Arsenal striker who ended Liverpool's double bid last season. Of the legacy of playing staff he will be leaving Shankly says, '. . . they have the strongest playing staff since I came here; you will need an international cap to get a game in Liverpool's reserves.'

DEFIANT MAZDA GOES FOR 3 NEW ROTOR CARS

Japan's Mazda motor firm is introducing 3 new rotary-engined cars in spite of other manufacturers' doubts about this type of power. British Leyland chief, Lord Stokes, is just one who believes the engine is a commercial 'non-starter' because it uses more petrol than a conventional power unit. Mazda say that in Britain 38% of their customers choose a rotary model. The 3 new cars are versions of the RX4: saloon (£2,215), coupé (£2,272), estate (£2,314), all including tax.

5 ROLLS-ROYCES AT ONLY 26

For the young Nordic-looking figure standing in the spotlight at the Royal Festival Hall it was the realization of a Walter Mitty-style fantasy. As if by command the 103 members of the London Symphony Orchestra put down their instruments and gave him the kind of standing ovation they usually reserve for the likes of Menuhin or Rubinstein.

The applause was even more extraordinary when you consider that Rick Wakeman is a rock musician whose dreams of playing with the LSO were shattered 4 years ago when he left the Royal College of Music convinced he was a second-rate pianist. Today he is the world's most successful symphonic composer – his work during the last year has grossed £8m in record sales – the trappings of which include no less than 5 Rolls-Royces. The son of a trumpeter in the Billy Cotton Band, Rick, 26, played in pubs and clubs after leaving the Royal College. He joined The Strawbs before moving to a group called simply Yes. Now, after 2 hit solo albums, *The Six Wives of Henry the Eighth* and *Journey to the Centre of the Earth*, he has left the group to star in his own right.

HOW 2 BROTHERS FOUND THE FLAWS IN BRITAIN AND TURNED THEM INTO A FORTUNE

The more inefficient British industry becomes the more profits there are to be taken. Typical of the kind of firm which is now thriving is Brutus which is run by 2 young brothers, Alan and Keith Freedman. Every day crates of shirts and jeans which have been made, packed and despatched in Hong Kong are sent to shops throughout Britain. Although wages in Hong Kong are now nearing British levels and the cost of the raw materials is the same throughout the world, the brothers still find it worthwhile to go to Hong Kong, pay the freight charges and 20% import duty just to get enough goods quickly. 'If we waited for British manufacturers, our designs would be out of fashion by the time they made delivery,' said 25-year-old Alan. The brothers do not regard themselves as unpatriotic. 'British manufacturers are 10 years behind the times,' said Alan. 'We have built up a business out of their misfortune and we are millionaires as a result.'

Cheek-to-cheek champions Chris Evert and Jimmy Connors open the Wimbledon ball.

PAY PATIENTS ORDERED OUT

The Socialist campaign against private medicine took a new turn last night when private patients at Charing Cross Hospital were transferred to open wards after union members forced the hospital to close its fee-paying wing. Mrs Esther Brookstone of NUPE said, 'There is a massive feeling of resentment by all of us at the existence of 2 standards of medicine within one hospital. . . the sight of Daimlers and Rolls-Royces parked outside the hospital is a constant source of irritation to us.' Private patients pay £174 a week for their room, meals and nursing; surgical and medical fees are extra. The cost of a private patient to the Health Service at this hospital is about £136 a week. The Government is committed to phasing out private medicine from the Health Service. At present 4,527 pay-beds are reserved for private patients, 1% of the total number in state hospitals.

David Bedford winning the AA 10,000 metres at Crystal Palace.

STAY AS WE ARE, PLEADS SCHOEN

West German Manager Helmut Schoen turned from the most triumphant moment of his life to warn FIFA that the World Cup will be ruined if they pursue their plan for 20 finalists in 1978. After his country's victory over Holland in the Olympic Stadium Schoen said, '. . . both ourselves and Holland were very tired today at the end of a competition for 16 finalists. If in the future 20 teams play, it will be impossible for them – there will be too many games. The World Cup will suffer badly.'

BRITAIN PROBES WAVE POWER

The possibility of using sea waves to meet Britain's growing power demand is being investigated by the Department of Energy. Experts estimate that wave power around Britain's coast could provide up to 2/3 of the present peak demand for electricity. The idea is to float special tanks about 1 mile offshore; the movement of the waves produces enough energy to pump water ashore to operate generators. The snag is that electricity from wave generators would cost 2 to 3 times as much as that from nuclear power stations, now regarded as the cheapest form of generation.

SHOPS CASH IN ON SUGAR CRISIS

Hundreds of shopkeepers are cashing in on the sugar shortage by charging up to 18p for a 2lb bag which usually costs 11½p. Supplies to shops and supermarkets are 40% down on normal and panic buying by housewives has made the situation worse. The shortage has been caused by a cut in deliveries from the West Indies. Most of the big supermarket chains have introduced a strict rationing system to prevent panic buying. Some small shops have been insisting that customers could buy sugar only if they spent at least £1 on other groceries.

THE MOMENT THE WHISTLE BLEW ON THE LIONS. . .

A split second after this picture was taken Fergus Slattery grounded the ball for what should have been an historic rugby try. It didn't count because of an error by the referee in the final test between South Africa and the British Lions. He had blown his whistle a split second before believing – wrongly – that Piet Cronje, whose legs are beneath the ball in the picture, could continue to prevent Slattery touching down at the end of this move in the third minute of injury time. After the match, which ended in a 13–13 draw, both the referee and Cronje admitted the error which deprived the Lions of a clean sweep of tour victories, a record unparalleled this century.

CYPRUS – IT'S ALL-OUT WAR

7 hours after Greek Cypriot rebels claimed to have killed Archbishop Makarios in his blazing palace, he was said to be still alive and organizing resistance to the new regime. As tanks rumbled through Nicosia pro-Makarios forces throughout the island were reported in heavy fighting with the Greek-officered National Guard, the unit which originally attacked the presidential palace. The official Cyprus Radio declared, 'The National Guard this morning took over authority in Cyprus. This step was taken to put an end to civil strife among Greek Cypriots. Long live the Greek Cypriot people.'

JENKINS STOPS FORCE-FEEDING IN PRISONS

Prisoners who go on hunger strike will no longer be force-fed to keep them alive. This major policy change was announced yesterday by Home Secretary Mr Roy Jenkins. Future practice should be that prisoners refusing to accept any form of nourishment would be examined to ensure that their capacity for rational judgement was unimpaired. Mr Jenkins has decided on the move after the controversy over the Price sisters and other Irish terrorists who went on hunger strike earlier this year in an effort to force the Government to send them to Ulster to serve their jail terms for the London car bombings. Force-feeding has been controversial ever since it was introduced 70 years ago. Doctors and prison officers have condemned it as barbaric but until now it has been a firm idea that the State has a duty to keep prisoners alive.

DAY BY DAY

1 July
General Juan Perón, President of Argentina, dies, aged 78, 2 days after his wife was sworn in as interim President.

4 July
Don Revie becomes England's Manager.

5 July
Chris Evert of the USA wins the Wimbledon ladies' singles title. Her fiancé Jimmy Connors wins the men's championship the following day.

Romantic novelist Georgette Heyer dies, aged 71.

7 July
West Germany beats Holland 2–1 in the World Cup Final.

9 July
Mr Christopher Mayhew, Labour MP for Woolwich East since 1951, joins the Liberal party.

10 July
Energy Secretary Mr Eric Varley announces that future nuclear power stations will use British steam-generating heavy water reactors and not the American pressurized water reactors.

12 July
John Ehrlichman, former advisor to President Nixon, is found guilty of conspiracy and perjury.

18 July
Trade Secretary Mr Peter Shore announces the abandonment of plans to build a third London airport at Maplin.

20 July
Turkish forces invade Cyprus.

22 July
Chancellor Mr Denis Healey announces a reduction in VAT from 10% to 8%.

Greece and Turkey agree to a cease-fire in Cyprus.

23 July
The military Government in Athens recalls Mr Constantine Karamanlis to form a new civilian cabinet.

25 July
The Industrial Relations Court and the Pay Board are abolished.

27 July
A House of Representatives committee votes to recommend that President Nixon be impeached.

31 July
The Government announces plans for nationalizing 32 firms in the shipping industry.

The Lions have no doubt that Slattery has scored a try in the final Test against the Springboks.

LITTLE BLUE BAGS WORTH THEIR SALT

Little blue bags of salt are making a comeback in packets of Smiths Potato Crisps – by popular request. The blue bags were dropped 9 years ago when the crisps became pre-salted. Smiths said it was too expensive to employ people to put one in each packet and moisture sometimes made the salt soggy. Now Smiths has put the salt in an airtight blue sachet.

AUG 1974

WAR ON THE HOME FRONT

The still unannounced general election burst into life last night as Labour unleashed an onslaught on Tory plans to help home-seekers and rate-payers. Environment Secretary Anthony Crosland rushed into action within hours of an announcement by his shadow Mrs Margaret Thatcher that the Tories will cut mortgage rates to 9.5%, give cash grants to first-time home-buyers, let council tenants buy their houses as of right and abolish the present rating system. Mr Crosland labelled the scheme 'Margaret's mid-summer madness' and 'hopelessly expensive'. Mrs Thatcher said last night that the scheme would not be cheap. It was a question of where one spent government money, she said, 'and we know it is needed in housing'.

James Caan faces death on the track in Norman Jewison's Rollerball.

NORTH SEA PETROL ON SALE IN 3 MONTHS

Motorists will be able to fill up with petrol made from North Sea oil within the next 3 months. About 35,000 tons of crude oil will come ashore every 5 days but as the tanker loads will be small in terms of refinery capacity the North Sea oil will be processed with whatever other oil happens to be going through the refinery at the time. The first all-North Sea petrol will not be available until crude from BP's Forties Field is piped ashore next spring. Some motorists are already buying petrol made partly from North Sea sources. Conoco, who market Jet petrol, are making about 1.5 million gallons a month from North Sea gas. The gas contains a condensate – a light oil – that is processed into petrol. Britain should be self-sufficient in oil supplies within 6 years.

BUT WAIT, WHAT'S BERT DOING AMONG THE BEATLES?

Beatlemania is about to burst once again on an otherwise dreary London scene. Like last time it comes from Liverpool and trails the names of John, Paul, George and Ringo, but this time they are joined by Bert. *John, Paul, George, Ringo. . . And Bert* is indeed the title of a new musical opening tomorrow. Wildly acclaimed in its native city it explores the careers of the fab 4 using their own music. 4 unknown actors from the Liverpool Everyman Theatre, Trevor Eve as McCartney, Philip Joseph as Harrison, Bernard Hill as Lennon and Antony Sher as Starr impersonate the originals, but to avoid odious comparisons their songs are sung by Barbara Dixon. Author Willie Russell's play aims to do a lot more than simply retell the story of the group. Bert, played by George Costigan, is a fictional character who once played with the boys but dropped out even before Peter Best and Stuart Sutcliffe. 'I used Bert to show that whatever happens to you in life you can't escape yourself,' says Willie Russell. 'That's the real tragedy – if that's not too big a word – for what became of the Beatles.'

SCAMPI MEN BLAME FANNY

TV cookery expert Fanny Cradock was blamed by angry scampi fishermen yesterday for causing a collapse of their market. The crew of many of the boats which form the Ayr prawning fleet face ruin because they cannot sell their catch. Many say it is Fanny Cradock's fault because on TV earlier this year she showed housewives how to make ersatz scampi using cheap monkfish; she claimed that the difference in flavour was almost undetectable.

Daily Mail
FRIDAY, AUGUST 9, 1974
4p

HEALEY'S NEW TAXES Pages 10, 11

Gerald Ford is ready to take over as the President makes his momentous decision

NIXON GOES

By WILLIAM LOWTHER Washington Correspondent

the wake of the greatest litical scandal in history, hard Milhous Nixon yesterday was on the brink of resignation as the 37th President of the ited States.

Today he is expected to hand over power President Gerald Ford.

was going on national television at nine tonight Washington time to tell the nation of decision made

Having made his decision Mr Nixon decided to stay silent on the details until he had spoken directly to the nation.

It was dull and muggy in Washington as crowds began gathering outside the White House and Mr Nixon ended his 341st and final day of power.

After making his decision Mr Nixon went to bed for a few hours. But he was up early and at 11 a.m. called Vice-President Ford to the Oval office.

Dilemma

According to Washington sources, Mr Nixon told him that he was resigning and that power would be handed over on Friday afternoon.

Mr Ford is an old and loyal Nixon friend. Their 70-minute meeting is said to have been very emotional.

As it ended, Mr Ford crossed the street to the executive office building and conferred with his chief aide.

tion. It is thought likely to be 66-year-old Nelson A. Rockefeller, former Governor of New York.

Wednesday must have been a terrible 24 hours for Mr Nixon. Throughout the day Republican supporter after Republican supporter called on him to quit. Even his best friends were pressing him to quit.

By the evening, he was exhausted. Normally a formal and unemotional man, Mr Nixon held a family dinner in the White House. For probably the first time in his Presidency, he sat down at the dinner table in his shirt sleeves.

There was just his wife, Pat, daughter and son-in-law Julie and David Eisenhower, and daughter and son-in-law Tricia and Edward Cox.

The President had still not decided.

His two sons-in-law told him he had no option. He had to get out.

No emotion

GEORGE RAFT TOLD: KEEP OUT OF BRITAIN

Hollywood film star George Raft, banned from Britain since 1967, has been told that he still cannot enter the country, even for a 2-week visit. Raft, now 78, wanted to come here later this year to promote his biography but Home Secretary Mr Roy Jenkins, who first declared Raft a prohibited immigrant 7 years ago, has again refused him entry. In 1970 Raft denied associations with the Mafia after being called before a New York grand jury.

HOW AUNTY EDNA HIT PETER IN A FROZEN ATTIC. . .

The discovery of a new native comic novelist is as rare as the sighting of a new British breeding bird. There has been excited agreement behind the critical binoculars lately on the subject of Peter Tinniswood. His 3 books to date represent instalments in the saga of the Brandon family. Peter Tinniswood was working in Sheffield as a journalist when the Brandons hit him, complete with their philosophy. The first paragraph came by itself – he doesn't know where from. 'When Aunty Edna fell off a bus she fell on her pate and remained unconscious for 63 days. At the end of that period they had a funeral.' The third book, *Except You're A Bird*, has just won the Winifred Holtby Award.

The face of '74. Lauren Hutton is the most celebrated and highest paid model of the day.

NOW – ADS AT ARSENAL

Arsenal is to break with a 61-year Highbury tradition and allow advertisements round its pitch. Arsenal has also doubled the price of its programme to 10p – another indication it is worried about the mounting cost of running a top club. Last season the average home gate dropped from 40,000 to 30,000, just below the figure needed to break even. £100,000 a year is needed just to maintain Highbury in its existing state.

GEE! THEY'VE GOT A NEW MARILYN – THE GIRL FROM THE BEEFBURGER ADVERT

Blonde Sandra Dickinson, who plays the dumb gangster's moll in a TV advertisement for beefburgers, is to portray Marilyn Monroe in *Legend*, a play about the last three months in the star's life. The producer chose 25-year-old Sandra because of her likeness to Monroe, her baby-doll voice and her personality. In the beefburger advertisement, Sandra plays the dumb blonde diner in a restaurant who, when surrounded by a mob of gangsters carrying guns in cases, provides the punchline 'Gee, they've got a band.' The role was originally taken by actress Joan Collins but because of a delay to sort out legal difficulties over the content of the production she was unable to carry on. The play has been written by David Butler, who wrote the TV series *Black Beauty*.

GIANT HOLIDAY FIRM CRASHES

The giant holiday firm Court Line, which owns Clarksons and Horizon Holidays, last night announced that they have ceased trading. A spokesman said steps were being taken to go into liquidation. Court has been in financial difficulties since the beginning of the year because of the fuel crisis and the slump in holiday bookings. There is thought to be no prospect of British Airways or any other airline taking over Court or its fleet of 14 jets.

SWITCH OFF STARTS BABY BOOM

A baby boom is about to hit the maternity wards because of those blacked-out TV screens last winter. The first night of early closing on television, imposed because of the power crisis, was 18 December. Hospitals all over Britain report that maternity bookings are up for the last week in September and the early part of October, just 9 months later. Reaction from the Family Planning Association: 'People have lost the art of entertaining themselves, so when their ready-made entertainment fails, they resort to the oldest form of recreation of all.'

Gerald Ford becomes the 38th US President.

MONEY TROUBLES DRIVE OUT THE TYCOON MP

The brief and troubled political career of Mr Jeffrey Archer, 34-year-old tycoon and Tory MP, crumpled amid 'severe financial problems'. After less than 5 years at Westminster, dogged by controversy about his ambitions and sometimes spectacular commercial ventures, Mr Archer announced that he will not fight his seat at Louth, Lincolnshire at the next election.

SEPT 1974

A ROAD TO END CAR ACCIDENTS

Britain has developed a radical new accident saver – a road where the entire surface has the tread pattern similar to that on a car tyre. The design should stop skidding and cut spray hazards on wet roads, according to scientists at Dunlop and Birmingham University who have spent 7 years evolving the surface, which cannot become polished or slippery.

FASTER THAN A BULLET!

The world's most secret plane hurtled across the Atlantic in an incredible 1 hour 55 minutes and 42 seconds yesterday. The 2,000-m.p.h. Lockheed SR-71, America's latest spy plane, blasted off from Beale in California and flew most of its journey 15 miles above the earth. SR-71, nicknamed Blackbird, covered an average of 3,100 feet per second – 3 times the speed of sound and faster than the muzzle velocity of a rifle bullet.

WOMEN GET THEIR CHARTER

Women will be guaranteed equal treatment in almost every walk of life under White Paper proposals announced by Home Secretary Mr Roy Jenkins yesterday. Anyone who refuses a woman a job or a mortgage or a pint of beer just because she is a woman will face legal action and so will anyone who refuses to employ a man as a secretary just because he is a man. If Labour is returned at the next election the plans should become law in a year's time, when the Equal Pay laws come into force.

There would be some exceptions, however. The Army won't have to employ dolly-girls in the front line and the Church won't have to ordain women priests; work in private houses and firms with fewer than 10 employees will also be excluded. Jobs such as modelling, where a person's sex can be a genuine occupational qualification, would be outside the new laws; single-sex schools would escape too. The act would also set up an Equal Opportunities Commission with offices throughout Britain to see everyone gets a fair deal.

PARDON FOR NIXON

President Ford has ended the great American tragedy of Richard Milhous Nixon. In a hurried but solemn ceremony the President stepped in yesterday to shield his former boss from imminent criminal prosecution by granting him 'full, free and absolute pardon'. Mr Ford acted just in time to stop Mr Nixon from being charged with a series of crimes mainly concerned with obstruction of justice in the Watergate scandal.

'TOM THUMB' MENACE OF NEW DRUG

A Home Office pathologist warned yesterday of a new drug known as 'Angel Dust' which triggers hallucinations of being dwarf sized. An addict also believes he can hide in tiny crevices and pass through keyholes. The drug, phencycladine, is normally used by vets to tranquillize large animals such as rhinoceroses. Its effects include a feeling of weightlessness and a sense of flying. The drug, which is apparently used quite widely in the United States, is reported as being sold by pushers as 'peace pills'.

THE GOLDEN TREBLE

Britain triumphantly closed the week's European Athletic Championships in Rome last night. Brendan Foster, the 26-year-old Recreational Manager from Gateshead, slashed the championship record in winning the 5,000 metres in 13 minutes 17.2 seconds after leading from start to finish. Ian Thompson, leading the marathon almost throughout, was only 8 seconds off the championship mark with 2 hours 13 minutes 18.8 seconds. The 4 x 400-metre squad of Glen Cohen, Bill Hartley, Alan Pascoe and David Jenkins was a mere 1 second off a record in taking the relay title in 3 minutes 3.3 seconds.

NOW CHILDREN GET THEIR OWN TV NEWS

Children are to have their own television news bulletins 4 times a week, the BBC announced yesterday. *John Craven's Newsround* began as a twice weekly experiment; now it will run for 10 minutes every afternoon from Monday to Thursday, starting next week. Part of a massive wooing of young viewers by the BBC this winter is a remake of the children's classic *The Secret Garden*. Also coming back are new series of *Captain Pugwash*, *The Wombles* and *The Magic Roundabout*.

ENOCH CHOSEN TO STAND FOR ULSTER SEAT

Enoch Powell's political exile ended last night when he won acceptance as the Unionist candidate for South Down. His selection virtually assures his return to Westminster in the next election. Mr Powell's latest broadside at his party's policies on Ulster and Europe came as he claimed Conservatives had done more damage to the interests of Northern Ireland than the Labour Government had before 1970 or since February.

CON MEN KNOCK OUT THE KUNG FU YOUNGSTERS

Crooks are cashing in on the big kung fu craze. Youngsters who want to learn the Oriental martial art are getting from some clubs a demonstration of the art of the British conman. Boys attracted by the films of kung fu stars like Bruce Lee are being enrolled by 'clubs' and paying as much as £10 to sign on for a course of lessons, but when they turn up they find no instructors and no club.

Daredevil Evel Knievel prepares for a Wembley show in which he plans to leap over a row of lorries on his 750 cc Harley-Davidson. He is reported to have made £2m in his failed attempt to jump Snake River Canyon in Idaho.

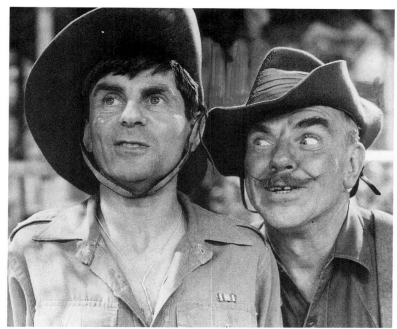

BSM Williams (Windsor Davies, right) gives a word of advice to Bdr. Beaumont (Melvyn Hayes) in It Ain't Half Hot Mum.

THE FILM STAR WHO WON 3 OSCARS

Walter Brennan, the only actor to win 3 Academy Awards, has died aged 80. A family spokesman said Brennan had a lung illness which had been aggravated by smog. Born in Massachusetts, Brennan went to Hollywood in 1923, often making the rounds of the studios with another struggling actor, Gary Cooper. Even then Brennan knew what image meant to Hollywood. 'If they paid me $10 a day I was Walter Brennan; if the cheque was $7.50 they got Walter Andrews; for anything less than that my billing was Philip Space.' He never had much to say about acting. His acceptance speech for his first Academy Award for *Come and Get It* in 1936 was 'Thank you'; for *Kentucky* in 1938 it was 'Thank you very much'; and for *The Westerner* in 1940, 'Thank you very, very much.'

LEEDS SACK CLOUGH AFTER 44 DAYS

Brian Clough was sacked last night after 44 days as Leeds United Manager. The parting came at a meeting at the Elland Road ground between Clough, his solicitor and Chairman Manny Cussins. The sacking comes hours after the *Daily Mail* revealed that Leeds players had passed a vote of no-confidence in Clough in a dramatic dressing-room scene. Leeds' Eire international Johnny Giles will be appointed Manager today.

THE BORN LAUGHTER-MAKER

Coco once said that there were only 11 clowns left in the world. Now there are only 10. The laughable figure with size 24 boots, baggy pants, ping-pong-ball nose and checked suit died yesterday in a Peterborough hospital: he had been ill with acute bronchitis. He was born Nicholia Polialoff in the property room of a theatre in the Ukraine where his father worked. No one knows how long ago that was, for he always kept his age a secret. He came to Britain in 1929 to work with Bertram Mills for 4 weeks and stayed with them for 40 years. His love for children went beyond the Big Top; his travels teaching them road safety led to the OBE in 1963.

NEW THREAT TO AVENGER

The Japanese Mitsubishi Colt cars, which forced Chrysler Avengers out of the American market, are going on sale in Britain in the next few weeks. The firm has decided to market its range of 9 Colt cars independently of Chrysler UK. In America Chrysler and Mitsubishi have a marketing agreement under which Chrysler has distribution and sales rights for Mitsubishi cars. Now Mitsubishi is to launch the Colt in direct competition with the Chrysler Avenger in Britain. The Colt range will start at about £1,400 for the Lancer while the top-of-the-range Galant Coupé will cost about £2,200.

IT'S POWER TO THE PARENTS

Parents are more worried about school standards now than at any time in recent history, Tory Education Spokesman Mr Norman St John-Stevas said yesterday. He was giving details of a parents' charter which the Conservatives promised to introduce if they win the election. Mr St John-Stevas claims it is the most important Tory education statement for 30 years. The charter promises to:

- change the law to force local councils to pay more attention to parents' wishes.
- set up appeal committees for parents who are dissatisfied with schooling.
- promote parents onto school governing and managing bodies.
- encourage, possibly force, schools to set up Parent-Teacher Associations.
- encourage schools to publish their records and achievements.
- extend choice of schools by widening catchment areas.

DAY BY DAY

1 Sept
A US helicopter crashes at Farnborough Air Show, killing both crew members.

4 Sept
A report into the manslaughter of 7-year-old Maria Colwell by her stepfather criticizes the local authority after Maria was taken from her foster parents and returned to her mother.

11 Sept
6 Territorial Army paratroopers are drowned when they are accidentally dropped into the Kiel Canal during a NATO night exercise.

12 Sept
Emperor Haile Selassie of Ethiopia is deposed and a military government under Lieutenant-General Aman Andom is formed.

17 Sept
6 hostages, held captive in the French Embassy in The Hague for 4 days, are released after their captors, 3 Japanese terrorists, collect a £125,000 ransom. With another Japanese terrorist, who was released from a French prison, the 4 are flown out of Holland.

18 Sept
The Prime Minister announces that a general election will be held on 10 October.

The Japanese terrorists surrender in Damascus.

21 Sept
More than 8,000 people are reported to have died in floods caused by hurricanes in Honduras.

22 Sept
Lord Chalfont, former Foreign Office Minister, resigns from the Labour party, blaming left-wing influences in the party.

26 Sept
Mr Roy Jenkins, the Home Secretary, says he would resign from a Labour Government which took Britain out of the EEC. Yesterday, Prices Secretary Mrs Shirley Williams said she would not remain in politics if a referendum were in favour of withdrawal.

30 Sept
General António Spínola resigns as President of Portugal and is succeeded by General Francisco da Costa Gomes.

THE WOMAN WHO WROTE 3 BESTSELLERS

Jacqueline Susann, the world's best-selling author, has died in a New York hospital. Miss Susann, who was 53, had had cancer for 12 years, a secret she kept from the public until the end. Her books probably earned her more than £10m. *Valley of the Dolls* was her first novel, written in 1966. It rocketed her to international fame and, with sales of more than 17 million copies, still holds a place in the *Guinness Book of Records*. With her second novel, *The Love Machine*, written 3 years later, and *Once Is Enough*, her final novel published last year, she became the first author to write 3 consecutive number 1 bestsellers.

BEETHOVEN GETS A NATURAL BREAK

TV adverts which feature classical music as part of their sales jingles are bringing the work of top composers to pop-orientated fans. But there's a twist: the fans know the music by the product rather than the title. Cheshire priest Father John McLeigh says his nephews and nieces know snatches of classics as well as they know Donny Osmond's latest hit but he says, 'I have been puzzled trying to interpret their requests for the chocolate advert which turned out to be Beethoven's Pastoral; the cigar advert which is Mozart's Twenty-First or the Hovis advert which is Dvořák's New World. I recently delighted my 8-year-old niece by playing Mozart's Jupiter, then I discovered she knew it as the latest Wombles Minuet.'

Mr and Mrs Wilson at No. 10 after the general election.

The wrecked front of the Horse and Groom public house in Guildford.

IRA WAR ON THE WOMEN

The IRA went to the sleepy Surrey town of Guildford this weekend and declared war on Britain's girl soldiers. They killed 2 teenage members of the WRAC and wounded 11 others. The 2 pubs hit by the explosions – the Horse and Groom in North Street and the Seven Stars in Swan Lane – were popular with young WRAC recruits training at the Queen Elizabeth Barracks at Guildford, the only military establishment in the town. 19-year-old Ann Hamilton, who joined up 4 weeks ago, died while having a drink at the Horse and Groom; so did Carolyn Slater, a WRAC for 24 days. 2 soldiers, William Forsyth, aged 18, and 17-year-old John Hunter, also died on their first night out since starting basic training at Pirbright for the Scots Guards. 1 civilian was also killed. Altogether 65 people were injured in the 2 blasts 200 yards apart.

I WANT TO WIN THE LOT, SAYS £144,000 MILLER

Californian-born Johnny Miller's triumph in the Kaiser Open boosted his season's golf earnings to £144,000 and broke the record of £135,000 held by Jack Nicklaus. Miller, 27-year-old Mormon who gives 10% of his earnings to the Church, has now won 8 tournaments this season, equalling Arnold Palmer's 1960 record, but he still trails the 18 victories collected by Byron Nelson in 1945.

The Coronation St girls win a football competition and a holiday for two in Bermuda. The rules are bent to allow all eight to go. The holiday scenes were shot somewhat less exotically in Majorca.

IT'S ALL GO AS £60,000 NEAL JOINS LIVERPOOL IN 3-MINUTE DEAL

Phil Neal reported for training with Fourth Division Northampton yesterday morning and by mid-afternoon he was a Liverpool player. The 23-year-old defender admitted he was 'flabbergasted' to be given the chance of the £60,000 move to Anfield. His negotiations with Liverpool Manager Bob Paisley took just 3 minutes to complete. He is Paisley's first signing since replacing Bill Shankly as Manager at the start of the season.

SAVUNDRA FIGHTS ON TO CLEAR HIS NAME

Doctor Emil Savundra, the Ceylon-born financier who swindled 400,000 British motorists, was freed yesterday after 6½ years in jail. The man who was convicted for the Fire, Auto and Marine insurance fraud said that he was innocent and planned to take his case to the European Commission on Human Rights in Strasbourg. Doctor Savundra served a 10-year sentence – most of it spent in the hospital wing of Wormwood Scrubs suffering from diabetes and a heart condition – less full remission.

BRAZILIAN FITTIPALDI IS WORLD NUMBER 1 DRIVER

32-year-old Brazilian Emerson Fittipaldi became the new World Champion racing driver when he finished fourth in the United States Grand Prix. Clay Regazzoni and Jody Scheckter, his 2 rivals for the title, held by the now retired Jackie Stewart, both had mechanical trouble during the 200-mile event.

'£5,000 IS ALL I GET...'

Gordon Honeycombe complained last night that he was paid only about £5,000 a year to read the news on Independent Television. He did not doubt reports that some newsreaders earned £10,000 but pointed out that this was made up by personal appearances which he did for free. Mr Honeycombe, 38, was speaking during a break from picket-line duties outside ITN's West End studios where journalists have been on strike for a 30% rise to bring them into line with BBC rates. He said, 'I feel I am worth more in that I actually read more news for ITN than any other newscaster and I probably appear on the ITV national network more than anyone else in television.'

SAVE OUR STILTON

An SOS to 'Save Our Stilton' is being sent to the Agriculture Minister Mr Fred Peart. Mr John Farr, Tory MP for Harborough, Leicestershire, warned yesterday that Blue Stilton is in danger of disappearing because it is not subsidized like other English cheeses. It is considered strictly for the quality market, Mr Farr said, but 'subsidies should be right across the cheese board'.

Stan Bowles and Alan Ball tangle during a 2-2 draw between Arsenal and QPR at Highbury.

NOV 1974

EARL MISSING AS POLICE SEEK NANNY'S KILLER

The Countess of Lucan lay heavily sedated in hospital last night as detectives tried to trace her husband after the savage murder of her children's nanny. Police say they want to find the Earl of Lucan to tell him of the night of terror at his wife's Belgravia home. Lady Lucan, who separated from her husband 2 years ago, was beaten during the attack on Mrs Sandra Rivett on Thursday night. Last night Lord Lucan, the seventh earl, had not appeared at his usual haunts among the high-society gambling clubs of Mayfair.

BOMBING: 5 HELD AT PORT

5 men who are suspected of the Birmingham pub bomb outrage were under strong police guard last night. The 5 were detained 100 miles from the city, only 2½ hours after the first explosion on Thursday evening. They were held at the railway station at Heysham Harbour, Lancashire – a port which has a sea link with Belfast – after a police operation that virtually sealed off the whole of England. A police escort took them back to Birmingham where 19 people were killed and 184 injured when a vicious new type of IRA bomb blasted 2 public houses.

Detectives were waiting when the suspect IRA gang, all with Birmingham addresses, stepped off a boat-train which pulled into Heysham at 10.45 p.m. The 5 men had rail tickets with consecutive numbers issued at Birmingham's New Street Station – only a stone's throw from the bomb blasts – for the 7.55 p.m. train to Crewe. The train left New Street 21 minutes before the first bomb exploded. The suspects, who were given routine nitrate tests to show whether they had handled explosives, have lived in Birmingham for between 5 and 11 years. A senior police spokesman in Heysham said, 'The question of any charges is a matter for the West Midlands force; the matter is now out of our hands.'

PUB BOMBERS STRIKE AGAIN

More than 20 people were injured last night when terrorists struck again in a soldiers' pub – this time in London. A bomb believed to be several pounds of gelignite ripped through a crowded bar near Woolwich Barracks. It is thought to have been placed inside the pub itself, the King's Arms in Frances Street, London SE. The pub is a few hundred yards from the barracks used by the Royal Artillery.

The blackened stonework and falling rafters of the Mulberry Bush pub give some idea of the appalling devastation caused by the IRA bombs.

BOOTSIE AND SPORT IN LABOUR TV ROW. THE BBC PUT ITS FOOT DOWN

The BBC was adamant that a Labour party broadcast tonight by Mrs Shirley Williams couldn't go out at 10 p.m. and interrupt *Sports Night*; it should go out at 9 p.m. At that ITV put its foot down. *Bootsie and Snudge* goes out at 8.30. It builds up a big audience which would fade away if the Labour party came on at 9. Now the BBC and ITV plan to show the party political broadcast at different times – breaking the tradition that they are transmitted on all channels simultaneously.

Fans crowd round Queen, currently top of the charts with their single 'Killer Queen'.

Romance is in the air for Clara (Pauline Collins) and C.D. (John Alderton) in LWT's No Honestly.

MYSTERY OF THE VANISHING EX-MINISTER DEEPENS

Mystery last night surrounded the disappearance of ex-Cabinet Minister John Stonehouse when 2 Miami Beach guards told police, 'He didn't go swimming off our beach.' The guards were on duty at the beach owned by the Fontainebleau Hotel when Mr Stonehouse was thought to have gone swimming and vanished. Mr Stonehouse, 49, was staying at the hotel with business associate Mr James Charlton. The 2 men were in Miami in connection with their exporting company Global Imex and London Capital Securities, a private bank. Mr Charlton denied rumours that Mr Stonehouse, Labour MP for Walsall North and former Minister of Posts and Telecommunications, was in financial trouble. Last night Mrs Barbara Stonehouse was awaiting news of her husband.

NOW MRS THATCHER ENTERS ARENA

Mrs Margaret Thatcher is to fight Mr Edward Heath for the leadership of the Conservative party. Yesterday she became the first candidate to declare herself, thus blowing the leadership race wide open. It will now be almost impossible for Mr William Whitelaw not to agree to fight as well. Mrs Thatcher becomes the first woman in the history of British politics to make a serious attempt to head one of the major political parties.

NOW ANNELINE TAKES OVER AS MISS WORLD MARK 2

Miss South Africa, Anneline Kriel, the girl many people said should have been Miss World, took over the crown 5 days late last night. She replaced Miss United Kingdom, unmarried mother Helen Morgan, who resigned because of rumours that she was involved in the break-up of a marriage.

A FIRST-NIGHT SACK FOR MARY URE

Actress Mary Ure was sacked from the leading role of the play *Love For Love* which opened on Broadway last night. Director Mr How Prince refused to comment but told another member of the cast that the actress 'didn't communicate with the audience'. Miss Ure, wife of playwright Robert Shaw, was replaced by her understudy Glenn Close, a 22-year-old college graduate.

Not exactly 007. David Jason plays the spy game for laughs in The Top Secret Life Of Edgar Briggs.

DAY BY DAY

4 Nov
Judith Ward, formerly a private in the WRAC, is jailed for 30 years for her part in the M62 coach explosion which killed 12 people.

5 Nov
Welsh farmers block the railway line in Anglesey in protest against beef imports from Ireland.

7 Nov
Sir Alec Douglas-Home, who renounced his hereditary peerage in 1963, is awarded a life peerage.

The Government announces that tokens worth 20p a week are to be issued to pensioners from December to March for the purchase of beef or veal.

8 Nov
Ronald Milhench is jailed for 3 years for forgery, attempted fraud and firearms offences. He forged Mr Harold Wilson's signature on a letter which he tried to sell to Associated Newspapers.

11 Nov
The new Covent Garden market opens at Nine Elms, Battersea.

12 Nov
VAT on petrol is increased from 8% to 25% in a Budget introduced by Mr Healey.

15 Nov
Dr Michael Ramsey retires as Archbishop of Canterbury.

17 Nov
Mr Erskine Childers, President of Ireland, dies suddenly, aged 68. He was the fourth and only Protestant President of the Irish Republic.

Mr Constantine Karamanlis's conservative New Democracy party is returned in Greece's first general election after 7 years of military rule.

21 Nov
Peter Shilton becomes the world's most expensive goalkeeper as Stoke signs him from Leicester for £340,000.

22 Nov
Britain's Helen Morgan becomes Miss World.

4 Arab terrorists hijack a British Airways VC10 at Dubai and force it to fly to Tunis. The crew is later released after 7 Palestinians are freed from prisons in Cairo and The Hague.

29 Nov
Cearbhall O'Dalaigh is named as the new Eire President.

IRA BANNED

Home Secretary Mr Roy Jenkins yesterday brought in sweeping and draconian measures to drive Irish terrorists from the shores of Great Britain. Within minutes of his doing so the need for such legislation once again became self-evident as 3 bombs exploded in London – in Piccadilly, Victoria and at King's Cross. So sweeping are Mr Jenkins's proposals to drive out the IRA that he will even be able to issue 'exclusion orders' for the arrest and expulsion without trial from the mainland of people – even UK citizens – who have not been resident for more than 20 years. Proved membership of the IRA will now carry up to 5 years' jail.

DEC 1974

ASTON MARTIN TO CLOSE

Aston Martin, one of the greatest names in motoring, is to die because directors have decided to reject an offer of government cash. The conditions laid down by Industry Secretary Mr Anthony Benn 'just could not be met', said an Aston Martin director last night. The company is to go into voluntary liquidation today, killed by inflation and the economic crisis.

FAULTLESS KLAMMER

Austria's 20-year-old Franz Klammer gave a faultless display of alpine ski racing to win the downhill at the World Cup meeting in Val d'Isère, France, yesterday. Klammer's time of 2 minutes 3.19 seconds for the 2,298-metre run with its 915-metre drop was almost 3.5 seconds faster than the course record set 3 seasons ago.

OLD PEOPLE 'WANT CASH, NOT TOKENS'

An MP called yesterday for an end to the 'patronizing principle' of butter coupons and beef tokens for old age pensioners. Mr Robert McCrindle, Tory member for Brentwood and Ongar, advocating more cash instead of vouchers for OAPs said, 'I have long regretted the tendency of governments to treat pensioners as a separate society to be singled out either for pity or charity. The truth is that they wish neither. . .' Meanwhile Shadow Treasury Minister Mrs Margaret Thatcher was urged to open her larder for inspection by Britain's National Housewives' Association. The organization which attacked her for hoarding after she admitted saving stocks of tinned food has also invited her to visit Derby to inspect old people's larders 'to see how ordinary people have to live'.

'It is a store cupboard not a hoard in any sense', asserts Tory First Lady Margaret Thatcher.

Swinging perilously towards safety: Paul Newman and Steve McQueen in Towering Inferno.

IT'S HUNT THE LOAF TODAY

Shops already desperately short of bread will run out this morning as the bakers' dispute over pay worsens. The 33,000 who work for the big bakery chains which produce 75% of supplies for England and Wales were walking out at 6 a.m. The Bakers' Union, which wants a basic wage of £40 a week with no Sunday working and a fourth week's holiday, has already imposed a Sunday work ban which meant there was very little bread yesterday. About 200 bakeries belonging to the 3 big chains – Allied Breweries, Rank Hovis McDougall and Spillers French – and around 40 large independent firms will close down.

BOMB BLASTS SELFRIDGES

Terrorists struck at the heart of the West End last night when a huge car bomb exploded outside Selfridges. At least 3 people were injured – a young couple and a policewoman. Police were alerted by a telephoned warning and were able to clear many people from the area. The blast was heard and felt over a wide area of central London as far away as Marylebone, the House of Commons and Fleet Street.

CHANCE FOR STERLING AS KING CONTEH ABDICATES

World Light Heavyweight Champion John Conteh has given up his British title. He has been forced into the position because the Boxing Board has nominated Maxie Smith of Stockton-on-Tees to challenge him. Conteh cannot defend without putting his world title at stake. He has already relinquished his European crown, a title which has gone to Italy's Dominico Adinolsi. His latest decision could open the door for his best friend Bunny Sterling who has now proved himself a top contender in 2 weight divisions. Sterling was yesterday named to meet Maurice Hope for the British Middleweight title he once held but which is now vacant.

Mr Mackay sends Fletcher and Godber out of prison in a working party in Porridge. *(L. to r.) Fulton Mackay, Ronnie Barker and Richard Beckinsale.*

QUIET MICK QUITS THE ROLLING STONES

Guitarist Mick Taylor stunned millions of Rolling Stones fans yesterday by quitting the group. Taylor, 25, who replaced Brian Jones in the world's top pop group in 1969, announced that he wanted to expand his career in other directions. Among possible contenders to fill the vacancy are Ron Wood, lead guitarist with Rod Stewart's group The Faces, Mick Ronson, David Bowie's former lead guitarist, and Paul Kossoff, son of TV personality David Kossoff who was a regular member of the group Free. Last night Taylor was with Jack Bruce, bass guitarist of the legendary Cream pop group. The couple are planning to form a new band.

SLOW DOWN AND PAY UP

Motorists bear the brunt of government measures to save energy, it was announced yesterday. From Saturday midnight the speed limit on ordinary 70-m.p.h. roads goes down to 50. The 70-m.p.h. limit for motorways stays and a 60-m.p.h. limit is to be introduced for dual carriageways. Energy Secretary Mr Eric Varley told the Commons that the Government would load the next round of oil price increases mainly onto petrol and limit its use by price. By Christmas petrol is expected to go up by 9p to 71½p a gallon.

ATKINSON IGNORES CONTRACT DISPUTE TO HELP KETTERING

Ron Atkinson begins his job as Manager of Fourth Division Cambridge United this morning – then returns to Kettering tonight to take charge of their first-round FA Cup replay with Swansea. Despite the threat of legal action over his departure from the Southern League club Atkinson said last night, 'I shall be giving 100% for Kettering.' Kettering threatened to sue for compensation because they claim Atkinson's contract does not expire until the end of 1976. Atkinson and Cambridge insist that his contract finishes at the end of the month. Atkinson says he was offered a 2-year extension but 'signed nothing'.

VANITY TRAPS LITTLEJOHN THE RUNAWAY 'SPY'

Kenneth Littlejohn who claimed to be a British 'spy' against the IRA was trapped by his own vanity yesterday, 275 days after he escaped from jail. He was arrested in Birmingham – where 2 weeks ago he was unable to resist giving a newspaper interview. Littlejohn, jailed for 20 years for taking part in a £67,000 bank robbery in the Irish Republic, escaped from Mountjoy Prison in Dublin last March. In the interview he said he was going to hunt down IRA bombers in England and form an assassination squad to kill the terrorists. Littlejohn, 33, has always maintained that he was under British Secret Service orders to infiltrate the IRA.

COFFEE MORNING TAX PUTS NSPCC DEEPER IN RED

One of Britain's biggest charities, the National Society for Prevention of Cruelty to Children, is facing 'formidable' financial difficulties. It was disclosed yesterday that the society has already spent £135,000 more than its income this year. Part of this was £65,000 in annual VAT payments which NSPCC Director the Revd Arthur Morton described as 'monstrous'. Of the tax which was even levied on coffee mornings in private homes to raise money he said, 'VAT on coffee mornings does have an adverse psychological effect as well as an adverse financial effect.'

STOKES FIXES £50m DEAL

Lord Stokes, boss of beleaguered British Leyland, pulled off a £50m gatecrash into the Arab world in Cairo yesterday. British Leyland will start building a factory outside Cairo in 1975 that will produce 10,000 Land Rovers a year. For more than 20 years British Leyland has been on an Arab blacklist because of its trade with Israel. To complete the deal Lord Stokes had to satisfy the Arabs that dealing with Israel had ceased.

(L. to r.) Patsy Smart, Gordon Jackson, Angela Baddeley and Jean Marsh in Upstairs, Downstairs. *The series was inspired by stories about life as a servant told to Miss Marsh by her mother.*

JAN 1975

CURRY WINS THE SILVER FOR BRITAIN

Britain's John Curry gave a thrilling free-skating display to take the silver medal in the men's individual event at the European Championships in Copenhagen last night. He was beaten only by a brilliant performance from Russian Vladimir Kovalev who earned his country's first men's individual title.

And it's a happy New Year from him. . . The Two Ronnies, Messrs. Barker and Corbett.

AT LAST IT'S SIR CHARLIE

Charlie Chaplin is knighted in today's Honours List and so is another leading laughter-maker, P. G. Wodehouse, 93-year-old creator of Jeeves and Bertie Wooster and author of more than 90 humorous masterpieces. West Indian cricketer Gary Sobers and Dr Roger Bannister, the first man to run the mile in under 4 minutes, are also among the new knights.

Other honours include the award of Companion of Honour to Mr Jack Ashley – a rare tribute to a sitting MP. Mr Ashley has continued to represent Stoke-on-Trent even though he is now deaf. Jockey Lester Piggott, who has ridden 3,000 winners and won the Derby 6 times, gets the OBE; so do Willie Ormond, Scotland's soccer team boss, Bill Nicholson, ex-Spurs Manager and World Cup Final referee Jack Taylor. Showjumper Ann Moore and keepfit expert Eileen Fowler are among new MBEs. On the showbusiness side George Mitchell, creator of the Black and White Minstrels, is awarded an OBE and *Upstairs Downstairs* star Angela Baddeley, who plays Mrs Bridges, gets a CBE.

CAN THIS BULLET HIT THE TARGET?

It has the profile of 0.5lb of Cheddar and it is, they say, 'the shape of things to come'. It carries 2 people and the fairly critical responsibility for the coming shape of British Leyland Motors. The TR7 – or 'bullet' – is a nimble, wedge-shaped hard-top intended to challenge the Japanese- and German-dominated American sports-car market. It is the first British car ever launched and sold exclusively in a foreign country – it will not be available in Britain for at least a year – and it will be given the biggest ever promotion of any British car anywhere in the world.

£40m MOTHBALLS FOR THE CHANNEL TUNNEL

The Channel Tunnel was laid to rest in the Commons yesterday – at a cost of £40m. That is the amount to be paid in compensation to the companies who have already constructed 5 miles of access tunnels. Environment Secretary Mr Anthony Crosland said he held out some prospect that the scheme had only been put into mothballs for 10 or 15 years – by which time the wealth from North Sea Oil could give a new reality to the fantastically expensive project. He told MPs that he still believed the tunnel would be built 'in my lifetime'. He is 57.

I WILL WEAR CRASH HELMET – GREIG

Tony Greig plans to wear a protective batting helmet when Australia plays in the World Cup and 4 tests in England next summer. The day after Australia recaptured the Ashes with a bombardment of bouncers from Dennis Lillee and Jeff Thomson, England's 6 foot 7½ inch all-rounder said, 'When I get home I'm going to see if I can't design something to protect my skull.' In the 30s 'Patsy' Hendren batted in a crash helmet against a West Indies bumper trio of Constantine, Martindale and Griffith.

TOP GRAMMAR SCHOOL SAYS, 'WE GO IT ALONE'

Manchester Grammar School, one of the most famous routes to Oxbridge for working-class boys, is to go independent. The decision was forced onto the school by Labour's proposal to end the direct grant to 174 grammar schools. Most will be deciding in the next few months whether to risk going independent at a time of soaring inflation or to join the state comprehensive system. Present fees at Manchester Grammar are £351. What parents pay is on a sliding scale depending on their income. Those earning less than £1,000 a year pay no fees; those earning above about £6,500 pay the full fees. Manchester will go independent when the direct grant is withdrawn, probably by September next year. Fees for new entrants will jump to £460 and there will be no subsidies for any parent.

NEW TEST FOR BATSMAN BISHOP

David Sheppard, Bishop of Woolwich and former England cricket star, is to be the new Bishop of Liverpool. At 45 he will be the youngest Diocesan Bishop in the Church of England. As a cricketer David Sheppard played for England 22 times between 1950 and 1963. In 1968 when MCC did not pick Basil d'Oliveira to play against South Africa for fear he would not be welcome David Sheppard led the protests and the tour was cancelled. 12 years ago in a test at Melbourne, Sheppard, who had made 0 in the first innings, dropped a vital catch off Fred Trueman. The forthright Trueman said through gritted teeth, 'Put your hands together in the accustomed manner, Rev, and you might just hold on to the next one.' He went on to make 113 in the second innings. In Liverpool he succeeds the Right Reverend Stuart Blanch who is to be Archbishop of York when Dr Donald Coggan moves to Canterbury.

LABOUR'S NEW GIRL JOINS THE WHIPS

Margaret Jackson got a £2,750 rise yesterday and a new job – as a Labour Whip in the House of Commons. She is the third woman whip. Attractive 32-year-old Miss Jackson, who ousted Labour rebel Mr Dick Taverne at Lincoln in the October general election, joins Miss Betty Boothroyd as an assistant Government Whip. In the Lords the Chief Labour Whip is Baroness Llewellyn Davies. Miss Jackson, who will get £7,000 in her new job, compared with her previous MP's pay of £4,250, said last night, 'The more women are given jobs the more likely they will be taken seriously.' On Mrs Thatcher's bid for the Tory leadership she added, 'Well, anything that breaks fresh ground makes it easier for the women following.'

Rock superstars Led Zeppelin with Manager Peter Grant (centre).

LED ZEPPELIN WILL ROCK FLORIDA WITH THE BIGGEST SOUND SYSTEM IN HISTORY

The biggest, brightest and loudest pop concert of them all is soon to shatter the peace of West Palm Beach in Florida. Over 150,000 fans will be able to see and hear – perfectly – the British rock group Led Zeppelin up to a mile away. The concert will use a synchronized 70,000 watt sound system, said to be the biggest in history, to eliminate the normal problems of distortion and echoing. 310,000 watts' worth of lighting effects will also be the biggest ever seen at a concert.

But why all this for a group which has never even had a single in the British Top Ten? Led Zeppelin may not be big at home but it is one of our hottest exports. In America it has become something of a phenomenon; there have been riots this week in New York as fans fought for tickets for its shows. In the past Led Zeppelin has grossed more than £150,000 at a single concert. The biggest concert in the world should break that record, too.

BROTHER PLEADS FOR KIDNAPPED HEIRESS

The brother of kidnapped 17-year-old Lesley Whittle pleaded with her kidnappers for her safe return yesterday. Coach-firm boss Mr Ronald Whittle had carried out the demand in the £50,000 ransom note – to wait by 3 phone boxes in Kidderminster town centre between 6 p.m. and 1 a.m. – but no one turned up and nobody rang. Lesley vanished early on Tuesday morning from her home in Highley, Shropshire.

DAY BY DAY

1 Jan
Former Attorney General John Mitchell and Mr Nixon's aides H.R. Haldeman and John Ehrlichman are found guilty of conspiracy to obstruct justice. They are later sentenced to between 30 months and 8 years imprisonment for their part in the Watergate cover-up.

5 Jan
Part of the Tasman Bridge at Hobart crashes into the River Derwent after being rammed by a 7,200-ton freighter. The ship sinks with the loss of 5 lives; 8 people who were driving across the bridge are drowned.

9 Jan
Australia regain the Ashes after beating England by 171 runs in the fourth test at Sydney.

11 Jan
Russian spaceship *Soyuz 17* is launched and the following day docks with space station *Salyut 4*, which was put into orbit on 26 December. *Soyuz 17* returns to earth on 9 February.

13 Jan
Mr John Stonehouse indicates his intention of resigning as MP for Walsall North but is later advised by his Australian lawyer not to sign the official resignation document.

Restrictions on heating for non-domestic consumers and a ban on the use of electricity for illuminating advertising signs during daylight come into force.

Bunny Johnson, Jamaican-born boxer living in Birmingham, takes the British heavyweight title by knocking out Danny McAlinden in the ninth round of their championship fight in London.

20 Jan
6 members of the National Graphical Association are refused a High Court injunction restraining the *Daily Express*, *The Times*, the *Evening News* and the *Evening Standard* from issuing dismissal notices. The employers claimed that their contracts were broken after failure to give an undertaking not to continue industrial action in support of a 40p a week differential.

22 Jan
Charity stamps are sold by the Post Office for the first time. The stamps cost 6p: 4½p for first-class letter rate and 1½p to be divided among various charities.

24 Jan
Dr Donald Coggan is enthroned as 101st Archbishop of Canterbury.

29 Jan
Television licences are increased to £18 for colour and £8 for black and white sets.

JUDGES OPEN SOCCER'S DOOR FOR THE FOREIGN STARS

Foreign footballers are legally free to play in English soccer as the result of a judgement just given in the European Economic Community's highest court. The ruling made it clear that FA restrictions on the employment by English clubs of players from other Common Market countries are illegal, according to the Treaty of Rome. An FA rule prevents any foreign player from entering the English professional game without a 2-year residential qualification. FA Secretary Fred Croker said last night that no move was imminent to throw out this rule.

'STOP MAGGIE THATCHER'

Mrs Margaret Thatcher's bid for the Tory leadership is gathering so much momentum that near panic has broken out among the party's top people. The anti-Thatcher forces are now banking on a theory that even if Mr Heath fails to win the necessary confidence vote, he will mobilize enough support to block Mrs Thatcher. If Mr Heath is not ahead on the first ballot enormous pressure will be exerted to persuade him to step down in favour of a 'compromise' candidate. This must be Mr Whitelaw, and if he does not stand then Mr Jim Prior will, if only to head off a Thatcher coup by the right wing of the party. This is the hasty strategy devised in the face of Mrs Thatcher's unexpectedly successful bid for the leadership. It remains to be seen whether it will work.

UPROAR AS REBEL MPs WIN FIGHT FOR PENSIONERS

Pandemonium broke out in the Commons last night when a revolt by Labour MPs led to an embarrassing defeat for the Government – and a resignation. 9 Labour rebels joined forces with Tories and Liberals to demand the relaxation of the rule under which pensions are cut if the pensioner earns over £13 a week. It was the Government's first defeat in the Commons since the October general election. Within minutes of the vote Mr George Cunningham, Labour MP for Islington South and Finsbury, who has been a leading campaigner to get rid of the earnings rules altogether, resigned as Parliamentary Private Secretary to Education Secretary Mr Reg Prentice.

Young Tories Liz Jones and Gill Archer support Edward Heath's re-election as Tory part Leader.

FOREST MOVE FOR CLOUGH

Brian Clough will be back in football next week as the new Manager of Nottingham Forest – if he wants the job. The door opened yesterday when Allan Brown, Forest's Manager for the past 14 months, was sacked and walked into unemployment declaring 'it's obvious they want Cloughie, so good luck to them'.

FEB 1975

WHY THEY'RE SPENDING £22,000 TO PLAY NOUGHTS AND CROSSES

A big money quiz show is to replace *The Golden Shot* on ITV this summer. The show, *Celebrity Squares*, looks like a lavish version of the *Criss Cross Quiz* game axed by ITV 8 years ago. A giant 18-foot-high noughts and crosses board will be built in the studio at a cost of £22,000. In each of the 9 squares will sit a showbiz celebrity. Contestants will pick a square and the celebrity has to answer a question. Then the contestant decides whether the answer is right or wrong. The quiz is actually an anglicized version of *Hollywood Squares*, which has been running on American TV every day for 9 years.

Gary Glitter: One of the first stars to appear on ITV's innovative pop show Supersonic.

'IF ONLY MRS PANKHURST WERE HERE'

85-year-old former suffragette Mrs Nina Popplewell raised a glass of sherry last night and said, 'I'm not a Conservative but I think we should all celebrate.' She added, 'It's going to be hard for Mrs Thatcher, though, harder than for a man. If you're a woman you have got to be so much better at everything.' The Suffragettes' Fellowship still meets annually on Mrs Pankhurst's birthday, 14 July, and Mrs Pankhurst's niece, Mrs Enid Goulden Bach, is its chairman. Her comment about Mrs Thatcher's victory: 'There's nothing to make a fuss about; history is littered with the names of women who should have got to the top and whose talents were wasted.'

I WILL PAY THE TRIPLE KILLER

The brother of kidnapped heiress Lesley Whittle volunteered yesterday to go alone to meet the Black Panther, the most dangerous criminal in Britain, in an attempt to save the girl's life. Mr Whittle wants to meet the killer – nicknamed the Black Panther because of the black clothes and hood he wears during raids – to hand over the £50,000 ransom demanded for the safe return of 17-year-old Lesley. Mr Ronald Whittle made his offer although he knows the kidnapper has already murdered 3 times. Detectives are certain that he is the gunman who shot dead 3 postmasters during raids on sub-post offices and also gunned down a security guard.

An injured passenger is brought up after the crash at Moorgate station.

CAR TESTS GETTING TOUGHER

A stiffer annual test for cars is to be introduced by the Government soon. It will cost the motorist nearly double – £3 instead of £1.64. Extra tests will include chassis corrosion and shock absorbers as specific checks – until now they have been looked at only if they affect steering and safety. Screen washers and wipers will be checked for the first time and headlights will be tested for beam angle – at present they only have to be working. The new test is expected to be introduced this summer and then be stiffened still further in 1979 when all testing will be done off road.

VW CHALLENGES THE MINI WITH ITS 55-m.p.g. POLO

Volkswagen yesterday challenged for a slice of the Mini market when it unveiled its new model, the Polo. It is a high-economy, scaled-down version of its already popular Golf. The Polo will be launched at the Geneva Motor Show next month and will be on sale in Britain in the summer. VW says the price will also compete directly with the Mini, which costs from £1,099 including tax.

Jack Nicholson, Josip Elic and Will Sampson in Miloš Forman's award winning One Flew Over the Cuckoo's Nest.

BUT THE TORIES AREN'T THE ONLY ONES WITH A VITAL POLL

Playboy Club employees voted last night to decide whether they want a union to fight for them officially. At present 265 bunnies, croupiers and caterers are members of the Transport and General Workers' Union, but the Club does not negotiate with it. There was quite a lot at stake. Playboy's British boss Victor Lownes made it clear he would cut perks like staff parties, free meals and hairdos if the majority joined up. The result of the ballot: 422 to 192 against.

THE GREAT PORT FIDDLE

Interpol has been called in to investigate a port wine fiddle involving millions of bottles. It is feared that the whole of Portugal's non-vintage port production for 1971 and 1972 has been fortified with synthetic alcohol made from coal and oil products instead of the traditional grape brandy. The Portuguese were quick to emphasize that the contaminated port does not taste any different nor is it in any way a risk to health. The scandal, which came to light after routine tests in West German laboratories, could mean a great financial loss to wine merchants as the port cannot be marketed as a 'quality' wine, according to Common Market regulations.

Max Boyce is enjoying phenomenal success. His Live At Treorchy *album is riding high in the charts with sales of 120,000; EMI had said they would be pleased with 4000. One of the tracks, 'Hymns and Arias' has been adopted as the battle song of Welsh rugby supporters.*

Margaret Thatcher on air with Jimmy Young.

Now cool Maggie plans new purge

LABOUR'S CIVIL WAR BEGINS

Mr Harold Wilson said yes to Europe yesterday – and instant civil war broke out in the Cabinet. 7 senior ministers will now be fighting to stay out while the Premier leads the stay-in campaign. The 7 are: Trade Secretary Peter Shore, Industry Secretary Tony Benn, Social Services Secretary Barbara Castle, Employment Secretary Michael Foot, Energy Secretary Eric Varley, Scottish Secretary Willie Ross and Planning Minister John Silkin.

IT'S SCOTLAND THE RAVE! BY ANNE NIGHTINGALE

Scottish rock musicians are suddenly the hottest names anywhere. Most triumphant of all is the Average White Band from Dundee which currently celebrates a rare double, topping both the singles and album charts in America. From Edinburgh there's Pilot, a band which topped the British charts last month with 'January'. For Pilot's song-writing team of David Paton and Billy Lyall the band's success means that they're now challenging another Scottish outfit of which they were once a part – the Bay City Rollers.

Perhaps the most unpredictable success of all has happened for Billy Connolly, the dynamic, earthy Glasgow comedian. Once with the Humblebums, Billy found that his spoken introductions were getting better audience reactions than his singing, so gradually he spoke more and sang less. It has taken Alex Harvey 20 years to become an overnight success. With his current outfit, the Sensational Alex Harvey Band, this 40-year-old Glaswegian has now become the rage of the American rock scene. 3 years ago his brother Les, guitarist with Stone The Crows, was electrocuted on stage in Wales.

LESLEY FOUND STRANGLED

Yesterday, the body of 17-year-old Lesley Whittle was found lying in a few inches of water 60 feet down a reservoir shaft at a lonely beauty spot near Kidsgrove, Staffordshire. She had been strangled with wire – the fourth victim of the Black Panther, one of the most callous killers in the history of modern crime. With the discovery, one of the biggest ever kidnap hunts was dramatically transformed into an intense nationwide murder hunt. Police believe the body had been there for several weeks.

BEATEN BRITAIN TURNS TO SLADE

The BBC is now convinced that a Top 10 group must sing for Britain in next year's *Eurovision Song Contest*. This follows the success of a group with a discotheque sound for the second year running in Saturday's contest in Stockholm. Britain's entry from The Shadows came second behind the Dutch group Teach-In with 'Ding-A-Dong'. In fact the BBC did ask Slade to sing in Stockholm but at the time the group was too busy working on its film *Slade in Flame*.

GO-AHEAD FOR OIL RUSH

The Government last night lifted the threat to full development of North Sea Oil by fixing the special tax at 45% – lower than anybody expected. The Government was worried by repeated threats from the oil giants, many of them American-owned, that they would pull out altogether if they were not allowed to make good profits. Many had held up development work until the tax was fixed, prompting an angry response from some Labour left-wingers. Mr Dennis Skinner (Bolsover) said, 'This is little short of a sell-out to the blackmail by the oil companies.'

AND THE NEXT OBJECT IS. . . THE SACK

For Norman Hackforth the next object on *Twenty Questions* is the sack. After 18 years as the Radio 4 panel game's original Mystery Voice and 10 years on the panel itself he has been told his services are no longer required. Out with him go Peter Glaze, Peter Jones and Joy Adamson, who have been on the panel since 1950. The only survivor is founder member Anona Winn. In come satirist William Rushton, cricket commentator Brian Johnston and actress Bettine Le Beau. Taking over as chairman will be Terry Wogan; he follows Stuart McPherson, Gilbert Harding, Kenneth Horne and Peter Jones in that role. 'It is nice that people don't think of me as just a disc jockey,' said Mr Wogan.

Slade rehearsing at home.

T HITS BRITAIN

T means Trevira. This is the message that Hoechst is spreading with the launch of a massive new advertising campaign. Trevira, Europe's most advanced polyester fibre, has gained rapid recognition on the UK market since its début in 1967. The brand awareness among the A, B and C1 socio-economic groups has increased to a high level and the Trevira label has been received as a symbol of quality by the public. It is now an accepted brand name in both men's and women's fashion.

'I have promised to be faithful.' Rod Stewart with Britt Ekland.

IT'S A KNOCK OUT FOR TV 'CHEATS'

The organizers of television's oddball olympics *It's A Knock Out* are clamping down on gamesmanship and professionalism. Officials from the countries which stage the international version, *Jeux Sans Frontières*, have decided that a draw must be made to decide which team member takes part in a particular game. In past heats 1 team used a professional limbo dancer to go under hurdles; other teams have drafted in top athletes like Robbie Brightwell and Anne Packer and Leeds soccer star Johnny Giles.

THE BIRTH-CONTROL REVOLUTION

Family doctors are to provide a free contraceptive service for all women and girls, married or single, from July. The Government announced yesterday that it has settled a year-long wrangle with the doctors about how much they should be paid for the service, the first completely free universally available one in Western Europe. The fees are: £3.50 a year for each woman for whom the pill or the Dutch cap is prescribed and £10 for fitting an intra-uterine device like the loop or the coil. The scheme has no lower age limit, though doctors have the right to refuse contraception for any individual patient. It will be left to the doctors' discretion whether to do so for girls under 16, the age of consent. The GPs are refusing to provide free condoms for men; they say these are 'non-medical' devices.

RUGBY SKIPPER QUITS AT 16 IN FAVOUR OF SOCCER

Russell Osman captains England's schoolboys in today's Rugby Union International against Wales at Twickenham and then at 16 will retire from the game. Russell is giving up rugby to concentrate on soccer when he leaves Burton-On-Trent Grammar School in July. For the past 5 years rugby has dominated Russell's sporting activity, soccer being limited to an average of a dozen games a season. Several top clubs were interested in the youngster but Ipswich signed him on the recommendation of Tom Robson, Ipswich Manager Bobby Robson's brother, who lives near Russell's home.

THE RED FLAG FLIES OVER DA NANG

The Viet Cong flag today flies over Da Nang, second largest city in South Vietnam. One of the first buildings on which it was hoisted was the former headquarters of the American marines, who landed 10 years ago to be greeted rapturously as liberators. Communist tanks rumbled through the city, eyed with suspicion and fear by those South Vietnamese who failed to get away in the last panic-stricken rush. The North Vietnamese, who control virtually all of the upper half of Vietnam, are now free to thrust southward into the military region that includes Saigon.

John Stonehouse is arrested in Melbourne on an extradition warrant.

John Conteh

A SCHOOL REPORT TO DISTURB EVERY PARENT

A major drive to rid schools of illiteracy is proposed in a report published yesterday. A committee, chaired by Sir Alan Bullock, says evidence points to a decline in the literacy standard of 7- and 11-year-olds in the last 10 years. The report, entitled *A Language For Life*, concludes: 'Standards are not satisfying present-day requirements. . . it is not only employers who express dissatisfaction; further and higher education institutions often remark on the inability of their entrants to write correct and coherent English.' The report's main recommendations include:

- improved teacher training to ensure that all teachers know how to teach reading and English.
- a detailed reading policy in every school.
- better screening methods and more help for slow readers.
- big increases in the tuition available for adult illiterates.

The committee refused to back any particular reading scheme or method, and members were divided about the controversial Initial Teaching Alphabet. They discovered that this system, which uses a new phonetic spelling, was used in about 1 school in 10. The report says that the system can be successful in the right teachers' hands.

IT'S RADIO WESTMINSTER

MPs last night agreed to Parliament's being broadcast on radio as an experiment, but they again turned down television. The radio try-out will be for 4 weeks, probably soon after Easter – in time for the important Common Market referendum debate. Although the move to bring in TV has failed for the fourth time in 9 years, its supporters hope that a successful radio experiment will lead MPs to think again. Opposition Leader Mrs Margaret Thatcher led those voting against TV.

APR 1975

DISASTER – BUT AIR LIFT GOES ON

A stunned President Ford yesterday pledged that America's Operation Babylift from Vietnam goes on despite the fateful beginning when a plane carrying orphans crashed in flames. The President said that the tragedy, in which it is feared half the 243 children aboard died, 'must not deter us from offering new hope to the living'. The plane was a C5A Galaxy Cargo Jet, the biggest in the world, making the first flight from Saigon in the operation to ferry out 2,000 orphans who have adoptive homes waiting in America.

Daily Mail

WEDNESDAY, APRIL 30, 1975   6p

MONEY MAIL TODAY

Frightened, abandoned and waiting for its fate... that is Saigon as 30 years of war reach a climax with a Dunkirk in the Sky

THE END

JOHN EDWARDS
Mail man on the spot reports from Saigon

THE Americans went out the way only they could.

They staged an aerial spectacular, a Dunkirk in the sky that went on all day and deep into the flare-ridden night. It was the biggest one-way trip in air history.

They went in their king-sized choppers'... Green Giants... Hueys and Chinooks. And they went fast, loading and pushing their way into the big birds, with the curses of the Vietnamese ringing in their ears.

It was farewell from the broken, abandoned army of the Republic of Vietnam with fusillades of automatic fire, triggered as much in contempt as in anger.

Now there's nobody left in town more. Except the Vietnamese for whom there's no way out.

They crouch in a Saigon like it has never been—still and frightened. Abandoned and waiting for its fate.

Pleading

What that fate will be we will know few days or hours when the new ns arrive. Big Minh's government national surrender are desperately

Stairway to safety... Americans and refugees clamber to an airlift helicopter

TIME FOR A SHOPPING SPREE

Britain's biggest-ever shopping stampede will start today because the Chancellor's new 25% VAT rate on luxury goods does not take effect until 1 May. This gives shoppers time to take advantage of the old 8% VAT rate on goods like fur coats, cameras, hi-fi and colour televisions. Many retailers were predicting a boom fortnight until the change comes into effect. However, one boss commented, 'This is the biggest closing-down sale the world has ever seen... come 1 May the boom will be over, factories will go on short time because demand will have been met for many months to come.'

NEW LIMIT AT DEAD-END STATIONS

Tube drivers have been ordered to slow trains to 15 m.p.h. when entering stations like Moorgate. There are 65 dead-end stations in London's Underground system. At Moorgate the driver Leslie Newson's train hit the buffers at an estimated 35–40 m.p.h. Now drivers are being ordered to stop outside at a signal until they know it is safe to proceed. Meanwhile a fourth expert has been called in to try to solve the riddle of whether Newson, who was killed in the Moorgate disaster, had been drinking.

Edward Heath speaking in favour of EEC membership at a Tory meeting on the Common Market; seated left is Margaret Thatcher.

FROM REP TO RICHES – THE FILM *CINDERELLA*

As Cinderella stories go, it's not a bad one. Unknown actress is spotted in a provincial pantomime by a big movie producer. From 200 auditioned she lands the starring role in a £2m musical version of *Cinderella* which will undoubtedly be the most expensive British film of 1975. It's the sort of story film publicists dream of and it has all come true for Gemma Craven. Now her name will go above Dame Edith Evans, Margaret Lockwood and Christopher Gable when the credits roll. Director Bryan Forbes said, 'In 30 years I have never seen a better first take at a screen test. She is magic.'

VAUXHALL GOES FOR A WORLD BEATER – AT 54P A GALLON

A new car being developed by Vauxhall to run on diesel fuel could become the country's most outstanding economy model. Diesel cars have not caught on with private motorists because they are noisy, sluggish and expensive to buy, but Vauxhall hopes to iron out many of the faults. Vauxhall has just launched its high-economy petrol-engined Chevette, a 2-door saloon powered by a 1256cc Viva engine; the same engine is being modified to become the world's smallest mass-produced diesel engine, as small as 1 litre.

British Leyland is also developing diesel engines. A spokesman said last night, 'We've got a diesel engine or two on the shelf because we think it prudent; when North Sea Oil starts coming ashore it will produce relatively more diesel fuel than petrol.' Diesel fuel, carrying less tax than petrol, costs between 54 and 56p a gallon; petrol costs up to 76p.

ITV ORDERS OFF CLOUGH AND CO

ITV's panel of football pundits has been given the boot from ITV's coverage of this year's FA Cup Final. Since the panel was first assembled for the 1970 World Cup it has included Brian Clough, Malcolm Allison, Jackie Charlton, Derek Dougan and Pat Crerand. Mr John Bromley, *World of Sport* Executive Producer, said yesterday, 'As a group of people the panel has talked itself out; it is our view that such a panel has now had its day.'

Going to work on an egg. . . Butch Wilkins, captain of relegation strugglers Chelsea.

HAIL THE CONQUERORS!

For Phnom Penh, its brave defenders battered and bewildered by 3½ months of bitter siege, the end came swiftly yesterday. Only time will tell if the end has come mercifully. For the Khmer Rouge, whose victory was built on terror tactics as much as skilful strategy, were expected to wreak bloody vengeance on the obstinate city. Yesterday white flags and banners blossomed from every office building and shop as the jubilant Khmer Rouge moved among the people. There were signs that at long last Cambodian had tired of killing Cambodian; some insurgent troops actually embraced their enemies. Last night, however, there were fears that the Khmer Rouge would soon show that they had not moved in as peaceful liberators. The occupation of the capital was only a few hours old when a rebel radio went on the air to warn 'We enter Phnom Penh as conquerors; we have not come here to speak about peace with traitors.'

Meg and Hugh (Noele Gordon and John Bentley) outside the Birmingham Register Office after their wedding in Crossroads.

SMOKING BEAGLES CARRY ON PUFFING, SAYS HEAD OF ICI

Animal lovers yesterday failed to stop ICI using beagle dogs for research into cigarette smoking. Responding to complaints from some shareholders at the company's annual meeting, retiring Chairman Sir Jack Callard insisted that there was no alternative to using animals to discover if a new smoking material was toxic to humans. Shouts of 'Rubbish' greeted Sir Jack's statement that the dogs did not suffer any cruelty and were not distressed. He said that several thousand animals, mostly rats and mice, were used in experiments; there were 48 dogs involved in smoking tests. Spike Milligan joined an angry band of animal lovers in a protest outside the Dorchester Hotel, London, where the meeting was held.

THE FIRST DR WHO DIES

Actor William Hartnell, television's original Dr Who, died in hospital yesterday. He was 67. Hartnell was a familiar face to 2 generations of Britons. It was at the age of 55 in 1963 that he became a hero to millions of children as the eccentric time traveller. At first there were predictions that the programme would run for only 6 weeks but Hartnell had the part for 3 years. Previously he had played a string of hard-nosed characters – NCOs, foremen and others – leading to the part of Sergeant Major Bullimore in ITV's *The Army Game*.

DEATH TRAP GRAND PRIX

The motor race the drivers wanted to ban ended appallingly yesterday with just the kind of tragedy they feared. 4 people were killed at the Spanish Grand Prix when a car bounced 40 feet in the air off one of the Barcelona circuit's controversial safety barriers and landed in the crowd. It was because of the condition of the barriers that all but one of the drivers refused to practise on Friday, saying the circuit was a death trap for them and the spectators.

England and Newcastle footballer Malcolm MacDonald becomes the first player to score 5 goals for England at Wembley.

DAY BY DAY

3 Apr
President Ford, whose plans for military aid to South Vietnam were vetoed by Congress, announces the intention to airlift orphaned children to the US.

5 Apr
The Grand National is won by L'Escargot. Red Rum, winner for the past 2 years, finishes second. Chinese Nationalist leader Chiang Kai-shek dies, aged 87.

9 Apr
The House of Commons votes in favour of a government motion recommending continued membership of the EEC by a majority of 226. Mr Eric Heffer is dismissed as Minister of State for Industry for defying a Cabinet ruling that ministers should not speak against the Government's recommendation in Parliament. Of the 170 MPs who voted against the motion, 145 were Labour.

10 Apr
The Government announces that the referendum on EEC membership will take place on 5 June.

13 Apr
Jack Nicklaus wins the US Masters Golf Championship for a record fifth time.

15 Apr
VAT on luxury goods raised from 8% to 25% and road fund licences up from £25 to £40 are among the measures in Mr Healey's Budget.

16 Apr
Malcolm MacDonald becomes the first player to score 5 goals for England at Wembley when England beat Cyprus 5–0.

23 Apr
The House of Commons votes against the Government's plan for a national declaration of the EEC referendum result and in favour of a county by county result.

24 Apr
It is announced that the Government is to take a majority shareholding in British Leyland.

25 Apr
The West German Embassy in Stockholm is blown up by terrorists after their demand for the release of 26 members of the Baader-Meinhof gang held in German prisons was refused.

In the first free elections in Portugal for 50 years the 3 main non-Communist parties win a large majority in the new Assembly.

30 Apr
The South Vietnamese Government announces an unconditional surrender to the Vietcong.

OH BROTHER, LOOK WHAT THEY'RE IN FOR NOW. . .

The Brothers comes back for another series minus 2 of its leading ladies from past programmes – Ann has finally walked out on Brian and Jill has been killed in a car crash. But there is a new girl; next month fiery redhead Kate O'Mara will join the board of Hammond Brothers.

MAY 1975

BAY CITY ROLLERS RIOT: 100 HURT

40 girls had to be rescued from a lake yesterday after they plunged in to follow their pop idols the Bay City Rollers. Another 100 fans were injured during the BBC-sponsored Fun Day at Mallory Park, Leicestershire, which featured pop and motor racing by disc jockeys. When the chart-topping Bay City Rollers were ferried across a lake from an island in the centre of the racetrack they were mobbed. The Rollers have had 6 hit records in 16 months to become the teenyboppers' favourite group. 'Bye Bye Baby', which topped the charts last month, has sold 1 million records.

EX-BLACK POWER CHIEF MICHAEL X IS EXECUTED

Michael Malik, who as Michael X dominated London's Black Power movement, was hanged for murder yesterday. His execution at the Royal Jail, Port of Spain, Trinidad, marked the end of a 3-year fight to save him from the gallows. His final appeal was rejected by the Privy Council in London early this month. On Wednesday the Queen signed the order allowing the execution. Trinidad-born Malik fled from Britain in 1971 to escape robbery and blackmail charges after 20 years in the country.

BABOON KEPT A BABY ALIVE

Doctors linked a baby's heart, lungs and kidneys to a baboon in an attempt to save his life. 13-month-old Scott Malloy, critically ill with a congenital heart defect, was kept alive for 16 hours before the strain of maintaining 2 circulatory systems killed the baboon; Scott died shortly afterwards at Harefield Hospital, Middlesex. The operation was led by the hospital's chief cardio-thoracic surgeon, Mr Magdy Yacoub, who was one of the pioneers in Mr Donald Ross's heart-swap team. The baboon was chosen because it has similar organs to man and man can function with baboon blood.

Eric Faulkner (left) and Les McKeown of the Bay City Rollers.

A WINNING DUO

Sharing top billing at the Ivor Novello Awards in London were Vera Lynn, still remembered as the Forces Sweetheart, and Lynsey de Paul, who wasn't even born when the hit of the day was 'We'll Meet Again'. Vera's award was for 'outstanding services to the British musical industry'. Lynsey received hers as the composer of 'No, Honestly', written for the TV comedy series, which was named the best among film, radio or television themes. The best-selling record was 'Tiger Feet', written by Nicky Chinn and Mike Chapman.

LUDMILLA 'WAS NOT READY'

The shock defeat of Russia's world champion gymnast Ludmilla Turischeva in the European Championships in Norway was due to lack of training through injury, says her coach. It was her first defeat in international events in 5 years. Ludmilla's main rival in Soviet gymnastics, Olga Korbut, did not compete because of a leg injury. Her stand-in, Nelli Kim, was second overall behind 13-year-old Rumanian Nadia Comaneci.

BAYI MILE BEST YET

Filbert Bayi cut the world mile record to 3 minutes 51 seconds in Kingston, Jamaica, at the weekend and convinced top coaches that the 3-minute 50-second barrier can be broken this year. The Tanzanian clipped one tenth of a second off American Jim Ryun's 8-year-old mark and looked capable of being yards faster.

Mr Roy Jenkins, Home Secretary, speaking at the pro-Common Market 'Britain in Europe' conference in London's Waldorf Hotel; seated left is Lord (Vic) Feather.

PRESSES ROLL AT NEW DAILY

A teacher pushed the start button of a printing press last night and launched the *Scottish Daily News*. The teacher, who bought the first share in the workers' co-operative which is producing the paper, was one of a number of guests at last night's celebrations including Mr Wedgwood Benn, the Industry Minister, and millionaire publisher Mr Robert Maxwell. The paper, run by former Beaverbrook newspaper staff, has been launched 13 months after they were declared redundant when the company's Scottish printing operation was closed.

THATCHER PLAYS IT COOL ON EUROPE

Mrs Margaret Thatcher talked with French President Giscard D'Estaing yesterday on her first official visit as Leader of the Opposition to a foreign Head of State. If the French President hoped that she would use the opportunity to give a declaration of enthusiasm for the Common Market's long-range goals, he was disappointed. Mrs Thatcher was extremely cautious about expressing her views on an ultimate European Government or even the halfway step of economic and monetary union of the 9 countries.

IT'S ADOPTION LINE ANNA

Anna Ford starts a controversial new job this week, finding homes for thousands of unwanted children. The 32-year-old sociology graduate will present a new ITV programme – the first regular series offering children for adoption. 10 youngsters representing the 90,000 unwanted in Britain will be shown to viewers during the next 12 weeks. The new series, part of the Granada *Reports* programme, will be screened only in the North-west but will be monitored by TV producers all over the country.

F.A. Cup Final: Fulham 0 West Ham 2

COURT BATTLE OVER CUP BOOTS

Fulham's footballers will have to wait until just before the kick-off today to find out what boots they can wear in the FA Cup Final. Stylo Matchmakers International claims that the players broke an agreement to wear only its football boots this season. The Yorkshire firm applied in the High Court yesterday for an injunction restraining Fulham from wearing any other boots. The agreement also provided that if Fulham reached the Cup Final Stylo would pay them £2,000. This sum was actually paid to the club on 12 April. Last week Stylo learned that its boots were not being worn, that the players had no intention of wearing them for the Final, and the £2,000 had been returned. Mr Justice Walton adjourned the case to allow the players to be represented at 10.30 this morning.

LAW LORDS RULE ON RAPE

A man cannot be convicted of rape if he honestly believed the woman consented to intercourse – and it does not matter how unreasonable his belief was. This legal principle emerged yesterday in a House of Lords ruling on the 'mental element' of rape. Lord Cross of Chelsea said the question was whether a man could be said to have committed rape if he believed a woman was consenting to the intercourse 'and he would not have attempted to have it but for his belief, whatever his grounds for so believing'. Lord Cross said, 'I do not think that he can. Rape to my mind imports at least indifference as to the woman's consent.'

ONION WIZARD CRYING ALL THE WAY TO THE BANK

The man who took the tears out of peeling onions was wearing a £530,000 smile yesterday. That was the settlement for inventor Leslie Parsons after a 70-day High Court case. He had sued engineering firm Mather & Platt, claiming they had been incompetent in developing and marketing his onion-peeling machine. He began work on the invention 20 years ago and eventually developed a commercial machine which could top and tail onions and separate the skin. It was hailed as a breakthrough in the trade and widely patented.

THE BUBBLE BURSTS FOR BABYCHAM AND POMAGNE

Some of the sparkle went out of 2 British companies yesterday. A judge banned them from using the word champagne to promote their drinks of Pomagne and Babycham. Mr Justice Whitford also severely criticized the 2 firms – Bulmers of Hereford and Showerings of Shepton Mallet, Somerset – and said they hoped to deceive the British public into thinking that their products were real champagne. The 22-day hearing was the result of an action brought in 1970 by Bulmers and Showerings against 2 champagne houses, Bollinger and Champagne Lanson Père Et Fils, representing the Champagne area of France. The 2 British companies argued that the descriptions 'Champagne Perry' and 'Champagne Cider' had been used for so long that the champagne houses could no longer complain about their usage. Bulmers had used the word champagne for 100 years and Showerings for 35.

JUNE 1975

SECOND BRITON IN UGANDA FACES DEATH SENTENCE

A Ugandan military tribunal yesterday sentenced 61-year-old British lecturer Denis Hills to death by firing squad – and President Amin threatened the same fate for another Briton on trial. Amin warned that if Stanley Smolen, 38, is found guilty on the charge of hoarding cooking oil, he, too, would face the firing squad 'because his case of economic sabotage is as serious as treason'. The warning came hours after Mr Hills – suffering from cancer and given only a year to live by his doctor – was convicted of treason. His crime: a few sentences in the manuscript of an unpublished book called *The White Pumpkin*. The offensive words which sent General Amin into a rage were: 'Because of Amin all prejudices against the black man have arisen again to the surface. He has done harm to his people and, from his tiny territory, to the cause of Africa as a whole in that, governing like a village tyrant by fear, he has reimposed on Ugandans all the habits of submission and servility that one hoped Uhuru (freedom) was eroding.'

A COMIC GENIUS

Tom Sharpe gets on his bicycle at 6 every morning and cycles across Cambridge to write in a garden shed he rents for £13 a month. Not the usual picture of the writer at work but Tom Sharpe, hailed as a comic genius in the Waugh and Wodehouse tradition, considers his way of life infinitely preferable to 'those accursed Liberal Studies' he taught at the local technical college when he wrote his first book at the age of 40, 7 years ago. He is being supported financially by his publisher, Secker & Warburg, to enable him to write full-time. His last novel, *Blott on the Landscape*, made the bestseller lists. Next year's book is about 'a poor little guy who works at the tech' but he stresses it is not set in Cambridge. He has reason to affirm that none of the characters 'resemble real people, living or dead'. He has just had to pay undisclosed damages to television producer Christopher Cuthbertson over his novel *Porterhouse Blue*, set in an imaginary Cambridge college. He made up 'this incredible name' to represent – would you believe – a television producer.

Sybil Fawlty (Prunella Scales) and husband Basil (John Cleese) in Fawlty Towers.

FIRST NORTH SEA OIL FLOWS

Britain's motorists will be filling up with the first North Sea petrol in a few weeks. At 12.35 yesterday a valve was opened on the Transworld 58 rig sited in the Argyle Field 225 miles off Edinburgh and the first gallons of home-produced oil were pumped into a waiting tanker. In 5 days, with 12,000 tons aboard, the tanker will sail for the BP refinery on the Isle of Grain in the Thames Estuary; 15 days after unloading the petrol will be on sale at garage pumps.

GRAND PRIX CARS MUST CLIP WINGS

Racing cars are to have their wings clipped to take some of the danger out of Grand Prix events. The ban on wings, which starts next year, is being imposed to reduce speeds through corners, which have become 'too perilous'. The decision, announced by the ruling body of motor sport, the International Sporting Commission, means that drivers will have less grip through bends and will have to take them slower, though they will be faster down the straights.

Roy Jenkins speaking in a televised debate on Britain's first national referendum.

PROTESTORS WARNED

6 Sikh motor-cyclists wearing turbans, who headed a Coventry protest over the crash-helmet law, have been served with notices of intended prosecution by police for not wearing helmets.

Counting at Earls Court – like a gargantuan whist drive.

DAY BY DAY

1 June
Rhodesian police shoot dead 13 Africans during a riot in Salisbury outside a meeting of the African National Council Executive.

2 June
Snow stops play in county cricket matches at Buxton and Colchester. It is the first time for more than 80 years that sleet and snow is so widely reported in June.

4 June
Grundy wins the Derby.

5 June
The Suez Canal is reopened to shipping by President Sadat.
The first national referendum in Britain results in a 2 to 1 majority in favour of staying in the Common Market. Only 2 of the 68 voting areas, Shetland and the Western Isles, vote against continued membership.

9 June
Proceedings of the House of Commons are broadcast live for the first time on radio.

12 June
Greece applies for EEC membership.

19 June
A verdict of murder by the Earl of Lucan is returned at the inquest on Mrs Sandra Rivett, nanny to his 3 children.

21 June
The West Indies win the Prudential World Cup, beating Australia by 17 runs in the final at Lord's.

25 June
The Portuguese East African territory of Mozambique becomes independent.

26 June
Peter Bottomley, 30, wins the Woolwich West by-election for the Conservatives, leaving the Government with a majority of 1 – that 1 being the absent Mr John Stonehouse.

A state of emergency is declared in India and more than 670 political opponents of Mrs Gandhi are arrested following criticism of the Prime Minister after her conviction for electoral malpractices.

27 June
An Anglo-American-Canadian consortium buys the assets of Aston Martin for just over £1m.

28 June
Mrs Jacqueline Tabick is ordained the first woman rabbi in Britain.

HONOUR FOUGHT PROFUMO

John Profumo, centre of the most sensational sex and security scandal this century, today officially regained his self-respect. 12 years to the month that he quit in shame as Minister of War he has been honoured with the CBE. His name appears on the Queen's Birthday Honours List on the recommendation of Mr Harold Wilson for his work among the deprived of London's East End; it expresses the admiration of his former colleagues for the way he chose to pay back the debt he believed he owed society.

'VENGEANCE BOMBERS'

The IRA slaughtered 21 people in 2 pub explosions in Birmingham to avenge the death of 1 of their lieutenants, a jury was told yesterday. Even before their bombs went off, it was alleged, 5 members of a 'vengeance squad' were on their way home to their friend's funeral, playing cards and in 'a jolly mood' on the train to Belfast. The pub victims were sacrificed to 'commemorate' James McDade who blew himself up trying to wreck a telephone exchange, said the prosecution. It was while his body was being taken back to Ireland that the bombs were planted at the Mulberry Bush and the Tavern in the Town. Yesterday 9 Irishmen went on trial, 6 accused of murder.

AIR SEATS CAN BE SOLD TWICE

Airlines who deliberately overbook flights to make sure all seats are filled cannot be prosecuted under the Trade Descriptions Act, 3 High Court judges ruled yesterday. The verdict reverses a decision last year by magistrates at Stockport, Cheshire, when British Airways was fined £250. BA was taken to court by a businessman after a confirmed booking proved to be overbooked and he was forced to wait for the next flight. Lord Widgery, the Lord Chief Justice, said the act related to a false or misleading statement made about a service already given; an advance booking was a future promise of a service and the act did not apply.

COLIN COWDREY RETIRES

The end of the season brings a close to Colin Cowdrey's illustrious cricketing career. Cowdrey, 42 in December, played in more tests (114) and played more test innings (188) than any other cricketer; he also scored more runs (7,624) and held more catches (124). Wally Hammond (7,249 runs) and Sir Gary Sobers (117 catches) came nearest to him with the bat and in the field. He captained England 27 times and led Kent from 1957 to 1971 after making his début for the county in 1950. Cowdrey was awarded the CBE in 1972.

JULY 1975

A £6 GAMBLE ON BRITAIN

Harold Wilson yesterday produced a brand new device for enforcing his £6 pay limit – 'phantom' reserve statutory powers. Many had expected immediate legislation which the Government could invoke overnight to forbid individual pay settlements. Instead the Government will next week publish a draft bill but will not risk its Commons majority by asking MPs to make it law; that hurdle will only be attempted if 'the pay limit is endangered' by a union smashing the £6 barrier.

BACK HOME – TO THE CELLS

John Stonehouse and his secretary Mrs Sheila Buckley were back in Britain and behind bars last night. After their arrival from Australia Stonehouse was charged on 21 counts alleging forgery, fraud, theft and conspiracy. Mrs Buckley was accused on 5 charges of theft and 1 of conspiracy to defraud. It was the end of 7 months of bitter battling with Scotland Yard and the Australian and British Governments following Stonehouse's discovery and arrest in Melbourne on Christmas Eve after disappearing in Miami on 20 November.

HOW WILL THEY RATE ERIC AND ERN NOW?

After years of bickering over the reliability of each other's audience research methods, the BBC and ITV have at long last agreed to conduct joint research into our viewing and listening habits. A prime example of their wildly conflicting claims is the *Morecambe and Wise Show* screened on Christmas Day 1973. The BBC claimed it had an audience of 24.5 million; ITV said it was only seen by 16 million. Now, both organizations have agreed to a trial audience research method in which selected viewers will be asked to keep daily diaries of what they watched the night before. Until now the BBC has carried out its own research with street interviews, while ITV uses electronic meters attached to TV sets to arrive at their statistics.

WHODUNNIT? DETECTIVES HEMPEL AND HAGGERTY AT YOUR SERVICE

As detectives, blonde actress Anouska Hempel and actor Patrick Mower have impeccable records. Patrick won his colours in criminology as Detective Chief Inspector Haggerty of ITV's *Special Branch* and before that in the ITV *Callan* series. Anouska's record is less dramatic but more real. When valuable antiques were stolen from her London home earlier this year, she recovered them with a spot of do-it-yourself sleuthing. All of which explains why she and Patrick were automatic choices in a new series of Thames TV's crime quiz series *Whodunnit?*

The famous double act in their opening routine for The Morecambe and Wise Show.

Part of the terracotta army unearthed last year near the tomb of Qin Shi Huang in Shaanxi Province, China. The warriors, each bearing a different face, are said to have been made over 2000 years ago to protect the Emperor after his death.

THE WINNING WATER-BABE

Mike Hazelwood, 17-year-old part-time potato grower and European Junior Water-skiing Champion, is a leading member of Britain's latest group of sporting élite. At Ruislip Lido yesterday he helped Britain beat France and set a national record in the slalom – 4 buoys better than the 22 established by Paul Seaton. However, Seaton, the European Senior Champion, won the jumping and tricks events and so made a major contribution to Britain's victory.

THE HUNT FOR THE JACKAL

The Jackal is on the run. The international assassin whose murderous professionalism matches any fictional killer's, was being hunted across the world last night, 5 days after he brutally gunned down 3 men in Paris. His London lair, stocked with an arsenal of weapons, was raided yesterday by Scotland Yard as the full astonishing story of the man operating in the capital as Carlos Martinez began to emerge.

OH PETER! OH JANE! MS IS SO UPSET

Peter is a male chauvinist pig and the wretched Jane is brainwashed into being docile. The mythical brother and sister who star in the Ladybird series of books, used in hundreds of schools to teach children to read, are under attack by one of the country's biggest unions. The National and Local Government Officers' Association claims the books 'are well known for their sexist bias'. NALGO is also not keen on the Janet and John books, another series widely used in schools. A member of the working party that made the study, Ms (as she prefers) Ruth Lister, said, 'The books show the little boys doing traditionally adventurous things while the little girls stay at home helping Mummy with the housework.' Ms Lister is also unhappy about the middle-class settings of the 2 series. Peter and Jane particularly come under attack for living in a detached surburban house with integral garage complete with car, which Peter helps Daddy clean while Jane sits in the passenger seat.

BYE BYE, BIBA. IT'S MARKS & SPENCER NOW

The most beautiful department store in the world closes this autumn. The retail operation moving into Biba's Kensington High Street premises will be a far cry from the ostrich feathers and Art Nouveau: it will be dear old Marks & Sparks. The big surprise, however, is the announcement that Biba will continue to trade in a reduced area, probably on the ground floor. The thought of Biba and Marks & Spencer together seems startling – rather like putting a disco in the corner of the Athenaeum.

RED TAPE PUTS MILK DOWN THE DRAIN

A farmer yesterday blamed government red tape for forcing him to pour away 3,500 gallons of milk even though a national shortage is threatened. Mr Neil Cox, who farms near Henley-on-Thames, is 1 of 8,724 milk-producing farmers who joined a Common Market scheme which offered them cash grants if they switched from dairy herds to beef cattle. The farmers, who get about £100 for each cow sold, paid out of Government and Market funds, were given until last month to complete the switch; to collect their grants they had to stop selling milk on 30 June. Mr Cox has arranged to sell his herd, but not until 24 July. He may have to waste another 8,500 gallons before then. The milk that has already gone down the drain could have made 30 cwt. of cheese and earned Mr Cox more than £1,000. The scheme started in 1973 when most EEC countries had too much milk.

Arthur Ashe in action.

FALDO STAYS AN AMATEUR

Even though new English champion Nick Faldo's kind of talent is desperately needed in the professional ranks, he has no immediate plans to play for money. The 18-year-old giant from Welwyn Garden City, who is already being hailed as the 'new Oosty', intends to defend his amateur title next year. If there is any pressure to turn professional, then it could be because of the high price of amateur golf. He said after the final, 'I came to St Anne's at the beginning of the week with £108; I've £10 left and still haven't bought the petrol to get home.' Faldo is not the new Oosty. He is better than Peter Oosterhuis was at this age and even now 6 foot 3 Nick has the kind of text-book swing for which Oosty still searches.

THE LAW: POWERLESS TO MOVE INTRUDERS FROM YOUR HOME

The law on squatting which actually comes down on the side of the law-breakers is bizarre. The 1381 Forceable Entry Act, which says that a person can only enter a property 'in a peaceable and easy manner', applies to the owner of a property as well as the intruder. Squatters who manage to get into a house without using force, through an open window for example, cannot be legally ejected by force. The only offence they have committed is 'trespass', which is a civil matter and has nothing to do with the police. Only if squatters cause damage or steal from the house can the police act; even then the police always err on the side of caution. If they break into a house and find nothing damaged they themselves can be prosecuted by the squatters. The Law Commission is expected to recommend the repeal of the Forceable Entry Act, replacing it with prison sentences for people who enter property by force or who refuse to leave when ordered out by the owner.

Solicitor David Wiltshire was restoring a property in Bath when squatters moved in. Being aware of the Statute of Forceable Entry, he contacted a CID friend who put him in touch with a climber – legal slang for a burglar. When the squatters were out and the windows had been left open, the climber went up a drainpipe and let Mr Wiltshire in. He moved all the squatters' baggage outside and changed the locks in the house. He had, in effect, squatted on the squatters.

AT MIDNIGHT A MILLION PEOPLE LOST THEIR PAST

A disturbing new piece of legislation went onto the Statute Book at midnight last night. The title of the act could not be more benign, The Rehabilitation of Offenders Act, 1974. The intentions of those who framed it could not be more honourable – to give convicted felons the opportunity of wiping the slate clean. Quite simply it allows a person to keep secret past convictions provided they have gone straight for 10 years after receiving a prison sentence of less than 30 months. It means that a million people will be able to hide their past criminal convictions.

Mr Denis Hills taking his leave of President Amin on his return to Britain.

AUG 1975

JUST WATCH THAT SPACE, MR TARBUCK

How many motorists realize that they are breaking the law by repositioning digits on car number plates? For example, Jimmy Tarbuck, owner of COM 1C, could be fined if the figures on his Rolls-Royce number plate were changed to COMIC. Housewife Mrs Winifred Taylor has just been fined £5 for wrongly spaced registration marks. Her car number plate read 004 004; it should have been 00 4004. In fact she got off lightly; the maximum fine for such an offence is £100.

This is not the only odd law. Indicators have to 'wink' at the legal rate of 90 flashes per minute plus or minus 30, which is a complicated way of saying that they must operate at between 60 and 120 flashes per minute or you can be fined up to £100. Your car's headlights, dipped and main beam, must balance, meaning that bulbs on each side must be of equal power or you can be fined up to £100. The 1 mm legal minimum of tread must cover three-quarters of the width of each tyre or you could be fined up to £400 for each faulty tyre. Then, there is your licence: it must be signed by you or you can be fined up to £50.

LEYLAND DEAL IS SUICIDAL, SAYS MP

British Leyland's decision to supply equipment and skilled know-how to a new Korean firm of motor manufacturers – potential competitors – was denounced by an MP yesterday. Mr Douglas Hoyle, Labour MP for Nelson and Colne, called the deal with Hyundai Motors 'suicidal madness'. A BL spokesman pointed out that if BL hadn't accepted the contract it would probably have gone to the Japanese and Hyundai would have built their cars just the same.

THE DREAM THAT TURNED INTO A NIGHTMARE FOR BRITAIN

British motor-cycles were supreme throughout the world in 1960 when an ex-Japanese army mechanic called Honda had the nerve to offer an impudent intruder for sale: a 250cc machine called The Dream. The Dream became a forerunner of the nightmare flood of small-capacity Japanese motor-cycles which, by 1968, had almost taken over this section of the British market. Belated attempts to compete with the invaders were disastrous and by 1973 the British industry had been reduced to a 3-factory conglomerate of Norton, Villiers, Triumph. Even this was one factory too many and the Meriden factory was ordered to be closed down. The workers rebelled and finally persuaded Mr Benn to create a co-operative backed by £5m of tax-payers' money; but the Government dealt a near-fatal blow to the industry last night, deciding it was not worth spending £50m to keep NVT factories at Small Heath and Wolverhampton going.

BANNED – THOSE SEXY SMOKERS IN ADVERTS

Tobacco manufacturers have agreed to keep sex, glory and youth out of cigarette adverts. Under a new voluntary code announced yesterday, cigarettes must not be seen to make people better lovers, more courageous, more relaxed or better at their jobs. Smoking should not be seen as natural or non-smokers as abnormal, says the code. Famous people or social groups who attract special admiration should not feature in adverts and actors who do should clearly be over 25. Adjectives such as 'clean' or 'pure' will be banned and no more than half the people in any group seen on adverts should be smoking. The new code will not affect cigar- or pipe-smoking.

MUNICH DISASTER PILOT DIES

Captain James Thain, pilot of the Manchester United plane which crashed in Munich 17 years ago, died yesterday. He was 53. Captain Thain never flew again after the crash which killed 23 people, including 8 United players. He became a chicken farmer and died at his farmhouse in Berkshire. Captain Thain was sacked by BEA and lost his pilot's licence after the crash but fought to prove his theory that it was caused by slush on the runway. In June 1969 – 11 years and 4 enquiries later – he was vindicated by a House of Commons report which endorsed his theory.

ORIENT EXPRESS CASE ACE DIES

Agatha Christie has been concealing the death of her most famous detective, Hercule Poirot, since 1940 when the story in which it occurs was deposited in her publisher's vaults. Having been read only by Dame Agatha, Sir William Collins and her agent, the story, written at the peak of her career, will be published in September entitled *Curtain – Poirot's Last Case*.

The World's largest oil production platform being towed from Stavanger, Norway to the Shell/Esso Brent oilfield in the North Sea.

Chris Tarrant and Sally James, presenters on the anarchic Saturday morning kids show TISWAS *(Today is Saturday Wear A Smile).*

THE LION OF JUDAH DIES AT 83

Haile Selassie, former Emperor of Ethiopia, died yesterday, an almost forgotten figure in his own country. Ever since his overthrow by the military last September, after a reign of over 40 years, the 83-year-old Lion of Judah lived like a hermit in the palace overlooking Addis Ababa. Exiled in England after the Italian invasion of his country in 1934, he strode into the League of Nations with a dramatic challenge against the Fascist aggression. Its failure heralded the collapse of the League but the Emperor returned with the liberating British Forces in 1941 and dragged Ethiopia into the twentieth century with a series of political, educational and medical reforms. Unfortunately his blind spot was to let the land remain in a feudal state. His statues remained after his overthrow as a reminder of the symbol of history and legend surrounding an emperor descended from the Queen of Sheba and King Solomon.

BIRMINGHAM BOMBERS IN JAIL FOR LIFE

The 6 Provisional IRA men convicted of murdering 21 people in the Birmingham pub bombings went to jail last night with no prospect of ever coming out. Mr Justice Bridge, sentencing them to life imprisonment, made no recommendation of a minimum period they should serve. The perpetrators of Britain's worst act of urban terrorism took their sentences impassively at Lancaster Crown Court. They had heard the Jury Foreman, in an announcement lasting more than 12 minutes, say 'Guilty' 126 times – 1 for each of them on each of the 21 counts of murder. They also heard the Judge tell them: 'You all stand convicted of each of 21 counts on the clearest and most overwhelming evidence I have ever heard on the crime of murder.'

UNION THUG VANISHES

An abandoned car with a pair of white gloves neatly folded in the back seat today marks one of the most bizarre – and perhaps final – chapters of the notorious career of Jimmy Hoffa. Hoffa, 62, has dominated the American labour scene for more than 40 years. It is suspected that the former boss of the powerful American Teamsters' Union may have fallen foul of his own vicious methods and the corrupt organization he once headed.

NATIONWIDE SUE GETS LATE-NIGHT SHOW

After 10 years the BBC is bringing back a 5-times-a-week current affairs programme called *Tonight*. But unlike the original, which made TV personalities of Cliff Michelmore, Alan Whicker, Derek Hart and Fyfe Robertson, it will be a late-night show. It will have a young face – the team are all under 40 – and one of the regular presenters will be a woman. She is 29-year-old Sue Lawley, who has appeared on the *Nationwide* programme for 3 years. With her will be Dennis Tuohy, 38, one of the original anchormen of BBC2's *Line-Up* and Donald MacCormick, a 36-year-old Scot who has never before appeared on networked television. The new programme, which replaces *Midweek*, begins on 1 September.

WALKER CRACKS THE MILE RECORD

John Walker last night became the first man to run the mile inside 3 minutes 50 seconds. The New Zealander swept round the Gothenburg Track in Sweden in 3 minutes 49.4 seconds, slashing 1.6 seconds from the time set by Tanzania's Filbert Bayi in Jamaica last May.

LADY PENELOPE GOES SOLO

The voice behind the TV puppet Lady Penelope has parted from her husband and partner. Sylvia and Gerry Anderson have split up after working together producing puppet films for 16 years. The Andersons became Sir Lew Grade's biggest TV export earners. *Thunderbirds*, featuring International Rescue, was a big hit in the 60s. Blonde special agent Lady Penelope, whose lines were spoken by Sylvia Anderson, was the most popular character; she even had a magazine devoted to her adventures. 2 years ago they moved into Pinewood Studios to work on ATV's £2.5m space fiction series, *Space 1999*.

Noele Gordon as Meg Richardson owner of the Crossroads motel with the cook Shugie McFee (Angus Lennie).

SABOTEUR!

The captain of a works cricket team yesterday admitted sabotaging the pitch to wreck the Third Test Match and disappoint millions of people. Then, unabashed, he went off to enjoy a match himself. Colin Dean said it was he and 3 others who ruined the wicket at Leeds by digging holes in it and pouring motor oil on the turf. Their motive: publicity for a campaign against the conviction of Dean's brother-in-law East End mini-cab driver George Davis, who is serving 20 years in jail for armed robbery. The Test Match, in which Australia needed 225 to win on the last day with 7 wickets left, was abandoned as a draw. This means that Australia, 1 up in the series with 1 to play, keeps the Ashes.

DAY BY DAY

1 Aug
Mr Harold Wilson, with leaders of 34 other nations, signs in Helsinki the Final Act of the Conference on Security and Co-operation in Europe.

3 Aug
All 188 people on board a Boeing 707 flight from France to Morocco are killed as it crashes on its approach to Agadir Airport.

4 Aug
Queen Elizabeth the Queen Mother celebrates her 75th birthday.

9 Aug
Soviet composer Dmitri Shostakovich dies, aged 68.

12 Aug
An all-party House of Commons committee criticizes the Government's plan to invest £1,400m in British Leyland.

15 Aug
Sheikh Mujibur Rahman is killed during a coup by army officers in Bangladesh. Mr Khondaker Mushtaq Ahmad is sworn in as President.

20 Aug
A Viking unmanned spacecraft is launched from Cape Canaveral on a 10-month journey to Mars.

24 Aug
35 members of the public are chosen by ballot for a flight in Concorde. More than 500,000 people applied for places on the goodwill flight.

26 Aug
Robin Hobbs, playing for Essex against the Australians, scores 100 in 44 minutes, the fastest century for 55 years.

27 Aug
33 people are injured when a bomb explodes in a Caterham public house near the barracks of the Welsh Guards.

29 Aug
Irish statesman Eamon de Valera dies, aged 92.

SEPT 1975

Roy Schneider and Richard Dreyfuss in the water in a scene from Steven Spielberg's Jaws.

DEATH OF THE RYDER CUP

The Ryder Cup passed away yesterday, not just for another 2 years but almost certainly for ever. The last-rites of this contest, which has endured upon American goodwill for most of its 48 years, were performed before lunch with a humiliating defeat of Britain and Ireland. British golf has certainly forfeited any right to maintain a solitary challenge. The Americans favour a structure that would involve world-class talents such as Gary Player, Bob Charles, Jack Newton and Roberto De Vicenzo. This can be achieved quite simply by the deletion of the first 2 words in the qualification clause which says that 'native-born members of the British PGA' are eligible for Ryder Cup selection.

(The Laurel Valley match was the twenty-first for the Ryder Cup since it started in 1927. The United States has won 17, Britain and Ireland 3 (1929, 1933 and 1957) and one has been halved (1969).)

CZECH TENNIS GIRL DEFECTS

Czech tennis star Martina Navratilova said last night that she had defected to the West for love. . . of America. The fiery 18-year-old speaking at a Manhattan hotel denied that the prospect of earning a small fortune was a factor in her decision. Her tennis has so far earned her £50,000 but 20% of her purse goes back to the Communist Government in Prague. Her closest friend, sometime partner and former Wimbledon Champion Chris Evert, said, 'She's going to be a terrific force in women's tennis.'

NEW DEMOS AS FRANCO FACES THE WORLD'S FURY

Spain felt the backlash of world opinion yesterday over its execution of 5 guerillas. As riots broke out in the Basque town of Algorta – 2 of those executed were Basques – the Labour party issued a statement angrily condemning the Franco regime. However, Mr Reginald Maudling, Tory Spokesman on Foreign Affairs, pointed out that the 5 had been convicted of killing policemen, a crime for which the great majority of people in this country would think the death penalty quite suitable.

STUDENT NICHOLAS TURNS IN A SHOCKING THESIS

Student Nicholas Wilson's thesis made riveting reading: it said that a three-quarter ton concrete slab was liable to plunge into a chemistry laboratory and expansion gaps in concrete beams were 5 times the planned width of half an inch. As a result of the thesis – on Leeds University's £1m award-winning geology complex – a hundred supporting props have been installed and the university has called for a report from the structural engineers who worked on the 9-year-old building. Nicholas, however, will not know the examiners' verdict on his thesis until later this month.

Margo, Tom, Jerry and Barbara – characters in The Good Life, *a new BBC comedy series.*

COLOUR BAR CLUBS WILL BE OUTLAWED

Tough new measures to stamp out racial discrimination were unveiled in a White Paper by Home Secretary Mr Roy Jenkins yesterday. A major target will be to outlaw the colour bar in 'whites only' sports and social clubs. The new law will reverse House of Lords' judgements on the 1968 Race Act allowing such clubs to operate a race bar. About 4,000 working men's clubs and thousands of golf, tennis and other sports clubs are affected. A section of the Tory party has called in Mrs Thatcher to lead them in wholehearted opposition to the new proposals, which were 'objectionable and incapable of realization'. They would give immigrants a privileged status and make millions 'feel a minority in their own homeland'.

SCOTLAND BANS BILLY BREMNER FOR LIFE

Skipper Billy Bremner and 4 other Scottish internationals have been banned for life from playing for Scotland following reports of misbehaviour after Scotland defeated Denmark 1–0 last Wednesday. The other banned players are Joe Harper of Hibs, Willie Young and Arthur Graham of Aberdeen and Pat McCluskey of Celtic. The allegations are that after being ordered out of a Copenhagen nightclub and threatened with arrest, the players returned to their hotel, where 3 of them are said to have gone into the room of Scottish FA official Mr John McDonald and interfered with his belongings. Mr McDonald is reported to have laid Bremner out with a right hook. Bremner said at his Leeds home last night that he was 'staggered' by the ban.

HEIRESS PATTI HEARST HELD

Fugitive heiress Patti Hearst was arrested by the FBI in San Francisco yesterday. Earlier 2 members of the group which kidnapped Miss Hearst 19 months ago were also held. All were wanted on nearly 20 charges including kidnapping and illegal possession of automatic weapons. Miss Hearst was also believed to be involved in an armed bank raid in San Francisco.

£18,000 A YEAR TO MAKE 80P

A toll bridge across the River Cart at Inchinnan near Renfrew has been opened to let ships pass just 4 times in the past 3 years. The fees collected totalled 80p; it costs the tax-payers £18,000 a year to man the bridge 24 hours a day.

DAY BY DAY

3 Sept
The TUC conference in Blackpool votes 2 to 1 in favour of the Government's policy of limiting pay rises to £6 a week.

6 Sept
Nearly 3,000 people are reported dead in an earthquake centred at Lice in eastern Turkey.

14 Sept
Britain retains the Wightman Cup, the first time since 1925 that Britain has won the cup in America.

15 Sept
Leicestershire wins the County Cricket Championship for the first time.

16 Sept
The Prince of Wales attends Papua New Guinea's independence celebrations.

17 Sept
The High Court rules that a sterilization operation should not be carried out on an 11-year-old handicapped girl because it would deprive her 'of a basic human right – that of a woman to reproduce'. The girl's mother agreed to the operation.

24 Sept
The Government announces measures to reduce unemployment, including: a £30m grant to the Manpower Services Commission to create jobs in high unemployment areas; a subsidy of £5 a head for 6 months to companies recruiting young people without full-time jobs since leaving school; an extension of the £10-a-week subsidy to all firms keeping on redundant employees.

28 Sept
10 Territorial soldiers are drowned during a river exercise near Newark when their assault craft is swept over a weir.

29 Sept
Postage rates are increased to 8½p. and 6½p for first- and second-class letters respectively.

30 Sept
Former RAF pilot Alistair Steadman receives a 9-year prison sentence after being found guilty at Mold Crown Court of attempting to sell secret information to Russia.

Opportunity Knocks – *Hughie Green's television talent show returns for its 14th series.*

DIVERS DIED OF OVERHEATING ON NORTH SEA RIG

The deaths of 2 divers on a North Sea oil rig last week were caused by 'overheating' it was disclosed yesterday. It is thought to be the first case of hyperthermia in diving. Hyperthermia had never been considered a dangerous factor in diving, the more usual problem being hypothermia – heat loss. Experts in diving medicine and physiology are baffled by the deaths, which occurred after the men surfaced from a 390-foot dive.

COULD IT SOON BE A CASE OF 'MOVE OVER, BOB DYLAN'?

The rock press has labelled him the new Bob Dylan. He inspires the sort of pandemonium reminiscent of Mick Jagger, the Beatles and Elvis Presley. When *Rolling Stone's* Jon Landau caught his act in Boston, he proclaimed, 'I saw rock-and-roll's future and its name is Bruce Springsteen.' He promptly quit his job to co-produce the 25-year-old Messiah's third album, *Born To Run*, issued last week by Columbia.

AN EXAM NOBODY CAN FAIL

A new exam which hardly any 16-year-old can fail should replace the GCE O Level, a government advisory body has decided. The Schools Council proposal follows the scrapping this year of the whole idea of a pass or fail mark in the exam. Now the Council wants to introduce an exam with questions so easy that nearly every candidate will get a certificate with 1 of 7 grades marked on it; an eighth 'ungraded' category is reserved for those who have made no effort. The exam would be called the CEF (Certificate of Education Foundation) and would completely replace both the O Level and the easier CSE.

BRITON DIES AS CLIMBERS BEAT EVEREST AGAIN

Another triumph for the British Everest team has been marred by the death of one of its members. Climber and cameraman Mick Burke, 32, died during a second assault on the summit. Burke was part of a BBC team covering the expedition.

THE WORLD'S TOP 2

Doug Scott and Dougal Haston yesterday became the first men to climb Everest the hard way – up the south-west face. Lord Hunt, Chairman of the expedition's Management Committee and leader of the Hillary and Tenzing team which first conquered Everest in 1953, called it the 'last great challenge'.

OCT 1975

£20,000 FOR A 'CLOTHES' LINE'

When the town of Swansea was made a city the council decided that the rise in status should be commemorated. Internationally famous artist Kenneth Martin was commissioned, at a total cost of around £20,000, to design a tribute to the fight of the Swansea people in turning their war-blitzed town into a magnificent modern city. The resulting kinetic sculpture consists of a 20-foot-high pole with 4 electrically powered moving arms on top. The work has been described by opponents as 'a clothes' line'.

'Finally London is ready for Bruce Springsteen' ran the posters promoting his first UK concert. But Springsteen insists that they be taken down before his second gig as they are too much to live up to.

THIS SHOW'S NO JOKE

Equity has threatened to bar its members from working for London Weekend TV unless the comedy programme *A Joke's A Joke* is taken off the screen. The half-hour Saturday night show features amateurs telling gags in their workplaces. Professional comedians complain that most of the jokes are filched from them and that their livelihood is threatened because the material is overexposed. 3 instalments of the programme have so far been broadcast and a further 12 are ready for showing. LWT, which pays the amateur performers £5 to tell a joke, has offered Equity £1,000 but this has not been accepted.

NOBEL PEACE PRIZE FOR SAKHAROV

Andrei Sakharov, the grey-haired father of the Soviet hydrogen bomb who later turned against his brainchild, was awarded the Nobel Prize for Peace yesterday. It is the first time a Russian has won the award, which is worth £70,000. Doctor Sakharov, 54, is one of the most outspoken defenders of human rights in the Soviet Union.

NOW SPEND, SPEND VIVIEN LOSES HUSBAND NUMBER 5

Vivien Nicholson, who vowed to 'Spend, spend, spend,' after a pools win of £152,000 in 1961, has lost yet again in her search for love and happiness. After a night out her fifth husband collapsed and died, making her a widow for the third time at the age of 39. Police believe 32-year-old Gary Shaw, who married Vivien 8 weeks ago, died from a drugs overdose.

BEAUTIFUL AVENGER

The B1 Bomber will reach Moscow 4 hours after the Third World War is over. The ultimate 'no win' revenge weapon will only ensure that if America loses, most of the Russian people will die. The top speed of the B1 is estimated at more than 2,000 m.p.h. which is slow compared with intercontinental missiles. If total nuclear war is waged it will be fought in a series of half-hour battles – the time it takes these missiles to travel the 6,000 miles involved.

RUSSIANS FIND IT'S A ROCKY VENUS

Earthmen yesterday had their first view of the surface of Venus, the most mysterious planet in the solar system. A Russian spacecraft dropped through the dense, poisonous clouds that always mask the planet and relayed pictures to Earth which startled the scientists. Instead of the sandy desert they expected, the surface was covered with grey rocks and stones. Unique measurements taken of the swirling clouds which veil Venus to a depth of 20 miles may also throw light on the theory that they are made up of droplets of sulphuric acid. Tass, the Soviet newsagency, said the descent craft functioned for 53 minutes. This short period suggested that the equipment aboard may have failed in the intense heat and buckling pressure of the Venusian atmosphere. The planet's temperature is higher than the melting point of lead and the atmosphere some 60 times as heavy as Earth's.

HOW A LAW FOUND TRADERS' BLIND SPOT

Thousands of shopkeepers all over Britain could be in trouble because of an obscure 128-year-old law which states that blinds outside shops should be at least 8 feet from the ground. Over the years, many shopkeepers may have inadvertently broken this law but now they could face a crackdown following a test case in which a fruiterer was fined £10 for contravening the Town Police Clauses Act, 1847. The case was brought by Mr Alan Lambert, who complained that he had hit his head on a low blind outside the shop on more than one occasion.

NEW BLACK COMEDY

The first TV domestic comedy entirely about a coloured immigrant family is planned by London Weekend next year. *The Fosters*, which has an all-black cast, is about a West Indian family who live in a tower block in Streatham. The cast includes Lennie Henry, the 17-year-old comic from ITV's *New Faces*, who plays the Fosters' teenage son. Producer Stuart Allen, who made the *Love Thy Neighbour* series, said, 'There was some criticism of *Love Thy Neighbour* because it was said youngsters picked up racial words from it. It was accused of instilling prejudice. That cannot be said about *The Fosters*.'

'STOP THIS FOREIGN BRITISH CAR'

Vauxhall car workers were up in arms last night at their firm's decision to market a new car in Britain. The German-made car, assembled in Belgium and given a British-style front, will be called the Vauxhall Cavalier and is a version of the German Opel Manta and Ascona cars, launched a few weeks ago in West Germany. Both Opel and Vauxhall are part of America's General Motors, the world's biggest motor firm.

IT'S THE MOST EXPENSIVE PAPERBACK EVER – AND IT'S SURE TO BE A BESTSELLER

At £7.50 it is probably the most expensive paperback ever aimed at the populace but I doubt if there will be many unsold copies of the *Complete Pirelli Calendar* book. People have been known to pay £60 for one Pirelli calendar on the black market – and the firm gave them away to clients. This book gives the fruits of the whole 10 years' production. In that time, it has become the status symbol for the office wall, the Rolls-Royce of calendars, as David Niven points out in the introduction.

LOTUS HITS THE JACKPOT

Lotus chief Colin Chapman yesterday totted up £8.5m worth of orders for the 3 new models on display at the Motor Show: the Esprit at £5,800, the Eclat at £5,700 and the Elite at £7,800. Meanwhile Rolls-Royce put out an SOS for cigar lighters after 60 were stolen from the 5 models on display. Each car is fitted with 3 lighters.

PROFESSOR'S DOGS SNIFF OUT BOMBS

An animal psychology expert claims to have trained dogs to sniff out a letter bomb from a thousand envelopes. Professor Robert Lubow says he has trained the dogs to detect the scent of 4 different chemical substances which cover virtually the entire range of known explosives. In his experiments the dog presses a lever with his paw and gets a pellet of food as a reward if he sniffs an explosive substance. The dog has learned to press the lever only after having smelled the chemical. Professor Lubow says that certain rodents, rabbits or even pigs could be trained in the same way.

DEATH HITS THE *STREET*

Actor Graham Haberfield, who played Jerry Booth in *Coronation Street*, was found dead at his home yesterday. Police said they were sure 34-year-old Mr Haberfield died from natural causes. Illness had plagued the former Bristol Old Vic Theatre School pupil since he joined *Coronation Street* in 1962. No decision has been taken yet as to how the character will be written out of the programme. Mr Haberfield left the show several times but always returned. His biggest success outside the *Street* was as Winston, a loud-mouthed Manchester City fanatic in the ITV comedy series *The Dustbinmen*.

CLIFF SAYS, 'PLEASE BAN MY HAPPY HOOKER DISC'

Cliff Richard is trying to get his latest record banned from the air – because he has discovered it is not the simple love song he thought it was. Cliff believed the song, 'Honky Tonk Angels', was a tribute to love and the goodness of women, instead he's found out it's about the vice girls who operate in sleazy American bars. The singer has already succeeded in getting the record taken off the BBC's play list, even though they made it one of their records of the week. Cliff added, 'If the record is a hit and I'm asked to sing it, I will refuse unless all the words are changed.'

FRANCO'S RULE ENDS AS CARLOS TAKES OVER

The 36-year rule of General Franco, the West's most enduring dictator, was effectively ended last night. The Spanish Government announced that Prince Juan Carlos had taken over as temporary Head of State with full powers. As Franco's fight against a massive series of heart attacks entered its third week, the 37-year-old Prince, grandson of Alfonso XIII, Spain's last king until he was deposed in 1931, was installed under Article 11 of the Constitution. If Franco dies Juan Carlos will automatically be sworn in as the first king of Spain for 44 years. Even if the General survives it is unlikely that he will be well enough to rule again.

DAY BY DAY

1 Oct
The Lord Chief Justice, Lord Widgery, refuses to grant the Attorney General, Mr Samuel Silkin, an injunction to prevent the publication of the late Richard Crossman's diaries.

3 Oct
Dutch industrialist Dr Tiede Herrema is kidnapped near his home in Limerick by Provisional IRA members demanding the release of 3 prisoners, including Dr Rose Dugdale.

5 Oct
Spanish terrorists kill 3 policemen, bringing the total for the year to 18. A Basque barman, believed to have connections with the separatist group, is shot dead in reprisal the following day.

8 Oct
The Conservative party conference at Blackpool votes against any form of proportional representation in parliamentary elections.

9 Oct
A man is killed when a bomb explodes outside Green Park Underground station in London.

A soldier is killed as an army patrol vehicle is blown up near Crossmaglen.

11 Oct
David Broome wins a record 7 events in the Horse of the Year Show at Wembley.

13 Oct
Department of Trade statistics show that during its test programme Concorde exceeded the permitted noise limit at Heathrow on 27 out of 37 take-offs.

22 Oct
3 members of the Provisional IRA and an 18-year-old girl are sentenced to life imprisonment at the Central Criminal Court after being found guilty of the Guildford and Woolwich pub bombings last year.

26 Oct
A woman is killed when a locomotive rams the Aberdeen–London express, which broke down near Arbroath.

NOV 1975

CHEESE SAVES YOUR SMILE

If you want to keep an attractive smile say cheese at the end of meals. According to researchers at Newcastle University a piece of cheese can help prevent tooth decay by counteracting the acidic effect of a sweet course. Cheese, it seems, is at least as good for the teeth in rounding off a meal as the mouth-cleaning apple advised by dentists.

2-HOUR HOUSE

A family watched their new house being built yesterday – in 2 hours. The Tildesleys stood open-mouthed as the £10,500 house was delivered on the backs of 4 lorries. Every part of the house is put together in the factory, where 70 men work on a conveyor belt, as in car production. The finished product is simply dropped onto 7 concrete bases on site; the 4 sections are then bolted together and connections to the sewers, water, gas and electricity complete the job. A thorough inspection by surveyor Mr John Tophouse revealed no major problems though he pointed out, 'I wouldn't like to get a house built on a Friday afternoon; it could be as bad as buying a Friday afternoon car.'

PORTUGAL ABANDONS ANGOLA

Portugal abandoned the infant state of Angola last night to a bloody independence. After 500 years of neglectful rule Lisbon lowered its colours over the capital of Luanda, marking the end of a 13-year guerilla struggle with 6 million Africans. The country has slipped the shackles of a European ruler to carve out a doubtful future with bullets instead of brotherhood. Since the independence agreement was initiated by Portugal 10 months ago, a bitter civil war between 3 rival movements has claimed 30,000 lives.

CHRYSLER: IT'S YOURS

The Government can have Chrysler UK – for nothing. That is the astonishing offer being made to the Prime Minister by Chrysler International boss John J. Riccardo. The offer is designed to show that Chrysler is not trying to obtain money from the Government and is one of 3 alternatives put by Mr Riccardo. The others are a demand for virtually unlimited funds and a run-down of Chrysler's production and eventual end to car-making here. Mr Riccardo flies into London later this week to hear the Government's response.

GRACE ARCHER DIES AGAIN

It still ranks as radio's most famous fictional death – that September night in 1955 when Grace Archer was dragged from a blazing stable and died in her husband's arms. The young bride of 5 months had everything to live for when the BBC 'killed off' Grace, stunning the programme's 20 million followers. Yesterday, Grace and Phil – played by Ysanne Churchman and Norman Painting – went through it all again for posterity. It was all over in less than a minute but the recording finally completed the BBC's sound archives. For in the omnibus version including Grace's death her dying words at the end of the original episode were edited out.

Racing driver Graham Hill is killed when a plane piloted by him crashes in fog.

THE SUPER SOFT SELL

Who decides which albums reach the top of the charts? Not the record buyers, not the performers; the choice is made by the marketers. They invest the money that buys chart success. Before last March, Stylistics albums sold 35,000 copies to die-hard soul fans; with TV, *The Best of the Stylistics* has sold 850,000. The first big TV records were the compilation albums put out by K-Tel and Arcade about 3 years ago. Phonogram's Ken Mallifant decided to fight back by hiring an advertising agency, which came up with a novel concept of selling the music instead of the artist; showing up-market people using the music for a purpose such as enhancing their status. The 'product benefit' of the affluent dinner party in the Stylistics ad was swinging parties and a trendy lifestyle. A similar technique is being used for the new Peters and Lee album, *Favourites*. The ad shows family situations each illustrating the slogan: 'The one you give to the one you love.' As in the case of the Stylistics, Peters and Lee only appear musically, not in person.

SAD SECRET OF *UPSTAIRS DOWNSTAIRS*

The secret of how ITV is to end *Upstairs Downstairs* after 5 years at the top of the ratings has leaked out. James Bellamy, the young heart-throb of the series, is to be killed off after his cousin Georgina rejects his love and he falls heavily into debt. Viewers will see him die on 14 December and the following week, with the threat of the Bellamy home being sold off to pay debts, the series will finally fade from the screen.

GRAMMAR DON'T MATTER, DO IT?

Teachers who penalized children for incorrect spelling and bad grammar got a black mark yesterday. Correct English, said a university lecturer, is just a dialect. In a report, *Accent, Dialect and the School*, Dr Peter Trudgill of Reading University says, 'Grammar and spelling are largely a matter of opinion and teachers who insist on a "correct" version are unfairly penalizing the working class.' Examples of grammar from children in a working-class junior school included: 'I done that. . . Playing on me bike. . . Them men was 2 bankrobbers. . .' Doctor Trudgill says, 'These forms are not inferior to standard grammatical forms and they are not wrong.' Standard English need only be used when writing application forms, drafting reports, in business correspondence or official written work. There was no reason, for example, to ask children to use standard English in creative writing or in personal letters since no social advantages were likely to result from it.

MINTER TAKES TITLE

Alan Minter, bronze medal winner at the Munich Olympics in 1972, outpointed Kevin Finnegan to win the British Middleweight Championship at Wembley last night. 3 weeks ago Chris Finnegan regained the British Light Heavyweight title but Kevin could not make it a family double.

THE MAN WHO WAS *THE WORLD AT ONE*

William Hardcastle, known to millions of radio listeners as the voice of *The World At One*, died yesterday (10 November). He was 57. He stamped his personality on the Radio 4 news programme with his distinctive presentation for 10 years, having joined the programme at its inception in 1965.

RECORDS BOOK MAN MURDERED

Ross McWhirter, one of the twins who created the *Guinness Book of Records*, was found murdered yesterday, shot in the doorway of his home in Enfield, Middlesex. Detectives are linking the murder with Mr McWhirter's outspoken stance against IRA terrorism. He was heavily involved in extreme right-wing politics and was well aware that he was a possible target. Ross McWhirter and his twin brother, Norris, are household names, their bestselling *Guinness Book of Records* having been published for 22 years. Last year's edition itself set a record as the modern book with the largest sale in the world. Sales of more than 24 million pushed Doctor Spock's book on bringing up babies into second place.

BIGGEST HIT BOOK THIS YEAR

When ITN reporter Gerald Seymour next takes his microphone into Belfast he will do so with some trepidation – and £100,000 in his bank account. The money comes from the runaway success in America of his first novel, *Harry's Game*. Just published in this country, the book is likely to cause heated arguments on both sides of the conflict for 'sympathetic' treatment of the leading character, an IRA Provisional. As the *New York Times* pointed out when it acclaimed the book: 'It soon gets so we don't know whose side we ought to be on.'

CENSOR LETS CHILDREN SEE *JAWS*

Children as young as 5 will be able to go on their own to see *Jaws*, the film about a killer shark. Even though the censors admit that youngsters may find it 'disturbing' the British Board of Film Censors has given the film an A certificate which means that children under 14 do not have to be accompanied by an adult. A films are passed for general exhibition but, unlike U films, contain material which it is felt parents might not want their children to see.

DAY BY DAY

3 Nov
At Dyce, Aberdeenshire the Queen inaugurates the flow of oil from the BP Forties field.

4 Nov
9 men die following an explosion at a British Steel Corporation plant at Scunthorpe.

6 Nov
King Hassan of Morocco orders thousands to cross the border into Spanish Sahara to claim the territory. He orders their return 3 days later when they are 7 miles inside Spanish Sahara and within sight of Spanish guns.

7 Nov
Cardinal John Heenan, Archbishop of Westminster since 1963, dies, aged 70.

Dr Tiede Herrema is released when his captors, Provisional IRA members Eddie Gallagher and Marion Coyle, surrender to police.

8 Nov
The Scottish Daily News is published for the last time, 6 months after its launch by a workers' co-operative.

11 Nov
The Governor-General of Australia, Sir John Kerr, dismisses Labour Prime Minister Mr Gough Whitlam and asks Liberal party Leader Mr Malcolm Fraser to form a caretaker government until a general election can be held. The crisis arose because the Liberal and Country parties in the Senate, the upper house where they had a majority, blocked the Labour Government's Budget bills.

14 Nov
Spain agrees to withdraw from her Sahara colony in February 1976 and hand over the territory to Morocco and Mauritania.

20 Nov
General Franco dies, aged 82.

25 Nov
Swinau, a Dutch colony for more than 300 years, becomes an independent republic.

3 Royal Navy frigates are ordered to the disputed fishing grounds off Iceland to protect British trawlers.

27 Nov
A White Paper outlining the Government's plans for devolving powers to elected assemblies in Scotland and Wales is published. Scotland, but not Wales, is to have some legislative powers and both are to continue sending representatives to Westminster.

29 Nov
Racing driver Graham Hill is killed when a plane piloted by him crashes in fog near Elstree, Herts. The 5 other people in the plane are also killed.

In the New Zealand general election the National party, led by Mr Robert Muldoon, defeats Mr Wallace Rowlings's Labour administration, which has been in power since 1972.

RECORD LOAN

Britain is to borrow £975m from the International Monetary Fund, the largest single loan in the Fund's history, Chancellor Denis Healey announced last night.

DEC 1975

SETTLE NOW OR RISK BLOOD BATH, SMITH TOLD

White Rhodesians got their grimmest warning yet from Downing Street yesterday. The verdict of Mr David Ennals, Foreign Office Minister of State, on returning from talks in Africa was blunt: 'Europeans in Rhodesia should be under no illusions. Preparations for military action are already being made: several thousand are under training and more are joining every day. The consequences of an armed struggle are incalculable but its eventual outcome cannot be in doubt.' For the first time since UDI 10 years ago the British Government is convinced that time is running out for Premier Ian Smith and that the Africans are ready and able to win in a bloody showdown.

WHEN A WOMAN CAN'T SAY NO

No matter how much force or ill treatment a husband uses to have sex with his wife he is not guilty of rape, a jury heard yesterday. When a woman marries she gives away her right to say 'No', barrister Mr Nicholas Purnell said at the Old Bailey. 'It may come as some surprise in these days but this is the state of the law,' he said, but then went on to prosecute a husband with the very offence he had indicated was impossible because 'further processes of law' had revoked the marital right.

Mrs Elizabeth Ramprasad had taken matrimonial proceedings against her husband on the grounds of persistent cruelty; she had also obtained an injunction ordering him to leave the family home. But it was revealed yesterday that the injunction had expired when Ramprasad went back to the house and the incident happened. Mr Purnell said that because of this he did not intend to proceed with the prosecution. The judge agreed and formally directed the jury to find Ramprasad not guilty of rape. After the case Mrs Ramprasad said, 'My ex-husband has escaped justice because of a loophole in the law; I am just another battered wife.'

INTRODUCING GROVER

The Wombles are to be threatened by new TV rivals. *The Muppets* will introduce us to Hilda, Bert, Ernie, Biff and white-whiskered Grover, who is the oldest Muppet of them all. ITV hopes they will replace Uncle Bulgaria, Wellington and the rest of the BBC's Wombles as children's favourites. The Muppets, created by American puppeteer Jim Henson, first appeared in the educational pre-school TV series *Sesame Street* but now they are coming to Britain. They are to get a TV series of their own which begins production early in the new year.

Kermit and Miss Piggy from The Muppet Show.

AVENGERS RETURNS AFTER 7 YEARS

Actor Patrick McNee is dusting off his bowler and brolly to bring *The Avengers* back to television nearly 7 years after the last episode was made. McNee, now 53, has been signed to repeat the role of John Steed and the search is now on for an actress to follow in the energetic footsteps of Honor Blackman, Diana Rigg and Linda Thorson as Steed's assistant. 'She will be a stockings and suspenders girl,' said writer-producer Brian Clemens, who wrote the first *Avengers* story in 1961. The producers also plan for Steed to be given a second assistant – a man – in his fictional fight against crime.

CARS TO BE TESTED FOR M.P.G.

A standard miles-per-gallon test for all new cars is to be introduced by the Government in January 1977. Under the scheme, announced last night by Energy Secretary Mr Wedgwood Benn, manufacturers will have to submit all new cars to an independent fuel-economy test supervised by the Departments of Energy, Industry and Environment plus the Office of Fair Trading. At present each firm has its own testing procedure making it impossible for new car buyers to compare fuel consumption figures accurately.

EDELMAN DIES AND LABOUR LOSES LEAD

Labour MP Maurice Edelman, 64, died yesterday and now the Government faces a crucial by-election for his 'Chrysler' constituency. His seat at Coventry North-west, where he had a majority of 7,488 in the last election, is one of the most sensitive in the Midlands. If the American car firm had not been saved by the Government, Labour would almost certainly have lost the seat. Mr Edelman's death means that the Government has lost its 1-vote overall majority and is now level pegging with the combined opposition parties.

STORM AS PRISONERS GO FREE

As the last of Northern Ireland's detainees were freed from the Maze Prison, Tory fury was turned on the man who opened the gates, Ulster Secretary Merlyn Rees. Opposition leaders demanded an explanation for the decision, which had taken them by surprise. Shadow Ulster Secretary Mr Airey Neave said, 'He will have to take the consequences of his action, which I believe will be very dangerous.' Detention without trial was introduced in 1971 because the Government felt that witnesses were afraid to give evidence that would convict terrorists. Mr Rees now hopes to cripple the value of detention as a propaganda weapon and hit back at the IRA strictly through the courts.

PUTTING THE SQUEEZE ON TYRES

A British firm has discovered by accident a new process that could save millions of pounds by making every type of tyre last longer. Under traditional methods tyre makers 'stretch' the tread to cover the casing for both new and remould tyres. However, a Hampshire firm said yesterday that it had found that compressing the tread before bonding it made the tyres tougher. It claims the process gives the tyres twice the life of their traditionally made counterparts, along with a better grip, better petrol economy and less risk of punctures.

'HOUSE SOLD' SIGN BANKRUPTS MAN

A man with nearly £4,000 in the bank found himself made bankrupt over £9 yesterday because he refused to pay an estate agent for putting a 'Sold' sign outside his house. Mr John Stewart told Birmingham Bankruptcy Court that he had received the agent's £154 bill for the sale of his house but disputed the £9 on a point of principle. He said that the agents asked if they could put up the board after selling the house but he did not realize he was expected to pay for it. Last night Mr Stewart was waiting for the receiver to settle the bill from his frozen assets. A spokesman for the National Association of Estate Agents said, 'It is normal practice for estate agents to charge for "For Sale" signs but not for "Sold" boards.'

Police marksmen cover the Balcombe St flat where Mr and Mrs John Matthews are held hostage.

BRITISH PASSPORT EXPIRES

The British passport, with its navy blue cover and gold royal crest, is to go. In 2 years it is to be replaced by a 'Euro passport', a plastic-covered, claret-coloured document headed 'European Community', with 'United Kingdom' in smaller letters underneath. Agreement on the Community passport was reached in Rome yesterday by the Heads of all 9 governments, including Mr Wilson. Holders of the new passport will not normally have to show it when crossing EEC borders.

POLICE NAME SUSPECT HELD IN BLACK PANTHER SEARCH

A man will appear in court today charged in connection with the kidnapping and murder of 17-year-old heiress Lesley Whittle. He is 35-year-old odd-jobman Donald Neilson. Detectives who have been hunting the Black Panther fear angry scenes when Neilson is brought before the magistrates at Newcastle-Under-Lyme, Staffordshire. Neilson is married with an attractive daughter, Catherine, who is 3 years younger than Lesley. His arrest has shocked neighbours in Thornbury, a small suburb of Bradford, Yorkshire.

E.L.O. performing on LWT's pop show Supersonic.

THE END OF THE AFFAIR

Edward Woodward and actress Michelle Dotrice finally parted yesterday. He left for a reunion with his wife, she for her parents' house in Warwickshire. Their reluctant parting at the end of a 12-month secret love affair brought praise from Michelle's father, actor Roy Dotrice, for their 'courageous decision'. Michelle used to play with Edward Woodward's 2 children – his third child, Sarah, now 13, wasn't then born. When they met he was 28 and she was just 12.

JAN 1976

This is the dramatic moment the dangerous cat-and-mouse manoevering of the Cod War turned into a collision at sea. The Icelandic gunboat Thor has rammed her starboard bow into the stern of the British Frigate HMS Andomeda.

BOYS BEAT THE GRAND MASTERS

For the second time in 24 hours a British schoolboy has beaten a Russian chess Grand Master. The first victory was by 10-year-old Nigel Short from Lancashire, who checkmated the world's number 2, Victor Korchnoi. Victory number 2 came when 12-year-old Julian Hodgson from London beat another Grand Master, David Bronstein. Both Russians were playing simultaneous games, Korchnoi against 30 opponents and Bronstein against 21. Nigel, who is rated as one of Britain's best hopes for the future, was the only victor against Korchnoi, who won 21 games and drew 8.

WHITE ELEPHANT TROUBLE

A TV advertisement for beds in which painted elephants appear has angered RSPCA officials. The ad, featuring Frank Thornton, Captain Peacock of BBC's Are You Being Served? was intended to emphasize that not all January sales bargains were 'white elephants'. The Society has demanded an explanation over concerns that putting the elephants under hot lights might do them harm, pointing out that elephants lose heat through their skin, especially the ears. The agency concerned said that the paint had been tested before it was applied and a vet had been consulted.

MEET THE OTHER SMALL MAN IN BARKER'S LIFE

Ronnie Barker has found himself another diminutive TV comedy partner in the shape of David Jason. The 2 are teaming up for a new BBC situation-comedy series, Open All Hours, which goes into production next month for showing in the autumn. A spin-off from one of the Barker Comedy Playhouse programmes concerns the mishaps of a corner grocery shop with Barker as the grocer and Jason as his assistant. It is not the first time the 2 have appeared together. Jason played Dithers the geriatric gardener in Hark at Barker. Since then he has starred in the less than successful slapstick spy spoof, The Top Secret Life of Edgar Briggs, but this new series promises to give Jason, who has been heralded as a British Buster Keaton, the stardom that has so far eluded him.

AT LEAST I WASN'T LAST, SAYS MURIEL THE FIRST

Jockey Muriel Naughton made racing history yesterday but failed to achieve the first she really wanted. The 28-year-old housewife from Yorkshire became the first woman to race against men over the sticks and indeed the first woman to race at all under National Hunt Rules, but after being well up for most of the race she ended sixth of the 7 finishers.

THE BBC HATES TO PLAY YOU, BABY

A hit record has been banned by the BBC because it is too sexy. The record, 'Love to Love You, Baby', features heavy breathing and simulated sounds of love-making and was recorded by 25-year-old Donna Summer on her own in a studio.

AGATHA CHRISTIE DIES BUT SHOW GOES ON

As the 9,611th performance of The Mousetrap ended last night actor Brian McDermott stepped to the front of the stage and told the packed house that, with the news of Dame Agatha Christie's death a few hours earlier, it had seemed that her famous play might close for the first time in its history; but they knew that she would have wanted the show to go on. Outside, the neon lights of St Martin's Theatre were turned off and the lights were also dimmed at the Savoy Theatre, where another Christie play, Murder At The Vicarage, is running. Agatha Christie, created a dame in the 1971 Honours List, died aged 85 at her home in Wallingford, Oxfordshire. Over 55 prolific years she wrote 85 books – 77 of them crime novels – 17 plays and made an estimated £10m.

FIRST IN THE ACT

Ann Hunt is first in line to enforce the law on equal pay for women. Mrs Hunt is a £2,016-a-year stock controller at a decorating firm. John Fletcher, another stock controller at the same firm, gets £700 a year more. Last April Mrs Hunt asked Crown Decorations Products of Birmingham for equal pay and was turned down. On the day the Equal Pay Act became law she applied for a hearing before an industrial tribunal.

LISA THE RISING STAR

Lisa Harrow was named the most promising artiste yesterday by the Variety Club of Great Britain. The 28-year-old actress won the award for her performance in All Creatures Great and Small, a film about a country vet. She follows in the footsteps of Tom Courtney, Sarah Miles, Jenny Agutter, Polly James and Michael Crawford, who are all previous winners.

James Bolam as Jack Ford and Susan Jameson as Jessie Seaton in a new BBC series When the Boat comes In.

THORPE'S DAY OF ANGUISH

Jeremy Thorpe faced up to some of the most agonizing hours of his life last night as he attempted to safeguard his future as Liberal leader. A government report on a bank group which crashed with losses of £30m says that the 4 non-executive directors – Mr Thorpe was one – took an insufficient part in deciding policy. Even as Mr Thorpe was drawing up an answer in which he admitted 'an error of judgement' he suffered a further embarrassment. The defendant in an obscure court case in Devon, Mr Norman Scott, alleged that he had had a sexual relationship with Mr Thorpe. The Liberal leader immediately issued an emphatic denial. He said, 'It is well over 12 years since I last saw or spoke to Mr Scott; there is no truth in Mr Scott's wild allegations.'

NEW YEAR HONOURS

Harry Corbett, whose glove puppets Sooty and Sweep have entertained children for years, is awarded the OBE for his charity work; Harry H. Corbett, who played Harold Steptoe in the TV comedy series,' also receives the OBE; Richard Attenborough is knighted; opera soprano Janet Baker becomes a dame; comedian Alfred Marks, *Archers* scriptwriter and actor Norman Painting (he plays Phillip Archer) are made OBEs; cellist Jacqueline du Pré also receives an OBE.

LEBANON'S PREMIER QUITS AS CEASEFIRE COLLAPSES

Lebanese Prime Minister Rashid Karami resigned last night as fighting escalated in the civil war. His resignation plunged the country, which has been ravaged by 9 months of bloodshed, further into political crisis. Karami, a Muslim who headed a 6-man coalition cabinet of 3 Christians and 3 Muslims, said that the hoped-for ceasefire had not taken effect for even 1 hour. The subsequent fighting in Beirut between right-wing Christian phalangists and left-wing Muslims and Palestinians was among the fiercest of the war.

CONCORDE'S BIG DAY

This morning (21 January) a 14-year-old dream comes true. At 11.30 a.m. Concorde Alpha Alpha will leave Heathrow for Bahrain to inaugurate the world's first commercial supersonic passenger service. Simultaneously, 250 miles away at Charles de Gaulle Airport, Paris, the French Concorde will begin its departure for the flight to Rio. The Alpha Alpha flight includes the Duke of Kent and Trade Minister Mr Peter Shore and Energy Minister Mr Eric Varley. The 28 fare-paying passengers for the Alpha Alpha flight also include Viscount Leathers, who booked tickets for himself and his wife nearly 12 years ago. The cost of the return trip is £676.10.

LADY CHATTERLEY'S REAL LOVER DIES

Angelo Ravagli, Lady Chatterley's real lover, has died aged 84 in a luxury villa on the Italian Riviera. The real life 'Mellors' seduced Frieda Lawrence in 1925 when her husband D.H. Lawrence rented his parents' villa for a holiday. Lawrence discovered the pair, left Italy at once and wrote *Lady Chatterley's Lover* as a kind of literary revenge on his wife. In the book Lady Chatterley – a thin disguise for Lawrence's wife – is seduced by Mellors, the gamekeeper.

When Lawrence died in 1930 Ravagli wrote to Frieda and 3 weeks later the widow, then 51, arrived in Italy. Angelo left his Italian wife and went to New Mexico with Frieda where they lived together on a ranch bequeathed to D.H. Lawrence by an eccentric millionairess. In 1948 Angelo obtained an American divorce and married Frieda, which paved the way for another irony. When Frieda died 8 years later Angelo inherited a quarter of her estate, including the rights to *Lady Chatterley's Lover*. In the 1960s, when Lawrence's book was finally permitted to go on general sale after an obscenity charge against it at the Old Bailey was dismissed, Angelo became a rich man.

Starsky and Hutch – *an new all action police series set in Los Angeles.*

FEB 1976

Julie Covington as Dee, Rula Lenska as 'Q' and Charlotte Cornwall as Anna as the 'Little Ladies' in Rock Follies.

BRITONS DODGE SHELLS IN FALKLANDS CLASH

An unarmed British survey ship yesterday dodged shells from an Argentine destroyer in an extraordinary clash at sea 80 miles off the Falkland Isles. The victim was the *Shackleton*, which was engaged on a sea-bed research project. The Foreign Office said, 'The Argentine destroyer threatened to fire into the *Shackleton's* hull if she did not heave to. The *Shackleton* informed the warship that she was carrying explosives for scientific purposes and could explode if hit.' After radioing the Governor of the Falklands the captain was told to avoid being boarded by the Argentine navy but not to risk his ship and head at full speed for Port Stanley. One explanation for the astonishing incident was thought to be the growing obsession of Argentina to take over the British colony of the Falkland Isles and Argentinian suspicions of British vessels in the area.

IF YOUR CAR BREAKS DOWN TODAY, DON'T WORRY

A new code giving motorists a fair deal from car makers and garages comes into force today (2 February). Foreign car firms operating in Britain have also agreed to abide by the code, whose main provisions are: extended warranty to cover prolonged periods off the road for troublesome new cars; transfer of all warranties on all new cars so that if a car is sold during the guarantee period the warranty will pass to the buyer; warranty work to be carried out free, or as detailed, by any franchised dealer for that make of car. Also, car order forms must list all extra charges on top of a car's price so that the buyer knows exactly what he must pay, whilst used-car buyers will be able to demand a copy of the pre-sales inspection report. Firm quotes for repairs must be given and the repair work guaranteed against failure due to poor workmanship; and there must be low cost arbitration for dissatisfied customers.

GREATEST CON-MAN IN THE WORLD – HONESTLY

He was the man whose con tricks inspired the film *The Sting*. In 40 years Joseph 'Yellow Kid' Weill netted £4m. He lived by the maxim: 'You can never cheat an honest man; a truly honest man would never have fallen for any of my schemes.' Yesterday it was announced that the greatest con-man of them all has died in a Chicago nursing home aged 100. He once fired a shotgun loaded with gold dust pellets into the sides of an abandoned quarry and sold shares in his gold mine. In another scheme he rented an abandoned bank, hired billiard hall characters as tellers and filled money bags with lead – all to fool a soap magnate into making a large deposit. He died days before lawyers representing William Brannon, who wrote several books on Weill, planned to sue producers of *The Sting*. Brannon claimed the plot 'was stolen right out of the Kid's life'. In the nursing home, he had 1 inflexible rule: 'I never play bingo – it's a rip-off.'

WHY WIFE CANNOT ADOPT HER OWN SON

What is a 'reasonable' parent? Certainly not a homosexual, one judge ruled but in the Appeal Court yesterday 3 others decided that he was wrong. They allowed an appeal by a homosexual father to prevent his son from being adopted by his former wife and her new husband. Last April a County Court judge made an adoption order because he held that the father was unreasonable to withhold his consent. The mother and her husband wanted the 8-year-old boy, who lives with them, to break ties with his father, concerned about the boy learning of his father's homosexuality. The judge believed a reasonable father would have decided: I must protect my boy, even if it means parting from him for ever, so that he can be kept free from this danger. The Appeal Court gave the mother and her husband leave to petition the Lords on whether the test in this case should be what a heterosexual father would consider reasonable.

Artist L.S. Lowry with one of his favourite works.

ICE-COLD GOLDEN BOY

John Curry gave us precisely what he promised in Innsbruck last night – an exhibition in skating as a new modern art form and an Olympic gold medal as something akin to an afterthought. If Britain hadn't struck gold at the Winter Olympics for 12 years, we won this one by a street. The rest of the world could only marvel at the commanding brilliance of the 26-year-old bachelor, born in Birmingham but now based in the United States. For his rivals it was an exercise of total pointlessness.

THE IMMORTAL

Champions are men who deliver on the day; great champions are men who face crushing odds and still deliver on the day. Then there are immortal champions. They are men who face crushing odds and conquer with breathtaking brilliance and style. Such a champion is Franz Klammer, who yesterday hurled himself down 3,000 yards of solid ice on an Austrian mountain in 1 minute 45.73 seconds to win what has been proclaimed the greatest Olympic downhill ever.

FRIGATES GO INTO ACTION

Iceland was set to break off diplomatic relations last night as the Royal Navy headed back into the Cod War. The full-scale resumption of hostilities came after 2 gunboat attacks on British trawlers. Foreign Secretary James Callaghan sent 2 frigates back to the fishing grounds from points outside the disputed 200-mile limit. The attacks were regarded in Whitehall as deliberate provocation at a time when British officials were standing by to fly to Reykjavik for a last chance to reach a negotiated settlement.

PERIL IN BABY'S BOTTLE

Babies less than 6 months old should not be fed on National Dried Milk, the Government warned yesterday. Any evaporated or condensed milk sold as suitable for babies increases the risk of convulsions and fits, according to the Health Ministry. Instead of these, bottle-fed babies under 6 months old should be given the modified baby milk powders on the market. A Health Ministry working party has found that unmodified cow's milk powders and liquids contain too much sodium phosphate and protein concentration for very young babies. Reporting the findings, Junior Health Minister Mr Michael Meacher said the risks lessened as the babies grew and for this reason the Government did not intend to withdraw National Dried Milk.

BODIES OF EXECUTED BRITONS ARE 'FOUND'

The bodies of 14 British mercenaries executed by their own men are reported to have been found in Northern Angola. The claim has come from the leader of the Cuban-led MPLA, whose forces are advancing throughout the country. In Kinshasa the leader of the British mercenaries, 'Major' Norman Hall, revealed that only half of the executed men had so far been identified. Their bodies were left unburied for 5 days after they had been machine-gunned on the orders of the man they knew as Colonel Callan. Hall said of Callan, a Greek Cypriot whose real name was Costas Georgiou, 'He was completely kill crazy, an absolute madman.' He said he himself did not hear of the executions until 5 days later when he was visiting some men wounded in their fighting against the MPLA.

GETTING ROUND THE LAW

Advertisers in search of their elusive ideal requirement are finding that a tongue-in-cheek approach can land the staff they want when they are not supposed to discriminate between the sexes. One employer got almost exactly what he wanted – an attractive, mini-skirted receptionist – without actually breaking the Sex Discrimination Act. His advertisement read: 'What we really wanted was a mini-skirted, blue-eyed blonde but under the Sex Discrimination Act we cannot advertise for her so we'll just say that we require a receptionist.' The advertisement, quite within the bounds of the law, brought 60 replies, none of them from men. The successful applicant, 17-year-old Deborah Farden, said, 'I think the new act has advantages but it seems ridiculous when both sexes can apply for jobs which are obviously designed either for a man or for a woman.'

Roger Davis replaces Pete Duel in Alias Smith and Jones.

MAR 1976

BACK TO CIGARETTE CARDS

Cigarette cards are making a come-back after an absence of nearly 36 years. Rothmans revealed last night that the cards, depicting vintage cars, are to promote the reappearance of one of its most famous brands, Black Cat, last seen in 1959. A Rothmans' official stressed that there was no wish to encourage children to buy cigarettes just for the card collection; the company believed that the cards would be snapped up by adults.

PLAYER WINS £1,250 FOR SOCCER FOUL

A £1,250 award by the Criminal Injuries Compensation Board to an amateur footballer has made soccer history. It is the first time a football foul has been regarded as a criminal act of violence – and could open the way for a spate of similar claims at every level of competitive sport. A Football Association official said, 'It will spoil the game if everybody is worried about prosecutions.' The foul tackle occurred during a match between 2 firms of solicitors playing in the London Legal League.

THE RACE IS ON – AND IT'S JIM IN THE LEAD

After Harold Wilson had shattered the Cabinet, the Labour party and the country by announcing that he was resigning, it looked last night as though James Callaghan was leading the race to succeed him. Even though he is nearly 64 – 4 years older than Mr Wilson – Foreign Secretary Mr Callaghan looked far ahead of his 6 possible rivals. Mr Roy Jenkins, the Home Secretary and champion of Labour's moderate and right-wing MPs, is going to run. Another certain candidate is Environment Secretary Anthony Crosland, who could split the moderate vote wide open in a battle with Mr Jenkins. 3 others were hesitating last night: Chancellor Denis Healey, Prices Minister Mrs Shirley Williams and Employment Secretary Michael Foot. The other prominent left-winger, Anthony Wedgwood Benn, had yet to show his hand. Mr Wilson's total of nearly 8 years in Downing Street makes him the longest serving peace-time prime minister this century. His shock announcement, which wiped nearly £1,000m off the value of shares on the Stock Market, was one of the best kept secrets in a political regime famed for its leaks. He shared his plans with the Queen last December.

TV CAT DIES

Arthur, the TV (queen) cat who scooped food out of cans with her paw, has died. She was nearly 17. Arthur, who was owned by Spillers Foods, was the star of Kattomeat commercials for nearly 10 years.

TEST CASE WOMAN WINS EQUAL PAY RIGHTS

Working mother Mrs Valerie Perry has become the first woman to win a claim under the Equal Pay Act. Her victory means that her employers, Doulton Insulators of Tamworth, must scrap a job-grading system under which men were earning more. Mrs Perry told the tribunal that before the act came into force at the end of December, women at her factory used to do the same jobs as men for two-thirds the pay. Since the act, she claimed, jobs had been graded and in 3 months women had done only the B-grade jobs, which carried a piece-work rate one-third lower.

WILSON BEATEN AND MAGGIE TELLS HIM 'GO'

Disaster struck the Government last night when it was defeated by 28 votes on its proposals to cut public spending plans by £3,000m. The Wilson Government was hit by one of the biggest backbench revolts by left-wing MPs for years and pandemonium broke out as the Tories raised the roof in jubilant delight. Opposition Leader Mrs Margaret Thatcher called for the Wilson Cabinet's resignation, describing the defeat as 'unprecedented in modern times'.

THE LAST OF THE GREAT WARRIORS

Monty is dead. Long live his memory, for without doubt Montgomery was the last of the great British military heroes. However historians see him, whatever arguments tacticians hold over his battles, his name will always be linked in the nation's mind with those of Wellington and Nelson. Like them, Monty was the people's hero. Sitting in the turret of a tank in black beret and battle-dress he brought us what we needed most when we needed it most – victory. Bernard Law Montgomery died yesterday (24 March) aged 88.

Harold Wilson's cabinet gathered for a dinner to mark his departure from the Labour Leadership.

MARGARET AND SNOWDON TO PART?

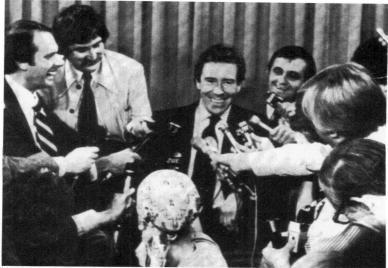

Lord Snowdon meets the press with a smile and a 'no comment' as news of the separation comes while he is in Australia with an exhibition of his photographs.

Buckingham Palace confirmed last night that Princess Margaret's troubled marriage had been discussed by the Royal Family. The Palace statement came after rumours that the Queen had been asked to give permission for a separation between Lord Snowdon and the Princess. It was being pointed out last night that a judicial separation was not the same as a divorce and was sometimes resorted to by people who have a religious objection to divorce. Under the Royal Marriages Act the Queen has to give permission for any member of the Royal Family to end their marriage.

FORD GIVES LOSER REAGAN THE CHANCE TO BOW OUT

President Ford, who clinched his party's nomination with a landslide victory in the Illinois Primary, has asked challenger, California Governor Ronald Reagan, to pull out of his hopeless battle for the presidency with the promise that he will hail the decision as a statesmanlike sacrifice in the name of party unity. For the Democrats, former Georgia Governor Jimmy Carter carried the day in Illinois with 48% of the vote. With his nearest rival, Alabama Governor George Wallace, polling 28%, the result confirms Carter as the front-running Democrat.

INTO BATTLE – BY BICYCLE

Angry Amabel is riding into battle, just like her famous ancestor the Duke of Wellington. Whereas the Iron Duke favoured horses, Amabel Wellesley-Colley will be riding on a bike. She intends to fight a summons for cycling in Hyde Park because she believes the ban on bicycles to be unconstitutional. She said yesterday, 'The police told me that bicycling on the footpath is contrary to park regulations dating back to 1872, but I believe that Rotten Row is a public right of way and it would take an Act of Parliament to forbid people to cycle along it.'

STORK AND BUTTER. . . NO COMPARISON

Even if you can't tell Stork margarine from butter you can't be told so on television. A High Court ruling yesterday means that it is now taboo for any margarine producer to even mention the word butter in the context of margarine – pending an appeal. The action was brought by the makers of Stork, the Unilever subsidiary Van Den Berghs & Jurgens, who sought a declaration that 3 advertising films did not contravene the margarine regulations in the 1967 Food and Drugs Act. The firm took the case because the television commercials had been banned by the Independent Broadcasting Authority after protests from the Butter Information Council. Mr Justice Whitford said that Stork compared in many respects with butter and it began advertising in 1931 on the basis that the 2 were similar, but the strict application of the regulations led him to conclude that the advertisements constituted an infringement.

HOW TO TOP THE POPS WITHOUT PLAYING A NOTE

All the pop fans wanted to see Kenny when their record made the charts. But when the group was invited to appear on *Top of the Pops*, its creators were in trouble for there wasn't any Kenny. Songwriters Bill Martin and Phil Coulter had used session musicians to record their hit number 'The Bump'. So the 2 men, who also wrote 'Puppet on a String', looked around for some young faces to fit their music. They found what they wanted in the cold storage department of a banana warehouse in Enfield, Middlesex. A group called Chuff was rehearsing there and the songwriters signed it up. Chuff became Kenny, appeared on the programme and shot to overnight success on the disc it didn't make.

A NEST PACKED WITH OSCARS

One Flew Over The Cuckoo's Nest has all but swept the board at Hollywood's Oscar awards, the first time in 42 years that a film has so dominated the ceremony. The moment of triumph was made all the more poignant when Louise Fletcher, who won the Best Actress Award for her portrayal of the tyrannical nurse, delivered her acceptance speech in sign language as well as words. Watching television at their home in Birmingham, Alabama were her parents, both deaf mutes. Jack Nicholson got the Best Actor Award after 4 unsuccessful Oscar nominations. He said delightedly, 'I guess this proves there are as many nuts in the Academy as anywhere else.' The film took 3 more Oscars: for Best Picture, Best Adapted Screenplay and Best Director, Miloš Forman.

APR 1976

PAN'S PEOPLE PASS ON

Pan's People, who revolutionized dancing on TV 10 years ago when they first featured on *Top of The Pops*, are to make their last appearance on 6 May. In their place comes a new group called Ruby Flipper. It will include 2 of the Pan girls, Sue Mehenick and Cherry Gillespie, and 3 male dancers. Ruth Pearson, one of the original line-up, will run the new group along with choreographer Flick Colby. The name is a loose combination of parts of the 2 girls' names.

DANGER SPRAYS

The potential health hazard caused by aerosols will be discussed in the Commons this week following an investigation into the effect on the atmosphere of gases used to pressurize the spray cans. British scientists have largely confirmed American findings that a propellent gas called fluorocarbon eats away at the ozone layer, the atmospheric belt 15 to 30 miles above the earth which protects everyone from dangerous ultra-violet rays. The effect of the gas is to thin out and neutralize this protection to a point where the rays could pierce the belt and expose everyone to the hazard of skin cancer. Some manufacturers have already started to use alternative harmless propellants in their sprays and at least 13 American states have banned the use of fluorocarbon.

VARRINGTON'S VODKA TONIC

The unlikely town of Warrington has been put firmly on the map, largely thanks to the brainwave of a vodka distillery executive and a group of men at the New Town Development Corporation. 'Varrington', which is how the advertising of the locally made vodka has irate Russian commissars pronouncing the name, got a further boost when a festival was launched as the Development Corporation unveiled its New Town plan. Warrington has even gone on the tourist map; French travel agents recently took in the distillery, Wigan Pier and Ma Boyle's oysters in Liverpool.

HOWARD HUGHES DIES IN PLANE

Howard Hughes, the 70-year-old legendary reclusive multi-millionaire, died yesterday on a plane taking him from Mexico to the US for hospital treatment. Hughes first made the headlines as a Hollywood playboy, then as a controversial film-maker, daredevil pilot and finally as the recluse with the Midas touch in the world of high finance. It all began with a unique drill bit until recently used on nearly every oil rig in the world, the rights to which he inherited from his father in 1923.

Harold Wilson leaves 10 Downing Street for the last time as Prime Minister.

'MURDER ME LIKE THIS'

One of television's top detectives is to be killed off. Steve Keller, who is played by Michael Douglas in the ITV police series *The Streets of San Francisco*, will be shot dead when the show returns to the screen. Michael, son of Hollywood star Kirk Douglas, has been working out his own 'murder' with the series' script-writers. He plans to spend more time behind the camera, having gained great prestige from the film *One Flew Over The Cuckoo's Nest*, which he co-produced. His father originally bought the play and starred in it on stage but could never get it made into a film so he turned it over to his son.

4 SACKED IN UNION DISPUTE

British Rail has sacked 4 people because they refused to join a trade union. The action follows a 'closed shop' agreement with the rail unions last August. Last November there were between 6,000 and 8,000 non-union workers among 250,000 employees. 'Now that the first dismissals have been effected, we hope the others will comply,' a BR spokesman commented.

DANGER ON THE IRONING BOARD

Housewives are being warned to look out for worn and frayed asbestos on ironing boards and oven doors. The warning is part of a campaign to protect the family from possible health hazards caused by asbestos dust. Following an agreement between the manufacturers and the Government, goods containing asbestos will from October carry a sign saying: 'Take care with asbestos. Breathing asbestos dust can damage health. Observe the safety rules.'

CURB THIS DANGER SPORT, SAY DOCTORS

Doctors, police and the gliding experts are calling for stricter controls on the new sport of hang-gliding to cut the number of accidents. They say too many people are being injured trying the sport in which the 'pilot' takes off on foot from a hillside and glides suspended from a kite-like wing.

ALL IN THE FAMILY

Mr Callaghan could be the first British prime minister to be interviewed on television by his son-in-law. His daughter Margaret is married to Peter Jay, presenter of *Weekend World* and economics editor of *The Times*.

CROSSROADS GETS LOST FOR 4 MILLION VIEWERS

Television chiefs are miffed that only one viewer out of an estimated 4 million bothered to complain when a whole episode of *Crossroads* was missed out. Viewers watching Granada, Southern, HTV and Scottish TV saw the next night's episode instead. ATV officials are furious because they claim the lost episode came at a crucial moment in the series. 'Nobody in those areas will know that Meg has disappeared. They won't know either that Jill and Stan are excited because their offer for a house has been accepted.' The mix-up occurred at Southern TV, which networks the series to the other 3 stations. Southern plans to drop an episode next month so that once again the whole country can watch the same story on the same day.

VCRs WILL REPEAT TV SPECTACULAR

The trick of making money from new technology is to note the gap between its invention and the time when it becomes commercially profitable. John Logie Baird invented television but died in 1946 worth only a few pounds. The next boom to watch for is in VCRs, Video Cassette Recorders. Most electrical shops agree that the boom is some way off yet but Currys are about to place their first order for VCRs. At around £500 it may seem a lot to pay for a new consumer toy, yet colour TV took off in the 60s when a set cost £260 – equal to £650 in today's money – and the story of black and white TV is similar. If any manufacturers make fortunes from VCRs they will not be British. Sony and the Dutch firm Philips effectively have the market sewn up between them.

Tommy Docherty, the Manchester United manager, with Dave Mackay, the Derby manager, after playing in a charity match.

Magpie presenters Mick Robertson, Jenny Hanley and Douglas Rae with winners in a Design a Road Safety Poster Competition.

FORD PLANS HYDROGEN CAR FOR THE 80s

A hydrogen-powered car is being developed by Ford with an engine which operates on the same principle as a household refrigerator. The new car's power unit is based on the Stirling engine, invented by a Scottish clergyman in the early 1800s. Long before the development of the petrol engine the Reverend Stirling had the idea of heating air so that it would expand and drive the pistons. The idea has worked successfully for large static engines but not – so far – for compact car engines which need brisk acceleration. Instead of air the Ford motor uses liquid hydrogen, which is heated using almost any fuel. To accelerate the car the hydrogen is simply pumped round faster. An experimental model is already giving about the same power as a 2-litre Cortina engine. Ford hopes the new unit will be powering cars by 1985.

END OF THE LINE FOR THE ONEDIN SCHOONER

The *Charlotte Rhodes*, the 73-year-old schooner known to millions through television's *Onedin Line*, sailed into the archives yesterday. After voyaging through 3 series the vessel has been declared unseaworthy by the Board of Trade. As the schooner completed her last day's filming for the fourth series near Exeter yesterday, the owners were planning to fight the ruling.

SID JAMES DIES ON STAGE

Sid James, one of Britain's best-known comedians, died last night after collapsing on stage with a heart attack. He slumped unconscious 10 minutes after the curtain rose at the Empire Theatre in Sunderland. 62-year-old Sid came to Britain from his native Johannesburg in 1946 after working as a boxer, truck-driver, dance instructor and diamond polisher. The man with the craggy face and gravel voice, who boasted the dirtiest laugh in showbusiness, appeared in 250 films, 30 of them in the *Carry On* series.

LABOUR MAJORITY VANISHES AS MINISTER DIES

The Government's overall majority of 1 was lost yesterday with the death of Brian O'Malley, Minister of State for Health and Social Security. The 46-year-old Rotherham MP's death will make little difference in the Commons; Labour has a lead of 40 over the Tories and the other minority parties seldom agree on concerted action.

'They peel them with their metal knives.' Cadbury's Smash advert.

MAY 1976

DUNN'S TITLE CHALLENGE ENDS IN A KNOCKOUT

Richard Dunn today joins the long list of fighters who have tried and failed to win the richest prize in sport, the World Heavyweight Championship. In the early hours of this morning (25 May), Yorkshire's 31-year-old Dunn became the fourth British boxer to be beaten by Muhammad Ali for the title. He was knocked out in the fifth round. Paratroop Sergeant Dunn's consolation is that he is a minimum of £65,000 richer; Ali took his income from fights to £16m.

EVERY CHILD'S DREAM SOLD FOR £4m

Hamleys, one of the world's top toy shops, has been saved from liquidation. Debenhams, the store group, is taking over the '10 floors of fun' in Regent Street in a deal worth £4,780,000. The previous owners, Lines Bros., went into liquidation in 1970. Hamleys began in 1760 when Cornishman William Hamley called the shop Noah's Ark and started by selling carved wooden boats and painted dolls.

Jeremy Thorpe is forced to quit as Liberal Leader over allegations of a homosexual affair. Jo Grimond takes over as an interim leader.

ITV GOES BACK TO VARIETY

Variety in the style of the old *Sunday Night At The London Palladium* is returning to ITV in the autumn. The new *Wednesday At Eight* will have all the ingredients of the old show with top international acts being introduced by a big-name compère. There will also be an audience participation game in the middle of each show called Name That Tune, replacing Beat the Clock. The game involves contestants guessing music titles for a big money prize. The original Palladium show ran for 12 years, reaching audiences of 22 million each Sunday and making stars out of compères like Bruce Forsyth and Norman Vaughan. It was revived briefly 2½ years ago with compères Jim Dale and Ted Rogers but was unable to recreate its old magic.

DAVIS BACK TO A HERO'S WELCOME

George Davis, the man whose innocence was proclaimed in whitewash on the street walls of London's East End, came home to a pop star's welcome after being released from Alberney Prison last night. He was a free man, though not yet officially an innocent one. He had served exactly 60 weeks of his 17-year sentence for robbery and wounding with intent to resist arrest. Home Secretary Mr Roy Jenkins decided to release him because an interim report by police into the circumstances of his arrest threw doubt onto the identification which resulted in his conviction. A secret witness came forward a month ago to back Davis's alibi with a story that was strong enough to make Mr Jenkins act.

Ronnie Wood and Mick Jagger on the Rolling Stones UK tour.

£75m FOR 12½p

The 12½p that Melvin Dumar gave to a hitchhiker may be worth £75m. The hiker was multi-millionaire Howard Hughes, who left a one-sixteenth share of his estimated £1,000m fortune to Mr Dumar. Mr Dumar said that he was driving to California in 1968 when he pulled over and saw a man lying on the side of the road, bleeding. He didn't believe the man was Howard Hughes but gave him a lift to Las Vegas. There, the man asked for some money and Mr Dumar gave him 25 cents, which was the last he heard about the incident until today. The will which could bring Mr Dumar his fortune was found mysteriously in a Mormon church office in Salt Lake City. A nationwide search had been conducted for a will since Hughes died of kidney failure on a plane journey last month.

WESTMINSTER'S BREAKING POINT

The death of an MP under strain from acute political controversy yesterday unleashed the tensions of minority Government into one of the most vicious Westminster rows for years. One Labour backbencher described as 'political assassination' the death of 67-year-old Hugh Delargey, Labour MP for Thurrock, Essex, and Chairman of the Commons Select Committee. His fatal collapse came 12 hours after he made the stormiest Commons speech of his life, insisting that the Government should retain a built-in majority on legislative committees, despite losing its overall majority in the House.

Motor cycling ace Barry Sheene checks his machine before a race at Brands Hatch.

'SMILE OR GET THE SACK'

Boutique manageress Joy Churm insisted that her girls give the customers service with a smile otherwise they would face the sack. 17-year-old Dawn Spiers didn't smile, and out she went. Assistant Manageress Andrea Swift, 18, was so upset that she walked out in anger. Yesterday, however, Miss Swift was awarded £135 compensation by an industrial tribunal for unfair dismissal. Dawn was unable to claim for her sacking because she had not been with the firm long enough. Mrs Churm, who gave the smile order at the Subway boutique in Wolverhampton, insisted, 'I did not dismiss this girl. I gave her the alternative and she left.'

THE LITTLE INNOCENT WHO GREW UP INTO A WOMAN OF TERROR

The name of Ulrike Meinhof will go down in history alongside Leila Khaled, Patti Hearst and Rose Dugdale, all of them women who grew up from innocent childhood into a life allied to guerilla gangs. At the age of 14, Ulrike Meinhof wanted to be a nun. She had always been an idealist, always wanting to change things. At first it was by non-violent means; the terror that Ulrike and her political sidekick Andreas Baader introduced into Germany started as an intellectual drive to change a society that many young Germans saw as a materialist and hedonistic hell. Yesterday, at the age of 41, she hanged herself with a strip of towel in a prison cell in Stuttgart. The leader of one of the world's most feared terrorist gangs, the Baader-Meinhof, was dead.

MAN JAILED FOR 'ENGLISH ONLY' SIGN

Robert Relf went to jail yesterday for refusing to take down a sign advertising his house for sale with the words 'to an English family'. Relf was jailed for an unspecified term for contempt of court, becoming the first man to go to prison for breaking the race relations laws.

THE LONG AND WINDING ROAD BACK TO THE TOP

When Paul McCartney emerged from a 2-year exile after the break-up of the Beatles, he couldn't face playing in front of a large critical crowd again, so he got into a van with his wife Linda and a few musicians and set off along the M1 in search of a gig. They saw a sign to Nottingham and sent the driver ahead to the university to ask if the students wanted Paul McCartney to play for them. The audience of 200 paid 50p each. At Madison Square Garden this week, the highlight of the Wings tour of America, an audience of 20,000 paid £100,000. The 2 shows, 5 years apart, are strangely linked. McCartney told how he had never forgotten the Beatles' most successful show when they filled Shay Stadium in New York with 55,000 youngsters. His ambition was always to go back to New York with his own band and put on a show that would equal or surpass that night a decade ago. The 30-date tour of America will gross £2m.

Laurence Olivier and Dustin Hoffman in Marathon Man.

DAY BY DAY

1 May
Southampton beats Manchester United 1–0 in the FA Cup Final.

The TV programme *Dixon of Dock Green* ends after running for more than 20 years in 434 episodes.

2 May
James Hunt of Great Britain is disqualified after winning the Spanish Grand Prix because his Formula One McLaren car was found to be five-eighths of an inch too wide. His appeal to the International Automobile Federation is upheld in July and he is reinstated as winner.

5 May
The Government and the TUC agree a new pay policy which would give minimum pay increases of £2.50 a week and a maximum of £4.

8 May
St Helens beats Widnes 20–5 in the Rugby League Challenge Cup Final.

11 May
The Bolivian Ambassador to France, General Joaquin Zenteno Anaya, is shot dead in Paris by a group calling itself the Che Guevara Brigade.

12 May
Mr Jo Grimond agrees to resume the leadership of the Liberal party until a permanent leader is chosen; he was previously Leader from 1956 until 1967.

19 May
A report by a House of Commons Select Committee on the 1974 Cyprus crisis criticizes the Government for not intervening militarily.

24 May
British Airways and Air France Concordes fly to Washington, inaugurating the first commercial supersonic flights to North America.

27 May
The Speaker suspends the sitting of the House of Commons for 20 minutes because of an uproar between members after the Government wins a division on the Shipbuilding and aircraft Nationalization Bill by 1 vote.

28 May
Mrs Thatcher says the Opposition would stop co-operation with the Government in providing pairs after Mr Callaghan had told her that he would not set aside the previous night's vote on shipbuilding nationalization which Conservatives claimed had been won after a Labour MP broke a pairing agreement.

POP STAR DIED FOR HIS MUSIC

Pop singer Keith Relf died for his music. Against doctors' orders he played the harmonica despite a chronic chest complaint, smoked 40 cigarettes a day and died with his guitar in his hands. The instrument was still plugged in and the 33-year-old may have been electrocuted. Relf, who topped the charts with his group the Yardbirds 10 years ago, was planning a comeback. Other members of the group – Jeff Beck, Jimmy Page and Eric Clapton – went on to become some of the biggest names in pop.

JUNE 1976

DEATH OF A TOUGH GUY AT 48

Tough guy actor Sir Stanley Baker lost the hardest fought battle of his career yesterday (28 June). Sir Stanley, who was knighted in Sir Harold Wilson's resignation honours, died in a Malaga hospital where he was convalescing after a major cancer operation earlier this year. The son of a Rhondda coal miner, he travelled to London at the age of 14 in response to an advertisement in a stage newspaper and went on to make many memorable films, including *The Cruel Sea*, *The Guns of Navarone* and *Zulu*.

BRITAIN WINS BATTLE OF HASTINGS

A second Battle of Hastings has been fought and won. This time, however, 909 years and 323 days after King Harold fell on Senlac Hill, our American allies were on hand to help the English to victory. A £690,000 bid from the Department of the Environment, which included a large sum donated by an American charitable foundation, beat off interest from overseas property developers to keep the historic 573-acre estate in British hands.

Battle of the burgers: teenagers munch their way through Big Macs as McDonalds eats its way into the British hamburger market.

TORIES WOO HOME BUYERS

A new Tory housing policy switching government aid from council housing to home-ownership offers the party a vote-winner pitched at the heart of Labour grass roots support. The package has three key elements:
- part house purchase: first-time house buyers would be able to raise mortgages for a portion of the property, the rest being taken up by building societies, which would get interest repayments on their stake direct from the Government. The part owner would have the right eventually to buy out their building society partners.
- half-price council houses: at the moment such houses are sold to tenants at a maximum discount of 20%. This would be increased to one-third, while tenants of 15 years' standing could be offered the chance to buy their houses at half the market price.
- mortgage deposit grants: this scheme salvaged from the last Tory manifesto, would allow the Government to pay a cash contribution to young couples saving mortgage deposits.

THE POP STAR GUNMAN

Rock star Roger Daltrey of The Who is to star in a film about gunman John McVicar, once Britain's most wanted man. The film will be based on a book McVicar wrote in prison after he was recaptured in London in 1970 after 18 months on the run from Durham Jail. He is now in Leicester Prison finishing a 26-year sentence he was serving for armed robbery. Daltrey last appeared on screen in 1975 as Franz Liszt in Ken Russell's *Lisztomania*.

NOW IT'S THE SON OF THE SAINT

Simon Templar, the Saint in ITV's hit series of the 60s, is to pass on his halo to his son. Actor Ian Ogilvy is to take over from Roger Moore to star in *Son of the Saint*, a new series beginning next year. Ogilvy, a 32-year-old Etonian, played the young poet who married Elizabeth Bellamy in *Upstairs Downstairs*. Moore will still be seen briefly at the start of each episode as an elderly Simon Templar introducing his son before walking off with a young blonde on his arm.

Daley Thompson, the youngest ever athlete to represent Britain, trains for the decathlon in the Montreal Olympics.

FRAMPTON AND THE FAIRY TALE

Peter Frampton was just 14 when he began his career as a rock guitarist, and his partner on the steps of the art block during the lunch-hour was schoolmate David Bowie. At 18 he was voted the face of '68 by teenagers all over the country in a nationwide poll. By then he had scored 3 Top Ten hits with his group the Herd. The face was angelic and he could certainly play guitar but sometimes he didn't bother to plug it in because he knew the girls would be screaming so much they couldn't hear it anyway.

Then, after 2 years of fame, he walked out of his group when he realized he was being ripped off and the face of '68 soon faded into an almost forgotten face of the 70s. He left for America and, after 5 years of constant touring, found last autumn that he was $100,000 in the red and was on the verge of giving up his attempt to be a solo star. Then, like an absurd fairy story, his LP recorded live at a concert at San Francisco started to sell and sell. In 4 months *Frampton Comes Alive* has sold 4 million copies at £3 each. It is still number 1 in America. Now, Peter Frampton, still only 26, is being hailed as the logical successor to Elton John, Led Zeppelin and all the other English rock idols who've won huge rewards after conquering America.

STARS OF STAGE, SCREEN. . . AND ADVERTS

As 'legitimate' acting work is hit by the recession many big names gratefully jump onto the advertisement bandwagon. Brigitte Bardot will soon be seen promoting Goya's new aftershave, Zendiq. Her biggest rival in this field is probably Henry Cooper, used for nearly 3 years to sell Brut 33 for Fabergé. Bruce Forsyth is thought to be the highest-paid actor in commercials in Britain, earning more than £100,000 for talking to housewives about Stork margarine. Orson Welles pops up to tell us about sherry; George Savalas – brother of Telly – munches Wimpy hamburgers in a last-ditch attempt to ward off the threat of the growing McDonald's chain.

The stars attract enormous fees for such appearances, though it can still work out cheaper for companies to use them. Most top actors are paid on a fixed sum basis, whereas 'unknowns' tend to get repeat fees for every showing. Gordon Jackson was extolling the virtues of the Trustee Savings Bank before *Upstairs Downstairs* made him an upmarket actor. Last November the IBA ruled that it would 'no longer be appropriate' for him to appear as his integrity was thought to influence people unduly. He is now back on our screens making Hudson-like judgements on shopping at Fine Fare supermarkets.

The star system for commercials was really launched nearly 10 years ago when Maxwell House in America paid Edward G. Robinson $50,000 for drinking their coffee. The final seal of approval for such work came with Olivier's performance for Polaroid – receiving $250,000 for a day's work on condition that the commercials would not be shown in Britain.

CLASS OF '76

They should have been in school. Instead they graduated in terror and death and hatred on the streets of Soweto, their black township outside Johannesburg. One schoolboy carries the body of another young pupil shot dead when South African police opened fire on rioters at the gates of the Phefeni Junior Secondary School. The riots arose out of a demonstration by thousands of black high-school pupils against being taught some subjects in Afrikaans – to them the language of oppression. By last night, as 300 police in riot gear struggled to contain the escalating rebellion, the death toll had risen to 7. It was South Africa's worst racial confrontation since 69 demonstrators were shot dead by police 16 years ago at Sharpeville.

Ilie Nastase in action at Wimbledon.

CINEMA MOGUL ZUKOR IS DEAD

Adolph Zukor, founder of Paramount Pictures, has died in Hollywood at the age of 103. Zukor's death closes the chapter of that weird and wonderful breed – part robber baron and part inspired entrepreneur – who built and dominated Hollywood during its halcyon half-century between 1910 and 1960. He was the last of the dreammakers, the men whose impact on the public by remote control to their film studios was incalculable. They were more powerful than presidents, more influential than economists and educationalists. Zukor, who was born in Hungary and emigrated to America when he was 16, created or groomed stars including Rudolf Valentino, Gloria Swanson, Marlene Dietrich, Mae West, Gary Cooper, Ray Milland, Bob Hope, Bing Crosby and Claudette Colbert.

South African Prime Minister John Vorster in pensive mood at talks in West Germany about the political situation in his country.

HOLIDAY SCROUNGERS

Jobless sun-seekers are getting all-in holidays at the tax-payer's expense. Many are causing havoc with bookings for self-catering holiday flats by taking them over and then squatting. Under a Department of Social Security job search scheme, unemployed people anywhere in the country can apply for jobs in other areas advertised through the national Job Centres. They are given an appointment card for an interview, the return rail fare and told to apply to the local Social Security Department in the new area for subsistence money. Unsuccessful applicants then have the option of staying on to seek other work. It is the 'growing army' of these people, say tourist officials, who are taking on holiday flatlets for a temporary stay and then refusing to leave when their time is up. Meanwhile, they sign on for social security and unemployment benefit in the area where they are staying. Tory MP Alan Clark has called the situation a 'disgrace' and said that he would be putting down a question in the House of Commons.

ICELAND CLAIMS, 'WE'VE WON COD WAR'

Iceland proudly boasted victory in the Cod War last night. Under an agreement signed in Oslo by Mr Anthony Crosland, the Foreign Secretary, British trawlers could be barred from fishing within 200 miles of Iceland's coast in 6 months' time. The consequences for Britain's fishing industry could be 'painful', Mr Crosland admitted. To have carried on fighting, however, would have ruined Britain's standing in the world. Mr Crosland regards the agreement, which allows Britain to catch up to 30,000 tons of fish – 85% of it cod – in the next 6 months, as 'the best which could be achieved this time'. But Icelandic Foreign Minister, Mr Einar Heustsson, hailed it as a famous victory for Iceland. He insisted it secured the acceptance of Iceland's 200-mile limit unilaterally announced last July.

JULY 1976

HIJACKERS FREE 47

Terrorists yesterday released 47 hostages from the hijacked Air France airliner, then renewed threats to blow up the plane and its remaining 210 captives. Those freed were mothers, children, old women and the sick, who were flown to Paris from Entebbe airport in Uganda. The terrorists – half a dozen young men and women of the Popular Front for the Liberation of Palestine – continued to hold the other passengers in a disused airport lounge.

The hijackers are demanding the release of 53 prisoners held in Europe, Israel and Kenya and have set a deadline of 1 p.m. today (1 July) for them to be flown to Entebbe. The hijacking began on Sunday (27 June) when the airline, *en route* from Israel to France, was seized over Greece, refuelled in Libya and flown to Uganda.

Welcome home! The pilot of one of the Israeli resue planes is carried shoulder high by admiring crowds at Ben Gurion Airport, Tel Aviv.

LEFT-HANDED PUPILS JUST AS BRIGHT

Teachers who believe that left-handed children are more clumsy than right-handers are wrong, according to the findings of a new national study. The report says that many left-handed children appear awkward because they have to use educational equipment designed for right-handed children. The National Children's Bureau, which carried out the survey among 11-year-olds, found that teachers also thought more left-handers were bad writers, that they had a tendency towards poor speech and were on average more difficult to understand.

LASSE THE GREATEST

Lasse Viren last night joined the immortals of sport. The 27-year-old Finnish policeman won the Olympic 5,000 metres gold medal to add to the 10,000 metres gold he had already collected – a repeat of his golden double at the 1972 Munich Games. Now he plans to win the Marathon for an astonishing Olympic treble that only Emil Zatopek has achieved.

TOP GROUP SACK THEIR ROCKER

The lead singer of Uriah Heep, one of Britain's most successful groups, has been sacked because he failed to move with the times. David Byron, who arrived on the pop scene via public school and the Stock Exchange, was told he was out of a job following months of disagreement over the group's future. Byron wanted to include more rock and roll; the rest preferred to play more contemporary music.

PARENTS FIGHT FOR GRAMMAR SCHOOLS

Defiant Tameside are taking on Whitehall in the High Court in a bid to retain their grammar schools. In an unprecedented case, councillors and parents have challenged the power of the Education Minister, Mr Fred Mulley, to order them to accept a completely comprehensive system. The scheme to go comprehensive this September was going ahead until 8 weeks ago when the Tories won power in the local elections and halted the Labour plans.

SHEENE CLINCHES TITLE

Britain's Barry Sheene is the new world 500cc motor-cycling champion, despite losing the Belgian Grand Prix to John Williams. Sheene's second place gave him an unbeatable 72 points in the championship.

Nadia Comaneci, who scored the first perfect score awarded in any apparatus event.

SCREEN COUPLE MARRY

A screen romance became reality yesterday when 26-year-old actress Liza Goddard married 33-year-old actor Colin Baker, who plays her fiancé in the BBC television series *The Brothers.* Liza plays April Winter to Colin's Paul Merroney and their screen wedding is planned for the autumn.

PRIMATE: CURB IMMIGRATION

The Archbishop of Canterbury has called for clear restrictions on the number of immigrants allowed into Britain. Seeking 'to help Christians to speak more clearly on race relations', Dr Donald Coggan said, 'The forces of law and order must be supported in their resistance to every kind of illegal immigration. There must be a clearly defined limit to the numbers of those allowed into this country. There are signs that our present legislation needs a careful look at this point.'

TURN OFF THE TAPS – BY LAW

The Cabinet decided yesterday (1 July) to rush through new drought laws to curb the use of water. The measures, to be outlined to the Commons today in an emergency statement by Planning Minister John Silkin, will restrict less essential users, such as golf courses and car washes, without turning off supplies in the home. At present, the Government can use the 1945 Water Act to ban hosepipes and sprinklers but under the 1958 Act a clampdown on industrial users is allowed only if domestic users in the same area are also subjected to strict curbs, with standpipes installed in the street. The Cabinet feels that some industrial users should have their supplies cut off without bringing in blanket restrictions.

Once it was a pond with ducks and boats; now he'd be better off flying a kite as the drought continues.

Liberal leadership candidate David Steel pictured at home with his wife Judy and children (l. to r.) Graeme, Rory and Catriona.

THE END FOR INVALID TRICYCLES

Invalid 3-wheel cars, which have been attacked on safety grounds, are to be phased out in favour of mobility allowances, Social Services Secretary Mr David Ennals announced in the Commons yesterday. The mobility allowance, now £5 per week, was introduced as an alternative to the familiar light-blue tricycle in September 1974.

BORIS THE CHEAT

Russia's Boris Onischenko was banned from the Olympics yesterday (19 July) after officials discovered his épée was wired to score a hit without touching his opponent. The 1971 world champion was fighting Britain's Jim Fox in the fencing section of the Modern Pentathlon. He lunged forward and the Briton stepped back untouched – then stood amazed as a light signalled a hit. Fox's immediate protest eventually led to the expulsion of the 38-year-old Munich silver medallist.

HERE IS THE NEWS ABOUT THE NEWSCASTER

ITN newscaster Gordon Honeycombe's new book – his fourth – is fighting its way to the top of the non-fiction bestselling list. Called *Red Watch*, it is a documentary novel based on what happened when 30 fire engines were called to a blazing Maida Vale hotel in December 1974. Honeycombe, 39, spends 16 days a month at ITN and the rest of the time writing in his Primrose Hill flat – not bad for someone who branded himself a failure at 27 and bought himself a one-way ticket to Australia. He was out of work at the time and, by his own admission, hadn't progressed as an actor in 2 years with the Royal Shakespeare Company, had had his first novel rejected and was living on tomato soup. Then he watched someone he'd been at Oxford with reading the news headlines and thought he could do the job better. He wrote to the editor of ITN and within 2 weeks was reading the national news.

TAIWAN OUT – AND NIGERIA FOLLOWS

The Olympic Games suffered a double blow last night (16 July) when the withdrawal of Taiwan was followed by a walk-out by Nigeria. The Nigerians were protesting against the participation of New Zealand, whose All Blacks rugby team is touring South Africa. Tanzania refused to send its athletes in the first place and last night, on the eve of the opening ceremony, other African countries were discussing with their governments whether to follow Nigeria's example. The official departure of the Nationalist Chinese came after the International Olympic Committee voted 58 – 2 that they could compete only under their island name of Taiwan, and not as the Republic of China.

Chilling reminders of the criminal career of Donald Neilson – one of his hoods, which would conceal all but his eyes, and his sawn-off shotgun.

DAY BY DAY

1 July
Donald Neilson is found guilty of murdering Lesley Whittle. 3 weeks later he is found guilty of murdering 3 sub-postmasters and sentenced to life imprisonment.

2 July
Chris Evert beats Evonne Cawley in the final of the Wimbledon women's singles.

3 July
Israeli troops raid Entebbe Airport, Uganda and free more than 100 hostages who have been held there for almost a week aboard the hijacked Air France airbus. In a raid lasting only 40 minutes 3 of the hostages, 1 Israeli commando and 20 Ugandan soldiers were killed. 7 hijackers were also killed, but 3 were believed to have escaped.

Bjorn Borg of Sweden wins the Wimbledon men's singles title, beating Romanian Ilie Nastase. He becomes Wimbledon's youngest post-war champion.

4 July
Celebrations to mark the bicentenary of American Independence are held throughout the United States.

7 July
Mr David Steel is elected Leader of the Liberal party with 12,541 votes compared with 7,032 for Mr John Pardoe.

10 July
4 mercenaries, 3 British and 1 American, are executed by firing squad in Luanda. President Neto of Angola has rejected all appeals for clemency, including one from the Queen.

15 July
Labour retains Thurrock in a by-election.

17 July
The Queen, accompanied by Prince Philip and Prince Andrew, opens the Olympic Games in Montreal. 19 African and Arab countries boycott the Games in protest at the New Zealand rugby team's tour of South Africa.

20 July
A Viking spacecraft lands on Mars and relays photographs of the planet's surface.

21 July
Mr Christopher Ewart-Biggs, British Ambassador to Ireland, and Miss Judith Cook, a private secretary, are killed when a bomb explodes under their car a few miles from Dublin.

22 July
Britain's first gold medal at the Olympics is won by the modern pentathlon team, Jim Fox, Adrian Parker and Danny Nightingale.

24 July
David Wilkie takes gold in the 200 metres breast stroke. He only won the silver in the 100 metres (20 July) in spite of breaking the world record; John Hencken took gold in that event.

28 July
Britain breaks off diplomatic relations with Uganda.

29 July
The end of Southend pier is destroyed by fire.

30 July
The High Court rules that Mr Peter Shore acted wrongly when he was Secretary of State for Trade in withdrawing the licence for Mr Freddie Laker to operate a cut price Skytrain air service to America.

AUG 1976

HOW THE MAN IN THE DIRTY MAC CLEANED UP

Peter Falk, known to 40 million viewers as Columbo, didn't start acting until he was 28. Today, the rumpled, restless little man with one eye has a contract that makes him the highest paid actor in TV. He lost his right eye at the age of 3 as the result of a tumour. He got a BA in Political Science and an MA in Public Administration and his first job was as an efficiency expert for the state of Connecticut. 19 years ago he was interviewed by Columbia Pictures tycoon Harry Cohen. When Falk enquired about money Cohen exploded: 'For the same price I can get an actor with 2 eyes!' These days, for a single episode of the detective series he gets £138,000. Columbo's popularity is such that he has Universal Studios at his mercy. He demands the best scripts, which he is able to rewrite before directing them. Falk created the character from a part that was originally designed for Bing Crosby.

HOW HARRY FINALLY SOLD A STORY – THE BIGGEST HIT SINCE *JAWS*

Jack Higgins earns Harry Patterson the price of a Rolls-Royce every fortnight. The fact that Patterson still drives the Scimitar he bought years ago when he adopted Higgins as his latest pseudonym and actually sold a novel or two emphasizes his late arrival into the big time. *The Eagle Has Landed* has brought him from a back-to-back in Belfast to a luxury home in Jersey via a gritty period in Leeds, where he wrote under half-a-dozen pseudonyms without selling a word. The author wryly reflects on the fact that all his earlier works are now eagerly being published in America under the name of Jack Higgins, when he couldn't get any of them published before. Sales of *Eagle* already exceed 5 million and it is due out shortly in paperback with orders exceeding anything since *Jaws*. His new novel, *Storm Warning*, comes out next week.

LEGEND UNDER THE HAMMER

Jensen Motors dies today (16 August). The famous luxury car firm, in business for 50 years, is to come under the auctioneer's hammer this week. Included in the sale will be the three last Jensen cars that will be built. No one is quite sure what a Jensen Interceptor – £10,764 in a dealer's showroom – might fetch in the knowledge that there will be no more to follow.

NIKI FIGHTS FOR HIS LIFE

World champion driver Niki Lauda was fighting for his life last night after his Ferrari crashed in flames on the track he described as 'too dangerous to drive on'. It happened when he hurtled into a steel guard rail on the second lap of the West German Grand Prix at the much-criticized Nurburgring circuit.

At last . . . John Walker exults in his 1,500-metre finish at the Olympic games in Montreal.

STONEHOUSE: 4 VERDICTS OF GUILTY

Runaway MP John Stonehouse has been found guilty on 4 of 19 charges involving forgery and theft. The jury were unable to reach unanimous verdicts on the other 15 charges Stonehouse faces – or the 6 charges his secretary Sheila Buckley jointly faces. The 51-year-old MP for Walsall North was found guilty of: making a forged passport application; stealing the proceeds of a banker's draft for $12,500; obtaining an American Express credit card by forgery; and attempting to enable Barbara Stonehouse to obtain £30,000 from the Royal Insurance Company. The jury will now be asked to consider majority verdicts on the remaining charges.

PAINTER DROPS A LINE: I'LL RETURN ONE DAY

While the art world has been trying to contact painter Tom Keating in connection with pictures attributed to Samuel Palmer, he has been riding around on his moped on holiday. Mr Keating, who has the reputation of being able to turn his brush to the style of many of the big names of the past 300 years, sent a card to a friend saying, 'I have travelled 750 miles. I will return one day.' The card was posted on 2 August. Since then Mr Keating has been named in a newspaper article concerning the authenticity of drawings accepted as originals by Palmer, the nineteenth-century master.

PATIENCE PAYS OFF FOR BIG-HITTING BOTHAM

Ian Botham, at 20 the youngest player in the Prudential Cup squad, will be England's youngest player since Brian Statham made his début in 1951 if he is chosen in any of the 3 one-day matches against the West Indies. A Somerset regular for the past 3 seasons, Botham had a soccer offer from Bert Head, then Manager of Crystal Palace, to go to Selhurst Park for a trial. 15-year-old Botham turned it down. 'Cricket is a more enjoyable life and lasts longer.' Botham is married to a Lincolnshire girl and lives in the John Wesley village of Epworth in the winter. He has a job there with a company that makes musical instruments. He will probably need leave of absence this winter as he is expected to tour India. West Indies Captain Clive Lloyd picked him out this week as one of England's most promising young players.

BY JINGLE IT'S A SINGLE!

It happens once every 5 years: the catchy little jingle that takes off and becomes a hit record. Presently stunning the pop world and delighting the ad men is the phenomenal success of David Dundas's jingle for Brutus jeans, called 'Jeans On'. The last time a commercial made good was back in 1971 when Coca Cola scored a smash hit with 'I'd Like To Teach The World To Sing'. David Dundas, a 31-year-old lord who started jingle writing last November, wrote the song that turned him into an overnight pop idol in just one afternoon.

Leonard Rossiter stars in The Fall and Rise of Reginald Perrin.

ALASTAIR SIM DIES AT 76

Alastair Sim, the actor who created the headmistress of St Trinians, has died aged 76. For more than 40 years his doleful eyes and voice of impending doom delighted theatre and cinema audiences. He played eccentric Scottish aristocrats, bumbling murderers, policemen, vicars, Scrooge, Captain Hook, Prospero. But it is as Miss Fritton that he will be best remembered. Sim's route into acting came through lecturing in elocution at Edinburgh University. His popularity secured his election as Rector there in 1946 in a landslide victory over future Prime Minister Harold Macmillan. He leaves a wife and daughter; actor George Cole, who played the spiv in the St Trinians films, is his adopted son.

PETE AND DUD'S 4-LETTER LP

In a move which will shock and alienate many of their fans Peter Cook and Dudley Moore have decided to release an LP which is littered with 4-letter expletives and could be construed as obscene. Called *Derek and Clive (Live)* the record was made without scripts 3 years ago in New York in a studio and before an audience at the Bottom Line Club in Greenwich Village. Island Records is releasing the record this week, confident that any prurient aspect will be outweighed by the humour of a yobbo extension of the Pete and Dud formula.

DAY BY DAY

2 Aug
German film director Fritz Lang dies, aged 85.

4 Aug
The first women's cricket match to be played at Lord's is between England and Australia. The English women's team wins by 8 wickets.

Lord Thomson of Fleet, who headed the group which owns *The Times* and the *Sunday Times*, dies, aged 82.

6 Aug
John Stonehouse, Labour MP for Walsall North, is found guilty on 18 of 19 charges involving theft and conspiracy and is sentenced to 7 years' imprisonment. His secretary, Mrs Sheila Buckley, is given a 2-year suspended sentence after being found guilty on 5 out of 6 charges.

17 Aug
The West Indies win the fifth test at the Oval to complete a 3–0 series victory over England. Viv Richards hit 291 in the match – the highest score ever by a West Indian in England and the thirteenth highest in test history. His aggregate from 4 tests – he missed one through illness – was 829 at an average of 118.

More than 3,000 people are killed when a severe earthquake, followed by tidal waves, strikes the southern Philippines.

18 Aug
The Republican party nominates President Ford as its candidate in the presidential election with 1,187 delegate votes. Mr Ronald Reagan receives 1,070 votes.

19 Aug
A letter is published in *The Times* from Mr Tom Keating admitting that he had imitated works of the Victorian painter Samuel Palmer as a protest against merchants who make capital out of artists. The authenticity of 13 Palmer paintings, one of which had been sold at auction a few years ago for £15,000, had been questioned.

25 Aug
M. Jacques Chirac resigns as Prime Minister of France and is succeeded by M. Raymond Barre.

30 Aug
More than 320 policemen and 131 civilians are injured when West Indian youths riot towards the end of the 3-day Caribbean carnival in Notting Hill, London.

24-year-old Viv Richards relaxes after his innings of 291 against England in the final Test at The Oval.

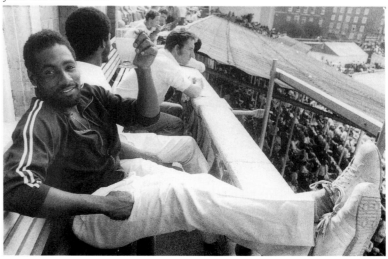

SEPT 1976

David Wilkie celebrating his triumphant return from Montreal where he won gold and silver for the 200- and 100-metres breaststroke respectively.

THE SAVING OF MR FIX-IT

A year ago Jeffrey Archer was shrugging his shoulders and telling the world he hadn't a bean. The Daimler had gone and the house in The Boltons – one of the most exclusive addresses in London – was up for sale. After a speculative business deal had gone disastrously wrong, he had even given up his seat as Tory MP for Louth, Lincolnshire. That was when he sat down to write a novel based on his business experiences. *Not A Penny More, Not A Penny Less* had, he says, 11 publishers chasing it and the film rights have been sold to America. He is confident that he will make half a million pounds as quickly as he lost the last half million. Mr Archer – known in the House of Commons as 'Mr Fix-it' for his high-powered fund-raising for charities – borrowed money to buy 50,000 shares in a Canadian company called Aquablast. The investment was in a 'magic pin' claimed to drastically reduce the poisonous fumes of a car's exhaust. The venture failed, Archer lost £400,000 and found himself with debts of £200,000 overnight. It was the advance on his book a year ago that pulled him back from the brink of bankruptcy.

Mao Tse-tung, Chairman of the Chinese Communist Party for 40 years, dies in Peking, aged 82.

HEATH CHALLENGE ON HOME RULE

Former Premier Mr Edward Heath last night put forward the idea of a referendum among the Scots on whether they wanted total independence or to remain in the United Kingdom. He warned that the Scottish and Welsh home rule issues could shake Britain's political reputation – and the pound – during the forthcoming parliamentary debate. It was vital for the main parties to agree a consensus line, said Mr Heath. 'Yet at this moment there are divisions inside the 2 major parties in Parliament, divisions north and south of the border, divisions between industrial and agricultural areas, divisions between town and country, divisions even within families on this issue.' Mr Heath said that he had no doubt of the outcome if a referendum were held: the Scots would opt to run their own affairs within the framework of the United Kingdom.

RETURN OF A CHAMP

World champion racing driver Niki Lauda said last night that he will enter the Italian Grand Prix on Sunday, just 6 weeks after he nearly died in a crash during the West German Grand Prix. If he is passed fit by the medical authorities he will return at Monza to defend his slender 2-point lead over Britain's James Hunt in this year's championship.

FULL SPEED AHEAD FOR SUPER TRAIN

Britain's world-beating train has been given the go-ahead by its drivers. ASLEF's decision that the new train should be manned by 2 men only at top speed – they had previously demanded such manning levels at all times – means that the 125-m.p.h. service will begin on 4 October. The high-speed train, called Inter-City 125 by British Rail, is pulled by a locomotive that recently reached 143 m.p.h. – a new world record for diesel trains. When it is introduced on the London–Edinburgh route, the travelling time will be 4½ hours, 1 hour less than at present.

TOP MODEL AGENT BOWS OUT

Cherry Marshall, the 'grandmother' of the modelling business, is to close down her world famous agency in Jermyn Street after more than 20 years. She became a top model at 23 and started the agency in 1954. Former Miss World Ann Sidney, actress Suzy Kendall and Beatle George Harrison's wife Patti Boyd are among those who have passed through her books. She discovered Paulene Stone, who later married actor Laurence Harvey, when she was just 16. Anthea Redfern of TV's *Generation Game* was also one of her girls. 53-year-old Cherry plans to continue her twice-weekly appearance in Southern TV's women's programme, *House Party*.

CAT'S EYES MAN DIES AT 86

Percy Shaw, the man who invented the cat's-eye road studs and became a millionaire on the strength of it, has died aged 86. Mr Shaw died at his house in the grounds of the Halifax factory which produces half a million cat's eyes a year. He got his famous idea when driving home on a foggy night 43 years ago. He worked on it till he achieved the breakthrough: a self-wiping device to stop mud from obscuring the reflectors.

US TO RE-OPEN KENNEDY CASE

The United States Congress voted yesterday (17 September) to re-open the enquiry into the assassination of President Kennedy in Dallas 13 years ago. There is increasing belief that the President's death was not the isolated work of a deranged killer but part of a conspiracy involving other murders. On top of doubts that the supposed assassin, Lee Harvey Oswald, could have fired 4 shots with such deadly accuracy in so short a time, pressure to re-open the case has been growing since the revelation that President Kennedy unknowingly shared a mistress with Mafia boss Sam Giancana. The woman involved, Mrs Judith Exner, gave evidence of her relationships with both men to a Senate committee; Giancana was murdered before he could appear. At the same time it was revealed that the CIA was involved in a plot with Mafia gunmen to assassinate Cuban leader Fidel Castro. A key figure in this was another friend of Mrs Exner's, Johnny Roselli, a West Coast Mafia leader. Last month Roselli, too, was assassinated. Oswald himself was murdered, while under arrest, by Jack Ruby, a nightclub owner with underworld connections.

TREASON CLAIM BY SACKED SCIENTIST

A scientist sacked for revealing defence secrets has accused his bosses of inciting him to commit treason. Mr Stephen Thornley, who was in charge of wind-tunnel tests on the new NATO Tornado aircraft, was fired after describing it in a letter to a newspaper as a sitting duck for enemy planes. He said his work showed that the top speed of the plane – a combat aircraft expected to be the lynchpin in NATO's air defences – was well below the makers' claims of twice the speed of sound. Mr Thornley, who is claiming that he was unfairly dismissed, said, 'For the Aircraft Research Association to suggest to an employee that he remain silent concerning a shortcoming in the national defence by reason of commercial security amounts to incitement to treason.'

MINTER HANGS ON

Alan Minter is still British middleweight champion, although those present at the Royal Albert Hall just couldn't believe it. They chanted the name of Kevin Finnegan, the former champion, who, for the second time in 10 months against Minter, was judged the loser by the narrowest of margins; half a point. Programmes, cartons and coins rained into the ring at the announcement of the decision which makes the Lonsdale Belt Minter's own property.

SEX TESTS AT WIMBLEDON?

Sex tests introduced into tennis for the United States Open 3 weeks ago are now compulsory for all members of the Women's Tennis Association. The next major step could be tests at Wimbledon, where the draw includes many players outside the Association. The issue arose over the case of Renée Richards, the father of a 4-year-old son, who tried to enter the women's singles at Forest Hills following a sex-change operation. She refused to take the chromosome test used in the Olympic Games.

The first of the 40,000 to have their water cut off because of the drought began queueing at street standpipes yesterday.

DEFIANT SALUTE TO MURDERED 14,000

Katyn has been called 'the crime without parallel'. Last Saturday (18 September), 36 years later, it finally got its memorial with the British Government discreetly turning its head away. Serving British officers were forbidden to attend the ceremony at Gunnersbury Cemetery, Hammersmith, in which the deaths of 14,500 Polish officers and men in 1940 were commemorated by an obelisk. Some 4,000 Poles were found in mass graves at Katyn in western Russia and it is widely believed that the murders were committed on Stalin's orders in an attempt to wipe out the ruling caste in Poland before it was taken over by the Soviet Union. The Russians have always denied this, accusing Nazi SS death squads of the murders. The Soviet Government has protested over the date on the memorial – 1940 – as this puts the blame firmly on the Russians; Nazi Germany had not then invaded Russia.

LASER SURGERY 'TOO DEAR'

A laser 'knife' which can give almost bloodless surgery has been shown to British doctors by its pioneer. But the doctors have told Professor Isaac Kaplan of Tel Aviv that they doubt whether the health service could afford the £35,000 instrument. The laser, also said to reduce post-operative pain, is already in use in 19 countries. Professor Kaplan said he hoped the doctors were being unduly pessimistic as, while laser surgery would never completely replace the scalpel, it had come to stay.

DAY BY DAY

1 Sept
A state of emergency is declared in the Irish Republic as a preliminary to the introduction of anti-terrorist legislation.

2 Sept
Middlesex wins the County Cricket Championship.

3 Sept
Prisoners who rioted at Hull Gaol for 2½ days, cause damage estimated at more than £1m.

9 Sept
Mao Tse-tung, Chairman of the Chinese Communist party for 40 years, dies in Peking, aged 82.

10 Sept
A British Airways Trident flying from London to Istanbul and a Yugoslav DC9 *en route* to Cologne from Split collide at 33,000 feet over Yugoslavia. All the 176 passengers and crew in both aircraft lose their lives.

11 Sept
The two-hundredth St Leger is won by the French horse Crow, ridden by Yves St Martin.

15 Sept
Parts of North Devon become the first areas of Britain to have mains water supplies cut off completely and standpipes brought into operation. The new Royal Exchange Theatre, built within the former cotton exchange, opens in Manchester.

20 Sept
A Turkish Airlines Boeing 727 with 154 passengers and crew crashes near Isparta. There are no survivors.

Foreign ministers of the 9 EEC members sign documents authorizing the introduction of direct elections to the European Parliament in 1978.

24 Sept
Mr Ian Smith announces his Government's acceptance of the proposals put to him by Dr Kissinger for a 2-year transition to Black majority rule in Rhodesia.

28 Sept
Muhammad Ali beats Ken Norton on points in a 15-round championship fight in New York.

WAR ON THE CHART CHEATS

Widespread changes in the way the pop charts are compiled are under way following an investigation into record rigging. An enquiry showed how companies have been able to buy their new releases into the charts for less than £2,000 by concentrated purchases at the 300 stores around the country that are used to determine the week's bestselling discs. It was revealed that the list of stores – supposedly a closely guarded secret – could be bought for £50.

And lo, there came a man from Whitehall. And his name was Denis Howell. And Denis found favour in the eyes of Jim. And Jim spake unto Denis, saying, 'Go thou, and where the earth is dry, make it wet, for thou shalt be my Minister for Drought.'

OCT 1976

IT'S SUPERNICK

The search for a screen Superman is over at last. He is Nick Nolte, 35, who has been chosen for the role following refusals from Robert Redford, Steve McQueen, James Caan and Paul Newman. As Nolte, who established himself in *Rich Man Poor Man*, reads the script in the Bahamas while filming with Jacqueline Bisset in *The Deep*, a carefully planned new Superman cult is being prepared in Hollywood. The decision to cast Nolte leaves 2 men particularly disappointed: the actor who wanted the part most but wasn't offered it is Ryan O'Neal; and the man who underwent extensive screen tests was Olympic decathlon champion, Bruce Jenner. Their failure might be a blessing in disguise, however. The man chosen to play Superman's father is likely to steal the show – none other than Marlon Brando.

UNHOLY ROW OVER TV'S REVD EMERY

Comedian Dick Emery's TV parson has clergyman Roy Alison hot under his dog-collar. He thought the use of the comic figure in a massive advertising campaign for Ladbroke's Spot Ball competition was in bad taste. Mr Alison complained to the Advertising Standards Authority about the slogan 'Is it wicked, my brethren? Not if you win a damned great jackpot, it isn't.' The Authority yesterday upheld the complaint.

James Hunt relaxing at home after becoming World Motor-Racing Champion.

GETAWAY WEEKEND WITH MR SPOCK

Around 400 people have just spent the weekend light years away from it all on board a starship a couple of centuries in the future. They beamed aboard a dream world where all troubles could be blamed on Klingons and all problems would be solved by Captain Kirk and Mr Spock. The down-to-earth location was the Dragonara Hotel in Leeds, where fans of television's *Star Trek* spent 2 days reliving favourite episodes, listening to sci-fi lectures and watching their heroes' adventures which had been banned by the BBC as unsuitable for children. There are 500,000 registered 'Trekkies' around the world and conventions in America attract up to 12,000 people.

SEVERIANO SPIKED BY RULES

Severiano Ballesteros marched angrily out of the Piccadilly World Matchplay Championship after the first round at Wentworth yesterday, convinced he had been the victim of an incorrect ruling. The 19-year-old Spaniard, top professional in Europe this season, was furious when the referee refused to allow him to tap down tufts of grass on the sixteenth green at a crucial moment in his match against defending champion Hale Irwin. Ballesteros claimed the tufts were spike marks which, under British rules, players are allowed to tap down. The referee disagreed, the tufts remained untouched and Ballesteros missed a vital putt. He lost the match 2 and 1.

NOW THE SWITCHED-ON TRAFFIC SERVICE

Commercial radio has beaten the BBC in the race to launch Britain's first automatic traffic information service. The scheme, to be run by the London Broadcasting Company, means that some motorists will be able to pick up traffic information on their car radios, even when the set is switched off or tuned to another station. Initially, the scheme will apply only to a team of guinea-pig drivers whose cars have been equipped with a £15 decoder device which will automatically signal them to switch on their radio when traffic information is due.

Mr Michael Foot is elected Deputy Leader of the Labour Party.

HE-E-E-Y! BUT CAN THE FONZ BEAT DOCTOR WHO?

It's a lot to ask of an 18-year-old Italian-American high-school dropout saddled with the nickname Fonzie, but on his leather-jacketed shoulders rests a large part of the task of snapping London Weekend Television's schedules out of their present torpor. In America the hip motor-bike-riding Fonzie can create mass hysteria with a click of his fingers. He is the latest cult hero there, receiving more fan mail than Redford and Newman. Can *Happy Days*, the 50s-style comedy show in which he stars, win viewers from *Doctor Who*, the BBC's lord of the Saturday tea-time slot? He just might. When the show started 2 years ago the Fonzie role was a small one, playing second string to Ron Howard, Donny Most and Anson Williams. But the reaction from viewers across the country was so fervent that he was soon promoted to the star. The craze has catapulted actor Henry Winkler into the top earning bracket of world TV stars.

Bruce Forsyth and Anthea Redfern celebrating the hundredth edition of The Generation Game.

WE'RE DYNAMITE!

2 blondes have made the difference between obscurity and phenomenal success for Fleetwood Mac. Long forgotten in Britain, their homeland, this 10-year-old group's last album has spent more than a year in the US Top 10 with sales of nearly 4 million.

On the face of it, those achievements are largely due to the 2 blondes in the band. It's 7 years since Christine McVie, then Christine Perfect, was voted Britain's top female singer by *Melody Maker*. Not long afterwards, she joined her husband, Fleetwood Mac's bass guitarist John McVie, whose fortunes were waning after enjoying 60s success. They got work in America but 2 years ago were almost wiped out when their former manager put another group on the road using the same name. The originals won the subsequent legal battle but ended up with low spirits and a confused image.

In the summer of 1975 their fortunes changed when their sound engineer introduced them to a young American couple, Lindsay Buckingham and Stevie Nicks, whose singing and composing talents were added to the band just 2 weeks before starting to record an album called simply *Fleetwood Mac*. The combination of Christine's soulful voice and Stevie's more energetic delivery turned out to be commercial dynamite. Next month sees the release of a new album, whose songs revolve around the break-up of long-standing relationships between both John and Christine and Lindsay and Stevie. It is called *Rumours*.

DAY BY DAY

3 Oct
In the West German general election Herr Helmut Schmidt's coalition Government is returned.

4 Oct
British Rail's first High Speed Train comes into service and makes the journey from Paddington to Bristol in 92 minutes, 4 minutes ahead of schedule.

6 Oct
The Prime Minister of Thailand, Seni Pramoj, is deposed in a military coup and Admiral Sangad Chalawoyo assumes power.

12 Oct
Joe Bugner regains the European, British and Commonwealth heavyweight boxing titles by knocking out Richard Dunn in the first round of a championship fight at Wembley.

The Prime Minister of China, Hua Kuo-feng, is appointed Chairman of the Chinese Communist party in succession to the late Mao Tse-tung.

14 Oct
Actress Dame Edith Evans dies, aged 88.

17 Oct
The Pope canonizes John Ogilvie, the first new Scottish saint to be proclaimed for more than 700 years. Princess Alexandra and Mr Angus Ogilvy, a descendant of John Ogilvie, are present at the ceremony.

21 Oct
Mr Michael Foot is elected Deputy Leader of the Labour party with 166 votes against 128 for Mrs Shirley Williams.

British publisher Sir William Collins dies, aged 76.

22 Oct
The Prince of Wales attends the final El Alamein reunion in London.

President O'Dalaigh of Ireland resigns after a dispute over his decision to refer new anti-terrorist legislation to the Supreme Court to test its constitutionality.

The House of Lords rejects the Government's bill which would enable the British Transport Docks Board to take over the port of Felixstowe.

24 Oct
James Hunt finishes third in the Japanese Grand Prix and becomes World Motor-racing Champion, snatching the title by 1 point from Niki Lauda, who withdrew from the race.

25 Oct
The National Theatre is opened officially by the Queen.

BOSS CAN ASK YOU TO WORK CHRISTMAS

Employers are entitled to ask staff to work on Christmas Day this year – and they don't have to pay a penny extra. The trouble is that Christmas Day and Boxing Day fall on Saturday and Sunday, with New Year's Day the following Saturday. The Government has switched the official bank holidays in England, Wales and Northern Ireland to Monday and Tuesday (27 and 28 December) and Monday 3 January.

BEWARE THE CULT OF THE CARROTT

Mr Jasper Carrott will request the pleasure of the company of the 35,000 football supporters who share his preference for Birmingham City at his own game next Saturday. Mr Carrott is paying £1,200 for the privilege of lending his name to the Birmingham v. Middlesbrough match and becomes the first individual to sponsor a First Division game. Last year the zany comedian had the nineteenth bestselling single in Britain, despite the fact that the BBC would only play the flip side because they objected to 2 words on his send-up of *The Magic Roundabout*.

MIGRANTS RAMPAGE OVER BIG YIN

Scots comedian Billy Connolly was forced off stage in a riot caused by drunken Scots migrants during a concert in Brisbane, Australia. The angry Scots were disappointed that Connolly, known as the Big Yin, wasn't a younger version of Andy Stewart. The riot followed shows in Melbourne and Sidney which have led to Connolly's being acclaimed as a new superstar. But in Brisbane, known in the south as the 'deep north' because of its conservatism, Connolly's bawdy humour was not appreciated.

Birmingham City supporter Jasper Carrott pays £1,200 for the privilege of becoming the first individual to sponsor a First Division game. Last year the zany comedian had the 19th best-selling single in Britain despite the fact that the BBC would play only the flip side because they objected to two words in his send-up of The Magic Roundabout.

BOFFIN'S JUMBO-SIZED BRAINCHILD

Everyone knows what a tennis racket looks like. . . or do they? In the United States more than 50,000 people, including some famous names, have switched to a new jumbo-sized racket which has a strung area 50% larger than usual. There are no regulations limiting either the size or weight of a tennis racket, merely the definition that it is 'an implement used to strike the ball'. You can use a cricket bat or dustbin lid if you feel it will improve your game. The new racket is called the Prince and will be available here early next year at a cost of £43. It is the brainchild of Howard Head, a former military aircraft structural designer working in the Physics Department at Princeton University. After the war it was Head who transformed the ski world with his metal skis, became a millionaire and took up tennis after retiring at 55. Feeling unhappy with the equipment, he took to his laboratory and the result is something looking more like a snow shoe than the sleek, oval-shaped rackets most of us know. The manufacturers claim it gives 'more accuracy for less effort' and has a 'sweet spot' 3½ times larger than that on the conventional design.

Mr Jimmy Carter wins the United States presidential election.

FADE-OUT FOR KATIE

Katie, the TV housewife, will no longer give a meal 'man appeal' by crumbling an Oxo into it. Brooke Bond Oxo, makers of the stock cube, have parted company with actress Mary Holland who played Katie in the adverts over an 18-year period. She receives a £5,000 handshake – on condition that she does not promote rival products for a year. Miss Holland has been dropped in favour of commercials showing several people crumbling imaginary Oxos. Her TV husband Philip, actor Peter Moynihan, was written out of the commercials in 1973 and is now a rowing instructor with the Inner London Education Authority.

RADIO RIOT PUTS ENOCH OFF THE AIR

The BBC's *Any Questions* radio programme was forced off the air in chaos last night because of a left-wing demonstration against Enoch Powell. Scuffles broke out and windows were smashed at the church in Basingstoke, Hampshire, from where the programme was being transmitted live. The demonstration, by a group calling itself the Basingstoke Anti-Fascist Committee, forced chairman David Jacobs and the team to retire for 19 minutes while order was restored. It was the first time *Any Questions* had been interrupted in such a fashion in 28 years.

THE QUEUE TO KILL A KILLER

Convicted murderer Gary Gilmore has been given a dramatic stay of execution. The news came as a grisly queue of volunteers was being vetted for his 5-man firing squad. Gilmore had himself persuaded the Supreme Court to let him 'die like a man' rather than spend a lifetime in jail. But the Governor of Utah has postponed the execution until a State Board of Pardons meets to decide whether to grant a further delay, allow the execution to take place or commute the sentence to life imprisonment. Utah allows those sentenced to death a choice between hanging and firing squad. 35-year-old Gilmore, who admitted killing a motel clerk, chose the latter and is demanding that the execution be carried out. 'I've been sentenced to die, I accept that. Let's do it,' he said.

The Northern Ireland Peace Campaign held their first march through London today when they marched from Hyde Park to Trafalgar Square. The photo shows (l. to r.) Mrs Ewart Biggs, Joan Baez, Mairead Corrigan, Dr Donald Coggan and Cardinal Basil Hume.

Chris and Fliss (David Ropes and Diane Keen) have their hands full in The Cuckoo Waltz.

SNOOKER KING MOUNTJOY JOINS MONEYMAKERS

Doug Mountjoy, Britain's newest world champion, flies home from South Africa today to start a lucrative career as a snooker professional. Mountjoy, a 34-year-old Welshman, begins his new career as a member of the 28-strong World Professional Billiards and Snooker Association after winning the world amateur title in Johannesburg.

GIRTON TOLD: MEN ARE ON THE WAY

Girton, the Cambridge women's college built 3 miles outside the city 103 years ago to minimize the risk of contact with male students, is to open its doors to men next year. 'They took it very calmly,' said mistress of the college Professor Brenda Ryman. Neither of the other 2 Cambridge women's colleges – Newnham and New Hall – nor Oxford's 5 have made any indication as to whether they will be following Girton's example.

ME AND MY HIGH VOICE – MAGGIE

Tory Leader Margaret Thatcher has spoken of how her voice becomes squeaky when she is nervous. Interviewed on Thames TV's *Good Afternoon* programme she refuted a suggestion by presenter Mary Parkinson that she had tried to make her voice more 'posh' over the years, though she admitted that she had tried to get it lower. The woman who has been dubbed the Iron Maiden also revealed that she writes in large letters at the top of her speeches 'Start low – relax.'

THE REAWAKENING OF SCAFFOLD

A 5-year-old who would not go to sleep is the inspiration behind a book, a record and the re-emergence of Scaffold, once one of Britain's most likeable pop groups. The youngster is Finn McGough, whose father Roger is as well known for his poetry as for his membership of the group. Finn is the boy behind Mr Noselighter, 'a nice old man with a candle instead of a nose', as McGough puts it. He was making up a bed-time story for his son, who insisted on hearing more about the character. The result was a book, published this week, followed by 2 songs. And who better to sing them than McGough, John Gorman and Mike McGear – Paul McCartney's brother – back together as a group after breaking up 3 years ago.

DAME FLORA DIES AT 98

Dame Flora MacLeod, the last person to have been born at Number 10 Downing Street, died yesterday (4 November), aged 98. Dame Flora was born when her grandfather was Chancellor of the Exchequer. In those days the Chancellor lived at Number 10.

BEN IS NAUGHTY 90

Playwright Ben Travers celebrated his ninetieth birthday yesterday (11 November). Sheila Hancock, star of *The Bed Before Yesterday*, a play he wrote last year, said, 'Ben is a genius; he understands women far more than men half or quarter his age.' Another of his plays, *Banana Ridge*, is also running in the West End at the moment. How could he write a sex play at his age? 'Well, I have a good memory,' he said.

BOSSY PAULINE GETS HER OWN SHOW AT 17

Actress Pauline Quirke is to star in her own television show – at 17. She last appeared on television as a sulky supermarket attendant in the ATV series *The Beasts*. Her new series for Thames Television is a children's programme called *Pauline's Quirkes*. Of her last series Pauline says, 'Sometimes we had an audience of 400 screaming girls. Fortunately I am bossy by nature and could keep them under control.'

DAY BY DAY

2 Nov
Mr Jimmy Carter, Democratic candidate, wins the United States presidential election with 51% of the popular vote and 297 electoral college votes. President Ford has 48% of the popular vote and 241 electoral college votes.

4 Nov
Labour loses the by-election at Workington and Walsall North to Conservatives and holds Newcastle Central with a reduced majority.

Delegates at the Rhodesia conference in Geneva are unable to agree on a date for independence. The British proposal of 1 March 1978 is rejected, African nationalists insisting on independence in 12 months and the Rhodesian Government wanting a 2-year transitional period.

15 Nov
The Government accepts the Opposition's amendment to the Dock Work Regulation Bill and agrees that dockers should have a monopoly of employment only within a half-mile, instead of a 5-mile radius.

Syrian peace-keeping forces move into Lebanon and occupy the whole of Beirut.

16 Nov
The House of Lords again votes to exclude ship-repairing companies from the bill to nationalize the aircraft and shipbuilding industries. Their earlier exclusion amendment to the bill had been rejected by the House of Commons.

18 Nov
Miss Jamaica, Cindy Breakspeare, Bob Marley's girlfriend, becomes Miss World.

19 Nov
Sir Basil Spence, architect of Coventry Cathedral, dies, aged 69.

22 Nov
Actor Rupert Davies, TV's Maigret, dies, aged 59.

24 Nov
An earthquake devastates the Turkish province of Van and more than 3,700 people are reported to have lost their lives.

26 Nov
African leaders at the Rhodesia conference in Geneva agree to a British proposal that independence should be not later than 1 March 1978.

28 Nov
The Australian dollar is devalued by 17.5%. 9 days later it is revalued by 2% and on 13 December by 1.3%.

29 Nov
The New Zealand dollar is devalued by 7%. On 20 December it is revalued by 2%.

30 Nov
The Scotland and Wales Bill, providing for elected assemblies in Edinburgh and Cardiff, is introduced in the House of Commons.

Glenn Hoddle, the Spurs midfield player tipped as a future international, shields the ball from Bristol City's Gary Collier.

DEC 1976

All is not well for Sheila Allen and Frank Finlay in LWT's Bouquet of Barbed Wire.

GOLDEN TREASURY OF REVD SCROPE DAVIES

A treasure chest of literary papers which could be worth £1m has been discovered at a London bank. The chest was lodged at the bank for safety 156 years ago by Reverend Scrope Davies, who, in addition to being a scholar and ordained clergyman, was also a womanizer, debtor and gambler. In January 1820 he tried to save himself from a £7,000 debt judgement by placing a bet that stood to win £20,000 at Newmarket races. The horse lost and, with his creditors closing in, Davies threw his personal papers into the chest and hurriedly left it at the bank before fleeing the country. The contents of the chest included original manuscripts entrusted to him by Byron and Shelley and drawings made by his naval officer brother while taking Napoleon to St Helena. His bank was eventually absorbed by Barclays and the chest had remained in the deposit room until a recent reorganization.

THE LAST BATH AT BATH

Sufferers from rheumatism and arthritis who have enjoyed the efficacy of Bath's natural hot springs – which send up 500 gallons daily at 120°F – may have bathed their last. The National Health Service yesterday in effect closed the unique facility by withdrawing its support for their maintenance. 2,000 rheumatism and arthritis sufferers used the springs every year, 95% of them through the NHS and the rest by paying around £4 for the privilege.

INSURANCE CHEAT DIES

Emil Savundra, the crooked insurance chief who left 400,000 British motorists stranded without cover after salting away £600,000 of their money, died yesterday (21 December), aged 53. The collapse of his company, Fire, Auto and Marine, began the landslide of cheap premium companies which went to the wall in the late 60s. Jailed for 8 years in 1968, Savundra was released after serving 6½ years at Wormwood Scrubs.

WHEN IT IS RIGHT TO END A LIFE

The Archbishop of Canterbury has controversially entered the debate over euthanasia. Dr Donald Coggan told doctors that in taking decisions to end the lives of terminally ill patients they should consider the interests not only of the patients but also of the Government and taxpayers. He accepted that he was treading on 'exceedingly dangerous ground' but emphasized that health service funds were not unlimited. He said, 'The prolongation of the life of one aged patient may in fact entail the deprivation of aid to others and even the shortening of their lives.' Dr Coggan said there was a large measure of agreement among Christians as to the wrongness of prolonging life of all those with terminal illnesses. Sir Rodney Smith, President of the Royal College of Surgeons, commented that when treating a patient a doctor should not be expected to add to his judgement the words 'How much does it cost?'

Shoppers begin queueing before dawn outside small independent bakeries as 3,000 London bread delivery drivers go on strike.

Clint Eastwood in The Outlaw Josey Wales.

PUNK GROUP IN TV STORM

Angry viewers have demanded the sacking of TV interviewer Bill Grundy after 4-letter words were used on his *Today* programme. They accused Grundy of encouraging the Sex Pistols group, who play music which they call punk rock, to use 'some of the dirtiest language ever heard on television'.

HOME RULE BY A LANDSLIDE

The Government has won a landslide majority for its plans for elected Scottish and Welsh assemblies – with the pledge of referenda in Scotland and Wales next autumn. Although the Government got backing for its plans to switch substantial power to Edinburgh and Cardiff, the vote – 292–247 – leaves the 2 major parties divided with rebels on both sides.

'FORGOTTEN' MATHIS HITS JACKPOT

A simple Italian melody has become a massive worldwide hit and provided a singer with his first number 1 in 15 years. The unlikely combination of an almost forgotten tune and 41-year-old Johnny Mathis – in chart terms an almost forgotten singer – has resulted in 'When a Child is Born' reaching the top spot this week. Obscure Italian pop composer Crio Dammico wrote the song 3 years ago but it was only when American lyricist Fred Jay spotted it this year that it was really launched on its way to the top.

NUCLEAR WORKMEN IN RADIATION SCARE

Dangerous radiation has been seeping into the soil at the Windscale nuclear power station. It was discovered by chance by workmen excavating for a new silo to store nuclear waste. Angry union leaders at the Cumbria plant – dubbed Britain's nuclear dustbin – are claiming that 'secretive' bosses breached safety agreements by not informing them of the leak, which was discovered in October, for 2 months. A spokesman for British Nuclear Fuels said the leak was 'very, very minor'.

MARVIN'S MISTRESS MAY COST HIM £250,000

Actor Lee Marvin may have to pay £250,000 to get rid of his mistress, Michelle Triola. In an historic ruling, the Californian Supreme Court has given her the right to be treated as a wife for the purpose of deciding her legal rights in a property settlement. 'I was called Mrs and I felt a Mrs. I washed dishes and Lee put out the garbage,' said Michelle of their 6-year relationship, during which she legally changed her name to Marvin.

HAMBURGER HAND-OVER

The debt-ridden Joe Lyons catering group has sold off the franchise for its 600 British Wimpy Bars. The buyers – for £7m – were United Biscuits, who also got Lyons' Golden Egg and Bakentake franchises as part of the deal. The sale comes at a time when the hamburger market is rapidly expanding. McDonald's, the giant American chain, are tentatively establishing themselves and, if they decide to make a full-scale invasion of the British market, 'Wimpy are in for a hell of a time,' according to one of their executives.

SINGLE WORD CAUSES STORM

TV chief Lady Plowden has come under attack for using an 8-letter word to dismiss the punk rock swearing on ITV earlier this month. Lady Plowden, head of the IBA, described the incident as a 'tiresome' mistake.

DAY BY DAY

2 Dec
The Queen opens the Museum of London at London Wall.

The Conservatives win the Cambridge by-election.

4 Dec
Lord Britten, Benjamin Britten the composer, dies, aged 63.

8 Dec
2 Conservative spokesmen on Scottish affairs, Mr Alick Buchanan-Smith and Mr Malcolm Rifkind, resign from the Shadow Cabinet in protest at Mrs Thatcher's decision to impose a 3-line whip against the Government's devolution bill.

13 Dec
New licensing laws come into force in Scotland, allowing public houses and hotels to close at 11 instead of 10 p.m.

A Pan Am Boeing 747 makes the longest non-stop passenger flight from Sydney to San Francisco in 13 hours 14 minutes.

15 Dec
The Prince of Wales leaves the Royal Navy after 5 years' service.

The Court of Appeal rules that the Secretary of State for Trade had exceeded his authority when he cancelled Laker Airways' licence to operate the Skytrain.

17 Dec
London's longest-running play *The Mousetrap* has its 10,000th performance.

21 Dec
Mr Reginald Prentice resigns as Minister for Overseas Development.

Creating a good impression. . . Sir Harold Wilson with Mike Yarwood.

JAN 1977

Robin Ellis and Angharad Rees as Ross and Demelza Poldark with Judy Geeson as Caroline and Michael Cadman as Dr Dwight Enys in a new series of Poldark.

GOLF AND SOCCER FEEL TAX PINCH

Rothmans last night pulled out of non-league soccer 3 months after withdrawing from the Piccadilly World Matchplay golf championship. The company warns that other tobacco firms could be reviewing their £2.5m annual sponsorship of British sport because of the effects of a new taxation system. End Product Tax will force all cigarette companies to pass on the cost of sponsorship and the tax has a multiplying effect whereby smokers could be paying up to 3 times the cost of the sponsorship itself in the form of higher prices. Manufacturers are paying EPT at 22% on the recommended selling price in addition to ordinary duty and VAT.

NOW IT'S THE 2-INCH TV

A British inventor unveiled the world's smallest television set yesterday. It has a 2-inch screen, weighs only 26.5 ounces and will fit into a large pocket. The black and white set, called the microvision, will be on sale next month at almost £200. The man behind its development is 36-year-old Mr Clive Sinclair, Managing Director of Sinclair Radionics. Mr Sinclair was also responsible for the world's first mini-calculator and the world's smallest radio.

DOCTOR BANS HOME BIRTH

A young mother-to-be claims she has been struck off her doctor's list because she wants to have her baby at home. 21-year-old Miranda Ward says that her GP was sympathetic to the idea of home birth at first but that his attitude changed after he received a letter from a consultant gynaecologist, who was against the idea. Mrs Ward and her husband have now called in a pressure group, the Society for Home Confinement, to help them find a doctor more sympathetic to their wishes.

CLAUDINE FOUND GUILTY

Claudine Longet, ex-wife of singer Andy Williams, has been found guilty of the negligent homicide of her lover, ski champion 'Spider' Sabich. The 35-year-old former showgirl was cleared, however, of the more serious charge of reckless manslaughter. Miss Longet, who claimed throughout the case that the .22 pistol which killed Sabich last March went off accidentally, could receive a 2-year sentence or a £3,000 fine, the maximum penalty for the lesser charge.

HIGNELL SCORES DOUBLE

Between studying Indian history and the Norman Conquest, Alastair Hignell manages to squeeze in a little sport. He plays rugby for Cambridge University and England and cricket for the University and Gloucestershire. Sport is so specialized now that a latter-day C.B. Fry – playing soccer and cricket for England and holding the world long jump record – seems unlikely. But 21-year-old Hignell is happy to try and knock down the theory that the age of the all-rounder is dead. He has played for England 6 times at rugby, but has yet to make it internationally at cricket. He modestly ducks the question of whether he could become another Mike Smith, who played for England in both sports.

A CAPITAL THAT FACES INVASION

The forgotten war in Cambodia rang alarm bells in the West last night as columns of invading Vietnamese tanks raced towards the capital of Phnom Penh. Premier Pol Pot, ruthless Communist who controls 7 million Cambodian survivors of his policy of genocide, broadcast a warning that the city might soon be abandoned. As his government and troops prepared to flee to the surrounding jungle he declared, 'We will never surrender.' One third of Cambodia is reported to have fallen to the massive Soviet-equipped Vietnamese force. The fear in the West is that Russia and China are fighting the war by proxy, for Peking has been supplying its Cambodian puppets with military aid. Cambodian rebels against Pol Pot's rule of blood and tears have been fighting alongside the invading force but they are not likely to be much happier under the Vietnamese yoke – the endless boatloads of refugees escaping its clutches bear testimony to that.

TOP OF THE COPS

2 of television's law-preserving heart-throbs are pounding an off-duty beat in the pop charts. David Soul, the blond partner in the *Starsky and Hutch* team, is enjoying his second week at number 1 with 'Don't Give Up On Us', while Dennis Waterman, Regan's much abused sidekick in *The Sweeney*, is hot on his trail with a song called 'I Will Glide'. Stratford Johns, the bullying Barlow of *Softly Softly*, may never have had a hit but his albums of easy listeners have achieved healthy sales. But it was Telly Savalas who really became top of the cops last year with a tear-jerking version of Bread's 'If'.

SURRENDER!

Amid international outrage and Arab glee, France yesterday laid on a first-class flight to freedom for the terrorist it dared not bring to justice. Abu Daoud, mastermind behind the massacre of 11 Israeli athletes at the 1972 Munich Olympics, arrived in Algeria last night to a VIP welcome. By then, Israel had recalled its Paris ambassador in protest and accused the French Government of a 'disgraceful surrender'. The British Government was said to be acutely embarrassed by France's action. There was no consultation with London, although the Common Market is supposed to have a concerted policy against terrorism.

ABBA top the album charts with Arrival.

THE STAR NO ONE WANTED TO KNOW

Like all the other streetwise kids in Manhattan's Hell's Kitchen, Sylvester Stallone grew up dreaming that he would be a champion fighter, Hollywood movie star and celebrated writer. Even when he had been expelled from 12 schools by the time he was 15, something told him that he was going to make it. Now, in perhaps the most extraordinary entertainment success story of the decade, Stallone has achieved all 3 of his ambitions. In 7 days last year he unleashed the frustrations and experiences of his life on the streets by writing a movie about boxing. The movie company liked the idea – but not him. Stallone was adamant that he would star or the deal was off. They offered him $150,000 not to take the part. He refused, even though he had only $104 in the bank. United Artists shrugged, put up $1m and surrounded Stallone with some of the best talent in the business in an attempt to prop him up. The entire picture, *Rocky*, was shot in less than a month. United Artists intends to nominate Stallone in the Best Actor category and probably for Best Writer, too. The film, which is making a fortune in America, arrives in England at the end of the year.

SUE'S BATTLING TO GIVE US A WONDER WIMBLEDON

In Wimbledon's centenary year dreams are being cherished of the greatest possible climax – a British champion. Sue Barker, the Devon 20-year-old ranked fourth in the world, is working flat out to turn wishful thinking into reality. She has already defeated every conceivable challenger for Chris Evert's title except the holder herself.

MURDERER GETS HIS WISH

Double murderer Gary Gilmore was executed by firing squad as he wished yesterday (17 January), with the agent who has the film rights as an official witness. It was in keeping with the whole affair, which was a ghastly farce to the end. Gilmore did not know for sure until minutes beforehand that he was indeed finally to die in America's first execution for nearly 10 years. The State Medical Examiner said that Gilmore lived for 2 minutes after the shots were fired – 4 bullets pierced his heart – though he said he was unable to tell whether Gilmore was sensing pain during that time.

SHEP THE CELEBRITY

Shep, the Border collie adored by millions of children who watch *Blue Peter*, yesterday went for a sculptor's sitting at Madame Tussaud's alongside presenter John Noakes. The last dog to appear at the famous waxworks was a Labrador that stood beside Sir Walter Scott.

'THESE BABIES NEED HELP'

A new fight to win compensation for children whose lives are ruined after whooping cough vaccination was launched last night. Labour MP Jack Ashley called for an 'urgent decision' from Social Services Minister David Ennals on government payments after pointing out that, following immunization against various diseases, there were 300 known cases of severe disorders in children, 182 of them after whooping cough vaccine. No absolute causal connection has yet been established and medical authorities are worried that concern over possible risks could undo all the benefits achieved by the vaccination programme in recent years. Before mass immunization was introduced in Britain in the 1950s there were an average 160 child deaths a year from the disease; this figure dropped to only 2 per year after the programme was fully implemented.

The parents of Jacqueline Eratt, who suffered brain damage following a whooping cough vaccination, plan to sue the Government, the first such case to come before the courts.

MINERS WIN PENSION FIGHT

Miners' leaders have won their battle for early retirement at 60. From August, men with 20 years' experience underground can retire at 62 with a tax-free handout of £500. The qualifying age will drop to 60 by 1979. The men will receive about 8% of normal wages up to the age of 65, after which they will move to a state pension, plus a Coal Board pension averaging £5.23 per week. Surface workers are not included in the scheme as yet. The package will now be put to Britain's 260,000 miners in a pithead ballot.

THE NEW MR EUROPE STICKS TO ENGLISH

On his first full day in office as 'Mr Europe' Roy Jenkins yesterday ruffled feathers of the Common Market's French-speaking nations. He said all the right things in his first speech as President of the European Commission, but refused to repeat them in French. Television crews from Paris, Luxembourg and Brussels were offended, though for the moment French remains comfortably king of the 6-language European castle.

President Jimmy Carter and his wife Rosalynn walk hand-in-hand down Pennsylvania Avenue, Washington, after he takes the oath of office.

FEB 1977

JIM PICKS A YOUNG ONE

A young doctor last night grabbed one of the most glittering prizes in British politics – a place in the Cabinet as Foreign Secretary. He is David Owen, Anthony Crosland's number 2 at the Foreign Office. At the age of 38 he becomes the youngest Foreign Secretary since Anthony Eden, who was 2 months younger when he was appointed in 1935. Dr Owen steps into the gap left by the death of Mr Crosland. The scale of his promotion is almost incredible. He leapfrogs Mr Michael Foot, Leader of the Commons, Mr Peter Shore, Environment Secretary, Energy's Mr Anthony Wedgwood Benn and Education's Mrs Shirley Williams. Dr Owen could not have imagined in his wildest dreams that he would become fifth ranking in the Cabinet when he was a brain specialist at St Thomas's Hospital, just across the bridge from Westminster. For the Labour party, a new star is born.

Anthony Crosland dies aged 58.

BUCK STOPS WITH JIMMY

Harry Truman's famous sign, 'The Buck Stops Here', is back on the President's desk in the White House for the first time in 27 years. Jimmy Carter has asked to borrow it for as long as he is in office.

Just like Daddy . . . Gareth Owen carries a case as he and his father, the new Foreign Secretary, Dr David Owen, step from their Limehouse home.

JENKINS HALTS CHEAP BUTTER

Roy Jenkins, British boss of the Common Market, has called a halt to the sale of cheap butter. From 6 p.m. on 25 February all exports of 'surplus' butter from EEC stocks were suspended indefinitely. His action came just 24 hours after it was revealed that the French were about to sell 75,000 tonnes of butter to Russia at the give-away price of 16½p per pound, compared with the 56p housewives pay in Britain. Exports of the surplus butter are subsidized to the extent of 48p per pound from Common Market funds and the Russian deal would have cost Market tax-payers £77m. Now, however, the chances are that Market housewives will enjoy cut-rate butter from the surpluses, which currently stand at more than 200,000 tonnes.

EXTRA YEAR IS FLOP – SHIRLEY

Education Secretary Shirley Williams conceded yesterday that many children were getting little benefit from their extra year at school. She risked falling foul of the left wing of her party by suggesting that 14- to 16-year-olds ought to be allowed to take part-time jobs. That looks remarkably similar to a proposal by Dr Rhodes Boyson, Tory Education Spokesman and pet hate of Labour educationalists. Dr Boyson said he believed that at 14 children should be able to take a new CSE-type course designed to meet the needs of industry instead of the academic course now offered; also, children should be allowed to leave at 15 if they have secured an apprenticeship or services cadetship.

PICK-A-BACK TAKE-OFF

A spacecraft that looks almost like a normal airliner hitched a ride on a jumbo yesterday. The scene was Edwards Air Base in California, where America's 75-ton space shuttle, *Enterprise*, was making its first test flight. In the early 80s the rocket-powered craft will be ready to blast off into space carrying supplies for orbiting astronauts. On its return, however, there will be no plummeting into the sea; it will land just like a conventional aircraft.

RUNDOWN ON FRIGHTENING NEW CULT

Many psychiatrists would like to ban a game described as 'insidious, morbid, gross and sick', which has swept the United States and seems certain to be introduced in Britain. It is called Death Race, and involves taking the wheel of a simulated racing car and attempting to massacre 'pedestrians' who appear on a screen before it. It is the most violent of a series of macabre games which have grown rapidly into a cult. Death Race has already been banned in some US cities.

JUDGE RULES AGAINST SLACKS IN COURT

A court reporter banned by a judge for wearing trousers turned up for yesterday's session in a below-the-knee skirt. But 22-year-old Gisele Albertine intends to report Judge Anwyl-Davies to the Equal Opportunities Commission, the first time a complaint against a court has been made. A spokesman for the Lord Chancellor's office said that a judge was the arbiter regarding the good order and dignity of his courtroom.

Returning to the screen The Survivors, *who remain after the collapse of industrial civilisation. Dennis Lill as Charles, Lucy Fleming as Jenny and John Abineri as Hubert.*

SCHOOL PARTY SEES HARE COURSING

A party of schoolchildren has been taken to watch a day's hare coursing, at which several kills are reported to have been made. A project on field sports and wildlife at Quarry Mount Middle School, Wallasey, Merseyside prompted the visit to Altcar, near Formby, Lancashire. One of the teachers said that the main aim of the project was to enable the children, who have already had a day's hunting with beagles, to make informed decisions regarding field sports. The trip, involving pupils aged 12 and 13, has brought protests from the League Against Cruel Sports.

MODERATES PREPARE TO KO LABOUR LEFT

A big Labour party counter-attack on the left is to be launched next week with the tacit support of the Prime Minister. Mr William Rodgers, the Cabinet's 48-year-old Transport Secretary, is all set to take on the mantle of Mr Roy Jenkins as leader of the right wing of the party. It is understood that Mr Rodgers, who organized Labour's campaign for democratic socialism in the early 60s, is being fully backed by Mr Callaghan and other leading moderates, such as Mrs Shirley Williams and Mr Anthony Crosland.

Richard Dreyfuss gives an Oscar-winning performance in Neil Simon's The Goodbye Girl, *also starring Marsha Mason.*

WANTED: SUPERGIRL TO FOLLOW LIZ

A British teenage girl with a love of horses is to be given the chance to follow the career of Elizabeth Taylor in a screen sequel to the classic *National Velvet.* It was the original 1944 movie which made 12-year-old Elizabeth Taylor the darling of millions. Now the same film company, MGM, is planning to launch another unknown actress in the sequel. The film, which is to be shot in England's West Country and written and directed by Bryan Forbes, is to be called *International Velvet.*

THE MAN WHO HAS TAKEN OVER WHERE EINSTEIN LEFT OFF

Dr Stephen Hawking is an astrophysicist of world repute and, at the age of 34, the youngest person ever to be elected a Fellow of the Royal Society. Yet, by a tragic irony, the man who dreams of turning the key that will unlock the very door of creation can't even manage to ask for a cup of tea and struggles to push a pen across a page. For 13 years he has suffered from a rare degenerative neuromotor disease which has increasingly disabled him. Dr Hawking's research into the 'black holes' of the universe has made him a star in his field. In simple terms, these are thought to be stars that have collapsed under their own gravity. Dr Hawking suggests that they may occasionally destroy themselves in violent explosions which could be as powerful as a billion tons of TNT. Astronomers previously thought that a black hole must continue its existence for ever, that it could not be destroyed without the destruction of the universe as a whole. In Dr Hawking's office a sticker proclaims: 'Black holes are out of sight.'

BOY JOCKEY WHO IS TOO GOOD

America's wonder boy jockey, 16-year-old Steve Cauthen, who has won more than $1m in purses in only 6 weeks, may be banned from racing today. The US Labor Department is claiming that a state law banning the hiring of children under 18 is being violated. The New York State Racing and Wagering Board takes issue with this view, regarding Cauthen, who comes from Walton, Kentucky, as an independent contractor and therefore only required to be 16. Cauthen, who has won 89 races, with 53 second places and 47 thirds in only 27 days of riding, has reached the $1m landmark faster than anyone in history.

DAY BY DAY

1 Feb
The National Union of Mineworkers votes in favour of accepting the proposal for retirement at 62 after 20 years' underground service.

5 Feb
The northern part of New York State around the city of Buffalo, which has already had 184 inches of snow this winter, is declared a disaster area.

6 Feb
The Queen celebrates the twenty-fifth anniversary of her accession to the throne.

9 Feb
Spain and the Soviet Union re-establish diplomatic relations after a 38-year breach caused by the Spanish Civil War.

4 members of the Provisional IRA are found guilty at the Old Bailey of 6 charges of murder, including that of Ross McWhirter, and of imprisoning John and Sheila Matthews in their Balcombe Street flat. They are each sentenced to life imprisonment with a recommendation that they should serve a minimum of 30 years.

14 Feb
A first edition of a Coverdale Bible is sold at Sotheby's for a record auction price of £30,000.

16 Feb
A British Rail passenger train makes a non-stop journey from Bristol to London at a record average speed of 99.5 m.p.h.

19 Feb
Mr Anthony Crosland, Secretary of State for Foreign and Commonwealth Affairs, dies, aged 58.

24 Feb
Peter Brooke holds City of London and Westminster South for the Conservatives in a by-election.

Steve Cauthen, America's boy wonder.

MAR 1977

570 KILLED AS HOLIDAY JUMBOS CRASH

BRIAN FAULKNER DIES IN HUNTING FALL

Former Ulster Premier Lord Faulkner's passion for hunting cost him his life yesterday. He was thrown from his horse while stag hunting in County Down. Lord Faulkner, who as Brian Faulkner led the Unionist majority in Stormont, was 56. He died sad and disillusioned after failing to realize his dream: the instilling of a new philosophy, devoid of religious bigotry and hatred, into the frenetic politics of Ulster.

BAN THIS TYRANT!

Furious MPs last night urged the Government to ban President Amin from Britain. Their anger followed the Ugandan leader's announcement that he would be coming to London in June 'whether Britain likes it or not'. He said that he would be bringing a delegation to attend the Commonwealth Heads of Government conference. One MP called on Home Secretary Merlyn Rees to bar what he called 'this bloodthirsty tyrant'; others have called for Uganda's expulsion from the Commonwealth.

At least 570 people were feared killed yesterday (27 March) when 2 jumbo jets collided and exploded at the holiday airport of Tenerife in the Canary Islands. The disaster, on a scale feared ever since the 300-ton Boeing 747s began flying commercially 8 years ago, happened in thick fog. A Dutch KLM jumbo was at full power just prior to take-off when a taxiing Pan Am jumbo turned onto the same runway. All 249 passengers on the Dutch plane were killed. Of the 386 on board the American jet, more than 300 were reported killed. These grim statistics add up to the world's worst plane disaster.

THE END OF THE LINE, LADIES

The last 'Ladies Only' compartments on British Rail trains are to be phased out. The decision signals the end of a tradition dating back almost a century, when separate accommodation was introduced following attacks on women. Only about 100 such compartments are left – all on the Eastern Region serving Essex commuters.

BANNER HITS THE QUEEN

A demonstrator yesterday hurled a banner at the Queen as she rode in an open Rolls-Royce through Sydney. The banner, which struck the Queen on the shoulder, bore the inscription: 'Independence For Australia.'

PUBS IN WINE FIDDLE

Pubs are being accused of a racket in sales of wine by the glass. Excessive profits – as high as 400% – are being made, according to the latest Egon Ronay Pub Guide. Generous landlords pour 5 glasses from a bottle; the worst profiteers squeeze out 10. The criticism comes only days after the announcement that Prices Secretary Mr Roy Hattersley is to take action aimed at curbing excessive pub profits on mixer drinks. The Government is also planning to introduce regulations to standardize measures for wine sold by the glass; at the moment the landlord serves as much, or as little, as he chooses.

US BANS SACCHARIN OVER CANCER SCARE

The United States and Canada banned the use of saccharin yesterday (9 March) because it is believed to cause cancer in laboratory animals. Saccharin has been the leading artificial sweetener since Cyclamates were banned by the Food and Drug Administration in 1969 as suspected cancer-causing agents. The British Government was panicked into applying a similar ban in this country, though the Food Additives Committee here will be reluctant to follow the US example on this occasion.

CUP FINAL HERO DIES

Soccer star Peter Houseman and his wife Sally have been killed in a car crash. The 31-year-old mid-field player had been with Oxford United since 1975 but his greatest triumphs came in a 13-year period at Chelsea, during which time he collected FA Cup and European Cup Winners' Cup medals.

BOXING COX

Being a boxing coxswain provides unusual weight problems for Oxford University's Colin Moynihan. For the boxing match against Cambridge last week he was selected at bantamweight, which meant increasing his weight to 8 stone 7. Since the bout, which he lost, he has been desperately trying to shed all the extra weight and more for Saturday's Boat Race. As coxswain he realizes he is 'dead weight' and the less there is of him, the less there is for others to pull.

Sabrina (Kate Jackson), Jill (Farrah Fawcett-Majors) and Kelly (Jaclyn Smith) as Charlie's Angels.

THE GREAT POKER GAME

The pistol the Liberals hold at the Government's head began to look more like a howitzer yesterday. Mr Steel and his followers piled demand on demand as their price for keeping Mr Callaghan in office. They want the abandonment of Socialist measures like worker representation at board level; a huge cut in income tax for everyone; a declaration that the Liberals will be consulted on future government policy. Mr Steel said he was less than optimistic that all his demands would be met, by which he meant Liberal ideas such as a Scottish Assembly with revenue-raising powers, a referendum on proportional representation and a massive switch from direct to indirect taxation. He said that he would give the Government until the last possible minute, before Wednesday's vote on the Tory motion of no confidence, to produce a deal.

NORAH OF *THE ARCHERS* DIES

Actress Julia Mark, who played barmaid Norah McAuley in *The Archers* on Radio 4, died yesterday (20 March). Miss Mark, 49, took a small part in the series when it began 26 years ago and had played Norah for 10 years. The part will not be written out of the series and auditions for a replacement are to be held immediately.

Graham Parker and his band The Rumour have a new album Heat Treatment *which is finding favour among devotees of the London pub and club scene.*

THE CREATURE BEING WIPED OUT BY MISTAKE

The otter, one of Britain's most fascinating and entertaining animals, is under sentence of death. There are estimated to be as few as 300 in English rivers, with numbers still declining, and the main culprit is man. He has killed them off, often unintentionally, by polluting the waters they inhabit, destroying their natural environment and turning the river banks into his playgrounds. Also, there are still 9 packs that actively hunt the otter every weekend from April till October. The Government is being pressed to put the otter on the list of endangered species.

CLASS APART

Ivan Reid, a lecturer at Bradford University, is the first researcher to analyse the vast range of government data stockpiled over the past decade. He has found that in spite of a considerable shift in wealth in that period, the style of life among the classes has hardly altered and an increase in wealth, at least initially, does not make working-class people into middle-class people. Mr Reid produces this picture of the archetypal middle class: compared with the working class they enjoy better health, live longer and have superior homes; they work shorter hours and have more disposable income; they spend longer in education, marry later in life, have fewer children and go to church more often; they also more frequently belong to clubs and political organizations.

AEROSOLS: STILL TOO MANY UNANSWERED QUESTIONS

5 million women spray lacquer from an aerosol onto their hair every day. Such sprays account for one third of the £180m now spent each year on more than 300 different types of aerosols on the market. All of which does not make up for the death of Joanna Rice in Solihull last week. Joanna, 11, sprayed on some lacquer while in the toilet and a few minutes later choked on her own vomit after inhaling the fumes. Joanna's death highlights the growing international controversy about the possible harmful effects that aerosols have, both on individuals and the environment. A strong lobby in the United States wants to see aerosols banned altogether.

DAY BY DAY

2 Mar
The Secretary of State for Industry, Mr Eric Varley, says that repair yards will not, after all, be included in the bill to nationalize the aircraft and shipbuilding industries.

4 Mar
Romania is struck by an earthquake and 1,570 people are reported to have lost their lives.

5 Mar
Welsh racing driver Tom Pryce is killed in the South African Grand Prix.

John Conteh retains the world light-heavyweight boxing title when he beats American Len Hutchings in the third round at Liverpool Stadium.

17 Mar
Australia beats England in the centenary test match at Melbourne by 45 runs, exactly the same margin by which Australia won the first test 100 years ago.

19 Mar
Oxford wins the Boat Race by 7 lengths.

22 Mar
Mrs Indira Gandhi resigns as Prime Minister of India after her Congress party is defeated in a general election by the Janata (People's) party.

23 Mar
A Commons motion of no confidence in the Government is defeated by 322 votes to 298. The Liberals vote in support of the Government after Mr Callaghan and Mr David Steel agree to set up a joint consultative committee to discuss policy and legislation.

24 Mar
Ball girls are employed at Wimbledon for the first time, breaking a 100-year tradition.

Mr Morarji Desai is sworn in as the new Prime Minister of India.

31 Mar
The Conservative candidate wins the Birmingham, Stechford by-election from Labour, the seat formerly held by Mr Roy Jenkins.

APR 1977

WILL HALEY'S STORY KEEP US ROOTED TO OUR SEATS?

The quest began with an ancestral memory, the name 'Kinte', handed down through generations. With little more than that writer Alex Haley set off on his 12-year genealogical safari, a black man in search of his past. The rest is now TV legend. *Roots* – 8 nights that shook America, touching the conscience of the whites and the pride of the blacks, the biggest event in TV history, as the Hollywood publicists proclaimed – attracted 3 out of 5 Americans, a vast audience of 130 million. The BBC obviously believes that the success can be repeated here.

BBC GOES 'QUAD'

The BBC is going quadrophonic. A year-long experiment of 4-soundtrack radio broadcasts starts on 30 April. Anyone who already has stereo radio will need an extra £100 worth of equipment, including 2 additional speakers, to receive them.

Woody Allen and Diane Keaton air their love affair in Annie Hall.

EVANS WINS UNION JOB

Mr Moss Evans is the new leader of Britain's biggest union, the 1.9-million-strong TGWU. His election as successor to Mr Jack Jones as General Secretary will be announced later this month. Mr Evans, the union's 51-year-old national organizer, is well ahead of the other candidates and will take over from Mr Jones next spring.

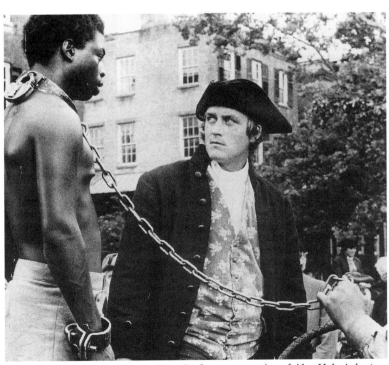

Levar Burton (left) plays Kunta Kinte in the screen version of Alex Haley's best-selling book, Roots.

'GO BACK TO REAL EXAMS'

School examiners want to see children really tested again with a tough new series of papers like the old School Certificate, dropped in 1951. The new exam would require children to pass at least 5 subjects at O level, including compulsory maths and English; those falling short of the 5-subject mark would receive a different certificate indicating their level of achievement. The plan has been put to Education Secretary Mrs Shirley Williams by the Associated Examining Board, whose Secretary, Mr Robert Childs, pointed out that any pupil could now tell an employer he had his certificate of secondary education 'even though the pupil has only obtained a very low grade in one obscure subject like ballet'.

FALKLAND FEARS OVER NEW TALKS

Fears of the Falkland Islands being sold out to Argentina rose last night after an announcement of negotiations between the British and Argentine governments. The talks, to be held in June, will for the first time focus on 'issues affecting the future of the islands', including sovereignty of the colony which has been under direct British rule for 150 years. The 1,900 islanders, some 400 miles from the Argentine coast, have repeatedly said they want to remain British, a declaration the Government has pledged to honour. Minister of State Mr Ted Rowlands said in a parliamentary answer, 'A major objective of the negotiations will be to achieve a stable, prosperous and politically durable future for the Islands.'

TORIES GO FOR 8 MILLION VOTERS

Mrs Thatcher is to make a big effort to win the votes of Britain's 8 million pensioners. A significant cause of discontent with the present Government is the way in which inflation erodes the value of savings. Pensions themselves may be inflation-proof, savings are not. As a prerequisite to lower taxes, more homes to let at rents fair to both tenant and landlord and an educational system which gives all children a grounding in basic subjects, the Tories will emphasize the need to curb inflation and boost production as the only way to improve the lot of everyone, young and old alike.

TIME TO STOP GHOST RIDERS

Whistling Jenny, winner of yesterday's 4.45 race at Lanark, must be the last horse to take the racing public for a ride. Top jockey Edward Hide rode the filly to victory in her first race, although it had been indicated in the press that she would be the mount of apprentice Derek Shaw. Hide's name had been against stablemate Earth Mover, who finished well down the field at 12–1. Such late changes are sanctioned by the Jockey Club, whose rules state that jockeys need not be declared until 45 minutes before a race.

DATSUN JOINS SUPERMINI BATTLE

Datsun, the Japanese firm that exports more cars to Britain than anyone else, is joining the supermini battle being fought by Ford and other leading manufacturers. Today sees the unveiling of the Cherry 100A F-11, a range of high economy small cars designed to compete with the VW Polo, Ford Fiesta, Fiat 127, Vauxhall Chevette and Peugeot 104.

MOTSON TO COVER FINAL

John Motson, BBC's *Match of the Day* soccer commentator, is to cover next month's FA Cup Final, taking over from David Coleman. The corporation has made it clear that 32-year-old Motson is not to be regarded as senior to Barry Davies, who has been asked to cover the European Cup Final by way of compensation. Motson joined BBC Radio in 1968 after working as a sports reporter on local newspapers. He made his TV *Match of the Day* début in 1971. Davies, 36, joined BBC TV in 1969 after 3 years with ITV.

PINK PANTHER'S PLOT THICKENS

Bumbling French policeman Inspector Clouseau is in trouble again – but this time it's fact, not fiction. A French court has seized a copy of his latest film exploits, *The Pink Panther Strikes Again*, because a top French cartoonist is claiming that the plot was stolen from him. René Gosciny, author of the Gallic series *Asterix*, has told a court that he sent a script called *The Master of the World* to Peter Sellers last year. The script was returned but M. Gosciny says that the basic elements from the plot have been used. The court is to investigate the alleged plagiarism.

Johnnie Rotten fronts the controversial Sex Pistols.

MARTIAL LAW IN PAKISTAN

Martial law was imposed on 3 of Pakistan's main cities last night (21 April). It was ordered by Prime Minister Bhutto to check 6 weeks of violence which has claimed more than 200 lives. Lahore, Karachi and Hyderabad have been flashpoint centres in the confrontation between Mr Bhutto and the Pakistan National Alliance which has been demanding his resignation, claiming that he rigged last month's general elections.

WE FIGHT, SAY SACKED 6

6 teachers facing the sack at the William Tyndale School, where the children ran wild, want the National Union of Teachers to strike in defence of their jobs. An enquiry has recommended that the 6, including headmaster Mr Terry Ellis, should be dismissed for indiscipline.

JONES BURIES CONTRACT

The Social Contract has failed, Mr Jack Jones, its principal architect, admitted yesterday. It has not curbed inflation, nor has it cut unemployment, and it was therefore necessary to return to free collective bargaining 'without destroying our trade union unity and our support of a Labour Government'.

BARBARA CASTLE TO QUIT

Barbara Castle, Labour's fiery red-head, is to leave the Commons. She will not stand for re-election to her Blackburn constituency, a seat she has held for 32 years, at the next general election. Mrs Castle, 65, introduced the breathalyser when she was Transport Minister and created an industrial storm with her 'In Place of Strife' policy when she was Employment Secretary. Her last Cabinet post as Social Services Secretary was fraught with controversy as she sought to abolish pay beds. Mrs Castle returned to the back benches following a Cabinet reshuffle in April last year.

LONDON FIRST FOR *EVITA*

The rock opera *Evita* is to be staged for the first time in London next year after a battle to lure the show to Broadway. Rock Follies star Julie Covington, who sings the part of Eva Perón on the record of *Evita*, looks certain to win the title role in the stage version. The musical, created by Andrew Lloyd Webber and Tim Rice, is being tipped as the biggest theatrical success since *Jesus Christ Superstar*, which they also wrote.

President and Mrs Carter applaud Egyptian President Anwar Sadat following a speech delivered at the White House.

DAY BY DAY

2 Apr
Red Rum wins the Grand National for the third time.

7 Apr
The Prime Minister of Israel, Mr Rabin, resigns as Leader of the Labour party after it becomes known that he and his wife have illegal American bank accounts. Under Israeli law he cannot resign the premiership of the interim Government until after the general election in May.

8 Apr
It is announced from Buckingham Palace that Princess Anne is expecting a baby in November.

13 Apr
Aston Villa wins the Football League Cup when it beats Everton 3–2 after extra time in the second replay.

18 Apr
President Carter speaks on television of the need for the American people to economize on the use of petrol and gas in order to avoid an energy crisis.

20 Apr
A 10-year-old boy sells an Anglo-Saxon sword at Christie's for £10,000; he had found the sword in a stream near Gilling West in Yorkshire.

24 Apr
Lucinda Prior-Palmer wins the 3-Day Event at Badminton for the third time.

27 Apr
Laurie Cunningham wins his first cap and scores as England beats Scotland in an under-21 international.

Robert Horne driving a Ferrari breaks the British land speed record for the flying mile with an average speed of 191.64 m.p.h. The previous record of 170.6 m.p.h. was set by Sir Malcolm Campbell in 1926.

28 Apr
In a by-election at Grimsby, Labour holds the seat with a majority of 520. The Conservative candidate wins Ashfield, formerly a Labour seat with a majority of 22,915, by 264 votes.

The Archbishop of Canterbury meets the Pope at the Vatican.

29 Apr
The British Aerospace Corporation, formed from Hawker Siddeley Aviation and Dynamics, the British Aircraft Corporation and Scottish Aviation, comes into operation.

TV WON'T WEAR IT

Derby County's sponsorship contract with Saab, the Swedish motor car company, may be worth £300,000 but the club has effectively wiped itself off British television screens. Both the BBC, whose charter does not permit such advertising deals, and ITV, whose own revenue is obviously eroded as a result, have been realistic enough to accept advertising as part of the modern sporting scene. Both channels drew the line at 'static' advertising: banners or hoardings around a stadium. What Derby is proposing is 'mobile' advertising – the display of a company's commercial insignia on a player's shirt. If the Football League and Football Association sanction such commercial sponsorship, games involving these clubs will not be televised.

MAY 1977

PROTEST OVER SEXY BOOK

A teachers' association is to protest about a novel which has been included in an O level course. The book, *Mr Sammler's Planet* by Saul Bellow, contains a reference to a man exposing himself and a girl saying she wanted sexual intercourse all night. 4-letter words are used in some passages. West Glamorgan's Director of Education said that any criticisms regarding parts of a syllabus would be investigated.

TORIES TO END RATES

The Tories have come up with the simplest answer of all to the owner-occupier's burden of ever-increasing rate bills – abolish the rates. A plan to do just that is nearing completion. The proposal is to raise the necessary cash through national direct and indirect taxation and distribute it to local authorities in annual grants. The plan is seen as an election winner.

Political storm brewing as Government ministers Denis Howell, Shirley Williams and Fred Mulley join pickets at the Grunwick film processing plant. The three are all members of Apex, the union at the centre of the 40-week-old dispute.

Women's campaign for Soviet Jewry demonstrate on behalf of Iosif Begun in London.

THE TWIST IN *OLIVER'S STORY*

When Erich Segal got stuck writing *Oliver's Story* he did not lack offers of help, especially from movie producers waiting to cash in on a lucrative sequel to *Love Story*. The first thing the studio wanted to know was who was going to die in the follow-up. When Segal replied that no one was, the producer sought to overcome the 'problem' by suggesting that Jenny's father be killed off. 'Everyone loves him; it'll be just great.' Segal's publishers, on the other hand, wanted Oliver's father to die. On the numerous offers he has had to write any picture in which anybody dies, the author reflects, 'I have become the mortician of literature.'

END OF FRANCE'S EMPIRE

France's last colony in Africa, Djibouti, goes to the polls tomorrow (8 May) for a referendum on independence. A 'yes' vote is so assured that France has already announced that it will pull out of the country on 27 June.

THE QUEEN STARTS UNITY STORM

The Queen yesterday made a personal appeal for national unity – and provoked a bitter backlash from some Scottish Nationalists. The Queen said that the complexities of modern administration and the feeling the metropolitan Government was too remote from people's lives had provided the background for discussion on devolution. Coming within hours of the Nationalists' triumph in the local elections, the remarks were described by Nationalist leaders as 'ill-advised' and 'unprecedented'.

Kerry Packer with Tony Greig.

WORLD'S TOP CRICKETERS TURN 'PIRATE'

In a player revolution unprecedented in sport, the world's top 34 test cricketers have secretly signed contracts to become freelance mercenaries. They are to play exhibition 'tests' for television, the first tour comprising an Australia versus the Rest of the World series. The 'tests' will be screened throughout Australia under an agreement signed with Kerry Packer, chairman of a huge media empire. Australian stars who have signed for the series include the Chappell brothers Greg and Ian, Denis Lillee and Jeff Thomson. The Rest of the World line-up includes: Tony Greig, Alan Knott, John Snow and Derek Underwood from England; Imran Khan, Mushtaq Mohammed, Majid Khan and Asif Iqbal from Pakistan; West Indians Viv Richards, Andy Roberts, Clive Lloyd and Michael Holding; and Barry Richards, Mike Procter, Graeme Pollock and Eddie Barlow of South Africa.

BRITAIN CALLS HALT TO ATOM PLANT PLAN

Plans for Britain's first commercial power station fuelled by plutonium have been deferred indefinitely. In a White Paper published yesterday the Government announced that there could be no go-ahead for the Fast Breeder power plants without extensive public debate. The problem with the new type of reactors is that they produce more plutonium than they require, thus leaving ever-increasing quantities of the fuel to be stockpiled safely; and plutonium is an essential ingredient in the making of nuclear weapons.

HELTER-SKELTER INTO SKATEBOARD SUMMER

What do enthusiastic surfers do when there is no surf to be had? Answer: they invent the skateboard, which provides all the thrills of riding the waves without relying on the elements. The sport, which began in America and is now sweeping the world, got off to a slow start – the film *Skater Dater* was made as long ago as 1966. It is not without its dangers: skateboarders are already banned in most Swedish cities and there have even been 11 deaths. Protective clothing is essential but the best way of averting most accidents is to take skateboarding off the streets. Enthusiasts here are pressing local authorities to provide skate parks similar to those which have appeared all over America.

GREEN SHIELD AXED BY TESCO

Tesco supermarkets are to give bigger discounts instead of Green Shield stamps. Green Shield chairman Mr Richard Tompkins confirmed that the contract, worth £18m a year, was not being renewed but declared that none of the company's 82 redemption centres would close. Tesco, which had been Green Shield's biggest customer, said that the demand for stamps was waning and the last would be given on 8 June. Tobacco firms and garages are experiencing a similar trend. A London petrol station is offering 30-fold Green Shield stamps or 14p off each gallon – equivalent to 150 stamps or paying only 81.8p – yet is finding that only salesmen whose petrol is paid for are requesting stamps.

BIGGEST SOCCER NIGHT FOR 9 YEARS

Liverpool are the football kings of Europe. In the greatest night for English soccer for 9 years they won the European Cup and wiped away the disappointment of their FA Cup Final defeat last Saturday. The 3–1 victory over Borussia Moenchengladbach in Rome was the first time an English team has won the trophy since Manchester United's triumph in 1968. The heroes on the night were 2 men who had just played their last match for the club. Kevin Keegan, on the verge of a £400,000 move to SV Hamburg, was at his world-class best while Tommy Smith, the 32-year-old veteran playing his last game after exactly 600 appearances, headed the crucial goal that put Liverpool 2–1 in front.

Tommy Docherty (l) and Laurie Brown of Man Utd. in training for the FA Cup Final against Liverpool.

JUNE 1977

Celebrations all over the country for the Queen's Silver Jubilee.

THE MAGNIFICENT 7 IN THE SKY

Although *Star Trek* is over and *Space 1999* irretrievably grounded, television science fiction receives another fillip with the news that the BBC is planning a new space saga. Set in the third century of the second calendar – a cunning way of disguising exactly when it all takes place – it's a space western entitled *Blake's Seven*, a kind of Magnificent Seven in the sky. The 7 – 4 men and 3 girls, as yet uncast – wage a guerilla war against the oppressive Galactic Federation. Due for screening next January it is all good *Boy's Own* hokum, which is exactly what its creator, Terry Nation, the man who invented Daleks, intends.

FUR GIANT TO CLOSE

Swears & Wells, Britain's largest chain of fur stores, is closing down because of changing fashions. A real fur coat no longer has snob value, while fun furs and synthetic leather coats have become socially acceptable.

BRAGG QUITS BBC

Melvyn Bragg is leaving the BBC to edit and present a new show for London Weekend Television. The new programme will replace *Aquarius*, ITV's main arts programme, and will feature items on the more popular branches of the arts – cinema, rock music and books.

US SCRAPS RAPE DEATH PENALTY

America's Supreme Court has ruled that never again will a man be executed for the crime of rape. The court, which has the last word in all American law, ruled that death is a 'disproportionate punishment' for rape and overturned a capital sentence imposed by a Georgia court on a man convicted of rape in 1974. No-one has been executed for the crime of rape since 1964. Had the court's 9 judges ruled in favour of allowing individual states to impose the death sentence for rape – as is the case at present – new laws giving states the right to execute for crimes such as kidnapping and terrorism would have been a possibility. It is thought that it will not be long before capital punishment is outlawed entirely.

BAN PUNK DISC, SAY MPs

MPs are urging record shops to boycott the Sex Pistols' latest single, which attacks the Queen. Although the group's version of 'God Save the Queen' has been banned by the BBC and most commercial radio stations, it is steadily climbing the charts. The song speaks of a Fascist regime turning the people into morons.

ROCKET MAN DIES

Dr Wernher von Braun, the brilliant German-born scientist whose V-2 rockets terrorized London in 1944 and who put America's first man on the moon, died yesterday (17 June) at the age of 65. Since his surrender to the Americans in 1945 the physicist has pioneered rocket development.

WIMBLEDON WAITS AND HOPES

If there is any fairness in football politics, Wimbledon will today become the tenth non-League club to be admitted to the Football League since the war. With 3 successive years as Southern League champions and a sound financial base, Wimbledon is in better shape than most Fourth Division clubs. 'What more can we do?' said Chairman Ron Noades. 'This is the fourth time Workington have had to apply for re-election. They won only 4 matches and got less than 20 points.' Under a new system only 2 non-League clubs are up for election this season: Wimbledon and Altrincham. A confident Noades added, 'I am sure we could become a First Division club in time because the potential here is fantastic.'

WHEN IS A PICKET NOT A PICKET?

The present law on picketing is set out in the 1974 Trade Union and Labour Relations Act but is so vague that no one knows exactly what a picketer is or what distinguishes him from an outside demonstrator. No limit on the number of pickets is laid down; the act merely states that peaceful picketing is lawful 'in contemplation of furtherance of a trade dispute'. Pickets may be posted at or near 'a place where another person works or carries on business'. They can also be posted at 'any other place where another person happens to be, not being a place where he resides'.

Black students in troubled Soweto signal their message to police.

DAY BY DAY

1 June
Lester Piggott, riding The Minstrel, wins the Derby for the eighth time.

4 June
Scottish supporters at Wembley, where they saw their team beat England 2–1, cause damage to the ground estimated at £15,000.

5 June
President James Mancham of Seychelles, in London for the Commonwealth Conference, is deposed and replaced by the Prime Minister Albert René.

6 June
At Windsor the Queen lights the first of a nationwide chain of over 100 bonfires.

10 June
British nationals in Uganda are forbidden to meet or travel in groups of more than 3, facing immediate arrest and imprisonment if they do so.

13 June
Inland postal charges are increased to 7p for a second-class letter and 9p for first class.

15 June
A Federal Appeal Court in New York declines to endorse a lower court's ruling that Concorde should be allowed to land at J. F. Kennedy Airport.

The first general election in Spain for over 40 years results in victory for Adolfo Suarez, the Prime Minister, and his Union of the Democratic Centre party.

16 June
In a communiqué at the close of their conference, Commonwealth leaders condemn 'the sustained disregard for the sanctity of human life and massive violations of human rights in Uganda'.

Mr Jack Lynch's Fianna Fáil party defeats the Fine Gael Labour coalition of Mr Liam Cosgrave, Prime Minister since 1973, in the Irish general election.

27 June
The French territory of the Afars and the Issas, on the east coast of Africa, becomes the independent republic of Djibouti.

The Government sells its 66,800,000 shares in British Petroleum, the largest ever single-share deal.

A 36-foot leather boat with a crew of 4 reaches Newfoundland 13 months after leaving Ireland. The voyage had been undertaken to show that sixth-century Irish monk, St Brendan, could have been the first European to sail to America.

RAPID RISE OF QUALIFIER McENROE

Top seed John McEnroe is expected to withdraw from Wimbledon's junior singles event. The 18-year-old American has reached the last 8 of the men's singles at senior level, the first qualifier to do so.

RACE LAW CAN MAKE IT FOURTH TIME LUCKY FOR BASIL

Basil Lewis has had 3 applications to join a Conservative Club rejected in spite of the fact that he is a Tory councillor. Any future application, however, will have the backing of the law; for Mr Lewis is black and the new Race Relations Act, which comes into effect today (13 June), makes it an offence to operate a colour bar in a private club. Such clubs were left free to continue discrimination under the old Race Relations Act of 1968. A new body, the Commission for Racial Equality, will enforce the new legislation and promote equal opportunity; it replaces the Race Relations Board.

WORLD CHIEF GUIDE DIES

More than 20 million scouts and girl guides in 100 countries will mourn the death of Olave, Lady Baden-Powell. The widow of Robert Baden-Powell, the founder of the scout and guide movement, died yesterday (26 June) aged 88. Olave St Clair Soames was only 23 when she met Lord Baden-Powell, the 55-year-old hero of Mafeking.

HOW SCIENTIST TOM ROCKED HIS WAY TO A FORTUNE

Every night after work mechanical engineer Tom Scholz locked up the laboratory, where he supervised some of the world's most advanced electrical equipment, and went home to tinker with old tape recorders rescued from refuse collectors. He was, in fact, recording an LP of rock music in which he played 4 instruments overdubbed onto tape. The result is one of America's most unexpected showbusiness success stories. In little more than 6 months the Boston LP has sold 3 million copies, produced 2 Top Ten hits on both sides of the Atlantic and looks as if it could earn Scholz £10m.

'He is the perfect golfing specimen' Peter Thompson on 22-year-old Greg Norman.

NO POLITICS FOR PREMIER'S DAUGHTER WHO BECAME PRESIDENT

Home at the moment for Benazir Bhutto is the cloistered calm of St Catherine's College, Oxford. By the end of the month, however, she will be embroiled in the excitement and danger of public life in strife-torn Pakistan, where her father Mr Ali Bhutto is Prime Minister. She will be joining her country's Foreign Service after 4 years at Oxford, during which time she won a degree in politics and philosophy and held the presidency of the union. The idea of entering the political arena has no appeal for 23-year-old Benazir, who, nevertheless, is a spirited defender of her father's somewhat tarnished reputation.

MP QUITS FOR TV JOB

Labour MP Brian Walden is quitting politics to take over Peter Jay's job as presenter of the ITV current affairs programme *Weekend World*. Mr Callaghan now faces yet another repercussion from the controversial appointment of Mr Jay, his son-in-law, as ambassador in Washington – a by-election at Mr Walden's Birmingham Ladywood constituency. An outspoken right-winger in the Labour party, Mr Walden described the offer as the 'chance of a lifetime'. Nevertheless, most of his colleagues had written off his political career. In 1974 he refused a ministerial appointment and last year he helped defeat the Government's Dock Work Regulation Bill.

PICTURES OF HATE

The Grunwick dispute has taken an ugly new turn with pickets brandishing a 'scabs gallery' – placards carrying pictures of workers who refused to join the strike. The dispute at the north London film-processing plant began last August over the sacking of a worker. 72 people walked out; more than 260 stayed on and they have enjoyed a 25% wage increase for their loyalty. The stoppage has been officially backed by the clerical union APEX, which the firm refuses to recognize.

JULY 1977

GRUNWICK BOSS LOSES CASE

Grunwick boss George Ward left the Lord Chief Justice's court yesterday an £8,000 loser. Lord Widgery had ruled that his film-developing firm should recognize the right of the white-collar union APEX to negotiate for his workers. Costs were awarded against Mr Ward – which is where the money went – although he said he would be appealing against the decision.

Engineering Union leader Mr Hugh Scanlon chats to a policeman outside the besieged Grunwick plant.

PISTOL HUNT FOR 'SON OF SAM'

New York police are trying to track down 28,000 guns in a bid to catch a mass killer who has murdered 5 people in less than a year. Police admit they have no description of the man but they do know that he uses a Bulldog .44-calibre pistol and are pursuing the remote hope than an investigation of known owners of such a weapon will provide a lead. The killer, who calls himself 'Son of Sam' and either leaves signed notes by his victims' bodies or sends them to newspapers, has so far foiled conventional police methods.

ROBSON THE FAVOURITE

Bobby Robson of Ipswich heads the queue of managers eager to stake their reputations on the England job which has defeated Don Revie, the toughest and most successful club boss of them all. Other serious contenders will be Jack Charlton, currently out of work after a successful period with Middlesbrough, and Brian Clough, who has masterminded Nottingham Forest's return to the First Division. Robson seems the most likely choice, however, with the grounding of a playing career as an England wing-half, a solid reputation as a coach, and the fact that he was the second choice after Revie in 1974. There is just a possibility that the FA might reorganize to prevent anyone else securing Revie's level of power. An elder statesman – perhaps West Ham's Ron Greenwood – could become general manager, working with an active young coach such as Crystal Palace's Terry Venables.

WILL VITAL MISTAKE LEAD TO RIPPER?

A vital difference has emerged between the original Jack the Ripper and his twentieth-century counterpart, who has killed 5 times since October 1975. Whereas none of the original Ripper's targets lived to tell the tale, police are hoping that the current killer's sixth victim – 42-year-old Maureen Long, found slashed last Sunday – will eventually help them spring the trap on the man who has terrorized the women who inhabit the twilight areas of Leeds and Bradford. A picture of the killer has already been built up: a man in his middle 30s, 6 feet tall and well made, with wiry blond hair, thick eyebrows and puffed cheeks.

GAY NEWS GUILTY OF BLASPHEMY

The homosexuals' newspaper *Gay News* was found guilty of blasphemous libel yesterday. In the first trial of its kind for 56 years the newspaper was convicted following the publication of a poem by Professor James Kirkup. The poem, entitled 'The Love That Dares to Speak its Name', was written as if by a homosexual Roman centurion describing his feelings towards Christ following the Crucifixion. The verdict will go down in legal history as the modern authority on blasphemy. The last such trial was in 1921 when a man named Gott published a pamphlet describing Christ as looking like a circus clown when he entered Jerusalem on a donkey. He, too, was found guilty.

ABORIGINES SUE FOR RETURN OF AUSTRALIA

200 years after Captain Cook claimed Australia from 'the noble savages' the Aborigines have begun moves to get back their country. In a High Court writ issued in Sydney yesterday, the world's oldest race is suing for 'British sovereignty proclaimed by Captain Cook in 1770 and all acts flowing from that' to be declared illegal. The Aborigines, who number 150,000, are claiming damages of £15,000m from the Australian and British Governments.

'BANNED' COMEDY BREAKS RECORD

A play which was once rejected by an Eastbourne theatre because its title was too *risqué* has become the world's longest running comedy. *No Sex Please – We're British*, now in its seventh year, broke the record previously held by *There's a Girl in my Soup* at the weekend when it reached 2,548 performances.

Arthur Scargill leads the Grunwick marchers.

Stepping out Punk-style.

BRITAIN BIDS FOR LAND RECORD

A Briton is planning to beat the world land speed record in a jet-engined car – and burst through the sound barrier at the same time. The present record is 631 m.p.h.; the speed of sound is 760 m.p.h. Richard Noble, a 32-year-old executive with the GKN engineering group, has persuaded the Defence Ministry to give him a jet engine from a Lightning fighter plane. It will be put into a 30-foot dragster car, to be called Thrust 3, which is designed to accelerate from 0 – 180 m.p.h. in only 3 seconds. For the driver it will be like taking off in a moon rocket. The present record was set by American Gary Gabelich on the Utah Salt Flats in 1970.

TORRID 20s OR SIZZLING 70s?

Yesterday's temperatures in the current mini-heatwave might have been portrayed as the torrid 20s by the centigrade-happy BBC but just about everyone else would rather stick to good old-fashioned Fahrenheit – the sweltering 70s. Try as the BBC might to get us thinking like Continentals by giving the temperature in centigrade, with Fahrenheit only as an afterthought, their policy doesn't seem to be working. Policeman Frank Evans typified the results of a survey with the comment, 'I know that 25 centigrade is hot. . . but I wouldn't be able to say for sure without spending hours working it out from the Fahrenheits.'

ARMY LEADER GIVES ELECTION VOW

Pakistan's generals took over the country yesterday (5 July) in a bloodless coup after Premier Zulfikar Ali Bhutto had destroyed the democratic system by an election fiddle that was totally unnecessary to keep him in power. Smouldering discontent over Mr Bhutto's rigging of the elections last March reached a climax in what the military called 'a spring clean-up' which has left General Zia ul-Haq in effective control. Explaining the coup, the General told the 75 million Pakistanis that military intervention had been undertaken to ensure that free and fair elections can take place as planned in October – then they will return to barracks.

BOTHAM IS TOPS!

England's young cricket hero Ian Botham captured 5 Australian wickets, including that of skipper Greg Chappell, on the first day of his first test match. The 21-year-old Somerset player's figures were 5 for 74. He served his apprenticeship on the MCC ground staff at Lord's but had only just joined when he had an offer from Crystal Palace that could have made him a professional footballer. 'It never really entered my head to make football my life,' says Botham of the decision that has been to English cricket's obvious benefit.

Virginia Wade celebrates her Jubilee year victory in the women's singles at Wimbledon.

James Hunt, winner of the British Grand Prix at Silverstone.

HE'S A SMASHER!

Love is. . . a 10lb 8 oz boy called Milo Casali. Milo was born to Kim Casali, creator of the *Love Is. . .* cartoon. Inspiration for Kim's world-famous cartoon, which is syndicated from Los Angeles to 60 countries, came from her love for her husband Roberto. When Roberto became fatally ill with cancer, Kim decided that, after his death, she wanted to add to the family they had already started. Roberto became an artificial insemination donor and, following his death last year, left Kim the legacy of a joyous pregnancy.

THE CITY THAT WENT BERSERK IN DARK

New York went crazy the night the lights went out. Looters went on the rampage after a bolt of lightning struck an electrical transformer and blacked out the entire city. 2,000 arrests were made as shops were plundered but 1 police officer observed that for every arrest dozens of others escaped.

AUG 1977

CARTER MOURNS ELVIS

'He was a symbol to the people the world over of the vitality, rebelliousness and good humour of this country'

From PHILIP FINN in New York

THE WORLD mourned Elvis Presley yesterday in a way no other popular entertainer has been mourned before.

The death of the king of rock 'n' roll brought grief to millions—and a tribute from President Jimmy Carter.

It is almost unheard of for a head of state to note the achievements of a singer.

But as hundreds of fans waited for a glimpse of their idol lying in state at his mansion in Memphis, Tennessee, President Carter said:

'Elvis Presley's death deprives our country of a part of itself. His music and his personality, fusing the styles of white country and black rhythm and blues, permanently changed the face of American popular culture.

White suit

'His following was immense and he was a symbol to the people the world over of the vitality, rebelliousness and good humour of this country.'

Mr Carter said Presley 'burst upon the scene more than 20 years ago with an impact that was unprecedented and it will probably never be equalled.'

President Carter said today, 42, who died on Tuesday of a heart attack after a strenuous game of squash, lay in a white suit from pop star Elton John,

Grief-stricken fans wait outside the Presley mansion yesterday: 'They're here to say goodbye'

The King is dead. President Carter said Presley 'burst upon the scene more than twenty years ago with an impact that was unprecedented and will probably never be equalled'.

U2 PILOT DIES IN CRASH

U2 spy pilot Gary Powers died a hero last night when the helicopter he was piloting crashed in California. Powers, who worked for a radio and television company, guided the crippled aircraft away from a populated area before it crashed, killing a TV cameraman as well as himself. It was in May 1960, when a summit meeting between Britain, America, Russia and France was being held in Paris, that Powers was shot down by the Russians. The U2 incident caused an international upheaval: President Eisenhower was forced to admit that the US was overflying Russia, while Premier Nikita Khrushchev threw one of his famous tantrums and cancelled the summit. Powers served 21 months of a 10-year sentence for spying before being freed in February 1962 in exchange for Russian agent Rudolf Abel, serving 30 years for espionage in the United States. The swap took place in the best espionage traditions on the middle of a Berlin bridge.

GOLDEN BOY OF SPEED

Michael Lee was 5 when his father took him to an aerodrome, sat him on an old Bantam motorbike and taught him to ride. Now, aged 18, Michael is Britain's youngest ever speedway champion. He is also becoming something of a cult figure in an increasingly popular sport. Speedway is taking over from pop concerts and films for its teenybopper following.

JAMIE FOLLOWS IN FATHER'S PETTICOAT

Jamie Leigh Curtis' parents are 2 of Hollywood's most celebrated stars – Tony Curtis and Janet Leigh. There is a certain irony in casting 18-year-old Jamie, an unknown actress, in the starring role of a TV remake of the film *Operation Petticoat*. Her father played the romantic lead in the film 18 years ago and Jamie remembers teasing her daddy over the love scenes with actress Dina Merrill, who starred in the part Jamie is now playing.

GOOD LIFE HOME FOR SALE

The TV home of the *Good Life* couple is up for sale. It's the 4-bedroomed detached house where the BBC filmed Tom and Barbara Good's exploits in self-sufficiency. In the series the outside scenes were shot in the gardens of 2 houses in Kew-ferry Road in Northwood, Middlesex. The Goods' house is being sold by real owners Michael and Elizabeth Mullins, though at £41,500 perhaps only those as well heeled as fictional neighbours Margo and Jerry Ledbetter will be able to afford it.

Bernard Hepton as Albert and Jan Francis as Yvette in the new BBC1 wartime drama series Secret Army.

BILLIONAIRESS!

A 9-year-old girl, whose greatest pleasure is feeding her 3 white mice, was playing on a Californian beach yesterday, unaware that she is one of the world's richest people. Lisa Marie Presley has emerged as the major beneficiary of her father's will, which some estimates have put as high as $1,000m. The singer's 62-year-old father Vernon and his 84-year-old grandmother Minnie Mae are the other beneficiaries but on their deaths all property and money reverts to the little girl when she reaches the age of 25.

'I'M GUILTY' POLANSKI COULD GET 50 YEARS

Film director Roman Polanski has admitted to unlawful intercourse with a 13-year-old girl, an offence that could put him in jail for up to 50 years. A judge in Santa Monica, California has ordered the 43-year-old film-maker to undergo psychiatric examination to decide if he is a mentally disordered sex offender.

The Space Shuttle Orbiter 'Enterprise' sits atop a modified 747 on the first of five unmanned flights.

MEET THE NEW ELVIS!

The new Elvis is a lean and lanky bespectacled former computer programmer who looks like an amalgam of Buddy Holly, Hank Marvin and Woody Allen. Elvis Costello is quite the unlikeliest rising rock star. He has nothing in common with Presley but is already a cult figure in London's rock sub-culture. His début album, *My Aim Is True*, confirms that he is close to establishing himself as the most exciting singer-songwriter of the New Wave.

Elvis Costello

BOOST FOR 'INSTANT' TV NEWS

Teletext – the TV 'news at a glance' system – has won the Government's seal of approval. Now, those with £500 to spare for the cost of fitting the system to a TV set will be able to select news, weather, travel reports and even what's on at the local cinema, on top of normal programmes. Trial transmissions have been going on since 1974 under the names Ceefax (BBC) and Oracle (ITV) with information superimposed on the screen. Now Home Secretary Merlyn Rees says he believes the systems are here to stay.

BAXTER LEAVES *TOMORROW*

Raymond Baxter has quit BBC's *Tomorrow's World* after nearly 13 years, in a row over its future. Baxter, 55, said the BBC wanted to depart from straightforward factual reporting and make the programme more investigative and campaigning.

CORNHILL CRASH

The immediate effect of the £1m injection into English cricket by the Cornhill Insurance group is to insulate Bob Woolmer, Derek Randall and Ian Botham from the temptations of Kerry Packer. Regular England players move into an assured £15–20,000-a-year bracket and, moral considerations apart, it will not pay to join the Australian circus. Tony Greig is fully committed to defection but Alan Knott and Derek Underwood have until 1 October to reconsider.

THE BLACK BISHOP

We called him the Black Bishop. The piety of his office and the violence of his politics were irreconcilable. Yet when Archbishop Makarios died yesterday (3 August) he had achieved the status of a respected Commonwealth senior statesman and a benign dictator for 17 years. Politically, the Cypriot President had led his country to independence and sought to free it from the influence of either Athens or Ankara. History will judge him on whether Greek and Turk are ever able to live together in a unified Cypriot community.

SALUTE THE MAN OF THE CENTURY!

Geoff Boycott became the hero of a sporting fairy tale in the test match against Australia yesterday (11 August). He became only the eighteenth cricketer in history to score 100 centuries and the first to achieve it in a test. For good measure he did it – with 110 not out – in front of his home Yorkshire crowd at Headingley.

DAY BY DAY

11 Aug
24-year-old David Berkowitz admits to being the killer 'Son of Sam'.

13 Aug
More than 100 people are injured in violent street battles in Lewisham when left-wing demonstrators try to break up a National Front march.

15 Aug
England wins the fourth test against the Australians and regains the Ashes.

18 Aug
Labour holds Birmingham, Ladywood, in a by-election caused by the resignation of Mr Brian Walden.

20 Aug
Groucho Marx dies, aged 86.

21 Aug
A 17-year-old Egyptian, Nasser El Sahzli, swims the Channel from Dover in a record time of 8 hours 45 minutes.

A Voyager unmanned spacecraft is launched from Cape Kennedy on course to Jupiter, Saturn and Uranus.

23 Aug
Mr Callaghan issues a statement denying a newspaper report that security forces had bugged 10 Downing Street while Sir Harold Wilson was Prime Minister.

25 Aug
Lord Justice Scarman's committee of enquiry into the Grunwick dispute recommends the firm to take back former workers who had gone on strike but who wished to be re-employed; *ex-gratia* payments should be made to those for whom there were no vacancies. The union, Apex, was criticized for permitting mass picketing which led to some civil disorder.

29 Aug
More than 50 arrests are made when gangs of youths engage in street battles at the end of the West Indian carnival in Notting Hill.

31 Aug
Mr Ian Smith's ruling Rhodesian Front party is returned in the Rhodesian general election.

A poor turn-out of pickets leaves police guarding empty pavements outside the Grunwick plant.

SEPT 1977

HAIN SWITCHES TO LABOUR

Peter Hain is leaving the Liberals and joining the Labour party. Mr Hain, 27-year-old former President of the Young Liberals who made his political mark in the late 60s and early 70s with militant anti-apartheid demonstrations, said the reason for the move was that the Liberal party had swung to the right and become 'more dogmatically anti-Socialist'.

THE PET EVERY CHILD KNEW IS DEAD

Petra, the TV dog loved by generations of *Blue Peter* viewers, is dead. Her owners at the BBC decided that she was too old and ill and, on the advice of a vet, she was put to sleep yesterday (14 September). Petra had clocked up more than 550 hours on TV in a remarkable career spanning 15 years.

Pro Lib-Lab pact Liberals voting during a stormy session of the Joint Liberal Assembly at Brighton.

FALDO HEADS MARCH OF YOUNG BRIGADE

There were jubilant scenes at Royal Lytham's last green as British golf fans cheered their new Ryder Cup hero, Nick Faldo. The 20-year-old apprentice professional, who defeated superstar Tom Watson, forms the nucleus of the new generation along with Peter Dawson, Mark James, Ken Brown and Howard Clark. The evidence was to be found in the last day singles in which Britain and Ireland tied 5–5 with the Americans, who claimed overall victory, however, with a score of 12½–7½.

I WILL NEVER GIVE IN

Grunwick boss George Ward has defiantly rejected the main recommendations of the Scarman Enquiry into the year-long dispute at his factory. In a letter to Employment Secretary Albert Booth he has made it clear that he would rather see his Grunwick plant go out of business than 'surrender to brute force'. Mr Ward rejects the recommendation that 95 dismissed strikers should be reinstated and refuses to compensate those 'who by their own actions terminated their employment'.

'HEADS MAY ROLL' OVER BIKO DEATH

Black political prisoner Steve Biko died of brutality or callous lack of care at the hands of South Africa's Security Police. This was the grim likelihood yesterday as Minister of Justice Jimmy Kruger said that the police had not told him of Biko's illness or hunger strike until after his death. Heads may roll in the Security Police over the incident, according to the Minister, taken aback by the force of local and world reaction at the death of a prisoner whose importance he and the South African Government had gravely underestimated. Across South Africa yesterday (18 September), thousands of black people held memorial services for the 30-year-old 'Martin Luther King of South Africa'.

DOOMWATCH WARNING OVER ANTARCTIC

Britain has warned against a rush to exploit the Antarctic's resources over fears that the world's weather pattern could be seriously upset. Underneath a mile of ice lie the prospects of an enormous bonanza in uranium, iron and other valuable minerals. There is also the possibility of between 50 and 100 million tons a year of krill, compared with the present total world catch of fish and shellfish of 60 to 70 million tons a year. But Minister of State Mr Ted Rowlands told a 13-nation conference in London that the Antarctic ice mass had been a regulating feature of the world's weather for some 10 to 15 million years longer than man had been on the planet. A clash over how to regulate exploitation splits the 13 nations. 7 – Argentina, Australia, Chile, France, New Zealand, Norway and the United Kingdom – claim parts of the continent. America and Russia make no claims and refuse to recognize others.

NEW *MAGPIE* MAN

Former dolphin trainer Tommy Boyd, 24, is to join Jenny Hanley and Mick Robertson as a presenter on the popular children's TV show, *Magpie*, when it returns to the screen next week.

ANNA STEPS INTO NEW *WORLD*

Raymond Baxter's place in the *Tomorrow's World* team is to be taken by Anna Ford, one of TV's new breed of thinking men's pin-ups who has a degree in economics and is a former President of the union at Manchester University. Since January, 33-year-old Anna has been a reporter on TV's *Man Alive* programme but next month joins Michael Rodd, William Woollard and Judith Hann in the show which presents the latest inventions and scientific discoveries.

The dreamy, wistful features of the singer who became the hottest property in the music business.

The barely recognisable 1275 Mini GT after the accident in which Bolan was killed instantly.

TENNIS GOES ELECTRONIC

Electronic line calling will be used in tennis for the first time in the Pernod Trophy, which begins at Edinburgh's Meadowbank Stadium next week. 'Subacall' is the invention of Dr David Supran and works by laying an activated tape on the edge of the white lines. If all the ball hits it the umpire receives a light signal on a small console while players and spectators will hear a bleep. The idea, aimed at eradicating bad calls, has been made possible only by a secret 7-year development of a new ball by Slazenger. It contains minute particles of stainless steel in the pile which releases the impulse on impact with the tape.

REPEAL 'EVIL' LAW, SAYS MP

Tory MP Mr Nicholas Fairbairn yesterday demanded the repeal of the Employment Protection Act, which he called 'absurd and evil'. He claimed the act made industry afraid to take on workers, thus keeping unemployment figures up and production down. The act says that anyone employed for more than 6 months must be regarded as permanent and protected by redundancy and unfair dismissal laws. Mr Fairbairn's attack followed claims that the Departments of Health and Employment are sacking casual workers every 26 weeks and re-appointing them a few days later, thereby placing them outside the protection of the act.

Gone but not forgotten: pop icon Marc Bolan.

SATELLITE EXPLODES: NOW THE BIG DELAY

Scientists admitted last night that Europe's first Telstar-type satellite will be delayed by at least a year following the explosion which destroyed the prototype during its first attempted launch. As the area around Cape Canaveral was searched for pieces of the £17m satellite, it seemed certain that the reason for the explosion was a fault in the American Thor Delta rocket, chartered for £10m to effect the launch. The satellite, built by European aerospace firms headed by Britain's Hawker Siddeley, was intended to carry 6,000 telephone circuits and was the forerunner of Europe's first commercial space satellite link.

STUDIES MUST WAIT FOR DOWNTON

A telephone call from Lord's on Saturday gave the first hint to 20-year-old Paul Downton that the impossible was about to happen. A voice asked whether the second year of his law degree could be deferred and he was subsequently told by Exeter University that he could resume the course in September 1978. Downton's emergence at international level marks the continuation of a long line of England wicket-keepers from Kent, for whom he has so far made 7 first-class appearances. He follows in the illustrious footsteps of Ames (1927–50), Godfrey Evans (1946–47) and Alan Knott (from 1964). With one appearance by 'Hopper' Levett in 1933, Kent's wicket-keepers have played in 233 tests since 1929.

MOSES SETS SUPERSTAR PACE

A superb display of 400-metre hurdling by 21-year-old Edwin Moses inaugurated the world's newest athletics spectacular in Düsseldorf last night. In the first track event of the World Cup, Moses strode to a seemingly effortless victory in 47.58 seconds, a faster time than that which brought him the gold medal in last year's Montreal Olympics and barely a tenth of a second outside the world record he set in June this year. It was precisely the kind of superstar start that this World Cup event, which could have such repercussions on the future shape of world sport, needed.

CHAMPION SKIER

Mike Hazelwood, 19-year-old potato farmer's son from Lincolnshire, was crowned world waterski champion in Milan yesterday (4 September). His silver medals in both the tricks and slalom events, followed by a fourth place in the jumps, added up to overall victory. It is 10 years since Janette Stewart-Wood won the equivalent women's gold medal for Britain.

DAY BY DAY

2 Sept
The Prices Commission reports an annual rate of inflation down to 11.7% compared with 20.9% in March.

3 Sept
Middlesex beats Glamorgan in the final of the Gillette Cup at Lord's.

8 Sept
Canadian Cindy Nicholas swims the Channel both ways non-stop in 19 hours 55 minutes, the first woman to do so.

9 Sept
Kent and Middlesex are joint winners of the County Cricket Championship. Both counties won their final game to snatch the title from Gloucestershire. It is the first tied championship since Surrey and Lancashire finished level in 1950.

13 Sept
Arthur Fagg, the only man to score 2 double centuries in a first-class match, dies, aged 62. He set the record of 244 and 202 not out in 1938 playing for Kent against Essex at Colchester. From 1959 Fagg was an outstanding umpire, officiating in 18 tests.

Peter Shilton moves from Stoke to Nottingham Forest in a £270,000 deal.

14 Sept
Rugby League *maestro* Jim Sullivan dies, aged 73. He played Rugby Union for Cardiff and the Barbarians at the age of 16. In 1921, at 17, he joined Wigan and dominated Rugby League for 25 years.

16 Sept
Miss Maria Callas, world-renowned opera singer, dies at her home in Paris, aged 53.

British rock musician Marc Bolan dies in a car crash, aged 29.

20 Sept
Victor, the collapsed giraffe at Marwell Zoological Park, dies under the strain of being winched onto his legs. His plight – doing the splits while mating – captured the imagination of the nation.

26 Sept
Following his arrest, George Davis is charged with 5 others in connection with a £50,000 bank raid in London.

Laker Skytrains begin a regular service between Gatwick and New York at a cost of £59 for the walk-on single fare.

28 Sept
The Liberal party assembly at Brighton endorses the alliance with the Government. Mr Cyril Smith, who disapproved of the Lib-Lab pact, resigns as the party's spokesman on employment.

29 Sept
The National Enterprise Board gives British Leyland a loan of £50m to help the company's day-to-day running costs.

Muhammad Ali retains the world heavyweight title after beating Ernie Shavers on points at Madison Square Garden, New York.

30 Sept
The controversial Drax B coal-fired power station in Yorkshire is given the go-ahead by the CEGB.

OCT 1977

IRISH ABANDON B-TEST

Hundreds of motorists facing drunk-driving charges have been reprieved following the decision by the Irish Republic to abandon breath tests. Believing that such tests were subject to too many legal loopholes, police there will revert to old-style methods such as walking white lines, picking up coins and drawing circles.

PREMIER TURNED PRISONER

7 months ago she was the most powerful woman in the world. Yesterday Mrs Indira Gandhi, autocratic ruler of one-seventh of the human race, was under arrest. She has been detained in a widespread investigation of massive corruption in her administration. Last March her Congress party, the only Government India had known in the 30 years since Independence, suffered a humiliating defeat in a general election. Since then accusations of her contemptuous and cynical abuse of power have been under investigation in an enquiry that has already resulted in the arrest of her son Sanjay and 10 close political associates.

THE NEW JOHNNY SPEIGHT?

Next month sees the arrival of urban guerilla Citizen Smith on our screens. The new comedy series, in which Robert Lindsay plays Wolfie Smith, leader of the Tooting Popular Front, highlights a fairy-tale story for 32-year-old writer John Sullivan. Not long ago he was cleaning carpets for a living while harbouring thoughts that he could improve on what the current comedy scene had to offer. After getting a job moving scenery he managed to corner top comedy producer Dennis Main Wilson. Not only was Sullivan's script accepted as a Comedy Playhouse but he was asked to write a whole series and is now hailed as a great new talent in comedy writing. (Dennis Main Wilson cast Cheryl Hall as Smith's girlfriend in the series – without realizing that she was married to Robert Lindsay.)

THE AYCKBOURN CONQUESTS

Until now Alan Ayckbourn, Britain's most prolifically successful playwright, has remained aloof from TV. Now his award-winning trilogy, *The Norman Conquests*, is making TV history. On his insistence it is being filmed in full and shown in 3 2-hour episodes, exactly as it was in the West End. The plays view a single traumatic weekend in the life of 1 family from 3 different perspectives. Ayckbourn comments, 'If I started writing for television I would be a novice; I see everything in terms of the theatre.'

BING DIES PLAYING GOLF

Bing Crosby, the world's best-loved entertainer, died yesterday (14 October). The 73-year-old was playing golf in Spain when he apparently suffered a heart attack. The song for which Bing is probably most famous, 'White Christmas', is listed in the *Guinness Book of Records* as the bestselling record ever.

FREDA WINS RIGHT TO CHANGE HER MIND

A woman's right to change her mind has been enshrined in law following a historic tribunal ruling. Mrs Freda Hughes first told the Area Health Authority that she would not want her old job back after having a baby. Later, however, she changed her mind but found that the job was no longer open to her. Her claim for breach of contract was at first rejected by Manchester Industrial Tribunal but her appeal to the Employment Arbitration Tribunal was successful and she has won compensation for wrongful dismissal. Reporting the case, Incomes Data Services commented, 'Companies must not rely on intentions voiced months before work ends.'

'NEW CIGARETTES WILL STAY'

The campaign to persuade Britons to smoke tobacco substitutes will go on. Manufacturers refused yesterday to write off the substitute cigarettes as a failure, although less than 3% of Britain's 20 million smokers have so far switched to the new brands.

DISGRACEFUL, SAYS LLOYD

David Lloyd yesterday described the international ban on double-strung tennis rackets as 'disgraceful' and 'a very backward step'. The British Davis Cup player, who won a tournament in Edinburgh using a double-strung racket only hours before the ban was imposed, added, 'It hasn't had a fair trial – now it never will.'

POP STARS DIE IN CRASH

3 members of the pop group Lynrd Skynrd were killed in a plane crash yesterday (21 October). Lead singer Ronnie Van Zant, guitarist Steve Gaines and Van Zant's sister, Cassie, who was a vocalist, were on their way to a concert date at Baton Rouge, Louisiana when their charter plane ran out of fuel. Voted one of the top 10 bands in the world, the group was created 10 years ago by friends living in Jacksonville, Florida, taking its unusual name from a teacher called Leonard Skinner, who frequently chided them for their appearance.

Wide lapels.

HOW SISTER MIRIAM BECAME MARY O'HARA AGAIN

The 12 years from 1962 to 1974 meant nothing to Mary O'Hara as she marooned herself joyously in a Worcestershire monastery. Before she became Sister Miriam she was regarded as a singer and harpist of rare quality. Then, 20 years ago, she felt she had to devote herself to God after her husband died of Hodgkins disease, a rare form of cancer. The girl who gave up her successful career at the age of 26 and whose albums continued to sell apace during her contemplative years, appears on the *Russell Harty Show* this week. Sister Miriam has become Mary O'Hara again.

Michael Edwardes arrives for work at Leyland.

BRITAIN GIVEN 'SPY IN CAB' DEADLINE

Britain has been given 30 days in which to order a tachograph – known as a 'spy in cab' – to be fitted to all long-distance lorries and buses. Under EEC regulations all such vehicles must be manned by 2-driver teams, a driver must not be behind the wheel more than 8 hours per day, and after 4 hours a 30-minute rest must be taken. The TGWU is opposed to tachographs, which monitor speeds and distances covered by a vehicle as well as times when it is stationary, claiming that the present log-book system is sufficient.

WHO NEEDS AN ORCHESTRA?

The most important word in the vocabulary of rock music today is Gizmo. It is a device which will revolutionize the performance of any electric guitar by enabling the guitarist to produce an unlimited range of sound effects, including those of an orchestra. It is the brainchild of Lol Creme and Kevin Godley, who quit 10CC last year to perfect their dream, and the first sample can be heard on their album, *Consequences*. The Gizmo goes on sale early next year.

ORDER OF MERIT FOR J.B.P.

The Grand Old Man of English Literature, John Boynton Priestley, has been appointed to the Order of Merit by the Queen. There are 3 other new members of the Order, which is personally chosen by the Queen for exceptional services to art, literature or science: choreographer Sir Frederick Ashton, Lord Todd of Trumpington, President of the Royal Society, and Lord Franks, academic and Chairman of a series of major government enquiries.

BOND MUSIC MAN TAKES BEATING

A High Court judge yesterday froze the British royalties of John Barry, composer of themes to such films as *Thunderball* and *Diamonds Are For Ever*. Barry, 42, formed a company in 1959 and, some 9 years later, launched another company in Guernsey to which the first advanced £246,000. A company formed in the Cayman Islands acquired the Guernsey company; this was in turn taken over by an American company. Mr Justice Templeman said that Barry, who owes £100,000 in tax, was the 'moving spirit' behind all of the company moves. The composer, who also wrote the *Born Free* theme, has been an elusive exile in the US for 7 years.

MP Reg Prentice resigns from the Labour Party and joins the Conservatives.

THE GREAT DASH TO DIVORCE

For every 2 marriages in England and Wales there is now 1 divorce. That startling figure, a product of the liberated 70s, compares with 1 divorce for every 7 or 8 marriages as recently as the mid 60s.

NOV 1977

UN BANS ARMS SALES TO SOUTH AFRICA

The United Nations Security Council yesterday imposed an arms embargo on South Africa – the first time any such action has been levied against a member country. The resolution, which takes effect immediately, follows controversy over the death of Steve Biko and was described as 'an historic occasion' by UN Secretary General Kurt Waldheim.

BUMPY FIRST RIDE FOR CONCORDSKI

Concordski, Russia's Tupolev 144 rival to Concorde, entered passenger service yesterday more than 6 years behind schedule. During the inaugural flight from Moscow to Alma Ata passengers, including the jet's designer Alexei Tupolev, had to shout to make themselves heard. The flight suffered from excessive noise levels even when the plane, travelling at speeds up to 1,250 m.p.h., was theoretically far outrunning its own sound.

THE HAND OF FRIENDSHIP

President Sadat yesterday offered the people of Israel the one thing they have longed for ever since they reached the Promised Land – a 'just and lasting peace' with their Arab neighbours. Addressing the Knesset, the Israeli Parliament, the Egyptian leader warned that there was a price for peace. His terms: total withdrawal from the occupied Arab territories and the establishment of the rights of the Palestinian people. Reacting angrily to the historic hand of friendship Arab hawks were screaming for President Sadat's political assassination.

CLEAN BOWLED

The cricketing establishment's ban on the stars of Kerry Packer's circus has been declared illegal. A High Court judge yesterday ruled that the 6 English Packer cricketers – Tony Greig, Alan Knott, Derek Underwood, Dennis Amiss, John Snow and Bob Woolmer – and the English-based overseas players such as Clive Lloyd and Mike Procter, could not be stopped from playing in county matches next season or in tests if selected.

Egypt's President Anwar Sadat addresses the Israeli Parliament. To his left are Knesset Speaker Yitzhak Shamir and President Ephraim Katzir.

TED RAY DIES

Ted Ray, king of repartee, died yesterday (8 November), aged 71. Ray – real name Charlie Olden – was a pillar of British entertainment since the late 1940s when his radio show *Ray's A Laugh* did the impossible by succeeding Tommy Handley's beloved *ITMA*. The show ran for 12 years.

THE HUNT FOR THE SUN

In theory the experiment of Dr Paul Rebut and his team should work. If successful they will have created a new sun and prove that the world can plug into an unlimited power supply. At the centre of the theory is nuclear fusion – joining atoms together instead of splitting them. The problem is that before they will combine the atoms must be heated to at least 100 million degrees centigrade. Other scientists working on nuclear fusion around the world have created such temperatures for a split second; Dr Rebut's team wants to generate 200 million degrees and maintain it for 20 seconds. The electricity they will use to achieve this would provide power for a city of 500,000 people. The first power plants providing electricity generated from the fusion process could be operating by 2030.

PISTOLS AD BANNED

TV and radio advertisements for the new punk rock LP by the Sex Pistols have been banned. The record, *Never Mind The Bollocks Here's The Sex Pistols*, has sold almost 200,000 copies within a few days of release and is already top of the album charts although Boots, W.H. Smith and Woolworths refuse to stock it.

BOOKER WINNER

Paul Scott, whose first novel was rejected by 17 publishers, has won this year's £5,000 Booker Prize for *Staying On*, a follow up to his *Raj Quartet*.

Steven Spielberg's Close Encounters of the Third Kind.

Elton John announces his decision to quit performing as the Chairmanship of Watford F.C. becomes virtually a full-time job.

'MASKED STAR' TO PLAY ELVIS

Former pop star P.J. Proby is to play Elvis Presley in a new West End musical. Welsh rock singer Shakin' Stevens will play the young Elvis, Proby will be the star in his thirties and a third actor/singer, as yet unnamed, will play Elvis in his later years. Proby, 39, who shocked pop fans a decade ago with a trouser-splitting act which led to a TV ban, auditioned for the part within a week of appearing masked on *Opportunity Knocks*, when he was voted last by a studio audience.

WHAT'S GOT 5 DOORS, 4 WHEELS AND 3 CYLINDERS?

Japan has launched a competitor for BL's new-generation Mini – a 60-m.p.g. 3-cylinder car. The revolutionary 993cc engine, said to be just as smooth as a conventional 4-cylinder unit, powers the Daihatsu, a new name in Britain. The firm is owned by the mighty Toyota company, and the new car is known in Japan as the Charade.

LEVI BEAT PANTS OFF MR WRANGLER

After a 7-year legal battle a federal judge has ruled that Wrangler jeans infringed the trademark of Levi Strauss. It all hinged on that tiny strip of leather bearing the Levi name over the right rear patch pocket, first used in 1936 and registered by Levi as a trademark 2 years later. Levi sued, claiming that Blue Bell, makers of Wranglers, started using the same placing for its Wrangler trademark in 1969. Judge Lloyd H. Burke placed an injunction on the use of a tab in the critical position, declaring that the Wrangler idea was 'designed to capitalize on a market previously developed by Levi Strauss'.

DECIMAL DANGER FOR DRIVERS

Thousands of motorists fall for an old dodge when they fill up at garages displaying signs such as '75.9p Each Full Gallon'. If the purchase includes part of a gallon that part could be at a far higher rate. Some critics want to ban garages from displaying petrol prices in 'catch penny' decimal places and have ½p as the minimum pricing step. But this would also make ½p the minimum difference between petrol grades. Within a couple of years we will be buying petrol in litres and, as there are 4.54 litres in a gallon, this would be equal to 2¼p per gallon if the ½p pricing step were introduced now and carried into decimalization. This is even more frightening when one considers that there is pressure in Whitehall to phase out the ½p coin. So to ban .9p petrol pricing could lead to increases of 4½p per gallon.

A WOMAN'S RIGHT TO SAY, 'GET OUT'

A battered woman can have her man thrown out of their home – even if he owns the house and they are not married. An historic Appeal Court judgement yesterday effectively liberates women from the nineteenth-century legal concept that property rights are sacred. The ruling followed the case of Jennifer Davis who had been subjected to extreme violence by her lover. The case hinged on whether the lover could be expelled from their joint tenancy council flat under the 1976 Domestic Violence and Matrimonial Proceedings Act. 2 previous Appeal Court rulings had found in favour of violent men because they had sole or joint rights to the property but Lord Denning declared these decisions 'erroneous'.

THE THIN GREEN LINE

From 9 o'clock this morning (14 November) it will be up to young servicemen and old Green Goddesses. Soldiers with as little as 1 day's training in fire fighting and obsolete civil defence fire engines put on stand-by 20 years ago were last night ready to take over from the 32,500 firemen due to strike today. The firemen want to be paid the average adult male worker's wage of £78.60 per week plus 10% to take account of the dangers of the job and their special skills. At present a fully qualified fireman with 5 years' experience earns £65.70. The firemen have been offered a 10% increase in line with government policy.

The Boomtown Rats led by Bob Geldof make the charts with their debut album.

DEC 1977

CROSSING THE CHANNEL ON FOOT

'L'Anglais Stupide.' That was how 2 French fishermen described John Webb after he landed in France from Folkestone, the first time anyone had ever windsurfed across the Channel. The mixture of surfing and sailing is the latest sporting craze to hit Britain. It took John 5 hours 10 minutes to make the 21-mile crossing.

PLAY IT AGAIN, BOGIE

Madness rules the charts every year over the Christmas period. Songs which would be ignored at any other time can become huge hits during the festive season. One of last year's surprises was 'On The Trail Of The Lonesome Pine' from a 1937 Laurel and Hardy film. The man responsible for digging it out, movie and music archivist Alan Werner, is trying for a repeat success with 'As Time Goes By'. The song, from the classic 1941 film, Casablanca, is performed by Dooley Wilson, who died in 1953. The voices of Bogart and Bergman are inserted melodramatically between the verses. However, the song faces competition from Paul McCartney and Wings with their bagpipe singalong, 'Mull of Kintyre'.

ALL-TIME TOP 10

Tim Rice, besotted with chart culture from an early age, is an expert in what he calls 'useless information'. Now he has written it all down in the newly published Guinness Book of British Hit Singles. It's taken him – together with younger brother Jo, DJ Paul Gambaccini and Thames Valley Radio's Mike Read – 3 years to assimilate all the information. 'We've left out opinion altogether and albums which I, frankly, find boring,' says Rice of the book which looks set to become the chart-follower's Bible.

PACT TORPEDOED

The Lib-Lab pact which has been keeping the Government afloat was hit by a political torpedo last night. The crisis followed a defeat in the Commons for a proportional representation system to elect Britain's members of the new European Parliament, an idea supported by Liberals. Although a majority of Labour MPs favoured PR, many Liberals felt they had not had the backing they deserved. 116 Labour MPs voted to keep the traditional first-past-the-post system and the idea of PR was defeated by 319–222.

TV STAR'S TRAGIC SECRET

Vi, the nosey neighbourhood gossip in the TV series Beryl's Lot, made millions laugh every week. But Barbara Mitchell, who played the acid-tongued Vi, was dying of cancer, a tragic secret known only to her husband and her agent. With Barbara's death yesterday (9 December) the tragic secret was finally revealed. The 48-year-old actress also starred in The Larkins, For The Love Of Ada, Please Sir and The Fenn Street Gang.

An egg-splattered Len Murray, TUC Secretary. Anger erupted outside the TUC headquarters after the TUC voted not to go against the government's pay guidelines.

A GLIMPSE OF CREATION

5 radio telescopes strung out over the Cambridgeshire countryside are receiving signals not only from unthinkable distances but also from the remote past. Astronomer Dr Simon Mitton says that the research has taken them 90% of the way to the beginning of the universe because of 2 quirks of natural law. One is that the galaxies are rushing away from each other at speeds which can be measured from their light or radio waves. Astronomers can thus calculate how far away these galaxies are. They can also work out the scale of the universe, so staggering that, measured in miles, it would need a figure containing 23 noughts. The second quirk concerns the comparative slowness of the speed of light. When we watched the astronauts on the moon we were actually seeing what they had done 1.5 seconds ago. Such a time-slip runs into millions and billions of years for remote parts of the universe. This has the advantage of turning astronomers' telescopes into time machines and it is now agreed that the beginning was the 'Big Bang' – an explosion of inconceivable violence that set the universe flying apart. The date they put on this is 20,000 million years ago.

MERRY ELECTRONIC CHRISTMAS

Electronic games are the big sellers this Christmas, ranging from TV games offering tennis, squash, football and cricket in black and white at £19.95 to computerized chess and backgammon at £150 and £225 respectively.

POLICE ACCUSED OF ACID TERROR

South Africa's security police have been accused of an indiscriminate acid attack on the daughter of Donald Woods, the banned editor of the Daily Dispatch. Soon after the ban T-shirts printed with pictures of Steve Biko, the black leader who died in police custody, were sent to his children. 5-year-old Mary screamed as she put hers on and the shirt was later discovered to be impregnated with a poisonous chemical. Investigations revealed that security police were opening Mr Woods' mail and one of their number almost certainly 'doctored' the garment.

Status Quo, rocketing into the charts with their new album Rockin' all over the World.

RECORD CHRISTMAS

The Morecambe and Wise Show, including a Cyrano de Bergerac sketch featuring Eric with the big nose and Penelope Keith as the girl who aroused his passions, attracted 28 million viewers, the highest figure for any TV show since the 1967 *Royal Variety Show*, which was watched by 31 million.

GREEN SHIELD CLOSES SHOPS

The Green Shield Stamp company, which has been operating for 20 years, is closing all its redemption centres. Nearly all centres will be combined with Argos discount stores, set up 4 years ago, where stamp holders will be able to redeem their collections. Both firms are owned by Mr Richard Tompkins.

WHEN MOTHERS CAN'T RETURN TO WORK

Women returning to work after having children are warned today that they may face the sack if it is proved that they are unable to do their job adequately and if the employer has tried to provide alternative work. Although a sacking solely on the grounds of pregnancy would be ruled unfair, several employers have successfully defended appeals against dismissal on the grounds of unsatisfactory performance after pregnancy. In one case a chemist's shop assistant was sacked because the job involved heavy lifting which she could no longer do after having her baby. As there was no lighter work available, the dismissal was upheld by an industrial tribunal.

A *STAR WARS* STAR IS BORN

Star Wars fever officially came to England when its star, 25-year-old Mark Hamill, arrived at Heathrow to promote a film which cost less than £4m to make and took £2m in its first 9 days in America, a box-office record. George Lucas, who produced and directed the film, gave each of the stars 1% of the profits so Hamill, who plays hero Luke Skywalker, is well on his way to being a millionaire. The film opened in New York in July and has already taken £70m in the US alone. Audiences in Britain, where most of the film was made, must wait until 27 December to catch the record-breaking space epic.

Actor Kenny Baker, just 3 foot 8 tall, can expect to be a big star in Britain soon. He plays the dalek-like robot R2D2 in *Star Wars*. He sat inside the skin-tight robot perched on a child's car seat and manoeuvred R2D2, who weighs about twice Kenny's 75lb, by rocking the device from side to side. He shares the discomfort of his role with actor Anthony Daniels, who plays fellow robot C3PO.

NEW PRESSURES FACING EVERY DRIVER

After the pound in your pocket it is now the pound in your tyre that's going metric. From January Britain is scrapping lb/inch^2 – the measure used since pneumatic tyres were invented nearly 70 years ago. The bar – equivalent to approximately 29.5 inches of mercury in a barometer – is part of the metric system being adopted by virtually every country.

CHEERIO, JOHNNIE

Johnnie Walker Red Label, the world's biggest selling Scotch, is being withdrawn from sale on the home market after 157 years. A Common Market ruling states that the same price must be charged for both export and home sales. Distillers were not prepared to cut the export price and decided that to increase prices in Britain by the necessary 60p would render the product uncompetitive.

DAY BY DAY

1 Dec
A report into losses by the Crown Agents for Overseas Governments amounting to £200m blames incompetence and bad accounting.

2 Dec
At the end of an inquest in Pretoria the magistrate rules that the security police were not responsible for the death of Steve Biko who died of brain injuries while in prison.

4 Dec
British troops arrive in Bermuda at the request of the Governor. Serious rioting has occurred in the capital, Hamilton, after the execution 2 days earlier of 2 black men convicted of murder.

Jean-Bédel Bokassa crowns himself Emperor of the Central African Empire in Bangui.

6 Dec
2 soldiers are killed when their Green Goddess fire engine overturns as they answer an emergency call in Manchester.

A new republic of Bophuthatswana, made up of 6 separate territories, becomes independent of South Africa. Other nations, including Britain, do not recognize the independence of the Bantustan homeland.

10 Dec
Mr Malcolm Fraser's Liberal–Country party coalition is returned in the Australian general election.

12 Dec
Lady Spencer-Churchill, widow of Sir Winston Churchill, dies at her London home, aged 92.

Women members are elected to the Jockey Club for the first time.

13 Dec
The Government's recommendation of a system of proportional representation in the first direct elections to the European Parliament is defeated in the House of Commons by 319 votes to 222.

14 Dec
5 Law Lords rule that the Advisory, Conciliation and Arbitration Service had abused its statutory powers in recommending that the clerical union, the Association of Professional, Executive, Clerical and Computer Staff should be recognized by the Grunwick film-processing laboratory when it had consulted only strikers and not those still at work at the laboratory.

16 Dec
The Queen opens the new extension of the Piccadilly tube from Hatton Cross to Heathrow.

20 Dec
The Prince of Wales is introduced as a member of the Privy Council.

21 Dec
Sir Reginald Rootes, car industry pioneer, dies, aged 86.

25 Dec
Sir Charles Chaplin, world-famous comedian, dies at his home in Switzerland, aged 88.

Cowley (Gordon Jackson), Bodie (Lewis Collins), and Doyle (Martin Shaw) in action as the crack anti-terrorist squad in The Professionals.

JAN 1978

David Byrne fronts Talking Heads who prepare to release their debut album Talking Heads 77.

CLEMMIE'S REVENGE

Lady Churchill destroyed the famous Graham Sutherland portrait of her husband before Sir Winston died, it was revealed last night. Sir Winston hated the portrait, presented to him by Parliament on his eightieth birthday in 1954. Lady Churchill promised that it would never be seen. The destruction of the painting – described by Sutherland last night as an act of vandalism – was revealed by Lady Churchill's executors. Sir Winston said of the painting, 'It makes me look half-witted, which I ain't.'

SKATEBOARD 'MENACES' IN COURT

Youngsters are being prosecuted for skateboarding on roads and pavements after an outcry from motorists and pedestrians faced with the hazardous consequences of the craze's Christmas bonanza. West Midlands police have brought charges against 20 teenagers under a 1950s bye-law originally designed to stop roller-skating on rights of way. The law states: 'No person shall skate by means of rollers or wheels to the danger of people on the highway.' Most local authorities have similar laws which would cover skateboarding.

GUN-FAN ROCK STAR KILLED

Rock star Terry Kath, lead singer with the Chicago group, shot himself dead when a party game went horribly wrong. 31-year-old Kath, for whom guns were a hobby, put what he thought was an unloaded gun to his head to frighten other guests. The gun contained 1 bullet, however, and he was killed instantly.

BRAGG'S BRAVE NEW WORLD

Melvyn Bragg, apostle of working-class culture, switches channels next week to launch London Weekend's successor to *Aquarius*, *The South Bank Show*. The first programme features an interview with Paul McCartney, a kind of icon of the new culture that the show is dedicated to.

AMONG THE NEW YEAR HONOURS

Union leader Jack Jones becomes a Companion of Honour; the 2 Ronnies – Corbett and Barker – receive OBEs; Walter Winterbottom, outgoing director of the Sports Council, is knighted; champion motor-cyclist Barry Sheene and sailor Clare Francis receive MBEs; cricketer Mike Brearley, rugby's Phil Bennett and showjumping commentator Dorian Williams all receive the OBE; TV scientist Dr Magnus Pike and actor Edward Woodward also receive OBEs; playwright Tom Stoppard receives a CBE; there are knighthoods for 'Hammer' of the Yard, Commissioner David McNee and Chief Constable Kenneth Newman, head of the Royal Ulster force.

POP GOES PAGANINI

In London's bed-sit land Julian Lloyd-Webber practises the cello by a small electric fire. Less than a mile away in Belgravia elder brother Andrew negotiates terms for his latest multi-million-pound musical. Both are stars and dominate the world of contemporary music but Julian earns a comparative pittance from his own remarkable talent and is unknown except to classical music enthusiasts. For years he has been badgering his brother to write something new and different for the cello. The result can be seen this week with the release of an album, *Variations On A Theme Of Paganini*, which also features the rock group Coliseum.

O, MR PRESIDENT

President Carter has made his third *faux pas* of his goodwill tour of the world. During talks in New Delhi with Indian Prime Minister Mr Morarji Desai, believing that the microphone was switched off, he whispered to Secretary of State Cyrus Vance that he wanted 'a cold and very blunt letter' sent to the Indian Premier concerning his country's nuclear policy. Since detonating an atomic bomb in 1974 India has resisted pressure to sign the non-proliferation treaty because of fears that the terms might inhibit peaceful atomic projects. The incident follows the President's comment to his hosts in Poland – thanks to a confused interpreter – that he 'desired them carnally'. The trouble started on the eve of Carter's departure from America when he shocked the Arab world by indicating that he was not in favour of an independent Palestine.

EVIL 'DAUGHTERS' OF RADON

Scientists have discovered that the home is a possible source of radiation that may cause 1 in every 100 deaths from lung cancer. The hazard comes from radon, a naturally occurring gas that seeps into the air in tiny quantities from soil and building materials. The particles are known as the short-lived 'daughters' of radon and experts are warning that home insulation not only traps the heat but also prevents the deadly gas from escaping.

The long-simmering feud between Rita Fairclough (Barbara Knox) and Elsie Howard (Patricia Phoenix) finally boils over in Coronation Street.

Vanessa Redgrave as Julia *and Jane Fonda as Lillian Hellman.*

DO-IT-YOURSELF SMOKERS KIT

A D-I-Y cigarette kit was launched yesterday to beat a Common Market tax. Its makers, Gallahers, who will market their brainchild under the trade name Custom, stress that it is not a 'roll your own' cigarette but a simple machine which can be used to make cheap, near perfect cigarettes in seconds. The kit cigarette has been launched because of the introduction of End Product Tax, a Common Market levy, on 1 January. EPT switches taxation from tobacco to finished cigarettes and will push up prices from 42p to almost 50p for 20 within the next fortnight. Unlike tobacco substitute, which has cost the tobacco companies millions of pounds and rates as the biggest flop in smoking history, the D-I-Y cigarette looks like being a winner.

DAY BY DAY

1 Jan
An Air India Boeing 747 explodes in mid-air after taking off from Bombay and crashes into the sea. All the 213 people on board lose their lives.

10 Jan
Liverpool pays Middlesbrough £352,000 for Graeme Souness, a new record cash deal between English clubs.

12 Jan
A delegate conference of the Fire Brigades Union votes to accept the employers' offer and to call off the 2-month-old strike.

13 Jan
The Building Societies' Association announces a reduction of 1% in the mortgage rate to 8.5%.

London Weekend Television is fined £50,000 by the High Court in Edinburgh for contempt of court in showing a programme containing references to a nursing sister who had been charged with obstructing the air supply to a patient and so prejudicing her chances of a fair trial.

Actor Michael Bates – star of *It Ain't 'Arf Hot Mum* and *Last of the Summer Wine* – dies, aged 57.

US politician Hubert Humphrey dies, aged 66.

18 Jan
The European Court of Human Rights clears Britain of charges, brought by the Irish Government, that treatment of 14 suspected terrorists in Northern Ireland 7 years ago amounted to torture, but the judges ruled that techniques of interrogation used for only a short time in 1971 were inhuman.

21 Jan
A Liberal party assembly at Blackpool votes in favour of the Lib–Lab pact continuing until the party leader, Mr David Steel, decides to end it.

22 Jan
English cricketer Herbert Sutcliffe dies, aged 83.

23 Jan
The Government is defeated in the House of Commons on a motion to devalue the green pound by 5%. A Conservative motion for a devaluation of 7.5% is carried. The green pound is the rate at which Common Market food prices are converted into sterling.

25 Jan
An Opposition amendment, making it necessary for 40% of the Scottish electorate to vote in favour of devolution before a separate assembly could be set up, is carried by 168 to 142.

29 Jan
4 motorists are found dead in their cars after the North of Scotland is swept by the worst blizzard for 30 years.

GOING FOR ANOTHER GOAL

Terry Venables will be spending the afternoon in the dug-out at Boothferry Park, not the kind of place you would expect to find James Hazell, the Cockney private eye who is the hero of a new TV series starting this week. Venables, Manager of Crystal Palace, who play at Hull City today, helped create Hazell and wrote 3 books about him with *Straw Dogs* author, Gordon Williams. 'The Hazell bit is because we wanted. . . a bit of femininity about him. You know how they talk in the East End: "duckie" and all that. . . Gordon supplies the 500-word descriptions of trees and things and I supply the dialogue.'

AUSSIES JUST RUN AND RUN

A group of Australian schoolboys has been shaking the foundation of British rugby with dazzling displays which have brought 10 victories over the past 5 weeks. Among the stars of the team are a trio of Aborigine brothers, Gary, Glen and Mark Ella.

16 CHILDREN FOR JOHN

Aspiring author John Knight has not had much success with his books but the real-life drama of his domestic situation is more sensational than anything in fiction. His wife, Carole, 33, will soon be having their ninth child. Less than 2 miles of Bodmin Moor separate Carole from John's mistress, Clare, 37, who is 7 months' pregnant with their seventh child. The women intend to deliver each other's babies and 41-year-old John says proudly, 'It's a perfectly happy arrangement; I'm a lucky man.' For the 2 newcomers he can expect rises on the £132 per week he already draws.

JUDGE McKINNON'S LAW

An Englishman's freedom of speech includes the liberty to make jokes about 'niggers, wogs and coons', according to a court ruling yesterday. John Read was acquitted at the Old Bailey of infringing the 1965 Race Relations Act after making a speech using just such language. The verdict, by an all-white jury, and particularly the summing up by Judge Neil McKinnon, has brought fierce criticism from MPs and community relations workers. The situation was complicated by the fact that since Read's speech, made in June 1976, a strengthened law on race relations has come into force. Although the trial took place this week it was conducted under the 1965 Act which states that the prosecution must prove that not only threatening, abusive or insulting words about a person's colour, race or creed have been used but that there was intent to stir up hatred against groups thus distinguished. Under the Race Relations Act of 1976 lack of intent is no defence.

Paul McCartney leaving Victoria Palace Theatre after seeing Annie.

Captainly words from England's Mike Brearley.

NIXON RETURNS

Richard Nixon returned to Washington yesterday, the city which was once the centre of his authority and shame. The disgraced President ended his 1,255 days of reclusive exile to honour cancer victim Senator Hubert Humphrey, the man whose dream it was to hold the power Nixon so shabbily flung away.

FEB 1978

'UNBORN BABY' WINS CASE

Legal history was made yesterday when the claims of an unborn child injured in a road accident were recognized. Michael Williams, who is now 6, was born 3 weeks prematurely with serious brain damage a day after his mother, Joyce, was the innocent party in a car crash.

VICE GIRLS JOIN 'RIPPER' HUNT

Vice girls have been asked to join the hunt for a 'Jack The Ripper' killer who has claimed 6 victims among prostitutes in West Yorkshire. Detectives have revealed that 18-year-old Helen Rytka, whose body was found last week in a Huddersfield timber yard, was the seventh victim. 'We are looking for a cunning psychopath,' said George Oldfield, West Yorkshire's Assistant Chief Constable, who is leading the enquiry.

Grange Hill, *a new series by Phil Redmond about children starting at a comprehensive school.*

SO THAT'S HOW TO WRITE A BESTSELLER

Can a bestseller be written to a formula? Robin Cook, a Boston eye surgeon, says it can. His book, *Coma*, has been selling at a considerably faster rate than either *Jaws* or *Star Wars* – over 4 million copies in 10 weeks. Before starting he read and analysed 200 successful mystery/thriller novels and entered their characteristics on a card index. 'I came up with about 25 recurrent tricks and I worked them all in,' says Cook.

He noticed that in mysteries the reader is presented with all the information required to solve them at the same rate as the hero, whereas in a thriller the reader knows more than the unsuspecting hero of the dangers that lie ahead. He decided to write a book that had both elements. *Coma* is about mysterious mishaps in the operating theatre at an American hospital and the first part of the novel is pure suspense. In the second half the heroine, a trainee doctor, unravels the mystery of the patients who are left permanently comatose following anaesthesia.

HOW NIXON STOPPED THE THIRD WORLD WAR

In the summer of 1969 the Soviet Union asked the United States to join it for an all-out pre-emptive nuclear strike against China. This devastating state secret is revealed by H.R. Haldeman, the former US President's Chief of Staff. Haldeman, who is serving a sentence for his part in the Watergate scandal, tells how the plan was rejected by President Nixon only for American Intelligence sources to reveal that the Kremlin had decided to go ahead with the plan alone. Haldeman describes how Nixon and his Foreign Affairs Advisor, Dr Henry Kissinger, frantically repaired 20 years of hostility between Washington and Peking to deter the Russians. A new era of Sino-American relations was opened up leading to President Nixon's visit to the Chinese capital and an understanding of a permanent alliance against Kremlin aggression.

STENMARK DOUBLE

Sweden's Ingemar Stenmark won the men's slalom title yesterday (5 February) and his second gold medal of the world ski championships in Garmisch. The 21-year-old, who had already won the Giant Slalom, becomes the fifth man to complete the Slalom Double.

POISON ORANGE AT MARKS

An orange poisoned with mercury was bought from a London branch of Marks & Spencer. The buyer spotted the tell-tale beads of silver on the flesh of the fruit when she cut into it. The orange alert began last week when consignments of Israeli fruit were found to be poisoned. Palestinian Arab terrorists claimed responsibility for injecting the fruit with liquid mercury.

A still from the Health Education Council's 'Exercise' TV commercial.

THE YOUNG CHALLENGERS

Jimmy White, a 15-year-old school-boy from Tooting, has never had a snooker lesson but within a year of becoming interested in the game at the age of 12 he was making his first century break. Last year he scored 118 in 4 minutes and 12 seconds, the kind of performance which has made him Britain's reigning boys' snooker and billiards champion. Tony Meo, 18, has scored 182 centuries, including a maximum 147. He recorded the maximum last year to become the youngest ever player to do so; it was a feat Joe Davis didn't achieve until he was 54.

SCIENTISTS SNIFF OUT TRUFFLE SECRETS

The myth surrounding that most mysterious and expensive of delicacies, the truffle, may have been exploded. Scientists in France, the home of the truffle, announced yesterday that they have artificially cultivated the mushroom nicknamed the 'black diamond'. The truffles were grown on specially treated trees planted only 3½ years ago, cutting the normal growing time by half. They grow underground attached to the roots of certain trees and have to be sniffed out by specially trained dogs. The only control to date has been to plant trees in fields where truffles have been collected before and then wait 7 years to see if new ones appeared. Attempts to 'produce' the truffle, known to date back at least 175 years, have failed until now.

ASTONISHING APOLOGY BY OWEN

Foreign Secretary Dr David Owen has offered an extraordinary apology to the Saudi Arabian royal family over the love affair that ended in a barbaric execution. Following reports that Princess Misha, 23, had been shot and her husband beheaded for defying marriage laws, the Foreign Office expressed its regret that such a tragedy should have occurred. Last night, however, the Saudi Government, angered by Whitehall's interference, said that the couple were unmarried and died for committing 'adulterous acts' in accordance with Islamic law. Within minutes of the apology Labour MPs were expressing their anger that Dr Owen 'should consider such an execution barbaric if the 2 persons were married but civilized if they were not'.

SMITH'S TRUMP CARD

Rhodesian leader Ian Smith has pulled off his greatest political coup since UDI. He reached agreement on an independence constitution with moderate black nationalist leaders. A new Government is to be formed 'within a few days' with blacks and whites in the Cabinet to prepare for the hand-over to black majority rule within 12 months. The clever part is that it gives whites a blocking vote of 28 seats in the proposed new 100-seat Parliament. The agreement, which is guaranteed for 10 years, is vehemently opposed, however, by the Patriotic Front leaders, Mr Joshua Nkomo and Mr Robert Mugabe, who command 40,000 black guerillas fighting the Smith regime.

DAY BY DAY

5 Feb
The John Lewis Partnership, which has 17 department stores and 64 Waitrose supermarkets, says that it is taking legal advice after learning that it had been put on the Government's blacklist for breaking the pay guidelines.

9 Feb
New and smaller £1 notes are issued with a portrait of Sir Isaac Newton on the reverse side.

A record transfer fee of £450,000 plus a levy of £45,000 is paid by Manchester United for Gordon McQueen of Leeds United.

13 Feb
A 12-volume second edition of Blaeu's *Atlas Major*, printed in 1667, is sold at Sotheby's for £38,000, a world record auction price for an atlas.

15 Feb
British Leyland announces plans to close the Triumph TR7 plant at Speke, resulting in about 3,000 redundancies. Workers at the plant had been on strike for 16 weeks in a dispute over new work schedules.

New Zealand beats England by 72 runs at Wellington for the first time in a test match.

Muhammad Ali loses his world heavyweight title when he is beaten on points by Leon Spinks at Las Vegas. Ali becomes the first World Heavyweight Champion to lose the title on points since Max Baer lost to Jim Braddock in 1935.

17 Feb
The monthly rate of inflation drops to 9.9%, the first time it has been below 10% since 1973.

24 Feb
The Secretary of State for Prices and Consumer Protection, Mr Roy Hattersley, says that compulsory powers will be used to force a reduction in the price of tea if the tea blenders do not make one voluntarily. The Prices Commission had earlier reported that tea should be 5p a quarter cheaper, but the tea companies rejected the report.

25 Feb
Princess Alice, Countess of Athlone, Queen Victoria's last surviving grandchild, celebrates her ninety-fifth birthday.

The Stranglers – *one of the most successful of the 'new wave' groups.*

SHOWROOM SIEGE FOR WESTERN CARS

Armed police had to be called in when western-built cars went on sale to the public in East Germany for the first time. Would-be buyers fought to place their orders for 10,000 VW Golf cars bought by the Communist regime recently in exchange for machine tools. The cars had been promised to the public at £8,000 and there were few applicants, even though the waiting list for an East German car is up to 7 years. Then, without explanation, the price was cut to £5,000, although the car sells in the West for £3,000.

MAR 1978

DEATH OF A GIANT

A fleet of ships was standing by along the south coast last night ready to help fight the worst oil-pollution threat ever known. The entire cargo of 230,000 tons of oil from the wrecked tanker *Amoco Cadiz* was threatening to pour into the sea and inundate the holiday beaches of Brittany. By last night there was an oil slick a mile wide and 16 miles long from the huge tanker, which was snapped in 2 on needle-sharp rocks a mile off the French coast near Ushant. British ships were ready to go to the aid of the French, if requested, under an agreement reached between the 2 countries after the *Torrey Canyon* disaster off Cornwall in 1967. The Liberian-registered American-owned tanker on charter to Shell was on her way from the Persian Gulf to Lyme Bay in Dorset.

UDI WRITTEN OFF

Under the glacial stare of a portrait of Cecil Rhodes Ian Smith yesterday (3 March) signed away 90 years of White rule. 'Independence Day' for a Black-ruled Rhodesia will be 31 December – 13 years after Mr Smith's unilateral declaration of independence.

THE TRUTH ABOUT PETROL COSTS

Motorists will soon be able to find out for the first time exactly how much different cars should cost them in petrol. The Government has tested 650 models and produced detailed figures showing which are the most economical. From 1 April, it will be illegal for new cars to be displayed in showrooms unless they carry labels indicating official fuel-consumption figures. The figures must also be included in car handbooks, advertisements and sales brochures. The tests cover simulated town driving, a constant 56 m.p.h. and, in some cases, a constant 75 m.p.h., though the test at the higher speed was voluntary. Some manufacturers, including Morgan and TVR, were excluded because of their small production figures. Taking an average of both town and distance-driving British cars fill 4 of the top 5 places in the small car class. They are: Mini 850 and 1000, Reliant Kitten and Ford Fiesta.

PAY VICTIM REGARDLESS OF BLAME

A new system of compensating accident victims regardless of blame has been proposed in a report from the Royal Commission on Civil Liability and Compensation for Personal Injury. Prime Minister Mr James Callaghan said the Government would look at the proposals but warned that the extra social security costs of £130m would have to be considered. The Commission argues that the overall cost of the measures would be small because of savings in court actions. 'No fault' compensation schemes could apply to vaccine-damaged children and people injured at work, the Commission says. In the Lords, Conservative spokesman Lord Hailsham expressed concern over the implication for the legal profession as a good deal of the profession's income was generated from cases of liability.

FALL OF THE GREAT WALLENDA

One of the world's great daredevils, tightrope walker Karl Wallenda, plunged 120 feet to his death while attempting the latest in a lifetime of stunts. A gust of wind swept the 73-year-old from a wire strung between 2 hotels in San Juan, Puerto Rico.

It's all in the eye of the beholder. This exhibition at Whitechapel Art Gallery featuring the work of Carl Andre prompts a mixed response. An arrangement of 4 blocks, each 12 in. by 12 in. by 36 in. costs £6,600.

DON'T CRY FOR ELAINE

An almost unknown actress has won the most coveted role in show-business. Elaine Paige is to play the title role in the Tim Rice/Andrew Lloyd-Webber musical, *Evita*. The search for an actress to play Eva Peron, wife of the Argentinian dictator, began when Julie Covington, who had a hit record with 'Don't Cry For Me, Argentina', taken from the show, turned down the part. 30-year-old Elaine's big chance comes after years of work in West End musicals such as *Hair* and *Billy* and TV serials such as *Crossroads*.

AN ACT OF WAR

Italy has declared war on left-wing terrorists after the kidnapping of Aldo Moro, the nation's elder statesman and probable next President. The 5 policemen assigned as bodyguard were shot dead by fanatical members of Italy's Red Brigade as Mr Moro was snatched in a Rome street on his way to work. The killers are demanding the release of their leader, Renato Curcio, and 48 of their comrades who are on trial for murder and subversion. A message to the news agencies minutes after the kidnap said, 'We have struck at the heart of the State. . . and this is only the beginning.'

DO YOU KNOW THE NEW CODE?

A new Highway Code has been launched and everyone is expected to learn it. It brings up to date the many rule changes that have taken place since the last code was published 9 years ago. It covers such things as pelican crossings and The Green Cross Code. Also Rules 31–33 state that cars should not have tinted or darkened glass; Rule 49 advises drivers to give way to buses trying to rejoin traffic after stopping; Rule 50 gives advice on how to drive in fog; Rules 77 and 91 explain bus lanes and mini-roundabouts respectively.

BRUNO GETS AN OFFER

The nationwide search by the Foley Boxing Club, Surrey for challengers to meet 15-year-old heavyweight Paul McDonald has unearthed some rare talent. One rival is 16-year-old Frank Bruno who today is leaving a GLC-run school in Sussex. Bruno does not hold an ABA medical card and so the meeting at the Foley gymnasium could only be on a sparring basis. The Secretary at the club Mr Richard Daykin said, 'The boy is very quick and very strong and, for a lad who has had no fights, has got a lot of ring sense.'

FAKED!

The famous photograph of Lee Harvey Oswald holding the gun used to assassinate President Kennedy is a fake, according to a British police forensic expert. Former Detective Superintendent Malcolm Thompson, who has been told he may be asked to give evidence before an American congressional committee, analysed photographs which purport to show Oswald carrying the murder weapon and which are said to have been taken by his wife, Marina, in their back yard in 1963. The photographs were produced by the FBI shortly after the assassination and Oswald claimed at the time that they were faked and that his face had been superimposed on someone else's body. An FBI expert assured the Warren Commission that the photographs were authentic. Mr Thompson now says that they are composites made of 3 photographs cut and pasted up before being re-photographed to produce the final prints. He said, 'In 30 years as a detective I have never seen such a blatant fake.'

CHICKEN PERIL

Housewives who serve roast chicken must beware not to dish up food poisoning at the same time. In a report out today scientists warn that a growing risk of bacterial contamination has accompanied the spread of factory farming. Intensive methods of breeding poultry, cattle and pigs mean that more of the meat that reaches the shops is infected with salmonella, according to the British Association for the Advancement of Science. The precautions suggested include thorough cleaning of surfaces and implements which have been in contact with uncooked meat; separation of cooked from raw meat; prompt cooling and storage of any uneaten meat which should be reheated to boiling point before consumption; thorough thawing of frozen poultry prior to cooking.

THE SHELDON SUCCESS FORMULA

Sidney Sheldon was over 50 when he began writing novels. Now, 4 books later, he has more than made up for lost time. His latest, *Bloodline*, which has the 3 basic Sheldon ingredients – glamour, intrigue and sex – looks certain to repeat in Britain the huge success it has already enjoyed in America.

In his early twenties Sheldon wrote for film, stage and television, and at 25 he had 3 musicals running on Broadway. Of his encounters with the censor he recalls the launching of a new TV series, *I Dream of Jeanie*, a fantasy comedy about a man who finds a girl genie in a bottle. The show was ready to run when an NBC executive commented: 'Jesus, this is about this half-naked girl living in a house with a bachelor. . .' and Sheldon received a 25-page memo.

DAY BY DAY

2 Mar
In the Ilford North by-election the Conservative candidate regains the seat which Labour won in the 1974 election.

Russia launches *Soyuz 28* with 2 cosmonauts, Alexei Gubarev and Czech Vladimir Remek. It is the first time anyone other than a Russian or an American has been in space. They return to earth on 10 March.

6 Mar
A report by Mr Justice Parker recommends that British Nuclear Fuels be allowed to build a nuclear reprocessing plant at Windscale in Cumbria.

8 Mar
Prison sentences are passed at Bristol Crown Court on 17 people who have been found guilty of making and marketing the drug LSD. Operation Julie was the code name for the investigation which resulted in the detection of an industry believed to be responsible for half the world's LSD supply.

14 Mar
The UN Security Council approves a resolution declaring that any internal settlement in Rhodesia is 'illegal and unacceptable'. Britain, the USA, France, Canada and West Germany abstain from voting.

16 Mar
Yuri Romanenko and Georgy Grechko in *Soyuz 27* return to earth after a record 96 days in space.

19 Mar
The coalition government of M. Raymond Barre is returned in the French general election.

22 Mar
Nottingham Forest wins the Football League Cup, beating Liverpool 1–0 in a replay at Old Trafford.

25 Mar
Oxford wins the Boat Race for the third year running. The Cambridge boat sank.

27 Mar
Broadcaster Wilfred Pickles dies, aged 73.

NOW IT CAN PAY DRIVERS TO ADVERTISE

A new way for motorists to cut the cost of driving has been imported from America. Just drive around with a slogan emblazoned on the family saloon and get a free respray, £6 a month and a bonus of up to £60 at the end of the contract. The motorists must cover a considerable mileage each week and keep their cars clean. So far the greatest interest has been from the cigarette firms, who are limited by law in their advertising, although even cars bearing a cigarette advertisement must also carry the government health warning.

Cheryl Champbell and Bob Hoskins in Pennies From Heaven.

APR 1978

The flood of refugees from Vietnam, the 'Boat People', continues to flow into Hong Kong.

TV BAN ON CONTEST WINNERS

The surprise winners of the *Eurovision Song Contest* have been banned from appearing on *Top of the Pops*. Israeli singer Izhar Cohen and his backing group Alphabeta were due to record the English version of their song '*A Ba Ni Bie*' for the show but the plan was vetoed by Equity because Israeli artists are not part of an EEC agreement on foreign performers and the record is not in the Top Thirty.

FINE EUROPE

Brian Lidbetter has joined the row over speeding fines after being ordered to pay £25 by Brighton magistrates. He exceeded the 30-m.p.h. limit by 15 m.p.h. and it was his first offence. This follows the resignation of Bootle JP Mrs Vera Bray, who took the drastic step in protest over the £15 fine imposed on Captain Mark Phillips for driving at 60 m.p.h. – double the limit – in Whitehall, an offence which came on top of a previous conviction. The Magistrates' Association recommends a speeding penalty of £1.50 for each mile per hour over the limit.

LEECHES MAKE A COMEBACK

Leeches, once regarded as a cure-all, are back in the blood-sucking business. They are being used on medical students to remove ugly bruises – after rugby matches, for example – at St Bartholomew's, London. Bart's records show that in 1837 no fewer than 96,300 leeches were used on 50,557 patients.

EASIER BORROWING

Britain's 2 biggest credit card companies, Access and Barclaycard, have scrapped the £30 limit on cash advances. Cardholders will now be able to borrow to the limit of their credit. Borrowers will pay no interest if their loans are repaid quickly – except for the handling charge of 2.5%. The changes have been made possible by Mr Healey's budget, which scrapped the £30 maximum cash advance.

WORLD'S FIRST LAB BABIES

A British doctor yesterday reported to have successfully implanted several women with the world's first 'test-tube' babies. Mr Patrick Steptoe, Senior Consultant Gynaecologist at Oldham General Hospital, was quoted last night as saying, 'We've not achieved babies yet but we have had pregnancies. . . I think you will very soon see this method passing into clinical application from the experimental stage.'

John Travolta in the film Saturday Night Fever.

CHURCH GIVES WAY ON DIVORCE

The Church of England is virtually certain to allow divorcees to remarry in church. At present the Church allows only a service of blessing after a Register Office wedding. This fundamental change in the Church's attitude to Britain's growing divorce problem would cause major controversy. It would also have significant constitutional implications, removing a major obstacle to a member of the Royal Family, such as Princess Margaret, marrying for a second time if she wishes.

BRITAIN LET US DOWN, SAY MANXMEN

The tiny Isle of Man was preparing to take on Britain and the rest of Europe yesterday after an international court said its birching law was 'degrading'. In Strasbourg the human rights court said the punishment – which can be inflicted on children between 10 and 14 and youths under 20 – should be stopped, and entrusted Britain with the task of enforcing the ruling. Many of the Island's 60,000 people were angry at the decision and blamed the British Government for failing to put their case properly.

BLACK WORLD CUP

Only 50 days from the opening of the eleventh World Cup disaster has overtaken the towering River Plate Stadium, where 9 matches, including the final, are due to be played. Instead of a lush green the playing surface became tar black after an unnamed groundsman put sea water on the grass. The salt contaminated the young grass roots and a scorching Argentinian sun cremated what was left. The hasty re-turfing process has left the pitch looking like a mosaic of curled-edge week-old sandwiches laid side by side, though the authorities believe it will be in excellent condition when the tournament starts.

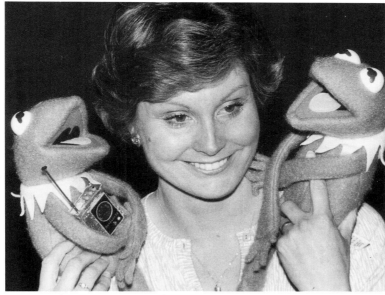

'I can see why Miss Piggy is so fond of him,' says Angela Rippon of Kermit as both receive Radio Industries Club awards.

BETTY FORD: I'M AN ALCOHOLIC

Mrs Betty Ford, wife of the former US President, yesterday admitted that she was addicted to alcohol and drugs. The ex-First Lady, who has been in Long Beach Naval Hospital for 12 days, said, 'I am grateful for this programme of recovery. I have found I am not only addicted to the medication I have been taking for arthritis but also to alcohol.'

IS ST JOHN A CHAUVINIST?

A woman is fighting a Cambridge men's college because it doesn't allow female dons. All men-only colleges may be forced to accept women dons if Dr Christine Hugh-Jones wins her industrial tribunal test case. Mrs Hugh-Jones' case rests on the claim that a college statute banning women is invalid and that fellowships constitute employment as laid down by the Sex Discrimination Act. The relevant statute, like that of all single-sex Oxbridge colleges, is laid down in the Oxford and Cambridge Act, 1923.

JONJO MAKES HISTORY

With 5 wins in 5 races at Perth yesterday Jonjo O'Neill leaped into National Hunt History, passing Ron Barry's record of 125 winners in a season over fences and hurdles. Yesterday's feat, which was last performed 10 years ago and represented a 764–1 accumulator, gave him the record with 6 weeks of the jumping season still to go. The 26-year-old jockey's phenomenal record now shows 129 wins from 445 mounts, on two-thirds of which he has been placed. A level pound stake on all his rides shows a profit of almost £100.

RECORD BRICKIE

Super brickie Andy Lundie, who earns £600 a week, set a new world record yesterday. In exactly 1 hour he built a wall 4 feet high and 45 feet long containing 1,414 bricks, shattering the existing record by more than 400 bricks. The wall borders a 5-bedroomed house which Mr Lundie built for a client in 9 working days.

A new series of the favourite cop show – Telly Savalas stars as Theo Kojak, with Dan Frazer as Frank McNeil.

PINHEAD MASTER BRAIN

A master brain the size of a pinhead is being introduced in kitchens, cars and industry to make life easier. It's a piece of electronics called a microprocessor, which can take the drudgery out of 1,001 daily chores, it is claimed. All you have to do is programme it, say the makers, Bosch of West Germany. The miniature 'brain', which contains thousands of switches capable of controlling mechanical functions in any piece of machinery, is now being offered to industry and motor firms throughout Europe at a cost of 'fractions of a pound for each mechanical unit'. Bosch say the microprocessor will 'add to the value of daily life' for the average family.

MAY 1978

IT LOOKS LIKE LA

A last-minute hitch between the International Olympic Committee and lawyers representing Los Angeles over who should bear the financial burden seems to have been resolved and saved the city's chances of staging the 1984 Olympic Games. But one piece of bad news for Los Angeles – the centre for synchronized swimming in the United States – was the decision that this event should not be added to the Olympic schedule.

RONO THE GREAT

Henry Rono, latest in a long list of brilliant Kenyan athletes, has claimed a place in sporting history by becoming the first man to hold world records for the 5,000 metres and the 3,000 metres steeplechase. Rono ran the steeplechase event in Seattle in 8 minutes 5.4 seconds, chipping 2.6 seconds off the old world mark. This follows the 4.5 seconds he sliced off the world 5,000 metres record held by New Zealander Dick Quax.

The bullet-riddled body of Italian Premier Aldo Moro is discovered in the back of a car in a Rome Street 54 days after being kidnapped by Red Brigade terrorists.

MAGGIE'S VICTORY

Another penny was cut off income tax last night as all the Opposition MPs combined to produce a knockout blow to the Budget. The Government crashed to an 8-vote defeat, a result which will reduce the standard rate of income tax from 34p to 33p. Amid the uproar Shadow Chancellor Sir Geoffrey Howe, calling for a general election, said, 'This is the first Government ever to be defeated on the crucial question of the basic rate of income tax. . .'

THE MOST UNLIKELY HEART-THROB OF 1978

In his crumpled jacket and rumpled waistcoat Rumpole of the Bailey views his new-found success as a TV cult figure after just 6 episodes with sardonic amusement. After playing Rumpole in a *Play of the Month*, actor Leo McKern, 58, suggested to its author John Mortimer the idea of a series. This meant breaking the habit of a lifetime for McKern – he refused the part of Maigret in a television series. A second series of Rumpole is planned, though McKern, star of *Ryan's Daughter*, *The Omen* and *A Man For All Seasons* among many films, says, 'Rumpole will be forgotten within 6 months.'

'Labour Isn't Working.' The Conservatives launch a huge poster campaign attacking the Government's record on employment.

THE REAL *CRÈME DE LA CRÈME*

'If only you small girls would listen to me I would make you the *crème de la crème*,' declared Miss Christina Kay 31 years before authoress Muriel Spark gave birth to Miss Jean Brodie. The character is strongly based on one of Muriel Spark's own teachers at the James Gillespie High School for Girls in Edinburgh. In the original class of 1930 Muriel Camberg sat with the other 10-year-old girls enthralled by the teacher who instructed them in the importance of goodness, truth and beauty. Christina Kay herself died during the Second World War.

STRANGE SPELL OF THE MOON PEOPLE

A mysterious card bearing the slogan 'Love People Freely' led 23-year-old Judy Salter to a ranch near San Francisco called Happylands. There, surrounded by the fanatical followers of Korean millionaire Sun Myung Moon, hailed by converts as Christ returned, Judy's adventure took on sinister overtones. She fell under the sway of the Moon people and her mother, Mrs Lyn Salter, is flying to California to try to rescue her. She believes her daughter is being brainwashed by the cult, which also goes under the name of the Unification Church.

STING CURE

Ivor Rice from St Austell, Cornwall had resigned himself to the fact that he was going blind. Then he heard about 70-year-old Mrs Julie Owen of Bromley, Kent, who has developed a treatment for blindness involving bee stings. Mr Rice started with 2 stings a day on his neck and head; now he is up to 10. He is so impressed with the improvement in his sight that he has asked his Liberal MP, Mr David Penhaligon, to inform Parliament about the treatment.

PILL ENDS NEED FOR OPERATIONS

A pill which will dissolve gallstones has been developed, it was announced yesterday. About 5.5 million people in Britain are affected by gallstones with about 1 million showing symptoms of illness. With a daily dose of the new drug Cherdol a higher proportion of stones shrink and eventually disappear, avoiding the need for a gall-bladder operation. The drug will not remove the need for surgery completely, however. Some gallstones are resistant to it while others are so large it could take up to 2 years for the drug to prove effective. Nevertheless, it is being hailed as a big medical breakthrough.

MAKE A DATE

Those with a penchant for figures will be eagerly awaiting the moment next Monday afternoon when the clock reaches 26 minutes to 1. For 60 seconds the date and time will be: 12.34 on the 5th day of the 6th month of 1978 or 12.34, 5. 6. 78. If they miss it they will have to wait until 12.34 and 5 seconds on 6 July, 1989 for another such phenomenon to occur. For 'upside-down' date freaks the big day will be 16 August 1991, when the date, erect or inverted, will read 16.8.91.

Isla St Clair and Larry Grayson in Britain's best-loved game show, The Generation Game.

BACK TO LIFE – THE DEEP FREEZE MICE

British scientists have brought back to life animals put in frozen suspended animation. Mice frozen more than 5 years ago were running round in a cage yesterday at the Royal Society in London. They were frozen in liquid nitrogen as 3-day-old embryos and stored at –196°C. Earlier this year they were thawed out and implanted into a female mouse and just over a month ago the litter was born. The long-term survival of embryos in cold storage showed that setting up frozen-embryo banks was now a reality, according to Dr David Whittingham of University College, London. The technique could have implications for humans. A couple could conceive any number of embryos during the wife's fertile years, put them into cold storage and then have them born by proxy later on in life.

FATHER'S RIGHTS DENIED

Joan Paton had an abortion last night, 5 hours after reluctantly making legal history when her husband's attempt to stop her was turned down by a High Court judge. Sir George Baker ruled that Mrs Paton's estranged husband had 'no rights whatever' under the Abortion Act. Outside the Liverpool court anti-abortionists demonstrated with placards reading: 'Equal Rights for Expectant Fathers', while pro-abortionists chanted that it was 'a woman's right to choose'.

THE END FOR GALTON AND SIMPSON

Galton and Simpson, the most successful comedy writing team in British TV, have split up. The 26-year partnership, which produced classics such as *Hancock's Half Hour* and *Steptoe and Son*, began by selling their jokes to the BBC at 10/- a time, which eventually brought them more than £2,000 a show. Ray Galton is planning a new partnership with Alf Garnett's creator, Johnny Speight.

RATES REPRIEVE

Home-owners dreading a rates revaluation have been reprieved until 1982. The last revaluation, in 1973, resulted in crippling rates increases, and, with councils desperate for extra cash, another one would almost certainly lead to bigger bills. The revaluation has been postponed because of a clash with the work of the Layfield Enquiry into local government finance.

Fleetwood Mac (l to r) John McVie, Christine McVie, Mick Fleetwood, Lindsay Buckingham and Stevie Nicks.

DAY BY DAY

1 May
The first May Day bank holiday in England and Wales.

6 May
Ipswich Town wins the FA Cup Final at Wembley 1–0 against Arsenal. In the Scottish Cup Final, Rangers beats Aberdeen 2–1.

7 May
Mr Moshe Dayan, Israeli Foreign Minister, addresses an audience of 15,000 people at a festival in Earls Court to celebrate the thirtieth birthday of the State of Israel.

9 May
The body of Aldo Moro, who was kidnapped by Red Brigade terrorists in March, is found in a stolen car in the centre of Rome.

The Government announces *ex gratia* payments of £10,000 to children damaged by whooping cough vaccine.

10 May
Another Conservative amendment to the Finance Bill to raise the threshold for higher rate income tax from £7,000 to £8,000 is carried by 2 votes.

Liverpool becomes the first British team to win the European Cup in 2 successive years when it beats Bruges 1–0.

13 May
Leeds beats St Helens 14–12 in the Rugby League Cup Final at Wembley.

15 May
Sir Robert Menzies, former Prime Minister of Australia, dies, aged 83.

17 May
Lord Selwyn-Lloyd, former Foreign Secretary and Speaker of the House of Commons, dies, aged 73.

18 May
Dr Yuri Orlov, a Russian nuclear physicist and campaigner for human rights, is sentenced to 7 years in a labour camp and 5 years' exile within the Soviet Union for agitating against the State.

25 May
Mr David Steel says that the Liberal party's pact with the Government will cease at the end of the present session of Parliament.

31 May
The Queen gives permission for Prince Michael of Kent to marry Baroness Marie-Christine von Reibnitz, a Roman Catholic whose first marriage was annulled.

George Robertson, 32, wins the Hamilton by-election for Labour.

BAN FOR *PRETTY BABY?*

A film about child prostitution now showing to packed American audiences may end up heavily cut by the British censor, and with the Protection of Children Bill due to become law by summer it could be banned altogether. The film is called *Pretty Baby* and stars 12-year-old Brooke Shields as a prostitute. She is never seen in physical contact with any of the men, though she does appear nude. On that point Brooke says emphatically, 'I won't do it again, though. I'm starting to get more conscious of myself.'

JUNE 1978

Two leading chat show hosts – Russell Harty appears on Michael Parkinson's show a few weeks after Parkinson's appearance on his show.

ANYONE FOR CRICKET?

The man who invented cricket's crash helmet – he prefers the term protective helmet – hopes that soon no self-respecting cricketer will go to the crease without one. Peter Benniman, the 50-year-old Smethwick businessman whose brainchild it is, expects current output of 75 a week to rise considerably. The idea sprang from Mr Benniman's association with batsman Dennis Amiss in 1976. They were in business together in a lawnmower repair service when Amiss was hit on the head by West Indian fast bowler Mike Holding. With most county sides already placing orders, Mr Benniman is confident the idea will catch on, and he points to a sporting analogy from the past: 'My uncle, Bernard Clarke, was the first person to introduce the golf trolley in this country after the war. People said it would never catch on.'

WHO WEARS THE TROUSERS?

9 women teachers who insist on wearing trousers could bring a comprehensive school to a halt today. The teachers – at Maiden Erlegh School, Reading – are threatening to arrive for duty wearing trousers, despite being banned from teaching for that very reason last week. Headmaster James Dunkley insists that teachers should set pupils a high standard where dress is concerned and that, he says, means women members of staff not wearing trousers in public.

IS THIS AN AIRCRAFT?

The problem of hang-gliders is being closely studied by Whitehall. Control of this fast-growing sport has been given a new urgency by the advent of powered hang-gliders. Last month David Cook from Suffolk made the first Channel crossing by a powered hang-glider but May also saw the first death involving such a machine. The Civil Aviation Authority, which is responsible for issuing certificates of air worthiness and registering all aircraft, is monitoring the situation closely.

LANDMARK COMMUNIST VISIT

President Nicolae Ceauşescu of Romania makes history today when he becomes the first Communist leader ever to make a state visit to Britain. In Romania the smiling face of Ceauşescu is everywhere: his speeches dominate the press, his red-covered books dominate the bookshops and the ubiquitous police have effectively silenced the dissident movement. He believes in strong leadership and even the smallest decisions sometimes need his approval – Romanians had to wait a day until they could read of the death of Chinese premier Chou En-lai.

While he is not an innately cruel man cruel results can follow from the system he heads. This was apparent in the aftermath of the earthquake which killed thousands in Bucharest last year. Ceauşescu ordered the rubble to be cleared as soon as possible and people watched in horror as the bulldozers scooped up debris where their relatives could still have been alive. The leader whose central aim is to propel Romania into the industrial age is a baffling and controversial character, flirting with the West while holding tight the Eastern system.

IT CANN'T BE RIGHT, CANN IT?

The familiar scene of a Scrabble dispute happened at the highest level yesterday. At the National Championships in London the word 'cannasta' was laid by Philip Nelkon's opponent. Philip challenged the word but was overruled, though he went on to take the title by a record 1,521 points in 3 games. The competition, whose originator is broadcaster Gyles Brandreth, suffered an even greater embarrassment 2 years ago when, just before the presentation of the trophy, it was noticed that it bore the inscription: 'Scribble Championship'.

THERESA TACKLES BOYS

Theresa Bennett, who was banned from playing for a boys' under-12 soccer team, beat the Football Association in court yesterday. A judge ruled that in the pre-puberty state the difference in the physical capabilities of boys and girls was marginal. Awarding Theresa £250 damages, the judge stated that Section 44 of the Sex Discrimination Act – which states that discrimination is not unlawful where the physical strength and stamina of the average woman would put her at a disadvantage to the average man – had been contravened.

Cyril Smith studies the form at the Miss Morecambe contest.

SCOTLAND GO OUT FIGHTING

Scotland found the team and the heart that could have terrorized the rest of the World Cup finalists too late last night. The mighty Dutch were swept aside 3–2 but a 3-goal win over the 1974 runners up was needed to take Scotland into the second-round groups in Argentina.

FATIMA KEEPS IT IN THE FAMILY

17-year-old Fatima Whitbread, who spent most of her childhood in orphanages until she was adopted 4 years ago by former British javelin champion, Margaret Whitbread, has been named for the same event at the Commonwealth Games in Edmonton.

SOCCER STAR BANNED

Soccer star Willie Johnston was sacked from Scotland's World Cup team last night, banned from playing for Scotland for life and ordered to be put on the first available plane home from Argentina. That was the penalty announced by the Scottish Football Association after Johnston, the man Scottish manager Ally Mac-Leod boasted could win him the World Cup, admitted taking two stimulant tablets before Saturday's game with Peru, which Scotland lost 3–1.

KID CAUTHEN LANDS TRIPLE CROWN

18-year-old Steve Cauthen made turf history when he became the youngest jockey ever to win the American Triple Crown. He won the Belmont Stakes on Affirmed to add to his Kentucky Derby and Preakness successes.

RECORD-BREAKER NAOMI

Lone yachtswoman Naomi James, 29, will today clip 2 days off Sir Francis Chichester's 274-day record when she enters Dartmouth harbour at the end of her round-the-world voyage.

WIGAN'S DREAM COMES TRUE

A football dream became reality yesterday when League soccer was restored to Wigan after forty-seven years. Veteran director Jack Farrimond was at the League's annual meeting in London, just as he had been thirty-four times before, for the crucial ballot and the place Wigan Athletic had been seeking since 1936. The club lost its League status through the demise of Wigan Borough in 1931. After a tie with Southport in the first ballot, Athletic were given the go-ahead for Fourth Division soccer from August. Southport went out for the first time since 1921.

THREE DIE IN TT

Three top motorcycle stars were killed in yesterday's TT races. The deaths of former British sidecar champion, Mac Hobson, his passenger, Ken Birch, and Swiss star, Ernst Trachsel, bring the total of fatalities at the infamous Isle of Man circuit to 120 since the TT races started in 1911. The 38-mile circuit was dropped from the World Championship calendar after the International Motorcycling Federation ruled it too dangerous in 1975.

GUY IS DEAD

Guy the Gorilla, London Zoo's biggest attraction, died unexpectedly yesterday at the age of 32. The strain of his 27-stone hulk at last proved too much for his heart. After having 8 teeth extracted he failed to come round from the anaesthetic. Future generations will, however, be able to see Guy, who entertained 60 million visitors in his lifetime, stuffed and preserved in the National History Museum.

DAY BY DAY

1 June
In the first test match against Pakistan at Edgbaston Chris Old takes a record 4 wickets in 5 balls.

3 June
Mr Freddie Laker receives a knighthood in the Birthday Honours. Miss Sue Ryder, founder of homes for the sick and disabled, is among 5 new life peers.

8 June
The Treasury announces a National Insurance surcharge of 2.5% to be paid by employers.

9 June
The Prince of Wales travels on the inaugural flight of the new helicopter service between Gatwick and Heathrow.

12 June
David Berkowitz is convicted of the 'Son of Sam' killings and is sentenced to over 275 years in prison.

13 June
The Israeli Army withdraws from occupied territory in southern Lebanon, handing over to right-wing Christian forces.

16 June
The Pope refuses permission for Prince Michael of Kent and his fiancée Baroness Marie-Christine von Reibnitz to marry in a Roman Catholic church. It is assumed that this is because Prince Michael had said that any children of the marriage would be brought up as Anglicans.

19 June
In the test match at Lord's England beats Pakistan by an innings and 120 runs. Ian Botham becomes the first man to score a century and take 8 wickets in 1 innings in a test.

25 June
Argentina wins the World Cup, defeating Holland 3–1 after extra time.

29 June
Princess Caroline of Monaco marries Philippe Junot in Monte Carlo.

30 June
Prince Michael of Kent and Baroness Marie-Christine von Reibnitz are married at a civil ceremony in Vienna.

Bob Crane, star of TV's *Hogan's Heroes*, is found murdered in his New York apartment.

Buenos Aires: Mario Kempes (on ground) scores the first of Argentina's goals in their 3–1 victory over Holland in the World Cup Final.

HIRED TO HAVE A BABY

A judge decided a child's future yesterday in a unique case arising from the bizarre possibilities of artificial insemination. On one side of the dispute was a couple so desperate to have a baby that they hired a vice girl to be impregnated with the husband's sperm; on the other was the girl who agreed to conceive the baby for them for £3,000. But when the time came to hand the boy over and receive the fee she refused to part with him. Under yesterday's High Court ruling, delivered by Mr Justice Comyn, the girl is to be allowed to keep the baby. The judge laid most of the blame squarely at the door of the couple, saying that they had behaved 'in a most selfish and irresponsible manner'.

JULY 1978

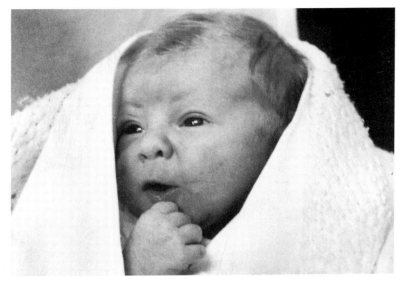

Louise Brown, the world's first test-tube baby.

WHY 225,000 WOMEN SHOULD SWITCH

A quarter of a million women in Britain today are protected against menopause problems because they are on Hormone Replacement Therapy. According to the latest statistics, however, only just over 10% of these women are using what is now regarded as the best and safest method. In the fertile years the ovaries produce first oestrogen, which builds up the lining of the womb, followed by progesterone in the second half of the cycle, which acts as a shedding trigger – menstruation – if conception has not taken place. For women experiencing the menopause many doctors have been content simply to prescribe oestrogen in a cycle of 3 weeks out of 4, believing that the week without taking the hormone would be sufficient to induce a complete shedding of the womb lining. Evidence now suggests an increased risk of uterine cancer in women on long-term oestrogen and recommends a 'combined method in which progesterone is also prescribed', effectively acting as a double trigger to induce the shedding process.

WOMEN'S LIBBERS TURN ON SUFFRAGETTES

Angry Women's Libbers yesterday disrupted a ceremony marking the golden anniversary of equal voting rights for women, which was being held near the Pankhurst statue in the gardens adjoining the House of Commons. Wearing suffragette colours of purple, green and white, the demonstrators descended on the ceremony to voice their dissent from a celebration of enfranchisement. 1 of the demonstrators declared that focusing on the voting issue diverted attention from the further changes still needed to improve the position of women in society. Suffragette Mrs Connie Lewcock, 84, said she fully understood the sentiments behind such banners as: 'The Vote Is A Con – Male Power Goes On.'

McVICAR BSc

John McVicar, the former armed robber who turned his back on crime to pursue an academic career from his prison cell, leaves jail for the university campus next week. The ex-thief once dubbed 'the most dangerous man in Britain' dug through brickwork from the shower of Durham Jail's top-security wing in 1968 and was at large for more than 2 years before being recaptured. He holds a BSc in sociology and the Parole Board has decided to free him so that he can study for a masters degree in the same subject. McVicar's provisional research thesis? A study of prison life and life in the Royal Navy: a comparison of isolated communities.

Wimbledon Ladies Singles champion, Martina Navratilova.

ELGAR NUMBER IS UP

'Land of Hope and Glory' will come to an end in 1984 and it will have nothing to do with George Orwell. Music publishers and instrument-makers Boosey & Hawkes own the rights to Elgar's most famous composition, which must be amongst their biggest earners. Many of Boosey's Elgar copyrights will expire in 1984.

BEAN FEAST

Hardly just like mother used to make, but Textured Vegetable Protein, made from soya beans, looks as though it is here to stay with annual consumption running at 20,000 tons. The Vegetable Protein Association laid on a buffet lunch in London yesterday to demonstrate how tasty the versatile bean can be. An Association spokesman said that at present TVP was mainly used as a meat extender, especially in schools, hospitals and prisons, but if food regulations were changed it could be used as a part substitute in processed meats like sausages.

CURTAIN FALLS AT BATLEY

The marriage between a Yorkshire mill town and the razzmatazz of showbusiness superstars has broken up. At the end of the month the curtain will fall on star cabaret at Batley, a move which proprietor Jimmy Corrigan blames on stars' demands for exorbitant fees, audiences becoming bored with the same performers and a shortage of new talent.

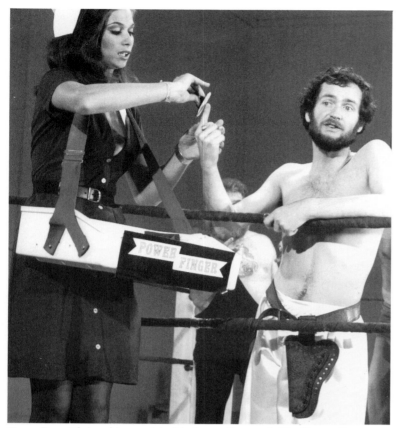

Kenny Everett brings his zany talent to the small screen in The Kenny Everett Video Show.

GEORGE DAVIS IS GUILTY

George Davis was back behind bars last night. Following a campaign to free him from a 17-year sentence 2 years ago, Davis was jailed for 15 years after admitting taking part in a raid on the Bank of Cyprus in London last September.

THE SHAPE OF THINGS TO COME

£1 coins for everyday use were struck yesterday for the first time since August 1914. For the moment they are for circulation only on the Isle of Man but currency experts believe similar coins will be replacing pound notes in the rest of Britain within 2 years. The coins are the exact size of gold sovereigns – slightly smaller than a 5p piece – which were withdrawn from circulation at the outbreak of the First World War. With today's pound having a purchasing power of just over a shilling, compared to the values of 64 years ago, the new coin may glister but it is only gold in colour. It is in fact nickel core covered with a complicated alloy which gives a precise magnetic reading to allow slot machines and others to check them against counterfeits. Although the Manx Government issues its own notes and coins, backed by sterling, their minters consulted the Treasury before settling on a design, a fair indication that it heralds the shape of things to come.

DAY BY DAY

6 July
Cardinal Basil Hume, Archbishop of Westminster, celebrates mass in the Crypt Chapel of the Palace of Westminster to commemorate the fifth centenary of the birth of Sir Thomas More. It is the first Roman Catholic mass celebrated in the palace since the Reformation.

7 July
The Duke and Duchess of Gloucester represent the Queen at the Solomon Islands' independence celebrations.

Martina Navratilova, a Czechoslovak exile, wins the Wimbledon Women's Singles Championship, beating Chris Evert in the final.

8 July
Bjorn Borg beats Jimmy Connors to become Wimbledon champion for the third successive year.

13 July
Russian dissident Alexander Ginsburg is found guilty of anti-Soviet agitation and propaganda and sentenced to 8 years in a labour camp. The next day another human rights activist, Anatoli Shcharansky, is sent to a labour camp for 13 years.

21 July
The Chancellor of the Exchequer, Mr Denis Healey, announces a pay rise guideline of 5% for the next 12 months.

24 July
The Government is defeated by 10 votes when the House of Commons rejects the Dock Labour Scheme.

26 July
The General Council of the TUC rejects the Government's proposal for pay increases to be limited to 5%.

30 July
A 13-year-old boy, Carl Benniston from Blackpool, becomes the youngest person to swim the English Channel. The previous day a 23-year-old American, Penny Dean, swam from Dover to Cap Gris Nez in a record time of 7 hours 42 minutes.

SNOOKER KING DIES

Joe Davis, undefeated snooker champion for 20 years and the man who lifted the game to its present popularity, died yesterday (10 July) aged 77. He was 4 times World Billiards Champion when he, Walter Lindrum, Clark McConachy and Tom Newman perfected the close cannon technique which robbed the game of its entertainment value. Davis saw and developed the potential of snooker and inaugurated the World Championships in 1926, winning the first of his titles the following year. It was mainly through him that the event, which carried a first prize of £6.10s in 1927, has blossomed to such as extent that this year's winner will pick up £7,500. Davis also made snooker history in 1955 when he achieved the first maximum 147 break under Championship conditions.

DRIVER'S PET HATE DIES

Lord Marples of Wallasey, the former Tory Transport Minister who became known as the man motorists love to hate, died in a Monte Carlo hospital yesterday (6 July), aged 70. He introduced yellow lines, parking meters, and gave the police powers to tow vehicles away. 'Marples' Law' became a national joke: 'If it moves, stop it, if it stops, fine it.'

MINTER KO VICTIM DIES

Italian boxer Angelo Jacopucci has died 2 days after being knocked out by Britain's Alan Minter in their European Middleweight title match. Jacopucci collapsed at Minter's celebration party 4 hours after the fight and, in spite of 2 brain operations, died without regaining consciousness.

YOUNG FLIER

Steve Cram, a 17-year-old Geordie schoolboy, ran the fastest mile for his age group yesterday to finish fourth in the Emsley Carr Mile at Crystal Palace. His time of 3 minutes 57.4 seconds was 1.6 seconds faster than that American Jim Ryun set 14 years ago when he was the same age.

MY BIG CHALLENGE

Osvaldo Ardiles, Argentina's World Cup mid-field man, has been speaking of his new career with Tottenham Hotspur. Ardiles, 25, signed along with Ricardo Villa by Spurs Manager Keith Burkinshaw in a sensational £700,000 double deal, regards the move as a great challenge. He is attending university and training to be a lawyer but, asked about his long-term plans after his 3-year contract expires, he said, 'If I like England, I might even want to stay.'

HOW THE SMURFS INVADED BRITAIN

In just a few weeks a variety of little gnome-like creatures has won its way into millions of British children's hearts. The Smurfs, selling for 36p at National Benzole garages and whose song is at number 2 in the hit parade, may be new here but they are actually quite ancient. Their prototype started life 20 years ago as a cartoon character called Schtroumpff, invented by Belgian artist Payo. The name changed in many European countries, eventually becoming Smurf in Holland, though the word means 'whatshisname' or 'thingummybob'. 7 years ago BP in Holland decided to use Smurfs as a promotion and they were so successful that National Benzole, part of the BP group, decided to introduce them here.

Bjorn Borg crushes Jimmy Connors 6–2 6–2 6–3 in one of the greatest Wimbledon finals.

AUG 1978

Grease is the word. A scene from the phenomenally successful film which spawned a string of hit songs.

KING OF THE BALLROOM IS DEAD

Victor Silvester, the ballroom maestro who set the world dancing to his slow, slow, quick, quick, slow tempo died yesterday (14 August) at the age of 78. For more than 50 years Silvester dominated the world of ballroom dancing. His records sold 50 million copies, bettered only by the Beatles, Bing Crosby and Elvis Presley. His book, *Modern Ballroom Dancing*, which he wrote 50 years ago 'because I was nearly dead broke', is now in its fifty-ninth edition.

DEATH OF THE POPE

The Pope died last night (6 August) after suffering 2 heart attacks at his summer palace outside Rome. Pope Paul VI, who was 80, was elected 15 years ago. After the first attack the Pope, who had been in poor health for some time, was given the sacrament of unction for the sick, which until 1965 was known as extreme unction. Pope Paul's Cardinal Secretary of State, Jean Villot, will take over as head of the Roman Catholic Church until a conclave is held to elect a successor.

POLICE POWERLESS IN NEW CRAZE

A new drug craze is catching on with youngsters, and the police cannot stop it. The pep pills are Diethylpropion, a drug not covered by the 1971 Misuse of Drugs Act. If police can find the sources of the pills, known as 'crazies' or 'blues', they can take action, as unauthorized drug production is illegal, though possession is not.

NEWS AMERICAN-STYLE COMES TO BRITAIN

Britain has taken another step towards becoming the fifty-second State of America with the arrival of the singing telegram girl. For £15 Eileen Battye, an employee of a company called Music Box, will sing anything anywhere anytime.

EL HIGGINS DIES

Henry Higgins, the first Englishman to become a fully fledged bullfighter, was killed in a hang-gliding accident yesterday (15 August).

MAKE MUSIC, MAKE MONEY

Every time you sing 'Happy Birthday To You' in a public place you are contributing to the gracious living of the nephews and nieces of 2 spinster schoolteachers in America. Although many people think the song has been around for centuries, it was actually written by Mildred and Patti Hill as recently as 1939. As Patti didn't die until 1946 the copyright doesn't expire until 1996 and tens of thousands of dollars are still pouring in to the sisters' relatives. 'Down At The Old Bull And Bush' and 'Any Old Iron' are other seemingly traditional songs that are still in copyright.

SCIENTISTS TO X-RAY SHROUD

The Holy Shroud, a strip of linen venerated as the burial cloth of Jesus, is to undergo X-ray tests. The Royal Family of Savoy, owners of the shroud, and the diocese of Turin have given the permission sought by scientists for years. The results of the tests may yield what the Roman Catholic Church has withheld from Christendom's most sacred and controversial relic – official recognition.

Jeremy Thorpe, charged with conspiring to murder Norman Scott.

'MASTERPIECE' NATIONAL

The National Theatre has scooped one of the country's top design awards made each year by the Royal Institute of British Architects. It will become 'a masterpiece of the seventies' along with 2 of the other award winners – the Herman Miller factory in Bath and the Sainsbury Centre for Visual Arts in Norwich.

WHEN WILL THEY COME CLEAN?

When a machine at a coin-operated cleaner's fouled up a woman's sweaters she naturally contacted the proprietor. He pointed to a notice which disclaimed responsibility for any loss or damage to customers' property however caused. These common enough notices in shops, dry-cleaners, restaurants and garages have, in fact, been illegal for the past 6 months. Under the Unfair Contract Terms Act 'You can't, by displaying a notice on a wall, get away with murder,' as David Tench, solicitor for *Which?*, puts it. Grievances not amicably settled between the parties should be pursued under the small claims section of the County Court, he advises.

CREDIT CALLS

The Post Office is considering a scheme for telephone calls on credit cards which would range in value from 50p to £50 with the value stored electronically on the card.

HEARTBROKEN

French screen lover Charles Boyer died yesterday (27 August) from a broken heart. 2 days before, his wife of 44 years, British-born former actress Patricia Patterson, had died. Boyer, who would have been 79 today, appeared in 50 romantic roles and was always remembered for the phrase 'Come wiz me to the casbah,' though he claimed that he never actually spoke the words – it was merely a publicity line coined for the 1938 film, *Algiers*.

DRIVE-INS OUT

In 1933 an office worker called Richard M. Hollingshead Junior did a most eccentric thing. He balanced a home-movie projector on his car's roof to screen holiday films against his garage door. From that sprang the great drive-in phenomenon. The world's first commercial drive-in cinema at Camden, New Jersey opened in June that year striking gold for Hollingshead and countless other competitors. Today, however, the seam threatens to peter out as outlets dwindle. With high land prices car parks can prove more profitable than evening-only entertainment, as one operator who has sold 3 sites this year pointed out. The sexual revolution has also played a part in the decline. The drive-in was once the favourite of courting couples; now it is regarded as 'uncool' or the mark of a lover too mean to rent a motel room.

KENYATTA DEAD

The future of Kenya was thrown into the balance yesterday with the death of Jomo Kenyatta (22 August). The man jailed by Britain as a Mau Mau terrorist leader had made Kenya one of the most stable countries in Africa for both Whites and Blacks. The nation of 16 million was stunned when the state radio announced that Kenyatta, president for 14 years, had died peacefully at the age of 89.

Peter Gabriel has released his second solo album.

UNKNOWN IN FAIRY TALE

It seemed like a fairy story when unknown actress Emma Samms was plucked from obscurity to star in a top film. John Dark, the man behind fantasy epics such as *Creatures The World Forgot* and *Warlords Of Atlantis*, chose Emma, who will be 18 this month, to play a princess in his latest film, *Arabian Adventure*.

BIRMINGHAM TO BRISTOL BY THE LEFT

John Perkins is the AA's specialist in bizarre enquiries. When a woman who had developed obsessive fears of turning right after being involved in an accident contacted the AA it was to John they referred. He worked out a route from Birmingham to Bristol that avoided the dreaded manoeuvre, and she didn't mind the fact that it added 100 miles to her journey. Other strange requests include: an agoraphobia sufferer who needed a holiday route flanked entirely by tall buildings or high hedges; an American funeral director checking out the British scene, who asked for a route covering every cemetery and crematorium between Land's End and John O'Groats (the route supplied weighed 7lb); a woman who asked him to identify a village she had seen in a dream. She described it so vividly that John traced it to a place in Warwickshire. John thinks he found the right one – the lady herself seemed satisfied with it.

HAPPY LANDINGS

The record-breaking Atlantic balloonists, Americans Max Anderson, Ben Abruzzo and Laurence Newman, made a triumphant landing in France last night (17 August). Their balloon, Double Eagle 2, touched down 60 miles north of Paris and 50 miles short of their target, Le Bourget, where Charles Lindbergh landed 51 years ago after his famous solo flight. It was not only the first Atlantic crossing by balloon but also the longest balloon flight.

DAY BY DAY

3 Aug
The Queen opens the eleventh Commonwealth Games in Edmonton, Alberta.

4 Aug
Liberal MP Jeremy Thorpe and 3 other men are charged at Minehead with conspiring to murder Norman Scott, a former male model. All 4 are remanded on bail.

Tests confirm that 4 patients in a Birmingham hospital, all of them pensioners, were suffering from botulism, a virulent form of food poisoning, after eating tinned salmon.

5 Aug
Sharron Davies wins the 200 metres individual swimming medley and the first gold medal for England in the Commonwealth Games.

7 Aug
Eddie Calvert, the Man with the Golden Trumpet, dies, aged 56.

10 Aug
The Chrysler Corporation of America announces that it has agreed to sell its European car manufacturing operations to the French Peugeot–Citroën group.

15 Aug
For the first time since March 1976 the value of the pound reaches $2 on the foreign exchange market.

16 Aug
The Ministry of Defence discloses that at least 9 more people working at the Atomic Weapons Research Establishment at Aldermaston have been found to have traces of plutonium in their bodies above the acceptable level. 3 women working in the laundry at Aldermaston had earlier been found to have traces of plutonium in their lungs.

21 Aug
President Nico Diederichs of South Africa dies in Cape Town, aged 74.

24 Aug
The Ministry of Defence announces the closure of all plutonium facilities at the Aldermaston Atomic Weapons Research Establishment until the staff concerned have been checked for contamination by plutonium dust.

26 Aug
Cardinal Albino Luciani, Patriarch of Venice, is elected Pope by the Sacred College of Cardinals and chooses to be called John Paul I.

28 Aug
Art experts say that some paintings attributed to John Constable are in fact the work of his son Lionel Constable.

THE GIRL WHO VANISHED INTO THIN AIR

An abandoned bicycle was the only clue yesterday to the mysterious disappearance of a 13-year-old newspaper girl. Genette Tate, who lived near the south Devon village of Sidmouth, had stopped just 3 minutes earlier to talk to 2 friends just around the corner from where she disappeared. They dawdled after her but when they turned the corner the bicycle was lying on the ground, newspapers scattered across the road, and Genette had vanished.

Ostensibly a children's show, the innovative Tiswas *format attracts a wide audience. Here, Ian 'Sludge' Lees, Chris Tarrant, John Gorman and Sylvester McCoy perform* The Bucket of Water Song.

SEPT 1978

Cyril Smith MP at the Liberal Party Conference at Southport.

DON'T DILLY-DALLY ON THE WAY

Mr Callaghan yesterday raised the curtain on the 1978 general election with a music hall turn. Speaking at the TUC conference, Mr Callaghan complained that political commentators had decided the date of the election already, but warned that that had been tried before in a famous old song. 'As far as I remember it went like this: "There was I, waiting at the church." Perhaps you recall how it went on.

' "All at once he sent me round a note
Here's the very note
This is what he wrote
I can't get away
To marry you today
My wife won't let me." '

To shouts of 'More', Mr Callaghan added that he had promised nobody that he would be at the altar in October. Tory party Chairman Lord Thorneycroft later retorted, 'Don't dilly-dally on the way, Jim.'
(Music hall expert Roy Hudd insists that the song, which Mr Callaghan attributed to Marie Lloyd, was in fact never sung by her; it was made famous by Vesta Victoria, he claims.)

Victoria Principal stars in Dallas, a new US soap centred round the oil business.

THE CARTER PEACE SHOW

Egypt and Israel yesterday took a historic step forward towards a peace treaty. After 13 days of wrangling President Sadat and Prime Minister Begin emerged from Camp David, President Carter's weekend retreat in Maryland, to announce agreement to an astonished world. A framework for peace in the Middle East, embodied in the signing of a treaty by the end of the year, has been agreed, though several key questions have been glossed over. Perhaps most important of these is the future of 50 Israeli settlement enclaves on the West Bank. Egypt insists that their withdrawal is essential to a peace treaty while Israel says the matter can be resolved by further negotiation.

PAN-AM BUYS 'FLY ME' AIRLINE

The airline that caused an international storm among feminists with its 'I'm Jane, Fly Me' adverts has been bought for £175m by Pan-American. If the deal to buy Miami-based National Airlines is approved by the US Civil Aeronautics Board and President Carter, Pan-Am will become the second biggest carrier anywhere. The biggest is America's United Airlines.

THE GREAT OIL STAIN

The Cabinet is to discuss what action to take over the sanctions-busting scandal of oil sales to Rhodesia. The publication of the *Bingham Report* yesterday confirms that from 1968 to 1975 Shell and BP were getting round the oil embargo against Rhodesia by an arrangement in which the French company Total supplied the Rhodesians and Shell and BP supplied an equivalent amount to Total.

TV's MR JINGLE TEAMS UP WITH ELTON

Elton John's millions of fans may be dismayed to learn that his next LP has been written by the singer of the Abbey National TV commercial. After dispensing with the talents of his long-term co-writer Bernie Taupin, the album marks the début of new partner 29-year-old Gary Osborne, whose previous hits include TV themes for Lucozade, Spangles and Ultra-Brite toothpaste. His best-known song is the ballad 'Amoureuse'; he also composed much of the current hit album *War of the Worlds* and is suing the record company for not publicizing the fact.

A news placard tells of the massive police hunt for the killers of 13-year-old newspaper boy, Carl Bridgewater. Carl was shot after disturbing intruders at Yew Tree Farm, near Kingswinford.

NEW STAR?

The *Daily Express* management has announced that it plans to launch a new national newspaper aimed at the bottom end of the market in competition with the *Daily Mirror* and the *Sun*. It is believed the title of the new publication will be the *Daily Star*.

MARGARINE WARNING

Top margarine manufacturers have been warned that they may be breaking the law by claiming their products are cholesterol-free. Analysts have discovered traces of the substance, which some doctors believe may be linked to heart disease, and the words 'Low Cholesterol' or 'Cholesterol Reduced' have been suggested as possible alternatives.

Blondie release their new album Parallel Lines.

SHAH CRUSHES RIOTERS

The bloodied streets of Tehran were silent last night as the Shah sheltered behind his guns and the people who have grown to hate him counted their dead. Tens of thousands of demonstrators had marched towards Parliament Square chanting 'Death to the Shah', following months of simmering protest by Muslim religious leaders at the 'Western decadence' of his oil-rich society. The first signs of trouble came early this year with the Muslims' condemnation of a liberalization programme including the importation of sexy and violent movies, more freedom for women and the trappings of a 1970s consumer society. The 58-year-old Shah, under the protection of the Imperial Guard, faces the worst crisis of his 25-year autocratic rule.

VORSTER QUITS

South African Premier John Vorster resigned yesterday (20 September) after 12 years in office. In that time he began the process of dismantling apartheid by measures such as removing segregation from sport and, to a large degree, from labour, education, the military and Civil Service. But Vorster always made it clear that he had no intention of abandoning the main pillars of apartheid, such as the laws that kept people of different races living in separate areas and those that forbade marriage and sex between whites and non-whites.

SECRET ROLLS

Locked in Chris Humberstone's workshop is the world's most secret Rolls-Royce – and he faces jail if he allows anyone a glimpse of it. Mr Humberstone converted a standard Silver Shadow for a client, giving it a new aluminium body and calling it a Panache. The result brought orders for similar versions and an injunction from Rolls-Royce, who is claiming breach of copyright. The company says it will continue to fight as long as the Panache carries any of its hallmarks, including the radiator, the Flying Lady and even the brake pedal, which bears the R-R insignia. Until the court hearing, which could take 2 years, Mr Humberstone has been ordered to keep the Panache under wraps. The case is causing anxiety in the car trade as a ruling in favour of Rolls would in theory also render illegal the customizing of Minis or Escorts.

WILD MAN MOON IS DEAD

Keith Moon, the wild man of pop, died yesterday (7 September) from a suspected drugs overdose. The 32-year-old drummer with The Who had been to Peppermint Park, a new hamburger restaurant in Covent Garden, to a party given by Paul McCartney in memory of Buddy Holly, who died 19 years ago at the height of his fame. Moon's last headline-hitting escapade was 2 months ago when he was thrown off a British Airways jet after trying to break into the pilot's cabin to play his drumsticks on the instrument panel.

GRANDMOTHER'S HOLOCAUST SUICIDE

For 40 years a Jewish grandmother was haunted by Nazi atrocities against her family. After watching the controversial television programme *Holocaust* frail Mrs Fanny Geddall, 81, killed herself. She left a note which said that after seeing 'that terrible programme' she wanted nothing more to do with the world.

ROCK ARTISTS WHO NEVER MAKE MUSIC

When the Rolling Stones illustrated the cover of their latest album, *Some Girls*, with unflattering portraits of Hollywood's female stars, 2 of those featured – Raquel Welch and Lucille Ball – swiftly contacted their lawyers. The result was that in the States Dolly Parton and Linda Ronstadt replaced their images.

This controversy over the art of packaging a record has once again fuelled intrigue over LP covers. Master designer Roger Dean has been offered up to £30,000 for originals of surrealistic paintings depicted on covers of albums by groups such as Yes. Warhol, who designed the Stones' *Sticky Fingers* cover, will command a similar fee. The Beatles' *Sergeant Pepper* album was probably responsible for provoking the importance now attached to sleeve design, which it is estimated can add 20% to sales. This means that on an album such as Pink Floyd's *Dark Side Of The Moon* sales of almost 1.5 million could be attributed to the cover design by Hipgnosis.

Police question bus passengers in the Aldwych area of London, where Bulgarian defector Georgi Markov is believed to have been stabbed.

THE SUB HUNTERS

A new long-range anti-submarine helicopter is being designed by Britain as an answer to the growing menace of the Soviet underwater fleet. Westland, the British helicopter firm, announced yesterday that work has begun on the project – code-named WG–34 – under a contract with the Ministry of Defence.

OCT 1978

A STAR IS BORN

Nigel Havers, Squire Paul Craddock in BBC's new Sunday serial *A Horseman Riding By*, is undoubtedly 1978's most attractive new male. An aristocrat on and off screen, Havers plays a Boer War veteran who finds fulfilment as a Devon squire. Ironically, Nigel's main rival as a pin-up is his old friend, Ian Ogilvy, who plays the Saint on ITV in direct competition to Nigel. Nigel's father is Sir Michael Havers QC, Conservative MP for Merton, Wimbledon and Shadow Attorney-General, and he has a brother who has followed the family tradition of entering the legal profession. Nigel stuck to his acting ambitions, however, and his greatest success to date has been 2 years as Billy Owen in *Mrs Dale's Diary*.

Is Deirdre (Anne Kirkbride) on the point of discovering the truth about husband Ray's (Neville Buswell) affair with Janice Stubbs?

TOMATOES WIN PLACE IN SUN

3 judges yesterday decided that Mr Herbert Allen's tomatoes had a legal right to sunshine. That means his neighbours, the Greenwoods, must move a high fence and caravan which have been casting a shadow over part of his greenhouse and preventing his tomatoes from ripening. The ruling was the first of its kind under the 'Ancient Lights' laws which apply to buildings used for at least 20 years. The judges ruled that the greenhouse was a building to which access of light applied under the 1832 Prescription Act.

Cardinal Karol Wojtyla, elected as the 264th pope, arriving at Rome.

THE IRON CURTAIN POPE

The bells of Rome's 500 churches rang out last night to welcome Pope John Paul II – one of the most astonishing elections in history. He is Polish Cardinal Karol Wojtyla, a former factory worker and resistance agent, the first non-Italian Pope for 400 years and the first ever from Poland. Cardinal Wojtyla chose to take the same name as his predecessor and within hours 300,000 Catholics crammed into St Peter's Square to cheer him.

QUEEN COMPLETES ANCESTOR'S JOB

The Queen completed a job begun 74 years ago by her great-grandfather with yesterday's service of dedication at Liverpool's new Anglican cathedral. In 1904 King Edward VII laid the foundation stone of the first Anglican cathedral to be consecrated in Britain since the thirteenth century. Yesterday (25 October) the Queen unveiled another stone to commemorate the end of the project. Rising to 318 feet, the neo-Gothic building is the largest enclosed space in the world.

HISTORIC ROPE TRICK

A retired physician has joined the hallowed ranks of those referred to with awe by sailors and the like. . . the men who invent knots. He has invented the Hunter's Bend. Dr Edward Hunter's knot, which he actually devised many years ago, is especially good for joining man-made fibres together. The knot, which is the first new design for 20 years, is a historic development in the field as it is regarded by experts as perfect. It meets all the classic criteria of being simple, easy to learn and straightforward to untie.

FATHER'S AFFAIR

Earl Mountbatten has publicly acknowledged that his father, Prince Louis, had an illegitimate daughter by actress Lillie Langtry. When Jeanne-Marie was born in 1881 it was assumed that the Prince of Wales was the father. The prince, one of her many lovers, was too gallant to deny the allegation. Jeanne-Marie's daughter, former BBC announcer Mary Malcolm, has actually interviewed Lord Mountbatten, though he was unaware at the time that he was talking to his niece.

THE IMPATIENT KILLERS

The Orkneys seal war enters its second week with the Norwegian hunters yet to make their first kill and the Government out-manoeuvred at every turn by protesters. The controversial cull has already been deferred 3 times by the Scottish Office, and there is now considerable dispute over the scientific evidence for it. It was supposed to have been established that mature grey seals eat 15lb of fish a day and that trawler fleets are being robbed of up to £20m-worth of code per year. Now it transpires that the consumption figures came from a study of zoo seals, and Greenpeace is asking the Government to cancel plans for this year's cull while all the scientific evidence is examined. The Norwegians' licence runs out in 2 weeks' time and, whatever happens, they will receive their £20,000 fee.

NO SHOTGUN DIVORCE FOR RAY

They have murdered Ernie Bishop, burnt Grace Archer and Val Barlow to death, killed off Carlos the chef and Martha Longhurst. Now, faced with competition for weekly butchery from *The Sweeney, Starsky and Hutch* and the like, the producers of the great British soap operas feel that death has lost its sting as a TV crowd-puller. So next month when Ray Langton walks out of the *Street* for good, there will be a tamer exit; he will disappear in the arms of his lover, Janice Stubbs. The softly softly exit has been perfected by *Emmerdale Farm* with only 1 major death – Peggy Skilbeck's – in 5 years.

HEATH BACKS JIM

Edward Heath finally turned his back on the Tory leadership of Margaret Thatcher last night. In a television interview the former prime minister endorsed the Labour Government's 5% pay limit and effectively put paid to any change of heart Mr Heath might have had of serving in a Thatcher Cabinet.

Morecambe and Wise team up with Regan and Carter (John Thaw and Dennis Waterman) for an episode of The Sweeney.

FAREWELL *ARK*

The *Ark Royal*, most powerful and biggest of our warships, is on its way to the breaker's yard. Built in 1943, without ever having fired a shot to kill, its last mission was to sail home from Gibraltar. On the journey it passed within miles of the old *Ark Royal* which was under 50 fathoms of sea with a U-boat torpedo hole in her side. On 4 December at a jetty in Devonport and with 960,000 miles on the clock, the boilers will be shut down for the last time. Senior engineer Lieutenant-Commander John Bolger, who will oversee the operation, said, 'I shan't be sorry. She's a bitch to keep going now.'

CHAPMAN WINS TAX BATTLE

Former Nottingham Forest Captain Sammy Chapman has won a battle for footballers everywhere over the taxing of testimonial benefits. Chapman, now with Shrewsbury, picked up £13,000 from his testimonial 18 months ago but lost £4,000 to the taxman. Now, after a year-long fight, he has won an appeal which will restore to him the money deducted in tax, although the action, unaided by the PFA, has cost him £1,000.

PUNK GIRL'S 'SUICIDE'

A theory that Sid Vicious' girlfriend committed 'hara-kiri' could be put forward when the 21-year-old former Sex Pistol is arraigned for murder in New York. Nancy Spungen was found in their hotel room with a hunting knife in her stomach. Detectives claim the Punk star – real name John Simon Ritchie – confessed to the stabbing, but on several occasions he has 'firmly denied' killing her.

PUNK BAND AXED

Punk band Sham 69 have been sacked from a new £2m film. Leader Jimmy Pursey said yesterday that he thought the reason the group had been dropped from the film *Quadrophenia* could be connected with the Sid Vicious murder charge. A spokesman for the film company said it was because the group's 2 numbers were not satisfactory for dancing. The film, backed by The Who and due for release next year, is set in 1964 in the Mods and Rockers era and shows 10 days in the life of a disillusioned Mod teenager.

Grandmaster in the making? 13-year-old Nigel Short from Atherton, near Manchester.

LIFELINE FOR REFUGEES

Britain has opened her heart and offered homes to nearly 350 exhausted, destitute and frightened people. The refugees, crammed into a leaking, 60-foot boat, were rescued by a British ship in the South China Sea as they made a do-or-die attempt to escape from Communist Vietnam. They had decided to follow thousands of other boat people who have set sail from Vietnam in the past 3 years determined to flee from Ho Chi Minh City – the new name for Saigon – in the hope of finding asylum.

SPORTS COUNCIL IN TOBACCO ROW

The Sports Council was in disarray last night after failing to reach a decision on the vexed question of sponsorship by tobacco companies. Rather than take the first steps towards severing sporting links with smoking by supporting the anti-tobacco resolution, the Council chose to pass the buck to individual governing bodies.

THALIDOMIDE MOTHER

Thalidomide victim Mrs Elaine Dale has become the mother of a perfectly formed baby girl. 18-year-old Elaine, who was born without arms, becomes Britain's second Thalidomide mother. Last year she became the first Thalidomide victim to pass a driving test.

FOR SALE: HUMPTY DUMPTY'S HOUSE

For around £60,000 the wall from which Humpty Dumpty took a tumble could be yours. Cawood Castle in Yorkshire, where Cardinal Wolsey was living when he fell from favour with Henry VIII, inspired the nursery rhyme that is still with us nearly 450 years later. Wolsey in fact did not die there but it seemed a shame to let the facts interfere with a good story.

NOV 1978

Bob Marley, in Britain to launch his new album Babylon By Bus.

CARS WILL BE NON-U

Cars will have a V plate when registration letters change next August. The current suffix letter is T but police have asked Swansea's Vehicle Licensing Centre not to use the letter U because of possible confusion with V. The decision means that the current suffix letter series will end in 1982 when it is expected that the letter indicating the year will be put at the front of the registration number starting at the beginning of the alphabet. The letters I and O were not used because of their confusion with numbers; Q was omitted because it is a special registration letter used at ports for licensing used cars; Z is also to be left out – it's a special registration mark for Northern Ireland vehicles.

RADIO FUN

If anyone's to blame for today's dreaded wavelength changes it's the Albanians. The whole of Europe is affected by the airwave carve-up, the first since 1948. The changes were made to accommodate 'emergent' broadcasting nations and give them a fair share of the increasingly overcrowded international frequencies. Britain lost out to Albania, which asked for and received one of our main frequencies – 464m medium wave, the current home of Radio 3. Radio 3 now moves to 247m, the current Radio 1 slot. Radio 1 moves to 275m and 285m medium wave. Radio 2 switches from long wave to 330m and 433m medium wave. Radio 4 transfers from medium wave to 1,500m long wave (the old Radio 2) and will blanket the country for the first time. Those who will be unhappy at the changes include about 100,000 people who have only long wave receivers and will no longer be able to receive Radio 2, while 500,000 have only medium wave and will miss Radio 4. A lot of car radios don't pick up long wave so they will lose Radio 4, too. Also in some places 247m reception is poor and the BBC recommends tuning to Radio 3 on VHF. Unfortunately, under two-thirds of the population owns VHF sets.

CALL FOR BAN ON SEX DRUG

The Home Office was urged last night to ban drugs which have produced bizarre side-effects on jailed sex offenders. Oestrogen – a female hormone – is used to reduce sexual urges but some prisoners have developed breasts which have had to be amputated; other risks include thrombosis and cancer. But the man who pioneered the use of such drugs at Dartmoor, Dr William Fitzgerald, said that his conscience was clear and that he had saved dozens of children from sexual assault. He added that the possible side-effects were explained and consent forms were signed. A former Broadmoor patient is, however, taking legal advice after developing a breast and claiming the risks were not fully explained.

'HE PLOTTED MURDER IN THE COMMONS'

The case of the century opened in Minehead, Somerset yesterday with a story of how Jeremy Thorpe plotted murder at the House of Commons. Thorpe, then Liberal Leader, was alleged to have discussed with fellow Liberal MP Peter Bessell ways of killing Norman Scott, with whom he was said to have had a homosexual relationship. Mr Bessell said airline pilot Andrew Newton was promised £10,000 to do the job. Newton, the court was told, lured Mr Scott to a lonely spot but when he pointed the gun at him 'either it jammed or he got cold feet'. The hearing continues.

MAN OF PRAYER WHO THREATENS THE SHAH

The fate of the Shah of Iran and the troubled country he rules is locked in the prayer-clasped hands of a bearded old man thousands of miles away in exile. As his land totters under mob violence and industrial anarchy observers await a final explosion that will precipitate the downfall of Mohammed Reza Pahlavi. The spark for this explosion could come from a small French farmhouse near Paris where 78-year-old Muslim mullah Ayatollah Ruhollah Khomeini plots the downfall of the peacock throne. Khomeini, the undisputed spiritual leader of Iran, has threatened to give the order for 'an armed popular struggle if the situation becomes intolerable for the people. . . for whom I cry'.

If Khomeini succeeds the troubled nation would take a giant backward step; the West would far prefer the Shah, with all his faults, to survive.

JULIET LAUNCHES BARD ON TV

Producer Cedric Messina, the man behind the BBC's £7m plan to screen all Shakespeare's plays, is looking for an actor to play King Lear. *Jaws* star Robert Shaw, who died 2 months ago, was to have taken the part. All 37 plays are due to be screened over the next 6 years, starting with *Romeo and Juliet* on 3 December.

Miss India, Kalpana Iyer, meets her hero Lord Mountbatten, the last viceroy of her country.

M FOR MYSTERY

They've sold over 50 million albums around the world – more than Rod Stewart, the Eagles or supergroup Led Zeppelin – yet their success has been built on little more than nursery rhymes. Half the nation can hum their Top 10 hits — 'Rasputin' is their seventh – without caring whom the voices belong to. It has certainly been the year of Boney M. They have dominated the charts as much as Abba did last year. It used to be that the music was secondary to the image as a formula for success but how many people know their names? The group was conceived 3 years ago by Frank Farion, the Doctor Frankenstein of the disco set. He cut a track called 'Baby, Do the Bump', using 3 backing singers whom he haphazardly named Boney M. When the record became a Euro hit he screened hundreds of applicants before teaming up singer and DJ Bobby Farrell with Marcia Barrett, Maizie Williams and Liz Mitchell.

THE LONGEST 6 MINUTES

6 minutes. . . that's the time it took to play the 2 games which changed the shape of world tennis and brought the Wightman Cup back to Britain for only the tenth time in 50 matches against the United States. With a score of 3 matches each, and 1 set all and 4 all in the final doubles rubber, Virginia Wade served to take the ninth game. 16-year-old Pam Shriver, partnered by Chris Evert served next, with Sue Barker delivering the bullet service return at 15–40 to win the match and a place in the history books.

Jeff Wayne's Album in the charts since its release five months ago.

DUMMY RUN AT ROYAL PERFORMANCE

The curtain at the London Palladium will rise next week on one of the strangest acts ever seen in a Royal Variety Performance – a tiny husband and wife team called the Krankies. At 4 foot 5 Janette Tough is so small she acts the part of a ventriloquist's doll sitting on husband Ian's knee and wearing a schoolboy outfit reminiscent of Jimmy Clitheroe. It is a comedy routine that is already earning them £2,000 a week in clubland. Ian, who at the age of 31 is the same age as Janette, though they are often mistaken for father and daughter, was an electrician at the Pavilion Theatre in Glasgow where Janette was a comedy stooge in a pantomime. They formed an act, originally mainly a singing duo before broadening into comedy, and married 3 years later. Next week's performance, which also stars Arthur Askey, Max Bygraves and Danny La Rue, marks Lord Delfont's departure from the show he has presented since 1958.

GRACIE STEALS SHOW

Gracie Fields left her home in Capri to make a surprise comeback at last night's Royal Variety Performance – and stole the show. In her tenth such appearance, which had been kept a closely guarded secret, she sang 'Sally', her signature tune for so many years. Afterwards she met the Queen Mother, who first saw Gracie in a Royal show in 1928.

VICTORY FOR GUILTY MEN

2 journalists and a former Intelligence Corps soldier stood convicted yesterday of breaking the Official Secrets Act. But they were freed from the Old Bailey for, despite what he regarded as grave offences, Mr Justice Mars-Jones decided against passing custodial sentences. Sentencing 34-year-old former soldier John Berry to 6 months' jail suspended for 2 years, the judge said that his disclosures about his work with signals intelligence might have imperilled lives, even though it seemed to be state and low-level information. The journalists, Crispin Aubrey, editor of *Time Out* magazine, and Duncan Campbell, who works for the *New Statesman*, were conditionally charged for receiving information knowing it to be secret. Referring to Section 2 of the 1911 act, under which the 3 were convicted, Defending Counsel Lord Jeremy Hutchinson QC commented, 'Perhaps 17 November 1978 will be remembered as positively the last appearance on the public stage of this raddled and discredited prima donna.'

DAY BY DAY

2 Nov
A new national newspaper, the *Daily Star*, is published by Express Newspapers for the first time. Printed in Manchester, it is intended for sale in the Midlands and the North of England.

Soviet cosmonauts Vladimir Kovalyonok and Alexander Ivanchenkov return to earth in *Soyuz 31* after a record 4½ months in space.

3 Nov
The Caribbean island of Dominica becomes an independent republic.

6 Nov
Mr John Davies, Conservative MP for Knutsford, resigns his seat in the House of Commons on health grounds.

8 Nov
The General Synod of the Church of England rejects a proposal to allow the ordination of women.

The Government's annual order for the renewal of sanctions against Rhodesia is carried in the House of Commons by a majority of 199. Against Shadow Cabinet advice, some Conservative MPs vote against sanctions. One such, Mr Winston Churchill, is later asked by Mrs Thatcher to resign his position as defence spokesman.

16 Nov
The transitional Government in Rhodesia decides to postpone the majority rule elections until April 1979.

20 Nov
The bodies of 912 members of the People's Temple are found at their headquarters in a jungle area of Guyana. All are believed to have committed suicide. The founder of the sect, Jim Jones, is also found dead.

21 Nov
Mr William Rodgers, Secretary of State for Transport, says that the Government plans to abolish the car tax by 1983 and to replace it with an increased tax on petrol.

22 Nov
Ford workers accept a 17% wage settlement and the strike which has lasted 9 weeks is called off.

24 Nov
Television licences are increased to £25 for colour and £10 for black and white sets.

28 Nov
The Battle of Britain Museum at Hendon is opened by Queen Elizabeth the Queen Mother.

Mr Healey, Chancellor of the Exchequer, says the Government will impose sanctions against the Ford Motor Company for breaking the 5% pay guidelines.

29 Nov
65 love letters by Lillie Langtry are sold at Christie's for £8,000.

AND A NEW FACE BEHIND THE NEWS

The BBC announced its first black radio newsreader yesterday, 3 months after she started doing the job. London-born Moira Stuart, 29, will read the news on Radio 4's first day of broadcasting on the new wavelength. It was felt that Moira should settle into the job before the official announcement was made.

DEC 1978

KEEGAN TAKES EUROPE AWARD

Kevin Keegan, 27-year-old former Liverpool forward now with Hamburg, has been named European Footballer of the Year. He becomes the fifth British player to take the award, the previous winners being Stanley Matthews (1956), Denis Law (1964), Bobby Charlton (1966) and George Best (1968).

NO, I WAS FIRST, SAYS JACK

Though it was Nottingham Forest's Viv Anderson who last week became the first coloured footballer to play for England, Jack Leslie recollects the day more than 50 years ago when he was picked to play for his country. From 1922 to 1934 Leslie played for Plymouth Argyle, part of a strike force old men in Devon pubs still discuss with awe. In 1925 he was informed by the manager that he had been selected for England. The bombshell came some days later when it was announced that Aston Villa's Billy Walker was playing instead. Leslie, now 77 and in charge of the boot room at West Ham, is convinced that his international career was peremptorily curtailed purely because of his colour. Plymouth, whose archives were destroyed in the blitz, has no documents on this bizarre piece of footballing history. But only this week Memory Man Leslie Welch said of Leslie in a radio broadcast, 'Part of the best left wing I ever saw, he'd have played for England scores of times but for his colour.'

Genesis line up without Peter Gabriel. And Then There Were Three is the year's chart success.

A DOG IS NOT A WEAPON

Magistrates yesterday threw out a charge against a man accused of carrying a weapon after learning that the 'weapon' was an Alsatian. Following the incident, which took place in Southend, the prosecution's case rested on evidence that the dog tried to bite a policeman because it had been trained to attack anyone in police uniform. Mr Jeremy Cole, representing the dog's owner, said, 'If a dog is an offensive weapon, then it's bad news for all dog owners.'

EAT, DRINK AND HAVE FAT BABIES

Would-be mothers who want slim children should go on a diet before they get pregnant. Fatness runs in families, Dr Alvin Eden, a leading child-care expert, warns today. But it isn't inherited: it's simply that if the mother and father eat a lot, the children will, too. 'Mothers should start fat-proofing their babies before they are conceived; pregnancy is not the time to diet.' A fat mother's baby is more likely to lay down excess fat cells during its last 3 months in the womb and these will stay with him all his life, says Dr Eden. The grown-up baby might shrink the cells by dieting but they are always ready to swell up again, making slimming far more difficult.

BABY TEST DANGERS

A test for abnormalities in babies while they are in the womb can damage or kill them, doctors have discovered. The procedure, called amniocentesis, involves puncturing the bag of fluid that cushions the baby to draw off a small amount for medical analysis. Many mothers-to-be have been seeking the test to try to avoid the heartbreak of having babies with spina bifida or mental handicap. A recent study, however, has shown that women who had the test suffered unwanted loss of their babies at more than twice the rate of those who did not.

INSULT THAT TURNED INTO A JOKE

When the phrase Male Chauvinist Pig was first coined by the Women's Lib movement, it was intended as a term of abuse, characterizing the worst type of man imaginable. Now, an enterprising MCP has made an industry out of the insult. 3 years ago publishing director John Wright started selling by mail order his now famous MCP tie. Following phenomenal sales he decided to branch out into goods such as cuff-links and whisky bearing the MCP logo. There is also an MCP diary, bound in pigskin, naturally.

Anna Ford joins News at Ten to become ITN's first woman newsreader. She dismisses comparisons between the BBC's Angela Rippon and herself.

The Deer Hunter. *Christopher Walken as a POW of the Viet Cong betrays the first signs that his mind is beginning to snap.*

THE GRAND OLD LADY OF ISRAEL DIES

Golda Meir, the former Prime Minister of Israel and one of the great Jewish personalities of the twentieth century, died yesterday (8 December), aged 80. The news plunged Israel into mourning and all radio networks switched over to solemn music. Born in 1898 in tsarist Russia, her father, a Kiev carpenter, barely earned enough to keep the family from starvation and 5 of her 8 brothers and sisters died in infancy. After migrating to America she decided in her teens to help fellow Jews build a home of their own. After graduating from a teacher training college in Milwaukee, she married and settled in Palestine in 1921. 4 months after Israel became a state in May 1948, she became the country's first ambassador when Prime Minister David Ben Gurion sent her to Moscow. Golda Meir announced her retirement in 1965 but 4 years later, when Premier Levi Eshkol died, she agreed to serve as a 'stop gap' prime minister but remained in office for 5 years.

THE MAN WHO BROKE THE SILENCE ON ABDICATION CRISIS

Ronald Harker last night watched on TV the effect of what happened after he unwittingly sparked the news of the abdication crisis. ITV's *Edward and Mrs Simpson* recalled the day in 1936 when, as a young reporter on the *Bradford Telegraph and Argus*, he covered a diocesan conference where the Bishop of Bradford, the Rt Revd Alfred Blunt, made a reference to the King. 'The benefit of the forthcoming coronation depends on the faith, prayer and self-dedication of the King himself, graces which he will so abundantly need if he is to do his duty faithfully. We hope he is aware of his need and some of us wish he gave more positive signs of his awareness.' The Bishop later denied he had been referring to Edward's marriage plans but within 24 hours of Harker's story going to press the unofficial news embargo was broken and the abdication crisis was rocking Britain.

BIG AXE FOR BRUCE

LWT is to axe Bruce Forsyth's *Big Night* at Christmas. They have decided that the £2.5m experiment, which was to transform Saturday night entertainment, has not worked, with viewing figures slumping from 15 million to less than 10 million.

DID 2 MEN SHOOT KENNEDY?

Evidence given yesterday (29 December) before an Assassinations Committee by 2 sound experts has given fresh credence to the conspiracy theory surrounding President Kennedy's death. Ernest Aschkenasy and Dr Mark Weiss are convinced that the third shot came from an area known as the 'grassy knoll', indicating the presence of a second assassin. Witnesses have spoken of a shot being fired from the small piece of parkland in front of and to the right of the car. Pictures show frightened people looking at the knoll and policemen running towards it. Now, the 2 experts, using a recording made when a police motor-cyclist travelling just behind the President's car accidentally left his microphone on, have deduced that the third and fourth shots were too close together to have come from the alleged assassin Oswald's rifle, which needed more than 2 seconds to reload. They were also able to tell by precise measurement of the 22 distinct echoes from the third shot that it came from the knoll.

CARTER'S CHINESE CRACKER!

President Carter has announced that formal diplomatic relations will be re-established with China on 1 January after a 31-year break. The Republican Chinese Government of Taiwan will no longer be recognized by the United States and all remaining American troops – about 2,000 – will be pulled out in the next 4 months.

EURO SHAMBLES

European unity was in a shambles last night over the Common Market's new currency plan. A summit to set up the scheme ended with Britain, Ireland and Italy refusing to commit themselves to it, leaving a rump of 6 led by West Germany and France to start the European Monetary System on 1 January. Mr Callaghan announced that, though the new scheme was 'a noble effort' it was not one for the pound sterling to join.

Christopher Reeves is man of steel in Superman.

JAN 1979

THE 7-YEAR REVENGE

A remote-controlled bomb yesterday (22 January) blew up the car carrying the man who masterminded the Munich Olympics massacre. It had taken Israeli secret agents nearly 7 years to exact their revenge on Ali Hassan Salameh for the murder of 11 of their nation's athletes. Salameh, code-named Abu Hassan, has been proclaimed a martyr of the Palestinian revolution.

SNIPER SHOOTS SCHOOLCHILDREN

A teenage girl taking shots at a school playground hit 12 people, killing the headmaster of the Cleveland Elementary School in San Diego, California, and a janitor. 16-year-old Brenda Spencer, who was last night barricaded in a house opposite the playground, explained the reason for her actions by telephone: 'I don't like Mondays. This livens up the day.'

London's 700,000 commuters are stranded as strike action over bonus pay affects the Southern Region.

PHEASANTS NOT BARBAROUS – PRINCE PHILIP

Prince Philip has made a rare defence of the Royal Family's hunting and shooting pursuits. In an interview in the *New Scientist* he said, 'I find it difficult to differentiate clearly between rearing chickens under factory conditions for slaughter and rearing pheasants for shooting. The fact that someone killing chickens in a slaughterhouse is paid for his work, whether he likes it or not, and that someone else likes to shoot pheasants without being paid does not really alter the case. If killing is immoral, whether you are paid for it or enjoy it really makes no difference.' Prince Philip was interviewed 4 days after hosting a shooting party at Sandringham with the Queen, Prince Charles and Prince Edward. Prince Charles took the opportunity to pass on a few tips to Lady Diana Spencer, 17-year-old sister of one of his favourite girlfriends, Lady Sarah.

SIMON FEVER IS CATCHING

The most coveted toy in America at the moment is an electronic game called simply Simon. Simon fever is raging, with Simon parties at homes lucky enough to have acquired the game, Simon challenges and a brisk black market in Simons. Launched late last year Simon looks like a plastic flying saucer with 4 panels that flash different colours, each matched by a musical tone. Players try to repeat an ever-increasing sequence by pushing the appropriate panels.

FAMILY FUN BEATS VIOLENCE AT BOX OFFICE

Sex and violence at the cinema are out; family entertainment is in. Of the top 20 British box-office films of 1978 only 3 carried X certificates, with 2 AA films; the rest – 6 Us and 10 As – were suitable for children. *Star Wars, Grease, Close Encounters of the Third Kind, The Rescuers* and *Revenge of the Pink Panther* swept the board. *Saturday Night Fever* received its X rating mainly because of its bad language. The other X certificate films were *The Gauntlet* and *The Stud*.

KEEP SMALLPOX LAB, SAYS WORLD HEALTH

The head of Britain's only remaining smallpox laboratory has been urged by the World Health Organisation to reconsider his decision to halt research. Professor Keith Dumbell has announced that, in view of the row over laboratory safety in Britain, 200 strains of live smallpox virus held at St Mary's Hospital in London would stay in deep freeze until the future of his high-security laboratory there had been decided. A WHO spokesman stressed the importance of the work carried out in the laboratory – 1 of only 10 in the world still holding the virus – as a means of ensuring that the world was free of smallpox. Professor Dumbell's announcement follows a smallpox virus escape at a Birmingham laboratory last autumn which killed medical school photographer Mrs Janet Parker.

The child within us . . . portrayed by Colin Welland, John Bird and Robin Ellis in Dennis Potter's Blue Remembered Hills.

ASSASSIN DEADLIER THAN THE COBRA

A plant poison twice as powerful as cobra venom killed umbrella victim Georgi Markov, an inquest heard yesterday (2 January). The 49-year-old Bulgarian defector, who died after being stabbed by an umbrella point last September, was injured with the poison ricin, against which there is no known antidote. Ricin comes from the seeds of the castor oil plant and was almost certainly contained in a metal ball fired into Mr Markov's leg from a weapon concealed in the umbrella. Who killed the BBC broadcaster remains a mystery, although those close to Mr Markov believe he died because of his outspoken remarks against the Bulgarian Communist regime.

TAKING A TIP FROM AGATHA

Ricin featured in one of Agatha Christie's early stories: *The House of Lurking Death.* However, the majority of her poisoning cases used better known substances such as cyanide (14), morphine (7) and digitalis (6).

ASHES SAFE

With the Ashes secure, following a 93-run victory in the fourth test, Mike Brearley has promised to go all out to crown his triumph in the 2 remaining matches. With an unassailable 3–1 lead following a 3–0 victory in 1977, Brearley has successfully defended the Ashes, a feat last performed by Sir Len Hutton, who won at home in 1953 and in Australia in 1954–5.

AMONG THE NEW YEAR HONOURS . . .

An OBE for Yorkshire vet James Alfred Wight who, as James Herriot, is a bestselling author; entertainers Tommy Steele and Olivia Newton-John also receive OBEs, as does actor Gordon Jackson. Donald Sinden receives the CBE; Joan Sutherland becomes a dame, as do Gracie Fields from showbusiness and Naomi James, single-handed round-the-world yachtswoman, while Hugh Scanlon from the trade union movement is made a lord. Jack Brabham, the former World Motor-racing Champion, receives a knighthood, while athletes Sonia Lannaman and Ian Stewart, swimmer Margaret Kelly and rally driver Roger Clark receive MBEs.

COMPUTER NAMES THOMSON FASTEST

Australian bowler Jeff Thomson is the fastest and most accurate in world cricket, according to the computer. Thomson scored highest in a test in which the world's top pace bowlers were invited to be measured. His fastest delivery was 91.86 m.p.h., well clear of Michael Holding (87.76 m.p.h.) and Imran Khan (86.77 m.p.h.). Each bowler was allowed 8 deliveries, the fastest of which was measured by camera and computer. The bowlers who completed the 'Top Ten' were: Garth Le Roux, Colin Croft, Andy Roberts, Dennis Lillee, Wayne Daniel, Len Pascoe and Richard Hadlee. Missing from the test were Australia's Rodney Hogg and Bob Willis.

KATHY JUMPS TO IT WITH US ARMY

Kathy Tayler has a great ambition – to become the world's finest all-round sportswoman. To help her achieve her goal 18-year-old Kathy from Reading joined the American Army for 3 months. The young pentathlon star is in training at Fort Sam Houston, Texas, which houses the training grounds of all the American hopefuls in the event. Kathy was 1 of the 4 girls who won the team title for Britain at the first women's world pentathlon championships last summer at Crystal Palace. Unfortunately, she must miss next year's Moscow Olympics – as yet there is no women's Olympic modern pentathlon.

NO CANNED MUSIC FOR NEW STAR

The pop world's latest sensation was resting last night after his first taste of stardom and a brush with the Musicians' Union. Metal Mickey, the singing robot, was stopped from miming to his first record – a version of the old Mudlarks song 'Lollipop' – on the ITV show *After Noon.* Human entertainers are not allowed to mime to records – they do it to specially recorded tapes – and the union didn't see why the electronically controlled robot should be any different. Compromise was reached when Thames TV agreed that Mickey could appear while the record was being played, but could not move his lips.

BRITAIN UNDER SIEGE

A state of emergency will be declared within 48 hours if the industrial chaos caused by the tanker and lorry driver strikes gets worse. Troops were standing by last night to control supplies of fuel and food. A grave situation is developing at the ports, where thousands of tons of perishable cargo are being held up by pickets. Prices Secretary Roy Hattersley has told the road haulage employers that even their present 15% offer to drivers is too much and if they yield to union demands totalling more than 20%, he could make an order to hold down prices.

FEB 1979

DRUGS KILL PUNK STAR SID VICIOUS

Punk rock star Sid Vicious, the inadequate youth who turned a tasteless pop gimmick into pathetic real life, died of a heroin overdose yesterday (2 February). His body was found after a party in his new girlfriend's New York apartment, held to celebrate his release from jail on bail – he had been accused of murdering his previous girlfriend, 'Nauseous Nancy' Spungen. 21-year-old Vicious, formerly John Ritchie from East London, was supposed to have been weaned off drugs while in custody.

SUZANNE'S BIG COVER-UP

Actress Suzanne Danielle has been suspended from the shooting of a controversial sex movie for refusing to appear naked. Suzanne, girlfriend of TV heart-throb Patrick Mower, may now lose the part, as an unknown American model, Sherrie Cronn, was being screen-tested to take over the lead role in the film *The World is Full of Married Men*. More than 30 minutes of the film, which was written by Jackie Collins and stars Carroll Baker and Tony Franciosa, has already been recorded at an estimated cost of £250,000.

Sid Vicious and Johnnie Rotten of the Sex Pistols.

WINNERS LOSE IN TRIPLE PHOTO

For the first time in more than 50 years of greyhound racing at London's White City there was a triple dead heat on Saturday (10 February). It was for second place and brought problems for Tote and punters alike. The Tote display boards were unable to show all the dividends and place punters collected less than their 10p stake on 2 of the dead-heaters. The pay-outs: Nameless Prince – 15p; Scintilla's Rock – 6p; Saucy Buck – 5p. The race, the William Hill Hurdles Championship Final, was won by West Mead Manor.

TV's favourite space travellers make the transition to the big screen in Star Trek – The Motion Picture.

TV SERIAL 'NOT FAIR'

A TV programme about life in a comprehensive school has upset some of the pupils at the school where it was filmed. BBC's *Grange Hill*, which was filmed largely at Kingsbury High School in London, has prompted pupils to complain that the programme makes them all look semi-literate trouble-makers.

MAUDLING: THE NEARLY MAN

Reginald Maudling, who died yesterday (14 February), had a knack of expounding complicated economic ideas in simple terms. It was probably this, plus a strong head for brandy, which led Churchill to make him his personal economic advisor. He became MP for Barnet, where he stayed for the whole of his time in the Commons, and quickly rose through the ministerial ranks. When Macmillan fell ill in 1963, Maudling missed his chance of becoming Tory Leader. In 1965, when Alec Douglas-Home resigned, he was beaten by a small margin by Edward Heath. It was then that he turned to business and found his way onto the boards of some ill-managed, even fraudulent companies, like the Real Estate Fund of America and the notorious Poulson enterprises. Though he was later exonerated from any complicity in the Poulson scandal, a select committee said that he should have declared his interest. Maudling made a comeback in 1975 as Shadow Foreign Minister but Mrs Thatcher dismissed him in November 1976 for failing to make enough speeches on behalf of the party.

PLAY IT COOL PLEA 'TURNED DOWN'

The American Government was furious yesterday (14 February) over the killing of its ambassador to Afghanistan. A State Department spokesman said the US embassy in Kabul had repeatedly urged the Afghan Government to exercise restraint and not try to free the kidnapped ambassador, Mr Adolph Dubbs, by force. Kabul radio said that the ambassador was shot by right-wing gunmen who were themselves killed by security forces.

JO CRUSHED BY LATEST PRODIGY

Jo Durie, the top-ranked British girl, no sooner discovered how to cope with the amazing Andrea Jaeger in the Pepsi Cola World Junior Championships in Boca West than she plunged to defeat. The 18-year-old British girl took the first set 6–1 but the 12-year-old American prodigy hit back to win by 2 sets to 1.

B.L. union man Derek 'Red Robbo' Robinson.

LORD KAGAN BIDS FOR ISRAELI CITIZENSHIP

Gannex raincoat tycoon Lord Kagan has offered to set up a huge denim factory in Israel if the Israelis grant him citizenship. The revelation is made in a *World in Action* programme to be shown tonight (12 February). Lord Kagan, a close friend of Sir Harold Wilson, faces tax charges in Britain and has been staying in Tel Aviv. A warrant has been issued for his arrest but the charges are not covered by an extradition agreement.

The first £1m signature takes Trevor Francis to Brian Clough's Nottingham Forest.

'UNFAIR' BROADCASTS BANNED

All party political broadcasts on ITV before the 1 March referendum on Scottish devolution were banned yesterday (16 February) by the IBA. The move followed a ruling in the Scottish Court of Session that broadcasts would not have maintained a proper balance. Labour 'Vote No' campaigners had complained that while the Labour party, the Scottish Nationalists and the Liberals would be urging a yes vote, the only party calling for a no would be the Tories. The BBC is said to be considering the implications of the ruling before making a decision on its broadcasts. Labour MP Leo Abse said that he would be contacting both television organizations to seek assurances that no party political broadcasts on the referendum would be made in Wales.

RETURN OF THE PROPHET

His hour of glory had come. After 15 embittered years in exile, Ayatollah Ruhollah Khomeini was home and an almost frightening power pulsated from him as, hands raised in prayer, he acknowledged the adulation of the millions. There was a frenzy on a scale unparalleled as 78-year-old Khomeini was driven through a seething mass of humanity. Tehran, which has seen intolerable bloodshed in recent days, could witness even more now that Khomeini has returned, determined to oust Premier Bakhtiar.

SURGEONS SPLIT OVER FIRST TUBES TRANSPLANT

2 surgeons were in disagreement last night over Britain's first Fallopian tubes transplant. Mr Peter Silverstone, who revealed that he had carried out the operation last October, suggested that it heralded new hope for childless women but one of the world's leading gynaecologists, Mr Robert Winston, said the technique used would not result in pregnancy. At least 9 previous Fallopian tube transplants worldwide have been unsuccessful. Mr Winston said the technique involved connecting the tubes and surrounding tissue but not the blood vessels. He was now preparing to carry out a transplant which would also connect the complex network of veins and arteries, believing the blood supply to be vital in establishing pregnancy.

Elaine Paige rehearses the part of the dying Evita.

WORLD'S BIGGEST CASINO FRAUD

The biggest casino fraud in history has been uncovered in the South of France. Interpol issued warrants for the arrest of up to 30 people after French police played thousands of make-believe games of roulette on computer in an attempt to justify mathematically the extraordinary luck of certain gamblers. They discovered that at the Siesta Club in Antibes tiny screws holding in place the partitions between the slots designating each number had been loosened slightly. The added suppleness given to the partitions had a tiny but important effect, allowing gang members to win huge sums when they consistently bet on a certain block of numbers.

A 'HOLY CAVALRY' RESCUES US EMBASSY

Ambassador William Sullivan surveyed his bullet-riddled American embassy in Tehran last night (14 February) and declared that it had been 'an interesting St Valentine's Day'. He had witnessed an invasion of US territory by Iranian guerillas, been physically abused and then rescued by followers of Ayatollah Khomeini. The guerillas, opposed to the creation of an Islamic republic, claimed they believed secret service agents were hiding in the embassy. Following the attack, in which 3 of the assault force were shot dead, US officials consulted the Iranian Government over the evacuation of Americans still in the country.

MAR 1979

POLL DISASTER FOR LABOUR

The devolution time bomb exploded in the Prime Minister's face yesterday (2 March) and left him at the mercy of Enoch Powell. The votes of the 7 Ulster Unionist MPs, who obey Mr Powell's commands, have now become Mr Callaghan's lifeline as he tries to weather the stunning rebuff from Scotland and Wales. Only a third of Scots voted for self-government – well below the 40% of the total electorate required under the Scotland Act – and all 8 Welsh counties gave a resounding no. The results were: Scotland – 33% yes; 31% no; 36% did not vote. Wales – 12% yes; 47% no; 41% did not vote. Devolution is now virtually dead; the big question is whether it will also mark the demise of the Callaghan Government.

BRADY IS PLAYERS' NO. 1

Liam Brady has been named Players' Footballer of the Year, beating Leeds and England mid-field star Tony Currie into second place with Spurs' Osvaldo Ardiles third. Honours in the Young Players' section went to West Bromwich Albion's Cyrille Regis, followed by team-mate Laurie Cunningham and Crystal Palace's Ken Sansom. Brady and Regis, born in French Guyana, are the first players from outside the United Kingdom to receive the awards.

EVERYBODY HISS

The nasty, good-for-nothing son of the landed gentry – that's dastardly Mark Russell, played by Steven Grives in ITV's *Flambards* – marks the return of the rotter who, amazingly, earns the admiration of millions. He is in the great British tradition of bullying braggarts that began with Flashman, the monster who roasted fags for fun in *Tom Brown's Schooldays*. With the possible exception of *The Forsyte Saga's* Soames, it is a tradition that has rarely been exploited by television. We have had Anthony Valentine as the loathsome Major Mohn in *Colditz*; currently there is JR in the American soap, *Dallas*, played by Larry Hagman.

The cult that has largely been ignored for so long has brought fame and fortune to George MacDonald Fraser, whose six *Flashman* novels are bestsellers in America. 'The interesting thing is, the further north you go, the more popular he is,' says the author. 'I suppose Flashman and the other rotters are pagan characters; they lack the Christian virtues of honour, fair play, charity towards the weak; they bully and brag just like the Anglo Saxons did . . .'

GOODBYE MALTA

A fireworks display tomorrow (31 March) will signal the end of 180 years of history in which British forces and the Maltese islanders shared the defence of the world's most natural fortress. HMS *London* will slip quietly away as Prime Minister Dom Mintoff has firmly told Her Majesty's Forces to find themselves somewhere else to defend.

Above: Mary Crosby and Larry Hagman in Dallas.
Miners leader Joe Gormley chats with his son Frank (right), who played a big part in the rescue operation that followed an explosion at Golborne pit, near Wigan.

Smiles all round outside the White House after the signing of the Middle East peace treaty (l to r) Egypt's President Anwar Sadat, President Carter and Israeli Prime Minister Menachen Begin.

'THE BOSS' FLEES SUN ISLE COUP

Left-wing rebels yesterday (13 March) overthrew the Government of the Commonwealth Caribbean island of Grenada. Prime Minister Sir Eric Gairy, known as 'the Boss' because of his rigid rule, has fled to New York and called on Britain and America to send in troops. The coup was led by lawyer Maurice Bishop and the new Government is expected to seek support from Cuba, but will not outwardly adopt Communism for fear of damaging the tourist industry. Sir Eric had controlled Grenada for almost 25 years and led the island to independence from Britain in 1974.

'ALL OUT' ALERT IN NUCLEAR LEAK

A radiation leak at a power plant yesterday (28 March) plunged Pennsylvania into a major nuclear scare. A state of emergency was declared as 500 workers were evacuated at the Three Mile Island plant near Harrisburg. Contingency plans to evacuate 10,000 people living a mile away were drawn up but the population was said to be in no immediate danger. Ironically, the emergency comes at a time when the controversial anti-nuclear film *The China Syndrome* is playing to packed houses. The film deals with just such an emergency and subsequent cover-up.

Mel Gibson stars in Mad Max.

THE MAN WHO THINKS ROUND CORNERS

Edward De Bono is the man who coined the phrase 'lateral thinking'. He believes his puzzles and games are fun and exercise our minds in ways that can be usefully applied to more relevant matters. It allowed him to think up the concept of the ventilated filter many years before it was marketed. He simply used to prick his cigarettes with an increasing number of pin holes so that he breathed in less and less smoke. Mayor Lindsay of New York once put the problem of traffic congestion to him. De Bono's suggestion was to encourage car sharing by giving each owner a free parking disc for a specific day. Another of his suggestions was free parking at meters as long as the car's lights were left on, so assuring very short stays. The latest of De Bono's 18 books, entitled *Future Positive*, is published this week.

500 FEARED DEAD AS KURD BATTLE RAGES

Heavy fighting has continued on the streets of Sanandaj and the death toll in this Kurdish city's war among Muslims has been put unofficially at 500 in just 3 days. Iranian Army troops have been besieged there for several days and the 'Voice of the Revolution' radio in Tehran claimed that the forces attacking the garrison were 'counter-revolutionaries'. The guerillas, who are fighting for their independence, have denied the claim. With Ayatollah Khomeini belonging to the Shi'ite sect of Islam while the Kurds are almost all of the rival Sunni branch, the prospects for peace appear bleak.

HOT ROCK POWER HOPE

Big cities could soon be using cheap power from the earth's core. Scientists at Harwell believe they have found vast reserves of hot water deep underground in some parts of Britain. A scheme to drill more than 2 miles below Southampton city centre has already been approved.

PUNCH-UP BLACKS OUT TV SHOW

The BBC show on which Britain's entry for the Eurovision Song Contest was to be chosen was wrecked when 200 technicians walked out. They were demanding the reinstatement of a colleague suspended following a fight in which a BBC executive was injured. The 12 entries, of which the Nolan Sisters were favourites, had to be played on tape to judges in the 14 BBC regional studios instead. The result: a relatively unknown Yorkshire group called Black Lace will represent Britain in Jerusalem on 31 March with a song called 'Mary Anne'.

MORK FEVER

Happy Days' producer/director Jerry Paris was desperate. Several top comedians had turned down the role of a visiting alien and he wearily auditioned the umpteenth bit-part performer mumbling, 'Think you can sit down like an alien would?' When Paris looked up, the unknown was balanced on his head, twanging his braces and spouting gibberish. That unknown was 26-year-old Robin Williams, and so successful was the *Happy Days* guest part as Mork from Ork that a spin-off series featuring the alien was created. *Mork and Mindy* – one of the biggest impact shows in American broadcasting history – was born. Now Britain is catching *Mork* fever with kids chanting, 'Nannu Nannu,' while adults, too, chuckle at the show's zaniness.

Mr Airey Neave MP is killed when a bomb rips his car apart as he is leaving the underground car park at the House of Commons.

PORRIDGE STAR FOUND DEAD

Television star Richard Beckinsale was found dead at his home yesterday (19 March). The 31-year-old actor who played Ronnie Barker's cell mate in the comedy series *Porridge* is believed to have had a heart attack.

ACTOR SEEKS HALF OF BIONIC WOMAN'S CASH

Actor Michael Brandon is demanding half of Bionic Woman Lindsay Wagner's 'substantial' fortune in a divorce suit. Under Californian law a 50–50 split of communal property is automatic in divorce cases, but this time it is the husband who is seeking 'a fair share'.

Rising Damp stars (l to r) Richard Beckinsale as Alan, Leonard Rossiter as Rigsby, Frances de la Tour as Ruth, and Don Warrington as Phillip.

APR 1979

EXTREMISTS GO TO WAR ON POLICE

A man died early today (24 April) after being injured during last night's riots in the West London suburb of Southall. The rioting centred round protests against an election meeting held by the National Front in Southall Town Hall in the middle of perhaps the most concentrated Asian community in Britain. The man who died was a schoolteacher in his thirties, Blair Peach, a New Zealander and a member of the Anti-Nazi League. Police said they were treating the case as a suspicious death.

PLAY IT STRAIT

After the excesses of the Sex Pistols and the Stranglers, America has rapidly become disenchanted with New Wave music. It seems a bad time for one of Britain's best new bands, Dire Straits, to make its attack on the US market. But the group's gimmick-free, exciting rock and roll has proved enormously successful, its 'Sultans of Swing' single and album reaching the Top Twenty on both sides of the Atlantic. The album has sold 4 million copies, generating around £10m; it was made for just £14,000, compared with £75,000 for a typical LP. Theirs is a classic rags-to-riches story: 20 months ago they were all struggling and out of work, living together in an £8-a-week London flat.

NEW MISS MARPLE

Award-winning actress Angela Lansbury is to star in *The Mirror Crack'd*, the third in EMI's big budget movies of the Agatha Christie whodunnits. The first, *Murder on the Orient Express*, starring Albert Finney, is the most successful picture ever produced with only British money. Last year's *Death on the Nile*, starring Peter Ustinov, looks set to be equally popular. Now Lord Delfont's company hopes to keep the money spinning with Dama Agatha's own favourite fictional creation and with Miss Lansbury, who is the granddaughter of George Lansbury, one of the founders of the Labour party.

LEYLAND GOES JAPANESE

British Leyland is negotiating with the Japanese Honda company to manufacture a middle-range car. The move is aimed at propping up BL's own struggling middle-range models – in particular the Dolomite – until a replacement, code-named LC 10, can be launched in about 3 years' time.

HOW A TYRANT'S CITY WAS TAKEN

Tanzanian troops marched into Kampala yesterday (11 April) to be met, not with guns, but flowers and kisses. Delighted residents saw the capture of the Ugandan capital as an end to the 8-year brutal reign of Idi Amin, who is believed to have fled to Jinja, the country's second-largest town.

Anyone for squash? (L to r) Jasper Carrott, Bernie Clifton and Leonard Rossiter at Wembley.

RIOTING SPREADS AS BHUTTO DIES

Police broke up riots in Rawalpindi yesterday (4 April) as a crowd chanted 'Death to Zia' – Pakistan's military ruler General Zia Ul-Haq – in protest against the Zulfikar Ali Bhutto. From his cell Bhutto had warned that his death would mean 'a conflagration' throughout the country. Worldwide pleas for clemency, including appeals from all 5 of Britain's prime ministers in the past 20 years, were ignored.

CHINA IN GAMES

China is back in the Olympics, following the International Olympic Committee's meeting in Montevideo. The 36–28 vote in China's favour came after Peking delegates said they would no longer oppose Taiwan's participation in the Games.

'BUTCHERS' RAVE OVER CONTI

Tom Conti has soared to international stardom after winning rave reviews for his Broadway début in *Whose Life Is It Anyway?* playing a paralysed road-accident victim, fighting for the right to die. He already had a cult following in the United States after TV screened *The Glittering Prizes* and *The Norman Conquests* but now the critics, the so-called 'Butchers of Broadway', and ordinary play-goers alike are acclaiming a performance in which he lies motionless on a hospital bed for 2 hours. The actor can enjoy the triumph for only 6 months, however. American Equity opposed his original selection and blacklisted him. The union lost the subsequent arbitration ruling but insisted that Conti be replaced by an American actor within 6 months.

I WAS PAID IN BRITAIN – STONES

Dwight Stones, the former world high-jump record holder, claims that he was given 'under the table' payments for appearing at British meetings. Stones is determined to expose 'shamateurism' in athletics, and there is to be an investigation of the allegations. But the way for athletics to rid itself of illegal payments is to follow the example of tennis by declaring itself open and paying star athletes their market value.

Pop singer Joe Jackson in the charts with his first album Look Sharp.

WHITE TIPPED FOR RECORD

Jimmy White, Tooting's 16-year-old snooker prodigy, goes to Helston, Cornwall hoping to break a record that had looked likely to last for ever. He plays Dave Martin in the final of the English Amateur Snooker Championship and, if he wins, he will become the youngest ever champion. Present holder is Rex Williams, now world professional billiards champion, who took the title in 1951 at the age of 17. Shortly after Williams' win, the minimum age for the championship was raised to 18; it was restored to 16 for this year's event.

'LIFE SUPPORT' CASE MAKES HISTORY

A man appeared in court yesterday (26 April) accused of murdering Carol Wilkinson, who was found unconscious after being attacked in October 1977. 60 hours later she was pronounced dead when doctors switched off a life-support machine. In a case that could make legal history an inquest jury has decided that she had been murdered by her attacker, which meant that her death was not attributed to the withdrawal of life support.

SMITH VOTES TO END WHITE RULE

In Salisbury's Rhodes Memorial Hall yesterday (19 April) Ian Smith cast his vote to give a black man the job he has held for 15 years. The man who vowed black majority rule would never arrive in '1,000 years' said he was pleased with the turnout – some 48% had already voted by halfway through the 5-day election in spite of threats of an African boycott. The terrorists who vowed to wreck the event have either abandoned their intention or bowed to the undeniable African desire to vote in a leader of their choice.

LUCINDA TAKES RECORD

Lucinda Prior-Palmer, riding Killaire, won the Badminton Horse Trials for a record fourth time yesterday (22 April).

SHOT – BUT NO ONE DARE BURY HIM

The bullet-riddled body of former premier Amir Abbus Hoveyda lies in a sealed room in Tehran's forensic medical institute. No friend or relative has yet dared to claim it and authorities at the city cemetery have refused to bury a man who, according to the Islamic court which sentenced him to death, 'declared war on God'. Hoveyda was the Shah's right-hand man for 13 years and his execution (7 April) has provoked worldwide revulsion.

WATT A CHAMP!

Jim Watt is world lightweight champion. At 32, an age when most boxers have retired, Watt gave a performance Glasgow will always remember last night (17 April), stopping Alfredo Pitalua in the twelfth round.

THE PARTY STARTING FROM SCRATCH

The man who founded Britain's newest political force was out among his livestock yesterday, practising what he will be preaching to the voters. Mr Tony Whittaker and his wife were successful solicitors before they fell for the Green revolution and launched the Ecology party. They sold their thriving law firm in Coventry in favour of 20 acres of Somerset countryside and the cause of self-sufficiency. Mr Whittaker hopes to become an MP by unseating former Liberal leader Jeremy Thorpe from his North Devon constituency. He has, he admits, little chance of winning, though all revolutions have to begin somewhere. He is one of 59 candidates of the Ecology party whose manifesto includes recycling and preservation of the earth's resources. The party hierarchy is working on a TV political broadcast in which it hopes to feature a cartoon character called Eco-man.

Uganda's President Amin ready to do battle with the invading Tanzanian forces.

DAY BY DAY

1 Apr
Iran is declared an Islamic republic by the Ayatollah Khomeini.

6 Apr
Reform of the House of Lords, a reduction in income tax, increased public spending and revision of the EEC Common Agricultural Policy are some of the points in the Labour party's election manifesto.

10 Apr
A British Rail high speed passenger train breaks a world record on the 94-mile journey from Paddington to Chippenham with a time of 50 minutes 31 seconds.

11 Apr
The Conservative party's election manifesto includes a cut in income tax, revision of the laws relating to trade union picketing, closed shops and government money to help pay for secret ballots, and denationalization of the shipbuilding and aerospace industries.

13 Apr
Mr Yusuf Lule is sworn in as the new President of Uganda.

16 Apr
2 passenger trains crash outside Paisley station near Glasgow, killing both drivers and 5 passengers.

22 Apr
Tanzanian forces capture Jinja, 50 miles from Kampala, where some troops loyal to Idi Amin had been holding out.

23 Apr
Lord Hunt, leader of the 1953 Everest Expedition, and Sir Paul Hasluck, former Governor-General of Australia, are appointed Knights of the Garter.

24 Apr
Bishop Abel Muzorewa's United African National Council wins 51 of the 72 African seats in Rhodesia's internal elections.

26 Apr
Europe's first jetfoil, the *Normandy Princess*, makes its inaugural trip from Brighton to Dieppe in 100 minutes.

27 Apr
The United States releases 2 convicted Russian spies in exchange for 5 Soviet dissidents, including Alexander Ginsburg and Edward Kuznetsov.

30 Apr
London Underground's new line, the Jubilee, is opened by the Prince of Wales.

PRUNELLA STILL HAS WHAT IT TAKES

At 63 Prunella Stack is still beautiful and lithe, a living tribute to the League of Health and Beauty exercises which she has practised religiously since she was 5. When she was 19 she was known throughout England as 'the perfect woman' – every girl in the 30s wanted to be like her. At 20 she headed the movement she and thousands of others believed in. Prunella recently led a course for a hundred League teachers training for the Jubilee celebration next spring.

MAY 1979

MAGGIE'S MEN FOR THE 80s

Mrs Thatcher has given government jobs to a group of Tory high-fliers picked out for possible stardom in the 80s. Among the more significant choices were: Nigel Lawson, 47, a former editor of the *Spectator*, as Financial Secretary to the Treasury; Leon Brittan, 39, barrister and former Tory spokesman on devolution, as Home Office Minister of State; Douglas Hurd, 49, former diplomat, thriller writer and Political Secretary to Edward Heath, as Foreign Office Minister of State; and Adam Butler, 47, son of Lord 'Rab' Butler, as Industry Minister of State.

THE BABY WHO MADE HISTORY

A healthy baby girl has been born to 29-year-old Mrs Margaret Martin in Auckland, New Zealand, though her survival is miraculous. Mrs Martin had a complete hysterectomy 8 months ago but must have had a newly fertilized egg in her body, doctors believe. The egg survived the operation and lodged into Mrs Martin's intestines, where it was nourished by the bowel's blood supply. A spokesman said that, although women without wombs had become pregnant, no foetus had ever survived before and it would probably never happen again.

Margaret Thatcher the new Prime Minister, with husband Denis at the entrance of Downing Street.

THE STAR WHO DROPPED A FAMILY BRICK

To most people in Britain the name Rossi is synonymous with ice cream jingles. To rock fans, however, the name is immediately associated with another kind of music – hard-driving pop. Intriguingly, the 2 are related. Francis Rossi, the inspiration behind Status Quo, is also a member of the Rossi ice cream family. His parents were sure he would follow into the family business but instead of taking out an ice cream van of his own, he spent his money on a guitar and it baffled everyone. Rossi says his family still thinks he made the wrong decision and is waiting for him to come to his senses. Rossi's father, Alberto, started the business after coming to Britain from Italy with his early partner, Charles Forte.

MAKE WAY FOR MACHINES, MISS SMITH

It is the typing pool versus the machine in offices today and the typists are losing. More and more bosses are ditching Miss Smith in favour of word processors. Already 30,000 jobs have gone in the big switch to the machines which are intelligent typewriters, able to memorize information, deal with large numbers of standard letters and handle office jobs like filing. They use the 'silicon chip' micro-circuit.

PICKFORD, THE FIRST SUPERSTAR, DIES

Mary Pickford, Hollywood's first screen darling, died last night (29 May) in Santa Monica hospital, California, aged 86. She made her first film in 1909 and the peak of her popularity came during the First World War, when she sold £2.5m worth of war bonds to Americans in a single day. She was once married to Douglas Fairbanks Snr and later married a co-star of several of her pictures, Buddy Rogers, who was at her bedside when she died. For the last 15 years she and her husband had lived a reclusive lifestyle at their lavish Beverly Hills home, called Pickfair. Although famous as 'America's Sweetheart', Miss Pickford was born in Canada in 1893. She was making more than £10,000 a week at the peak of her career and was the first woman to gain power in Hollywood when, in 1919, she became one of its 'Big 4' by forming United Artists along with Fairbanks, Charlie Chaplin and director D.W. Griffiths.

Arsenal's Alan Sunderland wheels away in jubilation after scoring the last gasp FA Cup winner against Man. Utd.

Diane Keaton and Woody Allen in Manhatten.

RELUCTANT HANDYMAN IS DIY MILLIONAIRE

David Quayle confesses to being nervous about changing a tap washer. But that hasn't stopped his becoming the nation's do-it-yourself king and a paper millionaire. It all began when the firm Mr Quayle worked for in the 60s sent him to Belgium, where he was impressed by the huge DIY self-service warehouses. Together with his brother-in-law Richard Block he formed a company in 1970 with capital of £80. B & Q was born.

The Jam backstage at The Rainbow in London.

£5m FOR ATOM WOMAN'S DEATH

A staggering £5,250,000 in damages was awarded yesterday (18 May) to the family of a girl who suffered through an atomic plant's negligence. The Federal Court of Oklahoma City found the Kerr-McGee Nuclear Corporation liable for the plutonium poisoning of 28-year-old laboratory technician Karen Silkwood. The case has sinister undertones, for Ms Silkwood, a union activist concerned with hazards at the now closed Cimarron plant in Oklahoma, was killed in a mysterious road crash in November 1975 while on her way to give a *New York Times* reporter documentary evidence on safety breaches and missing plutonium. Her body was found in the wreckage but the papers were missing. Local police decided that she had fallen asleep at the wheel, yet an accident expert hired by her family was convinced her car had been rammed by another vehicle. A week before her mysterious death, Ms Silkwood found that she herself had been contaminated by plutonium.

Stan Ogden is 57 today and he's not too pleased about it. Bernard Youens plays Stan, Jean Alexander is Hilda and Geoffrey Hughes is Eddie in Coronation Street.

THE SICKEST CRICKET EVER

Somerset captain Brian Rose defied a fair play plea from Lord's yesterday (24 May) and took a decision that made a mockery of one of Britain's knock-out competitions. He was warned over his plan to declare after only 1 over of the Benson & Hedges tie at Worcester to preserve Somerset's striking rate and guarantee it a place in the quarter finals. Worcestershire was allowed to win by 10 wickets, though its passage into the next stage of the competition will depend on other results. Angry Worcestershire officials refunded gate money after a game lasting only 20 minutes. Rose put the blame squarely on those who made the rules.

RAMPTON: POLICE CALLED IN

Police are to investigate allegations of torture and brutality to patients by staff at Rampton maximum security hospital in Nottinghamshire. The allegations are made in a Yorkshire TV documentary called *The Secret Hospital*, the first part of which is to be shown tonight (22 May).

IN STEP TOWARDS A SAFE WORLD

America and the Soviet Union have agreed to limit the nuclear arms race. Under the Strategic Arms Limitation Treaty (SALT 2), both sides will limit their intercontinental bombers and missiles to 2,400 until 1981 and then reduce that number to 2,250 until the agreement expires in 1985.

ARABS ARREST DEATH PARTY DOCTOR

A British girl plunged to her death from a fifth-floor window during a drinking party in Saudi Arabia where alcohol is forbidden. A young Dutchman who fell with her was impaled on railings below and also died. More than 20 guests, including an English doctor and his wife, were arrested under the anti-drink laws after the party last Saturday night (19 May). It was held at a flat near the Barbahksh Hospital in Jeddah, where the dead girl, 23-year-old Helen Smith from Yorkshire, worked as a nurse. Last night her family was trying to piece together her last hours.

A new folk hero for Llanelli, World Professional Snooker Champion Terry Griffiths.

JUNE 1979

JOHN WAYNE DIES

Since the film that finally won him an Oscar 10 years ago, the kind of battle John Wayne put up against disease has been described as 'true grit'. Like the cancer-stricken gunman J.B. Brooks he portrayed in his last film, *The Shootist*, he went out fighting yesterday (12 June).

TOURISTS IN BOMB TERROR

More bombs exploded on the Spanish holiday coast yesterday (29 June) as thousands of British tourists – targets of a terrorist campaign meant to scare them off – were flying to the Mediterranean sunshine. So far there have been no casualties but the Basque separatist group ETA is threatening more bombs unless the Spanish Government withdraws riot police from outside a prison near Madrid and transfers 100 Basque prisoners to jails in their homeland.

LAST STRAW AT LITTLE BIG HORN

Staring over the Black Hills of Dakota yesterday (14 June), Chief Elijah Whirlwind Horse refused to celebrate what any paleface would call the Red Indians' greatest triumph since Custer's Last Stand. More than a century after the rout at Little Big Horn, a United States court has awarded the Sioux nation about £50m for tribal land grabbed by President Ulysses S. Grant in 1877. But Whirlwind Horse, whose ancestors fought Custer's cavalrymen, did not regard it as a victory. With the case running for around 50 years it was the lawyers who would benefit; each Indian on the reservation would only receive about £900, he said. In 1863 the US Government signed a treaty with the Sioux, giving them the Black Hills area. 7 years later a Custer expedition found gold and President Grant hoped to blackmail the Sioux into allowing the prospecting rush by threatening to withhold vital food. Instead the Indians rose.

NOW HEAR ME, RUSSIA

From the heart of Communist Poland Pope John Paul II yesterday (3 June) spoke over the heads of his reluctant hosts to their masters in Russia. Abandoning his prepared speech and self-restraint he went on the political offensive with a plea for freedom. He said, 'There are Eastern ways and there are Western ways, and for 1,000 years we Poles have elected the Western ways.'

KINNOCK GETS TOP FRONT-BENCH JOB

Mr Callaghan has announced a major promotion for a young Labour left-winger. Mr Neil Kinnock, MP for Bedwellty, has been appointed Opposition Spokesman on Education with no previous front-bench experience. The 37-year-old Tribunite was elected last year to Labour's powerful National Executive.

THE RACE THAT GAVE THE WORLD A NEW WORD

Preparations are well under way for the 200th running of the Epsom Burberry. It might have been so named if the twelfth Earl of Derby had not won the toss of a coin against his old friend and racing rival Sir Charles Burberry. In 2 centuries the Derby has become not only a legend but a word. A young colt will on Wednesday, become an immortal name in the gallery of international sport. In just over 2.5 minutes he will have earned for his owner about £100,000, all because of a freakish groundswell of public rapture which turned the eighteenth-century equivalent of a pub bet into the Blue Riband of the racing calendar. The race has its own folklore: Running Rein, which won until he was discovered to be a 4-year-old; Mahmoud, winner of the fastest race (2 minutes 33.8 seconds); and Little Wonder, the smallest winner (14 hands 3¼ inches). Everyone seems to be agreed that Sea Bird was the greatest winner of all time.

Soap stars , literally

VORSTER TOPPLED

South Africa's President John Vorster resigned in disgrace yesterday (4 June), toppled by the biggest scandal in the country's history. He was found to have been involved in the bizarre 'Muldergate' affair, in which £45m of tax-payers' money was misappropriated. Premier P.W. Botha has reacted by introducing legislation to restrict investigation of government malpractices – the country's first blatant act of press censorship. The scandal, named after Information Minister Connie Mulder, involved the secret funding of a newspaper set up to support the Government, the bribing of foreign politicians and the establishment of 'front' organizations overseas to lobby for South Africa and its apartheid policies.

Norman Scott leaving the Old Bailey.

FREEDOM

Jeremy Thorpe won the 12 most vital votes of his life yesterday (22 June) – those of the jury which found him not guilty of conspiracy and incitement to murder. The verdict came 31 days after the trial began and 18 years after Jeremy Thorpe first met a male model called Norman Scott. In the most sensational political trial of the century David Holmes, John Le Mesurier and George Deakin were also acquitted of conspiracy to murder.

TV ENDS DOUBLING UP ON SPORT

The BBC and ITV have agreed not to screen the same sporting events on both channels at the same time. The deal marks the end of a 10-year battle over simultaneous coverage of major events which has infuriated some viewers, particularly women. The agreement came after the Football League accepted a £10m offer from the BBC and ITV to take turns in screening Saturday-night soccer. The 2 channels said they would extend co-operation to coverage of the Moscow Olympics, the European Football Championship next year and the World Cup in Spain in 1982. 2 matches will be shown simultaneously, however, the World Cup Final and the European Cup.

GOLFER SLIPS UP

Suzanne Parker, a former England girl golfer, wrote herself into the record books yesterday, much to her disgust. She took 45 strokes for the first 9 holes in the Carlsberg Women's Professional Tournament at Wolverhampton but, unfortunately, put that figure in the space provided for the ninth-hole score. Because the golfing authorities are such sticklers for the rules, the score for that hole must stand and her total for the round is an embarrassing 121.

THE CAR THAT'S MADE TO LAST FOR EVER

The car that lasts for ever is about to be made. It will not rust, will never need painting and, provided the engine can stand it, the car should run and run. The De Lorean will be air-conditioned, have a rear-mounted Renault V6 engine and tail panels that will swell back into shape if depressed. It is planned as a gull-winged 2-seater 120-m.p.h. sports car with a stainless steel chassis onto which is mounted a glass fibre one-piece bodyshell, which is then hung with stainless steel panels. The car is being made near Belfast with £53m of tax-payers' money. Although this means that every man, woman and child has, effectively, given £1 to the project, it is for export only. The man behind it – 54-year-old American John De Lorean, a former vice-chairman of General Motors – claims the British tax-payers will not lose out. A royalty of £185 per car is to be paid to the Government on each of the first 60,000 vehicles produced and £45 per car thereafter.

HELP AT THE TOUCH OF A BUTTON

Rubber Duck here, watch out for Black Ice and 2 Smoky Bears . . . That's the type of conversation you could hear if American-style Citizen's Band radio were operating in Britain. It is illegal here at the moment. Operators give themselves codenames and have nicknames for things they dislike. Black Ice is a police radar trap and policemen are Smoky Bears, for example. The radios can transmit up to 1 mile in towns and about 15 miles in flat country areas. Now an estimated 30,000 illegal operators in Britain are forcing the Government to consider whether CB radio should be allowed here. In America drivers take delight in beating speed traps using CB; and the police are happy because drivers are slowing down to the nationally disliked and widely disobeyed 55-m.p.h. speed limit. If it does come here it will not be cheap: Blaupunkt is Europe's only manufacturer and its unit costs around £250 plus up to £50 fitting charge, though it does contain a unique HELP system that could become a life-saving emergency service throughout Europe in the 80s.

HOWE'S THAT!

Chancellor Sir Geoffrey Howe fulfilled Tory election promises yesterday (12 June) with a dramatic budget designed to set Britain on the way to a more-pay, low-tax, high-incentive society. He cut the basic rate of income tax from 33% to 30%, with the higher rate being reduced from 83% to 60%; VAT was increased to one standard rate of 15% from 8% or 12.5%.

DAY BY DAY

1 June
Rhodesia becomes the new State of Zimbabwe –Rhodesia. Mr Ian Smith, Rhodesian Prime Minister for the past 15 years, is appointed Minister without portfolio in Bishop Muzorewa's Cabinet.

The TCCB expels Somerset from the Benson & Hedges Cup following its 7-ball declaration against Worcestershire (24 May).

2 June
The Duke of Kent flies to Peking to open the British Energy Exhibition. It is the first visit by a member of the Royal Family to China.

4 June
A Roman glass cup dating from about AD 300 is sold at Sotheby's for £572,000.

5 June
Dr Donald Coggan announces that he will retire as Archbishop of Canterbury in January 1980.

6 June
The two-hundredth Derby is won by Troy at 6–1, ridden by Willie Carson.

7 June
Conservatives win 60 seats in the first direct elections to the European Parliament, Labour 17 and Scottish Nationalists 1. Less than a third of the electorate votes in the election.

8 June
Couturier and court dressmaker Sir Norman Hartnell dies, aged 77.

12 June
An American cyclist, Bryan Allen, makes the first man-powered flight across the Channel by pedalling the *Gossamer Albatross* from Folkestone to Cap Gris Nez in 2 hours 50 minutes.

18 June
President Carter and President Brezhnev sign the American–Soviet Strategic Arms Limitation Treaty in Vienna.

23 June
The West Indies wins the Prudential World Cup, beating England by 92 runs in the final at Lord's.

CARTER URGES SOMOZA TO GIVE UP

President Carter has sent an emissary on a secret mission to try to persuade General Anastasio Somoza to resign as ruler of Nicaragua. With the Sandinista guerillas claiming to scent victory in their long fight to topple the General, America has suddenly begun to worry about the 'serious' regional implications of a change of regime. Somoza, head of a dynasty that has run Nicaragua for 43 years, is said to be in a concrete bunker in his presidential compound, confident that his National Guardsmen will eventually rout the guerillas.

A gaggle of the top comedy writers and performers.

JULY 1979

Test-tube baby Louise Brown celebrates her first birthday.

Trevor Eve plays 'Private Ear' Eddie Shoestring with Doran Godwin as Erica Bayliss.

BUY HALF AND RENT HALF

Sweeping new rights for council tenants were announced last night (27 July) as part of a big scheme to change the housing system. The most far-reaching proposal revealed by Housing Minister Mr John Stanley is a scheme to give council tenants the chance to buy a share of their homes with the option to buy the council's share at a later date. The package also cuts through the red tape which has stopped tenants decorating the outsides of their homes. They will also be able to take in lodgers in under-occupied homes.

CHILD'S PLAY

It may take an Act of Parliament to plug a loophole in the traffic laws opened up by Barry Pamplin. Mr Pamplin has avoided paying parking fines totalling £400 because the registered owner of his car is his 6-year-old son and, under Section 16 of the Children's and Young Persons' Act 1963, no child under 10 can be prosecuted. Mr Pamplin made his son the owner after discovering that only the 'keeper' of a vehicle, as the 1974 Road Traffic Act calls him, is liable to pay parking fines.

KRAY DECLARED INSANE

Gangland killer Ronald Kray has been declared a paranoid schizophrenic and is to be transferred to Broadmoor Hospital. Kray, 45, and twin brother Reggie are at present in Parkhurst Prison on the Isle of Wight, serving life sentences for murder.

HUNT FOR ATOM RUBBISH DUMPS

The first moves to create nuclear rubbish dumps in Britain were made yesterday (24 July). Environment Secretary Mr Michael Heseltine named 15 areas which contain the right kind of geological formations in which highly radioactive waste could be buried. But he stressed it would take 10 years of research before any sites were finally chosen and he left open the option of burying waste at sea. At the moment it is stored in special tanks at Windscale, Cumbria. By 1990 a plan to manufacture glass blocks to contain the waste will be in operation. These would be stored in water- or air-cooled vaults for some years before they were suitable for disposal, said Mr Heseltine.

SCARGILL'S ATOM WAR

Plans to build 5 more nuclear power plants are expected to bring massive protests. The first shots came yesterday (1 July) from Mr Arthur Scargill, the favourite to take over the leadership of the miners' union. 'We think Mrs Thatcher's declaration is taking Britain towards a nuclear disaster. We are moving lemming-like towards a nuclear holocaust.' The nuclear expansion, to be announced by the Government next month, is aimed at providing half the nation's power needs by the end of the 80s. At the moment there are 11 nuclear power stations supplying 14% of our electricity. British plants are Advanced Gas Cooled Reactors but some feel expansion could go ahead faster by using the American Pressurized Water Reactor.

BRITAIN ACTS ON WHALES

Britain is to join the international Save the Whale movement. This week the Government will officially ban the importation of sperm-whale oil and join the ranks of those nations fighting to save the earth's largest mammal from extinction. Britain has been importing £1.5m worth of whale oil each year, used mainly by tanners to soften and shape leather, often for women's shoes and handbags. 1,000 whales are killed annually simply to supply Britain. Pressure for the ban, which has already been implemented by America and New Zealand, has been going on for months, culminating in a rally in London yesterday (8 July) attended by Colin Welland, Joanna Lumley, Christopher Timothy, Spike Milligan and David Bellamy. Pressure in the Soviet Union and Japan, the countries responsible for most whale killing, is expected to increase as a result of Britain's becoming the third nation to implement a ban.

LIVERPOOL PUTS ITS SHIRTS ON HITACHI

League champion Liverpool has set a new trend in football's crusade to attract sponsorship by agreeing to become the first League club to carry a brand name on players' shirts. A deal with Japanese electronics giant Hitachi could lead the way for every other League club to tap a rich vein of much-needed revenue. Liverpool will wear their Hitachi shirts next season but only in games that are not televised.

Sebastian Coe sets a new world 800m mark of 1 min 42.33 sec.

A violent end for Coronation Street's Ernie Bishop (Stephen Hancock).

OUT GOES CHRYSLER – BACK COMES A NAME FROM THE GOOD OLD DAYS

Cars made by Chrysler Europe are to be known as Talbots from now on. The firm is taking a 'unique, unifying and truly European' name once famed for advanced auto-engineering in both Britain and France. The name change has been ordered by Peugeot-Citroën, which took over Chrysler Europe a year ago, to avoid confusion with the Chrysler Corporation in America. The new name recalls a period of automobile history when there were 2 independent Talbot car firms – Clement-Talbot Ltd in Britain and Automobiles Talbot in France. Rootes took control of the British firm in 1935 and, more than 23 years later, Simca bought its French namesake. Chrysler in turn acquired Simca in the early 60s and took over Rootes in Britain in 1964.

STEEL: I WON'T BACK ABORTION CHANGE

Liberal Leader David Steel has attacked plans to tighten abortion laws. Mr Steel, sponsor of the 1967 Abortion Act, said he will not support Tory MP John Corrie's bill, which seeks to reduce the time limit for abortions from 28 to 20 weeks. This, complained Mr Steel, had no medical backing, though he would have supported a reduction in the limit to 24 weeks. The Liberal Leader agreed that there had been concern over recent abortions near the 28-week mark. His statement coincides with an anti-Corrie bill campaign launched yesterday (10 July) by women's groups.

IT'S DOWN UNDER

After 6 years in space *Skylab* streaked back to earth yesterday (11 July) and dumped most of its 80 tons of molten metal into a watery grave. But up to 1,000 pieces of the giant space station rained down on Australia, mostly in sparsely populated desert areas and there were no reports of injury or damage. After fears that it might come to earth over Canada or the US, a last radio command was given sending the 118-foot machine on a wobbling course to reduce the friction of the atmosphere and add 40 minutes and a few thousand miles to its life. Britain's last chance of being hit was over by 11 a.m. but a number of West Country holiday-makers stayed in caves until they were convinced *Skylab* was down.

BATTERED WIVES TO GET COMPENSATION

For the first time battered wives are to be able to claim compensation for their injuries. In a change to the 1973 Powers of Criminal Courts Act compensation for family violence will be considered as long as the offender has been prosecuted for the assault. Under the new rule, which starts on 1 October on an experimental basis, the Criminal Injuries Board must be satisfied that the perpetrator of the assault will not benefit from the award.

MAGGIE FACES CRISIS IN AFRICA

A major new crisis for the Commonwealth – and a challenge to Mrs Thatcher – has blown up over Rhodesia. It follows demands from 5 African front-line states that:

– Britain should draft a new constitution for Zimbabwe/Rhodesia to 'wipe out white privileges once and for all'.
– Prime Minister Abel Muzorewa should be disowned.
– exiled Nationalists Robert Mugabe and Joshua Nkomo should be brought into new talks on Rhodesia's future.

The demands come from Zambia's President Kaunda, President Nyerere of Tanzania, Sir Seretse Khama of Botswana, President Neto of Angola and Mozambique's President Machel. The most serious Commonwealth crisis since South Africa was forced to walk out in 1961 stems from resentment against the hidden white power in the Army, police, civil service and judiciary behind the Muzorewa Government.

Ian Dury in his £3-a-week flat overlooking The Oval.

RIDERS WHO ARE OUT OF TUNE WITH THE LAW

Speed-crazy 16-year-old motorcyclists are making a mockery of the law by fitting 'hot-up' parts imported from Italy. It is legal to import, sell and fit the DIY kits, which cost £80, but it is illegal for a 16-year-old to use them until he has passed his driving test. He is restricted to a 50 cc machine – a moped – with a maximum speed of 30 m.p.h. until he has passed a moped driving test. At 16 a rider can obtain only a provisional moped licence; he must be 17 to obtain a motor-cycle provisional licence, enabling him to ride machines up to 250 cc. Untrained riders caught on a 'hotted-up' moped are being warned that they risk 12 months' disqualification before they even pass their test.

MY WORDS!

It has taken 100 people 10 years to compile the new Collins English Dictionary. There are 162,000 entries; 'A' alone had almost a column of definitions: 'a letter or vowel; a dialect word for "have"; a musical note with a frequency of 440 hertz; a symbol for an angstrom unit,' etc., etc. There were West Indian English words (jump-up: a Caribbean party); West African English words (day-clean: just after dawn); Australian English words (coming the raw prawn: attempting deception). The earliest lexicographer was Robert Cawdray, who, in 1504, wrote *An Alphabeticall for the Use of Gentle Women and Other Unlearned Persons*. That was just a list of 'hard' words. In the 1720s Samuel Bailey compiled the first dictionary listing every word in the language. Collins had noted that no full-length dictionary had been published in Britain since the 30s.

You might think the operation would have been a solemn affair but it was 'an absolute madhouse', according to editor Patrick Hanks. 'Have you ever heard 2 philosophy editors quarrelling over the meaning of the word "good"? We had one argument that went on all morning.'

Daily Mail
TUESDAY, AUGUST 28, 1979   9p (CHANNEL ISLANDS 10p)

MOUNTBATTEN SPECIAL ISSUE

MURDER OF LORD LOUIS

Mountbatten and 15 soldiers killed by IRA

Earl Mountbatten, victim of Ireland's Murderous Monday

Daily Mail Reporters

IN a day of unparalleled horror in Ireland, Lord Mountbatten of Burma, the Queen's cousin, and 15 British paratroopers were murdered by the IRA.

The killings were cowardly and callous.

Lord Mountbatten died when a bomb planted on his converted fishing boat exploded half a mile off Co. Sligo on the West coast of the Irish Republic.

His 14-year-old grandson, the Hon Nicholas Brabourne, also died in the blast and so did his boatman, Paul Maxwell, also 15.

Lord Mountbatten's daughter, Lady Patricia Brabourne, 55, her husband Lord Brabourne, 54, the Dowager Lady Brabourne, 82, and Nicholas's twin brother, Timothy, also were on board and were taken to hospital.

Last night the two women and Timothy were seriously ill in a hospital intensive care unit. Timothy was believed to be in danger of losing an eye. Lord Brabourne was said to be badly hurt and in a general surgical ward.

The Provisional IRA said similar radio-controlled bombs were used to

Turn to Page Two Col. 1

End of a legend: Mountbatten's body is taken from the boat which brought it to shore

Turn to Page Two Col. 1

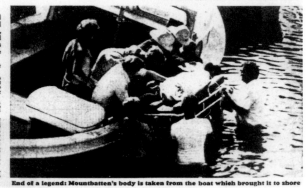

Lord Mountbatten died when a bomb planted on his converted fishing boat exploded half a mile off Co. Sligo on the West coast of the Irish Republic.

WANTED: £25,000 REWARD

Nazi hunter Simon Wiesenthal has for the first time put a price on a Nazi's head: £25,000 for SS doctor Josef Mengele. He said of the Auschwitz 'Angel of Death', 'He is number one on my most wanted list. . . Mengele is the most heinous of all the Nazis still at liberty and he must be found.' Paraguay has been Mengele's home for most of the time since the Second World War but the Supreme Court there has revoked his citizenship because he has been out of the country for more than 2 years. Mengele, now 68, is wanted in West Germany, which has extended its Statute of Limitations for war crimes, on charges of selecting 400,000 people, half of them children, for the gas chamber. He also performed bizarre experiments, including blinding prisoners while trying to change their dark eyes to 'Aryan' blue.

BRIGHTON BARES ALL

Brighton Council has agreed to have a nudist beach on the Sussex resort. For a trial period of 1 year, the British Naturist Council can go ahead with plans for a topless – and bottomless – beach east of Brighton's Palace Pier.

MASSACRE THREAT TO KURDS

Some 1,700 Iranian Revolutionary Guards, many disguised as Kurds, prepared last night (23 August) to attack Kurdish rebels who had earlier captured the town of Saqqez. Ayatollah Khomeini told the rebellious Kurds yesterday, 'If you continue your efforts against the people, you will suffer the consequences.' But outlawed Kurdish religious leader, Sheikh Ezzedin Hosseini, said, 'The Kurdish people will fight for their basic rights in a united Iran and will not stop for even a moment.'

Alec Guinness as George Smiley in the BBC's adaptation of John Le Carré's Tinker, Taylor, Soldier, Spy.

BEWARE OF KILLER HELMETS

The modern full-face helmet, as worn by over 1,000,000 motor-cyclists in Britain, could be a killer. Orthopaedic surgeon Mr Gordon Hadfield claims that many modern helmets are designed to fulfil riders' desires to imitate their heroes and not to protect them in accidents. He claims the helmets are so heavy they rotate the rider's head in a fall, increasing the risk of a broken neck. In 1 Surrey hospital in the past 18 months, 7 riders have been admitted dead, killed by their crash helmets. Investigations revealed that the chin area of their helmets broke on impact and jagged pieces of glass fibre stabbed them in the jugular vein or carotid artery, causing them to bleed to death.

PENALTY POINTS TO OUST TOTTING UP?

The Government is studying ways to introduce a penalty points system for motoring offences to help clear courts clogged by driving cases. Transport Minister Norman Fowler is looking at a German-style points system instead of the existing licence endorsements. At present, any motorist getting 3 endorsements within 3 years automatically loses his licence for 6 months, in addition to any disqualification for his third offence. In Germany the cases are virtually 'ticket offences' and a driver has to accumulate 18 points before he automatically loses his licence for 6 months. Speeding and jumping a red light carry a 2- or 3-point penalty, for example, while drunken driving carries 8 points – not enough to put a driver off the road automatically.

Guitarist Mark Knofler of Dire Straits in the charts with their second album Communique *after their first album became the fastest-selling debut album in the USA.*

A BITTER PILL FOR WOMEN'S LIB

A court yesterday (3 August) controversially defined the extra responsibility that a 70s girl takes on along with a supply of contraceptive pills and a liberated lifestyle. If she sleeps with a man then she, rather than he, is largely to blame if she becomes pregnant. At Ayr Sheriff Neil Sow QC awarded a young mother only £1 a week 'nominal maintenance' for her baby daughter against her former boyfriend. The decision has brought angry reactions from the National Council for One-parent Families, the National Women's Aid Federation and the Family Planning Association among others. A legal reaction came from Sir Melford Stevenson, a retired High Court judge, who said, 'This decision is quite fantastic; you can't apply contributory negligence to this sort of thing.'

SEBASTIAN THE GREAT

A story that a fiction writer would not dare risk became reality last night (15 August). Sebastian Coe broke the world 1,500 metres record in Zurich, his third world mark in 41 days, and put himself into the books as the greatest middle-distance runner the world has ever seen. His time was 3 minutes 32.03 seconds, 0.17 seconds faster than the mark set by Tanzanian Filbert Bayi at the Commonwealth Games in Christchurch in 1974.

FASTNET RACE OF DEATH

A sea disaster unparalleled in yachting history turned the Fastnet Race, the stern climax to Cowes Week, into awesome tragedy yesterday (14 August). Across hundreds of miles of ocean, some of the world's finest yachtsmen died or went missing in a sea whipped into frenzy by winds near hurricane force. In a matter of hours, many of the fleet of 335 boats were scattered, crippled or sunk. It was feared last night that the death toll could reach 30 or even higher. The Fastnet Race is the last of the 5 which decide the Admiral's Cup. It was first held in 1925 and has never before claimed a life.

MARS-BARRED

Sweet-toothed gelding No Bombs snatched a Mars bar from his stable boy on the way to the races and romped home by 8 lengths. But the horse then failed a routine dope test as traces of caffeine and theobromine were found and it has been revealed that the chocolate bar was to blame. Owing to the circumstances, the stewards waived what would have been a heavy fine but the disqualification stood. 'That's the most expensive Mars bar ever – it cost £4,064 in prize money,' said trainer Peter Easterby. A spokesman from the delighted Mars company confirmed that the 2 substances occurred naturally in all chocolate and, as they were mild stimulants, would make anyone run faster.

DAY BY DAY

1 Aug
Queen Elizabeth the Queen Mother is installed as Constable of Dover Castle and Lord Warden of the Cinque Ports, the first woman ever to hold the office.

4 Aug
South African Kevin Anderson becomes the youngest person to swim the English Channel. 24 hours later his record is broken by a boy from South London, Marcus Hooper, also 12 years old but 3 months younger than Kevin.

7 Aug
Increased bounty payments for volunteer reservists in the armed services are announced. The Territorial Army and Volunteer Reserve will also revert to its original title of Territorial Army.

8 Aug
Author Nicholas Monsarrat dies, aged 69.

9 Aug
For the second year running there is no award of the Bardic Chair at the National Eisteddfod at Caernarfon. The judges decide that the 13 entries submitted are not of sufficient merit.

14 Aug
Former Labour Minister John Stonehouse is released from prison on parole after serving just over 3 years of a 7-year sentence for theft, fraud and deception.

21 Aug
Essex wins the Schweppes County Cricket Championship for the first time.

24 Aug
A Russian jet is prevented from taking off for Moscow from New York because officials wish to make certain that Ludmila Vlasova Godunov, a prima ballerina with the Bolshoi, is returning of her own free will. Miss Vlasova's husband, Alexander Godunov, also a dancer with the Bolshoi, had earlier asked for political asylum. The aircraft is allowed to leave 3 days later after Miss Vlasova had convinced officials that she wished to return to the USSR.

27 Aug
18 soldiers die in bomb explosions when they are ambushed at Warrenpoint, Co. Down, the worst disaster for the Army in the 10 years it has been in Northern Ireland.

30 Aug
2 men, Francis McGirl from Co. Leitrim and Thomas McMahon from Co. Monaghan, are charged in Dublin with the murder of Earl Mountbatten.

The Caribbean island of Dominica is devastated by a hurricane. 1,000 people are killed.

DID MY TEAM WIN?

Heart-transplant patient Keith Castle came round from his operation with 1 big question on his lips, 'How did Fulham get on?' 52-year-old father of 4, Mr Castle, an artist from Wandsworth, was given the heart of 21-year-old Duncan Prestt, a golf professional who died in a car crash the day before the operation at Papworth Hospital, Cambridge. Mr Castle, whose operation was the sixth of its kind in Britain, received the good news when he awoke: Fulham had beaten Birmingham 4–3.

SEPT 1979

QUEEN TRACY

Tracy Austin became the youngest ever woman to win the US Open Tennis Championship when she beat 4-times winner Chris Lloyd in straight sets at Flushing Meadow yesterday (9 September). At 16 years 9 months she is 2 months younger than Mo Connolly when she won for the first time in the 50s.

'WOMEN WILL BECOME HOST MOTHERS'

Women could soon be bearing other women's children. There is no reason why a woman should not have an egg fertilized by her husband then implanted into another woman's womb, according to Mr Patrick Steptoe, Britain's test-tube baby pioneer. Mr Steptoe has said that he would carry out the delicate surgery on both host and donor mothers – but only for strictly medical reasons; he would not do so on purely social grounds. The technique would bring hope to thousands of women who are unable to bear children. Mr Steptoe admitted that there was still an element of science fiction about transferring an embryo from one woman to another; no one yet knew what the effect would be on the surrogate mother, who could be a close relative or complete stranger, when she had to hand over the baby she had borne.

Pope John Paul II at Drogheda during his historic visit to Ireland.

SHIRLEY DEFIES MILITANTS

Shirley Williams served notice on Labour's militant left yesterday that she would not be prepared to be an MP in a party dominated by their thinking. She singled out for particular attack the plans to make MPs liable to automatic re-election by their constituency parties. The proposal was an 'invitation to intimidation', she said. Mrs Williams, who lost her seat in the general election, also denounced proposals that the National Executive should draw up future manifestos, leaving the party leadership with no decisive voice and no veto.

THE THINKING CHILD'S MAGNUS PYKE

Johnny Ball is going to blow up his audience this afternoon. Children will find their chairs rising into the air as he explains how a hovercraft works. The *Play School* presenter has become a TV guru for children with *Think of a Number*, in which he has taken the traditionally dull subjects of mathematics and science and turned them into children's tea-time delights. As one small boy put it, 'He's the man who makes you feel numbers are friends.'

MAN WHO WILL HELP PUT MAGIC BACK INTO TALENT SHOWS

A Spanish magician from Morecambe with an act so clumsy that he makes Tommy Cooper look sophisticated will be unleashed on an unsuspecting public next month. The Great Soprendo will be one of 2,000 hopeful acts in *Rising Stars*, the show with a format which avoids the sneers of *New Faces* and the bogus condescending sincerity of *Opportunity Knocks*. Soprendo – alias Geoff Durham – is the boyfriend of Victoria Wood, probably Britain's most promising new playwright. Her recent ITV play *Talent* turned her into an overnight success as a writer and actress. Their approach to the talent-show business couldn't be more different: Victoria's play shows the seamy side of the talent market and she regards talent shows as the bottom of a hopeless pile of failure. Geoff, however, sees them as a ladder towards success.

MUSLIM MARRIAGE FOR CAT

Pop singer Cat Stevens is to marry a Turkish girl this week in an elaborate Muslim service at London's largest mosque in Regent's Park. Stevens, 31, embraced the Muslim religion 4 years ago and now calls himself Yusef Islam.

MODS MARCH BACK

The Mods, those clean-cut, parka-clad, Vespa-riding boys from the 60s, are back. With the success of The Who's film, *Quadrophenia*, the new Mods, with their shorn hair, sharp suits and Hush Puppies, are everywhere.

Fred Dibnah, steeplejack and demolition expert, gives an insight into his life and work.

READ THIS. . . AND FIND A TREASURE

Long after dark an unobserved artist, Kit Williams, set off on an extraordinary assignment – to bury gold and jewellery worth £5,000. Hidden somewhere in Britain, the treasure is today waiting to be found, and the key to its location lies in a remarkable fantasy called *Masquerade*. According to the publishers, the book's clues and riddles are as likely to be solved by a bright 10-year-old as an Oxford don.

POLISH DISSIDENTS FORM REBEL PARTY

Polish dissidents have announced the formation of a new political party in defiance of the Communists, who make up the only legal party in the country. The party – the Confederation of Independent Poland – is aimed at safeguarding the country's 'freedom and independence'. Launched at a rally in Warsaw to mark the fortieth anniversary of Hitler's attack on Poland which sparked off the Second World War, a spokesman said the party would be the first independent political movement to function openly there for more than 30 years.

THE SNEEZE FROM OUTER SPACE

There will be influenza showers over Cornwall with scattered measles over Wales – not a *Goon Show* script but a serious possibility if Sir Fred Hoyle is right. He believes that most diseases come, in the first place, from outer space, and are then scattered randomly by the weather. The eminent astronomer is not only telling doctors that they are looking for the origins of viruses in the wrong place, he is challenging the whole idea that we catch diseases from each other.

Other scientists have also been uneasy about the conventional theory. In an analysis published 3 years ago of the lethal 1917–19 flu epidemic, US doctor Louis Weinstein confessed himself astonished by the pattern. It was detected in Bombay and Boston on the same day, yet took 3 weeks to reach New York. In the 1948 flu epidemic in Sardinia, doctors identified cases where shepherds living in total isolation caught the disease at exactly the same time that it first appeared in neighbouring towns. Medical literature is full of such evidence, Hoyle declares.

ITALIAN BREAKS RECORD

Italy's Pietro Mennea set a world record of 19.72 seconds in the 200 metres at the World Student Games in Mexico City yesterday (12 September). His time clipped 0.11 seconds off the record set by America's Tommie Smith on the same track in the 1968 Olympic Games.

Terry (Dennis Waterman, right) works for wheeler-dealer Arthur (George Cole) in a new series, Minder, *soon to be broadcast.*

LAST POST FOR *REVEILLE*

Reveille, one of Britain's most popular weekly magazines, was 'killed' yesterday (7 September) because of a union dispute. The magazine was launched in 1940 for the armed forces, to whom it was free, under the patronage of Sir Winston Churchill.

OIL MAKES US ENVY OF WORLD

Britain has become self-sufficient in oil at least a year earlier than expected. However, half of the oil produced is exported as it is very light and of a particularly high quality; much of Britain's needs are for heavier crude oils which are cheaper. The effect of selling the quality oil and importing the cheaper grade is a dramatic boost to the country's balance of payments. By 1985 income from oil will reach almost £6,000m a year.

Sir James Goldsmith's Now! *magazine is launched.*

DAY BY DAY

2 Sept
Actor Sir Felix Aylmer dies, aged 90.

7 Sept
The Rt Revd Robert Runcie, Bishop of St Albans, is nominated to succeed Dr Donald Coggan as Archbishop of Canterbury in January 1980.

Actor Alan Browning, estranged husband of Pat Phoenix, dies, aged 53.

8 Sept
Somerset wins the Gillette Cup at Lord's and the next day becomes champion of the John Player League.

US actress Jean Seberg dies, aged 40.

10 Sept
The Rhodesia Constitutional Conference, under the chairmanship of Lord Carrington, opens at Lancaster House. Bishop Abel Muzorewa leads the delegation representing the Salisbury Government which includes Mr Ian Smith. Mr Nkomo and Mr Mugabe head the delegation representing the Patriotic Front.

11 Sept
A report by a committee, under the chairmanship of Dame Margaret Miles, enquiring into pregnancy at school, recommends that the law on age of consent which forbids sexual relations under the age of 16 should be repealed.

12 Sept
Sir Keith Joseph, Secretary of State for Industry, announces plans to split the Post Office into 2 separate corporations, one for postal and giro services and the other for telecommunications.

16 Sept
Nur Mohammad Taraki is overthrown as President of Afghanistan and the Prime Minister, Hafizullah Amin, takes over the presidency.

18 Sept
Inner London becomes the first local authority in Britain to outlaw the use of the cane. Its aim is to abolish all forms of corporal punishment from February 1981.

21 Sept
2 adults and a 2-year-old boy are killed when an RAF Harrier jump jet, after colliding in mid-air with another Harrier, crashes onto 3 houses at Wisbech in Cambridgeshire. Both pilots eject and parachute to safety.

Emperor Bokassa of the Central African Empire is deposed by his nephew David Dacko.

24 Sept
Representatives of the Patriotic Front agree to the British proposal that 20% of the seats in the Zimbabwe Parliament should be reserved for whites.

A civilian government takes over in Ghana after 7 years of military rule and Dr Hilla Limann is sworn in as President.

26 Sept
Mrs Sally Oppenheim, Minister of State for Consumer Affairs, says no more compulsory metrication orders will be made and it will be up to retailers to decide whether to sell their goods in metric or imperial measure.

27 Sept
In the Manchester Central by-election, caused by the elevation to the peerage of Mr Harold Lever, the seat is retained for Labour by Mr Robert Litherland.

Dame Gracie Fields dies at her home in Capri, aged 81.

OCT 1979

DRINKS ON MOTORWAYS

Drink is to be sold at motorway service areas, provided drivers have a meal as well. It is part of a government plan to sell its stake in motorway services to private enterprise. The decision, announced by Transport Minister Mr Norman Fowler, has provoked angry reaction from the police and the Royal Society for the Prevention of Accidents.

HOME IN ONE!

Isao Aoki played the richest stroke in golfing history at the Suntory World Matchplay Championship at Wentworth. The 37-year-old Japanese number 1 won himself a 2-bedroomed flat worth £55,000 for his hole-in-one at the Par 3 second hole. Bovis, who is doing the construction work, will not be losing out much, however – it insured against the loss by placing a £1,000 bet with Ladbrokes at 40–1.

ROLL OVER, BEETHOVEN

Paul McCartney was dubbed the most successful composer of all time yesterday (24 October). The 37-year-old singer was honoured by the *Guinness Book of Records* for achieving 3 major entries: he has written 43 songs which have sold more than a million copies, accumulated 60 gold discs and amassed sales of 100 million albums and 100 million singles. The book's editor Mr Norris McWhirter presented Paul with a disc sprayed with rhodium, one of the world's rarest metals, costing twice as much as platinum. Mr McWhirter pointed out that the award was a quantitative evaluation of recorded music and was not meant as a snub to classical composers. The work of Beethoven and Strauss was non-copyright so sales had never been audited, he said.

TEENAGER TAKES SQUASH TITLE

Jehangir Khan of Pakistan became the youngest ever winner of the world amateur squash title in Melbourne yesterday (15 October) and immediately set his country a problem. The championships now move to Brisbane for the team event and the 15-year-old, who was unseeded when he beat Britain's Phil Kenyon to take the title, is only on the Pakistani team sheet as second reserve.

CHEERS FOR CASTRO

Fidel Castro received a standing ovation from a fortress-like United Nations yesterday (12 October) when he took the podium in the General Assembly for the first time in 19 years. There was deafening applause when the Cuban leader accused Zionism and imperialism of committing against the Palestinians crimes which paralleled 'the genocide the Nazis visited on the Hebrew people'.

'CANCER COCKTAIL' KILLER

Brilliant scientist Steve Harper has been convicted in the world's first case of 'murder by cancer'. He poisoned 5 members of his ex-girlfriend's family with a cancer-causing additive used in rocket fuel. A court in Omaha, Nebraska, heard that jealousy drove Harper to mix the substance with lemonade and milk. 2 of the family did die, though not his ex-girlfriend, who had not drunk the lethal brew.

GREAT VIDEO BOOM SLIPS A DISC

Video cassette recorders may be an idea whose time has gone. Video discs could be the next great leap forward. Philips and Magnavox already have machines on trial in America; they should reach Britain in 1981. The video discs look like silver long-playing records and are played on machines which plug into the TV set. Though programmes cannot be recorded onto video discs, they are much cheaper than VCRs. The disc player costs £360 in the US, against £500 – £650 for a VCR. The discs themselves sell for about the same as an LP record, are almost indestructible and give a sound quality comparable to the best hi-fi equipment.

AWARD FOR COTTON

Henry Cotton yesterday (8 October) became the first British golfer to earn the coveted Walter Hagen award for services to the sport on both sides of the Atlantic. The 72-year-old former public schoolboy, who broke social conventions in the 20s by becoming a professional golfer, shares the award with Argentinian Roberto de Vicenzo.

The Pretenders are a new band receiving a lot of critical acclaim. Chrissie Hynde is their lead singer.

THE FORCE BEHIND POLICE

When the Police first appeared on TV they were playing not guitars but pinball machines in a brassière advertisement. Brutus Jeans and Wrigleys Spearmint Gum were other products with which they were associated as, 18 months ago, they seemed to spend more time on commercials than on performing. But the biggest-selling new group have proved themselves talented musicians with their latest single, 'Message in a Bottle', topping the charts. In the early days it was only the royalties from bit-parts in the ads which enabled them to keep going. In spite of their youthful image, the group is made up of veterans: 33-year-old guitarist Andy Summers used to play with David Essex and was shortlisted to join the Rolling Stones; drummer Stewart Copeland, son of the CIA's chief of operations in the Middle East, Miles Copeland, has played with Curved Air; lead singer Gordon Sumner, known as Sting, is a comparative newcomer, having spent 5 years teaching at a primary school before joining Police. The group's first album, *Outlandos D'Amour*, was made for less than £3,000, showing a massive profit for themselves and their record company.

POUND IS FREED AT LAST

40 years of foreign currency exchange controls and restrictions were wiped out last night (23 October). From today, people and companies can buy as much foreign currency as they like for any purpose; such purchases will not be recorded in people's passports. All that remains of exchange controls is a restriction on sending money to Rhodesia, part of the sanctions policy which Chancellor Sir Geoffrey Howe hopes will not be needed for long. Exchange controls were introduced at the start of the Second World War and 'have now outlived their usefulness', said Sir Geoffrey.

DAY BY DAY

1 Oct
Nigeria returns to civilian rule and Alhaji Shehu Shagari is sworn in as the new President.

The United States returns control of the 553-square-mile Canal Zone to Panama.

2 Oct
At the Labour Party Conference in Brighton a motion that all Labour MPs should be subject to reselection by their constituency parties between each general election is carried against the advice of Mr Callaghan.

3 Oct
Mr Mota Singh is sworn in as a Crown Court recorder, the first Sikh judge in England.

Delegates at the Labour Party Conference vote in favour of future election manifestoes being the responsibility of the national executive instead of members of Parliament.

6 Oct
Pope John Paul II becomes the first Pope ever to visit the White House when he meets President Carter at the end of his week's visit to the United States.

11 Oct
Doctor Godfrey Hounsfield, inventor of the EMI body scanner, is named as joint winner of the Nobel Prize for Medicine and Physiology.

18 Oct
The Queen opens the new Lyric Theatre in Hammersmith.

21 Oct
General Moshe Dayan resigns as Israel's Foreign Secretary because he does not agree with his country's policy on Palestinian autonomy.

Agreement is finally reached between the management and unions of Times Newspapers on the questions of uninterrupted production, a new disputes procedure, and on pay and hours. Publication of *The Times*, *Sunday Times* and 3 supplements has been suspended since November 1978.

24 Oct
Figures published by the Department of Employment show a total of 23,685,000 working days have already been lost this year due to strikes and stoppages, the highest number since the General Strike of 1926.

26 Oct
President Park of South Korea is shot dead at a dinner party in Seoul.

27 Oct
The Duke of Gloucester represents the Queen at the independence celebrations of the Caribbean island of St Vincent.

28 Oct
Chairman Hua Kuoi-feng arrives in Britain for a 6-day visit; he is the first Leader of Communist China to come to the United Kingdom.

30 Oct
British air engineer Sir Barnes Wallis dies, aged 92.

CHURCH SPLIT ON HOMOSEXUALS

The Church of England was still hopelessly divided yesterday (18 October) over whether homosexuals should be treated as normal Christians or unreformed sinners. A new report takes a charitable view of people living in what it calls 'loving, faithful and permanent' relationships, who have up to now been ostracized, but it stops short of condoning homosexual marriage. The report does, however, recommend that the homosexual age of consent should be reduced from 21 to 18. The Church's Board of Social Responsibility has publicly dissociated itself from the report's findings.

THE DROP-OUT SUPERSTAR

A year ago Gary Numan spent his days at Slough Job Centre or collecting his £19.75 dole and his evenings singing pop standards in London pubs. Today, at 21, he has twice achieved the distinction of having his singles and albums topping the charts simultaneously. In 3 months Numan has leaped from obscurity to become the hottest name in pop with music based on a Germanic electronic sound with menacing sythesizers. Teenagers dress like him and try to imitate his expressions and robotic movements. Expelled from grammar school, secondary modern and technical college without a CSE or O level to his credit, Numan's phenomenal rise was a calculated one: 'I've been watching the pop market since I was 17. I was aware of the gaps. I was watching what people wanted and what they were getting and the 2 weren't meeting.'

SCHOOL 'DOLE' TO END

A plan to stop the payment of social security money to teenagers as soon as they leave school and to students on vacation is being urgently studied by the Government. One possibility being considered is that school leavers would not qualify for the £14-a-week benefit until after the 6-week summer holiday, rather than in a few days as at present. The move, part of the Tories' shake-up of the Welfare State way of life, comes on top of the scrapping of a Labour government scheme which guaranteed that 16–19-year-olds who could not get jobs would be paid benefit if they took a further education course or began industrial training. Industry Secretary Sir Keith Joseph wants to go even further: he has made it clear he would like to see student grants replaced by a loan system, though he pointed out, 'I cannot persuade any of my colleagues on this; this is a very personal view.'

Kane (John Hurt) explores an underground chamber in the derelict ship in Alien.

NOV 1979

DUMPING DISCO

The most amazing new sound in pop today is that of disco records being broken. In America and Britain it has become fashionable for adolescents to hold 'dump disco' parties in which all the old Donna Summer and Bee Gees records are smashed. Disco, for 2 years the most influential musical force, is dying, following a dramatic slump in sales. Even the title of a movie starring the Village People has been changed from *Disco Dancing* to *Can't Stop the Music* as EMI thought the word might jeopardize the film's success.

SCHOOL SELLS A-BOMB PILOT'S LOG

A debt-ridden village school in Wicklow, Ireland is to auction a pilot's flight manual of the first A-bomb raid on Japan. This historic record of the Hiroshima raid has been given to the school by US Air-force General Paul Tibbets, the man who flew the plane. It was on 6 August 1945 that General Tibbets, now 65, flew the B-29 Flying Fortress, named *Enola Gay* after his mother, on its grim operation to drop the 4.5-ton bomb. He gave the unique records to the school after being asked for a donation by historian Gordon Thomas, who has known the General for some years and who has 2 children at the school. General Tibbets had previously refused large cash offers for the unique record.

DOOMSDAY MISTAKE THAT SHOOK AMERICA

British and American defence chiefs believed that a nuclear alert could not be given by mistake. They were wrong. A heart-stopping scare in America on Friday (9 November) proves that even the most sophisticated defence systems are not faultless. US and Canadian interceptor jets were scrambled when the main computer at Air Defense Command in Colorado Springs signalled a full-scale Russian attack. The Pentagon is doing its best to play down the affair, pointing out that 'only a very short time' elapsed before it was determined that the attack was a phoney.

SAFER PILL SOON

A new low-risk contraceptive pill should be available on prescription within a year. The new pill, produced by the German-based drug firm Schering, makes use of a breakthrough in scientific understanding of the dangerous mechanisms in existing oral contraceptives. Recent scares over circulatory disorders associated with the pill had been blamed on high oestrogen levels. Now there is evidence that excessive progestogen reduces the body's ability to clear harmful fat particles from the blood. The new pill, which has yet to be given a trade name, contains more oestrogen than current pills, while making a huge cut in the progestogen content. This represents a reversal in the direction in which other pills had been moving.

COLOUR US BLUE!

England is considering wearing all blue for the 1-day cricket internationals in Australia. After a poor fielding performance in its first appearance under floodlights yesterday (8 November) it is having second thoughts about its insistence on sticking to all white.

JOYCE GRENFELL DIES

Joyce Grenfell, one of England's most treasured institutions, died from cancer yesterday (30 November). The 69-year-old star, famous for her inimitable portrayal of a range of comic characters and her acutely observed monologues, appeared on television only 3 days ago in a filmed tribute to her aunt, Lady Astor.

Above: Village People

The Clash

HOSTAGES OF REVENGE

A mob of students stormed the American embassy in Tehran yesterday (4 November) and seized up to 100 hostages. Their demand: that the deposed and ill Shah should be extradited from the US to stand trial. The occupation had the support of Ayatollah Khomeini, according to a spokesman. The students claimed the hostages were being well treated; nevertheless, the volatile and bloodthirsty nature of the Iranian revolution is such that anything could happen, especially in view of the hysteria for revenge against the Shah, who is in a New York hospital.

QUEEN OF THE MARATHON AT 42

Joyce Smith, the remarkable 42-year-old Watford mother of 2, yesterday (18 November) became the Women's World Marathon Champion in Tokyo with a time of 2 hours 37 minutes 48 seconds. Until 3 seasons ago women were barred from racing marathons but some girls gatecrashed men's events to prove they were capable of competing. The world's best time for a women's marathon is 2 hours 27 minutes 33 seconds by Norway's Grete Waitz, who did not compete in Tokyo.

TRAITOR AT THE QUEEN'S RIGHT HAND

Anthony Blunt, knighted for his work as surveyor of the Queen's art collection, was officially exposed yesterday (15 November) as the 'Fourth Man' in the Burgess, Philby and Maclean spy scandal. After the dramatic news was revealed by Mrs Thatcher in the Commons, Blunt was peremptorily stripped of his knighthood by the Queen. By that time Blunt had packed his bags and left his London flat, alerted by the security services that the secret he had shared with the Establishment for 15 years was about to be revealed. The big question now was whether he would seek refuge in the Soviet Union.

Gail Potter (Helen Worth) and Brian Tilsley (Chris Quinten) tie the knot in Coronation Street.

PEN THAT WORRIES THE BANKS

The makers of a ball pen which has ink that can be rubbed out are confident the invention will keep them laughing all the way to the bank. But the banks are less than happy about the pen, claimed to be 'the greatest technological breakthrough in writing instruments for thirty years'. They say the pen is the greatest invitation to fraud this century and already Barclays has banned its staff from using it at work. The bank is also sending out millions of warning notices to customers, advising them not to sign cheques with the erasable pen. The pen, which is made by Papermate and sells for £1.39, has ink which does not become permanent for up to 24 hours.

START A NEW PARTY

Roy Jenkins has urged Labour moderates to form a new centre coalition free of union influence. The former Home Secretary, now President of the European Commission, made the plea when he delivered the Richard Dimbleby Lecture on TV last night (22 November). Mr Jenkins said he was in favour of the stimulus of the free market economy without the brutality of unrestricted distribution of rewards or indifference to unemployment. He also urged proportional representation as a means of bringing about the consensus politics which could, he argued, put an end to Britain's economic decline. Asked whether a party which splits would be electorally damaged, Mr Jenkins said, ' . . . if it saw a new grouping with cohesion and relevant policies it might be more attracted by this new reality than by old labels which had become increasingly irrelevant'.

SETTING A NEW TRACK RECORD

Hi-fi enthusiasts will welcome what is being hailed as the greatest breakthrough of the decade: 'digital' albums. They look exactly the same as any other LP and can be played on any good record system. The difference is in the sound quality, which makes ordinary albums as outdated as 78s. There is virtually no distortion achieved by recordings which are in digital code. The sounds are converted into numbers and are therefore not subject to any impairment of quality; with an orthodox 'analogue' album, sounds are recorded by magnetic wave on tape. The next step will be digital turntables which may use a laser beam instead of a stylus. Philips intends marketing such a disc – 6 inches in diameter – within a decade.

DOOM TOWN

The proud steel town of Corby was under sentence of death last night (1 November). The guillotine will fall early next year with the loss of 5,500 jobs; 1 in 3 working men in the town will become unemployed.

Frustration for Kevin Keegan at a fogbound Wembley as England's European Championship qualifying match against Bulgaria is postponed.

DEC 1979

POP GOES BANGOR FOR CHRISTMAS

A record by an obscure Kentish folk group called Fiddlers' Dram looks set to be number 1 for Christmas. With its lolloping sing-along rhythm and 'beer and skittles' atmosphere, 'Day Trip to Bangor' – a 'do-it-yourself' song written and recorded by enthusiastic amateurs – has cornered this year's novelty market.

WIVES WIN TAX RIGHTS

The tax-man is to stop treating married women as mere adjuncts to their husbands. In future, wives will be contacted direct about their tax affairs. Until now, the Inland Revenue has written to married women only in response to letters from them; correspondence has normally been addressed to the husband.

The Russians go into Afghanistan.

LYNCH'S 'I QUIT' WORRIES BRITAIN

A meeting in Dublin tomorrow to elect a successor to Irish Premier Jack Lynch will be watched with anxiety in both London and Northern Ireland. Mr Lynch's resignation yesterday (5 December) after 13 years at the head of the Fianna Fáil party – 9 of them in power – could leave the way open to a more Republican leadership in Ireland. Front-runner to succeed him is Health Minister Mr Charles Haughey, though Finance Minister Mr George Colley would be more likely to follow Mr Lynch's line of security co-operation with the British along the Ulster border. The 62-year-old Prime Minister has come under increasing criticism from within his own party since an agreement in September to allow British Army helicopters 5 miles into Irish air space when in hot pursuit of IRA suspects. This move hardened the already pro-Republican stand of some of his party.

MISSILE PLAN 'GETS THE GREEN LIGHT'

The plan to site hundreds of NATO nuclear missiles across Europe is said to have been unofficially approved. The tactical weapons, 464 Cruise and 108 Pershing missiles, will be deployed mainly in Britain, Italy and West Germany. Belgium and Holland have objected to the plan; Denmark and Norway, who won't have missiles on their soil, are also uneasy. The American-built missiles will counter Russia's new SS20 inter-continental nuclear weapons.

McQUEEN RIDES AGAIN

Steve McQueen is back. The bloated recluse is now slim, mean and hungry, ready once again to challenge Newman, Redford and De Niro for the title of top male film star. He plays Tom Horn, the legendary westerner who helped capture the Indian chief Geronimo. The slimmed-down action man is a far cry from the McQueen of the $3m flop, Chekhov's *An Enemy of the People*. After completing *Horn* and a film called *The Hunter*, he has revealed he will not even consider a script unless he is guaranteed £2.5m plus 15% of the profits.

REDS EXECUTE AFGHAN LEADERS

Less than 48 hours after a massive air-lift of Soviet troops and tanks into Afghanistan, the country's Government was toppled yesterday (27 December) and a pro-Kremlin supporter, Babrak Karmal, took over. The man who was overthrown, President Hafizullah Amin, was said to have been executed for 'crimes against the Afghan people'. The Kremlin's operation, observed with alarm in London and Washington, had sinister undertones of developing into a Russian Vietnam amid a bitter backlash from the Afghan Muslims. The new head of the Kabul Government had been Afghan Ambassador in Prague, an ironic reminder of the Soviet invasion of Czechoslovakia.

THE FLAMES OF HATE

The American embassy in Arab-extremist Libya was sacked and burned yesterday (1 December). It was the latest manifestation of international Muslim mob hatred against the US and one more blow to President Carter as he struggled with the apparently insoluble problem of how to secure the release of the 49 hostages who have been held in Iran for 4 weeks.

NEW STAR ON SUNDAY

Derek Batey, compère of ITV's *Mr & Mrs* show, is to take charge of a replacement for *Stars on Sunday*. The new programme, *Your Hundred Best Hymns*, does away with its forerunner's plastic fonts, extravagant trimmings and big name guests to concentrate on hymns and Bible readings.

Would-be taxi driver Chris (Mick Ford) must first aquire The Knowledge.

Definitely Not The 9 O'Clock News *as delivered by (l. to r.) Rowan Atkinson, Pamela Stephenson, Griff Rhys-Jones and Mel Smith.*

DAY BY DAY

3 Dec
11 young people are crushed to death in a stampede to get into the Cincinnati Coliseum, Ohio for a rock concert by The Who.

5 Nov
Mr Jack Lynch announces his retirement as Prime Minister of the Irish Republic; he is succeeded by Mr Charles Haughey.

12 Dec
Lord Soames arrives in Salisbury to become the new British Governor of Southern Rhodesia.

13 Dec
Former England Manager Don Revie wins his case in the High Court against the Football Association. The judge lifts the 10-year ban imposed by the FA, but criticizes Mr Revie for the way in which he resigned as England Manager in order to take over a United Arab Emirates football team.

15 Dec
The deposed Shah of Iran and the Empress Farah fly from Texas to the Panamanian island of Contadora to take up residence at the invitation of the President of Panama.

17 Dec
The Secretary of State for Trade, Mr John Nott, announces the Government's decision on Stansted as the site for London's third airport.

18 Dec
Stanley Barrett becomes the first man to break the sound barrier on land when in his rocket car he achieves a speed of 739.666 m.p.h. on a dried-up lake in California.

21 Dec
The UN Security Council lifts the diplomatic and economic sanctions it had imposed on Rhodesia in 1966.

25 Dec
The Queen's Christmas message is sent to Rhodesia for the first time in 14 years.

THE DAY THE EARTH MOVED

Britain's worst earthquake for 50 years jolted parts of the country out of the holiday mood yesterday (26 December). The shaken area stretched from Kendal in the Lake District as far north as Aberdeen and west as Ulster. It measured around 5 on the Richter Scale. No one was injured in the 30-second tremor, though there was considerable structural damage. Families rushed from their homes as the earth roared 'like a thousand express trains', as one witness put it. Within minutes police switchboards were jammed with terrified callers fearing a nuclear attack.

Don Revie wins a High Court case against the FA.

IT'S 'YES' TO PEACE

Lord Carrington shook hands on a peace agreement with the Rhodesians last night (5 December) after the guerilla leaders finally accepted terms for a cease-fire. A British governor – expected to be Lord Soames – will fly to Salisbury within days to take charge of the country and formally end the 14-year rebellion. He will remain in Zimbabwe/Rhodesia until the Union Jack comes down at independence early in March.

GOODBYE TO BRITAIN'S MR BOXING

Jack Israel Solomons, one of the 3 great promoters in the history of boxing, has died. He was born with 5 fingers and a thumb on each hand and had the extra ones amputated when he was a baby. He had his first professional fight at 15 but gave it up 2 years later after being knocked out cold. At 31 he began the career which made him famous, losing £295 on his first London promotion. It was after the war, starting with Jack London vs Bruce Woodcock, that he became Mr Boxing, a worthy successor to Tex Rickard, promoter of Jack Dempsey vs Georges Carpentier, and Mike Jacobs who ruled during the career of Joe Louis. His shows with Woodcock and Mills, Turpin and Downes were unforgettable theatrical affairs. When rival promoter Harry Levene heard the news of Solomons' death he said, 'My next show is at Wembley in March.'

WHITELAW: NO CRUELTY

The Home Secretary has denied that his plans for 'short, sharp shock' punishment for young offenders will involve cruelty. Labour MP Mr Robert Kilroy-Silk challenged Mr Whitelaw's plans, saying that a 1952 experiment showed that the 'tough regime' approach did nothing to reduce crime. He then asked if the regime would also apply to girls, to which the Home Secretary, who has decided to introduce 2 centres to try out his new approach, replied that there were no such plans.

HOLIDAY HOMES BURNED

Police feared last night (13 December) that they could be facing a new outbreak of attacks by Welsh Nationalist extremists after 4 empty holiday cottages were destroyed by fire. All were owned by English families.

DISC FIRMS SUE OVER HOME TAPES

Britain's major record companies are suing the Japanese electronics giant Toshiba over an advert which, they claim, encourages people to make illegal tape recordings. The action, by the British Phonographic Industry, is part of a tough new campaign aimed at curbing home taping which, it is claimed, will cost the record companies £150m in lost sales this year. The controversial advertisement is for a radio cassette recorder which 'has 2 microphones so it records in stereo as well as from the FM waveband, turntable or live music'. A BPI spokesman said, 'There seems to be a general misguided view among the public that it is all right to tape material at home from records as long as you don't sell it, but it is piracy.' Toshiba has agreed to drop the line from all future advertisements.

Francis Ford Coppola's Apocalypse Now.

FACTS & FIGURES

THE 4 MAIN OFFICES OF STATE

	Prime Minister	Home Secretary	Foreign Secretary	Chancellor of the Exchequer
Conservative Government (70–74)	E. Heath 19.6.70	R. Maudling 20.6.70	Sir A. Douglas-Home 20.6.70	I. Macleod 20.6.70
		R. Carr 18.7.72		A. Barber 25.7.70
Labour Government (74–79)	H. Wilson 4.3.74	R. Jenkins 5.3.74	J. Callaghan 5.3.74	D. Healey 5.3.74
	J. Callaghan 5.4.76	M. Rees 10.9.76	A. Crosland 8.4.76	
			D. Owen 21.2.77	
Conservative Government (79–)	M. Thatcher 4.5.79	W. Whitelaw 5.5.79	Lord Carrington 5.5.79	Sir G. Howe 5.5.79

GENERAL ELECTION RESULTS

PARTY	VOTES	% TOTAL VOTE	SEATS
1970 – Thursday, 18 June			
Con	13,145,123	46.4	330
Lab	12,179,341	43.0	287
Lib	2,117,035	7.5	6
Other	903,299	3.1	7
1974 – Thursday, 28 February			
Con	11,868,906	37.9	297
Lab	11,639,243	37.1	301
Lib	6,063,470	19.3	14
Other	1,762,047	5.7	23
1974 – Thursday, 10 October			
Con	10,464,817	35.8	277
Lab	11,457,079	39.2	319
Lib	5,346,754	18.3	13
Other	1,920,528	6.7	26
1979 – Thursday, 3 May			
Con	13,697,690	43.9	339
Lab	11,532,148	36.9	269
Lib	4,313,811	13.8	11
Other	1,676,366	5.4	16

OLD AGE PENSION

Date	Maximum rate for single person
Jan 70	100/–
Sept 71	£6.00
Oct 72	£6.75
Oct 73	£7.35
July 74	£10.00
April 75	£11.60
Nov 75	£13.30
Nov 76	£15.30
Nov 77	£17.50
Nov 78	£19.50
Nov 79	£23.30

PRICES AND WAGES

(1970 = 100)

Year	Retail Price	Weekly Earnings	Real Weekly Earnings
1970	100	100	100
1971	109.4	111.2	101.6
1972	117.3	125.5	107.0
1973	128.0	142.5	111.3
1974	148.4	167.8	113.1
1975	184.5	212.3	115.1
1976	214.9	245.3	114.1
1977	249.1	270.2	108.5
1978	269.7	309.3	114.7
1979	305.9	357.6	116.9

THE YEARS OF UPS AND DOWNS

BRITAIN experienced a revolution in trends over the decade. The birth rate went down but the rate of illegitimate births went up and abortions increased dramatically.

The divorce rate shot up as the Divorce Law Reform Act took effect. The marriage rate went down and the death rate remained static. The population of England and Wales increased to its highest ever level.

UP	1970	1979
Abortions	86,565	142,343
Illegitimate births	64,744	69,467
Divorces	58,239	129,053
Consumer expenditure on alcohol (including beer, wine and spirits)	£3.6 billion	£5.3 billion
Home owners	9.3 million	11.1 million

DOWN	1970	1979
Birth rate (per thousand population)	16.4	12.1
Manual workers' weekly hours	41.3	39.9

INCOME TAX

Year	Income Tax Rate	Purchasing Power of £ (1900 = 20/–)
1970	7/9 in £	2/8
1971	38.75%	12½p
1972	38.75%	11½p
1973	30%	10½p
1974	33%	9p
1975	35%	7½p
1976	35%	6½p
1977	34%	5½p
1978	33%	5p
1979	30%	4½p

CABINET MAKE-UP

Date	Party	Prime Minister	Cabinet Size	Aristocrats	Middle Class	Working Class	Public School All	Public School Eton	University Educated All	University Educated Oxbridge
Jun 70	Con	Heath	18	4	14	–	15	4	15	15
Mar 74	Lab	Wilson	21	1	16	4	7	–	16	11
Apr 76	Lab	Callaghan	22	1	13	7	7	–	15	10
May 79	Con	Thatcher	22	3	19	–	20	6	18	17

THE CHARTS

MOST WEEKS ON CHART FOR EACH YEAR

1970	Elvis Presley (59)
1971	Elvis Presley (66)
1972	T Rex (58)
1973	David Bowie (55)
1974	Wombles (65)
1975	Mud (45)
1976	Rod Stewart (48)
1977	Elvis Presley (51)
1978	Boney M (54)
1979	Abba (43)
	Blondie (43)
	Chic (43)

SINGLES

The most successful singles artists of the 70s by category:

MALE VOCAL	GROUPS	FEMALE VOCAL
1 Elvis Presley	1 E.L.O.	1 Diana Ross
2 Elton John	Slade	2 Donna Summer
3 David Bowie	3 Showaddywaddy	3 Suzi Quatro
4 Cliff Richard	4 ABBA	4 Olivia Newton-John
5 Rod Stewart	5 T Rex	5 Tina Charles
6 Gary Glitter	6 Hot Chocolate	6 Dana
7 Stevie Wonder	7 Stylistics	7 Lynsey De Paul
8 David Essex	8 Status Quo	8 Kiki Dee
Gilbert O'Sullivan	9 Mud	9 Shirley Bassey
10 Barry White	10 Sweet	10 Gloria Gaynor

Lists are based on the number of singles released in the 1970s to reach the top 40 (excluding re-issues and re-entries). Where more than one artist achieved the same number of top 40 successes, those which made the top 10 decided the order.

Led Zeppelin released 7 albums in the 1970s: they all reached No 1. Rod Stewart also notched up the same number of top spot albums from his 11 releases. Abba took 3rd place in the battle of the No 1s with 5 consecutive releases reaching the top slot.

TOTAL WEEKS AT NO 1 BY AN ALBUM RELEASED IN THE 1970s

(including compilation albums but excluding various artists)

41 Weeks ..... *Bridge Over Troubled Water* – Simon & Garfunkel
17 Weeks ..... *The Singles 1969–1973* – The Carpenters
11 Weeks ..... *Greatest Hits* – Elton John
11 Weeks ..... *Greatest Hits* – Abba
10 Weeks ..... *20 Golden Greats* – The Beach Boys
10 Weeks ..... *Arrival* – Abba
9 Weeks ..... *The Best of the Stylistics* – The Stylistics
8 Weeks ..... *Electric Warrior* – T Rex
7 Weeks ..... *Band on the Run* – Wings
7 Weeks ..... *20 Golden Greats* – Diana Ross and the Supremes
7 Weeks ..... *The Album* – Abba
7 Weeks ..... *Atlantic Crossing* – Rod Stewart

TOP 10 MOST SUCCESSFUL ALBUMS RELEASED IN THE 70s

(by virtue of number of weeks on chart to date)

Rumours – Fleetwood Mac
Bat Out Of Hell – Meat Loaf
Bridge Over Troubled Water – Simon & Garfunkel
Dark Side of The Moon – Pink Floyd
Greatest Hits – Simon & Garfunkel
Tubular Bells – Mike Oldfield
Jeff Wayne's War of the Worlds – Jeff Wayne
The Rise and Fall of Ziggy Stardust and the Spiders from Mars – David Bowie
Off the Wall – Michael Jackson
Manilow Magic – Barry Manilow

SOLO BEATLES

The early 70s saw the break-up of the group who dominated the previous decade. As a solo artist Paul McCartney was by far the most successful of the four, his first release – *Another Day* – reached No 2 in 1971; *My Love*, also a Top 10 hit, was the first Wings success. In all, he scored 20 Top 40 hits before the decade was out, 14 of them going Top 10 and *Mull of Kintyre* (1977/78) reaching No 1, one of the biggest selling singles of all time.

John Lennon made the Top 40 8 times during the 70s. *Happy Xmas (War is Over)* was his highest placed single in this time, reaching No 4 as one of the Christmas hits of 1972. It improved on this position 8 Christmases later reaching the No 2 slot, in one of its 5 chart runs. *Imagine* went one better in 1980/81, having reached No 6 on its first release in 1975.

George Harrison's first solo hit, *My Sweet Lord,* occupied the No 1 spot for 5 weeks in 1971, later becoming the subject of a legal wrangle over its similarity to The Chiffons hit of 1963 – *He's So Fine*. Only 4 more Top 40 hits followed.

Ringo Starr also had early successes; between 1971 and 1974 he enjoyed 5 Top 40 hits, 4 of them going Top 10 with *Back off Boogaloo* denied No 1 spot mainly due to the Royal Scots Dragoon Guards' version of *Amazing Grace*. *Only You* (1974/5) reaching No 28 was his last chart success of the decade.

THE NO 1 SINGLES ARTISTS

Abba take top spot with 7 No 1s during the 70s. Slade reached the top 6 times, Rod Stewart on 5 occasions. The Osmonds also had 5 No 1s between them in various guises.

Boney M, whose hit single Rivers of Babylon *spent more consecutive weeks on the chart than any other.*

STRAIGHT IN AT NUMBER ONE

Only 4 singles went straight to the top spot in the 1970s, all of them in 1973.

Cum On Feel The Noize............Slade
Skweeze Me Pleeze Me..............Slade
I Love You Love Me Love..........Gary Glitter
Merry Xmas Everybody............Slade

MOST TOP 10 HIT ALBUMS RELEASED BY AN ARTIST IN THE 1970s

David Bowie 13
Elton John 12
Elvis Presley.. 11
Bob Dylan 11
Paul McCartney 10
Rolling Stones.. 10
Rod Stewart 9
Status Quo 9
Yes 8
The Who 8

MOST WEEKS ON CHART IN THE 1970s (Consecutive)

*40 Weeks ..... *Rivers of Babylon/Brown Girl in the Ring* – Boney M
*39 Weeks ..... *Tie a Yellow Ribbon Round The Old Oak Tree* – Dawn
*34 Weeks ..... *Chirpy Chirpy Cheep Cheep* – Middle of the Road
 32 Weeks ..... *Amazing Grace* – Judy Collins
 31 Weeks ..... *And I Love You So* – Perry Como
*27 Weeks ..... *Knock Three Times* – Dawn
*27 Weeks ..... *Grandad* – Clive Dunn
 27 Weeks ..... *Big Six* – Judge Dread
*26 Weeks ..... *You're The One That I Want* – John Travolta & Olivia Newton-John
*24 Weeks ..... *Long Haired Lover From Liverpool* – Little Jimmy Osmond
*24 Weeks ..... *Welcome Home* – Peters & Lee
*24 Weeks ..... *Amazing Grace* – Royal Scots Dragoon Guards

*These records reached No 1 during their chart run

LONGEST AT NO 1 IN THE 1970s

9 Weeks ..... *Bohemian Rhapsody* – Queen (1975/76)
You're The One That I Want – John Travolta & Olivia Newton-John (1978)
Mull of Kintyre – Wings (1977/78)

7 Weeks ..... *In The Summertime* – Mungo Jerry (1970)
Summer Nights – John Travolta & Olivia Newton-John (1978)

6 Weeks ..... *The Wonder of You* – Elvis Presley (1970)
Band of Gold – Freda Payne (1970)
I Hear Your Knockin' – Dave Edmunds (1970)
Hot Love – T Rex (1971)
Bye Bye Baby – Bay City Rollers (1975)
Save Your Kisses For Me – Brotherhood of Man (1976)
Don't Go Breaking My Heart – Elton John & Kiki Dee (1976)
Dancing Queen – Abba (1976)
Bright Eyes – Art Garfunkel (1979)

David Bowie: *most top 10 hit albums.*

FILM AND TELEVISION

The Godfather: 'best film' award for 1972.

TOP 10 MONEY-MAKING FILMS OF THE DECADE

(based on total reported North American box-office receipts)

1 *Star Wars*, 1977
2 *Jaws*, 1975
3 *Grease*, 1978
4 *The Exorcist*, 1973
5 *The Godfather*, 1972
6 *Superman – the Movie*, 1979
7 *The Sting*, 1973
8 *Close Encounters of the Third Kind*, 1977
9 *Saturday Night Fever*, 1977
10 *National Lampoon's Animal House*, 1978

THE REDIFFUSION STAR AWARDS

(Presented by Rediffusion Television Limited)

'Harlequin' Award for Children's Programmes

1970	*Vision On*
1971	*Follyfoot*
1972	*The Intruder*
1973	*Ragtime*
1974	*Rainbow*
	Soldier and Me
1975	*Newsround Extra*
	Ballet Shoes
1976	*John Craven's Newsround*
	Multi-Coloured Swapshop
1977	*Go with Noakes*
	The All Star Record Breakers
1978	*Grange Hill*
	Think of a Number
1979	*Grange Hill*
	The Book Tower

TOP BOX OFFICE STARS OF THE 70S

1 Clint Eastwood
2 Burt Reynolds
3 Barbra Streisand
4 Robert Redford
5 Paul Newman
6 Steve McQueen
7 John Wayne
8 Woody Allen
9 Dustin Hoffman
10 Al Pacino

AWARDS FOR 'BEST FILM'

Year	Oscar	British Academy Award
1970	*Patton*	*Butch Cassidy and the Sundance Kid*
1971	*The French Connection*	*Sunday, Bloody Sunday*
1972	*The Godfather*	*Cabaret*
1973	*The Sting*	*Day for Night*
1974	*The Godfather, Part 2*	*Lacombe Lucien*
1975	*One Flew Over the Cuckoo's Nest*	*Alice Doesn't Live Here Any More*
1976	*Rocky*	*One Flew Over the Cuckoo's Nest*
1977	*Annie Hall*	*Annie Hall*
1978	*The Deer Hunter*	*Julia*
1979	*Kramer vs Kramer*	*Manhattan*

Year	Best Actor Oscar	Best Actress Oscar
1970	George C. Scott, *Patton*	Glenda Jackson, *Women in Love*
1971	Gene Hackman, *The French Connection*	Jane Fonda, *Klute*
1972	Marlon Brando, *The Godfather*	Liza Minnelli, *Cabaret*
1973	Jack Lemmon, *Save the Tiger*	Glenda Jackson, *A Touch of Class*
1974	Art Carney, *Harry and Tonto*	Ellen Burstyn, *Alice Doesn't Live Here Any More*
1975	Jack Nicholson, *One Flew Over the Cuckoo's Nest*	Louise Fletcher, *One Flew Over the Cuckoo's Nest*
1976	Peter Finch, *Network*	Faye Dunaway, *Network*
1977	Richard Dreyfuss, *The Goodbye Girl*	Diane Keaton, *Annie Hall*
1978	Jon Voight, *Coming Home*	Jane Fonda, *Coming Home*
1979	Dustin Hoffman, *Kramer vs Kramer*	Sally Field, *Norma Rae*

THE BRITISH ACADEMY OF FILM AND TELEVISION ARTS AWARDS

Year	Best Light Entertainment Programme
1970	*Dad's Army*
1971	*The Benny Hill Show*
1972	*Monty Python's Flying Circus*
1973	*The Stanley Baxter Big Picture Show*
1974	*The Stanley Baxter Moving Picture Show*
1975	*The Two Ronnies*
1976	*The Muppet Show*
1977	*The Morecambe and Wise Christmas Show*
1978	*The Kenny Everett Video Show*
1979	*Ripping Yarns*

Best Comedy Series

(From 1969–1980 this category was titled 'Best Situation Comedy Series')

Year	
1970	Not awarded
1971	Not awarded
1972	*My Wife Next Door*
1973	*Whatever Happened to the Likely Lads*
1974	*Porridge*
1975	*Fawlty Towers*
1976	*Porridge* (Special)
1977	*Rising Damp*
1978	*Going Straight*
1979	*Fawlty Towers*

Year	Best Factual Series
1970	Not awarded
1971	*World in Action*
1972	*Horizon*
1973	*World in Action*
1974	*Horizon*
1975	*Disappearing World*
1976	*Sailor*
1977	*The South African Experience*
1978	*The Voyage of Charles Darwin*
1979	*Circuit 11 Miami*

Year	Best Documentary Programme
1970	*The Tribe that Hides from Man*
1971	Not awarded
1972	*The Making of a Natural History Film (Horizon)*
1973	*Last Night Another Soldier . . .*
1974	*Beauty, Bonny, Daisy, Violet, Grace and Geoffrey Morton*
1975	*Johnny Go Home*
1976	*The Rescue (Sailor)*
1977	*Casualty (Hospital)*
1978	*The Warlords (Opium)*
1979	*Fred Dibnah, Steeplejack*

Year	Best Drama Series
1970	Not awarded
1971	*Upstairs Downstairs*
1972	*Country Matters*
1973	*Upstairs Downstairs*
1974	*South Riding*
1975	*Edward the Seventh*
1976	*Rock Follies*
1977	*Madame Curie*
1978	*Edward and Mrs Simpson*
1979	*Testament of Youth*

Year	The Best Single Play(s)/Drama
1970	*The Lie*
1971	*Edna, the Inebriate Woman*
1972	*Stockers Copper*
1973	*Kisses at Fifty*
1974	*Antony and Cleopatra*
1975	*The Evacuees*
1976	*Bar-mitzvah Boy*
1977	*Spend, Spend, Spend*
1978	*Licking Hitler*
1979	*Blue Remembered Hills*

Year	Best Light Entertainment Performance
1970	Eric Morecambe/Ernie Wise, *The Morecambe and Wise Show*
1971	Ronnie Corbett/Ronnie Barker, *The Two Ronnies*
1972	Eric Morecambe/Ernie Wise, *The Morecambe and Wise Show*
1973	Eric Morecambe/Ernie Wise, *The Morecambe and Wise Show*
1974	Stanley Baxter, *The Stanley Baxter Moving Picture Show*
1975	Ronnie Barker, *Porridge*
1976	Penelope Keith, *The Good Life*
1977	Ronnie Barker, *Porridge/The Two Ronnies*
1978	Ronnie Barker, *Going Straight/The Two Ronnies*
1979	John Cleese, *Fawlty Towers*

Year	Best Actor
1970	Keith Michell, *The Six Wives of Henry VIII/An Ideal Husband*
1971	John Le Mesurier, *Traitor*
1972	Anthony Hopkins, *War and Peace*
1973	Frank Finlay, *The Adventures of Don Quixote/Candide/The Death of Adolf Hitler*
1974	Peter Barkworth, *Crown Matrimonial*
1975	John Hurt, *The Naked Civil Servant/Nijinsky – God of the Dance*
1976	Derek Jacobi, *I Claudius*
1977	Peter Barkworth, *Professional Foul/The Country Party*
1978	Edward Fox, *Edward and Mrs Simpson*
1979	Alec Guinness, *Tinker, Tailor, Soldier, Spy*

Year	Best Actress
1970	Annette Crosbie, *Catherine of Aragon (The Six Wives of Henry VIII)*
1971	Patricia Hayes, *Edna the Inebriate Woman*
1972	Billie Whitelaw, *The Sextet*
1973	Celia Johnson, *Mrs Palfrey at the Claremont*
1974	Lee Remick, *Jennie*
1975	Annette Crosbie, *Edward the Seventh*
1976	Sian Phillips, *I Claudius/How Green was my Valley*
1977	Penelope Keith, *The Norman Conquests*
1978	Francesca Annis, *Lillie/The Comedy of Errors*
1979	Cheryl Campbell, *Testament of Youth/The Duke of Wellington/Malice Aforethought*

SPORT

RUGBY LEAGUE CHALLENGE CUP WINNERS

1970	Castleford
1971	Leigh
1972	St Helens
1973	Featherstone Rovers
1974	Warrington
1975	Widnes
1976	St Helens
1977	Leeds
1978	Leeds
1979	Widnes

RUGBY UNION COUNTY CHAMPIONSHIP WINNERS

1970	Staffordshire
1971	Surrey
1972	Gloucestershire
1973	Lancashire
1974	Gloucestershire
1975	Gloucestershire
1976	Gloucestershire
1977	Lancashire
1978	North Midlands
1979	Middlesex

RUGBY LEAGUE CHAMPIONSHIP PLAY-OFF WINNERS

1970	St Helens
1971	St Helens
1972	Leeds
1973	Dewsbury
1973/74*	Salford
1974/75	St Helens
1975/76	Salford
1976/77	Featherstone Rovers
1977/78	Widnes
1978/79	Hull Kingston Rovers

*The present 2-division system started in the 1973/74 season.

OPEN GOLF CHAMPIONS

1970	Jack Nicklaus
1971	Lee Trevino
1972	Lee Trevino
1973	Tom Weiskopf
1974	Gary Player
1975	Tom Watson
1976	Johnny Miller
1977	Tom Watson
1978	Jack Nicklaus
1979	Severiano Ballesteros

WORLD MOTOR-RACING CHAMPIONS

1970	Jochen Rindt (Austria)
1971	Jackie Stewart (UK)
1972	Emerson Fittipaldi (Brazil)
1973	Jackie Stewart (UK)
1974	Emerson Fittipaldi (Brazil)
1975	Niki Lauda (Austria)
1976	James Hunt (UK)
1977	Niki Lauda (Austria)
1978	Mario Andretti (USA)
1979	Jody Scheckter (S. Africa)

WORLD MOTOR-CYCLE CHAMPIONS

1970	Giacomo Agostini (Italy)
1971	Giacomo Agostini (Italy)
1972	Giacomo Agostini (Italy)
1973	Phil Read (UK)
1974	Phil Read (UK)
1975	Giacomo Agostini (Italy)
1976	Barry Sheene (UK)
1977	Barry Sheene (UK)
1978	Kenny Roberts (USA)
1979	Kenny Roberts (USA)

WORLD SNOOKER CHAMPIONS

1970	Ray Reardon
1971	John Spencer
1972	Alex Higgins
1973	Ray Reardon
1974	Ray Reardon
1975	Ray Reardon
1976	Ray Reardon
1977	John Spencer
1978	Ray Reardon
1979	Terry Griffiths

BBC SPORTS PERSONALITY OF THE YEAR

1970	Henry Cooper
1971	Princess Anne
1972	Mary Peters
1973	Jackie Stewart
1974	Brendan Foster
1975	David Steele
1976	John Curry
1977	Virginia Wade
1978	Steve Ovett
1979	Sebastian Coe

DERBY WINNERS

1970	Nijinsky – Lester Piggott
1971	Mill Reef – Geoff Lewis
1972	Roberto – Lester Piggott
1973	Morston – Eddie Hide
1974	Snow Knight – Brian Taylor
1975	Grundy – Pat Eddery
1976	Empery – Lester Piggott
1977	The Minstrel – Lester Piggott
1978	Shirley Heights – Greville Starkey
1979	Troy – Willie Carson

GRAND NATIONAL WINNERS

1970	Gay Trip – Pat Taaffe
1971	Specify – John Cook
1972	Well To Do – Graham Thorner
1973	Red Rum – Brian Fletcher
1974	Red Rum – Brian Fletcher
1975	L'Escargot – Tommy Carberry
1976	Rag Trade – John Burke
1977	Red Rum – Tommy Stack
1978	Lucius – Bob Davies
1979	Rubstic – Maurice Barnes

SCOTTISH LEAGUE CHAMPIONS

Division 1 Champions

1969/70	Celtic
1970/71	Celtic
1971/72	Celtic
1972/73	Celtic
1973/74	Celtic
1974/75	Rangers

Premier League Champions

1975/76	Rangers
1976/77	Celtic
1977/78	Rangers
1978/79	Celtic

SCOTTISH CUP WINNERS

1970	Aberdeen
1971	Celtic
1972	Celtic
1973	Rangers
1974	Celtic
1975	Celtic
1976	Rangers
1977	Celtic
1978	Rangers
1979	Rangers

COUNTY CRICKET CHAMPIONS

1970	Kent
1971	Surrey
1972	Warwickshire
1973	Hampshire
1974	Worcestershire
1975	Leicestershire
1976	Middlesex
1977	Middlesex
1978	Kent
1979	Essex

GILLETTE CUP WINNERS

1970	Lancashire
1971	Lancashire
1972	Lancashire
1973	Gloucestershire
1974	Kent
1975	Lancashire
1976	Northamptonshire
1977	Middlesex
1978	Sussex
1979	Somerset

LEAGUE CHAMPIONS

1969/70	Everton
1970/71	Arsenal
1971/72	Derby County
1972/73	Liverpool
1973/74	Leeds United
1974/75	Derby County
1975/76	Liverpool
1976/77	Liverpool
1977/78	Nottingham Forest
1978/79	Liverpool

FA CUP WINNERS

1970	Chelsea
1971	Arsenal
1972	Leeds
1973	Sunderland
1974	Liverpool
1975	West Ham United
1976	Southampton
1977	Manchester United
1978	Ipswich Town
1979	Arsenal

LEAGUE CUP WINNERS

1970	Manchester City
1971	Tottenham Hotspur
1972	Stoke City
1973	Tottenham Hotspur
1974	Wolverhampton Wanderers
1975	Aston Villa
1976	Manchester City
1977	Aston Villa
1978	Nottingham Forest
1979	Nottingham Forest

QUOTES OF THE DECADE

'Ladies and gentlemen, I stand before you tonight in my green chiffon evening gown, my face softly made up, my fair hair gently waved . . . the Iron Lady of the western world. ME? A Cold War warrior? Well, yes – if that is how they wish to interpret my defence of values and freedoms fundamental to our way of life.'

Margaret Thatcher speaking in her Finchley constituency (31.1.76) referring to a report in the Soviet newspaper *Red Star*.

●

'Crisis? What Crisis?'

Sun headline 11.1.79 referring to Mr Callaghan's dismissive comments concerning widespread strike action.

●

'I want to earn an honest living.'

Ronald Biggs, 1974.

●

'There are going to be no dramatic changes in Rhodesia.'

Ian Smith, 1975.

●

'The Scots don't want to play in Belfast. We may have to compromise on this one and meet them halfway.'

Harry Cavan, Irish soccer official, 29.12.79.

●

'If you pay peanuts you get monkeys.'

Sir James Goldsmith about paying top salaries on his magazine *Now!* 1979.

●

'We know the air is unfit to breathe and our food is unfit to eat – and we sit watching our TVs while some local newscaster tells us that today we had 15 homicides and 63 violent crimes, as if that's the way it's supposed to be . . . It's like everything everywhere is going crazy.'

Peter Finch in *Network*, 1976.

●

'Hey, don't knock masturbation. It's sex with someone I love.'

Woody Allen in *Annie Hall*, 1977.

'The simple belief in automatic material progress by means of scientific discovery is a tragic myth of our age.'

Sir Bernard Lovell, 1975.

●

'An ounce of emotion is equal to a ton of facts.'

John Junor, 1979.

●

'The Pope's got great charisma. I'd like to sign him up.'

Lord Grade, 1979.

●

'The chaos affecting everyone today . . . is so all-pervading that it cannot be ignored, yet so shattering that it can only be approached through comedy. Tragedy demands firm foundations; today we are dancing among the ruins.'

British playwright David Campton, 1977.

●

'What becomes nostalgic is trash. What doesn't is meaningful.'

George Melly, 1975.

●

'That was a great game of golf, fellas.'

Bing Crosby's last words, 1977.

●

'My father made him an offer he couldn't refuse.'

Al Pacino in *The Godfather*, 1972.

●

'You can't reheat a soufflé.'

Paul McCartney discounting rumours of a Beatles reunion, 1977.

●

'One man's wage increase is another man's price increase.'

Harold Wilson, 1970.

●

'That part of his speech was rather like being savaged by a dead sheep.'

Denis Healey replying to a parliamentary attack by Sir Geoffrey Howe, 14.6.78.

INTO THE 80s

'We have been through 10 difficult, dangerous years and their problems are still with us. They will not go away because the calendar changes . . . There are signs of a new spirit, of co-operation, of a more realistic approach to our problems. Let this spirit rise high, for it will signify, more certainly than anything else, that our country is on the way forward again to prosperity – to be shared fairly, as in a family.'

Mrs Thatcher's New Year message,
Evening Standard, 13.12.79.

'Tory ministers are like those eighteenth-century quacks who applied leeches to the patient's body to suck more of his blood even when he was dying of anaemia.'

Mr Callaghan's New Year message,
Evening Standard, 31.12.79

'We are being given the opportunity of facing apparent disaster with a creative ingenuity which will make the 80s one of the greatest eras ever of technological invention.

'And most of this invention will be stimulated by the needs of peace, not of war. There is not going to be a world war.'

Anthony Burgess, *Daily Mail*, 31.12.79

'In America, Bobby Clampett and John Cook; in Ireland, Ronan Rafferty; from Australia, Wayne Grady and Greg Norman. I think Nick Faldo and Sandy Lyle have the capacity to be champions.'

Peter Allis on the golfing stars of the 80s,
Daily Mail, 20.12.79.

'. . . a comprehensive national system of trunk roads on which commercial traffic and private cars can move freely and safely and on which congestion and the frustration and economic costs it creates will have been virtually eliminated.'

From the White Paper *Roads for the Future*, 1977.

'I don't see how we can talk with Mrs Thatcher . . . I will say to the lads, come on, get your snouts in the trough.'

NUR leader Sid Weighell, *Daily Mail*, 10.4.79.

'In Europe I think that Ivan Lendl of Czechoslovakia is the most promising player.'

Buster Mottram, on tennis in the 80s,
Daily Mail, 22.12.79.

'Half a million doesn't go far nowadays.'

Lord 'Rab' Butler on being asked what he would do with the money the Queen paid him for Gatcombe Park, which she bought for her daughter,
Daily Mail, 31.12.79.

'I hate having to memorize things for TV. I prefer the spontaneity and intimacy of radio.'

Terry Wogan, interviewed in the *Daily Mail*, 24.12.79.

'I can envisage a time in the not-too-distant future when the makers of a big movie, a Bond film for example, will put it straight into the shops in cassette form. The returns will be much greater than going into cinemas. They will offer it to the cinemas next, and to the TV companies last of all . . . I can envisage BBC Enterprises putting cassettes of our programmes into the shops.'

Robin Scott, Deputy Managing Director of BBC TV on the threat of home video, *Daily Mail*, 17.12.79.

'The motorway/trunk-road programme with all its ramifications, poses a consummate evil and constitutes the greatest threat to the interests of this nation in all its history . . . The more highways we build, the more we generate traffic to fill them, the greater the congestion and snare-ups, and thus the more highways we require to build.'

John Tyme (Motorways vs Democracy, 1978).

Circa 1975

Tim Hill, a teacher and writer, is married with two children and lives in Paignton, Devon.